THE
CONSTITUTIONAL
HISTORY OF ENGLAND

THE
CONSTITUTIONAL
HISTORY OF ENGLAND

A COURSE OF LECTURES
DELIVERED BY

F. W. MAITLAND

CAMBRIDGE
AT THE UNIVERSITY PRESS

PUBLISHED BY
THE SYNDICS OF THE CAMBRIDGE UNIVERSITY PRESS

Bentley House, 200 Euston Road, London, N.W. 1
American Branch: 32 East 57th Street, New York 22, N.Y.

First Edition 1908
Reprinted 1909
1911
1913
1919
1920
1926
1931
1941
1946
1948
1950
1955
1961
1963
1965
1968
1974

First printed in Great Britain at the University Press, Cambridge
Reprinted in United States of America

PREFACE

" I have written a course of lectures in six months on Constitutional History. Do I publish it? No." The lectures written in six months, which Professor Maitland told the Cambridge Law Club would not be published, were delivered during the Michaelmas term of 1887 and the Lent term of 1888, and were specially designed for the needs of undergraduates of the University of Cambridge reading for the Law Tripos. The last word of the last lecture was written on April 7, 1888.

Let us observe the date. Maitland had been recalled to Cambridge as Reader in English Law in 1883 and this is one of his early courses of academic lectures delivered before his election to the Downing Chair in the summer of 1888. It was written seven years before the appearance of the History of English Law, nine years before Domesday Book and Beyond, ten years before Township and Borough, twelve years before the Introduction to Gierke's Political Theories of the Middle Ages. From internal evidence it would seem that some of the earlier lectures were composed before the completion of Bracton's Note Book in 1887. Much of the ground which is here covered was afterwards traversed with greater deliberation and more elaborate scrutiny; some part of the journey Maitland had never the leisure to retrace. Yet the student of his work will find in these early discourses many of the seminal ideas which were subsequently developed in the History of English Law, and here, as elsewhere, will admire the union of high speculative power with exact and comprehensive knowledge of detail. This volume then is not a specimen of Maitland's polished and mature work; it does not claim to be based upon original research; for much of his information the Reader of English Law was confessedly content to draw upon the classical text-books, Hallam, Stubbs, Dicey, Anson, the study of which he frequently commends to the attention of his audience. Yet although the manuscript was laid aside, and the larger theme was abandoned for more special researches into medieval law, the author would sometimes admit that, did time allow, the course of lectures upon Constitutional History might be worked up into a shape worthy of publication.

There is much to be said against printing work which was not intended for the press, and I should not have ventured to recommend the publication of these lectures but for three compelling reasons. The first is that the lectures cannot detract from Maitland's reputation; but must, on the contrary, if possible, enhance it, showing, as they do, that the profound student was also a brilliant populariser of knowledge. The second is that the lectures contain several new and original ideas, which Maitland had no opportunity of expressing in his later work and which we cannot afford to lose. The third is that there is no book, to my knowledge, which provides so good an introduction to the study of English Constitutional History or which is likely to be more highly valued by practical teachers of the subject at our Universities. I can vouch good and lawful men to warranty. Professor Dicey, Sir Courtenay Ilbert and Mr C. R. L. Fletcher were kind enough to look over the manuscript and concurred in urging its publication.

The editor's part has been insignificant. The lectures are printed as they were delivered, and there has been no attempt to rewrite, expand or compress wherever the manuscript was fairly written out. In a few places however the manuscript took the form of brief notes which have been expanded with as strict an economy of words as is consistent with grammar. In one place the substance of a missing page was happily recovered from notebooks kindly lent to the editor by Dr Pierce Higgins of Downing College and Mr A. H. Chaytor of Clare College. For the references and remarks in the footnotes the editor is responsible, save where they are followed by the initials of the author. The references to the Statutes have been verified.

Help has been generously given by many friends, in particular by Sir Courtenay Ilbert, who has contributed many valuable suggestions with reference to the last section of the volume. The editor will be grateful to his readers for any further suggestions by means of which a second edition of the book, should one be called for, may be made more fully worthy of the author and the subject.

H. A. L. FISHER.

NEW COLLEGE, OXFORD.
May 1908.

ANALYSIS[1]

Outline of the course. Sketch of public law at five periods, (I) 1307, (II) 1509, (III) 1625, (IV) 1702, (V) the present day. Reasons for this choice of periods. The first and last sketches will be the most thorough.

PERIOD I.

ENGLISH PUBLIC LAW AT THE DEATH OF EDWARD I.

A. *General Characteristics of English Law and Review of Legislation.*

(i) Before 1066. Dooms of the kings and witan; substratum of traditional law (folk right); local customs; theory of the three laws, West Saxon, Mercian, Danish; formalism of traditional law; Roman law unknown; influence of the church; characteristics of the dooms
Pages 1—6

(ii) 1066—1154. What law had the Normans? Survival of English law; confirmations by William I and Henry I. Law books: *Leges Edwardi, Willelmi, Henrici Primi*; fusion of English and Norman (Frankish) law. Genuine laws of William I; charters of Henry I and Stephen; Domesday Book . . . **6—10**

(iii) 1154—1215. Henry II as a legislator; Constitutions of Clarendon (1164); growth of Canon law; study of Roman law; 'assizes'; possessory assizes and grand assize; assizes of Clarendon (1166) and Northampton (1176). Law books: Glanvill (circ. 1188); *Dialogus de Scaccario*; the first Plea Roll (1194) . . **10—14**

---

[1] Printed copies of this analysis or syllabus were supplied to those who attended the course of lectures. A few slight changes have been made, where the order of topics in the lectures does not correspond with that laid down in the analysis.

E. *Administration of Justice.*

The courts are (1) communal, (2) feudal, (3) royal, central and permanent, (4) royal, local and temporary (visitatorial), (5) ecclesiastical. General principles as to their competence.

Growth of royal jurisdiction :—

F. *Retrospect of Feudalism.*

PERIOD II.

SKETCH OF PUBLIC LAW AT THE DEATH OF HENRY VII.

A. *Parliament.*

1. *Its Constitution.*

History of the three estates.

(i) Clergy:—bishops, abbots; non-attendance of clerical proctors.

(ii) Lords:—the dukes, marquises, viscounts. Peerage by patent and peerage by writ. Barony by tenure. Number of peers. Idea of 'peerage'; right to trial by peers admitted, but within narrow limits. Court of the High Steward. The peerage not a caste. Preponderance in the House of Lords of lords spiritual.

(iii) Commons:—Number of members. The county franchise; the forty shilling freehold. Number of boroughs represented. The borough franchises. Wages of members.

Arrangement of Parliament in two houses; when effected. Functions of the two houses. Wording of the writs . **165—177**

2. *Frequency and Duration of Parliaments.*

Annual Parliaments. Statutes of 1330 and 1362. Intermissions of Parliaments become commoner under Edward IV . **177—178**

3. *Business of Parliament.*

We must not start with a theory of parliamentary sovereignty; such a theory the outcome of struggles **179**

(i) Taxation:—here the need of Parliaments is established. Direct taxation without consent of Parliament becomes impossible. History of indirect taxation. Benevolences. Parliamentary taxation; taxation of clerical estate. Money grants to be initiated by the Commons: form of grants. Tonnage and poundage. Wealth of Henry VII. Change in the king's financial position. Purveyance and preemption. Audit of accounts and appropriation of supplies

179—184

(ii) Legislation. Changes in the legislative formula. Original equality of commons and clergy. Declaration of 1322. Gradual coordination of lords and commons. *Magna concilia.* Legislation by the king's Council; ordaining and dispensing powers. Forms of bill and statute. Royal dissent. Growing bulk of statute law: character of the statutes . . . . . . **184—190**

---

¹ Maitland appended a note to the effect that these subjects would be treated 'if time serves.' Time did not serve, but the Legal History of the Reformation is briefly summarised later—pp. 506—13.

PERIOD V.

Sketch of public law at the present day (1887–8).

Preliminary.

1. Though concerned chiefly with England we must remember that England is no longer a state but is a part of the United Kingdom.

Incorporation of Wales in England. Union with Scotland; 'personal union' in 1603; legislative union in 1707; scheme of the union; the 'fundamental conditions.' Relation of Ireland to England in Middle Ages; Poynings' law; questions as to authority of English statutes and judicial power of English House of Lords; Act of 1719; Act of 1783 freeing Irish Parliament from subjection; union of 1801; articles of the union. No federation of three kingdoms, but a complete merger in the United Kingdom of Great Britain and Ireland.

Colonies and Dependencies; general principles as to laws in force in them; subjection to legislature of Great Britain and Ireland; taxation of the American colonies. Abolition of slavery and other instances of legislation for colonies. Colonial constitutions; crown colonies and self-governing colonies; wide powers of legislation given to colonial assemblies.

Distinguish institutions which are merely English, from those common to Great Britain or to the United Kingdom or to all the king's dominions; e.g. there is no English Parliament, no English nationality, but English courts of law, English domicile.

Now it becomes important to distinguish carefully rules of law from rules which however punctually observed are rules of 'positive morality,' 'customs or conventions of the constitution,' 'constitutional understandings'; these are much interwoven; reason of this, our conservatism of form . . . . 330—343

A. *The Sovereign Body.*

I. *The kingship*; statutory settlement of succession; queens; queens' husbands. 'The king never dies.' Coronation oath; declaration against Popery; king must 'join in communion with' English church. Royal Marriage Act. No legal mode of deposing king.

Infant and incapable kings; common law makes no provision; king never legally incapable; minorities provided for by occasional statutes; events of 1788 and 1810 when George III was insane; great seal used without king's assent . . . . 343—346

II. *The House of Lords.* Lords Spiritual; legislation as to the new bishoprics. Irish bishops have come and gone. Mode of appointing bishops.

Lords Temporal; increase of numbers; representatives of Scottish and Irish peers; mode of making peers . . . 347—351

III. *The House of Commons.* (1) Fluctuation in number; the Acts of Union . . . . 351—352

Historical Review. Revolution settlement; large prerogatives left to William III which he was expected to exercise. Position of Privy Council and growth of Cabinet. How the Cabinet was legally possible. Attempt (1700) to stop by statute the growth of an inner council; repealed 1705 . . . . . . 387—390

History of the great officers; chancellor, treasurer, keeper of privy seal, president of council, secretaries of state, chancellor of exchequer, admiral; treasury and admiralty in commission. These or some of these form an irregular inner council, with whose concurrence a king can exercise prerogatives; they have the seals; importance of the seals of office; no need to summon other councillors 390—394

Cabinet government of modern type slowly evolved; king ceases to be present at cabinet meeting; solidarity of cabinet slowly established (1) political unanimity, (2) common responsibility to Parliament (though not to the law), (3) submission to a 'Prime Minister.' Gradual retirement of king behind his Ministers, who are now expected to be in Parliament; he ought to take their advice, and choose them in accordance with wishes of Parliament (later, of House of Commons). All this 'extra-legal.' King's legal powers have not been diminished; on the contrary since the establishment of ministerial system have vastly grown owing to modern statutes. King's own sign manual or consent given at a (formal) meeting of Privy Council necessary for countless purposes. Other powers given to this or that high officer (cabinet minister). Distinguish prerogatives (i.e. common law powers) from statutory powers of king

394—400

Present State. (1) Necessary existence of Privy Council. (2) Its legal constitution. (3) And actual composition. (4) King may consult such privy councillors as he pleases and this is legally a meeting of the Privy Council. (5) Large powers of king in Council. (6) Necessary that king should have certain high officers (e.g. two Lords of the treasury, otherwise he cannot lawfully get the money that Parliament has voted). (7) Customary composition of the 'Cabinet' out of these high officers; as a body it has no legal powers. (8) But almost every member has large legal powers. (9) Customary composition of 'Ministry.' (10) Solidarity of Ministry, maintained by customary rules as to resignation and acceptance of office, but not recognized by law; ultimate sanction a refusal of supplies. (11) Legal tenure of high offices during king's pleasure. Choice of Prime Minister. (12) Relation of Cabinet to the Privy Council;

formal meetings of Privy Council (i.e. of king with a few ministers and sometimes a royal duke, or officer of household), at which king's powers are exercised in accordance with policy of Cabinet. (13) Many, but not all, royal powers must be exercised by Order in Council; but every (or almost every) exercise of royal power requires authentication by some high officer.   Form of an Order in Council. Classification of delegated powers   .   .   .   .   **400—407**

Of some of the high officers and their legal powers.   (1) The Lords of the Treasury, (2) the Secretaries of State; large legal powers in governing England of (Home) Secretary.   (5) Board of Trade.   (6) Local Government Board.   (7) Education Department, etc.   Illustration of actual working of government system   **407—414**

Object of illustrating these statutory powers :—Blackstone's statement that the high officers (e.g. secretaries) have few (if any) legal powers of their own, has become utterly untrue, though still repeated by text writers.   The old theory (never very true) that 'legislative power is in king and Parliament, executive power in king' now requires serious modifications.   Many powers of great importance are given by statute not to the king but to some high officer—e.g. power of making rules for the government of police given to Secretary of State.   The requisite harmony between those who have these powers is obtained by the (extra-legal) organization of the Cabinet. Our law now knows not so much 'the executive power' as many executive (better, governmental) powers.   This is obscured by talk about 'the Crown'; 'the Crown' is often a cover for ignorance; the king has powers and the high officers have powers, but the crown lies in the Tower.

Difficulties as to limits of king's prerogative powers; because instead of them new statutory powers are used; but a prerogative does not become obsolete by disuse and the clear words of a statute are necessary to take it away   .   .   .   .   .   **415—421**

C. *Classification of the Powers of the Crown.*

Shall deal with many in subsequent sections; but here (1) recall powers relating to constitution, assembling and dissolving of Parliament and turning bills into statute; (not correct to speak of king as having a 'veto'; he must actively assent; assent last refused by Anne); (2) note power of making war or peace; question as to power of ceding territory; power to make treaties, but treaty does not alter English law; illustration, extradition treaties; ambassadors; aliens; (3) appointment of offices .   .   .   .   .   **422—430**

G. *The Police System.*

H. *Social Affairs and Local Government.*

J. *The Church.*

PERIOD I.

English Public Law at the Death of Edward the First.

A. *General characteristics of English law and review of legislation.*

i. *Before* 1066.

The oldest English laws that have come down to us are those of Ethelbert, king of Kent, and we have good reason for believing that they were the first English laws that were ever put into writing. Ethelbert became king in 560 and died in 616. The laws that we have must have been published after he had received the Christian faith ; we may attribute them to the year 600 or thereabouts. Thus the history of English law may be said to begin just about the time when the history of Roman law—we will not say comes to an end, for in a certain sense it has never come to an end—but comes to a well marked period :—the reign of Ethelbert overlaps the reign of Justinian. Not only are Ethelbert's the earliest English laws, but they seem to be the earliest laws ever written in any Teutonic tongue. It is true that on the continent the German nations which overwhelmed the Roman Empire had already felt the impulse to put their laws in writing ; the *Lex Salica*, for example, the law of the Salian Franks, is considerably older than anything that we Englishmen have to show, but it is written in Latin, and for centuries Latin continued to be the legal language of the new kingdoms. But our earliest laws are written in English, or Anglo-Saxon, and until the Norman Conquest all laws were written in English, though

Latin was commonly used for many legal documents, conveyances of land and the like. Seemingly it was the contact
with Roman civilization in the form of Christianity which
raised the desire for written laws. Beda, who died in 735,
says that Ethelbert put his laws in writing ' juxta exempla
Romanorum.' It is possible that some collection of ecclesiastical canons served as a model. We do well to remember
that the oldest laws that we have, however barbarous they
may seem, are none the less Christian laws. ' God's property
and the church's 12-fold. A bishop's property 11-fold. A
priest's property 9-fold. A deacon's property 6-fold. A clerk's
property 3-fold ':—this is the first utterance of English law.
This it is well to remember, for it should prevent any glib talk
about primitive institutions : Teutonic law (for what is true of
England is true also of the continent) when it is first set in
writing has already ceased to be primitive ; it is already
Christian, and so close is the connection between law and
religion, that we may well believe that it has already undergone a great change.

We have two more sets of Kentish laws, a set from Hlothar
and Eadric, who seem to have been joint kings of the
Kentings, which we may date in 680 or thereabouts, and a set
from Wihtræd, which comes from 700 or thereabouts. Wessex
takes up the tale ; in 690 or thereabouts king Ine, with the
counsel and consent of the wise, published a set of laws.
Then we have a gap of two centuries, the greatest gap in our
legal history. The laws of Alfred, which come next in order,
may be attributed to 890 or thereabouts. They show us that
during the two last centuries there had been no great change
in the character of law or the legal structure of society.
Alfred disclaims all pretension of being an innovator, he will
but set down the best principles that he has been able to find
in the laws of Ethelbert, of Ine and of the Mercian king,
Offa. The laws of Offa of Mercia, who died in 796, have not
come down to us.

Beginning with Alfred's we now have a continuous series
of laws covering the whole of the tenth century and extending into the eleventh, laws from Edward the Elder, Æthelstan,
Edmund, Edgar, and Ethelred ; the series is brought to an end

by a long and comprehensive set of laws coming from our great Danish king, Canute. We have no one law that can be ascribed to Edward the Confessor, who, however, in after days acquired the fame of having been a great legislator.

These Anglo-Saxon laws or dooms—as they call themselves—after having lain hid in MS. for several centuries, were dug up in the sixteenth century as antiquarian curiosities. Lambard published some of them in 1568 under the title Archaionomia. In 1840 they were published for the Record Commissioners with a modern English translation under the title *Ancient Laws and Institutes of England*; they were again published in 1865 with a German translation by Dr Reinhold Schmid[1]. These editions contain, besides the dooms, a few brief statements of customary law, forms of oaths and the like. The whole material can be printed in about 160 octavo pages. We have nothing from this period that can be called a treatise on law, and we have but very few accounts of litigation. On the other hand we have a large number of private legal documents, conveyances of lands, or land books as they were called, leases, wills and so forth; these were collected and printed by J. M. Kemble in his *Codex Diplomaticus Ævi Saxonici*.

I have spoken of 'sets of laws' and have refrained from using the word code. Once or twice it would seem as if an attempt had been made to state the existing law; but in general these laws seem to be new laws, additions to the law that is already in force; we may compare them to our modern statutes and like our statutes they pre-suppose a body of existing law. I will not say that they pre-suppose 'common law,' because I think that the phrase implies law common to the whole kingdom, and how much law there was common to the whole kingdom in the days before the Norman Conquest is a very difficult question. In the twelfth century, some time after the Conquest, it was the established theory that England was or had been divided between three laws, the West-Saxon, the Mercian and the Danish. The old laws themselves notice this distinction in a casual way; but we have little means of telling how deep it went. It is highly

---

[1] The best edition is now that of F. Liebermann, *Die Gesetze der Angelsachsen*, 2 vols., Halle, 1903 and 1906.

probable, however, that a great variety of local customs was growing up in England, when the Norman Conquest checked the growth. Originally there may have been considerable differences between the laws of the various tribes of Angles, Saxons and Jutes that invaded Britain, and the Danes must have brought with them a new supply of new customs. But this would not be all; the courts of justice, as we shall presently see, were local courts, courts of shires and of hundreds; resort to any central tribunal, to the king and his wise men seems to have been rare, and this localization of justice must have engendered a variety of local laws. Law was transmitted by oral tradition and the men of one shire would know nothing and care nothing for the tradition of another shire.

The written laws issued by the king and the wise cover but a small part of the whole field of law. They deal chiefly with matters of national importance, in particular with the preservation of the peace. To keep the peace is the legislator's first object, and is not easy. The family bond is strong; an act of violence will too often lead to a blood feud, a private war. To force the injured man or the slain man's kinsfolk to accept a money composition instead of resorting to reprisals is a main aim for the law giver. Hence these dooms often take the form of tariffs—so much is to be paid for slaying an eorl, so much for a ceorl, so much for a broken finger, so much for a broken leg. Another aim is to make men mindful of their police duties, to organize them for the pursuit of robbers and murderers, to fine them if they neglect such duties. But of what we may call private law we hear little or nothing—of property, contract or the like. It is easy to ask very simple questions about inheritance and so forth to which no certain answer can be given, and like enough there were many different local customs. There was as yet no body of professional lawyers, law was not yet a subject for speculation; it was the right and duty of the free man to attend the court of his hundred and his shire, and to give his judgment there. This must not, however, lead us to believe that law was a simple affair, that it consisted of just the great primary rules of what we think natural justice. In all probability it was very complicated and very formal; exactly the right words must be used, the due solemnities must be punctually performed. An ancient popular court with a traditional law was no court of equity; forms and ceremonies and solemn poetical phrases are the things which stick in the popular memory and can be handed down from father to son.

A great deal has been done by modern scholars and a great deal more may yet be done towards reconstructing the Anglo-Saxon legal system. Besides the primary sources of information that I have mentioned, the evidence of Caesar and Tacitus, the kindred laws of other German tribes and books written in England after the Conquest may be cautiously employed for the purpose: but for reasons already given I do not think that this matter can be profitably studied by beginners; we must work backwards from the known to the unknown, from the certain to the uncertain, and when we see very confident assertions about the details of Anglo-Saxon law we shall do well to be sceptical. One point however of considerable importance seems pretty clear, namely, that the influence of Roman jurisprudence was hardly felt. There is no one passage in the dooms which betrays any knowledge of the Roman law books. German scholars are in the habit of appealing to these Anglo-Saxon dooms as to the purest monuments of pure Germanic law; they can find nothing so pure upon the continent. But we must not exaggerate this truth. Roman jurisprudence did not survive in Britain, but the traditions of Roman civilization were of great importance. The main force which made for the improvement of law was the church, and the church if it was Catholic was also Roman. Thus, for example, at a quite early time we find the Anglo-Saxons making wills. This practice we may safely say is due to the church:— the church is the great recipient of testamentary gifts. We may further say that the will is a Roman institution; that these Anglo-Saxons would not be making wills, if there had been no Rome, no world-wide Roman Empire; but of any knowledge of the Roman law of wills, even of so much of it as is contained in the Institutes we may safely acquit them. Suppose a party of English missionaries to go preaching to the heathen, they would inevitably carry with them a great deal of English law although they might be utterly unable to answer the simplest examination paper about it; for instance they would know that written wills can be made, and they would think that written wills should take effect, though they might well not know how many witnesses our law requires, or whether a will is revoked by marriage. In some such way the church, Catholic and Roman, carried with it wherever it went the tradition of the older civilization, carried with it Roman institutions, such as the will, but in a popularized and vulgarized form.

I have spoken of the Anglo-Saxon dooms as the dooms of this king and of that, but we ought to observe, even in passing, and though this matter must come before us again, that no English king takes on himself to legislate without the counsel and consent of his wise men. Legislative formulae are of great importance to us, for we have to trace the growth of that form of words in which our Queen and Parliament legislate for us to-day. Here is the preface of the laws of Wihtræd: 'In the reign of the most clement king of the Kentish men, Wihtræd, there was assembled a deliberative convention of the great men: there was Birhtwald, Archbishop of Britain, and the fore-named king, and the Bishop of Rochester, Gybmund by name; and every degree of the church of that province spoke in unison with the obedient people. There the great men decreed these dooms with the suffrages of all, and added them to the customary laws of the Kentish men';—and so on until the end of the period, until the laws of Canute: "This is the ordinance that king Canute, king of all England, and king of the Danes and Norwegians, decreed, with the counsel of his ' witan ' to the honour and behoof of himself."

ii. 1066–1154.

The Norman Conquest is an event of the utmost importance in the history of English law; still we must not suppose that English law was swept away or superseded by Norman law. We must not suppose that the Normans had any compact body of laws to bring with them. They can have had but

very little if any written law of their own ; in this respect they
were far behind the English.

Since 912 these Norsemen had held a corner of what had
once formed a part of the great Frank kingdom; but their
dukes had been practically independent, owing little more
than a nominal allegiance to the kings of the French.   They
had adopted the religion and language of the conquered, and
we must believe that what settled law there was in Normandy
was rather Frankish than Norse.   They were an aristocracy
of Scandinavian conquerors ruling over a body of Romance-
speaking Kelts.   No one of their dukes had been a great
legislator.   Such written law as there was must have already
been of great antiquity, the Lex Salica and the capitularies of
the Frankish kings, and how far these were really in force, we
cannot say.   The hold of the dukes upon their vassals had
been precarious; but probably some traditions of strong and
settled government survived from the times of the Carlovings.
For instance, that practice of summoning a body of neighbours
to swear to royal and other rights which is the germ of trial
by jury, appears in England so soon as the Normans have
conquered the country, and it can be clearly traced to the
courts of the Frankish kings.

There is no Norman law book that can be traced beyond
the very last years of the twelfth century ; there is none so old
as our own Glanvill.   Really we know very little of Norman law
as it was in the middle of the tenth century.   It cannot have
been very unlike the contemporary English law—the Frankish
capitularies are very like our English dooms, and the East of
England was full of men of Norse descent.   We must not
therefore think of William as bringing with him a novel
system of jurisprudence.

The proofs of the survival of English law can be briefly
summarised.   In the first place one of the very few legislative
acts of William the Conqueror of which we can be certain, is
that he confirmed the English laws.   'This I will and order
that all shall have and hold the law of king Edward as to
lands and all other things with these additions which I have
established for the good of the English people.'   Then again,
after the misrule of Rufus, Henry I on his accession (1100)

confirmed the English law : ' I give you back king Edward's law with those improvements whereby my father improved it by the counsel of his barons.' Secondly, these confirmations of Edward's law seem to have set several different persons on an attempt to restate what Edward's law had been. We have three collections of laws known respectively as the *Leges Edwardi Confessoris*, *Leges Willelmi Primi*, *Leges Henrici Primi*. These are apparently the work of private persons ; we cannot fix the date of any of them with any great certainty. The most valuable is the *Leges Henrici Primi*, which has been ascribed to as late a date as the reign of Henry II, but which the most recent investigations assign to that of Henry I. It is a book of some size, very obscure and disorderly. The author has borrowed freely from foreign sources, from the *Lex Salica*, the capitularies of the Frankish kings, and from collections of ecclesiastical canons—one little passage has been traced to the Theodosian Code ; but the main part of the book consists of passages from the Anglo-Saxon dooms translated into Latin, and the author evidently thinks that these are, or ought to be, still regarded as the law of the land. The picture given us by this book is that of an ancient system which has undergone a very severe shock. So the compiler of the *Leges Edwardi Confessoris* has borrowed largely from the old dooms. His book did much to popularize the notion that the Confessor was a great legislator. In after times he became the hero of many legal myths ; but as already said there is no one law that can be attributed to him. The demand for Edward's law which was conceded by William and by Henry I was not a demand for laws made by Edward ; it was merely a demand for the good old law, the law which prevailed here before England fell under the domination of the Conqueror[1]. Thirdly, Domesday book, the record of the great survey made in the years 1085-6—the greatest legal monument of the Conqueror's reign—shows us that the Norman landowners were conceived as stepping into the exact place of the English owners whose forfeited lands had come to their hands; the Norman repre-

---

[1] For a fuller account of the law-books of the Norman period see Pollock and Maitland, *History of English Law*, 2nd edn. vol. I, pp. 97—110. Stubbs, *Lectures on Early English History*, 37—133.

sents an English antecessor whose rights and duties have fallen upon him. The same conclusion is put before us by the charters of the Norman kings, the documents whereby they grant lands to their followers. It is in English words that they convey jurisdictions and privileges : the Norman lord is to have *sac* and *soc, thol* and *theam, infangthief* and *outfang-thief*,—rights which have been enjoyed by Englishmen, rights which can only be described in the English language.

At the same time it must be admitted that there has been a large infusion of Norman ideas. Occasionally, though but rarely, we can place our finger on a rule or an institution and say 'This is not English.' Such is the case with trial by battle, such is the case with the sworn inquest of neighbours which comes to be trial by jury. More often we can say that a new idea, a new theory, has been introduced from abroad, this as we shall hereafter see is the case with what we call feudalism. But still more often we can only say that a new meaning, a new importance, has been given to an old institution. The valuable thing that the Norman Conquest gives us is a strong kingship which makes for national unity.

No one of the Norman kings, among whom we will include Stephen, was a great legislator. The genuine laws of William the Conqueror are few ; of most of them we shall speak by and by. The two most important are that by which he severs the ecclesiastical jurisdiction from the temporal, and that by which he insists that every man, no matter of whom he holds his land, is the king's man and owes allegiance to the king. From the lawless Rufus we have no law. Henry the First on his accession (1100) purchases the support of the people by an important charter—important in itself, for it is a landmark in constitutional history, important also as the model for Magna Carta. Stephen also has to issue a charter, but it is of less value, for it is more general in its terms. It is as administrators rather than as legislators that William the First and Henry the First are active. The making of Domesday, the great rate book of the kingdom, is a magnificent exploit, an exploit which has no parallel in the history of Europe, an exploit only possible in a conquered country. Under Henry the First national finance becomes an orderly system, a system of which an orderly written record is kept. The sheriff's accounts for 1132 are still extant on what is called the Pipe Roll of 31 Hen. I; this is one of our most valuable sources of information. It has been casually preserved; it is not until the beginning of Henry II's reign that we get a regular series of such records. To illustrate the Norman reigns we have also a few unofficial records of litigation. These have been printed by Mr Bigelow in his *Placita Anglo-Normannica*. The genuine laws of William I and the Charter of Henry I will be found in Stubbs' *Select Charters*. The so-called *Leges Edwardi Confessoris, Willelmi Conquestoris*, and *Henrici Primi* are among the Ancient Laws published by the Record Commissioners[1].

iii. *Henry II* (1154–89), *Richard* (1189–99), *John* (1199–1216).

The reign of Henry II is of great importance in legal history; he was a great legislator and a great administrator. Some of his laws and ordinances we have, they have been casually preserved by chroniclers; others we have lost. The time had not yet come when all laws would be carefully and officially recorded. At his coronation or soon afterwards he issued a charter, confirming in general terms the liberties granted by his grandfather, Henry I. The next monument that we have of his legislation consists of the Constitutions of Clarendon issued in 1164. Henry's quarrel with Becket was the occasion of them. They deal with the border land between the temporal and the ecclesiastical jurisdictions, defining the province of the spiritual courts. During the anarchy of Stephen's reign the civil, as contrasted with the ecclesiastical, organization of society had been well-nigh dissolved—the church had gained in power as the state became feeble. Henry endeavoured to restore what he held to be the ancient boundary, to maintain the old barriers against the pretensions of the clergy. These Constitutions are the result. To some

[1] The *Leges Edwardi Confessoris* and the *Leges Henrici Primi* may now be read in Liebermann's *Gesetze der Angelsachsen*. For a full and valuable commentary on the latter document see Stubbs, *Lectures on Early English History*, 143—65. For the *Leges Willelmi* see Stubbs, *Select Charters*, p. 84.

extent Henry failed: the murder of the Archbishop shocked the world, and shocked him, and he was obliged to surrender several of the points for which he had contended. Nevertheless in the main he was successful; by the action of the royal court which now becomes steady and vigorous a line was drawn between the temporal and the spiritual spheres, though it was not exactly the line which Henry tried to define, and though for a century and more after his death there was still a debateable border land. The Canon law was just taking shape, a law for ecclesiastical matters common to all Europe. One great stage in its development is marked by the *Decretum Gratiani*, the work of a Bolognese monk, composed, it is believed, between 1139 and 1142, i.e. in our King Stephen's reign. The decrees of ecclesiastical councils, ancient and modern, genuine and spurious, were being elaborated into a great system of jurisprudence. The classical Roman law, which for some time past had become the subject of serious study, was a model for this new system. We have to remember that throughout the subsequent ages Canon law administered by ecclesiastical courts regulated for all Englishmen some of the most important affairs of life. It did not merely define the discipline of the clergy—all matters relating to marriages and to testaments fell to its share. A great deal of the ordinary private law even of our own day can only be understood if we remember this. The fundamental distinction that we draw between real and personal property, to take one example, is the abiding outcome of the division of the field of law into two departments, the secular and the spiritual. Why do we still couple 'probate' with 'divorce'? Merely because both matrimonial and testamentary causes belonged to the church courts.

We have just mentioned the revived study of Roman law. In Southern Europe Roman law had never perished: it had survived the dark ages in a barbarized and vulgarized form. Then in the eleventh century men began to turn once more to the classical texts. The new study spread rapidly. In 1143 Archbishop Theobald brought hither in his train one Vacarius, a Lombard lawyer. He lectured in England on Roman law; it seems that Stephen silenced him; Stephen had quarrelled with the clergy. But he did not labour in vain; the influence of Roman law is apparent in some of Henry's reforms, and it has even been conjectured that Henry as a youth had sat at the feet of Vacarius[1]. To the early part of his reign we owe certain measures of the utmost importance. The text of the ordinances or assizes whereby they were accomplished we have lost. An assize (*assisa*) seems to mean in the first instance a sitting, a session for example of the king and his barons; then the name is transferred to an ordinance made at such a session—we have the Assize of Clarendon, the Assize of Northampton, and, to look abroad, the Assizes of Jerusalem; then again it is transferred to any institution which is created by such an ordinance. Henry by some ordinance that we have lost took under his royal protection the possession, or seisin as it was called, of all freeholders. The vast importance of this step we shall better understand hereafter. He provided in his own court remedies for all who were disturbed in their possession. These remedies were the possessory assizes of novel disseisin and mort d'ancestor; there was a third assize of darein presentment which dealt with the right of presenting to churches. Doubtless these possessory actions were suggested by, though they were not copied from, the Roman *interdicta*. The distinction between a possessory and a proprietary action was firmly grasped; proprietary actions still went to the feudal courts while the king himself now undertook to protect possession. All this will become more intelligible hereafter. But if the thought of protecting possession or something different from property was of Roman origin, the machinery employed for this purpose was of a kind unknown to the Romans, it was, we may say, a trial by jury. This new procedure gradually spreads from these possessory actions to all other actions. Henry himself extended it to proprietary actions for land—in the form of the grand assize. The person sued might refuse trial by battle and have the question 'Who has the best right to this land?' submitted to a body of his neighbours sworn to tell the truth. More of this by and by

[1] For a fuller account see Pollock and Maitland, *History of English Law*, vol. 1, pp. 118—9.

when we come to the history of trial by jury; our present point is that by providing new remedies in his own court Henry centralized English justice. From his time onwards the importance of the local tribunals began to wane; the king's own court became ever more and more a court of first instance for all men and all causes. The consequence of this was a rapid development of law common to the whole land; local variations are gradually suppressed; we come to have a common law. This common law is enforced throughout the land by itinerant justices, professional administrators of the law, all trained in one school. During the latter part of Henry's reign the counties are habitually visited by such justices.

By the Assize of Clarendon in 1166 reissued with amendments at Northampton in 1176 Henry began a great reform of criminal procedure. Practically, we may say, he introduced the germs of trial by jury: the old modes of trial, the ordeals and the judicial combat, begin to yield before the oath of a body of witnesses. From 1181 we have the Assize of Arms which reorganizes the ancient military force and thus establishes a counterpoise to feudalism. From 1184 we have the Assize of Woodstock, which for the first time defines the king's rights in his forests. The establishment of an orderly method of taxation and the decline of feudalism as a political force are marked by the first collection of a scutage in 1159— personal service in the army may be commuted for a money payment—and by the first taxation of personal property, the Saladin tithe of 1188.

Two great books illustrate the legal activity of the reign. The *Dialogus de Scaccario* describes minutely the proceedings of the Royal Exchequer. It was written by Richard Fitz Neal, Bishop of London and Treasurer of the Exchequer. The other book is a Treatise on the Laws of England, commonly attributed to Ranulf Glanvill, who became chief justiciar (prime minister and chief justice we may say) in 1180. This book, known to lawyers as 'Glanvill,' was written in the very last years of the reign, 1187–9. It is the first of our classical text books. It gives us an accurate picture of the working of the royal court. The law contained in it is mostly land law: as yet it is with land that the royal court is chiefly concerned. We can see that Roman law has been exercising a subtle influence; the writer knows something of the Institutes and occasionally copies their words; but in the main the king's court has been working out a law for itself. It is only with the king's court that the writer deals. The customs which prevail in the local courts are, he says, so many, so various, so confused, that to put them in writing would be impossible. However by the action of the royal court a certain province has been reclaimed from local custom for common law; that province is 'land-holding' about which there are already many uniform rules. The book thus marks an important stage in the development of common law[1].

Henry's reign finished, we look onwards to Magna Carta. Under Richard the tradition of orderly administration, of the concentration of justice in the king's court was maintained. Richard himself was an absentee king; he never was in this country save on two occasions and then but for a few months; the country was governed by justiciars, by men trained in the school of Henry II. Our materials for legal history now begin to accumulate rapidly. Not that there is much that can be called legislation; but it now becomes the practice to keep an official record of the business done in the king's court. Our earliest judicial records come from the year 1194; thenceforward we have the means of knowing accurately what cases come before the king's justices and how they are decided. During the first half of John's reign the country was decently governed, though the legislative and reforming activity of his father's day has ceased. But then John casts off all restraints, becomes involved in a great quarrel with the church, in another with the baronage, unites the whole nation against him, and at length in 1215 is forced to grant the great charter.

iv. *Henry III* (1216–72).

The great charter, from whatever point of view we regard it, is of course a document of the utmost importance[2]. The

---

[1] Pollock and Maitland, *History of English Law*, vol. 1, pp. 161—7.

[2] An admirable commentary on Magna Carta was published by W. S. McKechnie in 1905.

first thing that strikes one on looking at it is that it is a very
long document—and a good deal of its importance consists in
this, that it is minute and detailed. It is intensely practical ;
it is no declaration in mere general terms of the rights of
Englishmen, still less of the rights of men ; it goes through
the grievances of the time one by one and promises redress.
It is a definite statement of law upon a great number of
miscellaneous points. In many cases, so far as we can now
judge, the law that it states is not new law ; it represents the
practice of Henry II's reign. The cry has been not that the
law should be altered, but that it should be observed, in
particular, that it should be observed by the king. Hence-
forward matters are not to be left to vague promises ; the
king's rights and their limits are to be set down in black and
white. Apart from the actual contents of the charter, which
we must notice from time to time hereafter, we ought to
notice that the issue of so long, so detailed, so practical a
document, means that there is to be a reign of law.

Now Magna Carta came to be reckoned as the beginning
of English statute law ; it was printed as the first of the
statutes of the realm. But to explain this we have first
to remark that of Magna Carta there are several editions.
We have four versions of the charter, that of 1215, that
of 1216, that of 1217 and that of 1225, and between them
there are important differences. Several clauses which were
contained in the charter of 1215 were omitted in that of 1216
and were never again inserted. It seems to have been thought
unadvisable to bind the young king to some of the more
stringent conditions to which John had been subjected. The
charter of 1217 again differs from that of 1216. Substantially
it is in 1217 that the charter takes its final form; still it is the
charter of 1225 which is the Magna Carta of all future times.
That there were four versions is a fact to be carefully remembered ; it is never enough to refer to Magna Carta without
saying which edition of it you mean. As we shall hereafter
see, the whole history of parliament might have been very
different, had not a certain clause been omitted from the
charter of 1216 and all subsequent versions—a clause defining
the common council of the realm.

Now the charter of 1225 came to be reckoned as the beginning of our statute law. This in part is due to accidents. The lawyers of the later middle ages had no occasion to go behind that instrument; the earlier ordinances so far as they had not become obsolete had worked themselves into the common law; but every word of the charter was still of great importance. So when the time for printing came Magna Carta, i.e. the charter of 1225, took its place at the beginning of the statute book. It was constantly confirmed; Henry confirmed it in 1237; Edward confirmed it in 1297—thenceforward down to the days of Henry IV it was repeatedly confirmed; Coke reckons thirty-two confirmations. It was one thing to obtain the charter, another to get it observed. It was a fetter on the king, a fetter from which a king would free himself whenever he could; and the nation has to pay money over and over again to procure a confirmation of the charter:—that the king is bound by his ancestors' concessions is a principle that is but slowly established.

Magna Carta then, however ill it may be observed, constitutes what for the time is a considerable body of definitely enacted law. From the long reign of Henry III we have not much other legislation; legislation is as yet by no means a common event. The interest of the reign is to be found not so much in the laws that are made but in the struggle for a parliament. Gradually, as we shall see hereafter, the idea of what the national assembly should be is undergoing a change; it is ceasing to be that of a feudal assembly of barons, it is becoming that of an assembly of the three estates of the realm—clergy, lords and commons; the summoning of knights of the shire in 1254, and of representative burgesses in 1264 are the great landmarks. Still there are two important legislative acts. The first of these is known as the Statute of Merton made in 1236. It contains provisions which are in force at the present moment. Among its other noticeable clauses, we come across the famous declaration of the barons that they will not change the laws of England. They have been asked by the clergy to consent that children born before the marriage of their parents should be deemed legitimate:— their reply is '*Nolumus leges Angliae mutare.*' Between this

and the next great act, there occurs the great crisis which we
know as the Barons' War. The discontent of the nation with
Henry's faithlessness and extravagance comes to a head in
1258. After stormy years of quarrelling, a leader is found in
De Montfort ; the insurgents are victorious at Lewes (14 May,
1264), and then defeated at Evesham (4 Aug. 1265). But a
great deal of what they wanted is gained. The statute made
at Marlborough in 1267, commonly called the Statute of Marlbridge, chiefly consists of a re-enactment of certain concessions
which had been obtained from the king during the revolutionary period, concessions which we know as the Provisions
of Westminster of 1259[1]. The grievances redressed in this
instance are for the most part the grievances of the smaller
landowners.

But it is not only or even chiefly by means of legislation
that English law has been growing. The reign of Henry III
is the time when a great part of the common law takes definite
shape—in particular the land law. The king's court has been
steadily at work evolving common law ; that law is carried
through the length and breadth of the kingdom by the itinerant
justices. As yet the judges have a free hand—they can invent
new remedies to meet new cases. Towards the end of the
reign indeed complaints of this grow loud. It is more and
more seen that to invent new remedies is in effect to make
new laws ; that the judges while professing to declare the law
are in reality making law ;—and it is more and more felt that
for new laws the consent of the estates of the realm, at all
events of the baronage, is necessary. But law, judge-made
law if we like to call it so, has been growing apace. The
justices have been learned men, mostly ecclesiastics, men
not ignorant of Canon Law and Roman Law. A great law
book is the outcome[2]. Henry of Bratton, or Bracton as he is
commonly called, died in 1268 ; for twenty years he had been
a judge. Sometime between 1250 and 1260 he wrote his
treatise on the Laws of England. He owed a great deal to
the work of an Italian lawyer, Azo of Bologna, and we can
plainly see that the study of Roman law has had a powerful

---

[1] Printed in Stubbs' *Select Charters*, pp. 400—5.
[2] Pollock and Maitland, *History of English Law*, vol. I, pp. 206—10.

influence on the growth of English law:—it has set men to think seriously and rationally of English law as a whole, to try to set it in order and represent it as an organized body of connected principles[1]. But the substance of Bracton's work is English. He cites no less than 500 decisions of the king's judges. English law, we see, is already becoming what we now call 'case law'—a decided case is an 'authority' which ought to be followed when a similar case arises. We see also that the growth of English law, especially land law, has been very rapid. Glanvill's book looks very small and meagre when placed beside Bracton's full and comprehensive treatise. We may indeed regard the reign of Henry III as a golden age of judge-made law: the king's court is rapidly becoming the regular court for all causes of any great importance, except those which belong to the ecclesiastical courts, and as yet the judges are not hampered by many statutes or by the jealousy of a parliament which will neither amend the law nor suffer others to amend it. Also we now hear very little of local customs deviating from the common law; as the old local courts give way before the rising power of the king's court, so local customs give way to common law. The king's court gains in power and influence because its procedure is more summary, more rational, more modern than the procedure of the local courts. Their procedure is never improved, it remains archaic; meanwhile the royal court is introducing trial by jury; all the older modes of trial are giving way before this new mode. In 1215 the Lateran Council forbad the clergy any longer to take part in the ordeal. In England the ordeal was at once abolished, and the whole province of criminal law was thus thrown open to trial by jury.

v. *Edward the First* (1272–1307).

Edward I has been called 'the English Justinian.' The suggested comparison is not very happy; it is something like a comparison between childhood and second childhood. Justinian, we may say, did his best to give final immutable form to a system which had already seen its best days, which had

---

[1] *Select Passages from the Works of Bracton and Azo*, ed. F. W. Maitland (Selden Society), 1895—with a brilliant introduction.

already become too elaborate for those who lived under it. Edward, taking the whole nation into his counsels, legislated for a nation which was only just beginning to have a great legal system of its own. Still it is very natural that we should seek some form of words which will mark the fact that Edward's reign is an unique period in the history of our law. Sir M. Hale, writing late in the seventeenth century, says that more was done in the first thirteen years of that reign to settle and establish the distributive justice of the kingdom, than in all the ages since that time put together. We can hardly say so much as this; still we may say that the legislative activity of those thirteen years remains unique until the reign of William IV; for anything with which we may compare Edward's statutes we must look forward from his day to the days of the Reform Bill. Now Hale, I think, hits the mark when he says that more was done *to settle and establish the distributive justice of the kingdom* in Edward's reign than in subsequent ages[1]. The main characteristic of Edward's statutes is that they interfere at countless points with the ordinary course of law between subject and subject. They do more than this—many clauses of the greatest importance deal with what we should call public law—but the characteristic which makes them unique is that they enter the domain of private law and make vast changes in it. For ages after Edward's day king and parliament left private law and civil procedure, criminal law and criminal procedure, pretty much to themselves. Piles of statutes are heaped up—parliament attempts to regulate all trades and all professions, to settle what dresses men may wear, what food they may eat—ordains that they must be buried in wool—but we may turn page after page of the statute book of any century from the fourteenth to the eighteenth, both inclusive, without finding any change of note made in the law of property, or the law of contract, or the law about thefts and murders, or the law as to how property may be recovered or contracts may be enforced, or the law as to how persons accused of theft or murder may be punished. Consequently in Hale's day and in Blackstone's

---

[1] *The History of the Common Law of England*, 4th edn., 1779, p. 152.

day, a lawyer whose business lay with the common affairs of
daily life had to keep the statutes of Edward I constantly in
his mind ; a few statutes of Henry VIII, of Elizabeth, of
Charles II he had to remember, but there were large tracts
of past history which had not supplied one single law which
was of any importance to him in the ordinary course of his
business. To a certain extent this is true even now, even after
the vigorous legislation of the last sixty years.   There are at
least two statutes of Edward I which you will have to know
well—the *De donis conditionalibus* and the *Quia emptores
terrarum*—these still are pillars of our land law; to pull them
away without providing some substitute would be to bring
the whole fabric to confusion.   It is well to remember the
dates of the great statutes.

> 1275.   Stat. Westminster, I.
> 1278.   Stat. Gloucester.
> 1284.   Stat. of Wales.
> 1285.   Stat. Westminster, II.
>   Stat. Winchester.
> 1290.   Stat. Westminster, III.
> 1297.   Confirmatio Cartarum, with new articles.

But Edward was not merely a great legislator, he was
a great administrator also, a great organizer.   Take any
institution that exists at the end of the Middle Ages, any
that exists in 1800—be it parliament, or privy council, or any
of the courts of law—we can trace it back through a series
of definite changes as far as Edward's reign, but if we go
back further the object that we have had in view begins to
disappear, its outlines begin to be blurred, we pass as it were
from sunlight to moonlight, we cannot be certain whether that
which we see is really that for which we have been looking.
Shall we call this court that is sitting, the King's Bench, or
the Council, or the Parliament? it seems to be all and yet to
be none of these.   In Edward's day all becomes definite—
there is the Parliament of the three estates, there is the King's
Council, there are the well known courts of law.   Words
have become appropriated—the king in parliament can make
statutes; the king in council can make ordinances ; a statute

is one thing, an ordinance is another. It is for this reason
that any one who would study the constitution of older times,
should first make certain that he knows the constitution as it
is under Edward I.

The vigorous legislation of the time has an important
consequence in checking the growth of unenacted law. Hence-
forward the common law grows much more slowly than under
Henry III. Its growth is hampered at every turn by statute—
the judges are checked by the now admitted principle that
changes in the law are not to be made without the consent
of parliament. Law continues to grow, but it can grow but
slowly; the judges are forced to have recourse to fictions and
evasions because the highroad of judge-made law has been
barred. Two law books come to us from Edward's reign,
Britton and Fleta, both written in 1290 or thereabouts; Britton in French, Fleta in Latin; both are little better than poor
epitomes of Bracton's work, epitomes which take notice of
the changes introduced by the great statutes. We learn from
them an important fact:—it is plain that English lawyers are
no longer studying Roman law. There can be no doubt that
under Henry III Roman law was slowly gaining ground in
England. To any further Romanization of English law, a
stop was put by Edward's legislation. The whole field of law
was now so much covered by statute, that the study of Roman
law had become useless. About the same time, we no longer
find ecclesiastics sitting in the royal courts; Bracton was an
ecclesiastic, an archdeacon, and the great judges whose decisions he cites were ecclesiastics—Martin Pateshull became
Dean of St Paul's, William Raleigh became Bishop of Winchester. But the opinion steadily grew among the clergy that
ecclesiastics should not sit in lay tribunals. The consequence
is that from the beginning of Edward's reign, English law
becomes always more insular, and English lawyers become
more and more utterly ignorant of any law but their own.
Thus English law was saved from Romanism; by this we
lost much—but we gained much also. The loss, we may say,
was juristic; if our lawyers had known more of Roman law,
our law—in particular our land law—would never have become
the unprincipled labyrinth that it became;—the gain, we

may say, was constitutional, was political:—Roman law here as elsewhere would sooner or later have brought absolutism in its train. It should be added that the rapid growth of the common law under Henry III was connected both as cause and as effect with the growth of a large class of English lawyers. From the beginning of Edward's reign, it is a large and a powerful class—and it is from among the members of this class that the king chooses his judges. And now a new form of legal literature appears. From 1292 we get our first law report—the first of the Year Books. The Year Books are reports of discussions which took place in court—of the arguments of counsel and the opinions of the judges. The series extends from Edward I to Henry VIII. Together with the text-books of Glanvill, Bracton, Britton and Fleta, they are the great source of all our information as to the common law and not only are they a source of information, but the cases reported in them were regarded as authorities—indeed they are so regarded even at the present day—if an occasion arises upon which they could be appropriately cited:—but this of course seldom happens, for the whole field of common law is pretty well covered by much more modern authorities. Still we note that from the middle of the thirteenth century our common law has been case law, that from 1292 onwards we have law reports, that from 1194 onwards we have plea-rolls[1].

This term common law, which we have been using, needs some explanation. I think that it comes into use in or shortly after the reign of Edward the First. The word 'common' of course is not opposed to 'uncommon': rather it means 'general,' and the contrast to common law is special law. Common law is in the first place unenacted law; thus it is distinguished from statutes and ordinances. In the second place, it is common to the whole land; thus it is distinguished from local customs. In the third place, it is the law of the temporal courts; thus it is distinguished from ecclesiastical

---

[1] Five volumes of the Year Books of Edward I, and thirteen volumes of the Year Books of Edward III, are published in the Rolls Series. The Selden Society has undertaken the publication of the Year Books of Edward II. The first three volumes, edited by Maitland, have already appeared, with introductions of the greatest interest and importance.

law, the law of the Courts Christian, courts which throughout the Middle Ages take cognisance of many matters which we should consider temporal matters—in particular marriages and testaments. Common law is in theory traditional law—that which has always been law and still is law, in so far as it has not been overridden by statute or ordinance. In older ages, while the local courts were still powerful, law was really preserved by oral tradition among the free men who sat as judges in these courts. In the twelfth and thirteenth century as the king's court throws open its doors wider and wider for more and more business, the knowledge of the law becomes more and more the possession of a learned class of professional lawyers, in particular of the king's justices. Already in John's reign they claim to be *juris periti*. More and more common law is gradually evolved as ever new cases arise; but the judges are not conceived as making new law—they have no right or power to do that—rather they are but declaring what has always been law.

B. *The Land-System.*

It may seem strange that we begin our survey of public law by examining the system of landed property, for proprietary rights we may say are clearly a topic of private law. That is true in our own day, though even now it is impossible for us fully to understand our modern public law unless we know something of our law of property:—for instance the right to vote in elections for members of Parliament is clearly a right given by public law, but directly we ask, Who have this right?—we have to speak of freeholders, copyholders, leaseholders and so forth, to use terms which have no meaning to those who do not know some little of our law of landed property. But if this be true of our own day, it is far truer of the Middle Ages. What is meant by the word 'feudalism' we shall understand more fully hereafter—but here we may describe 'feudalism' as a state of society in which all or a great part of public rights and duties are inextricably interwoven with the tenure of land, in which the whole governmental system—financial, military, judicial—is part of the law of private property. I do not mean that feudalism so complete as this is ever found—much less that we find it in England,—we shall see that in this country the feudal movement was checked at an early date:—but still it is utterly impossible to speak of our medieval constitution except in terms of our medieval land law. Let us then briefly survey the land law of Edward I's time—briefly, and having regard to its public importance; when you come to study real property law you will have to examine the same system more closely and from another point of view[1].

We must start with this:—All land is held of the king. The person who has the right to live on the land and to cultivate it, is a tenant. He holds that land of some one who is his lord. If that some one be the king, then the tenant is one of the king's tenants in chief, or tenants in capite. But between the tenant and the king there may stand many persons; A may hold the land of B, who holds of C, who holds of D, and so forth until we come to Z who holds immediately of the king, who is one of the king's tenants in capite. Each of the persons who stands between A and the king is a mesne, i.e. intermediate, lord; as regards those who stand below him he is lord, as regards those who stand above him he is tenant. Thus take a short series; A holds of B and B holds of the king; here B is lord of A, but tenant of the king.

Such is the actual arrangement. With it is connected the theory that at some past time all lands were the king's to do what he liked with. He gave land to Z (one of his great barons) and his heirs in return for certain services, Z then gave part of it to Y, Y to X, and so on until we come to the lowest tenant, to A who now has the right to enjoy the land and take the fruits thereof. This process of creating new tenancies is called subinfeudation. At the moment at which we have placed ourselves, that of Edward's death in 1307, a new measure has very lately been taken to put a stop to this process,—the statute *Quia emptores terrarum* passed in 1290:

[1] The subject of this section is treated with greater fullness in the *History of English Law*, vol. I, pp. 229—406.

more of this hereafter.   In passing let us warn ourselves not
to accept this legal theory that there was a time when all
land was the king's to do what he liked with as describing a
historical truth ; at present we note that it has become the
theory.   No one therefore, save the king, has land that he
does not hold of some one else—every other person has
some superior, some lord : the formula is *tenet terram illam
de B.*

Now in every case the tenant in respect of the land owes
some service to the lord—this in theory is the return he makes
to his lord for the land—he holds by some tenure (*tenura*) by
some mode of holding.   Gradually these tenures have been
classified :—we may reckon six tenures, (1) frankalmoign,
(2) knight service, (3) grand serjeanty, (4) petty serjeanty,
(5) free socage, (6) villeinage.

(1)   I mention frankalmoign first ; it can be very briefly
dismissed, but is instructive as showing how far the theory of
tenure has been pressed.   Sometimes religious bodies and
religious persons, monasteries, bishops, parsons, hold land for
which they do no earthly service to the lord.   They are said to
hold by way of free alms, free charity, *per liberam elemosynam*,
in frankalmoign.   The theory of tenure however is saved by
the doctrine that they owe spiritual service, that they are
bound to pray for the soul of the donor who has given them
this land, and this duty can be enforced by spiritual censures
in the ecclesiastical courts.   Do not think that a monastery
or a bishop can hold by no other than this easy tenure ; on
the contrary, though a large part of England is held by
ecclesiastics, tenure in frankalmoign is somewhat exceptional
—the ecclesiastics often hold by military service.

(2)   By far the greater part of England is held of the king
by military service, by knight service ; in some way or another
it has come to be mapped out in knight's fees.   We cannot
say that a particular acreage of land or land of a particular
value constitutes a knight's fee (*feodum militis*); but it seems
as if there had been a vague theory that a knight's fee should
normally be worth £20 a year or thereabouts.   But in Edward's
day we can say, that whether owing to some general rule or to
bargains made in each particular case, it has become settled

that this particular territory owes the service of one knight, that it is *feodum militis*, while another has not been split into single knight's fees but owes altogether the service of five or of ten knights.

The service due from a single knight's fee is that of one fully armed horseman to serve in the king's army for 40 days in the year in time of war. We notice however that there has been constant quarrelling between king and barons as to the definition of this service. Can the tenant be forced to serve in foreign parts? As a matter of fact they have done so: but in 1213 they refused to follow John to France and so forced on the grant of the Charter, and very lately, in 1297, they have refused to follow Edward to France and so forced on the confirmation of the Charter. That they are obliged to serve against the Scots and the Welsh is not doubted.

The tenant by knight's service, whether he holds of the king or of some mesne lord must do homage to his lord and must swear fealty. The act of homage is this—the tenant kneels before his lord and holds his hands between the hands of his lord, and says, 'I become your man from this day forward of life and limb and of earthly worship, and unto you shall be true and faithful and bear to you faith for the tenements that I hold of you'—then, if the lord be not the king, he adds these noteworthy words, 'saving the faith that I owe to the king.' Then the lord kisses his man. Fealty is sworn thus, with hand on book, 'Hear this my lord that I shall be faithful and true unto you and faith to you shall bear for the lands that I hold of you, and that I shall lawfully do to you the customs and services which I ought to do, so help me God and his saints.' The act of homage constitutes an extremely sacred bond between lord and man—the bond of fealty is not so close—and an oath of fealty must be sworn in many cases in which homage need not be done. The nature of these bonds we shall consider at large by and by—happily for England they became rather moral than legal bonds.

As a consequence of holding by knight's service the tenant is subject to many burdens which we know as the incidents of military tenure: it is usual to reckon seven; each of them has its own history.

(*a*) Aids. There has been a doctrine of vague extent that the lord can legitimately demand aid (*auxilium*) from his tenant when he is in need of money. The aid has been considered as a free-will offering, but one which ought not to be refused when the demand is reasonable. Gradually the demand has been limited by law. In the charter of 1215 John was compelled to promise that he would exact no aid without the common counsel of the realm save in three cases, namely in order to make his eldest son a knight, in order to marry his eldest daughter, and in order to redeem his body from captivity and then only a reasonable aid. The same restriction was placed upon the mesne lords. These clauses however were omitted from a charter of 1216. In 1297 however Edward I was obliged to promise that he would take no aids save by the common consent of the realm, saving the ancient aids. In 1275 (St. West. I. c. 36) the amount of aid for knighting the lord's son or marrying his daughter was fixed at 20 shillings for the knight's fee, and the same sum for every estate in socage of £20 annual value.

(*b*) If the tenant in knight service having an inheritable estate died leaving an heir of full age, that heir owed a relief for his land—*relevium*—a sum due on his taking up the fallen inheritance—*relevat hereditatem*. This has been a sore point of contention between the king and his barons, between them and their vassals ;—the lord has been in the habit of getting what he can on such an occasion, even of forcing the heir to buy the land at nearly its full price. Gradually the law has become more definite. The relief for the knight's fee is 100 shillings, but the holder of a barony (a term to be explained hereafter) pays £100; the socager pays one year's rent. This was already the law of Glanvill's time ; it was confirmed by the charter (1215, c. 2).

But (*c*) the lords have contended for a certain or uncertain right of holding the land of the dead tenant until the heir shall offer homage and pay relief :—this right is that of taking the first seisin after the tenant's death, the right of primer seisin. In this case law has gone against the lords; it lis established by the Statute of Marlborough (1267, c. 16) that the lord may not seize the land, he may but make a formal entry upon it in order to preserve evidence of his lordship. Law, however, has not had the same measure for the king as for other lords—the king has a right of primer seisin—he may keep the heir of his tenant out for a year—or what comes to the same thing, he can in addition to the relief extort one year's profit of the land.

(*d*) On the other hand there are rights of the lord which have steadily grown and which the law has now sanctioned. If the heir of the military tenant is under the age of twenty-one, being male, or fourteen, being female, the lord is entitled to wardship—to wardship of the body of his tenant, to wardship of the land also. This means that he can enjoy the lands for his own profit until the boy attains twenty-one or the girl fourteen. He is bound to maintain the child and he must not commit waste, but within these limits he may do what he likes with the land and take the profits to his own use—and this profitable right is a vendible commodity: wardships are freely bought and sold. Here again we find that the king has peculiar rights—prerogative rights they are called. Generally, if the child holds of two lords, each lord gets the wardship of those lands that are holden of him; but if one lord be the king, then he gets a wardship of all the lands, of whomsoever they be holden.

(*e*) Connected with the right of wardship is the right of marriage. This we can see has steadily grown as we trace it from the charter of Henry I to the charters of John and Henry III and the Statute of Merton (1236). It comes to this, that the lord can dispose of the ward's marriage, can sell his ward in marriage. The only limit to this is that the match must be an equal one; the ward is not to be disparaged, married to one who is not his or her peer. At first apparently all that the lord claims is that his female tenant shall not marry without his consent—a demand which is reasonable enough while the military tenures are great realities:—my female tenant must not carry the land which she holds of me to a husband who is my enemy. But the right has grown far beyond this reason:—it is now extended to males as well as females, and the marriage of every ward is a vendible commodity.

(*f*) Fines on alienation. Here the law has on the whole taken the side of the tenant. We can produce no text of English law which says that the leave of the lord is necessary to an alienation by the tenant. The tenant cannot indeed compel his lord to accept a new tenant in his place ; but he can create a new tenancy ; B holds of A, B can give the land to C to hold of him, B. We do not find it laid down that the consent of A was necessary for this ; the royal judges, like all lawyers, seem to have favoured free alienation :—but we do find that the consent of the lords is commonly asked, and we do find that the view taken by the lords is that their consent is necessary. This is a battle-field during the thirteenth century ; the greater lords are opposed to free alienation, the tenants wish for it ; the royal judges take the side of the tenants, except against the king. In 1290 a definite settlement is arrived at by the famous *Quia emptores terrarum.* That statute you must some day study as part of our existing law of real property. What it does is roughly speaking this, it concedes free alienation to all except the king's tenants in chief ; on the other hand it puts a final stop to the process of subinfeudation ; B holds of A, B wants to sell his land to C— he wants to convey it to C and his heirs ; he can do so without A's consent, but C is not to hold of B, he is to hold of A. A tenant may substitute another person in his place—but the creation of a new tenure is impossible—or rather, I must be exact though the words may be unintelligible to you—the creation of a new tenure in fee simple is impossible. The liberty of alienation however is not yet conceded to the king's tenants in chief ; the law has one measure for the king another for other lords. If one of the tenants in capite alienates without the king's consent, this is a forfeiture of the land ; it is Edward the Third's day before this severity was relaxed and a fine of one-third of the yearly value of the land took the place of the forfeiture.

(*g*) Escheat. If the tenant died without an heir the land escheated, that is, fell back to the lord—it became his to do what he pleased with. As you have been hitherto reading more Roman than English law, I had better say that the English heir was and is to this day a very different person from the Roman *haeres*. Before the Conquest the church had introduced the testament or last will, and lands or at all events some lands as well as goods could be given by will. But at the Conquest the will of lands disappears. The maxim is laid down in Glanvill—Only God can make an heir, not man. The English heir therefore never succeeds under a will. This is so even at the present day, though since the Restoration, 1660, lands have been freely alienable by will. To this day the heir is a person who succeeds on an intestacy—he who takes land under a will is a devisee: but at the time of which we are speaking, Edward I's day, the will of lands was still in the distant future. But a failure of heirs is not the only cause for an escheat, if the tenant commits any of those grave crimes that are known as felonies—there is an escheat; he loses the land, no heir of his can succeed him, the lord takes the land for good and all.

Such in brief were the incidents of tenure by knight's service.

(3) Grand serjeanty (*magna serjeantia*) differed but little from this. The tenant instead of being bound to serve as a knight for forty days in the wars, was bound to do some peculiar service for the king—to carry his banner, or his sword, to lead the vanguard or the rear guard, to be his champion, the constable or marshall of his army, or the like. In almost all respects this tenure had all those incidents which we have just described.

(4) Tenure in petty serjeanty came in after-time to be regarded as but a variation of tenure in socage. Its characteristic was the obligation to provide the king with warlike implements, a sword, a lance, or the like. It maintains its place in the catalogue of tenures merely because it was but slowly that the line was drawn between petty serjeanty and grand serjeanty. It was established by Magna Carta that where the service though of a warlike nature consisted merely in providing weapons, and not in fighting—then wardship and marriage were not due— hence a line was drawn between the grand serjeanties which in all important respects were like knight service—and the petty serjeanties which were almost the same as socage[1].

[1] For Maitland's later views on serjeanties see *History of English Law*, vol. I, pp. 282—90. 'The central notion seems what we may call servantship...the tenant by serjeanty is steward, marshal, constable, chamberlain, usher, cook, forester, falconer, dog-keeper, messenger, esquire; he is more or less of a menial servant.'

(5)   Postponing to a more convenient season the etymology
of the term socage, we find that tenure in free socage is a
tenure by some fixed service which is not military : that is
not the full explanation, but will serve for the present.   The
service of the socager generally consists of a rent payable
either in money or in agricultural produce ; very often he is
also bound to do a certain amount of ploughing for his lord—
to plough three days a year or the like :—this is so common
that lawyers already believe, what is not historically true, that
the term socage is connected with the word sock, which means
a ploughshare.   Now socage tenure involved some, but not
all, of those burdens of which we have lately spoken—the
socager swore the oath of fealty, though he did not usually do
homage ; he had to pay the three aids—the aid for knighting
the lord's son, marrying the lord's daughter, redeeming the
lord from captivity—in the first two of these cases he paid
20 shillings for land of the annual value of £20 ; by way
of relief he paid one year's rent ; if he held of the king in
chief, the king was entitled to a primer seisin ; if he held of
the king in chief he could not alienate without license ; his
land escheated to the lord if he died without an heir or
committed felony.   On the other hand socage tenure did not
involve the two worst burdens of feudalism ; the wardship and
marriage of the socager's heir did not belong to the lord.   If
he left an heir under fourteen the next relative to whom the
land could not descend was guardian, but when the heir
attained fourteen (that was full age as regards socage) the
guardian had to account to him for the profits of the land.

We must not be led into speaking as though the distinctions between these various kinds of tenures were distinctions
between various kinds of lands.   The self-same piece of land
might at one and the same time be held by knight service or
by socage.   For instance A has held of the king by military
service, but he has enfeoffed B to hold of him in socage ; the
military service due from A to the king is a burden on the
land ; if A will not perform it, then a distress can be made on
the land and B's goods may be taken ; but as between A and
B, it is A not B who is bound to do the service, or to pay the
scutage ; A must indemnify B, if the king compels B to pay

the scutage; as between A and B, B is only bound to pay the fixed rent, to do the ploughing or the like. By far the greater part of the lands of England are, I take it, held of the king by military service; to find land held immediately of the king by socage tenure is comparatively rare, but there seem to be considerable tracts which are held of the king by frank-almoign. The greater part of England therefore is held by military service, but then a great part of this is held by socage—the tenants in chief hold by knight's service, but many of their sub-tenants hold by socage. Such is the state of things in Edward's day; but as we have lately seen, in 1290 a stop was put to the process of subinfeudation—a new tenure of an estate in fee simple can no longer be created—no new rungs can be put into the feudal ladder. How far the process had really gone, it is difficult to say, but I think that pretty often the lords and tenants stood three or four deep—we may pretty often find that D holds of C who holds of B who holds of A who holds of the king. By means of subinfeudation free socage has become a far commoner tenure than it was in the twelfth century; the lords have found it profitable to grant out their lands in return for fixed rents.

One other remark of great importance must be made—military service is due to none but the king; this it is which makes English feudalism a very different thing from French feudalism. Suppose that A, a great lord, held 10 knight's fees of the king, he might grant one of these to B and stipulate that B should do the military service due from that fee: B then will hold of A by military service; if B neglects to do the service, then A has legal means of redress: B is bound to A to do the service; still the service is due not to A, but to the king; it is service to be done for the king in the national army; it is not service to be done for A in A's quarrels. This makes English feudalism a very different thing from continental feudalism: elsewhere we may find the tenant bound to fight for his lord in his lord's quarrels, bound even to fight for his immediate lord against that lord's lord; here in England, however strong may be the feeling that this ought to be so, that the man is bound to espouse his lord's quarrels, still that feeling is not represented by law—rather it is repressed by law :—the only quarrel in which any one is bound to fight is the king's quarrel, the only force in which any one is bound to serve is the king's force; our kings have been powerful enough to bring about this very desirable result.

(6) Villeinage. A very large part of England, by whatever tenure it may be holden of the king, is ultimately held in villeinage. The word *villenagium* is used in what seems to us a confusing way to cover two different things, first a personal status and secondly a tenure. There is a very large class of persons who are personally unfree. The technical term whereby they are described is *nativi*, which means born serfs or bondsmen—thus A is the *nativus* of B; but not unfrequently they are spoken of as *servi* and as *villani*. They are unfree, but we must not call them slaves; they are not rightless; the law does not treat them as things, it treats them as persons; still they are unfree; they must not leave their lord's land; if they do he may recapture them and bring them back; the law will aid him in this; it gives him an action for recovering the body of his *nativus*, an action *de nativo habendo*. Generally, if not always, the *nativus* has land which he holds in villeinage, which he holds by villein services. He has land, but how far he can be said to have a right in this land is a difficult question. One thing is clear— the king's courts do not protect that right against his lord. If the lord capriciously chooses to eject him, he has no remedy against his lord in the king's courts. We find however that he is conceived to hold his land by perfectly definite services and that this is not merely the theory of the villeins, but the theory of the lords also. This we learn from the surveys which religious houses made of their manors. In such surveys we find thousands of entries of this kind—A.B. holds a virgate of land; for this he is bound to do certain services, e.g. he is bound to work three days a week on the lord's land, and five days a week in autumn; what is to be deemed a day's work is often minutely defined—thus, if he be set to thrash, he must thrash such and such a quantity; if he be set to ditch, he must ditch so many yards in a day—in general everything is very definitely expressed. How far he can be said to be protected in his holding so long as he does these his due

services is a question which we cannot raise without first speaking of the manorial courts; but as already said, the king's courts give him no protection against his lord. Then very generally we find it said that he is prohibited from selling his ox or his horse without the lord's leave, also that he may not give his daughter in marriage without the lord's leave, or at all events may not give her in marriage outside the manor; in many cases however the sum that he must pay for the lord's license is a fixed sum. The king's courts however do not protect his movable goods against his lord, any more than they protect his land against his lord: the lord may at any time seize the chattels of his *nativi*. Again the lord may imprison the body of his *nativus*; the king's courts give no redress; but against maiming and death at the lord's hand they give protection; the life and limb of every man, be he free or unfree, are in the king's protection; to slay or to maim him is a felony. Also it is becoming more and more the theory and the fact that the king's courts will protect the *nativus*, his body, his goods, and his lands against every one except his lord. The status of the *nativus* is coming to be more and more regarded as a mere relationship between him and his lord, a relationship which in no wise concerns third persons, less and less as a status thrust upon the *nativus* by public law which stamps him as a person who has but imperfect rights.

But again, we find that a man may well hold land in villeinage and yet be no *nativus*. He is a free man, he may leave the land if he pleases, he cannot be captured and brought back, his chattels are fully his own, the lord may not seize them. Bracton often puts it thus: '*tenementum non mutat statum*'—the tenure of villeinage is different from the status of villeinage—this man holds land in villeinage, but personally he is no villein. However such a tenant in villeinage has as yet no right in the land which the royal courts will protect against the lord. Their doctrine is that the land is the lord's land, that the tenant is merely a tenant at the lord's will, whom the lord can at any time eject. On the other hand, as already said, we find it conceived, even by the lords themselves, that their *tenentes in villenagio*, even their *nativi*, held by perfectly definite services—so many day's work per week, ploughings, harrowings, reapings and so forth to be done on the lord's own demesne lands. We find too that these *tenentes in villenagio* do in fact alienate their lands; they cannot do this without the lord's license; they yield up, surrender the land into the lord's hand, who then grants it to the new tenant. We find also that at least in some cases the tenant's rights are considered as inheritable; thus we find it said in the manorial surveys that the heir of the tenant in villeinage must pay this or that sum to the lord for leave to enter on his ancestor's land. How far such a tenant can be said to have any legal right in his land as against his lord we cannot decide at present; he certainly seems to be conceived as having what we should call a moral right; but the first thing to understand is that he has no right in the land as against his lord that is protected by the royal courts. This is so in the days of Edward the First and for a long century afterwards[1].

It now becomes possible to fix the meaning of a term that we shall have often to use, viz. a *freeholder*. Ever since the days of Henry the Second the king's own courts have afforded protection to both the possession and the property which any one has in a *liberum tenementum*. Gradually a great mass of law has been developed as to the meaning of this term. In the first place it excludes the tenants in villeinage—*liberum tenementum* is contrasted with *villanum tenementum*. If a person holds in frankalmoign, by knight's service, by grand or petty serjeanty, or in free socage, he has a freehold, and is a freeholder; not so he who holds in villeinage. What exactly was the test which originally distinguished free socage from villeinage, it is now very difficult to see. Any uncertainty in the agricultural service seems to have been enough to stamp the tenure as villein[2]. The tenant in free socage was often bound to do a certain amount of ploughing on the lord's land; but generally he owed no week work, was not bound to work for the lord so many days in every week as the tenant in villeinage commonly was. When once the line was drawn,

---

[1] For an elaborate discussion on the status of the villein, *History of English Law*, vol. I, pp. 412—32.

[2] The test of villeinage is discussed by Vinogradoff, *Economic Journal*, vol. X (1901), p. 308 ff.

however, it was of the utmost importance; once decided that the tenure was freehold, it was perfectly protected in the king's own court; once decided that it was villein tenure, then the king's courts treated it as though it were merely a tenancy at the lord's will. *Villanum tenementum* is thus the first contrast to *liberum tenementum.*

But the evolution of new forms of landholding provided a new contrast. Since the Norman Conquest a practice had grown up of letting land for terms of years, in general short terms. The lessee, 'the termor,' who had such a lease was at first considered as having no right in the land, no real right, as we should say no right *in rem*. He had merely a personal right good against his lessor—his lessor had contracted that he, paying his rent, should enjoy the land for a term of years; on that contract he had an action against his lessor. If a stranger ejected him, he had no action against that stranger; the lessor might sue the stranger for entering *his* (the lessor's) land; but the lessee had only an action on the contract against his lord. While such was the case the lessee was not conceived to have *liberum tenementum*, he had no *tenementum* at all; he had but a right *in personam*; he was no freeholder. The word freeholder therefore excluded not only the tenant in villeinage, but also the termor, the person who had a right to enjoy land limited to some fixed term of years. Before the reign of Edward the First, the situation had been greatly changed; the king's court had by degrees given a large, though not as yet a complete, measure of protection to the termor against the world at large: it had in fact turned the *jus in personam* into a *jus in rem*. Nevertheless the old nomenclature with its important political consequences was still maintained—the termor was no freeholder, he had no place in the county court, and therefore no vote in the election of knights of the shire—no, not until 1832. A freeholder must hold land at least for the life of himself or of some other person. He may have, as the phrase goes, a greater estate than this, he may have an inheritable estate, one which will descend to his heirs, or to a limited class of heirs, the heirs of his body—but this at least he must have. He who holds for a fixed term of years however long, a thousand years or more, is no freeholder.

The distinction gets emphasized in another way. Whatever may have been the law or various local customs of inheritance which prevailed here before the Conquest, we may be fairly certain that primogeniture was unknown; that if a man left several sons, his whole property, land and chattels, were *as a general rule* divided among them all—though it is very probable that land, especially land held on servile conditions, often went to the youngest son. Primogeniture creeps in with the Conquest: very gradually a set of rules of inheritance giving the whole land to the eldest male whenever there are males of equal degree was elaborated, and very slowly it was extended from the lands of military tenants to other lands: that the land of the military tenant should not be divisible is very intelligible. Before the end of Edward the First's reign the primogenitary rules had been extended to socage tenure—this had been a slow process, but gradually it had become established that he who contended that the inheritance should be divided among all males of equal degree had to prove his case. Other systems endured merely as local customs: in Kent the inheritance was still heritable among sons, and very commonly a tenement held in villeinage descended to the youngest son[1]. But the gradual introduction of primogeniture, together with the principle that lands could not be left by will and the activity of the ecclesiastical courts combined to set a deep gulf between what came to be called real and what came to be called personal property. An explanation of these two terms would take us too far afield—but seize this principle, that for freehold and for chattels there came to be two distinct systems of succession. The freehold (with which no ecclesiastical court may meddle) descends to the heir, and only by force of some local custom can it be the subject of a last will. The chattels can be left by will; of all testamentary matters the ecclesiastical courts have cognizance; if there is an intestacy the heir does not get the chattels; they are distributed by the ecclesiastical courts. But further the term of years, the right of a lessee to whom land has been let for a term of years, is for this purpose a chattel; it is assimi-

---

[1] For the custom of Borough English, as it was called, see *History of English Law*, vol. I, p. 647, and vol. II, pp. 279—80.

lated to movable goods; it is a new creation, and the ecclesiastical courts have successfully asserted that it can be disposed of by will—the term of years is a chattel and personal property. All this you will of course have to study much more thoroughly hereafter. The distinction between real and personal property is still an elementary distinction of profound importance at the present day. But it was necessary to say some little about it, for the word freeholder must be constantly in our mouths.

In the Middle Ages land law is the basis of all public law. You will already have observed how the system of tenure provides the king with an army and with a revenue—men owe military service by reason of tenure, they pay aids, reliefs, scutages by reason of tenure, by reason of tenure the king gets profitable wardships, and marriages, and escheats—he is the supreme and ultimate landlord. But the influence of tenure does not stop here; the judicial system is influenced by tenure, the parliamentary system is influenced by tenure. Every lord claims a right to hold a court of and for his tenants. This is an important principle, but we can hardly speak of its working until we have spoken of the courts older than feudalism—the courts of the shire and the hundred which continue to exist during the feudal period.

Now if we suppose a quite perfect feudal arrangement, then all courts, all judicial and governmental organization, should be determined by tenure. The king as highest landlord should have a court of his tenants in chief; they would sit as judges therein, and they again would be the king's advisers; it would be with their counsel and consent that the king would impose taxes and make laws. Then again each of these tenants in chief would have his court of sub-vassals, who again would have their courts. Further the sole connection between the king and these sub-vassals would be a mediate connection, only through their lord would he control them. C who held of B who held of A who held of the king would not be the king's man or have any place in a court or assembly over which the king presided; he would not even be A's man; he would never meet or sit along with A's tenants on a footing of legal equality; he would owe no fealty or homage to any one but his immediate lord, namely, B. This ideal of a perfectly feudalized society was pretty fully realized in France; no immediate bond bound the vassals of the Duke of Normandy to the king of the French; they were bound to the Duke, and the Duke to the king. Happily this ideal is but very imperfectly realized in England, this we must constantly notice; but we ought carefully to keep this ideal in mind, for there have been powerful forces making for its realization and they have had to be met not only by laws, but also by the sword.

C. *Divisions of the Realm and Local Government.*

(i) England is divided into counties or shires. For the most part these units are already of very ancient date; though some of the Northern counties, in particular Lancashire, have been formed since the Norman Conquest. Already in Edward's day the arrangement is in most respects that which at present exists. Many, perhaps most, of these divisions are in their origin not divisions into which a kingdom of England has been carved, but are units which once were independent states but have coalesced to form the kingdom of England; Kent, Sussex, Essex, Middlesex, Surrey have had kings of their own; Norfolk and Suffolk are the settlements of North Folk and South Folk. As these old states by conquest fall together into one great state, some part of their primitive organization is left to them; to use a modern phrase, they are mediatized; in some cases the old dynasty of kings became for a while a dynasty of under-kings, *sub-reguli*. In other cases the shire may have been a division carved out of a larger whole, and organized on the model of one of these mediatized kingdoms. At any rate before the Norman Conquest each shire had its shire moot, which was a court of justice and to some extent also a governmental assembly for the shire. In it the ealdorman had presided. The ealdorman had been a national officer appointed by the king and the national assembly. The title ealdorman had, however, been giving way to that of eorl, and the office had been tending to become a hereditary office.

Every shire had by no means necessarily an ealdorman or eorl to itself; Canute had divided the kingdom into four great earldoms; but down to the time of the Conquest, this officer had been the chief man of every shire that lay within its territory, the president of its court, the leader of its forces. He received a third part of the profits arising from the shire moot, the third penny of the county, as it was afterwards called. Along with the ealdorman in the shire moot, the bishop had sat; it was not until after the Norman Conquest that a firm line was drawn between temporal and ecclesiastical causes, the two had been heard together in the ancient courts. But from a very remote period, the shire had had another officer, namely the shire reeve, or as we say, sheriff. He seems from the first to have been a royal officer, appointed by the king, and representing the royal authority. The ealdorman seems to have been considered as a national leader, the sheriff as a royal steward or bailiff, chiefly concerned with the protection of the king's interests. The shire moot had seemingly been held but twice in the year. There seems little doubt that originally every freeman of the shire had been entitled and bound to attend it, but long before the Norman Conquest this right and duty seems to have been confined to the free land-owners. The process whereby land-owning had taken the place of personal freedom as a political qualification will come before us hereafter, but we had better at once make a remark which is necessary if we are to understand medieval history. The right of attending courts and assemblies was not a coveted right; we must think of it rather as a burdensome duty, a duty which men will evade if they possibly can. We see the class of landless freemen getting gradually excluded from all participation in public business; but where we are apt to see a disfranchising process, a deprivation of political rights, they saw only a relief from public burdens, the burden of attending court or being fined for non-attendance.

Now the Norman Conquest had not destroyed the shire or the shire moot. There was a change of names. The French district which seemed most analogous to the English shire was the *comitatus*, the county, the district which had been subject to the *comes* or count, and so the English shire became a county. And the earl became in Latin documents, the *comes*. But this title or dignity was but seldom conferred by William or by his sons, and the earl of Norman times has about him but little of the character of a public officer or the ruler of a province. The dignity was hereditary, though the heir did not acquire full possession of it until he was invested by the king, until he was girt with the sword of the county. He like his English predecessor was entitled to the third penny of the county; but for the rest he seems from the Conquest onwards to be rather a great nobleman, who usually holds large lands in the shire, than a public officer. To this the palatine earldoms are exceptions. The earl of Chester becomes almost a sovereign prince, so does the bishop of Durham; but on the whole the Norman kings seem to have seen the danger of allowing official power and jurisdiction to become hereditary in the houses of the great feudatories :— it was not by means of earls, but by means of sheriffs, that they will govern the counties. After the Conquest, that ancient officer, the sheriff, becomes in Latin documents the *vicecomes*, the vice-count; that was the continental title which seemed best suited to describe him; but this must not induce us to think of him as one who derives his power from the earl, or who in any way represents the earl: from first to last the sheriff is distinctively a royal official, a representative of kingly power—and as the Norman Conquest greatly increased the kingly power, so it greatly increased the power of the sheriff. Even here the tendency, so marked in the Middle Ages, of every office to become hereditary, to become property, was felt, and just in a very few cases the shrievalty did become hereditary; but on the whole the kings succeeded well in maintaining their hold over the sheriffs, in treating them simply as their officers and representatives. The sheriffs held their offices at the king's will. In 1170 Henry II dismissed all the sheriffs of England and put others in their stead. The sheriff had in truth become a provincial viceroy; all the affairs of the shire—fiscal, military, governmental, its justice and police—were under his control, and he was the president of the county court.

For the Conquest had not destroyed the shire moot. It became the county court. The Norman kings seem to have seen its value as a counterpoise to feudalism. To a certain extent the feudal principle that all public rights and duties are connected with land holding had, even before the Conquest, modified the constitution of the ancient assembly, it had become an assembly of free land-owners. After the Conquest the qualification became more definite; the freeholder was entitled and was bound to be present. But a court formed by all the freeholders of a shire is not, you will see, a court formed upon feudal lines. In such an assembly the tenants in chief of the crown have to meet their own vassals on a footing of legal equality; a tenant may find himself sitting as the peer of his own lord. This retention of the old courts is of vast importance in the history of parliament. In Henry I's day the county court was held, as in the days of the Confessor, twice a year. More frequent assemblies seem to have become necessary. By the charter of 1217, it is ordered that the county court shall not meet more often than once a month; monthly sessions seem to have been common.

For a long time after the Conquest the county court remained what it was before the Conquest, the great ordinary court of litigation for all the men of the shire. The growth of the feudal courts (of which hereafter) had to some extent diverted business from it; on the other hand, the king used it as a check on the feudal courts. At the petition of a suitor suggesting that he could not get justice from the lord's court, the king would direct the sheriff to intervene and remove the case into the county court. Gradually, however, the county court began to lose its importance as a judicial tribunal. This was due, however, not to the rivalry of the feudal courts, but to the ever growing vigour of the king's own court, which began to throw open its doors to all suitors. Of this concentration of justice something has been said already and more must be said hereafter. But by the end of Edward I's reign, the king's own courts had already practically become courts of first instance for all matters of much importance. The county court had jurisdiction in personal actions (i.e.

actions in which land or rights connected with land were not claimed) up to 40 shillings, and jurisdiction in actions for land when default of justice was made in a feudal court, but in one way or another litigants could generally take their cases to the king's courts.

But while the county court was thus losing its high place as a judicial tribunal, it had been becoming the very foundation of the political constitution. When in the middle of the thirteenth century we find elected representatives called to form part of the national assembly, of a common council of the realm, or parliament, they are the representatives of the county courts. They are not the representatives of unorganized collections of men, they are the representatives, we might almost say, of corporations. The whole county is in theory represented by its court. So much is this the case that the language of the time draws no distinction between the two—the same word *comitatus* serves to describe both the county, the geographical district, and the assembly. The king in his financial necessities has treated with the counties, long before the counties were ordered to send representative knights to parliament. But the corporate nature of the county, the identity of the county and the county court is best brought out by entries on the judicial rolls, entries which enable us to see the county in the days of Richard and of John. The king's itinerant justices from time to time visit the counties; the whole county (*totus comitatus*), i.e. the body of freeholders, stands before them; it declares what the county has been doing since the last visitation; the county can give judgment; the county can give testimony; the county can be punished by fines and amercements when the county has done wrong; if the county has given false judgment, the county can be summoned to Westminster; four knights must be sent to represent it; he who has suffered by its false judgment may challenge the county to fight; and the county fights by the body of the county champion. Even the principle of election has been long growing before the day when the county is called on to elect members of parliament. In 1194, for example, coroners are first instituted; three knights and one clerk are to be

elected to keep the pleas of the crown[1]. These *custodes pla-
citorum coronae*, or coroners, are intended to act as checks
on the sheriff; they are elected by the county court. There
has even been a long struggle to make the sheriff an elected
officer, and at Edward's death this has for a moment been
a successful struggle; in 1300 he conceded the demand for
elective sheriffs. This concession, however, was withdrawn
very soon after his death. Of the representation of the county
court in parliament, we must speak hereafter; so also of its
jurisdiction as a court of justice; but we must learn to think
of the county as an organized unity which has long had a
common life, common rights and common duties. The idea
of a corporation had not yet made its way into English law;
we must wait for the fifteenth century for that; had it been
otherwise, in all probability the county of the thirteenth
century would have been recognized as constituting a corporation, a corporation governed by the body of freeholders
in the county court.

(ii) The county or shire is divided into hundreds. The
number of hundreds in a shire varies very greatly, and the
size of the hundreds also is very different in different
parts of England. Thus there are 5 in Leicestershire, 9 in
Bedfordshire, 17 in Cambridgeshire and 63 in Kent. This
division of the land into districts known as hundreds is
of very ancient date—in all probability it has existed ever
since the settlement of England by the German tribes. Similar
divisions known as hundreds are found in various parts of the
continent. It seems very probable that the German tribe was
for military and judicial purposes subdivided into groups, each
of 100 warriors, and that our English hundreds represent the
settlements of such groups. In some parts of England, in
the north-east, Yorkshire and Lincolnshire, the district is
called, not a hundred, but a wapentake—this is the name
both of the district and of its court or assembly, and seems

---

[1] The *Forma procedendi in placitis coronae regis* (*Select Charters*, p. 260) is
generally regarded as the origin of the coroner's office. Dr Gross (*History of the
Office of Coroner*, 1892, and *Select Cases from Coroners' Rolls*, 1896) claims to have
found earlier references. Maitland was unconvinced. See *Eng. Hist. Rev.* VIII,
758, and *History of English Law*, I, 519.

to point to the time when the assembly was still a body of armed warriors, who marked their approval by clashing their weapons. The hundred court or hundred moot of the Anglo-Saxon time seems to have been the court of ordinary jurisdiction for the men of the hundred; it, like the shire court, had both civil and criminal jurisdiction; the relation of the one to the other we do not exactly know, but perhaps a suitor was not entitled to go to the shire-moot, until the hundred moot had made default in justice. It was held twelve times a year.

The Conquest did not destroy the hundred court; the freeholders of the hundred were bound to attend it and to sit in it as judges. But in the twelfth and thirteenth centuries, it gradually lost business owing to that concentration of justice in the king's courts, of which mention has already been made. Before the end of Edward's reign, its competence in personal actions like that of the county court had been restricted to cases in which less than 40 shillings was at stake. But further, even before the Conquest, many of these courts had fallen into private hands; the notion that all jurisdiction is the king's had been formed, and the kings had freely given and sold the right of holding courts. To a great landowner this right was very profitable, it enabled him to keep his tenants in hand, and we must further remember that throughout the Middle Ages jurisdiction is a source of income—the lord of a court has a right to the numerous fines and forfeitures which arise out of the doing of justice. It is probable that in the thirteenth century most of the hundred courts had come into private hands. In 1278 Edward made a vigorous attempt to recover the jurisdictions which had become proprietary; he instituted a searching inquiry *quo warranto*, by what warrant, under what title, the lords were presuming to exercise a jurisdiction which prima facie belonged to the king; and his justices succeeded in recovering a great deal of the jurisdiction by insisting that only under written documents or by long prescription could a subject claim any larger jurisdiction than that of the ordinary manorial courts. The ordinary manorial courts, you will understand, had grown up under the influence of feudal ideas and existed side by side with the more ancient courts of the shire and the hundred. Also we must note that even when a hundred court had fallen into private hands, the king's officer, the sheriff, had at least generally the right to hold it twice a year for criminal cases. Twice a year it was the sheriff's turn to hold these courts, and a court so holden by him came to be known as the sheriff's tourn. When such courts as these were in private hands, they were generally called courts leet. The court baron and the customary court of the manor are the outcome of tenure; a court leet on the other hand has a certain criminal jurisdiction, jurisdiction in cases of petty offences, and it is not the outcome of tenure—it must have its origin in a royal grant, real or supposed; this doctrine Edward has succeeded in enforcing by means of his *quo warranto* inquiry[1].

In the general administration of the law, the hundred is an important unit. In particular it is important in the system of trial by jury introduced by Henry II. Each hundred is bound to present its malefactors; this is done by means of a jury of twelve. It is a responsible unit in the police system; from an early time, the hundred is bound to pursue criminals. Under the law of the Conqueror, if a man be found slain and the slayer be not produced, the hundred is fined, unless it can prove that the slain man was an Englishman; in other words, it pays a *murdrum* or murder fine unless there is a present-ment of Englishry. So again in Edward's day, the hundreds have lately been put under constables bound to see that the men of the hundred have proper armour for the pursuit of malefactors and the repelling of enemies. In very early times we hear a little of a hundred's ealdor, and it is possible that he was an elected president of the county; but after the Conquest, and probably before the Conquest, he has disap-peared; the sheriff appoints a serjeant or bailiff (*serviens, ballivus*) for each hundred, who presides over the court, unless that court be in private hands, and is bound to look after all the king's business within the hundred, the collection of taxes, fines, forfeitures and the like.

---

[1] For the whole subject of seigniorial jurisdiction, see *History of English Law*, vol. I, pp. 571—94.

(iii) The lowest unit in the governmental system is the township or vill; the Latin word used to describe the geographical district is *villa*, while *villata* describes the people of the *villa* regarded as a collective whole. The township as such has no court of its own, but it has many police duties to perform. It has duties in the apprehension of criminals, and can be fined for the neglect of them. When the king's justices visit the county, every township has to come before them. For this purpose, the township is represented by its reeve (*praepositus*) and four best men (*quatuor meliores homines*), and its opinion is constantly taken as to the guilt or innocence of accused persons. We constantly read that the township of (let us say) Trumpington (*villata de Trumpington*) says that A is guilty of the death of B, or the like;—if it says what is untrue, it is liable to be amerced. The representation of the townships in the local courts we can trace back to the time of Henry I; but in all probability it is of much higher antiquity[1].

Here it becomes necessary to take account of a principle that we largely noticed when speaking of feudal tenure. The jurisdictional constitution of England would have been a much simpler matter to describe had there not grown up by the side of the ancient courts of the shire and the hundred a newer set of courts expressive of a newer principle—feudal courts expressive of the principle that every lord has a right to hold a court of and for his tenants. The obligation of attending the lord's court, the obligation of doing suit of court, is one of the incidents of feudal tenure. This principle has been slowly growing up: but seems an admitted truth in the twelfth and thirteenth centuries.

We find that very generally these feudal courts are courts of manors; indeed the legal theory of later times asserts, though as I think without warrant, that only as part of a manor could such a court exist. Of the manor then we are compelled to say a few words. We find (I am speaking of

---

[1] It would appear from a note in the MS that Maitland went on to speak of the Township as a fiscal unit. What he may have said on this point may be gathered from *Domesday Book and Beyond*, p. 147; and the *History of English Law*, I, pp. 560—7.

Edward I's day) that England is full of manors. We cannot indeed say that the whole land is parcelled out into manors; our law has no such theory as that all land is part of some manor. Still manors there are in plenty. The name manor, *manerium*, has seemingly meant in the first instance merely an abiding place (*manerium a manendo*); it is closely connected with *mansio*; it has been used more or less vaguely to signify a landed estate; gradually it has gained a legal significance, it has come to imply the existence of a court. Now if we take a typical *manerium* of the time, we commonly find that there is in the first place a quantity of demesne land—land, that is, which the lord of the manor has in his own hand, which is in every sense his very own. Then there are lands which are held of him by freehold tenants, who owe him services: some of them perhaps are bound to do the military service due to the king, others pay him rent in money or in kind, and perhaps are bound to aid him in his ploughing: these are free socagers. Then there are the tenants in villeinage, who owe week work and so forth, and by whose services his demesne lands are cultivated. All these lands usually lie together, and very often the manor is coterminous with the township.

For the free tenants of his manor, the lord keeps a court; generally by the terms of their tenure they are bound to attend this court at stated intervals, e.g. in every third week; they owe suit to his court, *debent sectam ad curiam manerii*. This idea seems indeed to lie at the root of the term socage, it is that of seeking or following; the socagers, *sokemanni*, are bound to seek, follow, attend the court of the lord. The general principle seems for some time past to have been admitted into English law—that if a man has freehold tenants, he may hold a court for them; he may bind them by their tenures to do suit to his court. Such a court then becomes the proper court in which to demand any of the freehold land that is holden of the manor—if I claim against you land which, as we both admit, is holden of A, then I must begin my action in A's court, if A has one. But great inroads have been made upon this system of feudal justice. The hand of Henry II has been felt. The principle just expressed has not been abrogated, but its importance has been greatly curtailed. In one way and another it has become very possible for litigants to evade the manorial jurisdictions, to go straight to the king's court, or having just begun the action in the manor court to get it removed into the king's court by a royal writ. Still these courts exist, and in Edward's day have not yet ceased to do justice. Now such a court is constituted by the lord and his freeholders—they are the judges; he who owes suit of court is bound to go and sit there as a judge—a question relating to freehold land is decided by the peers of the tenure—the freeholder there gets the judgment of his peers, *judicium parium suorum*. In later times such a court is known as 'the court baron of the manor,' a phrase which seems at first merely to have meant the lord's court, *curia baronis*.

But then again the lord had what, at least in later times, was regarded as a distinct court for the tenants in villeinage. This was called the customary court, and the principle was established that in this court, unlike the court baron, the lord's steward was the only judge. I very much doubt whether this principle was established in the thirteenth century. Many important questions depend on this point; in particular the question how far the tenants in villeinage were protected in their holdings. If really the lord's steward was the only judge, then they were protected only by the lord's sense of justice: it was otherwise if they got the judgment of their *pares*. However you must know the orthodox theory that the lord's steward was the sole judge. It was in this so-called customary court that all transfers of the lands held in villeinage were effected:—A wishing to put B in his place, surrendered the land into the lord's hand, who admitted B as tenant; A being dead, the lord admitted B his heir. It became the practice to enrol all these proceedings; we have a few manor rolls from Henry III, a considerable number from Edward I. Copies of the entries relating to their lands were given to the tenants. Gradually, but this is not until a later day, the term tenant in villeinage gives way to tenant by copy of court roll, or copyholder; the copies of the court roll are the evidences of title that the tenant has. To look forward for a moment

in order to finish this matter:—about the middle of the fifteenth century the king's courts begin to protect the copyholder even against his lord; the services again become
commuted for money payments; after the discovery of
Mexico the value of money falls very rapidly, these payments
become trifling; at last the copyholder is almost as complete
an owner of land as is the freeholder:—but it is long indeed
before the distinction ceases to be of political importance—
not until 1832 does the copyholder vote for knights of the
shire. The tenure still exists, a horrible nuisance as you will
learn at large some day.

It should be noted that according to the orthodox legal
theory of the sixteenth century and of to-day, there can be no
manor without two freehold tenants, sufficient tenants, that is,
to constitute a court baron. Whether this theory be of ancient
date, I very much doubt; as a matter of fact, in the thirteenth
century there are many *maneria*, so-called in legal documents,
in which there are no tenants but tenants in villeinage.

Our kings have succeeded in asserting and maintaining the
principle that the feudal jurisdiction is a purely civil jurisdiction, that the fact of tenure does not give to the lord any
criminal or correctional jurisdiction over his tenants, or at least
over such of them as are free men. But as a matter of fact,
either by means of royal grants purchased from kings in want of
money, or by means of usurpations so ancient that they can no
longer be called in question, very many of the lords exercise
some of that criminal and police jurisdiction which as a rule
belongs to the hundred and county courts. In the language
of later law books, and to use a term the origin of which is
singularly obscure, they have established courts leet—courts
which take cognizance of petty misdemeanours. Such courts,
however, according to the legal theory of Edward's time, are no
natural outcome of tenure, like courts baron and customary
courts, but must be claimed by grant or prescription[1].

As a matter of fact, there is usually a close connection
between the manor and the township. Very usually the same
geographical district which from one point of view is a town-

---

[1] 'The lord might also hold a court for his honour, for all his immediate
tenants....The Abbot of Ramsey may bring to his court at Broughton his freehold
tenants from seven counties.' Pollock and Maitland, *History of English Law*,
vol. I, pp. 585—6.

ship, is from another point of view a manor. Recent historians see in the township a community which is far more ancient than the manor; a community which, so far as English history is concerned, we may call primitive; a group of men or of families bound together, very possibly by kinship, which cultivates land by a system of collective agriculture, which is or has been the owner of the land, which to a large extent regulates its own affairs, decides how the land shall be tilled, decides whether new members shall be admitted, has a township-moot in which such affairs are settled, though it has not what we should call a court of justice. In course of time, we are told, this primitive community has in general fallen under the dominion of a lord, has become a community of tenants, and usually of tenants who hold in villeinage, has become a manor. But still for the purposes of public law, in particular for what we may call police purposes, it is as a township, and not as a manor, that the state takes account of it, and when, as sometimes happens, the vill is not coincident with the manor, it is the township and not the manor that must answer to the state for the apprehension of criminals and so forth. The two organisms exist side by side; the older is not thoroughly absorbed in the newer.

All theories, however, as to the early history of manors and townships are beset by very great difficulties which at the present moment cannot be explained. What at present concerns us is that the state has fixed on the township, not the manor, as the unit responsible for good order. It is, I think, the theory of the thirteenth century and of later times that all England is divided into townships, that every bit of land lies in some vill, while it is not the theory that every acre of land must belong to some manor. Again, and this may help to explain the co-existence of township and manor, until lately, until 1290 it has been quite possible for landowners to create new manors; they could not be allowed to alter the police system of the country by the creation of new townships. On the other hand, as a matter of fact, it is difficult to find a township which is outside the manorial system; the township is represented, we have said, by its reeve and four best men, but the reeve is at least generally a manorial officer, a villein elected by his fellow villeins, who is answerable to the lord for looking after the manor, and seeing that his fellow villeins do their due services; to have served as reeve is indeed regarded as a presumptive proof of personal villeinage[1].

(iv) Under the name of *boroughs* a certain number of communities have attained to a higher stage of organization than that of the generality of townships. But this is a matter of degree ; at no time before the year 1835 can we say that the constitution of the various boroughs is the same throughout England, or even that it conforms to any one type. There hardly can be a history of the English borough, for each borough has its own history. That history largely depends on the charters that it has been able to obtain from the king or from other lords, and the liberality of the charter has depended on the price that the burghers were ready to pay for it ; municipal privileges were only to be obtained for valuable consideration. At the end of the thirteenth century, however, the time of which we are speaking, the privileges of the boroughs, the institutions which make it something different from a mere township, may be summed up under the following heads.

(*a*) Immunity from the jurisdiction of the ordinary local courts. The borough has aspired to be a hundred all by itself—to be exempt therefore out of the jurisdiction of any hundred court. When the king's justices visit the county, the borough is represented before it not by the reeve and four men, but by a jury of twelve, just as every hundred in the county is represented by a jury of twelve. Occasionally more extensive immunities have been conferred, the borough is exempted out of the jurisdiction of the county court. Some of the richer and larger boroughs have gone even further than this—it has been granted to them that their burgesses may sue and be sued only in their own courts, and thus one cannot sue a burgess even in the king's court.

(*b*) Coupled with this immunity is the privilege of having courts of its own, usually with the jurisdiction of a hundred court ; but the constitution of these courts varies greatly. In

---

[1] These views are substantially unchanged in the *History of English Law*, vol. I, pp. 594—634.

some cases the borough has already got itself free of the manorial system, and its courts are presided over by elected officers; in other cases the borough is still a manor and its court is the lord's court held under the presidency of his steward.

(*c*) Very frequently indeed the borough has by this time purchased the right of having its own elective officers—*ballivi, praepositi*, bailiffs or reeves, who stand on somewhat the same level as the bailiffs of the hundreds whom the sheriff appoints. Often again the burgesses have their own coroners, and in this respect are free from the organization of the county. In some cases the burgesses have already an elected mayor with ampler rights and powers than those of a bailiff or reeve.

(*d*) Very generally the burgesses have acquired the right to collect the taxes within the borough, and for this purpose to exclude the sheriff. For the ancient taxes they compound with a lump sum at the Exchequer—they are thus said to hold the borough in farm.

(*e*) Very generally also the borough constitution is interwoven with that of a merchant guild, an association of merchants which has by charter obtained the power of regulating trade. In some of the greater boroughs besides the merchant-guild, there are trade-guilds, or craft-guilds, the weavers' guild, the tailors' guild and so forth. A constitution in which the merchant-guild is the ruling body of the town, is gradually, and in very various stages, supplanting a more ancient constitution which was simply that of a privileged township or privileged manor.

The city of London resembles rather a shire than a township—already in Henry I's day it has got so far as to have sheriffs of its own, nay more, it holds the county of Middlesex in farm; its elective sheriffs act as sheriff of Middlesex[1]. To be utterly and totally exempt out of the shire organization, to be counties of themselves, to have sheriffs of their own, is one of the ends for which the more ambitious boroughs are striving, though in Edward I's day none save London has attained it.

---

[1] The Charter of Henry I to London is printed by Stubbs, *Select Charters*, p. 108.

Boroughs which are also bishop's sees are distinguished as cities (*civitates*), and their burgesses are citizens. The term city tells us no more than this, it does not point to any higher degree of municipal organization or independence than does the term borough (*burgus*).

In later times, in the fifteenth century and onwards, we can arrive at a legal definition of a borough; the notion of a corporation has then been formed, a fictitious person, a juristic person, which has rights and duties which are quite distinct from the rights and duties of its members. But this notion, though developed in the Canon Law, only made its way into English law by slow degrees[1]. The greater boroughs, however, of Edward's reign have already in substance attained to all or almost all of those distinctive characteristics which the later lawyers regarded as essential to corporate unity. These characteristics are five—the right of perpetual succession, the power to sue and be sued as a whole and by the corporate name, the power to hold lands, the right to use a common seal, and the power of making by-laws. Substantially these characteristics exist, but as yet they have not been worked into a theory by the conception of a fictitious person, who is immortal, who sues and is sued, who holds lands, has a seal of his own, who makes regulations for those natural persons of whom he is composed. The question what is the constitution of this fictitious person, how he is made up out of natural persons, has not yet arisen. The borough is as yet no more a corporation, no less, than is the township, the hundred, or the county; and if the borough may be spoken of as having rights and duties, as breaking the law and being punished, this is true also of the county, the hundred, and the township.

D. *Central Government.*

We turn to the central government, the king and his councils. This we are wont to regard as the main theme of constitutional law. We have here, however, postponed it,

[1] The idea is worked out in Maitland's *Township and Borough*, Cambridge, 1897.

for it can hardly be understood without some preliminary knowledge of the land law and of the local institutions. Now at the end of Edward's reign we find several different central institutions. In the first place there is the kingship; this is the centre of the centre. Then there is that assembly of the three estates of the realm, clergy, lords and commons, to which the name *parliamentum* is coming to be specifically appropriated. Then again the king has a council (*concilium*) which is distinct from parliament, and he has high officers of state, a chancellor, treasurer, constable, marshal and so forth. Then again he has courts, courts which in a peculiar sense are his courts: there is the King's Bench, the Common Bench, the Exchequer. All these now are distinct and have their different functions; but looking back a little way we see that they have not always been distinct, that a difference, for instance, between the king's council (*concilium Regis*) and the king's court (*curia Regis*) has but slowly been established. We will take therefore a brief retrospect of the history of our central institutions as a whole.

(i) *Before* 1066.

Among the German tribes described by Tacitus a kingship was by no means universal. In some cases the highest officers are *principes* elected by the tribe in its popular assembly; in other cases the tribe has already a *rex*; he also is elected, chosen it would seem because of his noble descent, but his power seems to be very limited. Our own forefathers when they first attacked the province of Britain seem to have had no kings; their leaders were ealdormen, in whom we may recognize the *principes* of Tacitus. But the kingship appears very soon; the process of conquering a new country would be very favourable to its development. The small states which were afterwards to coalesce into the kingdom of England, seem in other respects to have resembled the states described by Tacitus. Each had its popular assembly, the assembly of all free men, its *principes* or ealdormen elected in that assembly, and its king. The ealdorman presides over a *pagus* or district; the ealdormen, under the king's presidency, meet to determine the minor affairs of the state, but the weightier matters are discussed in the folk-moot:—*de minoribus rebus principes consultant, de majoribus omnes.*

Gradually by conquest greater kingdoms are formed, at last the English kingdom. The way for this was prepared by the acceptance of the Christian faith and the organization of an English church. The old state which has thus been absorbed in a larger state does not lose its unity, it now exists as a shire of the new kingdom; sometimes the members of its once royal house continue to be its ealdormen ; its folk-moot still exists, but now as a shire-moot, the county court of later days. The national assembly is not a folk-moot, not an assembly of the whole people, but a witenagemot, an assembly of the wise, the *sapientes.* This assembly when we look back at it seems a very unstable and indefinite body. It comprises the bishops, and towards the end of the period we often find a number of abbots present. It comprises also the ealdormen of the shires; their number varies according as the shires are administered singly or in groups. Besides these there are a number of persons who generally describe themselves as *ministri Regis,* or king's thanes, and this number increases as time goes on. It can never have been a very large assembly. 'In a witenagemot held at Luton in November, 931, were the 2 archbishops, 2 Welsh princes, 17 bishops, 15 ealdormen, 5 abbots and 59 *ministri.* In another, that of Winchester, in 934, were present the 2 archbishops, 4 Welsh kings, 17 bishops, 4 abbots, 12 ealdormen and 52 *ministri.* These are perhaps the fullest extant lists[1].' The question arises, who were these *ministri* or king's thanes ?

The *princeps* of Tacitus has around him a train of warlike companions (*comites*). It is the duty of all men to fight ; the host, as is often said, is the nation in arms ; but these *comites* are more especially bound to fight and to fight for their leader; this is their glory ; it gives them a high place in the estimation of the community. We can recognize them in the *gesith,* the companion, of our own kings, a name which gradually gives place to that of thane, or servant, in Latin *minister.* A nobility by service is thus formed, and the thegnhood begins

---

[1] Stubbs, *Constitutional History*, vol. I, § 52.

to be connected with the holding of land and to be hereditary. The unappropriated land, the land of the nation, the folk-land, forms a great fund whereout the king, with the consent of the wise, can reward his faithful followers[1]. The thane begins to look somewhat like the tenant by knight service of later times, and the king's thane (for an ealdorman may have thanes) begins to look like a tenant in chief. The definite idea of a military tenure, A *tenet de Rege per servicium unius militis*, is not formed before the Conquest; but to an extent, and in a manner that is now very dark to us, the military service due comes to be connected with and measured by landholding[2]. It is well to see that there were powerful economic causes in which this incipient feudalism had its roots. As agriculture becomes higher, as the distribution of property grows more unequal, as the art of war is developed, it becomes more and more convenient that some should fight while others till the soil: there is a division of labour, a specialization of employments. The work of feudalism goes on in the lowest strata of society as well as in the highest. While the king is gathering round him a body of armed vassals who are great landowners because they are vassals, the smaller men are putting themselves under the protection of lords, are content that their lords should do the necessary fighting while they till the lord's land. Dark as is the early history of the manor, we can see that before the Conquest England is covered by what in all substantial points are manors, though the term manor is brought hither by the Normans. Furthermore, in the interests of peace and justice, the state insists that every landless man shall have a lord, who will produce him in court in case he be accused. Slowly the relation of man and lord extends itself, and everywhere it is connected with land. The king's thanes then are coming to be the king's military tenants in chief.

---

[1] The term *folk-land* is now regarded not as denoting public land, but as 'land held without written title under customary law.' *History of English Law*, vol. I, p. 62. The point was proved by Mr Paul Vinogradoff in 1893. *Eng. Hist. Rev.* VIII, 1—17. This does not imply that there was no unappropriated land, only that it was not called *folk-land*.

[2] Maitland throws some light upon this dark question in *Domesday Book and Beyond*, pp. 307—9.

We cannot then arrive at any strict theory as to the constitution of the witenagemot. It is an assembly of the great folk; when there is a strong king on the throne it is pretty much in his power to say how it shall be constituted, to summon whom he will; when the king is weak, it is apt to become anarchical. It has even been contended by Mr Freeman that every free man had in theory a right to attend it[1]; but it is difficult to believe that a theory was maintained which was so flagrantly inconsistent with the actual facts. At all events it is clear that really this assembly was a small aristocratic body, tending always to become more aristocratic. The bishops constitute its most permanent and at times its most powerful element.

Such then is the national assembly, and at least on paper its powers seem vast; it can elect kings and depose them; the king and witan legislate; it is with the counsel and consent of the witan that the king publishes laws; the king and witan nominate the ealdormen and the bishops, make grants of the public lands, impose taxes, decide on peace and war, and form a tribunal of last resort for causes criminal and civil. It is a supreme legislative, governmental, and judicial assembly.

Such terms as these, however, may easily raise a false notion in modern minds. The whole business of a central government is as yet but small. Legislation is no common event; as already said, all the extant dooms of kings and witan would make but a small book. Taxation is still more uncommon, of anything that can be called by that name we hear nothing until late in the day. The rents and profits of the public lands, the profits of the courts, afford a sufficient revenue for such central government as there is. The Danegeld of Ethelred's reign is perhaps the first tax; in 991, 994, 1002, 1007, 1011, a tribute was raised to buy off the Danish invaders. Lastly, though we have clear proof that the witenagemot acted as a court of justice, it was no ordinary court for ordinary men; recourse to it was not encouraged; the normal courts were the local courts, and suitors were forbidden to seek the royal audience until justice had failed them in the hundred and the shire.

[1] *Essays*, 4th series, pp. 444—7.

Meanwhile the king's splendour grew as the extent of his territory grew. From being merely the nation's leader, he became the lord of all men, and we may almost say the lord of all land and lord of all justice. While as yet almost all offences can be atoned for by money payments, treason becomes an utterly inexpiable offence. The national land becomes always more and more the king's land, and the king's favour is thus the source of honour and of wealth. What is more, justice is regarded as being the king's, he can grant jurisdiction to whom he pleases, indeed a grant of land now usually involves a grant of jurisdiction ; the hundred courts come into private hands and manorial courts arise. This, the most dangerous element of feudalism, is rapidly developed towards the end of our period ; in particular Edward the Confessor seems to have been lavish in his grants of jurisdiction [1].

We have said, however, that the king's splendour grows, rather than that his power grows. Whether he will be powerful or no depends now very much on his own personal character. That lordship of land and of justice of which we have just spoken, may be as easily a cause of weakness as of strength. Every grant that he makes of land or of jurisdiction raises up a new vassal, and unless the king's hand be heavy upon his vassals they may become too strong for him ; he may end by being like the king of the French, *primus inter pares,* the nominal head of a turbulent baronage. The growth of large estates and private jurisdictions surrounds the great thanes with tenants and retainers bound to them by a close bond of fealty. Every man, it is true, can be called upon to swear allegiance to the king ; but the king is distant and the lord is near.

Even the fact that to the very end of the period the kingship is not strictly hereditary, but elective—that on the Confessor's death the witan can elect Harold—that a power also of deposing a king has been exercised as late as the days of Ethelred the Unready, is really rather a mark of constitutional weakness, of a dangerous feudalism, than of popular liberty:—

[1] *Domesday Book and Beyond,* p. 87 ff.

the crown itself may become the prize of the rebellious vassal. The really healthy element in the constitution as it stood on the eve of the Conquest lies here—that as yet no English king has taken on himself to legislate or to tax without the counsel and consent of a national assembly, an assembly of the wise, that is of the great. This is a valuable barrier against mere despotism, though what the national assembly shall be a strong king can decide for himself.

(ii) 1066–1154.

William of Normandy claimed the throne as the heir nominated by the Confessor. That title the English did not admit; it had not been law among them that a king might appoint his successor. Harold was chosen king. The battle of Hastings was fought. William proceeded to seek the recognition of the divided and dismayed witan. He was chosen and was crowned, swearing that he would hold fast right law, and utterly forbid rapine and unrighteous judgment. It is needful to remember that neither of his sons came to the throne by what we should think or even by what would then have been thought a good hereditary title, needful, for to this we probably owe the preservation of a certain form and semblance of free government. Rufus excluded Robert and was willing to make, though also to break, the most lavish promises. Henry again excluded Robert; he was hastily elected by a small knot of barons, took the oaths which Ethelred had taken, and purchased support by a charter of great importance, for it was the model on which the charter of 1215 was framed. 'Know ye,' it begins, 'that by the mercy of God and the common counsel of the barons of the whole realm of England I have been crowned king of the same realm.' Henry dead, the crown was seized by Stephen of Blois, to the exclusion, as we should say, of the Empress Matilda. He was obliged to make large promises at his coronation, and in 1136 to issue an important charter, important rather as a precedent than as anything else, for a strong party favoured the Empress and the feudal anarchy broke loose. In fact we may regard our Norman kings as despotic; when there is not despotism there is anarchy; still a certain semblance of another form of government is maintained, government by a king who rules with the counsel and consent of his barons.

Now the typical feudal king, if we may make such an abstraction, should have a court consisting of his immediate vassals, his tenants in chief. How much or how little he will be influenced by them, whether they will be utterly powerless or whether he will be but the first among equals is a different question—but such control over him as there is will be the control of a court thus formed. It would seem then according to this idea that the court of the English king should have consisted of his tenants in chief. But the tenants in chief were in England very numerous : this was the result of the Conquest and the subsequent grants of lands deemed forfeited —they were not just a few rulers and owners of vast provinces ; there were a large number who held single knight's fees and single manors holden directly of the king. This should be remembered, for it affects the constitution both of the House of Lords and of the House of Commons in later days. The body of military tenants in chief was from the beginning a very heterogeneous body. If it included great feudatories with vast possessions and numerous vassals, who might aspire to play the part of sovereign princes, it included also a large number of men who were by no means very rich or very powerful. This must have rendered it practically impossible that the king's court should have become a powerful definite body formed strictly on feudal lines. The Conqueror we find holds an ordinary court three times a year at the three great festivals. 'Thrice a year,' says the Saxon Chronicle, ' King William wore his crown every year he was in England ; at Easter he wore it at Winchester, at Pentecost at Westminster, and at Christmas at Gloucester ; and at these times all the men of England were with him—archbishops, bishops and abbots, earls, thegns and knights.' A similar usage was maintained by his sons though the rotation thus described was not strictly observed. When however we ask who actually attended ? still more if we ask who had a right to attend ? we get a very uncertain answer. The passage in the Chronicle to which I have just referred is a specimen of the vague statements which are all that we get—all the men of England were with him—archbishops, bishops and abbots, earls, thanes or knights ; often we are put off with some such word as *proceres*, which has a very uncertain sound. The archbishops, bishops and abbots attend by virtue of their official wisdom, but the theory seems always to gain ground that they are there because they hold baronies of the king—at any rate they become tenants in chief and so for them there is certainly a place. As to the other persons who come, so far as there is any legal theory, it must be that they are the tenants in chief. Probably it is fully acknowledged that the king may lawfully insist on the presence of every tenant in chief—probably it is the general opinion that every military tenant in chief has a right to be there. But we ought to remember that attendance at court is no coveted privilege. We must be careful not to introduce the notions of modern times in which a seat in parliament is eagerly desired. This would render a good deal of history unintelligible. For the smaller men attendance at court is a burden of which they are very ready to relieve themselves or be relieved, and this is true, be the court in question the hundred court, or the county court, or the king's court.

What seems to us from the modern point of view a valuable political right, seemed to those who had it an onerous obligation. The great baron again had no particular desire to be about his lord's court ; if, as was too often the case, he was not very faithful to his lord, his lord's court was the very last place in which he would wish to be. In point of fact we do not hear from the Norman reigns any assertion of an individual's right to attend the court. The king insists on bringing around him the most powerful of his tenants in chief, and such meetings are to him a source of strength. As Mr Dicey has pointed out in his Essay on the Privy Council it is the strong king who habitually brings his magnates round him. He thus keeps his eye upon them, and it strengthens his hands in dealing with the refractory that his measures are taken with the counsel and consent of their peers.

Under the Norman kings counsel and consent may have been little more than formality, and the king may have exercised the power of summoning only such of his tenants

in chief as he pleased—still such few legislative acts as we
have from this period are done with the counsel and consent
of the great.   Thus the ordinance which removed the bishops
from the secular courts and recognized their spiritual jurisdiction was made with the counsel of the archbishops, bishops,
abbots, and all the princes of the kingdom.   But anything
that could be called legislation was seemingly very rare.   The
right of the council to join in taxation was perhaps admitted
in theory.   Henry the First speaks of an aid which had been
granted to him by his barons : but there is nothing to show
that any such consent was asked when the Danegeld was
levied as repeatedly it was, and the king exercised the power
of tallaging his demesne lands of his own free will.   A court
of this nature was again the highest court of judicature, for
the great cases and the great men.   It was in such courts that
the king nominated bishops until the right of canonical election
was conceded by Henry I, and even then the election took place
in the royal court.   The ceremony of conferring earldoms and
knighthood and receiving homage were performed there ;
questions of general policy, of peace and war, of royal marriages
and so forth seem to have been debated.

But a smaller body collects round the king, a body of
administrators selected from the ranks of the baronage and
of the clergy.   At its head stands the chief-justiciar, the king's
right-hand man, his viceroy when the king is, as often he is,
in his foreign dominions.   There is also the king's chancellor,
the head of a body of clerks who do all the secretarial work ;
there are the great officers of the royal household and others
whom the king has chosen.   Under Henry I this body becomes
organic ; the orderly routine of administration begins even to
be a check on the king's power ; Stephen discovers this when
he quarrels with the ministerial body.   This body when it sits
for financial purposes constitutes the Exchequer (*Scaccarium*),
so called from the chequered cloth which lies on the table,
convenient for the counting of money.   Also it forms a
council and court of law for the king, it is *curia Regis*, the
king's court, and its members are *justitiarii*, justiciars or justices
of this court.   Under Henry I they are sent into the counties
to collect taxes and to hold pleas ; they are then *justitiarii*

errantes, justitiarii itinerantes.   During the whole period the term *curia Regis* seems loosely used to cover both the sessions of this permanent body and the assembly of the tenants in chief; the former may perhaps be regarded as a standing committee of the latter.

(iii)   1154–1216.

The reigns of the first three kings of the Angevin house form another and a fairly definite period in the history of the national assembly—which ends with the Great Charter of 1215. In its fourteenth clause we obtain for the first time something that may be called a distinct definition of that body. The twelfth clause declares that no scutage or aid shall be imposed in our realm save by the common counsel of our realm, *nisi per commune consilium regni nostri*—except the three ordinary feudal aids for redeeming the king's body from captivity, for knighting his eldest son, and for marrying his eldest daughter.   There follows this—' And for the purpose of having the common counsel of the realm for assessing an aid except in the three cases aforesaid we will cause to be summoned the archbishops, bishops, abbots, earls and greater barons (*majores barones*) singly (*sigillatim*) by our letters ; and besides we will cause to be summoned by our sheriffs and bailiffs all those who hold of us in chief; for a certain day, that is to say, at a term of forty days at least ; and to a certain place ; and in all the letters of such summons we will express the cause of the summons.'   Leaving out of sight, for a time, the clerical members of this body, we see that the national assembly is an assembly of the king's tenants in chief.   But we see an important distinction ; while the archbishops, bishops, abbots, earls and greater barons are to be summoned severally by letters addressed to them directly, the other tenants in chief are to be summoned not by name but by general writs addressed to the sheriffs.   Now this distinction has been the subject of much disputation.   It is mentioned in the Charter as an already well understood distinction, as one already recognized in practice; the difficulty has been to find its foundation—what makes a man a *baro major*?   The principle cannot be found in feudal theory,

feudally all these persons stand on the same level, they are
tenants in chief whether they hold whole counties or single
knight's fees.   One small class may be definitely marked off,
namely the earls.   The earl of the Norman reigns is definitely
the successor of the earl of the days before the Conquest, who
again is the successor of the older ealdorman.   To a certain
extent under William and his sons the earldom was still an
office implying a considerable though somewhat vague power
in the county which gave to the earl his title : but it had become
less and less of an office, more and more of a mere dignity.
The royal policy had been to prevent great jurisdiction falling
into the hands of powerful nobles, and to rule the shires by
sheriffs strictly accountable to the king and removable at a
moment's notice.   The earls, however, are a quite distinct class
and a small class, for the title had not been lavishly given.
As to the title of baron (*baro*) the clause before us is quite
evidence enough, were there no other, that it was not
confined to those who were entitled to the special summons,
for this distinguishes not the *barones* but the *barones majores*.
It would seem that at this time the title baron covered all the
military tenants in chief of the crown.   This is in accordance
with the original meaning of the word—*baro* is simply man :
this meaning it long kept in our law French : husband and wife
are *baron* and *feme*; but *man* is the term opposed to *lord*;
the man does homage to his lord, *hominium* or *homagium*, from
homo a man; and it seems somewhat of an accident that while
we speak of the *homage* of a manorial court, meaning thereby
the body of tenants owing suit and service, we speak of the
baronage of the king's court ; the king's tenants in chief are
his *homines* and his *barones* also.   A line has then been drawn
which divides these persons into two classes :—this probably
is a result gradually attained by the practice of a century.
The greater men had paid their feudal dues directly to the
king's exchequer, the smaller had paid through the sheriff ;
the greater when serving in the army brought up their retainers
under their own banners, the smaller served under the sheriff ;
the greater were summoned to the king's court directly, the
smaller through the sheriff.   But when we ask what greater
and smaller mean, we can give no precise answer.   In particular

we cannot say that a certain definite extent or value of land was either necessary or sufficient to make a man entitled to the special summons. Then again in this same Magna Carta we find a distinction as to reliefs, the heir of the baron is to pay for an entire barony (*baronia*) a hundred pounds, or according to some copies a hundred marks, the heir of the knight holding in chief of the king is to pay a hundred shillings for the knight's fee. It seems that the *baro* who has a *baronia* in the one clause is the *baro major* who is to have a special summons in the other clause. The process of narrowing the import of the word baron to those who are entitled to the special summons goes on during the following century. Tenancy in chief is not sufficient now to give a man this title of *baro*; he may hold in chief and yet be merely *miles*. The estate of the baron is a barony, but though there may be a theory floating about that the barony is or should be related to the knight's fee as the mark is related to the shilling, that is to say, that the barony should consist of thirteen knight's fees and a third—still it seems certain that an estate of this value was neither necessary, nor in itself sufficient, to entitle the holder to the special summons. Certain particular estates had come to be regarded as baronies and to pay the heavier relief, we can say very little more.

During the period which ends with the charter we have little evidence as to the constitution of the national assembly. The earliest writ of summons that we have is one addressed to the Bishop of Salisbury in 1205; of general summonses sent out through the sheriffs we have none preserved; but very possibly throughout the reign of Henry the Second the assembly had been constituted after the fashion prescribed by the charter. During that reign councils had been frequent; Henry was a strong king, not afraid of meeting his vassals, with a policy of his own and a policy which required their support. Some great laws, I may remind you, were made in his reign, though the text of them has too often perished—the Constitutions of Clarendon, the Grand Assize, the Assizes of Clarendon and Northampton. He professedly legislates by the counsel and consent of the archbishops, bishops, barons, earls and nobles of England—by the petition and advice of his bishops and all his barons and so forth. The counsel and consent may still have been little more than a ceremony—the enacting power was with the king—and he could put in respite or dispense with the ordinances that were issued. The tyranny of John after the discipline of Henry was what was needed to turn this right of joining in legislation into a reality. In form the Charter is a Charter, a free grant by the king, in reality a code of reforming laws passed by the whole body of bishops and barons and thrust upon a reluctant king.

It is not very clear that in theory the consent of the national council had been necessary for taxation or that it had been in fact granted. Henry the Second takes a scutage or an aid or a carucage; the chroniclers do not say that the consent of his council or his court has been given or asked. The feudal theory that the man makes a free-will offering to relieve the wants of his lord seems to have subsisted; the consent which theory requires is rather a consent of the individual taxpayer than that of the national assembly. The notion that the majority of an assembly could bind a recalcitrant minority or could bind those who were not present had hardly been formed and would have been as unpopular as the notion that the king himself can extort just what he wants. We begin to hear of opposition to taxation: in 1163 Becket protests, in 1198 Bishop Hugh of Lincoln. But these protests of S. Thomas and S. Hugh are rather the protests of individuals who will not pay a tax to which they have not consented, than assertions that the power to tax is vested in the national assembly. The necessity however of extending taxation from land to movables occasions a new organization and a new order of ideas. The Saladin tithe of 1188 is perhaps the first attempt to tax personal property[1]. Henry obtained from a great national council a promise of a tithe for the crusade; the assessment in such a case could not be left to a transaction between the individual taxpayer and the royal officers, so Henry's favourite machinery, a jury of neighbours, was employed; in 1198 this plan was applied to the assessment of the carucage, the land tax levied on the carucate or plough-

---

[1] *Select Charters*, p. 160.

land which had superseded the Danegeld[1]. Thus taxation and representation are brought into connection—the individual is assessed by his neighbours, by a jury representing his parish, and so in some sort representing him. The idea that representation should accompany taxation gains ground as personal property is brought under contribution. In 1207 John attempted to exact a thirteenth of movable property. The bishops refused this on behalf of the clergy; John had to give up this plan of taxing them. The great crisis followed and the charter was won. No scutage or aid, save the three regular aids, was to be levied without the common consent of the realm. Other forms of taxation, taxes for example on movables, were not mentioned, nor could the national assembly, as defined in the fourteenth article, be considered as adequately representing all classes: it was an assembly of prelates and tenants in chief. This however was but a stage, and the principle that representation should accompany taxation was already outgrowing the terms in which for the moment it was defined. Already in 1213, two years before the charter, an assembly for the discussion of grievances had been held at S. Albans, to which were summoned not only the barons and bishops but also a body of representatives—four men and the reeve from each township on the royal demesne; already a few months later, on 7 Nov. 1213, John had summoned to a council at Oxford, four lawful men of every shire, *ad loquendum nobiscum de negotiis regni nostri.* These are the first recorded examples of the appearance of local representatives in the national assembly. Eighty years were yet to pass however before a representation of the commons or the communities of the realm would become for good and all a constituent element of that great council of the realm which had meanwhile gotten the name of a *Parliamentum.*

Meanwhile the administrative and judicial body, the *curia Regis* in its narrower sense, has been growing more definite and has been splitting up into various bodies with distinct functions, all under the control of the justiciar and the king. There is the Exchequer, a fiscal bureau, and court of law for all matters affecting the revenue—the judges in it

[1] *Select Charters*, pp. 256, 7.

still keep the title *barones Scaccarii*, although they are by no means always chosen from the ranks of the baronage. There is the Chancellor who keeps the king's great seal and who stands at the head of a clerical establishment, the royal chancery. There is now a small compact body of judges, justices of the king's court, professionally learned in the law. The judicial work has enormously increased owing to the law reforms of Henry II. This judicial body again is splitting into sections. One party of justices attends the king in his progresses, and here we see the beginning of the court of King's Bench, another sits term after term at Westminster and is going to be the Court of Common Pleas—for the Great Charter concedes that common pleas, i.e. suits between subject and subject, are not to follow the king's person, but are to be heard in some certain place. But a reserve of justice remains in the king to be exercised by him in the great council of the nation, or in some smaller council. Judicial visitations of the counties, eyres, *itinera*, have become very frequent—the royal courts are becoming the courts of first resort for most cases; but the old local courts are brought into connection with the king's courts by these visitations. When the justices in eyre come into the county, the whole county must come before them; every freeholder must be there or send excuse, every hundred, every borough, must be represented by its jury of twelve, every township by the reeve and four men[1].

(iv) 1216–95.

After 1215 the next great halting-place in the history of the national assembly is the year 1295. In the latter year there is, we may say definitely, a parliament; the great outlines have been drawn once for all. During these eighty eventful years a new principle has emerged and become dominant. The assembly contemplated by the first edition of the great charter is a feudal assembly. It may be questioned perhaps in what right the archbishops, bishops and abbots find a place there—whether as the heads of the national church or

---

[1] For an elaborate survey of the judicial system at the end of Henry II's reign see Maitland, *Select Pleas of the Crown* (Selden Soc.), Intr.

as great vassals of the king; they were both; but the assembly is a court of tenants in chief. Now we can hardly say that the clauses of the charter which require the consent of an assembly of this kind to the imposition of a scutage or aid ever became part of the law of the realm. They were not repeated in any later edition of the charter. Henry III at his coronation was a child in the hands of William Marshall the great Earl of Pembroke, *rector regis et regni*, the head of the English baronage, and the king's guardians and ministers may have thought it undesirable that their hands should be bound by such clauses at a moment of grave peril when the foreigner was in the realm, and bonds may have seemed needless. This is not to be regretted; had these clauses become a permanent part of the law Parliament might have formed itself on strictly feudal lines; we might have had the Scottish parliament instead of the English. As it was, the necessity for raising money forced the king to negotiate with all classes of his realm. Henry was a thriftless, shiftless king, always extravagant and always poor. The meetings of the national assembly during his reign were many. Probably they were summoned in accordance with the principle laid down in the charter of 1215, the major barons being summoned individually, the lesser tenants in chief by general writs addressed to the sheriff. To such an assembly, held on the occasion of the king's marriage in 1236, we owe the Statute of Merton. These meetings were realities; counsel and consent could no longer be taken for granted; under John the baronage had learned to act together as a whole. Demands for money are met by demands for reform—demands which sometimes seem startling even to us. From 1234 onwards Henry was trying to rule without great ministers, without justiciar, chancellor, or treasurer. The scheme which from time to time pleases the baronage is that of a small number of ministers or counsellors appointed by and answerable to the common council of the realm. Henry was lavish with promises which are always broken.

Meanwhile the representative principle was growing. The notion of the representation of a community by some of its members must have been old. Already in the *Leges Henrici*

Primi we find that in the local courts the townships are represented by the priest, the reeve and four of the best men[1]. This usage may already have been very old. Certainly at a little later date we find that the county court when summoned in all its fulness to meet the king's justices in their eyres comprises not only all the free tenants of the shire, but also a representation of the boroughs and townships, from every township four lawful men and the reeve, from every borough twelve lawful burgesses[2]. The whole system of trial by jury in its earliest form implies representations—a person is tried by the country, by the neighbourhood, *ponit se super patriam, super vicinetum.* The voice of the jurors is the verdict of the country, *veredictum patriae.* When we look at the eyre rolls of this time (there are plenty of rolls from the first years of Henry III) we are struck by the deep root which this notion has taken:—the whole county is present and can speak its mind, every hundred is present, every township—the hundred of Berkeley says this, the township (*villata*) of Stow says that; the county, the hundreds, the townships can be amerced and fined for neglect of their police duties or for saying what is false. But representation does not necessarily imply election by the represented; representatives may be chosen by a public officer or by lot. However in 1194 we find that the juries for the various hundreds are appointed thus: four lawful knights are elected from the county, who choose two lawful knights from each hundred, who again choose ten lawful knights from the hundred to make with themselves the twelve jurors for the hundred. The coroners again from the first moment of their institution in 1194 had been elected by the county. This local organization had, we have seen, been made use of for fiscal purposes; assessments to taxes on movables and even on land had been made by local juries. At an exceptional crisis in 1213 four lawful men with the reeve from the vills of the royal demesne had been called on to meet the bishops and barons, and in the same year four discreet men from each shire had been summoned *ad loquen-*

---

[1] *Select Charters*, p. 105, VII, 7.
[2] *ib.* p. 358.

dum nobiscum de negotiis regni nostri[1]. Throughout Henry's reign the use of local and representative machinery for the assessing and collecting of taxes granted by the assembly of barons and prelates becomes more constant and more important. Distinct progress is made in 1225, in 1232, in 1237. The documents you will find in the *Select Charters*[2]. In 1254 a great step was made. The king had gone to Gascony and was in sore need of money ; the regents, his wife and brother, summoned a great council to Westminster : to which each sheriff was to send four knights from his county, ' four lawful and discreet knights from your county whom the county shall have chosen for this purpose in the place of all and singular of the said counties to provide along with the knights from the other counties whom we have caused to be summoned for the same day what aid they will give to us in this our great necessity.' Representatives of the counties, representatives elected by the counties, then are summoned not merely to assess, but to grant an aid ; there is to be no dealing with each county separately ; all are to meet together and to provide together.

The great struggle which began in 1258 and ended with the battle of Evesham, 4 August 1265, did not carry the history of parliament much further. The Parliaments between that of 1254 and that of 1265—the word *parliamentum* was just coming into use, supplanting *colloquium* and other terms, and the assembly which forced the charter from John had recently been styled retrospectively *parliamentum Runimedae*—did not contain, so far as we know, any representatives of shires or boroughs. The national strivings have another end in view : a small council elected by the barons to control the king, ministers elected by and answerable to the baronage, the reform of a miscellaneous catalogue of abuses. Beginning with the parliament held at Oxford in 1258, the Mad Parliament, we have complicated paper constitutions of an oligarchic

---

[1] *Select Charters*, pp. 276, 287, and *Constitutional History*, vol. 1, § 154. Mr Davis [*Engl. Hist. Rev.* April 1905, pp. 289—90] argues that in the earlier case the jurors were summoned not to S. Albans but to their respective shire-courts.

[2] *Select Charters*, pp. 355—6, 360—2, 366—8.

character, some of which work for a while, from which the king frees himself when he can.   An important set of reforms redressing the grievances of the smaller tenants in chief was obtained in 1259, the Provisions of Oxford; but in the end it came to fighting.   When the parties were already arming in 1261, the chiefs of the provisional government summoned to an assembly at S. Albans three knights from each shire; Henry ordered the knights to be sent not to S. Albans, but to Windsor.   The battle of Lewes was won on 14 May, 1264. Almost immediately Simon of Montfort, who had the king in his hands, ordered the election of four knights to meet the king in parliament on 22 June.   At the end of the year he summoned the famous parliament of 1265.   As to bishops, abbots and barons only such were summoned as were friends of the party in power—only five earls, only eighteen barons.   But each sheriff had a writ to return two discreet knights for each shire, and a similar summons was sent to the cities and boroughs.   What was newest in this parliament was the presence of representatives of the cities and boroughs.   Soon followed the battle of Evesham.   There is nothing to prove that during the six last years of the reign the parliaments included representatives of shires or boroughs; but we cannot be quite certain of this; and proctors of the cathedral chapters were present at the Parliament of Winchester held immediately after the king's victory.   One of these parliaments, that of 1267, passed the great Statute of Marlborough or Marlbridge, which conceded many of the reforms for which the nation had clamoured.   It professes to have been enacted *convocatis discretioribus regni tam majoribus quam minoribus*.

The same doubt hangs over many of the early parliaments of Edward's reign, many of the parliaments which passed the famous statutes.   In 1273 a great assembly was held to take the oath of fealty to the new king; there came the archbishops and bishops, earls and barons, abbots and priors, and from each shire four knights, and from each city four citizens. The Statute of Westminster the First (1275) declares the assent of archbishops, bishops, abbots, priors, earls, barons, and the community of the land.   The Statute of Gloucester

(1278), the next great Act, was, as it says, made with the assent of the most discreet men both of high and low degree. In 1282 a curious expedient was tried ; the king was fighting in Wales; he caused two provincial councils to be summoned, that for the northern province, at York, that for the southern, at Northampton ; clergy and laity were summoned to each, four knights for each shire, two representatives for each town. This case was exceptional, and became no precedent. Another somewhat anomalous assemblage was held at Shrewsbury in 1283, with representatives of twenty-one selected towns and two knights of each shire. It is not certain that any representatives were present at the parliament of 1285, which enacted that great code which we know as the Statute of Westminster the Second; the very important Statute of Winchester in the same year (1285) is on the face of it merely the king's commandment, and we do not know that any representatives of the commons were present at its making. Again, in 1290, the Statute of Westminster III, the celebrated *Quia Emptores*, was enacted by the king at the instance of the magnates. Knights from the shires did attend that parliament, but the statute was passed a week before the day for which they were summoned. Two knights from each shire were summoned in 1294.

The next year gives us the model for all future parliaments. The archbishops and bishops are directed to bring the heads of their chapters, their archdeacons, one proctor for the clergy of each cathedral and two for the clergy of each diocese. Every sheriff is to cause two knights of each shire, two citizens of each city and two burgesses of each borough to be elected. Seven earls and forty-one barons are summoned by name. The clergy and baronage are summoned to treat, ordain and execute, the representatives of the commons are to bring full powers from those whom they represent to execute (*ad faciendum*) what should be ordained by common counsel. A body constituted in this manner is a parliament ; what the king enacts with the consent of such a body is a statute. Very soon indeed these two terms become specifically appropriated ; for a very short while they may be used in a laxer way :—parliament of course merely means a conference, a meeting at which there is to be talk, debate, deliberation. Now and again the name is given to meetings of the king's ordinary council, or to meetings which would afterwards have been called *magna concilia* as distinct from *parliamenta*—meetings of the prelates and barons to which representatives of the commons were not called—or again to some anomalous assemblages which were occasionally summoned. But very quickly indeed usage becomes fixed: a *parliamentum* is a body framed on the model of 1295, it is frequently, habitually, summoned, and with its consent the king can make *statuta*[1].

Thus before the end of the thirteenth century the national assembly is ceasing to be a feudal court; it is becoming an assembly of the estates of the realm, that is to say, according to the theory of the time, of all sorts and conditions of men. Against the once common mistake of calling the king one of the estates of the realm, I need hardly guard you; it has been sufficiently denounced. The three estates are clergy, barons, and commons, those who pray, those who fight, those who work; this seems to have been considered an exhaustive classification of the divers conditions of men. A similar idea seems to have been very prevalent throughout Western Christendom and to have given rise to assemblies of estates; but the institutions to which it gave rise varied with the histories and circumstances of the different nations. For instance it is particularly noticeable about the English parliament that the burghers do not form a separate estate. There was perhaps some tendency towards an arrangement which would have drawn a broad line of demarcation between them and the knights of the shire, some danger (for such we may consider it) that the king would be able to get money by negotiating with the merchants grants of customs, indirect taxes which would have fallen on the consumer. There were such negotiations in Edward the First's day; but the danger was counteracted; the whole mass of representative members sat together and voted together and represented but one estate, the commons of the realm.

[1] The growth of parliament under Edward I is traced by Stubbs, *Const. Hist.* vol. II, c. 15.

Of course one such assembly as that of 1295 might well have been a solitary event which the historian would note on passing as an anomaly. Taking our stand at the death of Edward in 1307 we are not entitled to say that the sovereign powers which formerly were exercised by the king, or by the king and his barons, have definitely been transferred to an assembly of estates[1]. It is only in the light of what was at that time future history, that the parliaments of Edward's last years have their vast importance. However, we know as a matter of fact that they did form precedents; that parliaments formed on the model of 1295 were constantly held during the coming centuries; that at last it was distinctly recognized that the sovereign power of the realm was vested in a king and a parliament constituted after this model. It is with such knowledge in our minds that we will examine the nature of this assembly.

The first of the three estates is that of the clergy. In the first place the bishops and a number of abbots are summoned by name. Their position is, we may say, somewhat ambiguous. The bishops were the heads of the clergy, the rulers of the church; but they were also tenants in chief of the crown, and held baronies. They had therefore a double claim to be present. There can be little doubt that their claim to be there as prelates of the church, apart from all question of baronial tenure, would have been fully admitted. In the first place there is a difference between the wording of the writs addressed to the temporal lords and that of the writs addressed to the bishops. Usually the lay baron is charged to come upon 'the faith and homage,' or the 'homage and allegiance whereby you are bound to us'; in the bishops' writs homage is not mentioned, though the bishops had to do homage for their temporal possessions; it is to their faith and love to which the king appeals. In the second place when a see is

---

[1] This proposition is amplified in Maitland's *Memoranda de Parliamento* (Rolls Series), 1893, a record of the parliament of 1305. 'A session of the King's Council is the core and essence of every *parliamentum*, the documents usually called parliamentary petitions are petitions to the king and his council, the auditors of the petitions are committees of the council, the rolls of parliament are the records of business done by the council, sometimes with, but much more often without, the concurrence of the estates of the realm.' Intr. p. lxxxviii.

vacant the guardian of the spiritualities of the see was summoned instead of the bishop ; that guardian was in some cases the archbishop, in others the cathedral chapter ; the barony of the vacant bishopric was not in his hands. However, the double right of the bishops provided abundant material for controversy in later times.

As to the abbots—whatever their original title may have been, it soon came to be regarded as title by baronial tenure. This was brought about by the abbots themselves ; they had few interests in national politics, and attendance was burdensome. They therefore insisted that they need not attend unless they held by military tenure. The number of them summoned very rapidly decreases : under Edward I it is as high as 72 ; under Edward III it has fallen to 27, where it remains until the monasteries are dissolved.

But the representation of the clerical estate was not to be completed by the presence of the prelates. The inferior clergy were to be represented. Gradually the principle of representation by elected proctors (*procuratores*) had been making its way into the purely ecclesiastical assemblies. Owing to the rivalry between Canterbury and York, there never came to be any one ecclesiastical assembly for the whole realm ; just for an occasional moment, under the authority of a papal legate, a body representing the clergy of all England might meet, but no such body became a permanent element in the government of the church. Gradually two convocations were formed, the one for Canterbury, the other for York. The growth of representation among the clergy was parallel with the growth of representation among the laity. The inferior clergy were directed to send proctors to represent them in the councils of the church. Towards the end of the thirteenth century the plan adopted in the province of Canterbury was that the parochial clergy of each diocese should be represented by two proctors, the clergy of each cathedral by one ; these elected proctors, together with the archbishop, bishop, abbots, priors, deans and archdeacons, constituted the convocation. In the northern province a slightly different rule prevailed.

Now one must carefully distinguish these provincial convocations from the representation of the clergy in parliament.

The convocations are two ecclesiastical assemblies summoned by the archbishops. Edward attempted to bring the clergy to parliament. The bishops are to bring with them to the national assembly the heads of their chapters, their archdeacons, one proctor for the clergy of each cathedral, and two proctors for the clergy of each diocese. The clause directing the bishops to do this is known, from its first words, as the *praemunientes* clause. It has been in use ever since, is in use even at the present day, though since the end of the fourteenth century it has been steadily disobeyed. The clergy did not like this plan of being mixed up with the laity. They were the holders of great wealth; they had to bear a large share of taxation—but they preferred to deal with the crown separately, to vote their taxes in their own provincial and purely ecclesiastical convocations. Thus they missed the chance of becoming a large element in what was going to be the sovereign body of the realm. Parliament, instead of being an assembly of the three estates, became an assembly of lords, spiritual and temporal, and commons. But this refusal of the clergy belongs to a later time than that of Edward I; Edward made the attempt to get them to meet the laity, so that he might deal with all estates of men concentrated in one assembly.

The history of the baronage, the second estate of the realm, is a matter of difficulty : controversy has raged around it, it has become the theme of a large literature. The difficulty has at least in part been created by the continued existence down to our own time of this estate, and the high value that men have come to set on a seat in the House of Lords. From time to time peerages are claimed by titles which rake up the whole mass of obscure constitutional antiquities, and a committee of privileges of the House of Lords is called on to import into very remote times some definite theory of the baronage, some theory much more definite than had been conceived by the men of those times. No statute of limitations bars the claim to a peerage, and occasionally claims based on very ancient facts have to be discussed and decided.

A word about the way in which such claims are settled. It seems admitted that the House of Lords has a right to

decide on the validity of a new creation, a right which, for
example, it exercised in 1856 when it decided that the patent
of life peerage granted to Baron Parke, Lord Wensleydale,
did not entitle him to sit in the House of Lords.   On the other
hand it seems certain that the House has no jurisdiction on
claims to an old peerage.   The power of deciding such claims
the crown has kept to itself.   As a matter of fact, in a case of
doubt it refers the matter to the House of Lords, which refers
it to a committee of privilege—the committee reports to the
House, the House communicates the resolution to the crown,
the crown acts upon it—the claimant is or is not summoned.
But this is constitutional usage, not law, as has been very
explicitly admitted by the lords in quite recent times[1].   Now
that this should be so even in our own day is, I think, very
instructive.   There is no law court into which the claimant of
a peerage can go to establish his claim.   Now-a-days this
means next to nothing ; if you think that by hereditary right
you are entitled to be summoned as a peer of the land to the
House of Lords, doubtless you will get your right.   But it
points to what has been very important, the power of the king
to determine the estate of the baronage.

Lawyers and antiquaries have been forced to seek for
a strict theory of the baronage, and have never been very
successful in finding one.   Doubtless, however, tenure is the
quarter to which we must look : the idea of nobility of blood
is not the foundation.   That idea does occur all Europe over
among the peoples of our own race if we go back far enough.
The distinction between eorl and ceorl is a distinction between
men who by birth are noble, and those who by birth are
perfectly free but still not noble ; and in the old dooms this
distinction finds sufficient expression, it can be measured in
numbers, the wergild of the noble is so many times that of the

---

[1] This was very explicitly admitted by Lord Campbell in the Wensleydale
case (Anson, *The Law and Custom of the Constitution.* Part I: Parliament.
3rd ed. p. 208), and again by Lord Chelmsford in the Wiltes case (1869, L. R. 4,
H. L. 126).   Lord Chelmsford went so far as to hold that a committee of privileges, hearing such a claim, is quite unlike a judicial tribunal in this respect, that
it is not bound by the resolutions of a previous committee ; it may give diametric-
ally opposite advice in one case to that which has been given in another ; it
pronounces no judgment, it merely gives advice.   F. W. M.

non-noble, the oath of the eorl will outweigh the oaths of so many ceorls. But for a long time before the Conquest the nobility of birth had been supplanted by a nobility of tenure and of office. The thane is noble because of his relation to the king, a relation intimately connected with the holding of land, and a nobility of tenants in chief, crown vassals, would be the natural outcome. But as already pointed out, the Norman Conquest put difficulties in the way of the formation of such a nobility. The aggregate body of tenants in chief was a very miscellaneous mass, including very great men, and men who might relatively be called very small, the tenant who discharged all feudal obligation by coming in person to the field, and he who was bound to bring twenty or fifty knights. The grades were many and small; there was no one place at which a hard line could be drawn ; and probably it suited the king very well that none should be drawn, that he should not be hemmed in by a close aristocracy ; against the great feudatories he relies on the smaller tenants in chief. The practice of the royal exchequer and of the royal army does in time draw a line ; on the one hand stand the *barones majores*, who deal directly with the exchequer, are summoned personally to the army or the council; on the other hand stand *barones minores, barones secundae dignitatis*, who deal with the sheriff, and are summoned through the sheriff; the lands which the former hold are recognized as forming baronies ; for the purpose of feudal dues they are treated as wholes, they pay a lump sum for the relief; those who have not baronies pay on each knight's fee. Finally the word *baro* becomes appropriated to tenants of the former class; the latter are *tenentes in capite* ; but the word *baro* is long used somewhat vaguely; the *barones* of one clause of the great charter seem to be the *barones majores* of another.

It has been contended by some that tenure by barony was a particular kind of tenure differing from tenure by knight service. The difficulty, however, has been to find in what respect these tenures differed. To say that the one implied the right to the special summons while the other did not explains nothing, and brings us back to the point whence we started, that tenure by barony is the tenure of those who are specially summoned. When the law of tenures attains its fully developed form and a systematic expression, we do not find tenure by barony as one of the *kinds* of tenure; Littleton (circ. 1480) does not make it a kind of tenure; a man may hold a barony, certain parcels of land have long ago been recognized as forming a barony, but he does not hold by barony, he holds by knight service or by grand serjeanty. In all private law the distinction has no place, it is utterly unlike the distinction between tenure by knight service and tenure by socage. This is a question which has been contested by Selden, Madox and other very learned persons. I will state the cautious conclusion of Dr Stubbs : ' Whether the baronial honour or qualification was created by the terms of the original grant of the fief, or by subsequent recognition, it is perhaps impossible to determine. As we do not possess anything like an early enfeoffment of a barony, it is safer to confine ourselves to the assertion that in whatever form the lands were acquired or bestowed, the special summons recognized the baronial character of the tenure, or in other words, that estate was a barony which entitled its owner to such special summons[1].' Thus we seem to be involved in a circle—Who is entitled to the special summons ? He who holds a barony. But what estate is a barony? One which entitles its owner to a special summons.

The next point is this:—In the course of the thirteenth century knights representing the shires are summoned to parliament. As this practice is introduced, so the practice directed by John's charter of summoning the minor tenants in chief by means of general writs addressed to the sheriffs—a practice which may have been more or less carefully observed during the reign of Henry III—was abandoned. The minor tenants in chief would be represented in parliament by the elected knights of the shire. Probably they were well content with this ; to attend at their own cost assemblies in which they had little or no weight was a burden. They fell definitely into the mass of the commons : there was no longer any political distinction between the tenants in chief who do not get the

---

[1] *Constitutional History*, vol. II, § 189.

special summons (and who have now altogether lost the name of barons) and the tenants of mesne lords.

The baronage then is the body of men who are summoned specially to parliament—they are summoned because they hold baronies, estates which have been recognized as baronies by the special summons, and by the baronial relief. Several questions arise at this point, which are difficult of solution. First, was the king restricted to the summoning of those who really held what had already been regarded as baronies? The answer seems to be that such must long have been the theory, but a vague theory by which the king was not very strictly bound. In the fourteenth century, as already remarked, a large number of abbots were relieved from the duty of attendance on the ground that they did not hold baronies. It is not known, however, that any temporal lord was ever relieved for a similar reason. On the other hand it is not known that the peers ever objected to the introduction into their midst of one who had no territorial barony—nor for a long time do we hear of anyone protesting that he has a right to be summoned merely because he holds a territorial barony. Probably the theory prevailed and was more or less regularly observed (how regularly is a difficult question, involving a terrible investigation of pedigrees) until in the reign of Henry VI the practice crept in of creating barons by letters patent. Not very long after this it becomes the definitely established doctrine that a writ of summons followed by an actual sitting in the House makes a peer, barony or no barony. This, however, left open the question whether the possession of a barony did not give the right to be summoned, and that question was hardly settled until our own day. During the Middle Ages lands could not be devised by will, the king's tenants *in capite* could not alienate without royal license, and no great absurdity could have resulted from the doctrine that the right to a summons could be conveyed along with the land. Certainly it seems to have been thought in the fifteenth century that the dignity might be made the subject of a family settlement, that the dignity along with the land might be entailed. But in 1669 the contrary was definitely laid down by the king in council on a claim to the barony of Fitzwalter. Barony by tenure was declared to have been discontinued for many ages, and not in being, and so not fit to be 'received or to admit any right of succession thereto.' The question was reopened in 1861 by the Berkeley Peerage case, and what was by this time generally understood to be law was adopted and applied. No one now can claim a seat in the House of Lords on the ground that he holds a land barony. With our modern freedom of alienation some very quaint results might have been produced by a contrary decision. He must claim under writ of summons or letters patent.

As regards barony by writ of summons there are still some questions which remain very open. It may be doubted whether Edward I in summoning a baron intended to bind himself and his successors to summon that man and his heirs to the end of time. But at least very soon it became the rule to summon those and the heirs of those who had already been summoned. Whether a writ of summons conveyed a hereditary right was a question very warmly discussed in the seventeenth century between Coke and Prynne. Prynne produced a long list of cases in which apparently a person who was summoned once, or more than once, was not again summoned, and in which the heirs of a person who was summoned were not summoned. Dr Stubbs says that on careful examination Prynne's list shrinks into very small proportions; most of them can be accounted for by the circumstances of the particular cases, such as minorities[1]. At any rate it became the orthodox doctrine that the crown may not withhold the writ from the heirs of a person who has been once summoned, and who has taken his seat. This was definitely decided in 1673 in the case of the Clifton barony[2]. It seems to have been considered law already in Coke's day[3]. In 1677 the Freshville case decided the point that it is not enough to show that one's ancestor has been summoned, one must show also that he took his seat. Until he takes his seat he is no peer. In this respect barony by writ differs from barony by patent.

---

[1] *Constitutional History*, III, § 751 note.
[2] Anson, *Parliament*, p. 196.
[3] Abergavenny's Case, 12 Rep. f. 70.

The patent itself makes a man a peer[1]. On the face of a writ, you will understand, there is nothing about any peerage, any future summonses, any summoning of heirs—heirs are not mentioned—simply A. B. is summoned to come to the next parliament. A distinct theory of hereditary right has gradually been developed, superseding an indistinct theory of right by tenure.

But besides the prelates and the barons there are other persons who are summoned by name, members of the king's council, in particular the judges, and these distinctly do not hold baronies and are not barons. In the parliaments of Edward's reign the royal council meets the estates of the realm. Edward probably had no idea of restraining himself from seeking the advice of any whose advice might be worth having. It is only very gradually and as a notion of a hereditary right of peerage grows, that these councillors are recognized as having no real place in the deliberations of parliament. They continue to be summoned, even at the present day the judges and the law officers of the crown are summoned by name to attend the parliament:—but before the end of the Middle Ages it became established doctrine that they had no votes, that they were not even to speak unless asked for their opinion. Thenceforward their attendance became little more than a form—but, as just said, a trace of it is retained at the present day :—the judges are summoned to parliament, there are places for them in the House of Lords, and that House has a right to compel their attendance and to take their opinion on matters of law, a right which it occasionally exercises even now though only when it is sitting as a court of law.

[1] The question seems still open whether to prove the summons and sitting of one's ancestor at any time, however remote, is sufficient. In one recent case (the de L'Isle Peerage) Lord Redesdale seems of opinion that the summons and sitting must have taken place on this side the year 1382. This year seems to be chosen because of a statute, 5 Ric. 2, stat. 2, cap. 4, which says that 'all and singular persons and commonalties which from henceforth shall have the summons of the parliament, shall come from henceforth to the parliaments in the manner as they are bound to do, and have been accustomed within the realm of England of old times.' I much doubt whether that statute was directed to making the peerage more hereditary than it was: it seems to have had quite another object. Dr Stubbs would go back as far as 1295, or even further, should earlier writs be discovered. It is a small point, but rather instructive. F. W. M.

It remains to speak of the commons of the realm—the third estate. And first of the word 'commons.' It seems to me that two ideas have been blended. The persons who enjoy no special privilege, who have no peculiar status as barons or clerks, are common men. But I do not believe that this was the notion present to the minds of those who first used the term 'the commons' in contrast to 'the barons' and 'the clergy.' I do not think that the word 'a commoner' as opposed to 'a peer' is old. 'The commons,' says Stubbs, 'are the communities or *universitates*, the organized bodies of freemen of the shires and towns, and the estate of the commons is the *communitas communitatum*, the general body into which for the purposes of parliament these communities are combined[1].' I may remind you of the French commune, and that the language of our law just at the time when parliament was taking shape was French. Any way the representatives who appeared in parliament were not representatives of inorganic collections of individuals, they represented shires and boroughs. It is a little too definite to say that they represented corporations aggregate—the idea of a corporation aggregate had not yet been formed by our law, and the English county has never become a corporation. Still this word is only a little too distinct. The county was already a highly organized entity. County and county court were one. The language of the time did not distinguish between the two—the county court is the *comitatus*—there is no such phrase in our books as *curia comitatus, curia de comitatu*. On the judicial rolls of the time complaints are not uncommon of what the county has done; the county has delivered a false judgment; the county by four representative knights comes into the king's court and denies that it has given a false judgment; the county even wages battle by its champion; if the county does not appear then the county is amerced. It is well to remember that all this had been so for a long time before the knights of the shire were summoned to parliament. In summoning the county to send representatives Henry, De Montfort and Edward were only putting old machinery to a new use. This helps us

---

[1] *Constitutional History*, vol. II, § 185.

to face a question which has often been discussed—namely, who elected the knights of the shire who came to the early parliaments. One answer has been, the king's tenants in chief —these minor tenants in chief who were not summoned by name. There is something to be said for it. The court of a feudal king should consist of tenants in chief—should have no sub-vassals in it. The assembly recognized or designed in John's charter was an assembly of this sort. It became impossible or useless to call up all the tenants in chief, so instead the lesser of them, those who had no special summons, were allowed or compelled to send representatives. The constituency then of the knight of the shire was an assembly, not of all freeholders, but of tenants in chief: only gradually as tenure becomes of less importance, and as the working of the *Quia Emptores* largely increases the number of tenants in chief, are the tenants of mesne lords admitted. But this doctrine has been very generally rejected by modern historians, by Hallam and by Stubbs. From the first the language used of the knights is that they are to be elected in full county court, by the assent of the whole county, *in pleno comitatu, per assensum totius comitatus*, and so forth. Such language had already a definite meaning, it had been constantly used for other purposes; it referred to the county court; the county court was not an assembly constructed on feudal lines ; it comprised the whole body of freehold tenants holding whether by mesne or by immediate tenure of the king. Those who have maintained the opposite opinion have been forced to imagine another county court, one attended only by the tenants *in capite*; to the existence of any such assembly no record bears witness ; such an assembly could not have been indicated by the well-known phrases *plenus comitatus, totus comitatus*. If it be urged that a representation of sub-vassals is opposed to the feudal spirit, the answer is that Edward's legislation is pervaded by a spirit which is anti-feudal, it strives to lessen the public, the political importance of tenure, to bring all classes into direct connection with king and parliament. This is, I believe, the general opinion at the present day—but it has some difficulties to overcome, for it seems clear from a series of petitions in the fourteenth century that the question as to who were to pay the wages of the knights of the shire was a somewhat open one. The tenants of mesne lords contended that they were not bound to contribute, but they do not, I believe, urge as a reason for this contention that they are not represented. It seems very possible that practice differed somewhat widely from legal theory, that the smaller tenants, socagers and so forth, did not often attend the county court, that the office of representative was by no means coveted, and that the election was *de facto* made by the great men. But it seems almost impossible to believe in the face of existing documents that the electoral body was not from the first the whole body of freeholders, the *totus comitatus*. The Act of 1430 (8 Hen. VI, c. 7), which regulated the county franchise for four centuries, was (as appears by the preamble) passed to prevent riotous and disorderly elections— it ordains that the electors are to be people dwelling in the county, whereof every one of them shall have free land or tenement to the value of 40 shillings by the year at the least above all charges. The elector must be a freeholder, a forty shilling freeholder—he must have free land or tenement, but no distinction is noticed between tenure of the king and tenure of a mesne lord, nor between military tenure and tenure by socage. Certainly this act and some others of the two previous reigns do not favour the belief that such distinctions had ever been of importance.

I have stated these two opinions, viz., that the persons who attended the county court for the election of representative knights were (*a*) the tenants in chief of the crown, (*b*) all the freeholders—and I have said that the latter is the opinion which now prevails. For my own part, however, I doubt whether either of them gives us the real truth—reasons for this doubt you can see, if you wish it, in the *English Historical Review* for July 1888. Perhaps I ought just to state what I believe to be the truth. It seems to me that the duty of attending the county court, the duty of going there to sit as a judge, was conceived as being in general incumbent upon all freeholders, but that it had become a burden annexed to particular parcels of land, so that when the number of freeholders was increased by subinfeudation the number of suits due to the county court was not thereby increased. This manor, or this township, or this tract of land which belongs to A, owes a suit to the county court. A enfeoffs B, C, D with parts of the land. The whole manor, township, or tract still owes one suit, must send one suitor, but it owes no more. Who shall do that suit is a matter that A, B, C, D can settle among themselves, and they do settle it among themselves by the terms of the feoffment. As regards the king or the sheriff they are all jointly and severally liable for the coming of one suitor, as between themselves they can determine who shall discharge the burden. So again in a case of inheritance—A holds land which owes a suit: he dies and it descends to his three daughters B, C, D : one or other of them must do the suit, and in general the burden falls on the eldest daughter.

It was in this manner that the county court, which met month by month as a court of law, was constituted. Those who were bound to come there were not necessarily tenants in chief, nor again were all the freeholders bound to come—the persons who were bound to come were those persons who by means of bargains between lords and tenants were answerable for that fixed amount of suit to which the court was entitled. The evidence of this consists in a large number of entries in documents of the thirteenth century, e.g. the Hundred Rolls, in which it is said that A or B does the suit to the county court for a whole manor or township. Of course it is conceivable that when the county court sat for the purpose of electing knights of the shire, other persons attended and were entitled to attend, besides the regular suitors who came month by month—perhaps all freeholders might come:—but I do not see the proof of it—such phrases as *plenus comitatus, totus comitatus* are constantly used of the county court as constituted for judicial purposes, the court which sat month by month, and my contention is that by no means every freeholder owed suit to that court.

A similar question has been raised about the boroughs. Were the boroughs which were directed to return representatives only the demesne boroughs of the crown or all the boroughs in the shire? Both Hallam and Stubbs have written in favour of the latter view. The election of burgesses to

represent the towns was not a matter altogether distinct from
the election of knights of the shire.   A writ was sent to the
sheriff of each county commanding him to procure the election
of two knights from his county, two citizens from every city,
two burgesses from every borough.   The election was probably
made in the boroughs and then reported to the county court ;
but all was under the direction of the sheriff of the county
until the fifteenth century, when a few towns succeeded in
getting made counties of themselves and having sheriffs of
their own.   Indeed, so late as 1872, no writ was addressed to
any officer of the borough ; the sheriff of the county, as of old,
was told to send two knights for the shire, two citizens for
every city, two burgesses for every borough.   See the writ
printed by Sir William Anson, where the sheriff of Middlesex
is to return not only two knights of the shire, but also two
citizens for the city of Westminster and two burgesses of
each of the boroughs of the Tower Hamlets, Finsbury, and
Marylebone[1].   But during the Middle Ages the cities and
boroughs were not thus named.   A considerable power seems
thus to have been left in the sheriff's hand.   What were
boroughs and what were not was to a certain extent ascertained by the ordinary course of justice.   Some boroughs,
but by no means all, had charters ; but when the justices in
eyre came to the county court, every borough was represented
by its twelve burgesses, while the common country village, *villata*, township was represented by the reeve and four best men.
In telling the sheriff, therefore, to return burgesses from every
borough, terms were used which had an ascertained meaning.
We do find the idea of tenure cropping up at times, as though
only the king's demesne boroughs had a right to be represented, or rather were bound to be represented.   But it is
difficult to make the facts correspond with any theory, and
certain that the boroughs on one pretext and another evaded
the duty of sending representatives and paying their wages
whenever they could.   There is one case in which a borough
(Torrington) actually obtained a charter absolving it from
the obligation.

[1] Anson, *Parliament*, pp. 57—8.

By whom were the representative burgesses elected? As regards Edward's day, and indeed much later times, our materials for answering this question are very scanty. The one thing that we can say with some certainty is that the qualification varied from borough to borough. When at last we get accurate information, we find that it varies very greatly. In this borough the franchise is extremely democratic, every person who has a hearth of his own may vote; in another, every one who contributes to the local rates, who pays scot and bears lot; in another, every one who has a free tenement. Elsewhere the franchise is confined to the members of a small civic oligarchy. We can say with some certainty also that the more democratic the qualification, the older it is. In Edward's day contribution to the local burdens may have often qualified a man to vote; in other cases tenure was important, he had to be a tenant of the manor constituted by the borough; in some cases, membership of the merchant guild may have been requisite; but the small close corporations belong to a later age. The important thing to notice is that this matter was decided by no general law; each borough was suffered to work out its own history in its own way, and to buy what privileges it could from the crown.

That notions of tenure had a considerable, though a restricted, influence on the constitution of parliament is shown by the history of the counties palatine. The county of Chester returned no knights until 1543; the county of Durham returned none until 1672.

At the time of which we are speaking (1307), the parliament of the three estates was by no means the only organ of government; indeed, as we have seen, it was only just coming into being. Most of the great statutes of the reign were made in assemblies of the older type, assemblies in which the commons and the inferior clergy were not represented. Such assemblies of prelates and barons were held in later times, and got the name of *Magna Concilia* which distinguished them from true *Parliamenta*; only by slow degrees was the line established between what could be done by a *Magnum Concilium* and what could be done by a *Parliamentum*.

But besides these grand councils, the king had a permanent council in constant session. This permanent or ordinary council had grown out of the *curia Regis* of earlier times; the word *curia* comes to be more and more definitely appropriated to a judicial body, and the judicial body becomes distinct from the administrative deliberative body to which the king looks for advice and aid in the daily task of government. A *concilium* as distinct from the *curia* first becomes prominent during the minority of Henry III—it acts as a council of regency. It is generally called simply *Concilium Regis*, as opposed to the *commune concilium regni*; its members are *magnates de concilio, conciliatores.* It seems to comprise the great officers of state, justiciar, chancellor, treasurer, some or all of the judges of the royal *curia*, and a number of bishops, barons and other members who in default of other title are simply councillors. The chroniclers now and again inform us that one person was made a member of the council and another dismissed; but (and this is noticeable) there is from the first something informal about its constitution;—it needs no formal document to make a man a member of the council; the king can take advice in what quarter he pleases, and the so-called councillor has no right to be consulted. Just while parliament is growing this council also is growing. The task of government becomes always more elaborate; it requires constant attention; it cannot possibly be accomplished by the king without the help or interference of a national assembly summoned from time to time. During Henry's reign the scheme of reform constantly put forward by the barons is that they should elect the council; Henry's councillors have too often been his hated foreign favourites. This scheme breaks down. Under Edward the council is a definite body; its members take an oath; they are sworn of the council—swearing to give good advice, to protect the king's interests, to do justice honestly, to take no gifts. Under Edward the relations of this king's council to the great council of the realm are still indefinite; all works so smoothly that there is no struggle, and consequently no definition. Both in his parliament and in his council the king legislates, taxes and judges—indeed it is often hard for us to say whether a given piece of work is, has or has not been sanctioned by the common council of the realm. Let us take these points separately—(1) legislation, (2) taxation, (3) judicature.

(1) That the king could not by himself or by the advice of a few chosen advisers make general laws for the whole realm seems an admitted principle. The most despotic of Edward's predecessors had not claimed such a power—it is with the counsel of prelates and barons that they legislate. On the other hand, that the commons or inferior clergy must share in legislation was not admitted, was not as yet even asserted. As already said, the great laws of the reign—laws which made the profoundest changes in all parts of the common law, laws which all subsequent generations have called statutes, statutes which are in force at the present moment—were made in assemblies in which the commons were not represented. But again it seems to have been allowed that there were regulations which might be made without the sanction of a national assembly of any kind. The king in his council could make, if not statutes, at least ordinances. Some even of what we now call the statutes of Edward I do not on their face claim any higher authority than that of the king and his council. Here is a fruitful source of difficulty for future times. Can any line be drawn between the province of the statute and the province of the ordinance? Under Edward all works so smoothly that the question is not raised. We can say no more than this—and it is vague enough—that important and permanent regulations which are conceived as altering the law of the land can only be made by statute, with the consent of prelates and barons. Minor regulations, temporary regulations, regulations which do not affect the nation at large can be made by ordinance.

(2) We turn to taxation, and may begin with a few general reflections as to past history. In the first place, the king had not been nearly so dependent on taxation as a modern government is. Indeed it is not until the very end of the Anglo-Saxon time that we hear of anything that can be called a tax, not until it is necessary to pay tribute to the Danes. Let us briefly reckon up the sources of income which the kings enjoyed after the Conquest. In the first place there

were the demesne lands of the crown. The remnant of the old folk land had become *terra Regis*, and this constituted the ancient demesne[1]. Then escheats and forfeitures were constantly bringing to the king's hand new demesne lands. Apart from his being the ultimate lord of all land, the king was the immediate lord of many manors—he was by far the largest landowner of the kingdom. Secondly, there were his feudal rights—rights which had steadily grown in some directions, if they had been diminished in others. The charter of 1215, by clauses which were never again repeated, forbad him to impose any scutage, or any aid save the three regular feudal aids, without the common counsel of the realm. The charter defined the amount to be paid for reliefs, but besides scutages, aids and reliefs, he was entitled to wardships and marriages—his rights in this direction had steadily grown, and these were profitable commodities. Thirdly, the profits of justice in the king's courts must have been very considerable. Under John the sale of justice had become scandalous. By the charter, he promised to sell justice to none—but without exactly selling justice, there was much profit to be made by judicial agencies : fees could be demanded from litigants, and in the course of proceedings, civil as well as criminal, numerous fines and amercements were inflicted. Fourthly, the king had many important rights to sell, in particular the right of jurisdiction, and though the more far-sighted of the kings dreaded and checked the growth of proprietary jurisdiction, there was always a temptation to barter the future for the present. The right to have a market was freely sold, and many similar rights. Pardons again were sold. The towns had to buy their privileges bit by bit. What is more, the grantee of any privilege had in practice to get the grant renewed by every successive king. That the king was bound by his ancestors' grants might be the law, but it was law that no prudent person would rely on. Offices too, even the highest offices of the realm, were at times freely bought and sold—this does not seem to have been thought disgraceful. Fifthly, a good deal could be made out of the church—when a bishop died the king took the temporalities, the lands, of the see into his own

[1] See p. 57.

hand, and was in no hurry to allow the see to be filled; this however was an abuse. Sixthly, the king had a right to tallage the tenants on his demesne lands, and on his demesne lands were found many of the most considerable towns. This seems the right rather of the landlord than of the king; other lords with the king's leave exercised a similar right over their tenants in villeinage. The tenants on the demesne lands had for the most part held in villeinage; the burghers had very generally bought themselves free of villein services in consideration of an annual rent, but the king had retained the right to impose a tallage from time to time—to impose a certain sum on the borough or the manor as a whole—or rather an uncertain sum, for we hear of no limit to the amount. Lastly, somehow or another, the process is obscure, the king had become entitled to certain customs duties: Magna Carta recognizes that there are certain ancient and right customs (*antiquae et rectae consuetudines*) which merchants can be called upon to pay, and with these it contrasts unjust exactions, or maletolts. To all this we may add that the obligations of tenure supplied the king with an army which could be called up in case of war.

Here we shall do well to note that at this time and for several centuries afterwards, no distinction was drawn between national revenue and royal revenue; the king's revenue was the king's revenue, no matter the source whence it came; it was his to spend or to save, as pleased him best; all was his pocket money; it is to later times that we must look for any machinery for compelling the king to spend his money upon national objects.

But large as had been the king's income, and free as he was to deal with it in his own way, it had not been found large enough. Direct taxes had been imposed: a land tax, for some time called Danegeld, afterwards carucage, a tax of so much on the carucate or plough-land; then as already said, under Henry the Second the taxation of movables begins. We can hardly say that for such taxation the theory of the twelfth century requires a decree of the national assembly; it but slowly enters mens' heads that the consent of a majority of an assembly, however representative, can be construed to be

the consent of all men:—rather the idea is that a tax ought
to be a voluntary gift of the individual taxpayer, and now
and again some prelate or baron is strong enough to protest
that he individually has not consented and will not pay. The
clauses of the charter of 1215, to which reference has so often
been made, mark a very definite step:—no scutage or aid
(save the three feudal aids) is to be imposed without the
counsel of the prelates and tenants in chief. But these clauses
are withdrawn; it seems to be thought hard that the child
Henry should be compelled to make this concession, particularly at a moment when a foreign enemy is within the
realm. However, these clauses are in fact observed; Henry,
though he sometimes extorts money in irregular ways, does
not attempt to tax without the common council of the realm.
This council is as yet but an assembly of prelates and
magnates; it grants him taxes on land and on movables,
but we can see a doubt growing as to how far it represents
all classes of men, how far the consent of the unrepresented
classes is necessary. Henry is driven to negotiate with the
inferior clergy, and with the merchants. In 1254 knights of
the shire are summoned to treat about a tax. That however
remains an isolated precedent, and the parliament summoned
by De Montfort can hardly be called a precedent at all. It is
not therefore until 1295 that a regular practice of summoning
the representatives of the commons and of the inferior clergy
begins[1]. Each estate now taxes itself; thus in 1295 the barons
and knights of the shire offered an eleventh, the burgesses a
seventh, the clergy a tenth. On this followed the great crisis
of 1297. The rather elaborate circumstances we must leave
undescribed; Edward was in great need of money: the pope
Boniface VIII had published the Bull *Clericis laicos* forbidding the clergy to pay taxes to any secular power; the
barons, again led by the Constable and Marshal, Bohun and
Bigot, refused to serve in Flanders, contending that they were
not bound to do so by their tenure; Edward seized the wool,
the staple commodity of England, and exacted an impost
on it; he also obtained the grant of an aid from an irregular
assembly. The barons armed against him, and he was forced

---

[1] For Edward I's earlier experiments in summoning parliaments see Stubbs,
Constitutional History, vol. II, § 213.

to withdraw from his position, to confirm the charters with certain additional articles. The exact form of those articles is of some importance. According to what in all probability is the authentic version of this *Confirmatio Cartarum*, he granted that the recent exactions, aids and prises should not be made precedents, that no such aids, tasks or prises should be taken for the future without the common consent of the realm, that no tax like that recently set on wool should be taken in future without the common consent of the realm, saving the ancient aids, prises and customs. We have also what seems to be either an imperfect abstract of this document, or else a document which records the demands of the barons. This in after times came to be known as a statute, *Statutum de Tallagio non concedendo*, though as just said in all probability it had no right to this name[1]. It goes somewhat further than the authentic version; it contains the word 'tallage' which the authentic version does not, it does not contain a saving clause for the king's ancient rights. 'No tallage or aid shall be taken without the will and consent of all the archbishops, bishops, prelates, earls, knights, burgesses and other free men of the realm.' Tallage, as we have seen, was the name given to an impost set by the king on his own demesne lands—in origin rather a right of the landlord than of the king. Edward, it seems pretty certain, did not consider that he had resigned this right; in 1304 he tallaged his demesne lands. But though this particular mode of raising money may thus have been left open by the letter, if not by the spirit of the law, we may fairly say that after 1295 the imposition of any direct tax without the common consent of the realm was against the very letter of the law. I say of any direct tax, because subsequent events showed that the question of indirect taxes, of customs duties and the like, had not been finally settled. And the common consent of the realm was now no vague phrase ; that consent had now its appropriate organ in a parliament of the three estates.

As to the administration of justice by the parliament and the council, we shall speak hereafter, but first a little should be said of the general position of the king. And first as to his title :—

[1] *Select Charters*, pp. 487—98.

The kingship had, I think, by this time become definitely hereditary.

Before the Conquest the English kingship was an elective kingship, but the usage hardening into law was for the great men, the witan, to elect some near kinsman of the dead king. We ought to recollect in this context that the then existing law as to private inheritance was not primogenitary; ordinarily at least a dead man's lands and his goods were partible among all his sons; all primogenitary rules were but slowly worked out long after the Norman Conquest. We learn from Glanvill that even at the end of the twelfth century one of the most elementary questions was still open—A has two sons, B and C, the elder, B, dies during A's lifetime, leaving a son, D; then A dies; who shall inherit, C or D? English law has not yet made up its mind about this very easy problem—for primogeniture is new. So we must not think of private law as setting a model for the succession to the kingship; much rather is it true that the succession to a kingship or other office became the model for the succession to land; primogeniture spreads from office to property. It is long after the Conquest before the notion that the kingship is strictly hereditary becomes firmly rooted. The Conqueror himself could not rely upon hereditary right; he relied rather on gift or devise. Edward had given him the kingdom. I believe that the notion that of right the crown should have gone to Edgar the Ætheling only makes its appearance late in the day. Neither Rufus nor Henry I could rely on hereditary right even according to the notions of the time; both had to seek election and to rely upon the support of the people. Stephen again was compelled to assert a title by election. Probably the succession of Henry the Third did much towards fixing the notion of hereditary right. John has been spoken of by modern writers as an usurper; some at least of his contemporaries treated him as an elected king. Matthew Paris (who died about fifty years afterwards) has put into the mouth of Hubert Walter, Archbishop of Canterbury, a speech made by him before crowning John—and we have other reason for believing that something of the sort was actually said. He distinctly said that no one could claim the crown by hereditary right—kinship to the late king would give a preference; it is natural and proper to elect a near kinsman, and we have elected Earl John[1]. The succession of Henry III, a boy of nine, on the death of his father (there was no one else to crown) is in many ways an important event. From this time forward the kingship is, I think, regarded by contemporaries as definitely hereditary. Then during a period of nearly two centuries the late king has always an obvious heir who succeeds him—Henry III, the three Edwards and Richard II follow each other in strictly correct order, though we have to remember that Edward the Second is deposed. Edward I was the first king who reigned before he was crowned.

Long before the Conquest the English kings had been crowned and anointed. Whether this ceremony was borrowed straight from the Old Testament or became ours by a more roundabout route seems uncertain; but clearly it was not considered to bestow upon the king any indefeasible title to the obedience of his subjects; the kings are easily put aside, and no bishop objects that the Lord's Anointed cannot be removed by earthly power; still a religious sanction is given to the relation between king and people. Also the king swears an oath. The oath taken by Ethelred the Unready we have, and it is in these terms, ' In the name of the Holy Trinity three things do I promise to this Christian people my subjects: first that God's church and all the Christian people of my realm hold true peace; secondly that I forbid all rapine and injustice to men of all conditions; thirdly that I promise and enjoin justice and mercy in all judgments, that the just and merciful God of his everlasting mercy may forgive us all[2].'

Coronation oaths are of considerable interest, since they throw light on the contemporary conception of the kingship. The oath of Ethelred may be taken as the model of the oaths sworn by king after king in the days after the Conquest. The Conqueror, we are told, swore that he would defend God's holy churches and their rulers, that he would 'rule the whole people with righteousness and royal providence, that he would estab-

---

[1] *Select Charters*, p. 271.
[2] Liebermann, *Gesetze der Angelsachsen*, vol. I, p. 217.

lish and hold fast right law, and utterly forbid rapine and
unrighteous judgment.' Rufus swore a like oath. The oath
of Henry I seems to have been precisely that of Ethelred. It
is probable that the oaths of Richard, John and Henry III
differed somewhat from this ancient form. They promised
to observe peace, to reverence the church and clergy, to
administer right justice to the people, to abolish evil laws and
customs, and to maintain the good. It is to be regretted
that about the oath of Edward I there is some doubt—to
be regretted because the oath of Edward II differs in an
important manner from that of Henry III—but a French
form has been preserved which is possibly that used by
Edward I, and it has these words—'and that he will cause
to be made in all his judgments equal and right justice with
discretion and mercy, and that he will grant to hold the laws
and customs of the realm which the people shall have made
and chosen (*que les gentes de people averont faitz et eslies*),
and will maintain and uphold them and will put out all bad
laws and customs[1].' The oath of Edward II is much more
definite and precise than anything that has yet come before
us. The king is thus catechized by the Archbishop:

Sir, will you grant and keep and by your oath confirm to
the people of England the laws and customs granted to them
by the ancient kings of England your righteous and godly
predecessors, and especially the laws, customs and privileges
granted to the clergy and people by the glorious King
S. Edward your predecessor? I grant and promise.

Sir, will you keep towards God and holy church and to
clergy and people peace and accord in God entirely after your
power? I will keep them.

Sir, will you cause to be done in all your judgments equal
and right justice and discretion in mercy and truth to your
power? I will so do.

Sir, do you grant to hold and keep the laws and righteous
customs which the community of your realm shall have chosen
(*quas vulgus elegerit—les quiels la communaute de vostre
roiaume aura esleu*), and will you defend and strengthen

---

[1] *Constitutional History*, vol. II, § 179 note.

them to the honour of God to the utmost of your power?
I grant and promise[1].

You will observe the promise to confirm the laws of Saint
Edward.   The Confessor has by this time become a myth—
a saint and hero of a golden age, of a good old time; but
there are documents going about purporting to give his laws,
which, if they contain many things inapplicable to these later
days and even unintelligible about wergilds and so forth,
contain also some far from pointless tales, as to how the
sheriffs were once elected by the people, and the like.   But
the main interest of the oath centres in the words *leges quas
vulgus elegerit—les quiels la communaute de vostre roiaume
aura esleu.*   Legislation, it is now considered, is the function
of the *communitas regni, universitas regni,* the whole body of
the realm concentrated in a parliament.

And now what was the king's legal position?   I think
that we may in the first place say with some certainty that
against him the law had no coercive process ; there was no
legal procedure whereby the king could either be punished or
compelled to make redress.   This has been denied on the
ground that in much later days a certain judge said that he
had seen a writ directed to Henry III—a writ beginning
Praecipe Regi Henrico—a writ of course proceeding theoretically from the king, telling the sheriff to order King Henry
to appear in court and answer a plaintiff in an action.   But
this story is now very generally disbelieved.   On the contrary,
from Henry III's reign we get both from Bracton and from
the Plea Rolls the most positive statements that the king
cannot be sued or punished.   In this meaning, the maxim
that the king can do no wrong is fully admitted.   If the king
breaks the law then the only remedy is a petition addressed
to him praying him that he will give redress.   On the other
hand, it is by no means admitted that the king is above the
law.   Bracton who, you will remember, was for twenty years
a judge under Henry III, repeats this very positively :—The
king is below no man, but he is below God and the law ; law
makes the king ; the king is bound to obey the law, though if

[1] *Constitutional History,* vol. II, § 249.

he break it, his punishment must be left to God[1].   Now to a student fresh from Austin's jurisprudence this may seem an absurd statement.   You put the dilemma, either the king is sovereign or no ; if he be sovereign then he is not legally below the law, his obligation to obey the law is at most a moral obligation ; on the other hand if he is below the law, then he is not sovereign, he is below some man or some body of men, he is bound for example to obey the commands of king and parliament, the true sovereign of the realm.   This may be a legitimate conclusion if in Austin's way we regard all law as command ; but it is very necessary for us to re-member that the men of the thirteenth century had no such notion of sovereignty, had not clearly marked off legal as distinct from moral and religious duties, had not therefore conceived that in every state there must be some man or some body of men above all law.   And well for us is it that this was so, for had they looked about for some such sovereign man or sovereign body as Austin's theory requires, there can be little doubt that our king would have become an absolute monarch, a true sovereign ruler in Austin's sense— the assembly of prelates and magnates was much too vague a body, and a body much too dependent for its constitution on the king's will to be recognized as the depositary of sovereign power.   No, we have to remember that when in the middle of the seventeenth century Hobbes put forward a theory of sovereignty which was substantially that of Bentham and of Austin, this was a new thing, and it shocked mankind.   Law had been conceived as existing independently of the will of any ruler, independently even of the will of God ; God himself was obedient to law ; the most glorious feat of his Omnipotence was to obey law :—so the king, he is below the law, though he is below no man ; no man can punish him if he breaks the law, but he must expect God's vengeance.

While we are speaking of this matter of sovereignty, it will be well to remember that our modern theories run counter to the deepest convictions of the Middle Ages—to their whole manner of regarding the relation between church and state.

[1] Bracton, *De Legibus Angliae* (Rolls Series), I, 38; *History of English Law*, vol. I, pp. 160—1, 500—1.

Though they may consist of the same units, though every man may have his place in both organisms, these two bodies are distinct. The state has its king or emperor, its laws, its legislative assemblies, its courts, its judges; the church has its pope, its prelates, its councils, its laws, its courts. That the church is in any sense below the state, no one will maintain; that the state is below the church is a more plausible doctrine; but the general conviction is that the two are independent, that neither derives its authority from the other. Obviously while men think thus, while they more or less consistently act upon this theory, they have no sovereign in Austin's sense; before the Reformation Austin's doctrine was impossible.

But to return. The troubles of Henry's reign, troubles which he brought upon himself by his shiftless faithless policy, give rise to other thoughts. Bracton himself in one place hints that possibly if the king does wrong and refuses justice the *universitas regni* represented by the barons may do justice in the king's name and in the king's court. In the printed text of Bracton's book there is a passage, probably interpolated by some annotator, which goes far beyond this, which declares that the king is not only below God and the law, but below his court, that is to say, below his earls and barons, for the earls (*comites*) are so called because they are the king's fellows (*socii*), and he who has a fellow has a master (*qui habet socium, habet magistrum*); they therefore are bound to set a bridle upon him and constrain him to do right[1]. This passage clearly was written during the time of revolt, the revolt which led to the battles of Lewes and of Evesham. The ideal of that revolt was a small council of magnates, chosen by the barons, whom the king would be bound to consult, who, if need be, would exercise the royal powers. That ideal was not realized—happily, I think we may say, for it was an oligarchical ideal. The law was left as it was, as it is at this very moment—that against the king law has no coercive power, it has no punishment for the king, it cannot compel him to make redress—or, as we say, the king can do no wrong. It was left to later ages to work out consistently the other side of our modern doctrine, namely, that though the king can neither be punished nor sued,

[1] Bracton, *De Legibus Angliae*, I, 268.

no other person, no servant of the king, is protected against the ordinary legal consequences of an unlawful act by the king's command.

The power of deposing a king is a somewhat different matter. The next century presents us with two cases of deposition, that of Edward II and that of Richard II. There was talk of deposing John, there was talk of deposing Henry III. Apparently the common opinion of the time was quite prepared for the deposition of a king who would not rule according to law—any notion of divine hereditary right not to be set aside by any earthly power does not belong to this age. But the only precedents for deposing a king belonged to an already remote time, and in all probability were but little known. The events of 1327 and 1399, though they prove clearly enough that the nation saw no harm in setting aside a bad or incompetent king, prove also that there was no legal machinery for doing this. We shall see this more clearly when these events come before us hereafter. The idea current in the thirteenth century is not so much that of a power to try your king and punish him, as that of a right of revolt, a right to make war upon your king. It is a feudal idea and a dangerous one; the vassal who cannot get justice out of his lord may renounce his fealty and his homage, may defy his lord, may, that is, renounce his affiance, his fealty. This is not the remedy of an oppressed nation, it is the remedy of an oppressed vassal.

This would naturally lead us to speak of feudalism as a political or anti-political force; that is a subject which we will still postpone; but a little more may here be added about the theory of the kingship. Already in Henry III's reign it is the doctrine of the royal judges, who would not be disposed to narrow unduly the scope of their master's powers, that the king cannot make laws without the consent of his prelates and barons. This is brought out by the treatment which a famous passage in the Institutes receives at their hands—*sed et quod principi placuit legis habet vigorem.* Now under Henry II, the writer whom we call Glanvill does, as it seems to me, hint that these words are true of the king of England; his words however are not very plain, and it is possible that

he did not wish them to be very plain; however he brings out
clearly the matter of fact that Henry legislates with the counsel
of the magnates, *consilio procerum*[1].   In Bracton we may see
a distinct step—he cites the words of the Institutes, but so as
to give them a quite new meaning; this I take to be a bit of
deliberate perverseness, something not far removed from a
jest; he knows that the words in their proper sense are not
true of King Henry—the law has made him king, it is by
virtue of the law that he reigns, and this law sets limits to the
placita principis[2]. Undoubtedly, however, during Henry III's
long reign a great deal of what we should call law making
was done without the assent of the national assembly.   The
common law grew very rapidly; it could grow very rapidly
because the opinions of the time conceded to the king or to
the king and his selected councillors a considerable power of
making new remedies—new modes of litigation, new forms
of action.   It is not at once seen that to give new remedies
is often enough to alter the substantive law of the land.
Gradually however this is seen, and complaints against these
new actions become loud, chiefly because they draw away
litigants from the feudal courts and from the ecclesiastical
courts.   Bracton writing towards the end of the reign has left
us a curious transitional doctrine. The king can make new
writs, new forms of action; in strictness such a writ requires
the consent of the magnates, at least if it concerns land (for
land is the subject of the feudal jurisdictions); still the consent
of the magnates may be taken for granted; they consent if
they do not expressly dissent; and after all it is the king's
duty to find a remedy for every wrong—his solemn sworn
duty.   Such a theory could hardly be permanent, and one of
the definite results attained by what we call the Barons' War
was that a limit was set to the king's writ-making power.   In
Edward's day we find it admitted that new writs cannot be
made without the action of the national assembly—they must

---

[1] *Tractatus de Legibus Angliae. Prologus.* "Leges namque Anglicanas, licet
non scriptas, Leges appellari non videtur absurdum (cum hoc ipsum lex fit 'quod
principi placet, legis habet vigorem') eas scilicet, quas super dubiis in consilio
definiendis, procerum quidem consilio, et principis accidente authoritate, constat
esse promulgatas."

[2] *De Legibus Angliae*, 1, 38.

be sanctioned by statute; indeed so strict has this rule become that in 1285 it requires a statute to permit the clerks in the King's Chancery to vary the old writs slightly so as to fit new cases as they arise, but only new cases which fall under rules of law already established and which require remedies which are already given. Henceforth the sphere for judge-made law is hemmed in by the existing remedies, the writs that have already been made; to introduce a new form of action requires a statute. Henceforth for nearly two centuries the growth of unenacted law is very slow indeed.

E. *Administration of Justice.*

This brings us to the administration of justice. We have already had occasion to speak of courts of various kinds. Some repetition is unavoidable. The further back we trace our history the more impossible is it for us to draw strict lines of demarcation between the various functions of the state: the same institution is a legislative assembly, a governmental council and a court of law; this is true of the witenagemot; it is true, though perhaps less true of the Curia of the Norman kings; traces of its truth are left in our own time; our highest court of law is to this day an assembly of prelates and nobles, of lords spiritual and temporal in parliament assembled; everywhere, as we pass from the ancient to the modern, we see what the fashionable philosophy calls differentiation. We will now take a brief review of the whole system of law courts as it stands in Edward the First's day.

There are we may say courts of four great kinds. (1) There are the very ancient courts of the shire and the hundred; these we may call popular courts, or still better, communal courts—they are courts which in time past have been constituted by the free men of the district; they are courts which are now constituted by the freeholders of the district: but a good many of the hundred courts have fallen into private hands. (2) There are the feudal courts, courts which have their origin in tenure, in the relation between man and lord; there is the manorial court baron for the freehold tenants of the manor, in which they sit as judges; there is the hall-moot or customary court of the manor for the tenants in villeinage, in which (at least according to the theory of later times) the lord's steward is the only judge. (3) There are the <u>king's own central courts</u>. (4) There are the <u>courts held by the king's itinerant justices</u>—visitatorial <u>courts</u>, we may for the moment call them. We leave out of sight the ecclesiastical courts, or courts Christian, though these were important courts for the laity as well as for the clergy.

Now the preliminary notions with which we ought to start are, I think, these:—(*a*) The communal courts of the shire and the hundred are, to start with, fully competent courts for all causes criminal as well as civil. The kings of the pre-Conquest period had apparently no desire to draw away justice from these courts. Over and over again they ordain that no one is to bring his suit before the king before justice has failed him in the hundred and the shire. We must not think of the witenagemot even as a court of appeal—to introduce the notion of an appeal from court to court is to introduce a far too modern conception. The suitor who comes before the king comes there not to get a mistake corrected but to lodge a complaint against his judges; they have wilfully denied him justice.

(*b*) By the side of the ancient courts there have grown up the feudal courts. This process had in all probability been going on for a century before the Conquest. After the Conquest the principle seems admitted that any lord who has tenants may, if he can, hold a court for them. In this disputes between tenants are adjudged; in particular if land is in dispute and both parties admit that the land is holden of this lord, then his court is the proper tribunal. A great deal of jurisdiction has thus been taken away from the communal courts, but jurisdiction of a civil kind. Mere tenure cannot give a criminal jurisdiction; if the lord has this, he has it by virtue of some grant from the king.

(*c*) After the Norman Conquest the <u>king's court has, we may say, three main functions</u>: (i) as of <u>old it is a court of last resort in case of default of justice, (ii) on feudal principle</u> it is a <u>court for the tenants in chief</u>, (iii) it is admitted that <u>there are certain causes in which the king has a special interest</u>

and which must come either before his own court or before a
court held by some officer of his:—these are the pleas of the
crown.

We have now to watch the growth of this royal jurisdiction
and will begin by speaking of the pleas of the crown.

Already before the Conquest we find that there are
certain criminal cases in which the king is conceived to have a
special interest. Thus in the Laws of Canute it is said ' These
are the rights which the king has over all men in Wessex—
mund-bryce, hâm-sôcne, forstal, flymena-fyrmðe and fyrd-wite[1].'
Apparently in case of any of these crimes no lord may presume
to exercise jurisdiction—unless it has been expressly granted
to him ; such cases must come before the king, or his officer
the sheriff, and the consequent forfeitures are specially the
king's. A word as to the nature of these crimes:—*mund-
bryce* is breach of the king's special peace or protection, this
as we shall soon see becomes a matter of the utmost moment ;
hâm-sôcne is housebreaking, the seeking of a man in his
house ; *forstal* seems to mean ambush ; *flymena-fyrmðe* the
receipt of outlaws ; *fyrd-wite* the fine for neglecting the summons to the army. In these cases, it is conceived there is
something more than ordinary crime, e.g. homicide or theft,
there is some injury to the king, some attack upon his own
peculiar rights.

The next list of pleas of the crown that we get is found in
the *Leges Henrici Primi* (1108–18, § 10). It is much longer
and so instructive that I will translate it : ' Breach of the king's
peace given by his hand or writ; danegeld; contempt of his
writs or precepts; death or injury done to his servants; treason
and breach of fealty ; every contempt or evil word against
him; [castle building—*castellatio trium scannorum*;] outlawry;
theft punishable with death ; murder ; counterfeiting his
money ; arson ; *hamsoken* ; *forestal* ; *fyrdwite* ; *flymena-
fyrmðe* ; premeditated assault ; robbery ; streetbreach ; taking
the king's land or money ; treasure trove ; shipwreck ; waif of
the sea ; rape ; forests ; reliefs of barons ; fighting in the king's
house or household ; breach of peace in the army ; neglecting
to repair castles or bridges ; neglecting a summons to the

[1] Liebermann, *Gesetze der Angelsachsen*, vol. I, p. 317.

army; receiving an excommunicate or outlaw; breach of surety; flight in battle; unjust judgment; default of justice; perverting the king's law[1].' It is a most disorderly list. The writer has apparently strung together all cases in which either in ancient or modern times the king has asserted a special interest. Observe how criminal cases are mixed up with the king's fiscal rights—by fiscal rights I mean such rights as that to treasure trove, to shipwreck and goods thrown up by the sea. This is very instructive; one of the chief motives that the king has for amplifying his rights is the want of money; the criminal is regarded as a source of income. It will strike you that by a little ingenuity on the part of royal judges almost all criminal cases and very many civil cases also can be brought within the terms of this comprehensive list. But you will further observe that no such generalization has yet been made, it is not yet said that all crime, or all serious crime, or all acts of violence are causes for royal cognizance.

There is one term, however, which occurs in both these lists which can be so extended as to cover a very large space—that is the *mund-bryce* of Canute's laws, which in the *Leges Henrici* appears as *infortio pacis regiae per manum vel breve datum.* Let us go back a little. The idea of law is from the first very closely connected with the idea of peace—he who breaks the peace, puts himself outside the law, he is outlaw. But besides the general peace which exists at all times and in all places, and which according to ancient ideas is the peace of the nation rather than of the king, every man has his own special peace and if you break that you injure him. Thus if you slay A in B's house, not only must you pay A's price or wergild to his kinsfolk, but you have broken B's peace and you will owe B a sum of money, the amount of which will vary with B's rank—you have broken B's peace or *mund*; the *mund* of an archbishop is worth so much, that of an ealdorman so much, and so forth. Like other men the king has his peace. In course of time, we may say, the king's peace devours all other peaces—but that has not been effected until near the end of the twelfth century. In the *Leges Edwardi Confessoris* (§ 12) which represent the law of the first half of the century,

---

[1] Liebermann, *Gesetze der Angelsachsen*, vol. I, p. 556.

the king's peace covers but certain times, places, and persons. *Pax Regis multiplex est*—the king's peace is manifold.   First there is that which he gives with his own hand.   Then there is the peace of his coronation day, and this extends eight days. Then the peace of the three great festivals, Christmas, Easter, Pentecost: each endures for eight days.   Then there is the peace of the four great highways—the four ancient Roman roads which run through England.   To commit a crime in one of these peaces is to offend directly against the king.

Before the end of the century there has been a great change, a great simplification ; apparently it has been effected thus :—Under the Norman kings, the mode of bringing a criminal to justice was called an appeal (*appellum*); this word is not used in our modern way to imply the going from one court to a superior court—but means an accusation of crime brought by the person who has been wronged—the person, e.g., whose goods have been stolen or who has been wounded. Well, the king's justices seem to have allowed any appellor to make use of the words ' in the king's peace ' whenever he pleased, and did not allow the appellee to take exception to these words—did not allow him to urge that though he might have committed theft or homicide still he had not broken the king's peace, since the deed was not done against a person, or at a time or place which was covered by the king's peace. Fictions of this kind are very common in our legal history, they are the means whereby the courts amplify their juris-diction.   Any deed of violence then, any use of criminal force, can be converted into a breach of the king's peace and be brought within the cognizance of the king's own court.

Further, under Henry II we find a new criminal procedure growing up by the side of the appeal, once a specially royal procedure—this is the procedure by way of presentment or indictment.   Under the Assize of Clarendon royal justices are sent throughout England, to inquire by the oaths of the neighbours of all robberies, and other violent misdeeds; those who are accused, presented, indicted by the sworn testimony of the neighbours, by the juries of the hundreds and the vills, are sent to the ordeal.   This is an immense step in the history of criminal law.   A crime is no longer regarded as a matter merely between the criminal and those who have directly suffered by his crime—it is a wrong against the nation, and the king as the nation's representative. This procedure by indictment the king keeps in his own hands; it is a specially royal procedure; those who are thus accused of crime must be brought before the king's own justices.

A parallel movement, the details of which are as yet very obscure, has been giving to all the graver crimes the character of felony[1]. The origin and original meaning of the word are disputed, but the best authorities now tell us that it is Celtic and carries at first the meaning of baseness; it is said to be connected with the Latin *fallere*, and our verb *to fail*. Be that as it may, two things seem fairly clear, (1) that the word came to us from France with the Normans, (2) that it then meant the specifically feudal crime, the most heinous of all crimes in the opinion of that age, the betrayal of one's lord, or treachery against one's lord. For some time it is thus used in England; thus in the *Leges Henrici* felony is still one crime among many. We observe two things about it, that it is a crime punished by death, and that it is a crime which causes an escheat of the land which the criminal holds. But before the end of the twelfth century we find that this word has lost its specific signification, that it has a wide meaning. Whenever an appeal is made, be it for homicide, or wounding, or theft, the appellor always states that it was done not only *in pace domini Regis*, but also *in felonia*. We even find that these words are absolutely essential; if they are not used the appeal is null. Here again, I take it, fiction has been at work—the judges have encouraged the use of this term, and have not allowed accused persons to protest that though there might be homicide, wounding or robbery, still there was no felony. Two motives made for this:—the old system of money compositions was breaking down; at the beginning of the twelfth century it is still in existence, though capital punishment has been gaining ground; at the end of the century it has disappeared—every crime of great gravity has become a capital offence. Secondly, the principle that felony is a cause of

[1] The subject is treated at length in the *History of English Law*, vol. I, pp. 303—5, vol. II, pp. 462—511.

escheat, made it very desirable in the king's eyes, and the eyes of the lords, that as many crimes as possible should be brought under this denomination. Thus all the graver crimes became felonies. We never get to a definition of felony; but we do get to a list of felonies.

I think we may say that from the beginning of the thirteenth century onwards, all causes that are regarded as criminal are pleas of the crown, *placita coronae*, save some petty offences which are still punished in the local courts, but even over these the sheriff is now regarded as exercising a royal jurisdiction. To this point we shall return once more; we have meanwhile to watch the growth of royal jurisdiction in civil causes.

This is by no means a simple matter; the process is very slow, and indeed even in the present century our civil procedure bore witness of a time when the king's court had not yet taken upon itself to act as a court of first instance in the ordinary disputes of ordinary people. We may, however, indicate six principles which serve to bring justice to the king's court.

(1) From the outset it is a court to which one may go, for default of justice in lower courts. Under the Norman kings we find that frequently a litigant, who in the ordinary course is going to sue in the court of a feudal lord, will go to the king in the first instance, and procure a writ, a mandate directing the lord, ordering him to do justice in his court to the applicant, and adding a threat, *quod nisi feceris vicecomes meus faciet*—if you won't do it my sheriff will—the action will be removed out of your court into the county court, and thence it can be removed into the king's own court. This is a writ *de recto tenendo*, a writ of right.

(2) Henry II must, it would seem, have ordained that no action for freehold land shall be begun in a manorial court without such a writ. I say he must have ordained it: we have no direct evidence of this: but Glanvill lays down the principle in the broadest terms, no one need answer for his freehold without the king's writ, a writ directing the lord to do right—and we can say pretty positively that this was not law before Henry's day. You will notice that it is a serious invasion on feudal principles; when freehold is at stake, the

lord cannot hold his court or do justice until the king sets him in motion—the jurisdiction may spring out of tenure, but it is not beyond royal control. The excuse for such an interference may lie in that royal protection of possession of which we are soon to speak.

(3) In an action for land in a manorial court begun by writ of right, Henry II by some ordinance, the words of which have not come down to us but which was known as the grand assize, enabled the holder of the land to refuse trial by battle and to put himself upon the oath of a body of twelve neighbours sworn to declare which of the two parties had the greater right to the land. This was called putting oneself on the grand assize ; and the body of sworn neighbours was known as the grand assize.

(4) Henry II, as we have before remarked, took seisin, possession as distinct from ownership, under his special protection—men who consider that land is unjustly withheld from them are not to help themselves ; there is to be no disseisin without a judgment. He who is thus disseised shall be put back into possession without any question as to his title. This protection of possession is, I think, closely connected with that extension of the king's peace which we have been watching. He who takes upon himself to eject another from his freehold, breaks the peace, and the peace is the king's. This possessory procedure the king keeps in his own hands—it is a royal matter, the feudal courts have nothing to do with it. Thus there grows up a large class of actions (the possessory assizes) relating to land, which are beyond the cognizance of any but the king's justices, and these justices take good care that the limits of these actions shall not be narrow ; perhaps indeed they are not always very careful to draw the line between disputes about possession which belong to them, and disputes about ownership which should go to the royal courts.

(5) If we turn back to the list of royal rights contained in the *Leges Henrici*, we find among them—*placitum brevium vel praeceptorum ejus contemptorum*—pleas touching the contempt of his writs or precepts. Now here is an idea of which great use can be made : B detains from A land or goods or

owes A a debt; this may not be a case for the royal jurisdiction—but suppose that the king issues a writ or precept ordering B to give up the land or goods or to pay the debt, and B disobeys this order, then at once the royal jurisdiction is attracted to the case. The king's chancellor begins to issue such writs with a liberal hand. A writ is sent to the sheriff in such words as these: Command B (*Praecipe* B) that justly and without delay he give up to A the land or the chattel or the money which, as A says, he unjustly detains from him, and if he will not do so command him to be before our court on such a day to answer why he hath not done it. Thus the dispute between A and B is brought within the sphere of the king's justice; if B is in the wrong he has been guilty of contemning the king's writ. Such writs in Henry II's time are freely sold to litigants: but this is somewhat too high-handed a proceeding to be stood, for in the case of land being thus demanded, the manorial courts are deprived of their legitimate jurisdiction. So we find that one of the concessions extorted from John by Magna Carta is this: The writ called *Praecipe* shall not be issued for the future, so as to deprive a free man of his court, i.e. so as to deprive the lord of the manor of cases which ought to come to his court, his court being one of his sources of income[1]. To a certain extent in cases of land this puts a check on the acquisitiveness of the royal court. But even as regards land, it is evaded in many different ways, in particular, by an extension of the possessory actions which make them serve the purpose of proprietary actions. As regards chattels and debts the king has a freer hand.

(6) The notion of the king's peace is by no means exhausted when it has comprehended the whole field of criminal law: mere civil wrongs, 'torts' as we call them, can be brought within it—a mere wrongful step upon your land, a mere wrongful touch to your goods or to your person can be regarded as a breach of the peace; any wrongful application of force, however slight, can be said to be made *vi et armis et contra pacem domini Regis*: in such cases there may be no felony and no intention to do what is wrong—I may believe the goods to be mine when they are yours, and carry them off

[1] M. C. c. 34. McKechnie, pp. 405—13.

in that belief ; still this may be called a breach of the peace. Hence in the thirteenth century a large class of writs grows up known as writs of trespass ; for a long time the procedure is regarded as half-civil, half-criminal: the vanquished defendant has not only to pay damages to the plaintiff, he has to pay a fine to the king for the breach of the peace. Gradually (but this is not until the end of the Middle Ages) the fine becomes an unreality : actions of trespass are regarded as purely civil actions—and in course of time this form of action and forms derived out of it are made to do duty instead of all, or almost all, the other forms.

Armed with these elastic principles it was easy for the king's courts to amplify their province. By the beginning of Edward's reign we may, I think, say that all serious obstacles to the royal jurisdiction had been removed. The royal courts had in one way and another become courts of first instance for almost all litigation. But the extremely active legislation of his reign and the growth of parliament set a limit to the invention of new actions. It was now recognized that there were a certain number of actions to which no addition could be made except by statute. There were a certain number of writs in the royal Chancery ; these were at the disposal of every subject ; they were to be had on payment of the customary fees ; they could not be denied ; by these writs actions were began, were originated ; they were *brevia originalia*, original writs. A certain power of varying the stereotyped forms was allowed by the Statute of Westminster II (1285), and of this in course of time some good use was made; but from Edward's day down to the middle of the present century the development of common law was fettered by this system of original writs—writs which had been devised for the purpose of bringing before the king's court litigation which in more ancient times would have gone to other tribunals.

But the king's court could not have succeeded in thus extending the sphere of its activity if it had not been able to offer to suitors advantages which they could not get elsewhere. Royal justice was a good article—that is to say, a masterful thing not to be resisted. There were many processes which the king could give which were not to be had in lower courts.

To describe some of these would take us too deeply into the technicalities of legislation. But there is one royal boon, *regale beneficium*, as Glanvill calls it, which has had a most important influence on the whole of our national history—trial by jury. In order to understand its history we must say a little about these modes of trial and of proof which in course of time gave way before it.

Now the first thing to note about the procedure in the courts before the Conquest is that proof comes after judgment. This may sound like a paradox. It may seem to us that the judgment must be the outcome of the proof. By proof the judges are convinced, and being convinced give judgment according to their conviction. But the old procedure does not accord with this to us very natural notion. Suppose two persons are litigating—A charges B with having done something unlawful—we find that the judgment takes this form, that it is for A (or as the case may be for B) to prove his case. The judgment decides who is to prove, what proof he is to produce—and what will be the consequence of his succeeding or failing to give the requisite proof. This matter becomes clearer when we consider the known means of proof. They are oaths and ordeals—and of oaths again there are several different kinds : there is the simple unsupported oath of the party, there is the oath of the party supported by compurgators or oath-helpers, and there is the oath of witnesses. We must look at these modes of proof a little more closely.

In some few cases A having brought some charge against B, it will be adjudged that B do prove his case simply by his own oath. This being so, B has to swear solemnly that he has not done that which is alleged against him. If he can do this then the charge against him fails. This may seem a very easy way of meeting an accusation, and such probably it was, and in but few cases would so simple a proof as this have been sufficient. Still even in this ceremony it was possible to fail : the swearer had to use exactly the right words, and a slip would be fatal to his cause. I have said that we have no text-book of Anglo-Saxon law. But one of the things that looks most like a text-book is a brief collection of the oaths to be sworn on different occasions. They are very formal and, as it seems, half-poetical. Probably the utmost accuracy was required of the swearer. Besides we should remember that an oath was very sacred. One may hope that in the course of history the respect for truth increases—but just for this reason, as it seems to me, the respect for an oath as such diminishes. We think that we ought to tell the truth, that this obligation is so strict that no adjuration, no imprecation can make it stricter. To reverence an oath as an oath is now the sign of a low morality. Not so in old time:—the appeal to God makes all the difference ; men will not forswear themselves though they will freely lie; between mere lying and the false oath there is a great gap. But generally a defendant was not allowed to meet a charge in a fashion quite so simple; he was required to swear, but to swear with compurgators. Now a compurgator or an oath-helper is a person who comes to support the oath of another by his own. For instance A charges B with a debt; it is adjudged that B do go to the proof with twelve oath-helpers. This being so then B will first swear in denial of the charge, and then his compurgators will swear that they believe his oath—'By God the oath is clean and unperjured that B hath sworn'—they swear not directly that B does not owe the money, they swear to a belief in his oath. Now this process of compurgation is found not only in Anglo-Saxon law, but in all the kindred laws of the German and Scandinavian nations, nor in these only, for the Welsh laws about compurgation are particularly full and particularly interesting. Occasionally we come across a requirement that the oath-helpers shall be of kin to the principal swearer, and this has led to some interesting speculations as to the origin of this procedure. Obviously if what were wanted was the testimony of impartial persons to the truthful character of the accused, one would not naturally seek this from his next of kin, who will very naturally stand by their kinsman. In days when the bond of blood-relationship was felt as very strict, when men were expected to espouse the quarrel and avenge the death of their kinsman, they can hardly have been thought the best witnesses to his honesty. It has therefore been thought by some (and if we may refer to the Welsh laws they will fully bear this out) that compurgation takes us back to a time when the family is an important unit in the legal system. Any charge which primarily affects an individual is secondarily a charge against the family to which he belongs:—that family is bound to make compensation for the wrongs that he does, and even to pay his debts if he will not pay them. But if this theory be true—and I think that there is much in its favour—our ancestors had passed out of this primitive condition before they appear in the light of clear history : the family was no longer so important, the state had a direct hold on the individual. It is but rarely that we hear of kinsmen as compurgators. Generally it is only required that the swearer shall produce good and lawful men to the requisite number. That number varies from case to case—sometimes it is as high as 48 ; but 12 is a very common number—a fatally common number, for it misleads the unwary into seeing a jury, where in truth there are but compurgators. But the system is very elaborate. For instance we find a sort of tariff of oaths—the oath of a thane is worth the oaths of six ceorls, and so forth. Again in cases of grave suspicion the swearer has to repeat the oath over and over again with different batches of compurgators. In comparatively recent times, the thirteenth and fourteenth centuries, compurgation still flourished in the city of London, which had obtained a chartered immunity from legal reforms:—we read how the Londoner may rebut a charge even of murder by an oath sworn with 36 compurgators—how, in another case, he must swear nine times before nine altars in nine churches. Then again in the Anglo-Saxon days we find that occasionally the judge names a number of men from among whom the defendant has to select his compurgators. This seems the outcome of an attempt to make the procedure more rational, to obtain impartial testimony. But normally the person who has to swear chooses his own compurgators, and if he produces good and lawful men, i.e. free men who have not forfeited their credibility by crime, this is enough. Then again the compurgatory oath is sometimes made more or less difficult by the requirement or non-requirement of perfect verbal accuracy—sometimes it is sworn *in verborum observanciis*, sometimes not—that is, sometimes a slip will be fatal, sometimes not. The oath with compurgators, made more or less onerous in these various ways according to an elaborate system of rules, seems the general proof of Anglo-Saxon law —both in the cases which we should call civil, and in those which we should call criminal. The man of unblemished reputation is in general entitled to clear himself of a charge in this manner: the man who has been repeatedly accused or who cannot find compurgators must go to the ordeal.

But the law knows of other witnesses besides compurgators —or if we do not choose to consider these compurgators as witnesses, then we must say that it knows of witnesses as distinguished from compurgators. But these witnesses, like compurgators, do not appear until after judgment—they do not come to persuade the court to give this or that judgment —they come there to fulfil the judgment already given to the effect that the plaintiff, or (as the case may be) defendant, do prove his case with witnesses. It has been adjudged that A do prove his assertion by witnesses: A brings his witnesses; they do not come to be examined; they come to swear, to swear up to a particular formula, to swear up to A's assertion—this is all that is required of them. They must be good and lawful men—but if they are this, then B cannot object to them, cannot question them; if he thinks them forsworn, then his remedy, if any, is against them—he must charge them with perjury. Their evidence is not put before the court as material for a judgment; judgment has been already given. To decide a dispute by weighing testimony, by cross-examining witnesses, by setting evidence against evidence and unravelling facts—this is modern; the ancient mode is to fall back at once on the supernatural, to allow one party or the other to appeal to Heaven—to leave the rest to 'whatever gods there be.' This 'formal one-sided witness procedure' (that is the best phrase that I can find for it) is not so common in Anglo-Saxon law as the procedure by compurgation—but there are occasions for it. For instance many transactions such as sales of goods are required to be completed in the presence of witnesses and official witnesses. This is part of the police system. The typical action of Anglo-Saxon law seems the action to recover stolen cattle—doubtless, cattle

lifting was an extremely common form of wrong-doing—
and many of the dooms are concerned with its prevention.
A man who buys cattle must buy them in the presence of the
official witnesses chosen for each hundred and borough, otherwise should he buy from one who is a thief, he is like to find
himself treated as a thief. And there are other purposes for
which witnesses may be produced ; but it seems that there is
no power to compel a person to come and give evidence unless
at the time when the event took place he was solemnly called
to bear witness of it. If something happens and you think
that hereafter you may need the testimony of the bystanders,
you must then and there call upon them to witness the fact,
otherwise you will have no power of compelling them to come
to court and prove your case. But the matter on which
I would chiefly insist is the one-sided character of procedure,
because here is the gulf—the, as it seems, insurmountable gulf
—between the Anglo-Saxon witnesses and the jurors of Henry
the Second's reign. The witness is called in by the party—
the party to whom the proof has been awarded—to swear up
to his case; the juror is called in by the sheriff or by the court
to swear to the truth whatever the truth may be.

The ordeal was used chiefly, though not, I think, exclusively, in the case of the graver charges, criminal charges as
we should call them. This of course is a direct and open
appeal to the supernatural, the case is too hard for man, so it
is left to the judgment of God. There seems little doubt that
ordeals were used by our forefathers in the days of their
heathenry, though unfortunately almost all our evidence comes
from a time when they have become Christian ceremonies
practised under the sanction of the church[1]. Four ordeals
are known to Anglo-Saxon law ; the ordeal of hot iron: the
accused is required to carry hot iron in his hand for nine steps,
his hand is then sealed up and the seal broken on the third
day, if the hand has festered then he is guilty, if not, innocent;
the ordeal of hot water: the accused is required to plunge his
hand into hot water, if the ordeal is simple, to the wrist, if
threefold, then to the cubit ; the ordeal of cold water: the
accused is thrown into water, if he sinks he is innocent, if he

---

[1] Liebermann, *Gesetze der Angelsachsen*, pp. 401—29.

floats he is guilty; the ordeal of the morsel: a piece of bread or of cheese an ounce in weight is given to the accused, having been solemnly adjured to stick in his throat if he is guilty. I do not wish to dwell on these antiquities, which are sufficiently described in many accessible books[1]. Certainly it is very difficult to understand how this system worked in practice.

One form of the ordeal seems to have been unused by the Anglo-Saxons, namely, trial by battle, the judicial duel. This is a very curious fact, for I believe that in all the kindred systems of law the duel has a place. Perhaps we may attribute this to the action of the church, for against this form of ordeal the church very early set its face, and in England the church was very strong, popular and national. At any rate this seems the fact—there is no mention of trial by battle in the Anglo-Saxon laws, and I believe no evidence that any such trial took place in England before the Norman Conquest. Besides we have an ordinance, I believe, an undoubtedly genuine ordinance of William the Conqueror, which treats the duel as the form of trial appropriate for Normans. Now this probably constituted the one great difference between the Norman and the Anglo-Saxon procedure. Compurgation and the other ordeals are common to both systems, but in the Norman many questions are decided by battle, while the place of the duel in the Anglo-Saxon system is filled partly by the other ordeals, partly by those very elaborate forms of compurgation of which I have spoken. I speak of trial by battle as an ordeal, and this it seems to be. In theory it is not an appeal to brute force, but an appeal to Heaven.

We cannot find the germ of trial by jury either in the Anglo-Saxon procedure, or in the ordinary procedure of the Norman courts. Still the germ must be found somewhere, and the research of these last days has gradually been concentrating itself on one particular point, the prerogative procedure of the court of the Frankish kings.

I cannot speak of this matter with any minuteness. It must suffice that the Franks had occupied provinces of the Roman Empire far more thoroughly Romanized than our own

---

[1] References may be found in what is now the best and most accessible of these books, *The History of English Law*, vol. II, p. 596.

country; that a powerful monarchy grew up, that the Frankish king became Roman Emperor. Already I have said something about the growth of kingship and kingly power in this country. Abroad the same process went on, but much more rapidly, fostered by imperial Roman traditions. The Frankish king seems to have inherited many of the powers of the Roman government, and among these many procedural prerogatives; the formal procedure of the old Germanic courts did not apply to him, he could dispense with it, could for his own purposes make use of speedier and more stringent processes. We see something of the same kind in the England of a much later day. In litigation the king enjoys all manner of advantages. What is more we find phrases used of the Frank king's court which incline us to say that it was in the old English sense a Court of Equity, as well as of Law—that is to say, when compared with the popular communal courts it seems unhampered, untrammelled by procedural rules, it can devise new expedients for doing justice, for eliciting the truth. Then we find further that these Frankish kings and emperors to protect their own rights, the rights of the crown, make use of a means of getting at the truth not employed by the older courts. For instance, there being question as to some land whether it be demesne of the crown or no, an order will be given to a public officer to inquire into this by the oaths of the neighbours. It seems that such *inquisitiones* (for such is the term usually employed) were frequently ordered for the ascertainment of crown rights. The crown thus places itself outside the ordinary formal procedure; for its own purposes it will make a short cut to the truth[1]. Nor is this all: these Frankish kings assume the power of granting to others the privileges which they themselves enjoy—in particular in granting to the religious houses which they have founded, an immunity from the formal procedure of the ancient courts:—if the title of the monastery to its lands be called in question, then the matter is to be tried by a royal judge; there is to be

---

[1] We are here forcibly reminded of our own inquests of office—the sheriff or the escheator summoning a jury to testify whether someone has died without an heir, or has forfeited his land, in order that the rights of the crown may be known and the land seised into the king's hand. F. W. M.

no judicial combat; the judge is to summon the neighbours, and by their oath the question is to be decided. Here seems to be just what we want as the germ of trial by jury. A body of neighbours is summoned by a public officer to testify the truth, be the truth what it may, about facts and rights presumably within their knowledge. Lastly, a somewhat similar process is used for the detection of crimes. Procedure by private accusation is found insufficient for the peace of the realm, and the king finds himself strong enough to order that the men of a district be sworn to accuse before royal officers, those who have been guilty of crime. These royal officers (*missi* they are called) sent out to receive such accusations and to hold inquisitions, remind us strongly of our own itinerant justices, and indeed it seems very likely that our *justiciarii itinerantes* are in spirit the direct descendants of the Frankish *missi*.

It is now very generally allowed that this is the quarter in which we must look for the first rudiments of trial by jury, the prerogative procedure of the courts of the Frankish kings and emperors. But it must at first sight seem a very strange thing that an institution, which in its origin was peculiarly Frankish, became in course of time distinctively English. In France this inquisition procedure perished, transplanted to England it grew and flourished, and became that trial by jury which after long centuries Frenchmen introduced into modern France as a foreign, an English institution. How was this?

The Frankish Empire, let us remember, went to wreck and ruin and feudal anarchy. But in one corner of its domain there settled a race whose distinguishing characteristic seems to have been a wonderful power of adapting itself to circumstances, of absorbing into its own life the best and strongest institutions of whatever race it conquered—Frankish, Italian, or English. The Normans conquered England; they had previously conquered Normandy: for 150 years or thereabouts they had been settled on Frankish territory. And in their civilization they had become Frankish; they had thrown aside their heathenry and become Christians; they had forgotten their Scandinavian tongue and learned the Romance language of those whom they conquered. The legal history of Normandy during those 150 years, from 912 to 1066, is particularly obscure, but it seems sufficiently proved that the Norman dukes assumed and exercised that power of ordering inquisitions which had been wielded by the Frankish kings, of establishing a special procedure by way of inquest for the ascertainment and protection of ducal rights, and of the rights of those to whom the duke had granted a special immunity from the formal procedure of the ordinary courts. We find, for example, ducal charters giving such privileges to religious houses, very similar to the charters of the Frankish kings.

Then so soon as England is conquered we find the Norman dukes, now kings of England, ordering inquisitions within their new domains. One of these is very famous, for it is the Doomsday inquest. The king sent out barons who made the great survey on the oath of the sheriff, and all the barons and Norman landowners of the shire, and of the priest, reeve and six villagers (*villani*) from every township. This was a fiscal inquisition on a very large scale; the prerogative procedure whereby the Frankish kings had protected the rights of the crown, ascertained the limits of the royal domain and so forth, was now applied to the whole of a conquered kingdom. This is a splendid and notorious instance, but it does not stand alone, and we find the Norman kings ordering inquisitions not merely to protect their own rights, but also to protect the rights of those who acquired this privilege— acquired it for the most part for valuable consideration, for such privileges are vendible. Thus we have a writ of the Conqueror himself, ordering an inquisition in favour of the church of Ely; a number of Englishmen who knew the state of the lands in question in the days of Edward the Confessor are to be chosen and are to swear what they know[1]. There are other instances of such writs.

Hitherto, whether we have looked at the Frank empire, the Norman duchy or the English kingdom, the inquisition by the oath of neighbours has appeared as something exceptional—a royal or ducal privilege, no part of the ordinary procedure of ordinary litigation: indeed it is rather a fiscal or

[1] *Liber Eliensis*, I, 256.

administrative, than a judicial institution. But in Normandy and in England it became a part of the ordinary procedure open to every litigant. This no doubt was the work of Henry II; of this we have ample evidence, though we have not in all cases the text of the ordinances whereby the work was accomplished. Let us see the various forms which the inquisition or inquest now assumes.

(1) In the first place we have the grand assize. When A demands land from B, B instead of fighting or obtaining a champion to fight for him, may put himself upon the grand assize of our lord the king. Four knights are then chosen by the parties and they elect twelve knights, who come before the king's justices to testify whether A or B hath the greater right to this land. These jurors or 'recognitors' you see are called in not as judges of fact who are to hear the evidence of witnesses, but as witnesses, and a strict line between questions of fact and questions of law has not yet been drawn—they speak as to rights, not merely as to facts.

Glanvill in a memorable passage brings out the character, the royal origin, of this new procedure[1]. The grand assize, he says, is a royal boon by which wholesome provision has been made for the lives of men and the integrity of the state, so that in maintaining their right to the possession of their freeholds the suitors may not be exposed to the doubtful issue of trial by battle. This institution (he adds) proceeds from the highest equity, for the right which after long delay can scarcely be said to be proved by battle, is by the beneficial use of this constitution more rapidly and more conveniently demonstrated. We have here then no popular institution growing up in the customary law of our race, but a royal boon, *regale quoddam beneficium*.

(2) Then again Henry institutes those possessory assizes which we have more than once mentioned. A person who has been ejected from possession of his freehold, who has been 'disseised,' can obtain a writ directing the sheriff to summon twelve men to testify before the king's justices whether there has been a disseisin or no. Here we approach one step nearer

---

[1] *De Legibus Angliae*, II, 7. *Select Charters*, p. 161.

to the trial by jury of later times;—the question submitted to these recognitors is more definitely a question of fact—has there been seisin and disseisin—not who has the greater right; but still these recognitors are summoned in as witnesses, as neighbours who are likely to know the facts.

(3) By the establishment of the grand assize and of the possessory assizes, a great step is made in the history of trial by jury. The royal process of ascertaining facts and rights by the sworn testimony of a body of neighbours is now placed at the disposal of ordinary litigants; partly this may be in the interests of justice, but also it is in the interest of a king consolidating his realm, struggling with feudalism, desirous of making himself the one fountain of justice. But as yet this procedure by inquisition or recognition has a very definite scope: it is appropriate to certain actions and only to certain actions, and the form of the recognition varies with the form of the action—thus in the grand assize four knights elected by the parties elect the twelve recognitors, in the possessory assizes the twelve recognitors are directly summoned by the sheriff. And the question for the recognitors is determined by the form of the action. Thus in the grand assize it is whether demandant or tenant hath the better right to hold the land; in the novel disseisin, it is whether the defendant unjustly and without judgment disseised the plaintiff. These assizes are the outcome of definite legislation, but the procedure by recognition, once made common, spreads beyond the original bounds—gradually and without legislation. We find plaintiffs and defendants in all manner of actions purchasing from the king the right to have a recognition or inquest to determine some disputed point. By slow degrees what has been a purchasable favour becomes an ordinary right, and the sum which the party has to pay to the king becomes less and less a variable price, more and more a definite tax or court fee fixed by custom. It is a slow process by which this recognition procedure makes head and displaces the older methods of proof, the unilateral witness, procedure and compurgation. There is no one moment at which we can say that it becomes law that questions of fact must go to a jury, to a body of sworn recognitors. In certain

forms of action, the older processes maintained their footing. Thus even in the present century, there were certain actions in which a defendant might have recourse to compurgation; and for this reason those actions were never brought: means had long ago been discovered of bringing other actions in their stead. However, the new procedure slowly became the rule, and the old procedure the exception; in general disputed questions would be settled by the oath of the country, would be settled by trial by jury—by a jury (*jurata*); gradually this word came into use and was contrasted with *assisa*. The word *assisa*, as already remarked, implies a positive ordinance; it is a procedure which, as we should say, is statutory, and you should understand that the old assizes might have been used and were occasionally used even in the present century. They were not abolished until 1833, but long before that had become uncommon, their work being done for the most part by less cumbrous and anti-quated machinery. But by the side of the assizes, there grew up the practice of sending to a body of recognitors questions of fact which arose out of the pleadings in an action; a body of jurors thus called in was a jury, *jurata*, as contrasted with an assize, *assisa*. In an assize, the very first step was to obtain a writ directing the sheriff to summon twelve men to answer a particular question, e.g. whether A disseised B; the question for the assize was formulated in the original writ. Take another action, e.g. an action of trespass; the original writ says nothing of any recognitors, nothing of any mode of trial; A is summoned to answer before the king's court why he assaulted and beat B; then A and B plead before the court until they come to an issue about some question of fact or question of law; if it be a question of fact, then a jury (*jurata*) is summoned to answer this question—a question which has arisen out of the pleadings—not a question formulated in the original writ.

(4) In dealing with civil, before criminal, procedure we have been following the historical order. What we are apt to think the very typical case of trial by jury, the trial of a man for crime by a petty jury after a grand jury has indicted him, is the last development of the institution which has been

under our examination. But we have first to speak of the
accusing jury, of what comes to be the grand jury of modern
times. Here again, it is an ordinance of Henry the Second
that establishes the procedure as normal. If any trace at all
of a jury, or of anything that is on its way to become a jury,
is to be found in the Anglo-Saxon laws, it is the trace of an
accusing jury. In one of the laws of Ethelred, we read how
in a particular case the twelve eldest thanes are to go out
and swear on the relic that they will accuse no innocent man
and conceal no guilty man. It is conceivable that this law
has a general import, and that by the end of the tenth century
it was part of the procedure of the local courts that a body of
neighbours should be sworn to present the crimes which
had come to their knowledge. But it is difficult for want of
continuous evidence to connect this law with the measures of
Henry the Second, and the meaning of Ethelred's law is much
disputed. On the other hand, as already said, the accusing
jury was an element in the procedure of the Frankish courts
under the Carolingian kings, and produced in Normandy
under the Norman dukes. It may be then that Henry reformed or revived an ancient English institution, but more
probably we have here another offshoot of the royal and
fiscal inquisition. To ascertain and protect the rights of the
crown is the main object, and it seems almost a by-end that
incidentally crime may thus be discovered and suppressed.
The itinerant judges are supplied with lists of inquiries
which they are to lay before juries representing the various
hundreds which they visit. These lists of inquiries are known
as articles of the eyre, *capitula itineris*, and in the main they
are fiscal inquiries; the royal revenue is the chief end in
view. The jurors are to swear as to what profits have fallen
to the crown, as to escheats, forfeitures, marriages, wardships,
widows, Jews, treasure trove and other sources of income;
also as to the misdoings of the sheriff and his bailiffs; also
as to murders, robberies and so forth, for crime also brings
money to the royal exchequer—for instance there are the
murder fines to be collected. It is not improbable that our
Norman kings occasionally directed inquisitions of this sort.
In Henry the Second's reign, under the Assizes of Clarendon

and Northampton, the presentation of crimes by twelve men representing each hundred was made a regular permanent procedure. The twelve sworn hundredors are to present crimes; the persons whom they accuse are to go to the ordeal; if they fail at the ordeal they are to be punished by mutilation. What is more, the Assize of Northampton betrays some mistrust of the efficacy of the ordeal as a means of eliciting the truth, for even if a person thus accused satisfies the test, and thus has the judgment of God in his favour, he is to abjure the realm, that is, he is to leave the realm swearing never to return. You observe that these twelve sworn hundredors are sworn accusers; their testimony is not conclusive; their oath does not lead to immediate condemnation; it leads to trial; it puts the accused on his trial; he must go to the ordeal. In short they are the ancestors of our grand jurors, not of our petty jurors, and their sworn accusation is an indictment. For the rise of the petty jury we must look elsewhere. But let us pause to remark that these measures of Henry the Second institute a new mode of procedure in criminal cases, they put the indictment by the side of the appeal. Thenceforward English law has two criminal procedures; there is the appeal—a private accusation brought by the person primarily wronged by the crime, the person, e.g., whose goods have been stolen, or the nearest kinsman of the murdered man; then there is the indictment—the sworn accusation of twelve men who have sworn to present the crimes committed within their hundred. These two modes of procedure live side by side until modern times; the appeal of felony was not abolished until 1819; the indictment we still have, though in course of time its real nature has undergone a great change.

(5) And now as to the petty jury or trying jury in criminal cases. We cannot trace this back to any positive ordinance; it makes its way into our procedure almost insensibly and that too at a comparatively recent time—by which I mean that the system of assizes and juries in civil cases was in full swing before it became common that persons accused of crimes should be tried by the oath of their neighbours. From the Norman Conquest onward the regular means of bringing a criminal to justice was the appeal, or

private accusation, and this led to trial by battle. Gradually, however, in the reigns of Henry II and his sons, we find that appellees can purchase from the king the privilege of having questions tried by an inquest of neighbours. At first the questions thus tried seem merely to be incidental questions arising out of the pleadings, as for instance, whether the appellee is a maimed man who need not fight, or is above the fighting age. The questions thus tried become in course of time more substantial and touch the real issue of guilt or innocence : thus the appellee sets up an *alibi* and obtains an inquest to prove this ; or again he asserts that the appellor is moved to the appeal by no honest motive, but by spite and hatred, and obtains an inquest to prove that this is no true appeal but is the outcome of *odium et atya*. Lastly, we find the appellor putting himself on an inquest for the whole question of guilt and innocence—*ponit se super patriam et de bono et de malo*—he puts himself on his country, i.e. on his neighbourhood for good and for ill. An article of the Great Charter (the meaning of which has been contested) seems to provide that thenceforward an appellee is to have a right to put himself upon an inquest without having to purchase this as a privilege from the king[1]. By the time when Bracton wrote (circ. 1250) it seems to be law that an appellee has two alternatives open to him ; he can defend himself by battle or he can put himself upon his country, occasionally (as e.g. if the appellor be beyond the fighting age) the appellee must be forced to put himself upon his country.

Thus much as to trial by jury in the case of an appeal ; but as already said Henry II established by the Assizes of Clarendon and Northampton another criminal procedure, namely the indictment. Now under these ordinances the person indicted went to the ordeal, but as already noted some distrust of the ordeal was already shown, for even if there was supernatural testimony in favour of innocence still the accused, *si fuerit de pessimo testimonio et publice diffamatus*, had to abjure the realm. Half a century later the ordeal went out of use. The Fourth Lateran Council, held in

---

[1] M. C. c. 36. McKechnie, pp. 417—27.

1215, prohibited the clergy from taking part in the ordeal, and thus in effect abolished it, for the ordeal was nothing if not a religious ceremony. We find the council of an English king (Henry the Third had just become king and was yet a boy) at once accepting the abolition as an accomplished fact and making provision for the new state of affairs. It seems to become law that a person indicted by the twelve hundredors must submit to be tried by an inquest of neighbours or else must remain in gaol. I think that during the first half of the thirteenth century some at least of the king's judges held that, even if the accused would not voluntarily put himself upon the oath of his neighbours, nevertheless he could be tried, an inquest could be sworn, and, if it made against him, he could be sentenced and punished. It seems to me that this was Bracton's opinion, but that he did not care to express himself very plainly. Doubtless there was a very strong feeling that to try a man by a jury, when he had not submitted to be so tried, was thoroughly unjust. We moderns, especially if we come to the subject with the too common belief that trial by jury is a process of popular customary origin of immemorial antiquity, the birthright of Englishmen and so forth, must find it hard to realize this sentiment, but, if we fail to do this, an important tract of legal history will be for us a stupid blank. The mere oaths of twelve sworn witnesses (remember that the jurors of the thirteenth century are witnesses) are not enough to fix a man with guilt, unless indeed he has voluntarily submitted his fate to this test; he ought to be allowed to demonstrate his innocence by supernatural means, by some such process as the ordeal or the judicial combat; God may be for him, though his neighbours be against him. It is interesting to find that this notion was not confined to England; Brunner has shown that it crops up in Normandy and in other parts of France—a man is not to be condemned on the evidence of his neighbours unless he has put himself upon their oath[1]. I think, as already said, that some of the judges of Henry III's reign had risen above this notion and sent to trial by jury men who distinctly and emphatically

---

[1] Brunner, *Schwurgerichte*, pp. 469—77.

refused trial; but before the end of the century it had become
established that the indicted person could not be sent to
trial unless he put himself upon his country.   He could not
be tried, but he could be tortured into saying the requisite
words; superstitions look odd when they have ceased to be
our own superstitions: it became law that an indicted person
who, when asked how he would be tried, stood mute of malice,
that is, refused to answer 'By God and my country,' might be
pressed and starved to death.   I need not give the details of
this, the *peine forte et dure*, but one should think of it whenever
one hears talk of trial by jury as of an obviously just institution.
Our ancestors did not think so.

At the end of Edward I's reign, the moment at which we
have placed ourselves, the situation therefore is this.   In all
civil actions, trial by jury—i.e. by a body of neighbour witnesses
—has become the usual mode of trial, though still in certain
cases, not very common, the defendant can have recourse to
compurgation or to trial by battle.   As to criminal cases—
a person appealed may if he pleases put himself upon a jury
instead of fighting; jurors also are sworn in to indict criminals,
the person thus indicted must consent to be tried by another
jury; if he will not consent, he is pressed or starved to death.
All jurors, however, are as yet witnesses, or sworn accusers;
the process which turns them into judges of fact, judges of
fact testified by others, by witnesses produced and examined
in their presence, has hardly yet begun.   The fact that jurors
are regarded as witnesses is brought out by this; in many
cases, and their number is increasing, the person against whom
the jurors have given a verdict may take proceedings against
the jurors for perjury: these proceedings are called an attaint;
the verdict of the twelve jurors is brought before a jury of
twenty-four, and if these twenty-four find that the verdict was
false, it is set aside and the twelve perjured jurors are heavily
punished.   Also we may remark that as yet it is hardly well
established that the jurors must give an unanimous verdict;
in old times the verdict of a majority has been accepted.

We have now taken account of the doctrines whereby the
royal jurisdiction had extended itself, and of the new institution,
regale beneficium, which had made royal justice preferable to

all other justice. We may now look at the courts as they stand in Edward's reign.

(*a*) The old local courts still exist; as a political assembly the county court is still of first-rate importance, it is this that is represented in parliament by the knights of the shire ; but as a court of law it has lost much of its importance.   Almost all civil causes of any great importance can now be begun in the king's court, where there can be trial by jury.   Nor is this all ; a statute has lately been passed, the Statute of Gloucester (1278), which has been construed to mean that no action for more than 40 shillings can be brought in these local courts[1]. The statute does not say this; what it says is very different, viz. that no action for less than 40 shillings is to be brought before the king's justice—apparently it was felt that the centralization of justice had already gone too far; it was a hardship for men to be brought to Westminster for less than 40 shillings.   However, the king's justices seem to have at once construed this to imply that suits for *more* than 40 shillings were not to be brought in the local courts.   Thus the competence of those courts was now restricted by a barrier, which grew narrower and narrower as the value of 40 shillings became less and less.   As to criminal proceedings the county court had lost its jurisdiction.   The first steps in appeals of felony were taken in the local courts, but those courts could *try* no cases in which there was talk of a breach of the king's peace.   Presentments also and indictments were taken in the local courts; but they could not try the indicted. Quite petty offences could be punished however by pecuniary amercements in the hundred court and the courts leet, that is, hundred courts which had fallen into private hands; but even in these cases the penal jurisdiction was now deemed to emanate from the king, and was exercised by his sheriff or by some lord claiming under royal grant.   The private penal jurisdictions Edward had tried to suppress by demanding that all those who claimed them should prove a title derived from the crown—they seldom extended beyond the hanging of a thief caught in the act with the stolen goods upon him.

---

[1] See, for a fuller account of the decline of manorial jurisdiction, Maitland, *Select Pleas of Manorial Courts* (Selden Society), Introduction.

(*b*) The manorial courts as regards freehold had perhaps not lost much in theory—it was still the rule that a proprietary action for land freehold of the manor should be begun in the manor court, but this rule, though sanctioned by Magna Carta, was easily and successfully evaded. My impression is that before the end of the thirteenth century it was a very rare thing for an action concerning freehold to be begun, tried, and ended in a manor court. But the king's courts had not yet undertaken to protect the tenant in villeinage against his lord or to regard him as having any right in his land. Disputes as to lands holden by villein services were still heard and determined by the customary court of the manor, and in such courts alienations were effected, the old tenant surrendering the land to the lord who admitted the new tenant.

(*c*) The king's court, as we have seen, has by Edward's time split itself up into three different courts of law, the King's Bench, the Court of Common Pleas and the Exchequer. The stages in this process can be dated, but we must not go into details. The last stage is reached when the office of chief justiciar was extinguished. This we may say happens at the end of Henry III's reign. In 1232 Henry dismissed Hubert de Burgh, who is the last chief justiciar in the sense of being the king's first minister and lieutenant-general. Henry was then under the influence of the foreign party, and he appointed one Stephen Segrave to the justiciarship: but two years afterwards the barons revolted against the foreigners and Segrave was dismissed. Henry then tried for many years to rule without a justiciar, without ministers. For a short time near the end of the reign there was again a justiciar, but in 1268, shortly before Henry's death, the office became empty and was never again filled up. Thenceforth each of the three courts had its chief justice—there was the chief justice of the King's Bench, the chief justice of the Common Pleas, the chief Baron of the Exchequer. The extinction of the chief justiciarship is important in many ways. It marks a stage in the separation of judicial from governmental functions: the head of the court of justice is no longer the prime minister. This leads to the rise of the chancellor; Edward's first minister, probably the chief adviser in his legislative scheme, is his chancellor,

Burnell. But from this time forward we may say there is a body of judges who are expected to be non-political, who are to hold the balance of justice evenly not merely between subject and subject, but also when the king himself is concerned. Still we must not, for a long time yet, think of the judges as enjoying any great degree of independence; they are still the king's servants; they hold their offices for centuries to come during the king's good pleasure, and occasions on which the royal will is allowed to interfere with the course of royal justice are but too frequent. Of each of these courts a word :—

(i) The King's Bench is theoretically a court held before the king himself, and for a long time yet, its justices journey about with the king. It is very clear that both John and Henry III did justice in person. The theory of the time saw no harm in this. Bracton explains that all justice flows from the king; it is merely because he has not strength enough and time enough that he delegates some of his powers to justices. It was but gradually that the king abandoned the practice of sitting in court; but in the fourteenth century it had, I think, become uncommon for him to do so. Still to the very end of its career in 1875 the King's Bench was theoretically a court held *coram ipso domino Rege*; any suitor ordered to come before it, was bidden to appear *coram nobis ubicunque fuerimus in Anglia*. As to its functions :—it was in the first place the central court for pleas of the crown. Criminal cases had to be begun in the counties in which the crime was committed, before those itinerant justices of whom hereafter; but the King's Bench had criminal jurisdiction as a court of first instance over the county in which it sat. But further it had a general superintendence over criminal justice; it could order that any criminal case should be removed from the courts of the itinerant judges and brought before it. Secondly, it had a large power of superintendence over all royal officers, sheriffs, and the like—would entertain complaints against them and bid them do their duties. Thirdly, it had a large civil jurisdiction; it could entertain any civil action in which the defendant was charged with a breach of the king's peace— and as I have already said, this idea of the king's peace had been so enormously extended that any unlawful use of force, however small, could be regarded as a breach of the king's peace and could be brought before the King's Bench. Not content with this it proceeded by means of fictions to steal business from the Common Pleas. A great deal of our legal history is to be explained by the fact that for centuries the judges were paid by fees; more business therefore meant more money, and they had a keen interest in attracting cases to their courts.

(ii) The Court of Common Pleas was the central court for all cases between subject and subject. The charter provided that such cases should not follow the king, but should be heard in some certain place; as a matter of fact, this court was seldom removed from Westminster. It had a concurrent jurisdiction with the King's Bench in actions of trespass in which mention was made of the king's peace, while all other civil cases belonged of right to it. In course of time, however, both the King's Bench and the Exchequer contrived to rob it of a great deal of work.

(iii) The Exchequer of Edward's reign was as yet a somewhat ambiguous institution—both a court of law and an administrative bureau. In its former capacity it heard suits relating to the royal revenue. In its latter it collected the revenue and paid it out. Gradually these functions were separated. The fiscal work, the receipt and collection of revenue, was under the control of the lord treasurer, assisted by the chancellor of the exchequer, while a chief baron and three or four other barons heard and determined the litigious proceedings, and in course of time stole a great deal of work from the court of common pleas. The separation in this financial department of the administrative from the judicial work took, however, a long time :—the modern treasury is an offshoot of the ancient exchequer, and down to 1875 the chancellor of the exchequer was entitled to sit as a judge along with the barons, and just for form's sake a newly appointed chancellor of the exchequer used to sit there and hear a case or two. The barons of the exchequer of Edward's day, and even of a much later time, were not as a rule professional lawyers.

Such were what came to be known as the three superior courts of common law:—this phrase 'of common law' has not as yet acquired one part of the meaning which it had in later times: for the present we hear nothing of any court of 'equity.'

The evolution of these definitely judicial bodies did not, however, exhaust the fount of royal justice. If all other courts failed the king might still do justice in his council or in his parliament. The king's court of the Norman reigns had been, we have seen, in theory a court of prelates and barons; it is not until we have come to the days of Henry II that we find a smaller group of professional judges doing the ordinary and rapidly increasing work of the *curia Regis*. We have seen also that during the thirteenth century there grows up a contrast between the king's permanent council (*concilium Regis*) and the great council of the nation (*commune concilium regni*). In either of these assemblies the king can do justice, and during the reign of Edward I the machinery of government works so easily, and there is (except at the one great crisis of 1297) so little opposition to the king, that men are not very careful to distinguish between these two bodies. We have noticed this as regards legislation; the contrast between statute and ordinance is not emphasized; of some of Edward's laws it is hard to say whether they proceed from the king in parliament or from the king in council. So with judicature; the errors of all inferior courts may be brought in the last resort for correction before the king in parliament or before the king in council. Looking a little forward we see that this work, the work of an ultimate court of error, becomes definitely the work of parliament, but is transacted only by that part of the parliament which is of ancient date. The representatives of the commons, though they make good their claim to share in all legislation, never take part in this judicial work. Thus the House of Lords, the assembly of prelates and barons, becomes the ultimate court of error—still in name and theory the jurisdiction is that of the king in parliament. On the other hand jurisdiction is also claimed for the king in council— a long and stormy history lies before this claim, the history of the Star Chamber, the history of the Court of Chancery; but for the present under Edward's just and steady rule all works well—there is no great need to distinguish between the permanent group of advisers and the occasional assembly of prelates and magnates—the one may be treated as a standing committee of the other.

(*d*) It remains to speak of the visitatorial courts :—

From an early time a great deal of the work of royal justice is done not by the central tribunal but by itinerant justices, sent out by royal commission to hear cases in the various counties. We hear of such judges in the reign of Henry I; their visitations become normal and systematic under the rule of Henry II. The king commissions justices to transact this and that judicial business in the various counties of England. These commissions take various forms more or less comprehensive. First, justices may be sent out *ad omnia placita*, that is, to entertain all manner of pleas belonging to the county in question. Justices acting under this comprehensive commission are known pre-eminently as justices in eyre—their journey is an *iter* or eyre. When such a commission is issued, then all the business belonging to the county in question which is pending in the king's court is adjourned out of that court into the eyre—so that if the parties to a suit would otherwise have been bound to appear before the Bench at Westminster and take some step in the action, they will now be bound to appear before the justices in eyre. Further, these justices are armed with lists of inquiries which they are to lay before jurors representing the various hundreds of the county and to which such jurors must return answer on oath. Such *capitula itineris*, articles of the eyre, relate chiefly to crimes and to royal rights—the criminal and financial inquiries seem curiously mixed up together—for in truth crimes are pleas of the crown, and a source of royal revenue. So the justices in eyre inquire of murders, robberies and other felonies, also of escheats, wardships, marriages and the like, also (and this must have been important business) of the illegal profits of sheriffs and other royal officers. The whole of the county is summoned to meet the justices. In fact the justices hold a very solemn meeting of the county court and do royal justice therein. Now eyres of this kind were made throughout the thirteenth century. It is said that they were usually made once in every seven years; but certainly this period was not strictly observed; the king could order an eyre when and where he pleased. An eyre seems to have been regarded as a sore burden on the county, the attendance of all freeholders was required, and the justices exercised large powers of fining and amercing the county, hundreds, townships and individuals for neglect of police duties, small infringements of royal rights and other minor misdoings. Complaints of the frequency of these eyres were often made. They seem to have gone out of use in the time of Edward III. As machinery for collecting revenue they were becoming unnecessary: the king was beginning to depend more and more on taxes granted by parliament, less and less on the profits of jurisdiction and the income derived from his feudal rights, escheats, wardships and so forth. Justice could be done in the counties under less comprehensive commissions, commissions of a purely judicial kind.

By this time, besides the commission for a general eyre there were three other commissions in use—commissions which are still in use at the present day. Of these a few words must be said.

(1) The Commission of Assize. We have seen that Henry II instituted certain actions for the protection of possession, the three possessory assizes of Novel Disseisin, Mort D'ancestor and Darrein Presentment. Justices were sent out to take these assizes, that is, to hear and determine these possessory actions. Evidently circuits under such a commission, unlike the general eyres, were popular. John was obliged to promise in the charter of 1215 that justices for this purpose should be sent four times a year—in the charter of 1217 this was changed to once a year. This promise seems to have been fairly well kept. At first it was the practice to commission as justices some four knights of the shire; but gradually during Henry III's reign this work falls more and more into the hands of the professional judges of the royal court. It becomes the practice to commission one of them and such knights of the county as he shall associate with himself. The opinion gains ground that such work cannot properly be left to amateurs, and divers statutes from the

end of the thirteenth and from the fourteenth century provide
that one of the justices hearing the assize must be a judge of
the King's Bench or Common Pleas or a serjeant at law.

Then in 1285 the Statute of Westminster II threw a great
deal of new work upon these justices of assize. By this time
trial by jury had become the common mode of trying actions
other than the assizes. When an action in one of the courts at
Westminster was ready for trial, when, that is, the parties by
their pleadings had raised some issue of fact, it had been the
practice to summon to Westminster a jury from the county to
which the case belonged—thus if it was a Cornish case the
sheriff of Cornwall would be directed to send jurors from
Cornwall. It is to me very surprising that Englishmen should
so long have borne this heavy burden. But so it was; we still
may read on the contemporary rolls how jurors from the re-
motest corners of England journeyed up to Westminster to give
their verdicts. But in 1285 it was ordained that the trial of such
actions should, at least as a general rule, take place before
the justices of assize. The court then in which the action was
depending, instead of bidding the sheriff send Cornishmen to
Westminster, would tell him to have the jurors at Westminster
on a certain day, unless before that day (*nisi prius*) justices of
assize should come into Cornwall. The same statute (West. II,
13 Edw. I, c. 30) directed that assizes should be taken thrice a
year, but at some time or another it became the practice to
send them only twice a year—only once a year into the four
northern counties. As a matter of course, then, the justices of
assize would come round before the day named in the writ, and
then the case would be tried at *nisi prius*. Now it is well to
understand that though as a matter of fact the justice of assize
sitting to try a case at *nisi prius* was usually one of the judges
of one of the three courts of common law, he sat there not
as such a judge but merely as a royal commissioner sent out
for this one occasion to take the assizes of a particular county.
For instance the queen (I am speaking of what happened
twelve years ago) might commission a judge of the Common
Pleas to take the Cambridgeshire assizes[1]. He would come

---

[1] i.e. before the Judicature Act of 1875 which amalgamated the three courts.

to Cambridge, and under the Statute of Westminster he would try with a jury all the Cambridgeshire actions which were ready for trial, no matter in which of the three courts they were depending. The court he held would not be the court of Common Pleas nor the King's Bench nor the Exchequer. He would be sitting as a royal commissioner, empowered to try these cases. His one business would be to preside at the trial. In general, though to this there were some statutory exceptions, he could not give judgment. The action was an action pending in one of the central courts, the Westminster courts, and it was for that court to give judgment.

(2) The Commission of Gaol Delivery. Even while eyres *ad omnia placita* were still in use we find commissions of gaol delivery. These can be traced to the very beginning of the thirteenth century. The king by such a commission directed certain justices to deliver a certain gaol ; that is to say, to try all the prisoners who were in that gaol. This must in times past have been comparatively light work, for accused persons were seldom imprisoned unless they were charged with homicide, and this commission did not, I think, authorize the taking of indictments against those who were not in gaol. Such commissions are still issued in very much their old form —they are directed to the judges of the Westminster courts, the serjeants, queen's counsel and circuit officers, and empower them or any two of them (of whom one must be a judge, serjeant or queen's counsel) to deliver the gaol.

(3) General Commissions of Oyer and Terminer are not, I think, so ancient; they come into use as the eyres are dropped. They are directed to the same persons as the commissions of gaol delivery, and usually, I believe, to some great noblemen, landowners of the district. They authorize these commissioners to hear and determine all felonies and other crimes in the county. According to the interpretation put upon these two commissions in modern times there is but little difference between them ; they authorize almost exactly the same things; but it seems to me clear that in old times the Oyer and Terminer was a far more comprehensive authority than the Gaol Delivery, since the latter did not empower the

commissioners to receive indictments against those who were
not in gaol.

Now the cases which came before justices sitting under
these two last-mentioned commissions were criminal cases,
pleas of the crown, and they were not, you should understand,
cases depending in courts at Westminster like the civil cases
heard at *nisi prius*. The whole procedure—indictment, pleading, trial—took place before the commissioners, and they could
pass judgment and sentence—and thus completely dispose of
the whole case.

The general result of this system of commissions was that
a great deal of royal justice was done not by the permanent
central courts, but in the counties, by commissioners sent out
just for that occasion. They could completely dispose of the
criminal business of the county, and could preside over the
trial by jury of civil actions depending in the central courts.
In course of time more and more of this circuit work was
done by the judges of the king's permanent courts. The
details of the system, which was still in working order but
a few years ago, you will have to learn at some future time:
the importance of it in the history of our law has been
immense; owing to this system is it that we have never had
powerful local tribunals and what follows from such tribunals,
a variety of provincial laws; and again it was under the
discipline of the eyres that the counties and boroughs learnt
the first rudiments of representative government.

F. *Retrospect of Feudalism.*

Before quitting the first of our historic periods it will be
well for us to take a brief review of what we call feudalism—
in the first place to come to some understanding about the
meaning of the word, and then to see how far England was
ever subject to what can properly be called a feudal system.
We shall thus have occasion to speak of the growth of that
system of land law which hitherto we have considered merely
as an existing fact.

And first we will observe that in this country any talk of a
feudal system is a comparatively new thing: I should say that

we do not hear of a feudal system until long after feudalism has ceased to exist. From the end of the seventeenth century onwards our English law grew up in wonderful isolation; it became very purely English and insular. Our lawyers seem to have known little and cared nothing about the law of foreign countries, nothing about Roman jurisprudence. Their English authorities were all sufficient for them, and neither our parliaments nor our courts were subjected to any foreign influence. Coke in his voluminous works has summed up for us the law of the later Middle Ages, but in all his books, unless I am mistaken, there is no word about the feudal system. If, we may say, he expounds that system in full detail so far as that system was English, he is quite unconscious that he is doing anything of the kind; he has no thought of a system common to the nations of Europe, he is speaking of our insular law. No, for 'a feudal system' we must turn from Coke to a contemporary of his, that learned and laborious antiquary, Sir Henry Spelman. Coke was born in 1552 and died in 1633; Spelman was born in 1562 and died in 1641: so they were just contemporaries. Now were an examiner to ask who introduced the feudal system into England? one very good answer, if properly explained, would be Henry Spelman, and if there followed the question, what was the feudal system? a good answer to that would be, an early essay in comparative jurisprudence. Spelman reading continental books saw that English law, for all its insularity, was a member of a great European family, a family between all the members of which there are strong family likenesses. This was for Englishmen a grand and a striking discovery; much that had seemed quite arbitrary in their old laws, now seemed explicable. They learned of feudal law as of a medieval *jus gentium*, a system common to all the nations of the West. The new learning was propagated among English lawyers by Sir Martin Wright; it was popularized and made orthodox by Blackstone in his easy attractive manner. If my examiner went on with his questions and asked me, when did the feudal system attain its most perfect development? I should answer, about the middle of the last century. It was then, I should add, that the notion of one grand idea and a few simple principles underlying the mass of medieval law, English and continental, was firmly grasped and used as a means of explaining all that seemed to need explanation in the old English law. Now this was an important step—this connecting of English with foreign law, this endeavour to find some general intelligible principles running through the terrible tangle of our old books. Most undoubtedly there was much in our old law which could be explained only by reference to ideas which had found a completer development beyond seas, and to Blackstone and to Wright, and above all to Spelman, we owe a heavy debt. But since Blackstone's day we have learned and unlearned many things about the Middle Ages. In particular we have learnt to see vast differences as well as striking resemblances, to distinguish countries and to distinguish times. If now we speak of the feudal system, it should be with a full understanding that the feudalism of France differs radically from the feudalism of England, that the feudalism of the thirteenth is very different from that of the eleventh century. The phrase has thus become for us so large and vague that it is quite possible to maintain that of all countries England was the most, or for the matter of that the least, feudalized ; that William the Conqueror introduced, or for the matter of that suppressed, the feudal system.

What do we mean by feudalism? Some such answer as the following is the best that I can give—A state of society in which the main social bond is the relation between lord and man, a relation implying on the lord's part protection and defence; on the man's part protection, service and reverence, the service including service in arms. This personal relation is inseparably involved in a proprietary relation, the tenure of land—the man holds land of the lord, the man's service is a burden on the land, the lord has important rights in the land, and (we may say) the full ownership of the land is split up between man and lord. The lord has jurisdiction over his men, holds courts for them, to which they owe suit. Jurisdiction is regarded as property, as a private right which the lord has over his land. The national organization is a system of these relationships : at the head there stands the king as lord of all, below him are his immediate vassals, or tenants in chief, who again are lords of tenants, who again may be lords of tenants, and so on, down to the lowest possessor of land. Lastly, as every other court consists of the lord's tenants, so the king's court consists of his tenants in chief, and so far as there is any constitutional control over the king it is exercised by the body of these tenants.

That seems our idea of a feudal state. It is vague, it can only be described in very abstract terms; the concrete actual realities to which it answers, the Germany, France, England of different centuries may differ from each other very widely. A state which has these characteristics may be a powerful compact centralized kingdom; it may be hardly more than a loose confederation of principalities, a practical denial of national unity.

Now towards such an organization English society had been making progress for centuries before the Norman Conquest—and, as it seems, with an ever increasing velocity. The general nature of the process I shall describe in the words of Stubbs.

'The general tendency of the movement may be described as a movement from the personal to the territorial organization, from a state of things in which personal freedom and political right were the leading ideas, to one in which personal freedom and political right had become so much bound up with the relations created by the possession of land, as to be actually subservient to it....The main steps are apparent. In the primitive German constitution the free man of pure blood is the fully qualified political unit; the king is the king of the race; the host is the people in arms; the peace is the national peace; the courts are the people in council; the land is the property of the race, and the free man has a right to his share. In the next stage the possession of land has become the badge of freedom; the free man is fully free because he possesses land, he does not possess the land because he is free; the host is the body of landowners in arms, the courts are the courts of the landowners. But the personal basis is not lost sight of: the landless man may still select his lord;

the hide is the provision of the family ; the peace implies the maintenance of rights and duties between man and man ; the full-free is the equal of the noble in all political respects. In a further stage the land becomes the sacramental tie of all public relations, the poor man depends on the rich, not as his chosen lord, but as the owner of the land that he cultivates, the lord of the court to which he does suit and service, the leader whom he is bound to follow to the host ; the great landowner has his own peace, and administers his own justice[1].'

If for one moment we trespass outside the bounds of legal history, we may, I think, observe that one main cause of this movement is economic. The distribution of wealth becomes more and more unequal. Conquest and feuds may have something to do with this, but we need not, indeed cannot, ascribe it chiefly to violence. The better the peace is kept, the better the law is administered, the more progress is made towards free contract and free alienation, the more rapidly will great inequalities become common. In a time when there is little manufacture this will mean that land will be unequally distributed ; land becomes amassed in the hands of the rich, and wealth breeds wealth. But the rich do not really want the land, they want the produce of land. They want their lands cultivated. What is more, they are willing to let out their lands on very permanent terms. There is no speculation, no buying to sell or selling to buy ; to grant out land for ever at a perpetual rent—to receive it on those terms is no imprudent bargain—no rise or fall in prices is anticipated. I think it is well to bear this in mind ; for there seems to me a tendency to lay too much stress on the military and political, too little on the economic side of feudalism. When considered it seems not unnatural that a society consisting of land*owners*, free and barbarous, should by quite peaceful causes become transmuted into a society of landlords and tenants. But if we may look to such abstract considerations for the cause, we must look elsewhere for the facts of feudalism.

Now that personal relation between lord and man which is one ingredient of feudalism, is indeed old ; we may see it

[1] *Constitutional History*, vol. I, § 69.

in the first page of the history of our race. It can be traced to the relation between the German *princeps* and his *comites* described by Tacitus. Attached to the chieftain by the closest ties is a body of warlike companions—in many cases the sons of nobles, ambitious of renown : he provides their equipment, entertains them at his board. In war they fight for him, at once his defenders and the rivals of his prowess. They are bound to protect him, perhaps they even swear to do so. The *comes* is a dependent, but such dependence is glorious ; such service is preferable to the most perfect freedom. It was under leaders surrounded by such bands of *comites* that England was conquered by the German tribes. The *comes* of Tacitus may be recognized in the *gesith* of the Anglo-Saxon laws, a name which gradually gives way to that of thegn, a word which to start with means simply servant. But at first we cannot call this a feudal institution; it seems utterly unconnected with any tenure of land. The *comes* is not a landowner or land-holder, he is an inmate of his leader's household. But in England the thegn does come to be a landowner. The folk-land, the national land not yet appropriated, seems regarded as the natural fund out of which rewards may be provided for those who in war or otherwise have deserved well of the state[1]. The king with the counsel and consent of his wise men confers land on his distinguished followers. In England thegnage tends to become territorial. It seems expected that a thegn will naturally be a large landowner. The process goes further—the large landowner is worthy of thegn right ; he who has five hides of land and certain other rights which seem to be rights of jurisdiction over his dependents is entitled to be deemed a thegn, and so receives certain privileges such as an increased wergild, or an increased value for his oath. Then again from the beginning, the thegn is the warrior ; all free men are bound to fight ; the army is the nation in arms ; but the thegn is specially bound to fight—bound to fight for his leader. As then the thegn becomes a large landowner, and as the large landowner as such comes to be regarded as worthy

[1] See p. 57.

of the privileges of the thegnage, so the special duty of fighting, and fighting for the king, comes to be a duty incumbent on the large landowners. We know too that the folk-land, the unappropriated land which according to the older idea had belonged to the nation, had been becoming more and more the king's demesne land in fact, if not in theory. Stubbs notices that from Alfred's time onwards the clause in the deeds granting this folk-land, which expresses the counsel and consent of the witan, becomes rarer though it never disappears altogether. The wise men rather witness the grant than authorize it. After the Conquest, all this folk-land became simply *terra Regis*, the king's demesne; but large as the change may seem to us, very possibly it was a change rather in terminology than in anything else; it was a recognition of what had well-nigh become an accomplished fact. The thegn then who has received a grant of such land and who is bound to military service—it takes but a small change of ideas, a change in the point of view from which the facts are seen, to regard him as holding land of the king by military service. Exactly wherein consisted the special military obligation of the thegn, we do not well know. According to the old order of ideas, every man was bound to serve in the national army, the king's thegns were bound to fight round him and for him. As the thegnage became connected with the possession of land—so that the owner of five hides was worthy of thegn-right—so, it would seem, a special obligation to serve and find soldiers was laid on the great landowners and in some way, which we cannot now precisely determine, was proportioned to their holdings. But to the last, to the day of the Conquest, the old national army could be called out, and it is very necessary to remember that the Conquest did not put an end to this; the old national army exists alongside of the feudal army.

But it is not only the king who has thegns—great men may have them: indeed it seems that a thegn may have lesser thegns dependent on him—just as in after-days the king's tenant *in capite* might have tenants holding of him by knight's service; still the idea of tenure is not the essence of thegnship. The history of the thegnship is brought out by laws concerning heriots. Now in its origin the heriot is the equipment of arms which the *princeps* has provided for the *comes*; on the death of the latter, it must be given back —the word just means equipment for the army. The thegn ceases to be a member of the household, becomes a land-owner and provides his own arms; but still on his death the heriot is rendered. It now takes the form of arms and money, due to the king on the thegn's death. Thus in the laws of Canute, on the death of a king's thegn four horses —two saddled, two unsaddled—two swords, four spears, as many shields, a helm, breastplate and 50 mancuses of gold are due[1]. This is important under the Norman kings: these heriots come to be regarded as reliefs, sums paid by the heir on his taking up the land which had been his ancestor's, a burden of tenure. The payment may remain the same, the mode of regarding it is different. Thus the way of feudalism is prepared.

This tie of man to lord was regarded as a tie of the most sacred kind. While many offences which we should think very grave can still be compounded with money, treason against the lord, be he the king or another lord, is a capital crime. This is laid down in the laws of Alfred, and to these laws there is a curious preface which shows the strength of the feeling. The king explains that after the nations had accepted the Christian faith, it was ordained by the wise men (spiritual and lay) that for almost every first offence a money payment might be accepted, save for treason to the lord for which no mercy should be shown, since God Almighty showed none to those who despised him, and Christ, God's son, adjudged none to those who sold him, and commanded that a lord should be loved as one's self. The crime of Judas is the crime of one who betrayed his lord[2].

This relation of man and lord we find in all parts of the social structure. To start with it is a relation into which men enter voluntarily. Then, however, we find the legis-lators requiring that men shall have lords. This rule is laid down in the laws of Athelstan (925–940)—every landless

---

[1] *Select Charters*, p. 74, Liebermann I, pp. 357—9.
[2] *Select Charters*, p. 62, Liebermann I, pp. 45—6.

man must have a lord: if he has not got one, one must be found for him by his kindred[1]. This we may regard as a police measure. The law has no hold on the landless man; too often he can break the law and laugh at it; there is nothing of his that you can take from him; escape from justice is easy; he must have a lord who will be bound to produce him in court should he be wanted. Thus positive legislation extends the relation of dependence; it is required that men must either have land or have lords. The landless man may still be fully free, may have political rights, but he is dependent. The change has begun which makes free-holding, and not personal freedom, the qualification for political rights. The landless man is represented in the courts by his lord; his lord begins to answer for him, he is losing his right to attend on his own behalf, to sit there as judge and declare the law.

Probably he finds this very convenient. Attendance at the courts is a sore burden for the poorer men; they would go there to little purpose, merely to see things settled for them by the richer folk; while as to their private rights the lord will look after these, for they are much implicated with his own rights. We can see that it must have been convenient to have a lord; for what the landless are bound to do by law, the smaller landowners do of their own free will; they commend themselves to lords. We learn from Domesday that in some parts of England this practice of commending oneself had become common, especially in the eastern counties. The smaller landowners had placed themselves in a relation of dependence on superior lords. What exactly was implied by this we do not know—and very possibly commendation meant different things in different cases—sometimes, it would seem, the dependent was still able to transfer himself and his land from one lord to another; sometimes being personally quite free, he could leave his lord but then must leave his land, and in such cases it is a delicate and a verbal question whether the land is his land or has become his lord's. No legislation had turned the smaller owners into tenants of other men's lands or even compelled them to have lords—

[1] *Select Charters*, p. 66, Liebermann I, p. 170.

the change had been brought about by the private acts of individuals and the result, as sketched for us by modern writers, is intricate and confused.

But very often indeed, something which we cannot but call a tenure of land, a holding by one man of another, must have been created in a simpler fashion. By means of grants of folk-land territories were being amassed in the hands of great men and religious houses[1]. These again granted out their land to cultivators. Generally such grants were of a permanent kind: grants to a man and his heirs, or grants to a man and a certain specified number of successive heirs in return for labour services, ploughings and reapings of the lord's own demesne lands, or rents payable in money or in kind. We do not find grants or leases for years—I believe that among all the Anglo-Saxon charters, there is but one specimen of such a bargain. Permanence is desired on both sides—there is no speculating for a rise or fall of prices or of rents. And here we have something very like the estate in fee simple of later law—the feudal division of complete ownership between lord and tenant. The cultivator has perhaps under the terms of the grant an estate that is to endure for ever, or at least so long as he has heirs; but the services are burdens on the land—very possibly if his heirs fail the land will again become the land of the giver, very possibly if the services fall into arrear, the giver may resume the land. We know very little about all this—for the titles of the smaller people, the cultivators of the land, were seldom evidenced by written instruments. But it is very probable that before the Norman Conquest, a large part of England was holden practically on the terms of that socage tenure that we find existing at a later day—the possessor of the land being bound to perform services more or less onerous in return for the land, to plough the lord's own land, to pay rent in money or in kind. All that seems wanting to turn such a possession into a tenure by one man of another is just the technical termi-

---

[1] Maitland would possibly have rewritten this sentence somewhat as follows: 'By means of royal and other books (or charters) superiorities over land were being conferred upon religious houses and great men.' *Domesday Book and Beyond*, pp. 226—58, 293—318.

nology—and to a uniform technical terminology Anglo-Saxon land law had not yet arrived. So far as we can now see, it had no theory of tenure.

We approach here a difficult subject—perhaps the most difficult in the history of English law—namely, the history of villeinage, the history of that servile land-holding which is brought to our notice in the books of the twelfth and thirteenth centuries. It seems highly probable that at the date of the Norman Conquest there was a large mass of unfree tenants cultivating lands on much the same terms as those which constitute the villeinage of later days. Slaves there most certainly were throughout the Anglo-Saxon period —the existence of a class of persons half-servile, half-free, is a more disputable point.

Another element of feudalism is plainly visible. For some time before the Norman Conquest—how long is a debated question—jurisdiction, the right to hold courts, had been passing into private hands. The doctrine had long been gaining ground that justice was the king's, that he could grant it to others, could grant to them the right of holding courts. Certain it is that Edward the Confessor had made such grants on a lavish scale. Our evidence chiefly consists of grants made to churches and religious houses—ecclesiastical bodies were careful to preserve their title deeds, and so they have come down to us—but there can be little doubt that similar grants were made to great lay landowners. England was fast becoming a land of private courts—courts in which the lord did justice among his dependents, those dependents being bound to come and sit there, and help in making of judgments. Nothing, I believe, is more the essence of all that we mean when we talk of feudalism than the private court—a court which can be inherited and sold along with land. Looking at this we may say that England was plunging into feudalism, and feudalism of a dangerous kind—for during the Confessor's reign the central power was growing weak, the great lords were growing strong. The facts of feudalism seem to be there—what is wanting is a theory which shall express those facts. That came to us from Normandy.

The Conqueror came from a land which had formed part of the territory of the Frankish Empire, and within that Empire the process which we have seen at work in England had gone on faster and further. The soil had long been Roman. The Frankish conquest of Gaul had differed essentially from the English conquest of Britain. It had been effected slowly by a German nation which had become Christian during the conquest. A large population of the old inhabitants—Celtic by blood, Roman in language and in law—became subject to Teutonic rulers. In England the small landowner was, at least generally, a free Englishman; in Gaul he was a conquered provincial. What is more, in course of time the Romance tongue prevailed in France over the German speech of the conquerors, and the customs of the Franks were impregnated by Roman law. This Roman influence is apparent at once when we compare our old dooms with the still older *Lex Salica*, the code of the Salian Franks; the former are written in Anglo-Saxon, the latter is written in Latin.

Now on the continent the history of feudalism centres round the *beneficium*, or, as it came to be called, the *feodum*. It is this, of course, which has given us the word *feudal*. The word *feodum* does not, I believe, occur before the end of the ninth century. It is derived from the German word for cattle, which, like the Roman *pecunia* derived from *pecus*, comes to mean money or property in general. It is somewhat curious that the two words which English lawyers very frequently contrast as quite opposed to each other, the *fee* and the *chattel*, should both refer us back to what is perhaps the oldest form of property, namely cattle, for *chattel* is from the low Latin *catallum, cattle*. But the *beneficium* was an old institution; it appears very soon after the German tribes overrun the Roman Empire. It is a gift of land made by the king out of his own estate, the grantee coming under a special obligation to be faithful—not, it seems, a promise of definite service, but a general promise to be faithful in consideration of the gift. Such grants were freely made by the Frankish kings to their great men. At first, it seems the grant was made merely for the life of the grantee. Gradually, however, the benefice assumed a hereditary character : it was considered that the heir of the dead beneficiary had a claim to a renewal of the benefice.   The hereditary character of the benefice is already recognized in a capitulary (an ordinance) of 877—two hundred years before the Norman Conquest.   All offices in the Middle Ages tend to become hereditary—the kingship tends to become, actually becomes, hereditary; our sheriffdoms tend to become hereditary, in a few cases actually become hereditary; the English peers gradually acquire a hereditary right to be called to meet the king in parliament. So also the *beneficium* or *feodum* became hereditary—and yet the heir did not at once step into his ancestor's shoes : he did not hold the fief until he had been invested, put in seisin by the king, and a payment fixed more or less by varying custom might be required of him on thus relieving or taking up the fallen inheritance.   This was the relief.

To express the rights thus created, a set of technical terms was developed :—the beneficiary or feudatory holds the land of his lord, the grantor—A *tenet terram de* B.   The full ownership (*dominium*) of the land is as it were broken up between A and B; or again, for the feudatory may grant out part of the land to be held of him, it may be broken up between A, B, and C, C holding of B and B of A, and so on, *ad infinitum.*

The genesis of this idea of tenure, of divided ownership, has been and still is very warmly disputed among continental writers.   I may refer you to the writings of Maine—*Ancient Law*, chap. viii (last part), and *Early Law and Custom*, chap. x. Very possibly some ideas of Roman law helped towards the result, but the result is a notion which is not Roman—that of a *dominium* split up between lord and tenant.

Then also jurisdiction passed into private hands—the king granted it out along with the land to be held of him.   The idea that jurisdiction is the king's property and may be alienated by him had become current in France earlier than in England, the kingship had been stronger, and from the middle of the ninth century onwards such grants became common. This, it is to be remembered, is the time when the great Frank Empire went to pieces—the central authority became little more than a name—the effective courts were the courts of the great proprietors. Also, it is to be remembered that this is the time when the Northmen subdued Normandy—the Norman duke became the vassal of the king of the French, became so by commendation—Duke Richard of Normandy commended himself to Hugh duke of the French, whose descendants became kings. But the king's power in Normandy was hardly more than nominal. A disciple of Austin would probably say that Normandy was an independent political community, though this was not quite the theory of the time. The process of feudalization had gone on within the duchy; the lords of Norman extraction dominated over a people of another blood and formed a powerful aristocracy—only the personal character, the heavy hand of the dukes, kept together the duchy as a whole.

William came from Normandy to claim the English crown which, as he alleged, was his by right as the heir whom the Confessor had chosen. It was his own personal right that he came to seek—no right that Normans had to England, but a right that he, William, had to be king of the English. The claim may have been, seemingly was, indefensible, but its nature should be remembered. To have asserted a title by victory would have encouraged very dangerous ideas: if the duke had fought and won, had not his earls and barons fought and won also? No, an air of legality was given to the whole affair—William succeeded to Edward's position. The Conquest threw into his hands a vast quantity of land. Those who fought against him were rebels, and their land was forfeited by their rebellion; each new outbreak led to fresh confiscations. His followers had to be rewarded, and they were rewarded liberally. But there was no general scramble: the new owners step into the places of old owners; a forfeiture and then a grant by the king is the link in the title. Still by means of a quiet assumption feudal tenure becomes universal. All land is held of the king.

It is, I suppose, of this that an English lawyer first thinks when he hears any talk of feudalism. For some centuries past all the feudalism that has been of importance in England has been merely land law, real property law, a part of private

law. Our land law we still say is feudal; all land is still held
of the king mediately or immediately; this is as true to-day
as it ever was. But the mere fact that it is true to-day shows
that a legal theory of this sort is not the essence of feudalism,
for no one would think of calling the England of our day
a feudal state. If we examine our notion of feudalism, does
it not seem this, that land law is not private law, that public
law is land law, that public and political rights and duties
of all sorts and kinds are intimately and quite inextricably
blended with rights in land? Such rights carry with them the
right to attend the common council or court of the realm, the
common council or court of the county; jurisdictions, military
duties, fiscal burdens are consequences of tenure; the constitution of parliament, of the law courts, of the army, all
seems as it were a sort of appendix to the law of real
property.

Now this theory that land in the last resort is held of the
king, becomes the theory of our law at the Norman Conquest.
It is assumed in Domesday Book, the outcome of that great
survey of which we are now keeping the 800th anniversary:
quietly assumed as the basis of the survey. On the other
hand we can say with certainty that before the Conquest this
was not the theory of English law. Towards such a theory
English law had been tending for a long while past, very
possibly the time was fast approaching when the logic of facts
would have generated this idea; the facts, the actual legal
relationships, were such that the wide principle 'all land held
in the last resort of the king' would not greatly disturb them.
Still this principle had not been evolved. It came to us from
abroad; but it came in the guise of a quiet assumption; no
law forced it upon the conquered country; no law was necessary; in Normandy lands were held of the Duke, the Duke
again held of the king; of course it was the same in England;
no other system was conceivable. The process of confiscation
gave the Conqueror abundant opportunity for making the
theory true in fact; the followers whom he rewarded with
forfeited lands would of course hold of him; the great English
landowners, whose lands were restored to them, would of
course hold of him. As to the smaller people, when looked at

from the point of view natural to a Norman, they were already tenants of the greater people, and when the greater people forfeited their rights, there was but a change of lords. This assumption was sometimes true enough, perhaps in other cases quite false; in many cases it would seem but the introduction of a new and simpler terminology; he who formerly was a land*owner* personally bound to a lord, became a land-tenant holding land of a lord. There was no legislation, and I believe that no chronicler refers to the introduction of this new theory. As to the later lawyers, Glanvill and Bracton, they never put it into words. They never state as a note-worthy fact that all land is held of the king; *of course* it is. This is very remarkable in Bracton's great treatise. His general learning about property he draws from the Roman books, and propounds in the language of Roman law. The ultimate tenant of land, the lowest freeholder in the feudal scale, is the owner of the land, he has *dominium rei, proprietatem,* he is *proprietarius*; but of course he holds of someone, *tenet de* some lord; if he holds of no other, then *tenet de domino rege*; there is nothing here that deserves explanation.

Now if feudalism consists only in this legal theory of tenure, then I believe we may say that of all European countries England was the most perfectly feudalized. Every inch of land was brought within it. The great shock of the Norman Conquest rendered the material very plastic; all could be brought under one idea. If for example we look at the law of medieval Germany, we find it otherwise; there is feudal land and non-feudal land, there are feudal holders and non-feudal owners side by side. There are two different bodies of law, *Landrecht* and *Lehnrecht*, Common Land Law and Feudal Law. We Englishmen can hardly translate these terms; our *Landrecht* is all *Lehnrecht*, all our land law is law about land holden by feudal tenure. But we must not forget to look at both sides of this truth; our *Lehnrecht* is *Landrecht*, law not for a particular class of persons holding military fiefs, but the general law of rights in land. This I think of great importance; the wide extension of the feudal idea deprives it of much of its most dangerous meaning; it does not create

a caste ; it has to serve for the tenant in socage, the agricultural classes as well as for the tenant by knight service.
Many things in our legal history are thus explained, for
instance, the growth of primogeniture. In origin it belongs to
a military system ; slowly it spread from the military tenants
to the socagers, it ceased to be the mark of a class, it became
common law[1]. How consistently the idea of tenure was carried
through the whole land law, and how little that theory might
mean, is best seen when we look at the tenure by frankalmoign. The monastery pays no rent, none of the ordinary
profits of tenure can accrue to the lord, for his tenant never
dies, never leaves an heir, never commits felony ; but to save
the theory he is still a tenant holding by the service of saying
prayers for the lord.

The Norman Conquest then introduces the general theory
of tenure—makes it the theory of the whole land law. Also it
draws tighter the bond which already is beginning to connect
military service with the holding of land. Still we must not
suppose that the Conqueror definitely apportioned the quan-
tum of military service to be exacted from his feudatories.
'We have,' says Stubbs, 'no light on the point from any
original grant made by the Conqueror to any lay follower;
but judging from the grants made to the churches we cannot
suppose it probable that such gifts were made on any expressed condition, or accepted with a distinct pledge to
provide a certain contingent of knights for the king's service.
The obligation of national defence was incumbent as of
old on all landowners, and the customary service of one
fully-armed man for each five hides was probably the rate
at which the newly endowed follower of the king would be
expected to discharge his duty. The wording of the
Doomsday survey does not imply that in this respect the
new military service differed from the old ; the land is
marked out, not into knight's fees, but into hides, and the
number of knights to be furnished by a particular feudatory
would be ascertained by inquiring the number of hides that he
held, without apportioning the particular acres that were to

---

[1] This idea is worked out in the *History of English Law*, vol. II, pp. 260—73.

maintain a particular knight[1].' This apportionment seems rather the result of the process of sub-infeudation. The great landowner whose wide estates oblige him to furnish a large body of knights parcels out the duty among his followers, definitely providing that A or B shall hold this parcel of land by the service of one knight or of three knights. The system seems hardly to have been worked into perfect detail until the feudal array was already losing some of its importance. The imposition of scutage in the reign of Henry II, the commutation of military service for money payment, makes every particular definite; the obligation can now be expressed in terms of pounds, shillings and pence. This district constitutes a knight's fee; this is a fifth of a knight's fee; when the scutage is two marks on a knight's fee this land pays two shillings, and so forth. No general plan is imposed[2].

As regards what are generally called the burdens or incidents of feudal tenure—here again we ought not to think of William the Conqueror bringing over with him a fully developed law. The state of the English law when it becomes manifest in the pages of Glanvill and Bracton is the result of a slow process which went on during the eleventh and twelfth centuries, and which gradually defined the rights of lord and tenant. This process one can trace as regards each separate burden—relief, marriage, wardship, aids, scutages, and so forth. The final result we have already sketched. Some of our ordinary text-books encourage the notion that originally the English feudatories were merely tenants for life, but that in course of time, to use the common phrase, 'fiefs became hereditary.' Now it is perfectly true that long ago such a process as this had gone on abroad. The *beneficium* or *feodum* as it came to be called, was, to start with, only a life estate; but already in the ninth century the claim of the heir to inherit or take up his father's fief had been generally admitted. There seems no doubt whatever that when the Conqueror gave English land to one of his great followers,

[1] *Constitutional History*, vol. I, § 96. The number of knights does not seem to have borne any close relation to the size of the tenant's estate. Round, *Feudal England*, p. 247 ff.

[2] For Maitland's developed views on scutage see *History of English Law*, vol. I, pp. 266—71, where it is proved that the tenant in chief could not commute his service.

the gift was in terms the gift of an hereditary estate—a gift to
the donee and his heirs. Still doubtless the past history of
the *beneficium* clung about the gift. The heir's claim, though
an admitted claim, was still rather a claim to be placed in his
ancestor's position, than a claim that by mere death and
inheritance he was already in that position. He had a right
to have the land, but the land was not as yet quite his. He
must do homage and swear fealty ; what is more, money may
be expected of him if he is to fill the position of his ancestor.
There is still something of grace and favour in letting him
hold what his father held. We know little of what was the
practice of the Conqueror himself; but it is plain that William
Rufus would have liked to treat the feudatories as mere life
tenants, to have insisted that the heir must repurchase the
father's land, even that the new bishop or abbot must repurchase the land held by his predecessor. He wished, we are
told, to be the heir of every man in England. His demands,
however, were clearly regarded as oppressive and illegal.
Henry I on his succession to the throne found it necessary
to renounce the evil customs of his brother. The coronation
charter in which he did this is one of the main landmarks
in the history of English feudalism—even in the history of
England. Thus in particular we have this clause: 'If any
of my earls, barons or other tenants shall die, his heir shall
not redeem (*redimet*, buy back) his land, but shall relieve
it (take up the inheritance) by a just and lawful relief.' This,
you will see, on the one hand declares in an emphatic way
that fiefs are hereditary, while on the other hand it declares
no less emphatically that a relief is due. The amount, however, is not fixed. It is to be remembered that something like
the relief had been paid in England before the Norman Conquest—namely the heriot—and though (as I have already said)
the heriot had originally been of a different nature (the return
of the thegn's military equipment to the lord who provides it)
it had come to look much like the foreign relief. The thegn
had become a landowner; bound by special obligation to serve
the king ; on his death arms and money were rendered to the
king:—a Norman accustomed to the beneficiary system would
see here a relief. It is now very generally supposed that

Ranulf Flambard, the minister of William Rufus (of whose doings the contemporary chroniclers complain very bitterly), had much to do with shaping this part of English feudalism. The just and lawful reliefs of Henry's charter may have been equivalent to the heriots, a tariff of which is given in the laws of Canute. But it took a century and more from the coronation of Henry I to reduce the king's claims within any very definite bounds. What I have said of reliefs may be said also of those extremely onerous burdens which we know as wardship and marriage. The Coronation Charter of Henry I makes large promises about them, and lays down rules which are considerably less heavy on the tenants than those which ultimately become the rules of the common law. From the accession of Henry I to the Magna Carta of 1215 these matters are very unsettled—the king gets what he can, often he can get much. At length the Great Charter wrung from John sets precise bounds to his rights, though as a matter of fact another half century goes by before the charter is very carefully observed, and even the Great Charter is not in all respects so favourable to the tenants as is the charter of Henry I : this in particular is the case as regards wardship and marriage—the king's rights as ultimately fixed are, to say the least, very ample.

What has been said of the king and his tenants in chief is true also of the barons and their tenants. Henry I at the opening of his reign was compelled to throw himself on the whole nation for its support. His charter carefully stipulates that his behaviour to his tenants is to be the model for their behaviour to their tenants. They are to take no more than a just and lawful relief, and are to be content with such rights of wardship and marriage as suffice for the king. The rising, again, which won the charter of 1215, was distinctly a national rising, and the rights which were secured to the tenants in chief as against the king, were secured as against them for their tenants. The period from 1066 to 1215 we may regard as the age during which the feudal burdens are defined, partly by charters obtained by the king, partly by the practice of the king's exchequer, which gradually develops into a regular routine ; but many points are unsettled, the king will take what he can get, his tenants will pay as little as possible—will now and then revolt. In Glanvill's time, to give one example, the relief due from a knight's fee was fixed at 100 shillings; for socage land, one year's rent. He goes on to say that as to baronies no certain rule has been laid down, for baronies are relieved *juxta voluntatem et misericordiam domini regis*[1].

Let us now recount the limitations which are set in this country to the development of what can properly be called a feudal system.

(1) First and foremost, it never becomes law that there is no political bond between men save the bond of tenure. William himself seems to have seen the danger. We read that in 1086 he came to Salisbury, 'and there came to him his witan and all the landowning men that were worth aught from over all England, whosesoever men they were, and all bowed themselves down to him and became his men, and swore oaths of fealty to him that they would be faithful to him against all other men.' He exacted an oath of fealty not merely from his own tenants, but from all the possessors of land, no matter whose men they were; they were to be faithful to him against all other men, even against their lords. This became fundamental law: we have before this seen its result; whenever homage or fealty was done to any mesne lord, the tenant expressly saved the faith that he owed to his lord the king. The oath of allegiance we find is exacted from all men; this exaction becomes part of the regular business of the local courts.

(2) English law never recognizes that any man is bound to fight for his lord. The sub-tenant who holds by military service is bound by his tenure to fight for the king; he is bound to follow his lord's banner, but only in the national army:—he is in nowise bound to espouse his lord's quarrels, least of all his quarrels with the king. Private war never becomes legal; it is a crime and a breach of the peace. Certainly there was a great deal of private war; certainly men felt it their duty to follow their lord against his enemies, even

---

[1] *Select Charters*, p. 163.

against the king; but this duty never succeeds in getting itself acknowledged as a legal duty. If that seems to you too natural to be worth mentioning, you should look at the history of France; there it was definitely regarded as law that in a just quarrel the vassal must follow his immediate lord, even against the king.

(3) Though the military tenures supply the king with an army, it never becomes law that those who are not bound by tenure need not fight. The old national force, officered by the sheriffs, does not cease to exist. Rufus had called it out for compulsory service; more than once it was called out against the Scots; in 1181 Henry II reorganized it by his Assize of Arms; it was reorganized again under Edward I by the Statute of Winchester in 1285; it is the militia of later days. Every man is bound to have arms suitable to his degree, down to the man who need but have bow and arrows. In this organization of the common folk under royal officers, there is all along a counterpoise to the military system of feudalism, and it serves the king well. The great families of the Conquest are at length pulverized between the hammer of the king and the anvil of the people.

(4) Taxation is not feudalized. The king for a while is strong enough to tax the nation, to tax the sub-tenants, to get straight at the mass of the people, their lands and their goods, without the intervention of their lords. When the time for putting a restraint upon his power comes, it is only for a brief while, if ever, the restraint of a purely feudal assembly of tenants in chief. The king deals with the smaller landowners in the county court, until at last the county court is represented at Westminster by knights of the shire. On the other hand, the king relying on the nation is strong enough to insist that the lords shall not tax their tenants without his consent.

(5) The administration of justice is never completely feudalized. The old local courts are kept alive, and are not feudal assemblies. The jurisdiction of the feudal courts is strictly limited; criminal jurisdiction they have none save by express royal grant, and the kings are on the whole chary of making such grants. Seldom, indeed, can any lord exercise

more than what on the continent would have been considered
justice of a very low degree. The two counties palatine are
exceptions; but one of these, Durham, is in the hands of
a bishop, and the appointment of bishops is practically in the
king's hands. As to Chester, our best representative of real
feudalism; about the middle of the thirteenth century a series
of lucky accidents brings the earldom into the king's own
hands. The king again, as we have seen, rapidly extends the
sphere of his own justice: before the middle of the thirteenth
century his courts have practically become courts of first
instance for the whole realm—from Henry II's day his
itinerant justices have been carrying a common law through
the land.

(6) The *Curia Regis*, which is to become the *commune
concilium regni*, never takes very definitely a feudal shape.
The body of tenants in chief is too large, too heterogeneous for
that. It is much in the king's power to summon whom he
will, to take the advice of whom he will. The tradition of
a council of witan is not lost. Only slowly does a body of
barons, or major barons, separate itself from the larger body
tenants in chief, and it long remains in the king's power
to decide who these major barons are, who shall be summoned
by name to his councils. The residue of the tenants in chief
is not keen about going to court; gradually it is lost in the
body of freeholders. When the time for a representative
parliament has come, the smaller tenants in chief are mixed
with their own sub-vassals, and the bodies which are represented by the knights of the shire are the county courts
in which all freeholders find a place. The model parliament
of 1295 follows closely on the great statute of 1290 (*Quia
Emptores*), which puts a stop to subinfeudation, and vastly
diminishes the public importance of tenure.

Speaking generally then, that ideal feudalism of which we
have spoken, an ideal which was pretty completely realized in
France during the tenth, eleventh and twelfth centuries, was
never realized in England. Owing to the Norman Conquest
one part of the theory was carried out in this country with
consistent and unexampled rigour; every square inch of land
was brought within the theory of tenure: English real property

law becomes a law of feudal tenures. In France, in Germany, allodial owners might be found : not one in England. Also the burdens of tenure were heavier here than elsewhere ; the doctrines of wardship and marriage were, I believe, severer here than in any other country in Europe. On the other hand our public law does not become feudal ; in every direction the force of feudalism is limited and checked by other ideas ; the public rights, the public duties of the Englishman are not conceived and cannot be conceived as the mere outcome of feudal compacts between man and lord.

PERIOD II.

PUBLIC LAW AT THE DEATH OF HENRY VII.

IT may seem strange to you that I should choose the year 1509 as our next point of view. Certainly it would be more in accordance with tradition were we to pause at 1399, the deposition of Richard II, the accession of the House of Lancaster; again at 1461, the accession of the House of York, and again at 1485, the accession of the House of Tudor. But for one thing our time is short. In the second place it is well to break with tradition even though that tradition be reasonable ; we ought to accustom ourselves to review our constitution from many different points of view, and I do not wish to repeat exactly what is in the books that you ought to read. In the third place a moment of crisis, when, so to speak, our constitution is thrown out of gear, does not seem the best moment at which to halt in order that we may inquire what the constitution is,—the end of the four and twenty peaceful years during which Henry VII governed England seems to me a time at which we may profitably place ourselves in order to survey the permanent results of the eventful two centuries which have elapsed since the death of Edward I. The internal English history of these two centuries is very largely a history of the relation between king and parliament; that relation has varied very much from time to time, it has varied with the character of the kings, the character of the parliaments, it has been affected by foreign wars and by civil wars; still there is a certain permanent outcome, a constitution, a body of public law. Our first duty must be to consider what a parliament is.

A.   *Parliament.*

I.   *Its Constitution.*

We find that the great precedent of 1295 has been followed, that assemblies modelled on the assembly of that year have been constantly holden, that these have quite definitely acquired the name of parliaments. Parliament is still, at least in theory, an assembly of the three estates ; we must examine its component parts.

(i)   *The Clergy*

In the first place the two archbishops and the eighteen bishops are there, and as of old it may still be questioned whether they are there as holding baronies or as the heads of the national church. The number of abbots has sunk to 27; in 1305 it was as high as 75; but the abbots have insisted that unless they hold territorial baronies they are not bound to attend; they have cared little for national politics; no abbot has made himself conspicuous as a states-man; in 1509 their doom is at hand. The inferior clergy are summoned by means of the *praemunientes* clause ; but they have systematically refrained from attending; they have preferred to vote their taxes in their convocations. In time their attendance has been required for the same purpose as that of the commons; they have been told to come *ad faciendum et consentiendum*; this was the form down to 1340; gradually it was supplanted by *ad consentiendum*, which in 1377 became the invariable form : a consent to legislation might be given by silence. We know that the clerical proctors did occasionally attend throughout the four-teenth century, but even when they appeared they apparently took but little part in the proceedings of the parliament.

(ii)   *The Lords Temporal.*

The lords temporal are now divided into various ranks. In 1307 we had only to speak of earls and barons ; but now above the earls there are marquesses and dukes, and between the earls and barons there are viscounts. The first English dukedom was created in 1337, when Edward III gave that dignity to the king's eldest son; the dukedoms of Lancaster, Clarence, Gloucester and York were bestowed upon members of the royal house, and in 1397 Richard II gave dukedoms to some who were not members of that house. He also made our first marquess, Robert de Vere, marquess of Dublin. The title of viscount was not given until the fifteenth century. These titles were imported from abroad. They were at first used in order to give some nobleman a precedence over his fellows. They have never given more than this, and have been legally unimportant. They never implied any territorial power or jurisdiction over the place whence the title was derived. Even the old title of earl though always taken from a county or county town had long ceased to imply anything of the sort. The creation of these new dignities had, however, an important effect on the usual mode of creating peers. The dukes, marquesses and so forth were created by patent, that is, by letters under the great seal definitely giving this rank to them and their heirs. Hitherto, as we have seen, barons had not been created in this way, the writ summoning him or his ancestors to a parliament was all that the baron could show. In 1387 Richard II created a baron by patent: this example was occasionally followed, and from 1446 onwards was regularly followed. We thus get to the law of our own day, that a peerage must be created in one of two ways, either by writ of summons or by letters patent, and it may save repetition hereafter if we now trace this matter to an end.

Since the fifteenth century a patent has been the regular means of creating a new peerage: it is now the means invariably used. Such a patent usually confers the peerage, barony, earldom, dukedom, or whatever it be upon a man and the heirs male of his body. The House of Lords in 1856 advised the crown that a patent which gave no more than a peerage for life would not entitle the grantee to be summoned to parliament. A peerage created by patent must be descendible, inheritable: at this moment I can say no more, because to go further would be to enter the domain of real property law; but you will read more of it in Sir William Anson's book[1]. I believe that it must be admitted that as a matter of fact ever since the practice of creating peers by

1 *Law and Custom of the Constitution. Parliament*, c. VI.

patent had been in use no distinct precedent could be found for an attempt to make a man a peer without giving him an inheritable right; the decision of 1856 in the Wensleydale peerage case was to the effect that this practice had begotten a rule of law. But secondly I may claim a peerage and a right to be summoned on the mere ground that an ancestor of mine, whose heir I am, was once summoned and took his seat. It is held that a mere writ of summons directed to A.B., if obeyed by him, confers on him a right descendible to his heirs. Whether the kings of the thirteenth and fourteenth centuries meant that this should be so, may well be doubted, but on the whole the practice of summoning the heir was regularly observed, and in the sixteenth century the rule that summons and sitting gives a descendible right was regarded as fixed. A peerage may descend to a woman, although in modern times the patent usually prevents this by mentioning the heirs male of the body, or the king can confer a peerage upon a woman. Thus a woman may be a peeress in her own right. No woman however has ever, says Dr Stubbs, sat in a full and proper parliament. The nearest approach to such a summons is that of four abbesses who in 1306 were cited to a great council held to grant an aid on the knighting of the Prince of Wales.

We have before referred to the complicated question of barony by tenure. In 1509 the problem had not yet presented itself in any very definite shape. There can be no doubt that it was the general impression among both lawyers and others that the right to the writ of summons was in many cases still annexed to the holding of certain lands forming a barony. Such land baronies however were so seldom alienated that the question had hardly arisen whether the alienee or the alienor's heir would have the better right to the summons. Freehold lands, we must remember, could not as yet be given by will. As lands became more easily alienable the question was forced to the front and the decision was that the right to the summons was not annexed to the property in the land, and consequently could not be alienated.

Even when some definite rules as to the right to a summons were being evolved, the number of lords summoned varied greatly owing to minorities, attainders, extinction of baronies and similar causes. Under Henry IV the number never exceeded 50, under Henry V it only once reached 40, under Henry VI it fell as low as 23 and reached 55, under Edward IV 50 was the maximum. The Wars of the Roses thinned the baronage, but not so much as is often supposed; only 29 lay peers were summoned to the first parliament of Henry VII, but in a few years the number again reached 40, though only five new peerages were created. It is well to remember this, for we are too apt to think of the House of Lords as an assembly of hereditary nobles. Throughout the Middle Ages the spiritual and non-hereditary peers must often have been in a majority; even when the number of abbots had sunk to 27 they, with the two archbishops and 28 bishops, could frequently have voted down the whole lay peerage.

We have been using the terms peers and peerage. These terms but gradually came into use during the fourteenth century. Originally of course *pares* only meant equals. A new significance is given to the term by a principle deeply imbedded in our old law, namely, that a man who is to be judged, must be judged by those who are at least his equals—the free man is not to be judged by villeins. Thus in *Leg. Hen. Prim.* 31 § 7, *Unusquisque per pares suos est judicandus*[1]. So in feudal courts the vassal is not to be judged by sub-vassals. Thus a man's *pares* came to mean those who, standing on the same level with him, are competent to be his judges—the body of judges is the *pares curiae*, the body of peers which sits in the court in question. This principle, as we all know, is solemnly sanctioned by Magna Carta: the free man is not to be arrested nor imprisoned, disseised of his freehold, nor in any wise destroyed: *nisi per legale judicium parium suorum vel per legem terrae*[2]. These words are apparently borrowed from the constitutions of German emperors. Do not be persuaded that they have reference to trial by jury; the verdict of a jury, the testimony of a body of neighbour

---

[1] *Select Charters*, p. 100.
[2] M. C. c. 39. *History of English Law*, vol. 1, pp. 391—4. McKechnie, pp. 436—59.

witnesses, was in no sense a *judicium*. The demand is of a quite different kind; the barons want a court of their equals—they are to be judged by barons. Theoretically the *curia Regis* had probably been such a court; practically it had become something very different, a tribunal constituted by a few royal servants, some at least of whom were not of baronial rank, but were mere clerks and professional lawyers. The struggle of the barons for a *judicium parium* is a long one; it can be traced through the thirteenth century and in the end it is not very successful; against it the king opposes the assertion that his justices are good enough judges for any man. Ultimately it succeeds thus far, that the lords get a right to trial by lords in case of treason and felony; that is all; if they are to be tried for any lesser crime, any misdemeanour, the king's justices shall try them, and all their civil litigation comes before the king's justices. Even as to treason and felony the demand seems to have been often disregarded. The modern principle that I have just laid down is in truth a compromise—only in case of treason or felony has the peer any privilege. It seems to have been settled in the course of the fourteenth century. It required a statute of 1422 to secure the same privilege for noblewomen. Further, it should be observed that even in case of felony or treason there is a distinction—the peer accused of such a crime was tried by his peers in parliament, if parliament were then sitting, and the assembled lords are in such a case judges of both fact and law; but if parliament were not sitting, he was tried by a select body of peers chosen by the Lord High Steward, in what came to be called a Court of the Lord High Steward. The steward's office had at an early time become hereditary in the house of Leicester; it fell in to Henry IV and was merged in the royal dignity; thenceforth if a steward was wanted for the trial of a peer he was appointed for the occasion by the king; he chose a small body of lords, seemingly 23 was the usual number. In such a case the lords thus summoned were considered only as judges of fact, the Lord High Steward laid down the law. Not until after the Revolution of 1688 was it made necessary that all peers should be summoned to form the High Steward's court, and then only in case of treason. It will probably strike you that the privilege of being tried by some lord nominated for the purpose by the king and a small selection of peers nominated by this royal nominee cannot have been a particularly valuable privilege, but this is all that the baronage got with all its strivings[1].

This privilege, however, served to define a class of peers or *pares*. It was not the only privilege of peerage. The peer enjoyed a certain freedom from arrest, he could not be arrested and imprisoned for debt, though he might be arrested and imprisoned upon a charge of felony or treason. It is well to observe how few were the privileges of peerage : how little of a caste was our estate of lords temporal. It became the fashion late in the day to talk of noble blood, of a man's blood being ennobled when he was called to parliament. But this is nonsense unless it be held that the ancestor's blood flows only to his heir, and unless the heir only begins to have his ancestor's blood in his veins when that ancestor dies. The sons and daughters of lords have from the first been commoners during their father's lifetime, and on his death only his heir becomes entitled to any legal privileges. Whatever social pre-eminence the families of peers may have, has no basis in our law : we have never had a *noblesse*. It has been asserted that bishops are not entitled to demand a trial by the House of Lords, on the ground that their blood is not noble. The House of Lords asserted this in 1692, and it is a very doubtful question what would now happen if a bishop committed felony or treason ; but as a matter of fact, so soon as the word 'peers' came into use, the bishops were regularly recognized as peers of the land, and it is in the case of Archbishop Stratford in 1341 that we find the earliest definite formulation of the principle that peers are to be tried in parliament.

It is well to remember that during the Middle Ages the king had considerable powers over the constitution of what

---

[1] For further light on this subject see L. O. Pike, *Constitutional History of the House of Lords*, c. X ; L. W. Vernon-Harcourt, *His Grace the Steward and Trial by Peers*, and *Law Quarterly Review*, vol. XXIII, pp. 442—7 and vol. XXIV, pp. 43—8.

had come to be the upper House of Parliament. As to the lay peerage, even though usage hardening into law may have obliged him to summon the heir of the late baron, he had a power, to which the law set no limit, of creating new peers. This power was not, I think, very freely exercised; the advantage of a picked House of Lords was counterbalanced by the danger of creating new noble houses which would be dangerous to their creator. Over the spiritual part of the peerage the royal power was at least as great. The manner in which bishops were made had a long and complicated history. Theoretically the bishop ought to have been elected by the cathedral chapters; the Great Charter promised that such elections should be free; practically, however, the making of a new bishop was an affair for the king and the pope; if they worked together they had their way; when they quarrelled sometimes one, sometimes the other, was successful. When a see fell vacant the king sent the chapter his licence to elect (*congé d'élire*), accompanied by a letter (letters recommendatory) nominating the person who was to be elected. Under Henry VI, a weak and pious king, the pope had his own way; he provided bishops, though such provisions were contrary to English Acts of Parliament. Under Henry VII the royal nominees were invariably chosen. As to the abbots they were elected by the monks, and neither king nor pope often interfered with the election. As already said, the abbots play no distinguished part in parliament or politics.

(iii) *The Commons.*

First let us consider the knights of the shire. There are 37 counties returning two members apiece; Chester and Durham are not yet represented. We have seen that from the first the representatives were to be elected in the full county court. As to the mode of election during the fourteenth century we know little more than this; though we may gather from complaints of the commons that often enough the influence of the sheriff was all-powerful. It is but gradually that the counties appreciate the privilege of being represented, or that the duty of representing the county is regarded as an honour. In 1406 (7 Hen. IV, c. 15) a statute directs that the election shall be made in the first county court holden after the receipt of the writ ; it is to be made in full county court.   In 1410 (11 Hen. IV, c. 1) the conduct of elections is placed under the cognizance of the justices of assize, and a penalty of £100 is demanded against a sheriff who makes an undue return.   In 1413 (1 Hen. V, c. 1) residence within the counties is made a qualification both for the electors and the elected.   From 1430 we have the important act (8 Hen. VI, c. 7) which regulated the county franchise for the next four centuries:—the electors are to be persons resident in the county, each of whom shall have freehold to the value of 40 shillings per annum at the least above all charges.   The act complains that elections have of late been made by 'very great, outrageous, and excessive number of people, of which most part was people of small substance and of no value, whereof every of them pretended a voice equivalent as to such election with the most worthy knights and esquires.'   To start with, this must have been what would in our eyes be a fairly high qualification : the great change in the value of money caused by the discovery of silver in America rendered it in course of time very low and very capricious ; the forty shilling freeholder had a vote, the copyholder, the leaseholder, had none, no matter how valuable his land might be.   In 1432 another statute explains that the qualifying freehold must be situate within the county.   The king at various times exercised a power of inserting clauses in the writs directed to the sheriff specifying the sort of persons who were to be chosen—generally they were to be two knights girt with swords ; this order, however, seems to have been pretty generally disobeyed, many of the so-called knights of the shire were not knights—in 1445 it is considered sufficient that they should be knights of the shire or notable squires, gentlemen of birth, capable of becoming knights ; no man of the degree of yeoman or below it is to be elected.

The number of knights of the shire was, we have seen, constant, that of the citizens and burgesses fluctuated, diminishing pretty steadily as time went on.   For the maximum number of the boroughs represented we must go back to Edward I when 166 was reached; during the first half of the fifteenth century it had fallen to 99. After 1445 it begins to increase a little, Henry VI added 8 new boroughs, Edward IV added or restored 5. It should be remarked that during the Middle Ages no writ was sent to the boroughs—the writ went to the sheriff of the county, commanding him to return two knights from his shire, two citizens from every city, two burgesses from every borough. It was much in his power therefore to decide what towns should be represented. The towns very often desired not to be represented. According to the regular practice a borough was taxed at a heavier rate than the shire —thus when a fifteenth was laid on the counties, a tenth was laid on the boroughs; also if a borough sent burgesses to parliament it had to pay their wages. In one case, that of Torrington, in 1368, we find a borough successfully petitioning the king that it may not be compelled to send members. It is very probable that other boroughs effected the same object by negotiations with the sheriff. A statute of 1382 (5 Ric. II, c. 4) denounces a punishment against the sheriff if he omits boroughs which have heretofore sent members. During the fifteenth century the privilege of being represented seems to have been a little more highly prized. We find the king conferring the right to send members upon new boroughs, or restoring it to boroughs which have been represented in former times. This power made it possible for the king to pack the House of Commons; but we do not find it liberally exercised until the reign of Mary. The first House of Commons of Henry VIII consisted of 298 members—74 members for the shires, 224 for the cities and boroughs. The number of borough members had largely exceeded that of the knights of the shire, nevertheless through the Middle Ages it is the knights of the shire who are the most active and independent element in the parliament; every movement proceeds from them—to them it is due that the House of Commons takes its place beside the House of Lords.

As to the qualification of electors in the boroughs, we have seen that from the first it had varied from borough to borough. Lapse of time had done nothing to make it more uniform; quite the reverse, no general law was made and

each borough was left to work out its own destiny by the aid
of charters purchased from the king. The only general
principle that can be laid down is this, that the later the
charter the more oligarchic is the constitution of the borough.
A few towns acquired the right of being counties of themselves, of having their own sheriffs, and being exempt from
the powers of the sheriff of the surrounding county. London
had acquired this privilege under Henry I—no other town
succeeded in getting it until Bristol became a county in 1373.
York followed in 1396 and then Newcastle, Norwich, Lincoln,
Hull, Southampton, Nottingham, Coventry, Canterbury. In
such cases the writs were sent to the sheriffs of these counties
corporate and in some of them the county qualification, the
forty shilling freehold, was adopted as the qualification for the
electors. In other boroughs the qualification varies between
a wide democracy and the narrowest oligarchy.

Long ago parliament had taken the shape familiar to us,
an assembly consisting of two houses which sit, debate, and
vote apart—the one containing the lords, spiritual and temporal, the other all the representatives of the commons. How
high this separation can be traced has been disputed; there
is no doubt that we can carry it back to the middle of the
fourteenth century:—as regards the preceding half century
there is some doubt, but Stubbs holds that very probably
from the very first moment the lords and commons sat apart.
In the later Middle Ages they certainly sat in separate buildings, the lords in the Parliament Chamber of the king's palace,
the commons generally in the Chapter House or the Refectory
of the Abbey of Westminster. Westminster had long ago
become the usual seat of parliament, though during the fourteenth and fifteenth centuries there were a not inconsiderable
number of sessions at York and other towns; it was for the
king to decide when and whether he would summon a parliament. It is a noticeable fact that at a very early time,
perhaps from the very beginning, the citizens and burgesses
sit together with the knights; there seems certainly for a
long while a feeling that as it is for the barons to tax themselves, and for the clergy to tax themselves, so the boroughs
should be taxed by burgesses and the county by knights of

the shire ; and as a matter of fact the boroughs and counties are usually taxed at different rates—a 10th is imposed on boroughs, a 15th on counties : nevertheless we soon find that the two sets of representatives act together—they are regarded as representing but one estate of men, the commons of the realm.

The members of the common's house were paid wages by their constituents ; the knights of the shire received four shillings a day, the burgesses two shillings ; in 1427 we find the townsmen of Cambridge making an agreement with their members to take one shilling.

It is worth looking at the words of the writs whereby a parliament is summoned ; they bring out the fact that the two houses had not originally been co-ordinate assemblies ; a lord is told that the king intends to hold a parliament at a certain place and time, *et ibidem vobiscum et cum ceteris prelatis, magnatibus, et proceribus regni nostri colloquium habere et tractatum* ; he is then enjoined, *in fide et ligeancia quibus nobis tenemini*, if he be a temporal lord, *in fide et dilectione*, if a spiritual lord to be present *cum praelatis, magnatibus, et proceribus praedictis super praedictis negotiis tractaturi, vestrumque consilium impensuri.* A writ to a judge or to another councillor who is not a peer omits the word *ceteris*—he is not one of the magnates or *proceres* of the kingdom, and the opinion is growing, as we have before said, that he had no vote, and indeed no voice in debate, but is simply to give his advice if that is wanted. But the function of the lords as distinguished from that of the commons is marked by the words *tractaturi vestrumque consilium impensuri* ; they are to treat with the king and give their counsel. The writ to the sheriff recites the king's intention of treating with the lords, the *prelati, magnates,* and *proceres,* and then directs the election of knights, citizens and burgesses who are to have power on behalf of their constituencies, county, cities, boroughs, to consent to and to do what may be determined by the common counsel of the kingdom—*ad faciendum et consentiendum hiis quae tunc ibidem de communi consilio regni nostri favente domino ordinari contigerit super negotiis antedictis.* They are not to treat with the king ; it is not their counsel that the king wants, it is their consent—an active consent which shall be extended to doing (*ad faciendum*) what shall be determined by the common counsel of the kingdom. As to the clergy, we have already seen that from the time of Richard II onwards the word *faciendum* drops out of the *praemunientes* clause—they will not come to parliament— their absence will be consent enough.

II. *Frequency and Duration of Parliament.*

Such then is a parliament:—but how far is it necessary that there should be parliaments, and have parliaments been frequently and regularly holden? The question of law is intimately connected with the question of fact. Starting with the assembly of 1295 parliaments soon become very frequent. Already in 1311 one of the ordinances decreed that there should be a parliament twice in every year; but this was part of a baronial scheme and it may be doubted whether more than an assembly of barons was desired; but when in 1322 Edward II had succeeded in casting off the yoke of the baronial ordainers, the ordinances were repealed on the plea that the consent of the estates had not been given. The parliament of that year, 1322, published the following note-worthy declaration, the first declaration we may say of the supremacy of a full representative parliament—'the matters which are to be established for the estate of our lord the king and of his heirs, and for the estate of the realm and of the people shall be treated, accorded and established in parliament by our lord the king and by the consent of the prelates, earls and barons, and the commonalty of the realm, according as ·hath been heretofore accustomed.' In 1330 at the beginning of the new reign we have a statute for annual parliaments (4 Edw. III, c. 14). It is accorded that a parliament shall be holden in every year, or more often if need be. There can, I think, be little doubt that these words require that there shall be a parliament at least in every year—if need be parliament may be held more often, but at least once a year it must be holden. The slight ambiguity of the phrase should be noticed —it becomes important hereafter. In 1362 (36 Edw. III, c. 10)

another statute ordains that 'a parliament shall be holden
every year, as another time was ordained by statute.' These
provisions were fairly well kept for a long while; but there
were no parliaments in 1364, 1367, 1370, between 1373–6,
1387, 1389, 1392, 1396, or between 1407–10. On the other
hand in a considerable number of years there were two
parliaments, in 1340 there were three, in 1328 four. Each of
these parliaments, you should understand, was a new parliament, involving a new election. The time was not yet when
the same parliament would be kept alive year after year by
means of prorogations. The frequency of parliaments, if
theoretically secured by the statutes just mentioned, was
practically secured by the king's need of money. He was
coming to be very dependent on supplies granted to him by
parliament, and seldom was a tax imposed for more than a
single year. Under Edward IV, however, parliaments grow
much less frequent; in his reign of twenty-two years he held
but six; five years passed without any parliament. A considerable revenue from the customs duties known as tonnage
and poundage had been granted to Henry V for his life; this
grant was repeated in the reign of Henry VI and of
Edward IV; Edward also had other means of getting
money, of which hereafter. Henry VII seems to have meant
to rule like his Lancastrian ancestors by means of constant parliaments; before 1498 he had held six parliaments;
thenceforward to the end of his reign there was but one
session, namely in 1504. The statutes of Edward III, however, remained on the statute book, and very important
they became at a future time. I am not sure, however, that
Edward IV and Henry VII were considered by their contemporaries to be breaking the law in not holding annual sessions,
however illegal might be the means which enabled them to
get on without parliament. From our present standpoint
then we see that the letter of the statute book probably
requires annual parliaments; we see, however, what is more
important than this, that for the last two centuries parliaments
have, as a matter of fact, been very frequent, though their
frequency has somewhat decreased of late years.

III. *Business of Parliament.*

And now for what purposes were parliaments necessary? It is with no general statement of the sovereignty (in the modern sense) of the body composed by the king, the lords and the representatives of the commons, that we must begin our answer. Such a theory there cannot be, at least to any good purpose, until a foundation of fact has been laid for it, until the body thus composed has habitually and exclusively exercised the powers of sovereignty. We have to see how this foundation of fact was gradually laid, and we have to remember that at the beginning of the fourteenth century the king in parliament was by no means the only possible claimant of sovereign power. Representatives of the commons had but newly been called to meet the prelates and barons. Looking back now it may seem to us quite possible that sovereignty will ultimately be found to be in the king and the baronage, or in the king and his council, or again in the king alone.

(i) The field of work in which the cooperation of a parliament seems most necessary is that of taxation. In 1297 the principle has been enounced that the common consent of the realm is necessary to the imposition of aids, prises, customs : saving the king's right to the ancient aids, prises and customs. The highroad of direct taxation is thus barred against the king, though at least one bypath is open. The right to tallage the demesne has not been surrendered, and in 1304 Edward I exercised that right. Edward II did the same in 1312, and so did Edward III in 1332. But on this occasion parliament remonstrated and the king had to give up his project. This seems the last attempt on the king's part to set a tallage. In 1340 (14 Edw. III, stat. 2, c. 1) a statute was obtained which declares that the people shall be no more charged or grieved to make any aid or sustain any charge, if it be not by the common consent of the prelates, earls, barons and other great men and commons of the realm and that in the parliament. Just at this time too the scutage, the composition for military service, was becoming unprofitable and obsolete, it belonged to an age which had passed away.

Aids for knighting the king's son and marrying his daughter could still be collected ; but the amount of these was fixed by statute in 1350, expressly applying to the king the rule laid down for other lords (1275), namely 20 shillings from the knight's fee, and 20 shillings from £20 worth of socage land. These were an insignificant resource. On the whole, therefore, before the middle of the fourteenth century it was definitely illegal for the king to impose a direct tax without the consent of parliament.

The history of indirect taxation is more complicated. However, customs on wool, wine and general merchandise were levied in the twelfth century. Magna Carta says that merchants are to be free from any 'maletolt' or unjust exaction, saving the ancient and right customs which are referred to as well known things. In 1275 parliament grants to Edward a certain definite custom on wool ; but during the reigns of the first two Edwards the regulation of the customs is still constantly in dispute between the king and the nation. There is considerable danger that the king will get his way ; it takes some little reflection to see that indirect taxes, such as customs duties, are taxes at all :—if the king can by negotiation, by grants of privileges, induce the merchants to grant him such dues, may he not do so—is not this a matter between them and him ? The commons however seem early to have seen to the bottom of this question. Edward III had to make important concessions. In 1362 (36 Edw. III, stat. 1, cap. 11) it is provided that no subsidy or other charge should be set upon wool by the merchants or by any one else without the assent of parliament. In 1371 (45 Edw. III, c. 4) no imposition or charge shall be set upon wools, woolfells or leather, without the assent of parliament. This was re-enacted in 1387 (11 Ric. II, c. 9) but with a saving of the king's ancient right. The legislation on this subject of indirect taxation is not quite so emphatically clear as that which forbad direct imposts—some loopholes were left—still we may say that before the end of the fourteenth century the contest was at an end. There were at least no obvious ways in which the king could tax the community without breaking the law. The Lancastrian kings seem to have admitted

this. Even Edward IV may be said to have admitted it;
in his reign it is that we begin to hear of benevolences,
extorted freewill offerings. A statute of the only parliament
of Richard III (1483, 1 Richard III, c. 2) was designed to
stop this gap. The commons complain of new and unlawful
inventions—of a new imposition called a benevolence—and
it is ordained that the subjects be in nowise charged by an
imposition called a benevolence or any such like charge, and
that such exactions shall be no example, but shall be damned
and annulled for ever.

Under the Tudors the danger is of a different kind—it is
not so much that the king will tax without parliamentary
consent, but that parliament will consent to just whatever the
king wants and will condone his illegal acts. Thus in 1491
Henry VII had recourse to a benevolence which brought him
in a large sum. Very possibly the act of Richard III was
considered null as being the act of a usurper, though it
remained upon the statute book. But at any rate the parliament of 1495 made this benevolence lawful *ex post facto*;
the king was empowered by statute to enforce the promises
of those who had promised money but not yet paid it. Such
an act, extremely dangerous as it was to the liberties of the
nation, was none the less a high exercise of parliamentary
sovereignty—parliament undertook to make legal what had
been illegal. That is one peculiarity of the Tudor time and a
very remarkable one; parliaments are so pliant to the king's
will that the king is very willing to acquiesce in every claim
that parliament may make to be part of the sovereign body
of the realm. All the statutes against taxation by virtue of
prerogative are left unrepealed upon the statute book, to bear
fruit in a future age—at present the king has no need to wish
them repealed.

But not only had parliament repeatedly asserted that
taxes were not to be imposed without its consent, it had also
exercised to the full a power of imposing taxes of all kinds,
both direct and indirect. Further as regards taxation, the
House of Commons had won a peculiar importance. We
have to remember that, to start with, there are in theory three
estates of the realm: (1) clergy, (2) lords, and (3) commons.

On this theory it would be reasonable that each estate should tax itself; and this for some time takes place—the clergy make a grant, the lords another, the commons another. But before the end of the fourteenth century the lords and commons join in a grant, and a formula is used which puts the commons (upon whom the bulk of taxation falls) into the foreground—the grant is made by the commons with the assent of the lords spiritual and temporal. This form appears in 1395 and becomes the rule. In 1407 Henry IV assented to the principle that money grants are to be initiated in the House of Commons, are not to be reported to the king until both Houses are agreed, and are to be reported by the Speaker of the Lower House. Thus a long step has already been made towards that exclusive control over taxation which the House of Commons claimed in later ages—the taxes upon the laity are granted by the commons with the lords' assent. On the laity—the clergy still tax themselves in their convocations and no act of the parliament is as yet requisite to give validity to such a tax; to this extent the theory of the three estates still prevails; as a matter of fact, however, the convocations pretty regularly follow the example of the commons, making a corresponding grant to that which the commons have made.

Another point of importance is this, that during the Middle Ages permanent taxes are very seldom imposed. In general a tax is granted just for this occasion only: the king is granted a tenth of movables, or a customs duty, or it may be a poll tax just to meet the present demands upon his resources. Sometimes taxes are granted for two or three years to come, but this is rare. This renders an annual parliament a practical necessity, particularly after the long war with France has begun: every year now the king wants money, and can only get it by summoning a parliament. His non-parliamentary revenue which comes from his demesne lands, his feudal rights and so forth, is quite insufficient to meet the drain of a war. Some of the customs duties were permanent taxes. In 1414 parliament granted to Henry V tonnage and poundage for his life. No similar grant for life was made to Henry VI until 1453—the 31st year of his reign

—but they were granted for life to Edward IV in 1465, to Richard III in 1484, and to Henry VII by his first parliament. Such repeated grants of permanent taxes were dangerous precedents, as we find when we come to the reign of Charles I.

Henry VII, it is said, left behind him a treasure of £1,800,000. Edward IV also had been rich. Their predecessors had been habitually poor. The Wars of the Roses were in a great degree due to the poverty of Henry VI—he could not afford to govern the country thoroughly. This change in the king's financial circumstances is of course a very important matter—it absolves him from the necessity of convoking parliament. In two-and-twenty years Edward IV held but six parliaments; Henry VII held but seven parliaments during his 24 years. Whence did he get his treasure? To a large extent it would seem from the escheats and forfeitures consequent on the Wars of the Roses; to a large extent also by pressing to their uttermost the crown's claims for fines. It was believed that his ministers, Empson and Dudley, had trumped up all manner of accusations for the purpose of swelling the revenue, and were guilty of unjust exactions under colour of the feudal rights to reliefs, wardships and marriage. At the beginning of the next reign they were sacrificed to the popular outcry.

One of the burdens which has lain heavy on the mass of the people has been that of purveyance and preemption, the right of the king and his servants to buy provisions at the lowest rate, to compel the owners to sell, and to pay at their own time—which often enough meant never. It was an admitted royal right; over and over again parliament had sought by statute to bring it within reasonable bounds and to prevent abuses of it. Legislation begins with Magna Carta and goes on through the Middle Ages; one sees in such legislation at once the admitted claim of parliament to set limits to royal rights, and on the other hand the extreme difficulty that there is in getting the king to observe any laws which make against his pecuniary interests.

In another direction parliament has interfered with finance. In the first place it has claimed the power to appropriate the supplies granted to the king, to say that they shall be spent in this or that manner. Already in 1348 the money is to be applied to the defence against the Scots, in 1353 to the prosecution of the war. In 1390 there is more elaborate appropriation out of the 40 shillings laid on the sack of wool, 10 shillings the king may have for his present needs, while the other 30 shillings are only to be expended in case of the continuance of the war. This practice is continued with increasing elaboration under the Lancastrian kings. But it is one thing to say that money shall only be spent in this way, another to prevent its being spent in other ways. Parliament begins to demand the production of the royal accounts; we hear of this in 1340 and 1341. In 1377 two persons are appointed by parliament to receive and expend the money voted for the war. In 1379 the king presented his accounts, and thenceforward treasurers of the subsidies were regularly appointed in parliament to account to the next parliament. In 1406 the commons were allowed to choose auditors; Henry IV told them that 'kings do not render accounts,' but in the next year he rendered them. But the principle had to be contested over and over again ; it was a principle of no value unless parliament had a will of its own which it would exert year by year—this the parliaments of Edward IV and Henry VII had not.

(ii) We turn from finance to the wider subject of legislation. First let us observe, what is of great importance, the legislative formula of a statute. In the reign of Henry VII it has come to be almost exactly what it is at the present moment. 'The king our sovereign Lord Henry VII at his Parliament holden at Westminster...by the assent of the Lords spiritual and temporal and the commons in the said parliament assembled and by the authority of the same parliament hath done to be made certain statutes and ordinances in manner and form following.' It is the king's act, done with the assent (sometimes the form runs 'advice and assent') of the lords spiritual and temporal and commons in parliament assembled and by the authority of the said parliament. These last words are pretty new, 'by the authority of the same parliament'; they occur, it is said, for the first time as a part of the preamble in 1433, although they occur in a more casual way as early as 1421. It is admitted therefore that a statute derives its authority from the whole parliament. Also we observe that the commons now stand on the same footing as the lords; their function in legislative work is of the same kind—they give advice, assent and authority. But this form has not always been used. Throughout the fourteenth century the commoners generally appear in a subordinate position—the statute is made by the king with the assent of the prelates, earls and barons, and at the request of the knights of the shire and commons in the said parliament : sometimes it is at the instance and special request of the commons—occasionally the assent of the commons is mentioned. This becomes more common in the fifteenth century ; in 1435 and 1436 we have 'by the advice and assent of the lords at the special request of the commons'; in 1439 'by the advice and assent of lords and commons'; and this form is used for several years. But in 1450 we revert to 'advice and assent of lords and request of commons'—we get the one form in 1455, the other in 1460. Throughout the reign of Edward IV the two are promiscuously used. It is not until the House of Tudor is on the throne and the Middle Ages are at an end that all trace of the original position of the commons has vanished. Nevertheless it had long been admitted that the assent of the commons was necessary in order to give to a legislative act the quality of a statute— that this was necessary at least if the law was to deal with temporal affairs.

Let us first take the point raised by these last words. We have to remember that at starting the commons could hardly claim any higher place than that of the clergy, and we must remember that the theory of the time partitioned human affairs into two provinces—spiritual and temporal. It must long have remained a doubtful question whether the king, with the advice of the lords, could not make a statute on the petition of the clergy, just as well as on the petition of the commons—if the statute deals with the state the voice of the commons must be heard, if with the church the voice of the clergy. Practically the clergy solved the difficulty by neglecting to accept the place that was offered them in the national assembly; but there are not wanting some signs that in the fourteenth century the accepted theory allowed the king to make a statute with the assent of the lords on a petition of the clergy without consulting the commons. In 1377, however, the commons definitely demanded that neither statute nor ordinance should be made on the petition of the clergy without the consent of the commons: this demand seems to have been tacitly conceded. Turning to the other side of the theory, it does not seem to have been very seriously contended that legislation approved by lords and commons required also the consent of the clergy; but still the practice of summoning them to parliament seems to have been maintained chiefly in order to prevent their asserting that they were not bound by laws to which they had not consented. The fact that the prelates were a majority in the House of Lords prevented collisions between church and state, and was a guarantee that the interests of the clergy would not be neglected. It is worth notice, however, that, from an early time, the lords spiritual and temporal were conceived as forming one body— a statute might be made though the prelates had voted against it. In 1351 they withheld their assent from the statute of Provisors; they are not mentioned in it as consenting parties, but still it was a statute.

And now to the larger question as to the whereabouts of legislative power. We have seen that already in 1322 the principle was announced that legislation required the consent of the prelates, earls, barons and commonalty of the realm. Such consent was necessary for a statute; and from that time onwards it seems an admitted principle that the consent of both houses was necessary for a statute: for a long time to come indeed the function assigned to the commons was, as we have seen, that of petitioning, not that of advising or assenting; but of course 'petition' is assent and something more. But then we have to notice that a statute was not the only known form of legislation; we have to distinguish it from an ordinance. Now from Edward I's day onwards a set of rolls known as statute rolls was kept. What was entered upon them was a statute, and by the beginning of Edward III's reign it was an established principle that nothing was to go on to the statute roll save what had received the consent of king, lords and commons. We cannot apply this to earlier times; we to this day receive as statutes many laws made by Edward I in assemblies to which, as far as we know, no representatives of the commons were summoned; it is exceedingly doubtful whether those two pillars of real property law, the *Quia Emptores* and the *De Donis Conditionalibus*, were made with the assent of any such representatives. However, the principle is conceded under Edward II. But although it be allowed that a statute may require the consent of both houses, this does not decide that in no other manner can laws be made. Beside the statute there might be room for ordinances made by the king with the advice of the lords, or made by the king in his council. 'Great councils,' *magna concilia*, are still held under Edward II and Edward III, meetings of the king and his council with the lords spiritual and temporal. Such assemblies, however, are chiefly held for deliberative purposes—they were not serious rivals for parliament; on the whole the royal will was likely to find the lords as intractable as the commons. The rival that parliament had seriously to fear was the king in council. Now it seems to have been admitted during the fourteenth century that the king in council enjoyed a certain amount—or rather an uncertain amount—of legislative power. He could not revoke or alter statutes; he did so on more than one occasion, but this was generally regarded as an abuse. But without revoking or overriding statutes there was still a field for legislation; regard being had to past history we cannot be surprised at this. We find that parliament acknowledges the existence of this subordinate legislative power, even on occasions desires that it may be used. A statute is regarded as a very solemn affair, not easily to be repealed; temporary legislation, legislation about details, should be by ordinance. As time goes on, however, the existence of two legislative powers leads to frequent disputes. Richard II presses the ordaining power beyond all bounds: 'What is the use,' asks a contemporary, 'of statutes made in parliament? They have no effect. The king and his privy council habitually alter and efface what has previously been established in parliament, not merely by the community but even by the nobility[1].' In 1389 the commons pray that the chancellor and council may not make ordinances contrary to common law and statute. The king answers that what has been done shall be done still, saving the king's prerogative. Richard had a theory of absolute monarchy, and he was deposed. One of the charges against him was that he had said that the laws were in his own mouth and often enough in his own breast. The Lancastrian kings were kings by Act of Parliament; they meant to rule and did rule by means of parliaments. Under them we hear few complaints about the ordaining power—they seem to have used it sparingly. At the close of the Middle Ages its limits are still very indefinite; in this lies one of the great dangers for future times. The king, it is clear, cannot revoke or override a statute, at least in a general fashion; but still by ordinances made in his council he has a certain power of adding to the law of the land. We have been obliged to say that he cannot override a statute in a general fashion. But here again is another danger—is there a dispensing power?—can the king exempt this or that person from the scope of a statute? That he has some such power it is difficult to deny; parliament has quietly submitted to its exercise; as regards certain statutes the king has habitually exercised it, has given his license to A.B. to do something forbidden by statute: in particular the anti-papal statutes have habitually been dispensed with, so have the statutes of mortmain which forbid religious bodies to acquire land. What is the limit to this power? It is hard to say. The question is made the more difficult by this, that very often the sanction established by the statute is some fine or forfeiture of which the king is to have the benefit— may not the king renounce this benefit in advance, may he not say that he will not exact it from A.B. if A.B. infringes the statute? It is difficult to say that he may not. Two indefinite powers, an ordaining and a dispensing power, are at the end of the Middle Ages part of the king's inheritance.

Another point connected with these last questions has been cleared up. Throughout the fourteenth century there is danger

[1] Walsingham, II, 48. Stubbs, *Constitutional History*, vol. II, § 292.

that though the king, with the lords' assent, grants the petition of the commons, the consequent statute will by no means do just what the commons want. The statute is not drawn up until after the parliament is dissolved; its form is settled in the king's council, and it may not correspond very closely with the petition. The commons over and over again protest against this; the petitions are tampered with before they are turned into statutes. In 1414 this point is conceded. The commons pray 'that there never be no law made and engrossed as statute and law neither by additions nor diminutions by no manner of term or terms the which should change the sentence and the intent asked.' The king in reply grants that from henceforth 'nothing be enacted to the petition of the commons contrary to their asking, whereby they should be bound without their assent[1].' Thus gradually the practice is introduced of sending up to the king not a petition but a bill drawn in the form of a statute, so that the king shall have nothing to do save to assent or dissent. This became the regular practice, and under Henry VII was adopted in most cases of importance[2].

It is needless to say that the king still retains and often exercises the power of refusing to legislate. A statute is still very really and truly the king's act. The form of assent has already become what it still is *le roy le veut*; the form of dissent is *le roy s'avisera*—a civil form of saying No, but a form not unfrequently used.

It should be remembered that legislative power is by this time a power that has been constantly and freely exercised. The statute book is already a bulky volume. King and parliament have taken upon themselves to interfere with every department of law—even to regulate the wages of labourers, the price of commodities, the dress which may be worn by men and women of different stations in life. The statutes of Edward III and Richard II have hardly the deep permanent interest which we find in the statutes of Edward I; they do not in the same way go to the very root of the

---

[1] *Rot. Parl.* vol. II, 22.

[2] The change took place about the end of the reign of Henry VI. Stubbs, *Constitutional History*, vol. II, § 290.

ordinary law, the land law, the law of civil procedure; still they are very miscellaneous and high-handed. Under the Lancastrian kings there is less legislation—this is one of the causes of their fall: the maintenance of peace and order is not sufficiently attended to—the great men are becoming too great for the law. The few parliaments of Edward IV do little. Under Henry VII, though parliaments are few, still they pass valuable statutes; it is recognized that a good deal of the medieval common law sadly needs amendment—there are new wants to be attended to—and above all order is to be re-established and preserved.

B. *The King and his Council.*

The succession to the throne has had a stormy history. Before the end of the fourteenth century two kings have been deposed, and one king has succeeded to the throne who, according to our ideas, had no hereditary right. A modern constitutional lawyer has no great difficulty with the case of Edward II, he can say that Edward resigned the kingdom and that he was at once succeeded by his rightful heir; if this be a precedent at all, it is a precedent for what should happen in case a king abdicates. Still there can, I think, be little doubt that the parliament which met in January, 1327, conceived that it had full power to depose a worthless king. It had been summoned in a way which was at least outwardly regular—the king was in fact a captive in the hands of Isabella and Mortimer—the great seal was in their power and the summons was issued in the king's name. The proceedings, however, were tumultuary. In the midst of a noisy mob it was resolved to reject the father in favour of the son. Articles justifying the deposition were drawn up— the charges are very vague and general, amounting to this, that Edward was incompetent and incorrigible[1]. His resignation was then procured. On the whole, as it seems to me, these proceedings, so far from strengthening the notion that a king might legally be deposed, demonstrated pretty clearly

---

[1] Stubbs, *Constitutional History*, vol. II, § 255.

that there was no body empowered by law to set the king aside. The device of issuing writs in the king's own name, to summon the parliament which is to depose him, the extortion of a formal resignation, make the case rather a precedent for revolution than a precedent for legal action[1].

We come now to the events of 1399. The deposition, for such for a moment we may call it, of Richard II, has, I think, a greater constitutional significance than the deposition of Edward II—that is to say, the complaints against him which found expression in a series of formal charges, are not vague complaints of badness and uselessness, but accuse him of having broken the law. He has tried to play the absolute monarch; he has been acting on a theory of the kingship which is contrary to our laws—he has said that the laws were in his own mouth and often in his own breast, that he by himself could change and frame the laws of the kingdom, that the life of every liegeman, his lands, tenements, goods and chattels, lay at his royal will without sentence of forfeiture, and he has acted on these sayings. The revolution, if such we call it, is in this case a protest against absolutism. We must not plunge into the general history of the time; the forms observed are what chiefly concern us. Henry of Lancaster had landed, the nation as a whole had determined that he should be king—Richard had no party, made no serious effort, delivered himself up to Henry, and offered to resign the crown. A parliament was then summoned, the writs being attested by Richard and the council. It was proposed that the king should execute a deed of resignation before the parliament met. It was objected that in such case the parliament would be dissolved so soon as it met by the act of resignation. The expedient was then adopted of issuing new writs on the day on which the resignation was declared, summoning the parliament to meet six days later.

---

[1] It will not be impertinent to mention that the idea of an heir inheriting, while yet his father is physically alive, was not unfamiliar to our medieval law. There was such a thing as civil death. If a man entered religion—that is to say became a monk—he died to the world; his heir at once inherited, his will took effect, and his executors might sue for debts that had been due to him. It might well be considered that a king who had abdicated was dead to the law. F. W. M.

Before the Parliament met Richard executed a formal deed of abdication, renouncing all royal rights, and absolving all his people from homage, fealty and allegiance, and declaring himself worthy to be deposed. On the meeting of parliament the deed was produced. The question was put whether it should be accepted. It was accepted. The long list of charges was read, and parliament voted that they formed a good ground for deposing the king and that *ex abundanti* they would proceed to depose him. A sentence was then drawn up and read declaring that Richard was deposed from all royal dignity and honour. Commissioners were then sent to read this sentence to him. Apparently it did not enter the heads of any concerned that the estates lawfully summoned could not depose a king for sufficient cause—though he had resigned, they put it to the vote whether his resignation should be accepted and *ex abundanti*, as they said, proceeded formally to depose him. Perhaps they feared to let the matter rest upon an act of resignation, for this might leave it open for Richard to say at some future time, and not without truth, that the act was not voluntary, but had been extorted from him by duress. Still the deposition could really stand on no better footing than the abdication; if Richard was coerced into resigning he was coerced into summoning the parliament, and only by virtue of the king's summons had the parliament which deposed him any legal being. This perhaps is the reason why very soon afterwards Richard disappears from the world.

Richard deposed, Henry formally claimed the crown as descended in the right line of descent from Henry III and as sent by God to recover his right, when the realm was in point to be undone for default of governance and undoing of the good laws. It was proposed and carried that he should be king. The fact that Henry IV should have, though in vague terms, asserted an hereditary right is certainly important —showing, as it does, that there was by this time a strong sentiment in favour of strict descent. He seems to have stooped to encouraging the story which had been trumped up that his ancestor, Edmund of Lancaster, was the firstborn son of Henry III—older therefore than Edward I. A title as heir to Richard II or Edward III he did not assert. Such an assertion would have opened a grave problem. Of course according to what became the orthodox legal theory the House of York had a better right. It traced its title to Lionel of Clarence, a son of Edward III, older than John of Gaunt, from whom Henry was descended—but then it had to trace this title through a woman, through Lionel's daughter Philippa. Now certainly the analogies of private law were by this time in favour of the daughter of an elder son. But it is to be remembered that a title to the crown of England had not yet been transmitted by a woman, except in the case of Henry II, whose right came to him through his mother the Empress. But in that case the only competitor was Stephen. Stephen himself claimed through a woman. It was quite possible therefore to contend that so long as there was a male claiming solely through males, no woman, and no man claiming through a woman, could be admitted. In favour of that doctrine Fortescue, chief justice under Henry VI, wrote an elaborate treatise; he was prepared to defend his master's title even as a matter of pure hereditary right. But Henry IV at his accession seems to have shrunk from raising this question; he sought to evade it by hinting at a title derived through his mother and Edmund of Lancaster from Henry III. However, it is to be noticed that in 1399 and for many years afterwards we hear nothing of the Yorkist claim, those who have what we regard as the best blood in their veins acquiesce cheerfully in the parliamentary settlement; the Earl of York lives in close friendship with Henry V. There is no impression, at least no general impression, that the transactions of 1399 were not perfectly lawful or that the parliamentary title of the Lancastrian kings is disputable. Had Henry V left a decently competent son, even had Henry VI married any woman but Margaret of Anjou, nothing might ever have been heard of the Yorkist title. It is only in the course of bitter political strife that Richard of York begins to put forward his title as heir to Edward III. At first he is only anxious as to what is to happen when Henry dies, as probably he will die without issue, for he has been married five years and has no son. This must open a disputable succession because the Beauforts have claims of a sort derived from John of Gaunt. The queen gave birth to a son, and, though not at once, the claim to be Henry's successor becomes a claim to supplant Henry. When in 1460 the Duke of York laid his pedigree before the lords with a formal demand for the crown, legitimism makes its first appearance in English history. A compromise was patched up for a while—Henry was to remain king, but the Duke was to succeed him. War broke out, the Duke was killed. His son Edward, Earl of March, seized the crown and sceptre and had himself proclaimed king Edward IV. He reckoned his reign from 4 March, 1461, the day on which he proclaimed himself king. There had been no formal election, no parliamentary recognition: he reigned by hereditary right. A parliament recognized the justice of the claim. The three Henrys became pretended kings, kings *de facto* but not *de jure*.

So far as I can understand it, the confusing struggle which we call the Wars of the Roses is not to any considerable extent a contest between opposite principles—it is a great faction fight in which the whole nation takes sides. Still the House of Lancaster was in a measure identified with a tradition of parliamentary government, had been placed on the throne to supplant a king who had a plan of absolute monarchy, had been obliged to rely on parliament and more especially on the commons, perhaps owed its fall to its having allowed both lords and commons to do what they pleased, to get on without government. On the other hand, the claim of the House of York was bound up with a claim to rule in defiance of statutes. It might be urged that the statutes were void as having never received the assent of any rightful king, but an assertion that the laws under which a nation has been living for the last half-century are not laws, because you or your ancestors did not assent to them, is practically an assertion that you have a right to rule in defiance of any laws however made.

It is fortunate for us that Edward IV did not leave a son old enough to step into his father's shoes, and that no sooner had the crown been acquired by the legitimist family than the succession was again disturbed by the crimes of Richard III. Henry VII had according to our ideas little that even by courtesy could be called hereditary right. Probably he would not have got the crown had he not undertaken to marry Elizabeth, the daughter of Edward IV. Still an hereditary right he did assert, and Stubbs has argued that according to the notions of the time the assertion was not absurd[1]. He was accounted to have reigned from the day of Bosworth; before his marriage parliament declared that the inheritance of the crown should rest and remain in the then sovereign lord, king Henry VII, and the heirs of his body; he refused to be king merely in right of his wife.

The king's powers we might consider under various heads, but repetition must be avoided. We have already seen that it is for him to summon parliament; parliament cannot meet unless he issues writs. Again he could prorogue parliament, suspend its sessions and dissolve parliament. We have seen too that the constitution of a parliament depended in no small degree upon his will; it was for him to create peers—but the hereditary principle was here a check on his power; the bishops were practically his nominees; he had assumed the power of granting to boroughs the right to send representatives; disputes over contested elections came before him and his council. His assent was absolutely necessary to every statute; besides this, he had a somewhat indeterminate power of making ordinances and dispensing with statutes. Certain things he certainly could not do; he could not repeal a statute, he could not impose a tax, it had become unlawful for him to meddle with the ordinary course of justice. He was bound by law—true the principle still held good, it holds good at the present day, that 'the king can do no wrong'—law had no coercive process against the king, he could not be sued or prosecuted; the only way of getting justice out of him was by a petition, an appeal to his conscience. But means had already been found to reconcile this royal immunity with ministerial responsibility—if he could not be sued or prosecuted his servants could be, and his command would shield no one who had broken the law. What is more,

---

[1] *Lectures on Medieval and Modern History*, pp. 342–5.

as we shall see, a procedure by way of impeachment had been evolved whereby parliament could bring home their responsibility to his ministers.

But then again, the executive or administrative or governmental power was the king's. You will be familiar with such terms as these, they pass current in modern political life and of course they have a meaning. When we have marked off the work of legislation, the imposing of general laws upon the community, and also the work of judicature, the hearing and determining criminal charges and civil actions, there yet remains a large sphere of action, which we indicate by such terms as these. *Governmental* seems to me the best of these terms; *executive* and *administrative* suggest that the work in question consists merely in executing or administrating the law, in putting the laws in force. But in truth a great deal remains to be done beyond putting the laws in force—no nation can be governed entirely by general rules. We can see this very plainly in our own day—but it is quite as true of the Middle Ages:—there must be rulers or officers who have discretionary powers, discretionary coercive powers, power to do or leave undone, power to command that this or that be done or left undone. The law marks out their spheres of action, the law (as we think) gives them their powers. I do not wish you to think that a definite theory to the effect that while legislative power resides in king and parliament, the so-called executive power is in the king alone, was a guiding theory of medieval politics. On the contrary, the line between what the king could do without a parliament, and what he could only do with the aid of parliament, was only drawn very gradually, and it fluctuated from time to time. On the one hand we find that the king has a certain, or perhaps we should say uncertain, power of making general ordinances which shall have the force of law. On the other hand even at an early time parliaments interfere with what a political theorist would consider to be purely executive or governmental work: for instance they are sometimes strong enough to dictate to the king who shall be his councillors—as we should say, they appoint the ministry. Such a power as that our modern parliaments do not openly exercise, but it was exercised in the Middle Ages. Again we find a parliament ordaining that the taxes shall be paid to two particular persons and be expended by them on the war. The production and audit of the royal accounts is also insisted on : this we cannot call legislative business. In short, the more we study our constitution whether in the present or the past, the less do we find it conform to any such plan as a philosopher might invent in his study.

Still parliament, even when the king is weak, leaves him a large field of action and expects him to be busy in it. A do-nothing king, or a king who is merely a moderator between contending parties, or a king who merely executes the expressed desires of parliament, is not the ideal king of the Middle Ages. He is the ruler of the nation, the commander of its armies and its fleets, the national treasure is his treasure, and in very general terms does parliament interfere with his expenditure ; it is for him to keep the peace, the peace is his peace ; all public officers, high and low, with but few exceptions are appointed by him, dismissible by him ; they hold their offices during his good pleasure—this is true of the high officers of state, the chancellor and treasurer, it is true of the justices of the king's courts, it is true of the sheriffs, it is expected of him that he will supervise the work of his servants, that he will call them to account, that he will dismiss them when they offend.

It is somewhat unsatisfactory work, this attempt to speak in general terms of a long and eventful period like the two centuries which divide the accession of Edward II from that of Henry VIII. Changes in the letter of the law are, it may be, few and gradual, but the real meaning of the kingship varies from decade to decade. The character of the king, the wants of the time, these decide not merely what he will do but what he can do : this we must learn by tracing history step by step,—by seeing that the kingship is practically a different thing in almost every reign ; it changes as we pass from Edward III to Richard II, again as we pass from Richard II to Henry IV, and so on. To watch this process in the detail of practice we have here no time, rather let us speak of theory, and theory we shall find is more permanent than practice. Richard II, there can be little doubt, not only determined

to act as though he were an absolute monarch, but had a
theory of absolute monarchy. He made 'a resolute attempt
not to evade but to destroy the limitations' which had been
imposed upon his predecessors, and he had a theory which
justified him in the attempt; such limitations were vain, idle
efforts to limit a limitless prerogative[1]. When he falls it is
not merely his practice but his theory that is condemned—
not merely has he been guilty of many illegalities, but he has
held himself above law: he has said that the laws are in his
own breast, that the lives, lands and goods of the subjects
are the king's—in short, *quod principi placuit legis habet
vigorem.* He is deposed, and it is as representatives of a
different theory—that of a king below the law—that the
House of Lancaster is to reign. The king, as Bracton had
said more than a century ago, has above him the law which
makes him king. This principle is stated repeatedly and
very clearly by the greatest English writer on law of the
fifteenth century. Sir John Fortescue was made chief justice
of the King's Bench in 1422 and he served the House of
Lancaster in good and evil fortune until all was lost. He
did not die until after 1476. His most famous work, *De
Laudibus Legum Angliae,* was written about 1469. In this
and in other treatises he keeps repeating that the king of
England is no absolute monarch. The state of France gives
him an opportunity of explaining by way of contrast what
he means. The king of France is an absolute monarch—
in France that saying of the civil law holds good, *quod
principi placuit legis habet vigorem.* But it is not so in
England. 'Ther bith ij kindes of kingdomes of the wich that
on is a lordship callid in laten *dominium regale* and that other
is callid *dominium politicum et regale.* And thai diversen in
that the first kynge may rule his peple bi suche lawes as he
makyth himself, and therefor he may sette uppon them tayles
and other imposicions, such as he woe hymself, without their
assent. The secounde king may not rule his peple bi other
lawes than such as thai assenten unto. And therefore he may
sett upon them non imposicions without thair own assent[2].'

---

[1] Stubbs, *Constitutional History*, vol. II, § 268.
[2] Fortescue, *Governance of England*, ed. Plummer, p. 109; cf. also *De
Laudibus,* cc. 34—7.

The kingdom of England is of this second kind. This doctrine Fortescue maintained even after the hopes of the Lancastrian party were at an end and he himself had made his peace with Edward IV—and I believe we may say that it was the generally accepted doctrine of the time. Edward, however arbitrary might be his acts, asserted no theoretic claim to be above the law. The same may be said of Henry VII. The danger during the whole Tudor period is not that the king will assert such a principle but that practically he will be able to get exactly what he wants by means of submissive and subservient parliaments. It is the fashion now to speak of Edward IV as beginning 'the New Monarchy,' and there is point enough in this title—but the legal limits of royal power erected in earlier centuries remain where they were. In the changed circumstances the king is beginning to find out that parliamentary institutions can be made the engines of his will.

We turn from the king to the king's council, the early history of which we have already traced[1]. The king had at his side a body of sworn councillors. During the fourteenth century this body becomes definitely distinct from parliament on the one hand, and from the Courts of Law on the other. The composition of the council depends as a general rule on the king's will, though occasionally parliament has interfered with it. We have the list of the council as it was in 1404 under Henry IV; it contains three bishops, nine peers, seven commoners, in all nineteen persons. They can be dismissed by the king whenever he pleases; they are sworn to advise the king according to the best of their cunning and discretion. They receive salaries of large amount. They meet constantly; the king is not usually present at their deliberations. The proceedings of the council are committed to writing; this begins at least as early as 1386—the proceedings from that year until 1460 have been printed by the Record Commissioners. The function of the council, we may say, is to advise the king upon every exercise of the royal power. Every sort of ordinance, licence, pardon that the king can issue is brought before the council. Sometimes parliament

---

[1] See p. 91, and Dicey's *Privy Council.*

trusts it with extraordinary powers of legislation and taxation, allows it to suspend or dispense with statutes, to raise loans, and the like. It is to the advice of the council that the king looks in all his financial difficulties, which are many.

But though the royal council has thus become a permanent part of the machinery of government, and a most important part, still it is, we may say, an unstable institution —that is, its real power is constantly changing from time to time. Under a strong king it is really no check upon his will; he can appoint it and he can dismiss it; he is not obliged to take its advice, he is not even obliged to ask its advice. This Henry VII has discovered; he does not bring the weightiest matters before the council, or does not do so until he has made up his own mind: the council then has to register foregone conclusions. But under weak kings it has been otherwise, and under infant kings the council has ruled England. It will be no digression therefore if we say a little of royal minorities.

Since the Norman Conquest there have been three cases. Henry III was nine years old when he began to reign; Richard II eleven years; Henry VI was but nine months. We have further to remember that during a considerable part of his reign Henry VI was perfectly imbecile. When Henry III succeeded to the throne there was no member of the royal house capable of urging any claim to be regent. This is an important fact, for it gave rise to an important precedent. The barons, in whose power the young king was, appointed William Marshall, Earl of Pembroke, *rector regis et regni*, and associated certain councillors with him. We have already seen how it is to this time that we can definitely trace the existence of a *concilium Regis* that is distinct from the *curia Regis*. Within three years the regent died. No-one was appointed to fill his place, but the government was carried on by the council, at the head of which stood Hubert de Burgh, the chief justiciar. Our public law had made great advances before the next case arose, the accession of Richard II. On his coronation the assembled magnates appointed no regent, but named a council of government. Before long, troubles set in and the king had to submit to the restraint of a council appointed by parliament; not until he was three-and-twenty was he able to free himself from this control. When Henry VI succeeded his father we hear of a definite claim to the regency. His uncle, the Duke of Gloucester, claimed the regency both as next of kin and under the will of the late king. But this claim was disallowed by the lords assembled in parliament; after searching for precedents they pronounced that he could not claim the regency on the score of relationship, and that Henry V could not dispose of the government of the kingdom by his will. An act of Parliament constituted the Duke of Bedford protector and defender of the realm and church of England. The assent of the king to this act of parliament must of course have been a mere fiction—he was but a few months old. This precedent sanctioned what has since been regarded as law, namely, that our law makes no provision for any regency, that the king's nearest kinsman has not as such any claim to be regent, that a king cannot by his will declare effectually who is to govern England after his death. If such a case arises parliament must provide for it. Further, the king, no matter how young he is, can give his assent to an act of parliament—this, it is true, may be a fictitious assent, but a king is bound by the acts of parliament done during his minority: obviously this doctrine has difficulties before it, with which however we are not at this moment concerned. 'During the minority of Henry VI the council was a real council of regency and by no means a mere consultative body in attendance on the protector. It defined its own power in the statement that upon it during the king's minority devolved the exercise and execution of all the powers of sovereignty[1].' But then when Henry came of age the council became once more a new instrument in the hands of the king, or of those who, for the time being, could gain an ascendancy over the king. In 1454 Henry became quite imbecile; it was impossible to get a word from him. The lords chose the Duke of York protector and defender of the realm; this resolution was embodied in an act to which the commons gave their

---

[1] Stubbs, *Constitutional History*, vol. III, § 689.

assent; the king had just sense enough to place the great seal in the hands of the Earl of Salisbury, and in this way the royal assent was given. In the next year the king recovered his senses, but in a few months he again fell ill, and the same ceremony of appointing a protector by act of parliament was enacted.

Under Edward IV and the Tudors the council ceases to be any real restraint upon the king. Its power, it is true, increases, but this merely means an increase of the royal power. It is powerful against all others, but weak against the king. It is but an assembly of the king's servants, whom he appoints and dismisses as pleases him best, whom he consults when it pleases him, and only when it pleases him. Henry VII, says Bacon, in his greatest business imparted himself to none, except it were to Morton and Fox. No law compelled him to ask advice; all the powers which any council could exercise were simply the king's powers, powers which the king himself might exercise if and when he pleased.

A certain limitation to this principle was found in the practice regarding the king's seals. From the Norman days onward the king's will had been signified by writs, charters, letters patent, letters close and so forth, sealed with the royal seal. No document without the king's seal could be regarded as an authentic expression of the king's command. The king's Great Seal was committed to the Chancellor—he was the head of the whole secretarial establishment, (as we now might say) the Secretary of State for all departments. When in the middle of the thirteenth century the chief justiciarship came to an end, the chancellorship grew in dignity and in power. During the later Middle Ages and far on through the Tudor time the chancellor is the king's first minister—prime minister. The possession of the royal seal makes his office of the first importance. Gradually we begin to hear of other seals besides the great seal. The chancellor has so much miscellaneous work to perform as a judge and otherwise, so much routine business requires the great seal, that for matters directly affecting the king a privy seal is in use. The king under his privy seal gives directions to the chancellor as to the use of the great seal. Then this privy seal is committed to the keeping of an officer, the Keeper of the Privy Seal. In course of time a yet more private secretary intervenes between the king and these high officers of state, namely, the king's clerk or king's secretary, as he comes to be called, who keeps the king's signet. In the Tudor time we find two king's secretaries, who before the end of that time are known as secretaries of state. A regular routine establishes itself— documents signed by the king's own hand, the royal sign manual, and countersigned by the secretary are sent to the keeper of the privy seal, as instructions for documents to be issued under the privy seal, and these again serve as instructions for the chancellor to issue documents bearing the great seal of the realm. This practice begets a certain ministerial responsibility for the king's acts. The law courts will not recognize any document as expressing the royal will unless it bears the great seal or at least the privy seal. This insures that some minister will have committed himself to that expression of the royal will. The ministers themselves are much concerned in the maintenance of this routine; they fear being called in question for the king's acts and having no proof that they are the king's acts. The chancellor fears to affix the great seal unless he has some document under the privy seal that he can produce as his warrant; the keeper of the privy seal is anxious to have the king's own handwriting attested by the king's secretary. For the king again this is a useful arrangement; it is the duty of these officers to remember the king's interests, to know how the king's affairs stand; as the king's affairs grow more manifold, division of labour becomes necessary; there must be an officer at the head of every department bound to see that the king is not cheated or prejudiced, and the danger of his interests being neglected is decreased, if in the ordinary course of business his letters have to pass through several different hands. Thus, even when there is on the throne a strong-willed king with a policy of his own, ministers are necessary to him. At present we may say this is a matter of convenience, but in this doctrine of the royal seals we can see the foundation for our modern doctrine of ministerial responsibility—that for every exercise of the royal power some minister is answerable.

C. *Administration of Justice.*

Hitherto we have said nothing of what in general estimation constitutes the most important side of the council's history, the history of its judicial powers; but to this we shall best come by first taking a short review of the administration of justice as a whole.

More and more the king's courts have become the only courts of the first importance. Of the feudal and the ancient communal courts we need say but very little; by one means and another business has been drawn away from them. That an action for freehold land should be begun in the court baron of the lord of whom the land is holden is a principle unrepealed—it remains indeed unrepealed until 1833[1]; but many ways of evading it have been devised by the ingenuity of lawyers, and it has in truth become a dead letter. We may indeed doubt whether in Henry VII's reign there are many courts baron which have more than a nominal existence.

Even the customary court of the manor has suffered a heavy blow. It was, you will remember, the court for those who, whether personally villeins or no, held their land by villein tenure. In Henry VII's day personal villeinage, owing to causes which we cannot here discuss, has practically become extinct. But further, and this is of great importance, the king's courts have at length decided to protect the tenant in villeinage in his holding. He is now getting a new name, derived from those copies of the court rolls which serve as evidence of his title; he is a tenant by copy of court roll, in shorter phrase a copyholder. At length the king's courts have decided that he shall no longer be left with merely such protection in his holding as the manorial courts afford—if the lord contrary to the custom of the manor turns him out, he shall have an action against his lord, an action of trespass in the king's courts. In 1457 we get a hint that this is so; in 1467, and again in 1481, it is definitely said that the copyholder can bring an action against his lord if ejected contrary to the manorial custom. The manorial custom thus becomes a recognized part of the law of the land, to be enforced in

---

[1] 3 and 4 Will. IV, c. 27.

the king's court. This of course was a serious blow to the manorial courts—contentious business was taken from them—anyone who claimed copyhold land instead of going to them would go to the king's courts, where he would get a more certain justice. A great deal of business remained, and still in theory remains, for the customary court to do. The copyholder when he wishes to convey his land must surrender it into the hands of the lord, who then admits a new tenant; such surrenders and admittances took place in court—in theory they took place in court until very lately—but all this business became more and more a matter of routine now that the king's courts had fully recognized the rights of the copyhold tenant. If the customary dues were paid the lord had no choice but to accept the surrender and admit the new tenant, and these surrenders and admittances were in fact accomplished in what only by fiction and figure of speech could be called a court—practically there was but a transaction between the tenant and the lord's steward. However, our present point is that before the end of Henry VII's day, owing rather to the ingenious devices of lawyers in search of business than to any legislation, the manorial courts had ceased to be of any great importance as tribunals for contentious business.

As regards what I have called the communal courts, we have seen that before the end of Edward I's reign a rule had been established which made them courts for small cases: they were not to entertain cases in which more than 40 shillings was at stake[1]. In Henry VII's time the county court was still held month by month, and the sum of 40 shillings had not yet become a trivial sum; but long before this the freeholders of the shire had been allowed to discharge their duty of appearing at the monthly court by sending their attorneys instead of coming in person, and it is very probable that the judicial business was practically transacted by the sheriff without much interference on the part of the freeholders or their representatives. Trial by jury has not, we see, made its way into the procedure of these courts; they still make use of the ancient system of compurgation.

[1] See p. 132.

But we have now to notice a new institution which has grown up since the days of Edward I, an institution which is to play a very large part both in the administration of justice and in local government, namely, the justices of the peace. In the thirteenth century we hear occasionally of knights of the shire being assigned, that is, appointed, to keep the peace—sometimes they seem to be elected by the county court. Their duty seems to be that of assisting, perhaps also of checking, the sheriff in his work of preserving the peace, arresting malefactors, and the like. Then immediately after the accession of Edward III a statute is passed (1327, 1 Edw. III, stat. 2, c. 16) to the effect that in every shire good and lawful men shall be assigned to keep the peace. In 1330 (4 Edw. III, c. 2) it is repeated that good and lawful men shall be assigned in every county to keep the peace; those who are indicted before them are to be imprisoned, and they are to send the indictments to the justices of gaol delivery. These *custodes pacis,* conservators of the peace, have therefore already power to receive indictments, the accusations preferred by juries, but they do not as yet try the indicted; they commit them to prison to take their trial before the king's judges on their circuits. In 1360 another step is taken. A statute (34 Edw. III, c. 1) repeats that in every county there shall be assigned for the keeping of the peace one lord and, with him, three or four of the most worthy of the county, with some learned in the law, and they are to have power to arrest malefactors, to receive indictments against them, and to hear and determine at the king's suit all manner of felonies and trespasses done in their county according to the law and customs of the realm. The conservators of the peace are now authorised not merely to receive indictments, but to try the indicted. Very soon after this, having been trusted with these high judicial powers, they come to be known as justices; they are no longer mere conservators of the peace, they are justices of the peace. In 1388 it is directed by statute that they are to hold their sessions four times a year—this is the origin of those Quarter Sessions of justices of the peace which are still held in our own day. Now this new institution soon becomes very popular with parliament and flourishes; parliament constantly adds to the powers of these justices; they are in truth men drawn from the same class of country gentlemen which supplies parliament with knights of the shire. For a long time there are persistent demands that the justices shall be elected by the freeholders; this demand finds expression in many petitions presented by parliament to Edward III. But on this point the king will not give way, he will keep the appointment of justices in the hands of himself and his council. It is so common now-a-days to regard our constitutional history as one long triumph of the elective principle, that it is well to notice that at two points this principle was persistently urged and finally defeated. Our ancestors wanted elected sheriffs, and they wanted elected justices of the peace; to this day our sheriffs and our justices are appointed by the king, and I do not suppose that one would wish them elected. The justices of the fourteenth century were paid wages—four shillings for each day of session; they were entitled to these wages until very lately; here again the great change in the value of money which took place in the sixteenth century has had important effects on our constitutional law. In Richard II's day a form of commission was settled which, in all the most material respects, is that still in use. The king assigns certain persons by name to be his justices in a particular county; he empowers every one of them to keep the peace and to arrest malefactors, and he empowers every two of them to hold sessions for the trial of indicted persons.

Now at the period with which we are dealing these are the main duties of the justices of the peace :—(1) they are to keep the peace by putting down riots, arresting offenders and so forth, and (2) in their quarter sessions they are to try indicted persons—the trial is a formal trial by jury. Their power extends over pretty well all indictable offences except treason only, but the more difficult cases they are directed to reserve for the king's judges on their circuits. These are their main duties, but parliament has been gradually adding many other duties of a very miscellaneous character. In particular, parliament has long been engaged on elaborate legislation about the rate of wages. We have to remember the Black Death of 1349, one of the greatest economic catastrophies in all history; the guess has been made that it destroyed not much less than half the population. It utterly unsettled the medieval system of agriculture and industry: wages of course rose enormously; parliament endeavoured by statute after statute to keep them down, to fix a legal rate of wages. This attempt produced many of the grievances which burst into flame in the revolt of 1381, 'one of the most portentous phenomena to be found in the whole of our history. But still parliament did not abandon the effort: to gain its end it endowed the justices of the peace, representatives of the landowning class, with very large powers of compelling men to work for the legal wage. After a while, in 1427, it even delegated to these justices the power of fixing the legal rate: the justices of the peace were the justices of labourers also— in our language they have not merely judicial powers, they have governmental powers also. And this matter of wages, though it is the most important, is by no means the only specimen of governmental duties cast upon the justices of the peace. More and more the quarter sessions of the peace begin to supplant the old county court as the real governing assembly of the shire; the old county court sinks into a mere tribunal for small civil suits. In 1494 we find that the justices have even got a control over the sheriff: by 11 Hen. VII, c. 15, they are empowered to entertain complaints against the sheriff as to extortions practised by him in the county court, and to convict him and his officers in a summary fashion. This power to convict persons in a summary fashion, that is to say, without trial by jury, is, we observe, being given to justices in a number of cases. The practice begins in the fifteenth century and becomes very usual in the sixteenth: parliament is discovering that for petty offences trial by jury is a much too elaborate procedure. An instance or two may be given :—

In 1433 (11 Hen. VI, c. 8) the justices are empowered to punish in a summary way those who use false weights or measures; in 1464 we have an elaborate statute (4 Edw. IV, c. 1) about the making of cloth, regulating matters between master and man; upon complaint made of any offence against this ordinance, the justices of the peace may send for the party and examine him, and if the party by examination or other due proof be found guilty he is to be fined; in 1477 (17 Edw. IV, c. 4) we have a similar statute about the making of tiles; in 1503 the justices are to punish those who take young herons from their nests—they are to call the suspected person before them and by their discretion examine him. The statutes, of which these are specimens, seldom lay down any rules of procedure, only it is made clear that there need not be trial by jury, and that the suspected persons may be questioned.

We see here then a yet young but very strong and healthy institution, one which has a great future before it. Country gentlemen commissioned by the king are to keep the peace of the shire, are to constitute a court of quarter sessions with high criminal jurisdiction, are to punish the pettier offences in a summary way, are to exercise miscellaneous governmental powers and police powers—to fix the legal rate of wages for example. They are to be substantial men. In 1439 a statute (18 Hen. VI, c. 11) says that they are to have lands or tenements to the value of £20 a year. At present their number is small, some six or eight for the shire: during the Tudor time it increases. The Tudor kings find here a useful institution for the purposes of their strong policy—for from the first a stern check has been kept upon these justices; not only have the courts of law been ready, perhaps eager, to notice any transgression by the justices of their statutory powers (for the old courts will not suffer any rivalry, and will put the narrowest construction upon any statute which authorizes any departure from the procedure of the common law), but also these justices are specially under the eye of the royal council. A statute of 1388 (12 Ric. II, c. 10), when giving them certain new powers of dealing with labourers, threatens them with punishment at the discretion of the king's council if they do not hold their sessions. We shall have much more to say of justices of the peace hereafter.

The three old courts—the three superior courts of common law, King's Bench, Common Pleas and Exchequer—have grown in power and dignity. The number of the judges is small, though it has not yet become fixed at the sacred twelve—and they are now erudite lawyers, men who have made their fame by practising at the bar. The line of demarcation between the provinces of these three courts is not so plain as once it was, for by the use of ingenious fictions the King's Bench has been stealing business from the Common Pleas, and the Exchequer is beginning to follow its example. But to one or the other of these three courts goes almost all of the civil litigation of the realm—all that the local courts are incompetent to entertain. The King's Bench is the supreme court for criminal cases, and the Exchequer still keeps its monopoly of all cases touching the royal revenue. These courts have by this time become purely judicial institutions, they have little or nothing to do with governmental work; it is their function to hear and determine causes according to the law of the land, and they are very conservative of all the formalities of their procedure. Already the Year Books contain vast masses of decided cases, and these cases are treated as binding authorities.

Then again the ambulatory or visitatorial courts have been maintained. Twice a year or so the counties are visited by justices, whose commissions enable them to deliver the gaols and to hear and determine all the criminal business, or all such part of it as is not disposed of by the justices of the peace at their quarter sessions—whose commissions enable them also to take the trial of civil cases which are depending in the king's courts at Westminster. A great deal of this work is done by the judges of the three common law courts—indeed, by statute, much of it must now be done by them—though other persons, landowners of the county, are associated with them in the commissions. The work of these itinerant justices has now become purely judicial work—to preside at trials, to hear and decide causes; they no longer, like their predecessors of the twelfth century, add to this duty that of looking after the royal revenue and conserving the king's interests. What is more, we no longer find that the whole county is summoned to meet them, with all its hundreds, boroughs and townships represented. A single grand jury now represents the county: the older plan had been found very burdensome, and seems to have been abandoned late in the fourteenth century

A great change has been coming over trial by jury since we last looked at it, and trial by jury has become of great importance in national history. The change has been a slow one, and it is hardly yet completed. Turning first to civil cases we may formulate the change thus:—the twelve jurors are ceasing to be witnesses and are becoming judges of fact; it is no longer the theory that before they come into court they will know the truth about the matters at issue, but when they come into court the parties put evidence before them, produce witnesses who testify in the judge's hearing. We see that this is so from a book already mentioned: Sir John Fortescue, *De Laudibus Legum Angliae*. He describes how ' each of the parties by themselves or their counsel in presence of the court, shall declare and lay open to the jury all and singular the matters and evidences whereby they think they may be able to inform the court concerning the point in question, after which each of the parties has a liberty to produce before the court all such witnesses as they please[1]'— in short, trial by jury is taking that form in which we now-a-days know it, the jurors try questions of fact. Still, in Fortescue's book the change is not yet perfect, he sometimes speaks of the jurors as though they were witnesses—they are drawn from the district in which the events took place, in order that they may bring their own knowledge to bear upon the question; if they give a false verdict they are liable to be attainted, the case can be tried over again by twenty-four jurors, and if the new verdict contradicts the old, the first jury of twelve is very severely punished. In civil cases this mode of trial has become almost universal, though there are still certain cases respecting property in land in which trial by battle can be claimed, and there are some other cases in which recourse is still had to compurgation.

The commonest procedure in civil cases involves the use of two juries, an indicting and a trying jury, or, as we say, a grand and a petty jury. The grand jury is a body of twenty-three persons representing the county, sworn to present criminals. In the past the theory has been that such a jury

[1] c. xxvi.

accuses men of its own knowledge, and, even in our own day, this form is preserved—an indictment even in our own day states that the jurors say upon their oaths that A, of malice aforethought did slay and murder B. As a matter of fact, however, what happens now is this—and we may perhaps carry back the change as far as Henry VII's day—some person who believes that A has committed a crime goes before the grand jury and profers a bill of indictment, a document stating that A has murdered B. The grand jurors hear the evidence for the prosecution, and if they think that this makes it probable that A is guilty, then without hearing any evidence for the defence they write on the bill 'a true bill,' and then A has to take his trial before a petty jury; if, however, they think that there is no ground for suspicion, they write 'no true bill'—the old phrase was 'Ignoramus'—we know nought of this—the bill is said to be ignored, and A goes free, though he is liable to be indicted another time for the same offence:—he has had no trial, and is not acquitted. A majority of the body of twenty-three grand jurors decides whether the bill shall be ignored or no. So much as to the grand jury.

In the present day, a person who has been indicted must, as a matter of course, stand his trial before a petty jury; he is tried, as we all know, by a jury of twelve, and the jurors are judges of fact—their verdict is based on the evidence of witnesses given before them in court. But in Henry VII's day this was not quite the case—an indicted person was not tried by jury unless he consented to be so tried, but this consent was extorted from him by torture, by the *peine forte et dure*. If, when asked 'how will you be tried?' he refused to say 'By God and my country,' if (as the phrase went) he stood mute of malice, he was pressed under heavy weights until he either died or said the necessary words. So late as 1658 a man was pressed to death, so late as 1726 a man was pressed into pleading, not until 1772 was the *peine forte et dure* abolished. This horrible process was a reminder that trial by jury was not native to English law—there had been a time when to convict a man of crime without allowing him to appeal to God by means of battle or ordeal, had seemed an impossible injustice. The reason why men were found hardy enough to submit to the terrible torture of being pressed to death, instead of escaping with a mere hanging, was this, that if they were convicted they forfeited lands and chattels, if they died unconvicted there was no forfeiture, and thus their families were not ruined.

Another point that we may note is that before Henry VII's day the law had come to demand unanimity of the jurors—unless the twelve agreed there could be no verdict. This rule, as we all know, prevails at the present day; but it only became fixed in the course of the later Middle Ages; it certainly looked at one time as if the law would be content with the verdict of a majority.

We have already seen that procedure by indictment had once been a novelty in English law—a novelty introduced by Henry II: it had taken its place beside the older procedure of an appeal by the party wronged[1]. In Henry VII's day this older alternative still existed, and was still in use—the appellee could either claim trial by battle, or submit to trial by jury. Trial by battle was, however, becoming very unusual. Appeals were not, however, abolished until 1819: their abolition was due to the fact that in 1818, in the celebrated case of *Ashford* v. *Thornton*, an appeal was brought, and the appellee claimed trial by battle—the appellor refused to fight.

It is necessary, in order to explain what follows, to understand that before the end of the Middle Ages trial by jury had taken a deep root in the English system, and had already become the theme of national boastings. Fortescue contrasts it favourably with the procedure of the French courts, where there was no jury, and where torture was freely employed. It is a very curious point in European history, that an institution which was once characteristically Frankish, became, in course of time, peculiarly English, and underwent, without losing its identity, the great change which turned the body of neighbour-witnesses into judges of the evidence given by other witnesses.

But to return to the courts—we have yet to speak of the judicial functions of the parliament, of the king in parliament. In this sense 'the king in parliament' comes to mean the House

See p. 128.

of Lords. In the fourteenth century, as we have already seen, we must regard the presence in parliament of representatives of the commons as something new. These newcomers gradually improve their position, they will not be mere granters of taxes, they claim to share in deliberation and in legislation. But now we have to note that they never obtain, hardly attempt to obtain, any share in the judicial work which from of old had been done by the king in the assembly of prelates and barons. The jurisdiction of the king in parliament remains the jurisdiction of the king with his prelates and barons; in other words, since the king does not himself take part in judicial proceedings (in the fourteenth century, to say the least, it is most unusual for him to do so, in the fifteenth century, as we learn from Fortescue, it is thought distinctly improper that he should do so), the jurisdiction of the king in parliament has come to mean the jurisdiction of the House of Lords. This we find is of three kinds.

(i) The House of Lords acts as a court for the trial of peers accused of treason or of felony. Of this we have said something already[1]. If the parliament be not sitting, the peer is tried by the Lord High Steward, assisted by a body of peers chosen by him. Very probably it is because this work of trying peers was one very principal field for the jurisdiction of parliament, that the commons took no part in the judicial work. At any rate, in 1399 the commons, fearing perhaps that they might be called in question touching some of the very irregular proceedings of Richard's reign, protested solemnly that they had no part in judicial work—the judgment of parliament was the judgment of the king and the lords; this protest established a permanent principle.

(ii) We have what is called the jurisdiction in error, the jurisdiction of the king and parliament as a court of error, a court which could correct the errors in law of all lower courts. This we may trace back far—the last resource for royal justice was the king surrounded by the magnates of the realm. We find it settled in the fifteenth century as a juris-diction to correct errors in matters of law, as contrasted with matters of fact. The notion of trying the same *facts* twice over, except by attainting the jury, is quite foreign to our

[1] See pp. 169—171.

medieval law—but if the king's courts of common law make errors in law, it remains for the House of Lords to correct those errors. During the fourteenth century this jurisdiction seems to have been freely used, but for some reason or another, not very easy to understand, it went out of use in the fifteenth century. Between Henry V and James I there are hardly any known cases of error being brought before the lords: however, this procedure, though for a time disused, had a great future before it, as we shall see hereafter.

(iii) The parliament, that is to say, the lords, had gradually abandoned all attempt to act as a court of first instance in criminal or civil cases, save when a peer was to be tried for felony or treason—but to this there was one great exception. They had entertained accusations both against peers and against commoners when preferred by the commons. Such accusations preferred by the commons to the lords came to be known as impeachments. The first case of what can definitely be called an impeachment, occurs in the Good Parliament of 1376; Lord Latimer, the king's chamberlain, and one Lyons, were impeached. In 1386 we have the impeachment of the Duke of Suffolk; some other cases follow rapidly during the troubled reign of Richard II. A few more cases followed, just sufficient to establish the outlines of a procedure—the last is in 1459. After this there is a long break from 1459 until this ancient weapon was furbished for a new use in 1621; during the interval parliaments were hardly in a position to impeach the king's ministers, for it was as a check upon the king's ministers that the impeachment was chiefly valuable, and came to be afterwards valued; smaller offenders could be left to their fate in the ordinary courts.

One other parliamentary process remains to be noticed— but it must be carefully distinguished from an impeachment— I mean an act of attainder or of pains and penalties. A statute, we say, can do anything—such acts as I have just mentioned are statutes, acts of parliament for putting a man to death, or otherwise punishing him without any trial at all. It is not a judicial act, it proceeds with the legislative authority of king, lords and commons. At the Coventry parliament of 1459 the Yorkist lords were attainted. Two years afterwards the turn for the Lancastrians comes, and Henry VI, his wife, and a large number of his supporters are attainted. In 1477 the Duke of Clarence was attainted—these were miserable precedents, acts of anarchy and of revenge. It was under Henry VIII, who could obtain anything from parliament, that the act of attainder came into common use : of this hereafter. But distinguish such an act, a statute passed by king, lords and commons, without any trial, without any judicial formalities, from the trial before the House of Lords of a person who has been impeached, i.e., formally accused by the commons.

We have yet to speak of the jurisdiction of the king's council, a matter with which it is difficult to deal, because it was constantly the subject of bitter controversy. We have seen that in Edward I's time the council exercised a jurisdiction, which it is somewhat difficult to mark off from that of the parliament ; the two work together so harmoniously that the council at times seems a standing committee of the parliament, or the parliament a particularly full and solemn meeting of the council. But this harmony is soon dispelled : throughout the fourteenth century there is constant conflict between the council and the parliament, and the latter seeks time after time to set limits to the judicial functions of the former. We may distinguish three different kinds of jurisdiction, (1) the power to correct the errors of the ordinary courts of law, (2) an original jurisdiction, jurisdiction as a court of first instance in criminal cases, (3) an original jurisdiction in civil cases.

(1) The first of these has the shortest history. The function of correcting the errors in law of the ordinary courts of law became definitely the function of the parliament (i.e., as we have seen, of the House of Lords), and the council had to forego it. In 1365 we have a case in which the judges of the Court of Common Pleas refused to pay any heed to the reversal by the council of a judgment of the justices of assize—the council, they said, is not a place in which judgments can be reversed[1]. Again in 1402 we have a statute (4 Hen. IV, c. 23) which shows that the council had been calling in question the judgments of the lower courts, had

---

[1] *Yearbooks*, vol. III, 39 Edw. III, f. 14.

not been regarding them as final—it is therefore ordained that after judgment the parties shall be in peace, until the judgment be reversed by attaint or by error.   However, without interfering with judgments already delivered, the council had a wide field of action, and it is over its jurisdiction as a court of first instance that controversy rages.

(2) Already in 1331 parliament attempts to put a stop to legal proceedings, other than those in the ordinary courts of law.   It is enacted (5 Edw. III, c. 9) that no man is to be attached by any accusation, nor forejudged of life or limb, nor his lands, tenements, goods or chattels seized into the king's hands, against the form of the Great Charter and the law of the land.   In 1351 we have a second statute (25 Edw. III, stat. 5, c. 4): ' None shall be taken by petition or suggestion made to our lord the king, or to his council, unless it be by indictment or presentment of good and lawful people of the same neighbourhood, where such deeds be done in due manner or by process made by writ original at the common law; and none shall be put out of his franchise or his freehold, unless he be duly brought in to answer, and forejudged of the same by the course of the law.'   Then again in 1354 (28 Edw. III, c. 3), 'no man of what estate or condition that he be, shall be put out of land or tenement, nor taken, nor imprisoned, nor disinherited, nor put to death without being brought in answer by due process of law.'   In 1363 and 1364 we have other statutes (37 Edw. III, c. 18; 38 Edw. III, c. 9) which denounce punishment against persons who make false suggestions to the king, statutes which seem to be aimed at the jurisdiction of the council.   Then again in 1368 (42 Edw. III, c. 3) we have the old story—it is established that ' no man be put to answer without presentment before justices, or matter of record, or by due process and writ original according to the old law of the land.'   But all these statutes which seem devised to curb the council, and to sanction the procedure of the common law courts, indictments and original writs, as the only legal procedure, have apparently but little immediate effect.   Under Henry IV and Henry V the commons are still petitioning against the jurisdiction of the council; but the king does not assent to their petitions.   They then become

silent; and it would seem that under the constitutional rule of the Lancastrian house, the jurisdiction of the council was not oppressively exercised. The series of statutes at which we have glanced remained unrepealed, if disregarded, during the whole of the Tudor period. They became of vast importance under the Stuarts, for they were the base for the contention that the Court of Star Chamber was no legal tribunal.

Still the convenience of a tribunal which was not bound down to a formal procedure (and we must remember that the procedure of the common law courts was extremely formal) made itself apparent from time to time, and we find parliament admitting that the council has a certain sphere of jurisdiction. This we may see in several different quarters. In 1351 parliament began its course of anti-Roman legislation; we have those statutes of Provisors and of Praemunire, which play a large part in the history of our church, statutes directed to excluding the interference of the Pope with English benefices. In 1363 (38 Edw. III, stat. 2, c. 2) we find parliament ordaining that persons who offend against these statutes are to answer for it before the council, and to be punished according to the discretion of the council. Lords and commons are in great earnest about this matter, and are therefore quite content that justice shall be done rapidly and without any dilatory formalities. In 1388 parliament is so very desirous that justices shall hold their quarter sessions for the enforcement of the statutes of labourers, that it (12 Ric. II, c. 10) enacts that if justices do not hold sessions they are to be punished according to the discretion of the king's council. In 1453 we find a temporary but very severe act (31 Hen. VI, c. 2), passed after Jack Cade's insurrection, which fully admits the lawfulness of writs directing persons guilty of riots, oppressions and extortions, to appear before the council. Contempt of such writs is to be severely punished by forfeiture; this is to endure for seven years. A more general admission we find in certain articles for the council of the infant king agreed to by parliament in 1430—all petitions to the council dealing with matters determinable by the common law are to be sent to the common law courts, unless the discretion of the council feel too great might on the one side, too great unmight on the other, or else other reasonable cause that shall move them[1].

If we place ourselves at the accession of Henry VII, and ask ourselves whether the criminal jurisdiction of the council was legal, we shall find it hard to come by a very definite answer. On the one hand there were statutes unrepealed which might be read as condemning it entirely. Our law knows not now, and knew not then, any such principle as that statutes can grow obsolete—a statute once enacted remains in force until it is repealed. Still it is a hard thing to pronounce illegal that which parliament and the great mass of the nation, including probably the judges, regard as legal; and it seems probable that at Henry's accession this was true of the council's jurisdiction. It was generally admitted that it could punish those offences which the courts of common law were incompetent to punish, offences falling short of felony (the council seems always to have shrunk from pronouncing the penalty of death) in particular, offences which consisted in an interference with the ordinary course of justice, riots, bribery of jurors, and so forth. It was, I think, felt that there were men who were too big for any court but the council: they would bribe jurors and even judges. The statutes to which we have referred were, we may say, protests in favour of trial by jury—but there are other statutes which show very plainly that trial by jury often meant the grossest injustice: there were men whom no jury would convict. This, I think, was admitted, and the remedy was seen in a reserve of extraordinary justice to be found as of old in the king and his immediate advisers, justice which could strike quickly and not have to strike again, justice which could strike even the most powerful offenders.

It is with this in our minds that we approach the statute of 1487 (3 Hen. VII, c. 1), which has been regarded as creating the Court of Star Chamber. It recites that certain offences are very common, riots, perjury, bribery of jurors, misconduct of sheriffs and some others of the same class; then it empowers

---

[1] Nicolas, *Proceedings and Ordinances of the Privy Council* IV, 61, § 111.

the chancellor, treasurer, and keeper of the privy seal, calling to them a bishop and a temporal lord of the council, and the two chief justices or other two justices in their absence, to call before them persons accused of these offences to examine them, and to punish them according to their demerits as they ought to be punished, if they were thereof convict in due order of law. The statute says nothing of the Star Chamber; but for a long time past a room in the palace of Westminster bearing that name had been commonly used by the council for its judicial sessions. It names, we observe, certain particular offences—and it names certain persons who are to hear the charges and punish the offenders. Now, in later times (of this we shall have to speak again) we find a tribunal which is known as the Court of Star Chamber; it is not exactly constituted on the lines marked out by the statute of Henry VII, and it does not confine itself to the offences mentioned in that statute. It consists apparently of the whole council, or of a committee of the council, and must have generally comprised all or most of the officers mentioned in the statute: chancellor, treasurer, keeper of the privy seal, two judges, one temporal lord of the council and one bishop; and though it does punish the offences mentioned in the statute, still 'it punishes many other offences as well—in short, it exercises a very comprehensive penal jurisdiction, practically an unlimited jurisdiction, or limited only by this, that it does not attempt to inflict the penalty of death. Under the Stuarts we have bitter controversy as to the legality of this court: if on the one hand it is regarded as created by the Act of 1487, then it habitually exceeds the powers which were entrusted to it by parliament: if on the other hand it be regarded as exercising a jurisdiction inherent in the king's council, then it may well be argued that it acts in direct defiance of those unrepealed statutes of Edward III's reign, of which we have already spoken[1].

To this point we must come back hereafter; let us now notice that Henry VII and his successors have ready to their hands a most efficient engine of government. The same body

[1] Reference may now be made to Leadam, *Select Cases in the Star Chamber* (Selden Society) 1902.

which issues ordinances, which controls the execution of the law and the administration of the state, acts also as a court of justice with a comprehensive penal jurisdiction—one day it can make an ordinance, and the next punish men for not obeying it.   Its jurisdiction it exercises without any lengthy formalities—there is no trial by jury before it—the accused person is examined on his oath, a procedure quite strange to the courts of common law, in which (as the phrase goes) no-one can be compelled to accuse himself.   And it uses torture. Fortescue, the Lancastrian chief justice, to whose writings we have more than once referred, speaks of torture as foreign to English law—this is one of the respects in which he extols the English law at the expense of continental law[1].   But in Edward IV's reign torture begins to make its appearance ; we hear of it in 1468.   It never becomes part of the procedure of the ordinary courts, but a free use is made of it by council, and the rack becomes one of our political institutions.   The judicial iniquities of Edward IV's reign are evil precedents for his successors.

(3)   We have been speaking in the main of the penal or criminal jurisdiction of the council.   But it had exercised a civil jurisdiction as well, and this has a history of its own. If in one direction we see the power of the council represented by the Court of Star Chamber, in another we see it represented by the Court of Chancery.

We must go back a little way.   Ever since the Norman Conquest every king has his chancellor, who has the custody of his great seal, and is at the head of the whole secretarial body of king's clerks.   When at the end of Henry III's reign there ceases any longer to be a chief justiciar, the chancellor becomes the king's first minister.   Robert Burnell, the chancellor, is Edward I's chief adviser.   The chancellor is almost always an ecclesiastic—there are a few instances of lay chancellors in the fourteenth century—generally he is a bishop.   In many different ways he has for a long time past been concerned in the administration of law.   In the first place it has been his duty, or that of his clerks, to draw up those royal writs (original writs) whereby actions are begun in the king's courts

---

[1] *De Laudibus Legum Angliae* c. xxi.

of common law. He has also had some judicial powers of his own—in particular, if it be asserted that the king has made a grant of what does not belong to him, it is for the chancellor to hear the matter, and if need be to advise the king to revoke his grant. Then again he has always been a member of the king's council, and what is more, the specially learned member—that he should be acquainted with canon law and Roman law, as well as with the common law of England, was very desirable. Naturally then if questions of law came before the council, the chancellor's opinion would be taken.

As the fourteenth century goes on we find that a good deal of civil litigation comes before the council in one way and another. Persons who think themselves injured and who think that, for some reason or another, they cannot get their rights by the ordinary means, are in the habit of petitioning the king, asking for some extraordinary relief. We must remember that besides the ordinary writs whereby actions at law were begun, writs which were obtained from the Chancery as a matter of course upon payment of the fixed fee, there was a certain power reserved to the Chancery of making new writs to suit new cases, of introducing modifications in the established forms. Sometimes the relief which a petitioner desired was of this kind; at other times he wanted more than this—he wanted that the council should send for his adversary and examine him upon oath. Various excuses for the king's interference are put forward—the suppliant is poor, old, sick; his adversary is rich and powerful, will bribe or intimidate the jurors, or has by accident or trick obtained some advantage of which he cannot be deprived by the ordinary courts. The tone of these petitions is very humble, they ask relief for the love of God and that peerless Princess his Mother, or for His sake who died on the Rood Tree on Good Friday. A common formula is—for the love of God and in the way of charity. Thus the petitioner admits that strictly speaking he is not entitled to what he asks—he asks a boon, a royal favour[1].

[1] *Select Cases in Chancery* (A.D. 1364—1471), ed. for the Selden Society by W. P. Baildon, 1896.

Now the series of statutes and petitions of parliament, to which we have already referred, seems to have been directed quite as much against the interference of the council in civil litigation as against its assumption of criminal jurisdiction—the view of parliament is that the courts of common law are sufficient. Gradually, in the fifteenth century, the council seems to have abandoned the attempt to interfere with cases in which there was a question which the courts of common law could decide, but it became apparent that there were cases in which no relief at all could be got from these courts, and yet cases in which according to the ideas of the time relief was due. I cannot say very much about this matter without plunging into the history of private law—still something ought to be said. It had for many reasons and in many cases become a common practice for a landowner (A) to convey his estate to some friend (B), upon the understanding that though that friend (B) was to be the legal owner of it, nevertheless (A) was to have all the advantages of ownership:—B was then said to hold the land 'to the use of A, or upon trust or in confidence for A.' This dodge, for such we may call it, was employed for a variety of purposes. Thus, for example, A has some reason to believe that he will be convicted of treason—during the Wars of the Roses many persons must have regarded this as highly probable—he desires to prevent his land being forfeited, he desires to provide for his family:—he conveys his land to B upon the understanding that B is to hold it upon trust for, or to the use of, him, A. Then A commits treason,—there is no land to be forfeited—the land is B's and B has committed no crime—still B is in honour bound to let A's heir have the use and enjoyment of the land. The same device was used for the purpose of evading the feudal burdens; the same device was used for defrauding creditors—the creditor comes to take A's land and finds that it is not A's but B's. The same device was largely used by the religious houses in order to evade the statutes of mortmain; they were prohibited from acquiring new lands—but there was nothing to prevent a man conveying land to X to be held by him upon trust for the monastery. The credit or blame of having invented these uses, or trusts, is commonly laid at the door of the religious houses. At any rate, in the early part of the fifteenth century this state of things became very common: B was the legal owner of the land, but he was bound in honour and conscience to let A have the profit of it and to do with it what A might direct. His obligation was as yet one unsanctioned by law—the courts of common law had refused to give A any remedy against B; they would not look behind B; B was the owner of the land and might do what he pleased with it regardless of A's wishes.

By this time (we are speaking of the early part of the fifteenth century) it had become so much the practice for the king's council to refer all petitions relating to civil cases to the chancellor—the king's chief legal adviser—that petitioners who wanted civil relief no longer addressed their complaints to the king, but addressed them to the chancellor, and the chancellor seems to have commonly dealt with them without bringing the matter before the king and council. Now this device of 'uses, trusts or confidences' of which we have just spoken provided the chancellor with a wide and open field of work. In Henry V's reign we find that the chancellor will enforce 'a use' (as it is called)—if B holds land to the use of A, the chancellor on the complaint of A will compel B to fulfil the understanding, will compel him to deal with the land as A directs—will put him in prison for contempt of court if he refuses to obey the decree:—though B is legally the owner of the land, it is considered unconscionable, inequitable, that he should disregard the trust that has been put in him—the chancellor steps in, in the name of equity and good conscience. No doubt this was convenient; if the chancellor had not given help, in course of time the common law courts would probably have had to modify their doctrines and to find some means of enforcing these 'uses.' But the common law was a cumbrous machine, and could not easily adapt itself to meet the new wants of new times. On the other hand the chancellor had a free hand, and it is by no means impossible that for a long time past the ecclesiastical courts (and the chancellor was an ecclesiastic) had been struggling to enforce these equitable obligations. At any rate when once it had become clear that the chancellor was willing and able to enforce them, a great mass of business was brought before him. It was found highly convenient to have land 'in use.' Parliament and the common lawyers do not like this equitable jurisdiction of the chancellor—sometimes they plan to take it away and to provide some substitute —but it justifies its existence by its convenience, and in the reign of Henry VII we must reckon the Court of Chancery as one of the established courts of justice, and it has an equitable jurisdiction; beside the common law there is growing up another mass of rules which is contrasted with the common law and which is known as equity.

The establishment of such a system of rules is an affair of time. Of the equity of the fifteenth century, even of the sixteenth, we know but little, for the proceedings in the chancery were not reported as those of the common law courts had been ever since the days of Edward I. But this fact alone is enough to suggest that the chancellors did not conceive themselves to be very strictly bound by rule, that each chancellor assumed a considerable liberty of deciding causes according to his own notions of right and wrong. Probably, however, the analogies of the common law and the ecclesiastical jurisprudence served as a guide. In course of time (this belongs rather to a subsequent stage of our history but should be mentioned here) the rules of equity became just as strict as the rules of common law—the chancellors held themselves bound to respect the principles to be found in the decisions of their predecessors—a decision was an authority for future decisions.

Thus it came about that until very lately, until 1875, we had alongside of the courts of common law, a court of equity, the Court of Chancery. I shall attempt to describe hereafter the sort of thing that equity was in the present century before the great change which abolished all our old courts and the sort of thing that it is at this moment. We are now dealing with past time and must think of the chancellors as having acquired a field of work which constantly grows. They are supplementing the meagre common law, they are enforcing duties which the common law does not enforce, e.g. they are enforcing those understandings known as uses or trusts, and they are giving remedies which the common law does not give, thus if a man will not fulfil his contract, all that a court of common law can do is to force him to pay damages for having broken it—but in some cases the Chancery will give the more appropriate remedy of compelling him (on pain of going to prison as a contemner of the court) to specifically perform his contract, to do exactly what he has promised. Then again the procedure of the Court of Chancery differed in many important respects from that of the courts of law; in particular, it examined the defendant on oath, it compelled him to disclose what he knew about the facts alleged against him. Popular the Court of Chancery never was, but the nation could not do without it—and so gradually our law acquired what for centuries was to be one of its leading peculiarities; it consisted of a body of rules known as common law supplemented by a body of rules known as equity, the one administered by the old courts, the other by the new Court of Chancery.

D. *General Characteristics of English Law.*

As time does not permit me to carry out the whole of my plan, I will this morning take notice of a few miscellaneous points which are of some importance[1]. And, in the first place, I turn to criminal law in general and the law of treason in particular.

At the head of all crimes stands high treason. In 1352 this crime was defined by a very famous statute. It recites that there had been doubts as to what was treason and proceeds to declare that treason is: if any compass or imagine the death of the king, his wife or their eldest son and heir, or violate the king's wife or his eldest unmarried daughter, or levy war against the king in his realm or be adherent to his enemies in his realm, giving to them aid and comfort in his realm or elsewhere, and if this shall be provably attainted by men of his [the accused person's] own condition. And if a man counterfeit the king's great or privy seal or his money, or bring false money into the realm, or slay the chancellor

---

[1] For the omitted topics see Analysis, p. xvii.

treasurer, or justices of the one bench or the other, justices 'being in their place doing their offices.' Omitting the rarer cases we may say that there are three main modes of treason: (1) imagining the king's death, i.e. forming an intention to kill the king and displaying this intention by some overt act, (2) levying war against the king, (3) adhering to the king's enemies. From 1352 to the present day this statute has formed the basis of the law of treason. However, in every time of political disorder new treasons have been created, which generally have been abolished when the danger has passed away. Thus in 1397, at the troubled close of Richard II's reign, it was made treason not merely to compass the death of the king, but to compass to depose him. Two years afterwards, when the House of Lancaster had succeeded to the throne, this statute was repealed. So in 1414 it was made treason to kill or rob persons having the king's safe-conduct; but this was repealed in 1442. No other new treason was created by statute during the fifteenth century; but the judges were discovering that the words of the Act of Edward III could be stretched. Then with the Reformation we have new statutory treasons: nine Acts of Henry VIII create new treasons—four directed against the supporters of the pope, five devoted towards maintaining the royal succession as it stood after the king's various marriages:—thus it was made treason to publish and pronounce by express writing or words that the king is an heretic, schismatic, tyrant, infidel or usurper; obstinately to refuse the oath abjuring the papal supremacy; to imagine to deprive the king of his title as supreme head of the church; to assert the validity of the king's marriage with Anne of Cleves. At the beginning of the next reign (1547) all these new treasons were swept away—but some new ones were created—in 1549 it was made treason for twelve or more persons to make a riot with intent to kill, take or kill any of the Privy Council. Then these were abolished in Mary's reign: but some new treasons were created, thus it was treason if any by express words shall pray that God would shorten the queen's life—or to affirm that Philip ought not to have the title of king jointly with the queen. Under Elizabeth, again, there were some new treasons, as for any Jesuit born in the queen's dominions to remain in the realm. But all along the statute of 1352 remained the normal measure of treason.

It was discovered, however, that its words were elastic enough. We have some extraordinary stories, for the truth of which I cannot vouch, of what under Edward IV was held treason by imagining the king's death. Thus Walter Walker, dwelling at the sign of the Crown, told his little child that if he would be quiet he would make him heir to the Crown—this was treason. Thomas Burdett had a white buck in his park, which in his absence was killed by Edward IV when hunting; Burdett expressed a wish that the buck were, horns and all, in the belly of him who counselled the king to do it—this was treason, though Markham, C. J., refused to be a party to so iniquitous a judgment[1]. Whether these stories be true or no, it certainly became established doctrine under the Tudors that an attempt manifested by some overt act to depose the king, or compel him by force to govern in a particular way, is an imagining of the king's death. In the case of Lord Essex, in 1600, the judges declared that in case a subject attempts to put himself into such strength that the king shall not be able to resist him, and to force and compel the king to govern otherwise than according to his own royal authority and direction, it is manifest rebellion, and in every rebellion the law intendeth as a consequence the compassing the death and deprivation of the king, as foreseeing that the rebel will never suffer the king to live or reign who might punish or take revenge of his treason or rebellion. So again the term 'levy war against the king' was extended so as to include riots for political objects; thus Coke holds that it is treason to assemble for the purpose of pulling down not this or that enclosure, but enclosures generally, and in the seventeenth century (1668) a riot for the purpose of pulling down brothels was held to be treason. Thus by the process of interpreting the statute of 1352 what came to be known as 'constructive treasons' were created. For the most part these interpretations remain law at the present day; it has become unusual to put this part of the law in force, riots are generally punished under statutes

---

[1] Stow's *Chronicle*, p. 430. See also Reeve, *History of English Law*, ed. Finlason, vol. III, p. 32 note.

merely as riots—but still in the main the so-called constructive treasons are still treasons.

One measure of improvement had been passed. A statute of 1552 (5 and 6 Edward VI) required that in cases of treason there should be two witnesses, who are to testify before the accused—our law had no such provision for the case of other crimes and has not at the present day.

Another statute of some importance was passed in 1494 (11 Hen. VII, c. 1): this provides in substance that obedience to a king *de facto* who is not also king *de jure* shall not after a restoration expose his adherents to the punishment of treason. This act carries on its face the stamp of the Wars of the Roses. It became of some importance in after times: it is said that Oliver Cromwell's supporters pressed him to accept the crown in order that they, in case of a restoration, might have that protection which this statute gives to those who obey a *de facto* king—obedience to a lord protector was not within the statute[1].

Next below treason stand the felonies. These consist (1) of the common law felonies, which consist of those crimes which had been considered as peculiarly grave at the time when our common law first took shape in the thirteenth century: homicide, arson, burglary, robbery, rape and larceny. Broadly speaking we may say that they were capital crimes, save petty larceny, stealing to less value than 12*d.* And (2) of certain crimes which have been made felony by statute—and which also are punishable by death. But in the course of the sixteenth century a new line is drawn through the felonies—some are clergyable, others are unclergyable. To go back for a moment to remote times: Henry II had failed in his attempt to bring the clergy under the ordinary criminal law of the realm. The clerk found guilty of crime could only be handed over to the bishop, who would do no more than degrade him from his orders. Owing perhaps to the excessive severity of the law, the doctrine got established that anyone who could read was a clerk: and thus any man who could read could commit felony with impunity

---

[1] Reference may also be made to Hallam, *Constitutional History*, vol. III, c. xv, and to Stephen's *History of Criminal Law*, vol. II, c. 23.

—women had no such immunity. As the Reformation approaches, statutes begin to interfere with this state of things. In 1496 a statute (12 Hen. VII, c. 7) deprived all but ordained clerks of benefit of clergy, in case of wilful murder. Other statutes follow which take away clergy from all men in particular cases—thus in 1536 certain piratical offences, in 1547 highway robbery, horse-stealing, stealing from churches, in 1576 rape—and so forth, and thus felonies are divided into two classes known as clergyable and unclergyable. Then again under an act of 1487 it was provided that a person not really in orders should have his clergy but once, and should be branded in the thumb, so that the fact of his conviction might be apparent. In 1622, just at the end of our period, women for the first time obtained a privilege equivalent to the benefit of clergy.

Below the felonies again stand the misdemeanours—minor crimes not punished with death, but punished in general by fine and imprisonment. Some are misdemeanours by common law; many are the outcome of statute. The term misdemeanour is gradually appropriated to describe these minor crimes. In the older books we find them called trespasses—but, as time goes on, trespass is the term appropriated to civil wrongs, while misdemeanour is appropriated to crimes not amounting to felony. The same act may be both trespass and misdemeanour; thus if A assaults B, this is a trespass against B, he can sue A for it in a civil court and recover damages, but also it is a misdemeanour; A can be indicted for it before a criminal court, and can be punished for it by fine or imprisonment, or both; the same act has civil consequences and penal consequences, it is a cause for civil action and also a punishable offence.

Treason, felonies, and misdemeanours are all indictable offences—every indictable offence falls under one of these three heads. Of criminal procedure we have already said something—the accused person is indicted by a grand jury and tried by a petty jury. The old procedure by way of appeal is fast dying out. In case of misdemeanour, but not of felony or treason, a person might be put upon his trial before a petty jury without any indictment by a grand jury, in case the king's attorney-general took up the case and filed what is called a criminal information. The origin of the criminal information is still obscure—it was occasionally employed under the Stuarts for the prosecution of political misdemeanours. The king's attorney-general informed the Court of King's Bench that the accused person had committed a crime, and then that person was subjected to trial before a petty jury. This was the procedure used in the famous case of Sir John Eliot, which will come before us hereafter.

An indicted person was not allowed to make his defence by counsel, and only by degrees was he gaining the power of calling witnesses to give evidence in his favour. In criminal cases the theory that the jury were witnesses had not entirely given way before the theory that they were judges of fact—the prisoner seems at all events to have had no power to compel unwilling witnesses to come and testify in his favour.

Then again below these indictable offences there was springing up a class of pettier offences, for which no general name had yet been found, offences which could be punished without trial by jury by justices of the peace. As yet they did not attract the attention of lawyers, and it is only in the eighteenth century that their number becomes considerable. However, from time to time a statute created such an offence —they were all of statutory origin: the justices of the peace themselves were of statutory origin. Thus taking up the statute book of James I, the following cases meet our eye— he who is guilty of tippling in an ale-house is to be fined ten shillings, the offence being proved by the oath of two witnesses before any one or more justice or justices of the peace; then, again, in 1604 we have a severe game law: it is made penal for persons who have not a certain amount of wealth to keep a greyhound or a setter—he who offends can be sent to gaol for three months on the offence being proved by two witnesses before two or more justices of the peace— and so forth. Parliament has undertaken to regulate divers trades and industries in a very elaborate way, and a breach of these regulations is often made an offence for which the offender can be subjected to a small fine or a short term of imprisonment by justices of the peace without any trial by jury. In short, what we in our day know as offences punishable upon summary conviction, as contrasted with indictable offences, are becoming not uncommon.

The justices of the peace have by this time become very important persons. They are attracting attention, and books are written about their duties, in particular that excellent book, Lambard's *Eirenarcha*. For every shire a number of country gentlemen are appointed justices of the peace by the king. The boroughs are often privileged by their charters to elect their own justices—sometimes the county justices have no jurisdiction over the borough, sometimes the county and borough justices have a concurrent jurisdiction: this depends on the wording of the borough charters. The duties of the justices have by this time become very miscellaneous. In the first place, four times a year they hold sessions of the peace for the county—quarter sessions—and there they exercise a high criminal jurisdiction: they can try almost all offenders: they try with a petty jury those who are indicted by a grand jury. In the second place, out of quarter sessions they exercise those statutory powers of summary trial of small offences of which I have just spoken. In the third place, we find already the germs of another function which has become very important in our own day, namely, the preliminary examination of prisoners accused of indictable offences. We now are accustomed to see a person accused of crime taken before a magistrate, who either commits him to prison until trial, or lets him out on bail until trial, or, holding that there is no case against him, dismisses the charge. The preliminary trial, for such we may call it, before the justice of the peace has grown up slowly—but we can see the germs of it in the sixteenth century. Ever since their institution in Edward III's reign the duty of seeing to the arrest of suspected persons has been passing out of the sheriff's hands into the hands of the justices—it is for the justices to bail the prisoner if by law he be entitled to bail, or to commit him to prison. Then acts of 1554 and 1555 directed the justices to examine the prisoner and his accusers, to put the examination into writing, and send it to the court before which the prisoner was to stand his trial. However, we must not suppose that this examination was very like that to which we are now accustomed. The object of it is not to hold an impartial inquiry into the guilt or innocence of the prisoner, and to set him free if there is no case against him, but rather to question him and to get up the case against him; the justice of the peace here plays the part rather of a public prosecutor than of a judge. Fourthly, the justices of the peace have acquired a control over the constabulary of the county. Arrests are now generally made not by the hue and cry as in old times, but by constables who are often empowered to make the arrest by warrants issued by the justices. The validity of such warrants is in Coke's day still a matter of some doubt, but in course of time their scope is widened. Often the first step in a prosecution is now an application to a justice for a warrant for the arrest of a suspected person. Fifthly, the justices have acquired powers which we may, I think, call governmental. In particular, the new Poor Law system instituted by the act of 1601 is placed under their control: so is the new highway system. Quarter sessions thus become not merely a criminal court for the county, but also a governmental assembly, a board with governmental and administrative powers. It thus takes the place of the old county court, which has sunk into being a court held by the sheriff or his under-sheriff for the decision of petty civil causes—chiefly cases of small debts. Parliamentary elections are still said to be held, as of old, in the county court; but probably a parliamentary election is the one occasion on which freeholders attend; the small judicial business of the court is transacted by the sheriff or his deputy.

A very noticeable feature in English history is the decline and fall of the sheriff, a decline and fall which goes on continuously for centuries. In the twelfth century he is little less than a provincial viceroy. All the affairs of the county: justice, police, fiscal matters, military matters, are under his control. Gradually he loses power: new institutions grow up around him and overshadow him. As to justice: first the king's itinerant judges, then the justices of the peace deprive him of judicial work: his county court becomes a court for petty debts: the functions of his tourn are now performed by justices of the peace with statutory power for punishing small offences: he may never be a justice in his own county. The control over the constabulary has slowly slipped from his fingers and is grasped by the justices of the peace. He is even losing his powers as a tax collector; parliament makes other provisions for this matter, and what he has still to do is very subordinate work. Lastly, he is no longer head of the county force, the *posse comitatus*. Under the Tudors the practice begins of appointing a permanent Lord-Lieutenant to command the military force, the militia it is coming to be called, of the shire.

One of the immediate causes of this decline and fall is that the sheriff has become an annual officer. In the fourteenth century the sheriff was well hated as the oppressor of the county: he had taken the county at a rent and tried to make the most out of it. Having failed, as we have before noted, in obtaining elected sheriffs, parliament set itself to obtain annual sheriffs, and ultimately succeeded. This took a series of statutes extending over near a century, from 1354 (28 Edw. III, c. 7) to 1444 (23 Hen. VI, c. 7). No matter what statute may say, the sheriffs remain in office ten and twelve years: however, in the fifteenth century this point is won. This seals the sheriff's fate: an officer who is to be the head of the police and of the military force cannot be an annual officer. He falls lower and lower until at last he has little more to do than to carry out the judgments of courts of justice—to seize the property of debtors, to seize their persons, to keep the county gaol, to hang felons. His office, once so profitable, becomes merely a burdensome, expensive task. The real work is done by an under-sheriff, but the sheriff is responsible for his conduct and must pay for his mistakes. Already in the seventeenth century it is difficult to get sheriffs —men avoid the office if they can; but they can be, and are, compelled to serve. The sheriff, I say, falls lower and lower in real power: his ceremonial dignity he retains—he is the greatest man in the county and should go to dinner before the Lord-Lieutenant.

The Lord-Lieutenant is originally a military officer; but

he becomes also the honorary head of the justices of the peace. From the first, one of the justices has been specially charged to keep the rolls, the records of the justices—he is the *custos rotulorum*. Generally the same person is appointed Lord-Lieutenant and *custos rotulorum*—and it is in the latter character rather than the former that he comes to be regarded as the first among the justices. Under Tudors and Stuarts the justices are kept well in hand by the king's council, and the Lord-Lieutenant is the person with whom the council carries on its correspondence. At least in later days justices of the peace are usually appointed on the recommendation of the Lord-Lieutenant, but he has no rule over them, he is merely the first among equals. The justices we remember are appointed by the king and hold their offices merely during his good pleasure. Still the office is regarded more and more as a permanent office from which a man should not lightly be dismissed.

Our last word shall be as to the constables. A constabulary in our modern sense, a force of men trained, drilled, uniformed, and paid there is not—our modern police force is very modern indeed. But it has become the law that every parish—or more strictly speaking every township—is bound to have its constable. The constable as we have said is originally a military officer—a petty officer in the county force; but then the county force, the *posse comitatus*, is as much concerned with making hue and cry after malefactors as with defensive warfare; this work falls more and more into the constable's hands, and as the militia becomes more military the constable becomes less military, more purely, in our terms, a police officer. In the seventeenth century he is still elected by his neighbours in the old local courts, in those districts in which such courts still exist: elsewhere and perhaps more generally he is appointed by the justices. Every capable inhabitant of the township can be appointed constable, unless there is some special cause for exemption. Remember that all, or almost all, of our old common law offices are compulsory offices—a person appointed cannot refuse them. To this day a man may be made sheriff or mayor of a borough against his will. Generally the person chosen as constable was allowed to find a respectable substitute—and this he could do for £5 or £10 : the office was annual. The constable had no salary, but he was entitled to demand certain fees for some part of his business. His chief business was the apprehension of malefactors, and for this purpose he was armed with certain powers additional to those which the ordinary man has : thus it was sometimes safe for a constable to make an arrest on suspicion, when it would not have been lawful for a private man. It is well to remember that the constable is an officer long known to our common law : a great part of the peculiar powers of the modern policeman are due to this—that he is a constable, and as such has all those powers with which for centuries past a constable has been entrusted by law. Gradually the constables come more and more under the control of the justices of the peace—in particular, it becomes less and less usual for arrests to be made without the warrant of justices, and in executing such warrants the constable has special protection.

Let me remind you in conclusion that there is one book for the vacation in which some profitable things may be found about Elizabethan justices and Elizabethan constables —if you cannot yet enjoy Lambard's *Eirenarcha*, you can at least enjoy Shallow and Silence, Dogberry and Verges.

PERIOD III.

Sketch of Public Law at the Death of James I.

THE next point at which we will take our stand is the death of James I and the quiet accession of Charles I. Let us once more remember that we are neglecting what certainly are the most obvious divisions of our history. The Tudor period is a distinct, well-marked period, and anyone who was writing the history of England would have to mark it as such. But we are not attempting any such task; rather we are purposely choosing unusual points of view in order that we may see familiar facts in new lights—our attempt is to supplement our books of history. And I want very much to bring out the fact that the history of our public law regarded as a whole is very continuous : the very greatest events that occur in it do not constitute what can fairly be termed revolutions. The Tudor monarchy is indeed something very different from the Lancastrian—the latter was a very limited monarchy, the former, if we regard its practical operation, seems almost unlimited. Still the difference, when we look into it, is found not so much in the nature of the institutions which exist as in the spirit in which they work : the same machinery of king, lords, commons, council, law courts, seems to bring out very different results. Again there is no one minute at which the change takes place—it is not like a change in law which must take place at some assignable date. The Tudor kingship differs from the Lancastrian kingship—but what are we to say of the two Yorkist kings? A distinguished modern historian prefers to make what he calls the New Monarchy begin not with Henry VII, but with

Edward IV—we have indeed an intermediate time. So again at the end of the period, before the death of James I, the relation of the parliament to the king is practically very different from what it was under Elizabeth: but the change has not been sudden; gradually for some time past parliaments have been becoming more independent: there has been no great change in the law, but there has been a slow change in the working of the law.

A. *Parliament.*

1. *Constitution of Parliament.*

There have been no very great changes in the constitution of parliament. We look first at the House of Lords. The parliaments of Henry VII had contained two archbishops, nineteen bishops, and twenty-eight abbots, in all forty-nine spiritual peers. After the dissolution of the monasteries in 1540 the abbots disappear, but six new bishoprics are founded, Oxford, Peterborough, Gloucester, Bristol, Chester and Westminster, and their occupants as a matter of course are summoned to the House of Lords though they hold no baronies. The bishopric of Westminster, however, had no long continuance: it was dissolved in 1550, so the number of spiritual peers fell to twenty-six. The number of the temporal peers does not increase rapidly during the Tudor reigns: a new peerage was seldom created, save when an old peerage was extinguished; during the whole period it fluctuates (on account of minorities and so forth) round fifty. Thus after the dissolution of the monasteries, the spiritual peers became a minority. A change comes with James I; he throws about peerages with a lavish hand: eighty-two lay peers sat in his first parliament, ninety-six in his last. Peers are now invariably created by letters patent definitely granting the dignity. The bishops have become distinctly royal nominees. Practically for a long time past the king had usually had his way about the appointment of bishops; his only competitor was the Pope—but the form of election by the cathedral chapters was maintained. In 1531 a statute, one of the first statutes directed against Rome, dealt with this matter: the king gives the chapter his licence to elect a bishop, but along with this *congé d'élire*, he sends letters recommending a candidate, and if he is not elected within twelve days then the king may appoint a bishop by letters patent. Capitular election is therefore but a solemn formality. In Edward VI's reign even the *congé d'élire* was abolished by statute; the bishops were to be appointed simply by the king's letters patent. The act which did this was of course repealed under Mary, and was not re-enacted by Elizabeth, who re-enacted the statute of her father's reign, which still is law. We observe therefore that over the constitution of the House of Lords the king has great powers : he practically appoints all the spiritual peers ; he can make as many new lay peerages as he pleases.

The House of Commons has considerably increased. By an act of 1535 (27 Hen. VIII, c. 26) Wales was brought fully within the system of English public law. Monmouthshire became an English county with two members, and two for the borough of Monmouth. Each of the twelve counties into which Wales was divided sent one member, and eleven Welsh boroughs sent each one member. By another act of 1543 (34 Hen. VIII, c. 13) two members were given to the county, two to the city of Chester ; thus this ancient palatinate was incorporated in the general body of the realm ; Durham remained unrepresented until after the Restoration. Thus thirty-one members were added. For a short time Calais was represented, but that last relic of the king's French possessions disappeared in Mary's reign. But this was by no means all : the king, we remember, had exercised the power of conferring on boroughs the right to send members. Hitherto this power had not been extensively used for the purpose of packing parliament, and Henry VIII used it but very sparingly : he gave the right to but five boroughs. Under Edward VI the power was lavishly used for political purposes : he thus added forty-eight members, Mary twenty-one, Elizabeth sixty, James twenty-seven. The number of burgesses in the lower house was thus vastly increased, and with it the power of the crown. When a new borough was created, and when a new charter was granted to an old borough, care was generally taken to vest the right of election not in the mass of the burgesses, but in a small select governing body—a mayor and council—nominated in the first instance by the crown, and afterwards self-elected. Meanwhile the qualification for the county franchise was not altered; it was still, under the act of Henry VI, the forty-shilling franchise, a qualification which, as the value of money fell, was becoming somewhat low and very capricious. The copyholder now often had just as valuable an estate as the freeholder; it was fully protected by the king's courts, and his ancient services had been commuted for money rents, which, as the value of money fell, became less and less burdensome—still he had no vote. Towards the end of our period we begin to see many signs that to be a member of parliament is coming to be an object of desire: contested elections are keenly fought. James I gave the right to be represented by two members to each of the two Universities.

The time has come when we can no longer speak of the clergy as forming for any practical purpose an estate of the realm. We have seen that they had neglected to obey the *praemunientes* clause, but had voted their taxes in their convocations. They still vote their taxes in convocation, but since 1540 the practice has grown up of passing an act of parliament to confirm the vote, as if it might be doubted whether the convocations could bind the clergy. We have to remember that the church can now no longer claim to be independent of the state. The clergy have been compelled to admit the royal supremacy. In 1534 the convocations were compelled to promise that they would make no new ecclesiastical canons without the king's licence and approval, and this principle was confirmed by act of parliament. Even then within the purely ecclesiastical sphere the convocations can do nothing without the royal assent, and the doctrine has grown up that such canons, even though they have the royal assent, are not binding on the laity[1].

2. *Privileges of Parliament.*

We have as yet said nothing of what are known as the privileges of parliament, but this subject can no longer be postponed, for it is becoming of first-rate importance. Under this head—privileges of parliament—it is, or was, usual to mix

---

[1] See pp. 511—3.

together several distinct matters.   Let us notice first two of
the usual sub-heads, (*a*) freedom of speech, and (*b*) freedom
from arrest.

(*a*)   During the Middle Ages the right of each house to
debate freely and without interference from the king or from
the other house seems to have been admitted and observed.
It is common in this context to mention the case of Thomas
Haxey; in 1397 a bill was laid before the commons and
accepted by them, which contained a bold attack on Richard II
and his courtiers.   The king took offence, demanded the name
of the person who introduced the bill; Haxey's name was
given up; the lords declared that anyone who stirred up
the commons to make such demands was a traitor; they
condemned Haxey to die, but the Archbishop claimed him as
a clerk, so he was not executed, and was soon afterwards
pardoned: in 1399, shortly after the accession of Henry IV,
the judgment was annulled on the petition of the commons
as contrary to their liberties.   One of the curious points about
this case is that Haxey, to all seeming, was not a member of
the House of Commons; it is thought that he may have been a
clerical proctor attending parliament under the *praemunientes*
clause.   Such an interference with the freedom of debate seems
to stand almost alone in our medieval history; but in 1376
Peter de la Mare, the Speaker, was thrown into prison for his
conduct in the Good Parliament, and remained in prison until
after the death of Edward III, when Richard released him;
again in 1453 the Speaker, Thomas Thorpe, was imprisoned—
the cause seems to have been his opposition to the Duke of
York; he was however prosecuted on a private pretext and
imprisoned.   This occurred during a prorogation.   When the
commons again met they demanded their Speaker—they
demanded of the king and lords that they might have their
ancient privilege; the lords however refused their petition
and determined that Thorpe should remain in prison.   Here,
though the real cause of arrest may have been conduct in
parliament, the arrest was made in a civil action under the
judgment of a court of law, and it bears therefore rather on
freedom from arrest than on freedom of speech.   A much
more important precedent occurred under Henry VIII in

1512. Strode, a member of the commons house, was imprisoned by the Stannary Court for having proposed certain bills in parliament to regulate the privilege of the tin miners. A statute was therefore passed declaring void the proceedings against him, and declaring in a general way that any proceedings against any member of the present parliament or of any future parliament for any speaking in parliament should be utterly void and of none effect. This was a statutory recognition of the freedom of debate. In Charles I's day the king's party had to contend that this was no general statute, but had reference only to the particular case of Strode; the judges in the famous case of Sir John Eliot upheld this contention; then in the Long Parliament the commons resolved that Strode's Act was a general act, and the lords concurred in this resolution: but all this still lies in the future. In 1541 for the first time the Speaker at the beginning of the session included freedom of speech as among the ancient and undoubted rights and privileges which the commons claimed of the king, and thenceforward it became the regular practice that the Speaker should demand this privilege. It is during the reign of Elizabeth that this privilege becomes a matter of contention, though the queen cleverly manages that disputes shall be compromised. In 1566 she prohibits the commons from discussing the succession to the crown, but then gives way, revokes the prohibition, and the commons are grateful. In 1571 Strickland, who has introduced some ecclesiastical bills, is called before the council and ordered not to appear again in parliament; the queen again gives way. In 1576 Peter Wentworth makes trenchant speeches about freedom of debate; the commons are against him, and themselves commit him to the Tower. The same fate befalls him in 1588. The commons acquiesce in the queen's command that they shall avoid religious topics. In 1593 she is very positive—members are only to vote 'Aye' or 'No,' and ecclesiastical matters are not to be discussed; one Morice is committed to prison for introducing an ecclesiastical bill. The commons seem during these years very submissive, especially about ecclesiastical matters: they seem to feel that the time is full of dangers, and that the queen understands religious matters better than they do themselves. With James on the throne circumstances have changed: in 1614, when he dissolves his second parliament, he commits four members to the Tower; in 1621 Sandys is committed, and James tells the commons pretty distinctly that their privileges exist by his sufferance. The result of this is the Protestation of 18 December, 1621: the commons declare that the privileges of parliament are the ancient and undoubted birthright of the subjects of England—that the commons may handle any subject, and enjoy a complete freedom of speech[1]. James sends for the journals of the commons, tears out the protest with his own hand, and dissolves parliament. On the whole, we see that when Charles comes to the throne there are plenty of materials for a conflagration.

(*b*) The topic of freedom from arrest is connected, as we have seen, with that of freedom of speech, but it is wider. Not only do members of parliament claim that they are not to be arrested for words spoken in the house, but they claim a general immunity from the ordinary law. We have here therefore to note that until very lately our law made a free use of imprisonment, not merely in criminal cases, but in civil cases also; a debtor against whom a judgment had been obtained could be imprisoned until he paid the debt—he could be taken in execution; but also a defendant in a civil action could very generally be imprisoned as soon as the action was begun, unless he found bail for his appearance in court. Now the lords from an early time seem to have enjoyed a considerable immunity from arrest except on criminal charges, and the representatives of the commons seem to have claimed a similar liberty during the session of parliament and for a certain time before and after the session reasonably necessary for their coming and going—exemption from arrest upon criminal charges, at least in case of treason, felony or breach of the peace, was not claimed. A statute of 11 Hen. VI, c. 11 (1433) gave some sanction to this privilege— he who assaulted a member attending parliament was to pay double damages. The privilege was invaded in Thorpe's case, and the invasion was sanctioned by the House of Lords: but the judges who were consulted expressed themselves very

---

[1] Prothero, *Constitutional Statutes and Documents*, p. 313.

positively as to its existence, and further made a declaration which was to be of great importance in the future, to the effect that the courts of law could not measure the privileges of parliament, these being matters which could only be determined by parliament itself. The houses, in particular the House of Commons, by degrees carried the principle further and further. In 1543, in Ferrer's case, they began a practice of sending their sergeant to deliver a member arrested for debt, and Henry VIII admitted the existence of the privilege. In 1575 they delivered one Smalley, a member's servant, arrested for debt. In 1603 they delivered Sir Thomas Shirley, who had been arrested for debt; this produced the passing of an act (1 Jas. I, c. 13), which, while it fully admitted and gave statutory sanction to the existence of the privilege, yet made certain provisions for the benefit of the creditor. In the seventeenth century this privilege grew to huge dimensions; it became almost impossible to get any justice out of a member of parliament, and limits had to be set to what had become an intolerable nuisance.

(*c*) Connected with these matters is the power (or if we please to call it so, the privilege) of each house to punish persons (whether they be members of it or no) for a contempt. Already in 1548 we find the commons committing John Storie, one of their members, to the Tower, probably for having spoken disrespectfully of Somerset the Protector. From 1581 we have Hall's case. Arthur Hall, member for Grantham, has published a book derogatory to the authority and power of the house; his punishment is severe; by an unanimous vote the commons expelled him, fined him 500 marks, and sent him to the Tower. In 1585 they expelled Dr Parry for having spoken too warmly. But they also took on themselves to punish those who were not members of the house. Not only did they commit to prison those who interfered with their immunity from arrest, but they also punished some who spoke against the house: thus in 1586 one Bland was fined for having used contumelious expressions against the House. But they have not been content with punishing persons who have insulted the house: in 1621 they condemned one Floyd, who had expressed his satisfaction in the success of the Catholic cause in Germany, to pay a fine of £1000 and to stand in the pillory.   The lords resented this assumption of judicial power, and the commons admitted that they were in the wrong—that they had no jurisdiction except when the privileges of their own house were infringed.   Floyd however did not profit by this: the lords condemned him to a fine of £5000 and whipping and branding, besides the pillory.   The story is disgraceful to both houses.   Here again it is evident enough that the constitution is not working peacefully; both the king and the two Houses of Parliament are ready to commit acts of very questionable legality.

3. *Jurisdiction of Parliament.*

This leads us to speak of the judicial functions of parliament—for it is sometimes reckoned among the 'privileges' of the House of Lords that the judicial power of parliament belongs to it.   Such a use of the word privilege is not very accurate or convenient—but nevertheless should be observed. This matter has already come before us in the past[1]; we have seen that the representatives of the commons never gained a share in the judicial work of the parliament—in 1 Hen. IV (1399) they had protested that they were not judges, and shortly before the occurrence of Floyd's case, after a search for precedents, they had come to the conclusion that they had no power to punish save for a contempt of their house; in Floyd's case they were reminded of these declarations and for a while attempted to evade them, but in the end gave way.   The judicial work of parliament, done by the House of Lords, we have on a former occasion brought under three heads.

(*a*)   As a court for correcting the errors in law of the ordinary law courts, the House of Lords did very little during the greater part of the period that is under our review: hardly a case of error is to be found between Henry IV and Elizabeth.   The infrequent sessions of parliament, the fact that the council had assumed a very wide power of judicature, may be the causes of this.   About 1580 however this, among other powers of the parliament, was revived; the lords began once more to hear cases of error, and a statute of 1585 distinctly

[1] p. 214 ff.

recognized their power to do so. A little later they began also to hear both civil and criminal cases as a court of first instance. For this they had but few precedents— it is said that they could find but one between 1403 and 1602. They did not, as we shall afterwards see, ultimately succeed in establishing their right to act as a court of first instance, but from about 1621 onwards until the civil war they did so act; and in the year 1625, at which we have placed ourselves, perhaps we ought to say that it is somewhat doubtful whether they may do so or no—here again is an open question raised by the renewed activity of parliament.

(*b*) That a peer charged with felony or treason ought to be tried by the House of Lords if that house be sitting, and if not then by the Court of the Lord High Steward is now an admitted principle; but such trials have been far from common.

(*c*) The procedure by way of impeachment has just been revived. It seems true to say that there is no case of an impeachment between that of the Duke of Suffolk in 1449 and that of Sir Giles Mompesson in 1621, which was at once followed by those of Mitchell, Bacon and others: Mompesson and Mitchell were commoners, impeached of fraud, violence and oppression. The impeachment of Bacon for bribery is still more important, for he, of course, was a minister of the king—he was chancellor. In 1624 the Earl of Middlesex, the Lord Treasurer, was impeached for bribery and other mis-demeanours. It is evident that parliament has unearthed a weapon of enormous importance. During the Tudor reigns, matters had stood differently; there was no talk of impeaching the ministers of Henry VIII, and when he had made up his mind to destroy an enemy or a too powerful servant he made use of an act of attainder. Cromwell had by the king's command obtained an opinion from the judges to the effect that by an act of attainder a man might lawfully be con-demned without a trial, though, they said, this would form a dangerous precedent. Under such an act it was that Cromwell himself perished. An act of attainder, you will remember, is in form not a judicial but a legislative act, a statute made by the king with the consent of lords and commons.

4. *Functions of the Commons in granting money.*

The function of originating money-bills is sometimes reckoned among the privileges of the House of Commons—at any rate it is the function of that house. We have seen it growing in the past—in particular we have noticed the state of things under Henry IV[1]. The matter becomes clearer during the period which we are now surveying. To grant subsidies is the function of the commons, but the grant requires the authority of a statute enacted by king, lords and commons. In 1593 the commons resent a message from the lords reminding them of the queen's want of money—the custom is that the offer of subsidies shall proceed from this house. But it is not until just after the end of our period that a definite formula is adopted which expresses the share of the two houses in the work. Under Elizabeth and James the lords and commons are sometimes said to grant the money—more frequently the commons are said to grant with the consent of the lords. In the first parliament of Charles I we get the formula that is still in use. An act is passed which recites that the commons have granted a tax, and then it is enacted by the king, by and with the advice and consent of the lords spiritual and temporal in parliament assembled and by the authority of the same, that the tax be imposed. It is not until after the Restoration that the commons begin to contend that the lords can make no alteration in a money bill, but must simply accept it, or simply reject it.

5. *Right to determine disputed Elections.*

The commons claim a right to determine all questions relating to the election of members of their house. Such questions in the past seem to have been determined by the king in council. Under Mary, however, we find the commons appointing a committee to inquire whether Mr Alexander Nowell, prebendary of Westminster, may be a member of this house; and it is declared next day that as he is a prebendary of Westminster and as such has a voice in convocation, he cannot be a member of this house, and that the queen's writ ought to issue for a new election. In 1586 the commons, in opposition to the queen, definitely insist that

[1] p. 182

it is for them to inquire into the circumstances of a disputed election—and from this time forward they frequently exercise this function and it seems admitted to be properly theirs[1].

6. *Parliamentary Procedure.*

It is during the period with which we are now dealing that the great outlines of parliamentary procedure, as we now know them, are drawn—the practice of reading bills three times, and so forth. Each house may manage its own affairs; there is no legislation as to its procedure, but gradually precedents are formed and respected and a mass of traditional rules is the outcome. In the House of Lords proxies are admitted; from an early time we find the king licensing bishops and barons to be present in parliament by proxy. In the sixteenth century it becomes the rule that the proxy must himself be a member of the house. This privilege of appointing a proxy seems never to have been extended to members of the lower house. Lords also who dissent from the action of the house exercise the right of entering formal protests upon its journals; this practice grows up in the sixteenth century; there is no similar practice among the commons. Each house conducts its business in privacy; the king, however, occasionally visits the House of Lords, and makes speeches there; a throne is set for him there; but his presence is not necessary, and in practice has become a somewhat rare event.

7. *Frequency and Duration of Parliaments.*

We can have little idea as to what a parliamentary constitution has really meant until we have considered how often parliament has met. We remember that under Edward IV and Henry VII parliaments have been becoming far less frequent than they were in the fourteenth and the first half of the fifteenth century. We remember also that there are statutes of Edward III yet unrepealed which seem plainly to mean that a parliament ought to be summoned at least once in every year.

Henry VIII in his thirty-eight years held nine parliaments. One of these, however, endured for nearly seven years—this

---

[1] The question was again raised in the Bucks. Election case (*Goodwin* v. *Fortescue* 1604). Gardiner, *History of England*, vol. I, pp. 167—70.

was the great Reformation parliament, which was summoned for 4 Nov. 1529 and was not dissolved until 4 April, 1536; it sat in 1529, 1530, 1531, 1532, 1533, twice in 1534 and once in 1536; a parliament with so long a life was a very new thing. There is only one long interval without a parliament, namely, from 22 Dec. 1515 to 15 April, 1523, an interval of more than seven years.

Edward VI reigned from 28 Jan. 1547 to 6 July, 1553—six and a half years. There were but two parliaments. The first was summoned for 4 Nov. 1547: it sat a second time in Nov. 1548, again in Jan. 1549, again in Nov. 1549, again in Jan. 1552, and it was dissolved 15 April, 1552—having lasted four and a half years. Another parliament was summoned for 1 March, 1553, and was dissolved at the end of the same month.

Mary reigned from 6 July, 1553 to 17 Nov. 1558—a little more than five years, and in those five years five parliaments were held.

Elizabeth reigned from 17 Nov. 1558 to 24 March, 1603—44½ years; ten parliaments were held. There is one long parliament and some long intervals. Parliament I lasted from 23 Jan. 1559 to 8 May, 1559. After an interval of three years and more Parliament II met on 11 Jan. 1563 and endured to 2 Jan. 1567, having lasted four years. After an interval of four years Parliament III met on 2 April, 1571, and lasted until May. Parliament IV lasted from 8 May, 1572 to 17 April, 1583—hard on eleven years. This is the longest parliament we have yet met with. But it held only three sessions—in 1572, 1576, 1581; it was prorogued on 24 April, 1581, and never met again for business, though by repeated prorogations its nominal life was prolonged for another two years. Parliament V was summoned for 23 Nov. 1584 and lasted with two sessions to 14 Sept. 1585. Parliament VI met on 15 Oct. 1586 and was dissolved on 23 March, 1588. Parliament VII met on 12 Nov. 1588 and was dissolved on 29 March, 1589. Then there is an interval of near four years. Parliament VIII met on 19 Feb. 1593 and was dissolved on 10 April, 1593. Another interval of four and a half years occurs. Parliament IX met on 24 Oct. 1597 and was dissolved on 9 Feb. 1598. Again there is an interval of four years. Parliament X met on 27 Oct. 1601 and was dissolved on 19 Dec. 1601. In March, 1603 the queen died.

James I reigned from 1 March, 1603 to 27 March, 1625—twenty-two years. Four parliaments were held. There is one long parliament of nearly seven years, and two considerable intervals. Parliament I met on 19 March, 1604 and was not dissolved until 9 February, 1611; it held five sessions, 19 March—7 July, 1604, 21 Jan.—27 May, 1606, 18 Nov. 1606—4 July, 1607, 9 February—23 July, 1610 and 16 Oct. 1610—9 February, 1611. After an interval of more than three years Parliament II, 'the addled Parliament,' met on 5 April, 1614 and was dissolved on 7 June of the same year. Six and a half years intervened. Then Parliament III met on 30 Jan. 1621 and was dissolved after two sessions on 8 Feb. 1622. Parliament IV met on 12 February, 1624 and was dissolved by the king's death on 27 March, 1625.

Looking back then we may say that although the statutes of Edward III's reign have not been observed and are very probably regarded as obsolete, parliaments have still been frequently holden. The king has not been able to get on for more than three or four years without calling a parliament. James managed to do without a parliament for near seven years, and he kept the same parliament alive for near seven years: for so long a life there was a precedent in Henry VIII's reign, and one of Elizabeth's parliaments lived eleven years. We find from what happens under Charles I that the nation would be content if a parliament met once in three years, and was never kept in existence for longer than three years. The long parliaments of Henry VIII, Elizabeth and James, no doubt had very important results—not only did they educate the commons to act together, but they familiarized the nation with the notion of parliament as of a permanent entity, in which the sovereignty of the realm might be vested: it is difficult to think of sovereignty being vested in so fleeting an affair as a medieval parliament, which exists for a month or two and disappears.

The principles which at the present day make it indispensably necessary that parliament should sit in every year were not yet in force; there was no standing army to be

legalized, and the king did not by any means always require a
grant of money in every year.   Each of the kings and queens
of our period has tonnage and poundage granted for life ;
parliament also often grants additional taxes which will
carry the king on for several years.   The king is now rich
as compared with his predecessors—the spoils of the monasteries have enriched him—the feudal sources of revenue are
very profitable—wardships, marriages and the like bring in
large sums.   Under James I there has been much talk of
buying up the king's feudal rights : the parties have not been
able to come to terms however—the king wanted in exchange
an income of £200,000.

B. *Relation of the King to Parliament.*

If now we look at the relation of the king to the parliament and ask whether parliament has lost or gained in power
we have a rather complicated answer to give.   On the one
hand there is no doubt that the parliaments of the Tudor
reigns, more especially those of Henry VIII's reign, were
extremely submissive, practically Henry could get them to
do what he wanted.   I need not instance his matrimonial affairs,
or the great religious revolution, the measures whereby he was
made head of the church ; the best instance is, I think, given
by the remission of his debts.   In the years between 1522–8 he
exacted heavy loans by a regular process not far removed
from compulsion; in 1529 parliament wiped out all the debts;
he had recourse to the same expedient in 1542, and the
parliament of 1543 whitewashed him once more.   It is
only towards the end of our period that parliament again
begins to act as an independent check upon the king, to
assert a will of its own; the parliaments of Elizabeth grumble,
the parliaments of James I more than once resist him and
defeat him.   How it came about that the earlier parliaments
had been so very tractable, it is hardly for us to inquire, for
this question lies beyond the legal domain ; the remembrance
of past anarchy had to do with it, the religious difficulties
had to do with it, foreign affairs had to do with it, the nation
desired a time of peace and of strong government.   We must,

I think, add that the nation was thoroughly frightened by Henry. But what does demand our notice is that this very tractability of parliaments serves in the end to save and to strengthen the parliamentary constitution; parliament is so tractable that the king is very willing that king in parliament should be recognized as supreme—it strengthens his hands that what he does should be the act of the whole nation. Let us then look at some of the more extraordinary exercises of this sovereign power of king in parliament. We have already referred to the acts which blotted out King Henry's debts— that surely is an extraordinary exercise of power. We have also spoken of acts of attainder—these also are extraordinary; without any pretence of legal trial a statute may be passed condemning a man to death, and no court of law will call its validity in question. But now look at the royal succession. Thrice over during Henry's reign was the succession arranged by act of parliament; the king's marriage with Katherine of Aragon was declared void, and his marriage with Anne Boleyn was declared valid; then the marriage with Anne Boleyn was declared void; then again both Mary the daughter of Katherine, and Elizabeth the daughter of Anne were treated as legitimate and placed in the succession; then in default of the heirs of his body, Henry was to have power to leave the crown by will to anyone he pleased—to anyone, not necessarily a member of the royal house. It is fairly certain that Henry did exercise this power given him by act of parliament, and devised the crown on the failure of the issue of his three children to the heirs of the body of his younger sister Mary, Duchess of Suffolk, postponing to them the descendants of his elder sister Margaret, Queen of Scots. In the first year of Elizabeth it was enacted by parliament that if any person should affirm that the queen could not with the assent of parliament make laws to settle the descent of the crown, he should be deemed a traitor. There can be no doubt that there was a very strong sentiment in favour of strict hereditary descent—that seems the explanation of the undisputed succession of James I. In all probability he succeeded to the throne in defiance of a will duly executed by Henry VIII under the power given to him by act of parliament ; nothing however seems to have been said of the will, and the house of Suffolk made no claim. James, as it seems to me, had good reason for supposing that he reigned by virtue of strict hereditary right ; he and his successors had at least an excuse for believing that such right could not be overridden by act of parliament. Still, as we have just seen, there were important precedents the other way—parliament had repeatedly and successfully regulated the succession to the throne.

A still better illustration, however, at once of the actual tractability of parliaments and of the theoretic supremacy of king in parliament is afforded by an act of 1539, which has been called the *Lex Regia* of England, and the most extraordinary act in the Statute Book—power was given to the king to make proclamations with the advice of his council, or a majority of his council, to make proclamations which should have the force of statutes ; the punishment for disobedience might be fine or unlimited imprisonment; it was not to extend to life, limb, or forfeiture. This act was repealed in the first year of Edward VI—you will at once see the importance of its enactment and its repeal; they seem distinctly to confirm the doctrine that the king is not supreme, king and parliament are supreme; statute is distinctly above ordinance or proclamation; statute may give to the king a subordinate legislative power, and what one statute has given another statute may take away.

There is a yet stronger illustration and this, though it is a rather elaborate story, is worth giving, for it is not generally known. The accession of an infant in the person of Edward VI had been foreseen. His father was given power by statute to appoint governors. He appointed his sixteen executors to form a governing council. They, when Henry was dead, elected Somerset to be Lord Protector, and very soon allowed him to take the whole power into his own hands. Now in 1536 Henry had procured the passing of a statute (28 Hen. VIII, c. 17) which was to enable future kings to rescind any acts of parliament that should be passed while they should be under the age of twenty-four. This act however was at once repealed on the accession of Edward VI, by a statute of 1547 (1 Edw. VI,

c. 11), the requisite royal assent being given by the Protector and the governing council.   The reason for revoking the act of 1536 was this, that it was drawn in such very wide terms that had Edward attained the age of twenty-four and revoked the statutes made while he was under that age, it might well have been contended that these statutes were not merely null and void for the future, but that they had all along been null and void, so that everything done under them which could not be justified by the common law would have been rendered illegal *ex post facto*.   The act of 1547 repealed this act; it gave the king power when he should attain twenty-four to rescind the statutes passed while he was under that age, but declared that such a repeal was not to have retrospective force.   On the whole, I know of no acts of parliament which better illustrate our notion of the absolute supremacy of a statute. A statute gives a king power to revoke statutes and even render them void *ab initio*; this cannot prevent another statute being passed during that king's minority (his assent being given by a council of regency which itself is the creature of a statute), which statute may repeal or modify the previous statute that gave a power of revoking statutes. The power of statute-making cannot be curtailed; no parliament can bind the hands of its successors with any legal bonds.

We might multiply illustrations.   Probably it was in the domain of religion that the men of the time saw what seemed to them the most conclusive proofs of the sovereignty of king in parliament.   Throughout the Middle Ages there was at least one limitation set to temporal sovereignty; it had no power in spiritual matters; the church was an organism distinct from the state.   But now statutes have gone to the very root of religion; the orthodox creed is a statutory creed and that creed has been changed more than once. Thus statute has given the most conclusive proof of its power.

Not only however do we find the supremacy of king in parliament admitted in fact, we find it proclaimed in theory. The Tudor kings are well content that this should be so. The following emphatic and remarkable passage occurs in

'The Commonwealth of England and the manner of government thereof'—a book published in 1589 by Sir Thomas Smith who was Secretary of State to Queen Elizabeth: 'The most high and absolute power of the realm of England consisteth in the parliament....That which is done by this consent is called firm, stable and *sanctum*, and is taken for law. The parliament abrogateth old laws, maketh new, giveth orders for things past and for things hereafter to be followed, changeth rights and possessions of private men, legitimateth bastards, establisheth forms of religion, altereth weights and measures, giveth forms of succession to the crown, defineth of doubtful rights, whereof is no law already made, appointeth subsidies, tailes, taxes, and impositions, giveth most free pardons and absolutions, restoreth in blood and name as the highest court, condemneth or absolveth them whom the prince will put to that trial. And to be short, all that ever the people of Rome might do either in *centuriatis comitiis* or *tributis*, the same may be done by the parliament of England which representeth and hath the power of the whole realm, both the head and body. For every Englishman is intended to be there present, either in person or by procuration and attorneys, of what preeminence, state, dignity or quality soever he be, from the prince, be he king or queen, to the lowest person of England. And the consent of the parliament is taken to be every man's consent[1].' That is a very memorable passage; the following century, we may say, was one long struggle as to where sovereignty should be, should it be in king and parliament or in king alone. There can be little doubt, I think, which party had history on its side, not merely remote history, but the history of the recent Tudor reigns; the absolute supremacy of the statute-making body, of king and parliament, had been both admitted in fact and acknowledged in theory.

Still it must candidly be admitted that the extent of the royal power was in many directions very ill defined. Before speaking of this it is necessary to refer to the council. The Tudor reigns are, we may say, the golden age of the council:

[1] Smith, *De Republica Anglorum*, ed. L. Alston (with a preface by F. W. Maitland), Cambridge, 1906, Bk. II, c. 1.

the council exercises enormous powers of the most various kinds; but it is not an independent body—as against the king it has little power or none at all, and when in the case of Edward VI the king is a boy, then the council raises up above itself a Lord Protector, who acts pretty much as a king *de facto*. In 1553 the council consists of forty members ; there are but four bishops and fourteen temporal peers; the rest are commoners, among whom are the two king's secretaries, who before the end of our period have gained the title 'the king's secretaries of state.' The large number of the commoners marks a great change; the government of the realm has slipped out of the hands of the nobles. In 1536 it is matter of complaint that the councillors are of humble birth. The king chooses capable commoners who will serve him well and who will not be independent. Again, the ecclesiastical members of the council have lost their independence ; if they represent the church, still it is a church of which the king is head. On the whole, the council seems to be just what the king would wish it to be, and he consults it or not, as pleases him best; many important negotiations Henry does not bring before his council at all. But to the king a council of able servants is a source of strength.

We must now look at the powers wielded by the king with the assistance of his council. We will bring the subject under four heads—(1) legislation, (2) taxation, (3) judicature, (4) administration.

(1)   It certainly seems to have been the common opinion that the king had a certain ordaining power. Regard being had to the past it was difficult to deny this; but what were its limits? Henry VIII, we have seen, obtained from parliament a statute giving to his proclamations issued with the consent of the majority of his council the force of statute law[1]. But then this act was repealed. Elizabeth, we find, freely issues proclamations : thus anabaptists are banished from the realm, Irishmen are commanded to depart into Ireland, the exportation of corn, money, and various commodities is prohibited. A proclamation in 1580 forbids the erection of houses within three miles of London under pain of imprisonment. The council frequently issued proclama-

[1] See p. 253.

tions to restrain the importation of books, and to regulate their sale—thus a censorship of the press was established. James I followed the example of his predecessor—in particular he issued frequent proclamations to forbid the increase of London. In 1610 the commons protested—' it is the indubitable right of the people of this kingdom not to be made subject to any punishment that shall extend to their lives, lands, bodies or goods, other than such as are ordained by the common laws of this land, or the statutes made by their common consent in parliament. Nevertheless it is apparent both that proclamations have been of late years much more frequent than heretofore, and that they are extended not only to the liberty, but also to the goods, inheritances and livelihood of men, some of them tending to alter some parts of the law and to make a new; other appointing punishments to be inflicted before lawful trial and conviction,' and so forth. ' By reason whereof there is a general fear conceived and spread among your majesty's people, that proclamations will, by degrees, grow up and increase to the strength and nature of laws[1].' To all this, and there is more of it, the only answer is that the proclamations shall go no further than is warranted by law.

Before this answer was given the great oracle of the law had been consulted. Coke, then Chief Justice of the Common Pleas, was summoned to the council, and the question was put to him, whether the king by proclamation might prohibit the erection of new buildings in London and the making of starch from wheat. He was pressed to answer in the affirmative. He refused to answer without consulting his brethren. He consulted with three judges, and they answered that the king cannot by his prerogative create any offence which was not one before, but the king may by proclamation admonish all his subjects that they keep the laws and do not offend them upon punishment to be inflicted by the law—neglect of a proclamation aggravates the offence; lastly, if an offence be not punishable in the Star Chamber, the prohibition of it by proclamation cannot make it so. This probably was sound law—that is to say, there was a distinct precedent for it

---

[1] *Somers' Tracts*, vol. II, p. 162. The protest is also printed by Hallam, *Constitutional History*, vol. I, pp. 327—8.

coming from the middle of the Tudor period. In Mary's reign the judges had delivered this opinion : 'The king, it is said, may make a proclamation *quoad terrorem populi*, to put them in fear of his displeasure, but not to impose any fine, forfeiture, or imprisonment : for no proclamation can make a new law, but only confirm and ratify an ancient one.' But though James I had the opinion of his judges against him, still he went on issuing proclamations. It is difficult for us to realize the state of things—that of the government constantly doing what the judges consider unlawful. The key is the Court of Star Chamber—the very council which has issued these proclamations enforces them as a legal tribunal, and as yet no one dares resist its judicial power.

(2) But of course it is one thing to say that the king has no general legislative power and another thing to say that there are no matters about which he can make valid ordinances: thus it may be in his power to regulate the importation and exportation of goods. We are thus led to speak of the taxing power. The highroad of direct taxation had long been barred to the king by very distinct statutes ; the case of customs duties was almost equally clear. It is said, and I believe with truth, that between the accession of the House of Lancaster and the reign of Mary there is no precedent for any duty imposed by the king. Edward IV had recourse to benevolences, Henry VII and Henry VIII to forced loans— but they did not attempt to impose taxes on merchandise[1]. However in 1557 Mary set a duty on cloths exported beyond seas, and afterwards a duty on the importation of French wines. It seems probable that at the beginning of Elizabeth's reign the opinion of the judges was taken by the council as to the legality of these impositions, and that their opinion was not favourable. The queen however did not abandon the impost, and she herself set an impost on sweet wines. James imposed a duty on currants over and above the tax which was set on them by the statute of tonnage and poundage. Bate refused to pay. The Court of Exchequer decided in the king's favour. It is difficult to understand the judgment as an exposition of law ; rather, I think, we must say that the

---

[1] Henry VIII was given power in 1534 (26 Hen. VIII, c. x) during his 'life natural' to repeal or revive acts relating to the importation and exportation of merchandise.

king succeeded in obtaining from the barons of the Exchequer
a declaration that there is a large sphere within which there
is no law except the king's will. 'The matter in question is
material matter of state, and ought to be ruled by the rules of
policy; and if so, the king has done well to execute his extraordinary power. All customs, old or new, are effects of
commerce with foreign nations; but commerce and affairs
with foreigners, war and peace, the admitting of foreign coin,
all treaties whatsoever, are made by the absolute power of the
king. The king may shut the ports altogether; therefore he
may take toll at the ports.' This seems the main thought of
the judgment. It seems that the opinion of the two Chief
Justices, Popham and Coke, was taken, though the case did
not come before them judicially. They would not go nearly so
far as the barons of the Exchequer. They said that the king
cannot set impositions upon imported goods at his pleasure,
but that he may do so for the good of the people—thus if
foreign princes set taxes on English goods the king may
retaliate. Their doctrine seems to have been that the king
may not set impositions merely for the sake of revenue, but
that he may do so for other ends, as for the protection of
English merchants : obviously this is an unstable doctrine.

The House of Commons in 1610 took up the matter. The
lawyers in that house, in particular Hakewill, very learnedly
disputed the judgment of the Exchequer, relying on the
statutes of the fourteenth century, and on the cessation of any
attempts to tax merchandise without parliamentary authority
from the reign of Richard II to the reign of Mary. They
carried a bill enacting that no imposition should be set
without the consent of parliament, but the lords rejected it.
The immediate consequence had been that in 1608 the king,
having the judgment in Bates's case at his back, issued a book
of rates imposing heavy duties upon almost every article of
merchandise. The subject was resumed in the short parliament of 1614; the commons passed a unanimous vote denying
the king's right of imposition. They refused to grant any
subsidy until this grievance should be redressed. James
dissolved the parliament[1].

[1] See Prothero, *Statutes and Constitutional Documents* (1559—1625), pp. 340—53.

A more serious step was now necessary if money was to be obtained. The king had recourse to benevolences. Letters were written to the sheriffs directing them to call upon persons of ability for contributions. The unrepealed statute of Richard III against 'exactions called benevolences' stood in the way. Still it was difficult to argue that the king may not accept a perfectly voluntary gift of money. To the end of the reign the impositions are exacted, though the commons from time to time protest against them.

The legal ground that they occupied was certainly strong, but we must not exaggerate its strength. They were obliged to concede the existence of prerogatives which, at least in our eyes, amount to a prerogative of extorting money. For instance, Hakewill in his famous argument over Bates's case admits that the king can debase the coinage, and as a matter of fact the kings have done this over and over again. The king's power over the coinage was certainly very great. Sir Matthew Hale, writing after the Restoration, is still of opinion that the king may debase the coinage. It is legal, though dishonourable. Even Blackstone is not certain that it is illegal[1]. This is one instance of the admitted powers of the king, powers whereby he could increase his revenue. Another instance, and one which becomes of importance in James's reign, is afforded by monopolies.

From the Conquest onwards the kings had exercised the right of granting and selling many valuable privileges—to name but one, though an important matter,—it was to charters purchased from the kings that the towns owed their privileges. Not unfrequently such privileges included privileges of trading —the right to hold a fair or a market could be granted by the king. So could the right to take toll for merchandise passing through the town. Such grants were common, and do not seem to have been in the least unpopular; it was the object of every town to obtain as comprehensive a grant as possible. Under the Tudors the practice of granting rights of exclusive trading assumed enormous proportions : letters patent giving the patentee the exclusive right of selling became common, and some very necessary articles such as salt, leather,

[1] Hale, *Pleas of the Crown*, vol. I, p. 194. Blackstone, *Commentaries*, vol. I, c. 7.

and coal had been made the subject of monopolies. In 1597 the commons begin to protest; these monopolies have become a grievous burden. In 1601 a bolder attack is made, and Elizabeth was induced to promise that the existing patents should be repealed and no more issued. The commons however do not seem to have been prepared to assert that all monopolies were illegal, or to separate those which were illegal from those which were not. James, disregarding Elizabeth's promise, made a copious use of monopolies for the purpose of obtaining a revenue. The commons grew bolder, asserted the illegality of all monopolies, and in the last parliament of the reign a declaratory act was passed—an act declaring not merely that grants of monopoly were to be illegal in the future, but also that they had been illegal in the past[1]. This is the greatest victory of the commons during the reign of James. An exception was made in favour of letters patent granting the exclusive right of using for a term of fourteen years any new manufacture to the first and true inventor thereof. Our modern patent law is the outcome of this exception.

(3) It is by means of the judicial power of the Court of Star Chamber that the king enforces his proclamations. We have already said something of this court[2]. Let us remember that a statute of 1487 (3 Hen. VII, c. 1) gave authority to certain persons to punish certain crimes. These persons are the chancellor and treasurer of England and the keeper of the privy seal, or two of them, calling to them a bishop and a temporal lord of the king's council and the two chief justices, or in their absence two other justices. The offences that they are to punish are riots, unlawful assemblies, bribery of jurors, misdoing of sheriffs, and some others which we may describe as interferences with the due course of justice. It is evidently contemplated by the statute that the accused persons will not be tried by jury. The statute does not mention the Star Chamber, but that is a room which the council has long used.

Now a difficulty meets us : long before the end of our period there exists what is known as the Court of Star Chamber. This however does not exactly correspond to the

---

[1] 21 James I, c. 3. The Act did not apply to monopolies. Gardiner, *History of England*, vol. v, p. 233, vol. VIII, pp. 71—5.

[2] See pp. 218—21.

court described by the statute of 1487—and that in two respects. (*a*) All the members of the council seem to have been members of it. James himself, at least upon some occasions, sat there in person and himself passed sentence. As many as twenty-five councillors are sometimes found sitting there. It had a great deal of work to do, and in term time sat three days a week. This brings us to the second point. (*b*) It did not confine itself to dealing with the crimes specified in the statute of 1487. Its jurisdiction over crime was practically unlimited, or limited only by this—that it did not pass sentence of death. We know it best as dealing with what may be called political crimes—sedition and the like ; but it dealt also with commoner offences—robbery, theft, and so forth. It dealt with some misdoings for which the common law had as yet no punishment, in particular with libels.

Now was this the court created by the statute of Henry VII? Under Charles I (for we must anticipate this much) the opinion had gained ground that it *was*, that consequently whatever it did beyond the sphere marked out by that statute was an unlawful usurpation of jurisdiction. When the time for abolishing it had come, it was abolished on this score. But the general opinion seems now to be that the jurisdiction of this Court of Star Chamber was in truth the jurisdiction which the king's council had exercised from a remote·time, despite all protests and all statutes made against it. The act of 1487 constituted a committee of the council to deal with certain crimes; this however did not deprive the council itself of any jurisdiction that it had. This committee seems to have been in existence as late as 1529, for a statute of that year (21 Hen. VIII, c. 20) adds to the committee the lord president of the council, an officer recently created ; but before the end of Henry VIII's reign this statutory committee seems to disappear, it is merged in the general body of the council.

There can, I think, be no doubt that under Elizabeth and James this court was regarded as perfectly legal—though there may have been doubts as to how it came to be legal, and it is said that Plowden, the great lawyer, asserted that it derived all its lawful authority from the statute of Henry VII. Coke speaks of it with great respect, and does not seem to share Plowden's doubts: 'It is the most honourable court (our parliament excepted) that is in the Christian world[1].' A statute of 1562 (5 Elizabeth c. 9) enumerates the King's Court of Star Chamber along with the Chancery as one of the known courts of the realm. The Chancery had by this time become a fully recognized court of justice, administering a mass of rules known as equity, and yet the origin of its jurisdiction was as obscure as that of the jurisdiction of the council in the Star Chamber: if there were ancient statutes against the one there were ancient statutes against the other also. There can, I think, be little doubt that the Star Chamber was useful and was felt to be useful. The criminal procedure of the ordinary courts was extremely rude; the Star Chamber examining the accused, and making no use of the jury, probably succeeded in punishing many crimes which would otherwise have gone unpunished. But that it was a tyrannical court, that it became more and more tyrannical, and under Charles I was guilty of great infamies is still more indubitable. It was a court of politicians enforcing a policy, not a court of judges administering the law. It was cruel in its punishments, and often had recourse to torture. It punished jurors for what it considered perverse verdicts; thus it controlled all the justice of the kingdom. The old process of attaint, of which we have before spoken, had long gone out of use, but in the Star Chamber the jurors had to fear a terrible tribunal which would resent a verdict against the king.

Other courts of a similar kind closely connected with the council had come into existence in divers parts of England. The Council of the North was erected by Henry VIII after the Catholic revolt of 1536 without any act of parliament[2]. It had a criminal jurisdiction in Yorkshire and the four more northern counties as to riots, conspiracies and acts of violence. It was also given a civil jurisdiction of an equitable kind, but in Elizabeth's reign the judges of the common law courts pronounced this illegal. Their doctrine seems to have been that without act of parliament the king might create a new

[1] *Institutes*, Part IV, cap. 5. See Prothero, *Statutes and Constitutional Documents* (1559—1625), pp. 401—3.

[2] See Lapsley, 'The Problem of the North' in *American Historical Review*, vol. V, pp. 440—66 (1900).

court to deal with matters known to the common law, but that he could not create a new court of equity. But its criminal jurisdiction the Council of the North maintained, and this it seems to have exercised according to the course of the Star Chamber.

The Court of the Council of Wales seems to have arisen under Edward IV, but its authority was acknowledged and confirmed by a statute of 1542 (34 Hen. VIII, c. 26). It was to have authority in Wales and the Welsh marches[1]. Under this latter denomination it seems to have considered that the four counties of Gloucester, Worcester, Hereford, and Salop, were included. We hear of protests against this extension under James I, and according to Coke the twelve judges held that these four counties were not within the scope of the council's power. However, the opinions of the judges were in vain : the question what was meant by the marches of Wales was a difficult question. In considering the position of these courts it is desirable to remember that the old local courts had become very useless as judicial tribunals; they could only entertain personal actions in which no more than forty shillings was claimed, and forty shillings had become a small sum. That concentration of justice in the Westminster courts of which we have so often spoken was producing evil effects—it made litigation about small matters very slow and very costly ; in many instances it must have amounted to a denial of justice. So there was room enough for new local courts. Men in general seem to have been very willing that these new local courts should exist, and the opposition of the common lawyers was to a large extent a selfish professional opposition, though it served in course of time to maintain the authority of parliament against stretches of the prerogative.

There was, however, one new court of great importance, whose powers they were inclined rather to magnify than to minimize—this was the Court of High Commission[2]. Time does not permit us to investigate the great religious changes of our period ; but, of course, the Reformation has an important

[1] For further information see Miss C. A. S. Skeel, *The Council in the Marches of Wales* (London, 1904).

[2] For the High Commission Court see Prothero, *Statutes and Constitutional Documents*, Intr.

legal side, it is effected by acts of parliament. The measures of Henry VIII and those of Edward VI placed the church under the headship of the king, he was recognized as head of the church. These measures were repealed by Mary. Most, but not all of them, were revived by the Act of Supremacy (1 Eliz. 1); she did not revive the act which asserted the king's headship of the church[1]. The ecclesiastical courts continued to exercise their jurisdiction, but above them was raised a court of royal commissioners. The Act of Supremacy empowers the queen to appoint any number of persons, being natural born subjects, to exercise under Her Majesty all manner of jurisdiction in anywise touching ecclesiastical matters. The words of the act (sec. 18) are extremely large, and the commissions issued under it became wider and wider. In 1583 the power of the commissioners has become very ample—there were forty-four commissioners, most of them laymen. In many matters affecting religion they had a discretionary power of fine and imprisonment; these powers could be exercised by any three members of the body, one of them being a bishop. Now this court had a distinctly statutory origin; there could be no ground whatever for questioning its legality. But in this instance the common lawyers were on the side of the crown; if they disliked the prerogative when it interfered with the course of the common law, they magnified it when exercised about ecclesiastical matters; they were glad enough to see their old rival, the spiritual jurisdiction, the humbled servant of the temporal power; they held that so absolute was the royal supremacy over all religious affairs, that even the ample words of the Act of Supremacy did not express its full extent; the high commissioners might do things that were not expressly authorized by the statute book. A little later, the lawyers, or at least some of them, turned round. Coke held that the act of Elizabeth did not give the commissioners power to fine or imprison the laity—the sole weapons that it could use were the old ecclesiastical weapons of censure, penance, excommunication. However, this power was *de facto* maintained, and was largely and oppressively

[1] For Elizabeth's title see Maitland, *Defender of the Faith, and so forth*, *English Historical Review*, Jan. 1900.

used under Charles I. To whatever quarter we look we see that he inherited a great number of difficulties in church and state—lawyers and parliaments were beginning to call in question the legality of the institutions whereby the Tudors had governed the country.

Again commissions had been exercised for the trial of offenders by martial law. In tracing their history we have to notice a verbal confusion. From a very early time the king's constable and marshall were the leaders of the king's army. These offices became hereditary and of no very great importance. However, as late as Edward I, it is the fact that Bohun and Bigod are the constable and marshall, which enables them to paralyze the king, by refusing to lead the army to France. The marshall's office is still in existence; the Duke of Norfolk is Earl Marshall of England. The constable's office fell into the royal family on the accession of the House of Lancaster —occasional grants of the office were made; but after Henry VII's time, the office seems only to have been granted for special occasions. Now as leaders of the army the constable and marshall seem to have had jurisdiction over offences committed in the army, especially when the army was in foreign parts, and in the fourteenth century we hear complaints of their attempting to enlarge their jurisdiction. Now as a matter of etymology, *marshall* has nothing whatever to do with *martial*—the marshall is the master of the horse—he is *marescallus*, *mareschalk*, a stable servant—while of course martial has to do with Mars, the god of war. Still, when first we hear of martial law in England, it is spelt indifferently *marshall* and *martial*, and it is quite clear that the two words were confused in the popular mind—the law administered by the constable and marshall was martial law. Towards the end of the Wars of the Roses we find very terrible powers of summary justice granted to the constable. In 1462 Edward IV empowers him to proceed in all cases of treason, 'summarily and plainly, without noise and show of judgment on simple inspection of fact.' A similar patent was granted to Lord Rivers in 1467. They show something very like a contempt for law—the constable is to exercise powers of almost unlimited extent, all statutes, ordinances, acts and restrictions to the contrary notwithstanding. This illegal tribunal, for such we may well call it, came to an end after the accession of the House of Tudor—the king had no need of it ; but an evil precedent had been set. Mary seems to have executed some of those taken in Wyatt's insurrection without regular trial. In 1588, when the Armada was approaching, Elizabeth issued a proclamation declaring that those who bring in traitorous libels or papal bulls against the queen, are to be proceeded against by martial law. In 1595 there had been riots in London ; the queen granted a commission for trying and executing the rebels according to the justice of martial law. There seems to be another precedent for such a commission in 1569, after the insurrection of the northern earls, when six hundred persons were, it is said, executed by the Earl of Sussex. James on several occasions issued such commissions : in 1617, 1620, 1624 ; they empower the commissioners to try men by the law called the law martial—even those who have been guilty of ordinary felonies. There can, I think, be no doubt that, according to the opinion of the lawyers of the time, such commissions were illegal. The government may put down force by force—but when there is no open rebellion, or when the rebellion is suppressed, it has no authority to direct the trial of prisoners, except in the ordinary courts and according to the known law of the land. As to what was this 'law called martial law' we know little, and probably there is little to be known ; it meant an improvised justice executed by soldiers.

It may seem to us very strange that there should have been in full play tribunals, the legality of which was very questionable, and other tribunals, the illegality of which could hardly be questioned. Why, we may ask, was not the question raised in some court of common law ? The answer seems to lie, at least partly, in the fact that the judges of the courts of common law were very distinctly the king's servants. It is needless to accuse them as a class of any disgraceful sub-serviency, though some of them were disgracefully subservient —but past history had made their position difficult. The king was the fountain of all justice ; they were but his deputies— this was the old theory, and to break with it was impossible. To hold, not that some isolated act of royal authority was illegal—but that the government of the country was being regularly conducted in illegal ways—this would have been a hard feat for the king's servants and deputies. The position of affairs may be best illustrated by some episodes in the career of one who has left his mark deep in the history of our law.

Edward Coke was born in 1552, and died in 1634. His books, which were soon treated as venerable authorities, consist of the Institutes in four parts—the first the celebrated commentary on Littleton's *Tenures* (1628), the second a commentary on various statutes ranging from Magna Carta to James I, the third an account of the criminal law, the fourth a treatise on the various courts (all published in 1641 and therefore posthumous)—and thirteen volumes of Reports (the first eleven, 1600–1615, the last two posthumous)—and there are some minor works. Certainly he was a very learned man : he knew his Year Books at a time when such knowledge was becoming uncommon—and by giving the results of his learning in English instead of debased French, he made himself for ages an ultimate authority about all matters of medieval common law: we are but slowly beginning to find out that he did not know everything. In 1593 he became Solicitor-General, in 1594 Attorney-General, in 1606 Chief Justice of the Common Pleas. We soon find him in opposition to the king. In 1605 Archbishop Bancroft had complained of the interference of the common law courts with the ecclesiastical tribunals ; the former were constantly issuing in the king's name prohibitions forbidding the courts Christian from entertaining cases which, as the common lawyers maintained, belonged to the lay courts. The king was inclined to take the archbishop's side : he sent for the judges, told them that they were his delegates, and that it was for him to decide to which court cases should go. 'Then' (this is Coke's account) 'the king said that he thought the law was founded upon reason, and that he and others had reason as well as the judges. To which it was answered by me that true it was that God had allowed His Majesty excellent science and great endowments of nature ; but His Majesty was not learned in the laws of his realm of England and causes which concern the life or inheritance or goods or fortunes of his subjects; they are not to be decided by natural reason, but by the artificial reason and judgment of law, which law is an act which requires long study and experience before that a man can attain to the cognizance of it; and that the law was the golden met-wand and measure to try the causes of the subjects, and which protected His Majesty in safety and peace. With which the king was greatly offended, and said that then he should be under the law, which was treason to affirm, as he said. To which I said that Bracton saith *quod Rex non debet esse sub homine set sub deo et lege*[1]. We see these old words of Bracton doing service again and again. The judges seem even to have told the king that no king after the Conquest had ever taken on himself to give judgment: if they said so, they said what was certainly untrue; but we see that it was difficult to assure James I that he was not in fact, what he was according to admitted theory, the highest judge in his realm.

Coke's next exploit is in 1611, when he and his brethren in the Common Pleas held that the Court of High Commission had no power to fine and imprison. The question turned on the meaning of the section in the Act of Supremacy, to which reference has already been made. The Common Pleas held that the Commission which authorized the infliction of fine and imprisonment was not itself authorized by the statute. The judges of that court, and those of the other two courts, were summoned before the council and examined seriatim. Coke refused to give way; but the other judges were not unanimous. The king promised that a less objectionable form of commission should be issued; and a new commission was issued with Coke's name in it—but he refused to sit, as he was not allowed to see the commission.

As regards the impositions of customs dues. The Court of Exchequer held this to be legal, and Coke agreed that it was legal if the imposition was intended for the good of the public, and not merely for the increase of the revenue. As regards the validity of proclamations in general, he and the rest of the judges were bolder; they declared that a proclamation could not create a new offence—but of this we have already spoken.

[1] Coke, *Reports*, XII, 65. Cf. Gardiner, *History of England*, vol. II, pp. 36—9.

In 1613 Coke was made Chief Justice of the King's Bench, seemingly in the hope that in a more exalted position he would prove more pliant. But the hope was vain. In Peacham's case he objected to the judges being asked singly and apart for their opinions as to a matter which was to come before them judicially. At a later day, when he was no longer a judge, he objected to the whole practice of consulting the judges about such matters—but at this time he merely objected to their being consulted one by one : as solicitor and attorney-general he had often himself asked the judges for their opinions. The practice, however evil it may seem in our eyes, was an old, well-established practice, and it was even possible to contend that the judges were bound by their oaths to give the king legal advice whenever he asked for it.

Then in 1615 Coke plunged into a controversy with the Court of Chancery, in which he was decisively worsted. For some time past the Chancery had claimed and exercised a power of ordering a person who had been successful in a court of law, to refrain from putting in force the judgment that he had obtained, on the ground that he had obtained it by fraud or other inequitable means. You will understand that the Chancery did not attempt to prohibit the courts of law from entertaining or deciding causes—it claimed no supervisory jurisdiction over them, such as the Court of King's Bench exercised over the local courts; but it did claim that if a person had obtained a judgment by inequitable means, by fraud or breach of trust, he might be enjoined from putting in force, from obtaining execution. Coke rebelled against this—and seems to have thought that anyone who went to the Chancery in such a case was guilty of the offence created by the Acts of Praemunire, that of going from the king's courts to another tribunal—acts which had been directed against the judicial power of the bishop of Rome. The matter was referred to the king, and he had the pleasure of deciding in favour of the Chancery, and thus maintaining his theory that he was the supreme arbiter when his judges differed. The victory of the Chancery was final and complete—and if we were to have a court of equity at all, it was a necessary victory.

Then in 1616 came the case of the *commendams*—Bishop

Neile of Lincoln had received two benefices from the king to be held *in commendam,* that is to say, together with his bishopric. An action was brought against him by two men, Colt and Glover, who contested the legality of the royal grant, and in the course of the proceedings it was reported to James that the counsel for the plaintiffs disputed the royal right to grant a *commendam.* Coke and his fellows received orders not to proceed with the hearing of an action in which the king's prerogative was questioned ; they answered that they were bound by their oaths not to regard such commands. The king sent for them, and they humbled themselves, with the exception of Coke—from whom no more could be got than that if such a command came he would do what an honest and just judge ought to do.

The intractable chief justice was forthwith dismissed. ' It is the common speech (says a contemporary) that four p's have overthrown him—that is pride, prohibitions, praemunire and prerogative[1].' In 1620 he appears in parliament as a leader on the popular side, and from that time until his death in 1634, did not a little to give the great struggle its peculiar character— a struggle of the common law against the king.

On several occasions during that struggle an important part is played by the writ of habeas corpus. We had better therefore see what that writ was, and we shall have to notice that even during the Tudor time there was considerable doubt as to its scope. From a very early time our kings had claimed to supervise all the justice of their realm. If anyone was imprisoned it was in the king's power to inquire the cause of the imprisonment. We ought to carry our thoughts back to a time when England was full of private prisons—the prisons of lords who claimed jurisdiction by royal grant or by prescription. At the suit of an imprisoned subject the king would send his writ to the keeper of the gaol, bidding him have the body of that subject before the king's court, to undergo and receive what that court should award. As happened in many other cases, this prerogative of the king came to be regarded as the right of the subject. During the

---

[1] Gardiner, *History of England*, vol. III, pp. 25—6.

later Middle Ages a writ of habeas corpus seems to have been granted in the royal chancery almost or quite as a matter of course; there were clerks very willing to increase their business, and there were judges very desirous of amplifying their jurisdiction. When the three courts of common law had become separate, this work of investigating the cause of an imprisonment belonged most properly to the King's Bench; but by means of fictions the other two courts followed its example, and issued and adjudicated upon writs of habeas corpus.

We ought further to know some little as to the imprisonment of persons accused, but not yet convicted of crime. Our early law seldom kept a man in prison before trial if he could find pledges, if he could find persons who would undertake for his production in court. According to Glanvill it is only in cases of homicide that it is usual to keep a man in prison instead of allowing him to find pledges. The law during the next century grew somewhat stricter. The Statute of Westminster I (1275, c. 12) defined the cases in which pledges are not to be allowed—persons taken for the death of a man, or by commandment of the king or of his justices, or for forest offences, or for certain other causes, are not to be replevied. This statute determined what offences are replevisable and what not until 1826, though a considerable mass of interpretation grew up around it, and certain particular offences were from time to time specially dealt with by statute. In 1275 the work of bailing or replevying prisoners was still done by the sheriff; gradually his powers in this respect were transferred to the justices of the peace. A person who felt himself aggrieved by the refusal of the sheriff or the justices of the peace to let him find pledges could by means of the writ of habeas corpus bring his case before one of the common law courts. These courts had also exercised a power of bailing prisoners whom the sheriff or the justices of the peace could not set free: for instance, the sheriff and justices of the peace could not set a man at liberty if he was accused of treason or of murder—they were distinctly forbidden to do so by the Statute of Westminster—but the King's Bench did not consider that the Statute limited *its* power of allowing bail, and it exercised a discretionary power of bailing even accused traitors and murderers.

We ought to notice, even though we cannot afford to explore the matter to the bottom, that there was a somewhat subtle distinction between replevying a prisoner and bailing a prisoner: both processes had much the same practical result—but the distinction gave ground for the contention that the power of bailing exercised by the King's Bench was not limited by the Statute of Westminster, which merely forbad sheriffs and others to replevy persons in certain particular cases. Now this small point became of great importance: one of the cases in which a man was not to be replevied was that of a person imprisoned by the commandment of the king: could then the courts of common law bail a prisoner who was imprisoned by the king's commandment? In the reign of Charles I, when the power of the council to commit to prison was the subject of hot controversy, it was asserted by the king's advocates, denied by the parliamentarians, that the power of the King's Bench was restricted by the Statute of Westminster. The argument of the king's opponents took this form—the court's power of bailing prisoners cannot be touched by the Statute of Westminster, for in that case it would never be able to bail an accused murderer: but indubitably it does bail accused murderers—therefore this statute refers merely to the action of sheriffs and similar officers. But further, and this matter concerns us more directly, a number of cases were produced in which the Court of King's Bench had bailed prisoners, when the cause of their commitment was stated to be the king's command. In answer to the writ of habeas corpus, the gaoler had returned that the prisoner was committed by the command of the king, or by the command of the king's council, and yet the court had liberated him upon bail. There was one clear case of this from 1344—the lieutenant of the Tower had returned that one J. B. was in prison by the king's command under his great seal: the court let him out on bail *quia videtur curiae breve praedictum sufficientem non esse causam praedicti J. B. in prisona retinendi*. The other cases come from the reigns of the Tudors and James I—in all there were eleven of them—the prisoners were liberated on bail, though the gaoler returned that they were imprisoned (in some cases) by command of the king, or (in others) by command of the king's council[1].

It seems that in Elizabeth's reign, in 1591 or thereabouts, the judges were consulted by the council as to the power of the queen, and of the council, to commit to prison. We have two versions of the answer that they gave, the one is in Anderson, *Reports*, vol. I, p. 297, the other in Hallam, chap. 5. Both are singularly obscure—perhaps they are intentionally obscure—and there is a considerable difference between them. The judges manage to evade saying distinctly whether they will or whether they will not bail prisoners when the return to the writ of habeas corpus simply says that the prisoner was committed by the command of the king or the command of the council. They evidently think (as it seems to me) that the cause of the commitment *ought to be* assigned, but what they will do, if it is not assigned, they do not say. In the struggle of Charles's reign both parties claimed that 'the resolution in Anderson' was favourable to them: to me it seems to show that the judges of Elizabeth's day felt themselves in a great difficulty—and the difficulty grew greater; Coke himself, when Chief Justice, held that one committed by the council was not bailable by any court in England; he afterwards recanted his opinion in parliament, saying that he had been misled by an inapposite precedent.

It should be clearly understood that the judges of this time did not question the power of the council to act judicially and to sentence to imprisonment,—the jurisdiction of the Court of Star Chamber was not in debate—nor did they question the power of the council to commit to prison persons suspected of crime. The doubt was merely this—whether if the council committed to prison, the courts of common law would be prevented from considering whether the suspected person ought to be bailed—was the king's command or the command

---

[1] Proceedings on the Habeas Corpus brought by Sir T. Darnel and others, 3 Charles I, 1627, *State Trials*, vol. III, pp. 1—59. John Bilston's case (18 Edw. III, Rot. 33) was quoted by Coke, 24 March 1627, in the Commons but does not appear to have been cited in court, ib. p. 69.

of the council a sufficient answer to the writ of habeas corpus? If the return was that the prisoner was sentenced to imprisonment by the Star Chamber there would have been no talk of setting him free; the doubt was as to persons who had not been tried: could the king prevent an investigation of their cases in a court of law, by telling the gaoler to return that they were imprisoned by the king's command?

Taking a general survey, everywhere we see difficulties before King Charles I. The system by which England has of late been governed is a questionable system, it is being questioned in parliament, it is being questioned in the law courts. The more men look back at history (and history is now being minutely examined for controversial purposes) the more they see that the constitution is not what it was under the Lancastrian kings—that the mode of government conflicts with unrepealed statutes, that there is at least plausible excuse for pronouncing a great deal of it illegal. Whether a wiser man than Charles could have averted or guided the coming storm, is a question over which we may well think; but everywhere we see that the storm is coming.

C. *History of the Army.*

The last topic with which we can deal before passing to a new period is the history of the army—a matter of which we have hitherto said too little. After the Conquest the feudal tenures had supplied the king with troops; but the feudal array was an extremely clumsy weapon. The tenant by knight service was only bound to serve for forty days in the year—and there was constant friction between the king and his barons as to the conditions of the service—were they bound to serve in Normandy? were they bound to serve in Germany?—on more than one famous occasion these questions were raised, and the embarrassed king had to make concessions. Already in 1159 Henry II took the first scutage, by way of composition for personal service[1]. It is explained that his object was to spare the lives of his subjects and get

---

[1] Traces of scutage have been found as early as the reign of Henry I. Round, *Feudal England*, p. 268. See McKechnie, *Magna Carta*, pp. 86—90.

his foreign wars fought for him by mercenaries. Towards the end of his reign, in 1181, he revived and reorganized the ancient national force by his Assize of Arms. Apparently the idea of such a force had never ceased to exist; it had never become law that military service, at all events defensive military service, was limited by the system of military tenure. Every man, according to his degree, is to have suitable weapons—even the poorest free man is to have his spear and helmet. A national force, organized by counties, was thus created.

Henry III reissued the assize in an amplified form, and it forms the base of one of his son's great statutes, the Statute of Winchester. Its date is 1285, so there is just a century between it and the Assize of Arms[1]. Every free man between the ages of fifteen and sixty is to have armour according to his wealth. There are five classes, ranging from him who has £15 of lands and 40 marks of goods, a habergeon, iron helmet, sword, knife and horse, down to him who is merely to have his bow and arrows. Twice a year the arms are to be viewed in each hundred by two elected officers called constables. These provisions occur in close connection with others enforcing the ancient duties of watch and ward, of hue and cry. If this national force is to be useful against the public enemy, it is to be useful also for police purposes, for apprehending malefactors and the like. Its officers you will observe are 'constables'—the title is originally a military title, which spreads downwards from the king's constable, who along with the king's marshall arrays and leads the royal forces. Even the lowest officers in the national force become constables; the constable of the township looks after the armour of the township, above him are the constables of the hundred; they again are below the constable, the high constable (as he comes to be called) of the county. The military duties of the constable of the township are from the first allied with the duty of keeping the peace and apprehending malefactors—the ancient village officers, the reeves, the headboroughs (chiefs of the frankpledge), become also the constables, and lose their older names.

[1] *Select Charters*, pp. 154—6, 469—74.

To return.   The obligation of this armed force, defined
by the Statute of Winchester, to take part in war offensive
or defensive, is for a long while very indefinite.   Of course it
could not be contended that the king might send every able-
bodied man out of the realm to serve in France.   We find
that Edward I commissions certain of his servants to choose
out a fixed number of able-bodied men from their respective
counties.   In other words, he issues commissions of array.
The forces thus levied he pays at his own cost.   The troops
from a county are under the command of a royal *capitaneus*
or captain, in whom we may see the forerunner of the lord-
lieutenant of later times.   The sheriff would naturally be
the head of the county force, and so in theory he remains ;
it is he who can raise the power of the county, the *posse
comitatus*, for the pursuit of malefactors ; but for actual
warfare an annual officer (and permanent sheriffs the country
will not stand) is not a good commander.   So the sheriff
loses his military functions at a time when the institution
of permanent justices of the peace is sapping many other of
his powers.   Commissions of array become common under
Edward II and Edward III, and the king does not always
pay the soldiers whom he levies—he expects the counties to
pay them ; the counties were required to provide arms not
prescribed by the Statute of Winchester, to pay the wages
of men outside of their own area and even outside of the
kingdom.   Complaints of this become loud.   In 1327 the
commons petition that they be not compelled to arm themselves at their own cost contrary to the Statute of Winchester,
or to serve beyond the limits of their counties, except at the
king's cost.   The petition was granted by statute (1 Edw. III,
stat. 2, c. 5) in this modified form.   'The king wills that
no man be charged to arm himself otherwise than he was
wont in the time of his (the king's) progenitors, and that no
man be compelled to go out of his shire, but where necessity
requireth and sudden coming of strange enemies into the
realm ; and then it shall be done as hath been used in
times past for the defence of the realm.'   But Edward had
to make a further concession.   By statute (25 Edw. III,
stat. 5, c. 8) it is accorded and assented that no man shall be

constrained to find men-at-arms, hobblers nor archers, other than those which hold by such services, if not by common assent and grant made by parliament. Apparently those statutes were habitually broken or evaded. In 1402 they were confirmed by statute (4 Hen. IV, c. 13), and they seem to have been observed during the Lancastrian reigns. The Welsh and Scottish wars of Henry VI were regarded as defensive, resistances of invasion, and the county forces could lawfully be called to meet them. The army whereby Henry V won his victories in France consisted partly of soldiers voluntarily enlisted who had the king's wages, partly of forces raised by lords who served the king by indenture, by special bargain. During the Wars of the Roses both sides used the king's name for commissions of array, and the country got thoroughly accustomed to intestine war, compulsory service, and extorted loans and benevolences. The statutes of Edward III remained on the statute book; so did the Statute of Winchester.

The Tudor despotism was not enforced by any standing army; that is one of the most noticeable things in the history of the time. One or two hundred yeomen of the guard and a few guards in the fortresses were the only soldiers that the king kept permanently in his pay. Commissions of array, however, were issued from time to time; the counties were compelled to provide soldiers even for foreign service, and the statutes of an earlier time seem to have been disregarded and perhaps forgotten. An important act of 1557 (4 and 5 Philip and Mary, c. 3) takes no notice of the old acts, but speaks of mustering and levying men to serve in the wars as a recognized legal practice, and, as it seems to me, implicitly sanctions impressment by means of commissions of array, even impressment for foreign service. Certain offences when committed by the soldiers when mustered and levied are to be tried by the king's lieutenant, 'the lord-lieutenant' as he is here called. The usage of appointing a permanent lord-lieutenant for each county is said to date from this reign.

Another statute of this same year 1557 (4 and 5 Philip and Mary, c. 2) expressly repealed so much of every statute of earlier date as concerned the finding or keeping of horse or armour; and it enacted a new scale of armour, which replaced that ordained by the Statute of Winchester. But this statute was itself repealed in 1603 by 1 James I, c. 25, an act which repealed in a wholesale fashion a large number of the Tudor statutes. No reason is given for the repeal; Hallam suggests that the accession to the English throne of the king of Scotland had removed the chief necessity for a defensive force. But the repeal had a perhaps unexpected effect. Until 1850 it was our law that if statute A be repealed by statute B, and then statute B be simply repealed by statute C, statute A is thus revived—so the Statute of Winchester came to life once more[1]. Then in the days of Charles I it became matter of hot debate whether the armed force which the old statutes created was at the king's disposal. This force was just acquiring the new name of militia, and the control over the militia became one of the chief points of controversy between crown and parliament.

Meanwhile no standing army is kept up; for foreign warfare a temporary army is got together partly by virtue of feudal obligation, partly by voluntary enlistment, partly by impressment. However, in James's reign we find that the troops are not always disbanded immediately on their return to England, and we find that commissions of martial law are issued for their governance. Thus at the end of the reign, December, 1624, there are troops at Dover. A commission is issued to the Mayor and others empowering them 'to proceed according to the justice of martial law against such soldiers... and other dissolute persons joining with them...as commit any robberies, felonies, mutinies or other outrages or mis-demeanours...and then to execute and cause to be put to death according to the law martial[2].' Of the very questionable legality of such commissions we have before spoken : here let us notice that only by such means could a standing army be held together. This, I think, has been the verdict of long experience, that an army cannot be kept together if its discipline is left to the ordinary common law. These com-missions, you will observe, went far beyond matters of military

---

[1] 13 and 14 Victoria, c. 21. 5.

[2] Pat. Roll, 22 Jac. I, part 4, printed in Prothero, *Statutes and Constitutional Documents* (1559—1625), pp. 398—9.

discipline—they empowered the commissioners to try soldiers 'and other dissolute' persons for robberies and other felonies, as well as for mutinies. The difficulty of keeping a standing army was, as James's successors found, a double difficulty— (1) that of maintaining any discipline without having recourse to illegal commissions, (2) that of paying troops without having recourse to illegal modes of raising money.

As regards the legality of pressing soldiers, we have this to remember in the king's favour, and it is too often forgotten, that the legality of pressing sailors seems to have been fully admitted. From an early time, certainly through the fourteenth century, we find that the king presses sailors and presses ships for transport and for naval warfare. This is done by means of commissions closely similar to the commissions of array. But while the commissions of arraying soldiers excited much opposition, and parliament was constantly petitioning about them and sometimes succeeded in getting statutes passed limiting the king's power, the pressing of sailors and ships seems not to have been a great grievance. All one hears by way of protest is that the sailors ought to be at the king's wages from the time when they are on board ship. A statute of 1378 (2 Ric. II, c. 4) distinctly recognizes the lawfulness of the practice—it speaks of sailors arrested and retained for the king's service, and provides a punishment for them if they run away. Many later statutes speak of pressing as a lawful process. There are several from the last century which do so by making exceptions; in these and those circumstances sailors are not to be impressed. No word in the Petition of Right or the Bill of Rights is directed against this prerogative; the class affected by it was, I suppose, too small to make its voice heard, or else the necessity of manning a navy was considered so great that the king's power was never called in question.

PERIOD IV.

Sketch of Public Law at the Death of William III.

We pass over an exciting time, and placing ourselves at the quiet accession of Queen Anne, we ask what have been the legal and permanent results of the great events—Rebellion, Restoration, Revolution. The chronological sequence of these events we certainly ought to know ; but we have not time for everything, and I think that we had better adopt an analytical rather than a historical treatment. What, then, is the constitution in 1702 ?

We can now say with some certainty that we have a composite sovereign body—the king, lords spiritual and temporal, and commons in parliament assembled. Let us first look at the constitution of each of these factors—how and by what right do they come to be what they are ?

A. *Constitution of the Kingship.*

And first of the king. His title is now a statutory title if it be a title at all. Of course it is the opinion of a considerable number of persons that his title is bad ; let us attempt to understand their opinion. Not to go back to the Middle Ages, to the parliamentary right of the House of Lancaster, the hereditary right of the House of York, we remember that Henry VIII came more than once to parliament for an act regulating the succession to the throne, even obtained an act enabling him in default of issue to leave the crown to whom he would. In Elizabeth's reign it was treason to affirm that the succession could not be settled by act of parliament. We have seen, however, that James, by the quiet consent of the nation, succeeded to the crown, though, if statutes on such a matter had any validity, the succession was probably illegal; probably Henry VIII, in exercise of a statutory power, had preferred the issue of his younger to those of his elder sister. There was much therefore in his own case to set James on thinking that the inheritance of the crown was divinely appointed and was not to be meddled with by act of parliament. He was succeeded by his son Charles I, and when Charles I was murdered he was immediately succeeded by his son Charles II. I put the matter in that way because that was in 1702, and is even now the legal view of the matter, and we must not allow any sympathies or antipathies to interfere with our statement of the law. In 1702 it was not questioned that the first Charles had been murdered, and that the second began to reign on 30 January, 1649. On 29 May, 1660, the king began to enjoy his own again, but it already was his own and he had been reigning for eleven years and more. All the acts of the Long Parliament which had not obtained the king's assent were simply void. At the Restoration no statute was passed to declare them void; they were obviously void as having been made without the royal assent, and no repeal was necessary. In 1702 no lawyer would have appealed to them as law, and no lawyer would do so at the present day: they have no place in our statute book. This theory had been pressed far. On 16 March, 1660, the remains of the Long Parliament had declared itself dissolved. Elections were held without the king's writ—no decisive measure had yet been taken for inviting Charles to England—and a parliament, afterwards known as 'the Convention Parliament,' consisting of a few lords and the newly-elected commons, assembled on 25 April. It at once proceeded to enter into negotiations with Charles; on 7 May the houses resolved that the king should be proclaimed; on the 24th he set sail; on the 26th he landed; on the 29th he met the parliament. An act was at once passed declaring that the Long Parliament was dissolved (it had never been dissolved by the king, and so there might be question as to its dissolution) and that the lords and commons now sitting at Westminster in this present parliament are the two houses of parliament notwithstanding the fact that they had not been summoned by the king's writ. Of course, however, if the king's writ of summons was necessary to the legal being of a parliament, this defect could not be remedied by a parliament which had come together without such writ—if it was not a true parliament, its own declaration could not make it so. This Convention Parliament sat on until December, 1660, and passed a number of acts. Another parliament met in May, 1661, and this of course was summoned by the king's writ in due form. It proceeded to pass an act confirming the acts of the Convention Parliament as though their validity might be questionable owing to the want of the king's writ. All therefore that was done at the Restoration was done on the theory that Charles II had reigned from the moment of his father's death.

Passing to the events of 1688 we see that it was extremely difficult for any lawyer to make out that what had then been done was lawful. What had happened was briefly this. In July, 1688, James had dissolved parliament, so that at the critical moment there was no parliament in existence. On 5 November William landed; on 11 December James fled from London and dropped the great seal into the Thames; on the 22nd he left the kingdom. William, Prince of Orange, invited an assembly. It was rapidly got together. He summoned the peers and such of the members of the parliaments of Charles II's reign (not James II) as were in London; the aldermen of London also were summoned. This, of course, the lawyer cannot but regard as a quite irregular assembly, called by one who is not, who does not profess to be king. The assembly met on 26 December, 1688, and it advised the Prince to summon a 'convention' of the estates of the realm. In accordance with this advice he invited the lords to come, and the counties and boroughs to send representatives to a convention on 22 January, 1689. The convention met. On 25 January the commons resolved that King James II having endeavoured to subvert the constitution of the kingdom by breaking the original contract between king and people, and by the advice of Jesuits and other wicked persons having violated the fundamental laws and having withdrawn himself out of the kingdom, has abdicated the government, and that the throne has thereby become vacant. After some hesitation, on 12 February the lords agreed to this resolution, and it was resolved that William and Mary should be proclaimed king and queen. On 13 February the Houses waited on William and Mary and tendered them the crown, accompanied by the Declaration of Rights. The crown was accepted. The convention, thereupon following the precedent of 1660, passed an act declaring itself to be the parliament of England, notwithstanding the want of proper writs of summons. This Convention Parliament was not dissolved until early in 1690, and passed many important acts, including the Bill of Rights, which incorporated the Declaration of Rights. A new parliament met on 22 March, 1690, and this of course was duly summoned by writs of the king and queen. It proceeded to declare by statute that the king and queen were king and queen, and that the statutes made by the convention were and are laws and statutes of the kingdom.

Now certainly it was very difficult for any lawyer to argue that there had not been a revolution. Those who conducted the revolution sought, and we may well say were wise in seeking, to make the revolution look as small as possible, to make it as like a legal proceeding, as by any stretch of ingenuity it could be made. But to make it out to be a perfectly legal act seems impossible. Had it failed, those who attempted it would have suffered as traitors, and I do not think that any lawyer can maintain that their execution would have been unlawful. The convention hit upon the word 'abdicated' as expressing James's action, and, according to the established legal reckoning, he abdicated on the 11 December, 1688, the day on which he dropped the great seal into the Thames. From that day until the day when William and Mary accepted the crown, 13 February, 1689, there was no king of England. Possibly the convention would better have expressed the truth if, like the parliament of Scotland, it had boldly said that James had forfeited the crown. But put it either way, it is difficult for a lawyer to regard the Convention Parliament as a lawfully constituted assembly. By whom was it summoned? Not by a king of England, but by a Prince of Orange. Even if we go back three centuries we find no precedent. The parliaments of 1327 and of 1399 were summoned by writs in the king's name under the great seal. Grant that parliament may depose a king, James was not deposed by parliament; grant that parliament may elect a king, William and Mary were not elected by parliament. If when the convention met it was no parliament, its own act could not turn it into a parliament. The act which declares it to be a parliament depends for its validity on the assent of William and Mary. The validity of that assent depends on their being king and queen; but how do they come to be king and queen? Indeed this statute very forcibly brings out the difficulty—an incurable defect. So again as to the confirming statute of 1690.

Do not think that I am arguing for the Jacobite cause. I am only endeavouring to show you how much purely legal strength that cause had. It seems to me that we must treat the Revolution as a revolution, a very necessary and wisely conducted revolution, but still a revolution. We cannot work it into our constitutional law.

Passing from this point, we notice that the tender of the crown was made to William and Mary jointly; but William had refused to reign merely in his wife's right—such as it was —and the declaration of the convention was that William and Mary were to hold the crown during their joint lives and the life of the survivor of them, that, however, the sole and full exercise of the regal power was to be in William during their joint lives, but was to be exercised in the names of William and Mary, and that after their deceases the crown should go to the issue of Mary, and in default of her issue to the Princess Anne and the heirs of her body, and for default of such issue to the heirs of the body of William. The Bill of Rights, passed in 1689, confirmed this settlement, adding a clause to the effect that any person who should hold communion with the See or Church of Rome or profess the Popish religion or marry a Papist should be incapable to inherit, possess or enjoy the crown and government of the realm, and that the crown should pass to the person next entitled. In 1700, after the death of Mary, William being childless, and Anne's son the Duke of Gloucester being dead, it became necessary to make a further settlement, and by the Act of Settlement (12 and 13 Will. III, c. 2) it was ordained that in default of issue of Mary, Anne, and William the crown should go to the Princess Sophia of Hanover and the heirs of her body being Protestants. She, a daughter of Elizabeth Queen of Bohemia, a daughter of James I, was the nearest heir according to the ordinary rules of inheritance, if Roman Catholics were excluded.

A new form of coronation oath has been provided. About the coronation oath there has been controversy. In the reign of Charles I it became known that the king had taken an oath which differed in some respects from the ancient form. That ancient form has come before us already. In it the king promised to hold and keep the laws and righteous customs which the community of the realm shall have chosen—*quas vulgus elegerit, les quels la communaute de vostre roiaume aura esleu.* Now at Charles's coronation the last question put to him had been this : 'Will you grant to hold and keep the laws and rightful customs which the communalty of this your kingdom have, and will you defend and uphold them to the honour of God as much as in you lieth?' This form, you will observe, does not assert the right of the people, the community of the realm, to choose its own laws : the king is to hold and keep the laws which the communalty *has.* Archbishop Laud was accused of having tampered with the oath. His defence seems on this point to have been quite sound. He had administered the oath in the terms in which it had come to him, the terms to which James I had sworn, the terms to which Elizabeth had sworn. As to Mary's oath I know nothing ; but a change had been made on the occasion of Edward VI's accession. He had sworn to make no new laws but such as should be to the honour and glory of God and to the good of the commonwealth, and that the same should be made by consent of his people as hath been accustomed.

But a change seems to have been made yet earlier. There is extant a copy of the coronation oath in which alterations have been made in the handwriting of Henry VIII[1]. The last

[1] A facsimile of the oath with Henry's corrections is given in *English Coronation Records*, ed. L. G. Wickham-Legg, pp. 240—1.

clause reads thus—I will note the changes made by the king's own hand—'And that he shall graunte to hold the laws and [approvyd] customes of the realm [lawfull and nott prejudicial to his Crowne or Imperiall duty], and to his power kepe them and affirm them which the [nobles and] people have made and chosen [with his consent].' The interpolations are very remarkable: they seem to point to the notion of an indefeasible royal power which laws cannot restrain ; the king will not bind himself to maintain laws prejudicial to his crown. Thus since the accession of Edward VI the terms of the oath seem to have varied—and Laud, I believe, successfully showed that he could not be charged with any insidious alterations[1]. But the meaning of the more ancient form, the form of Edward II's oath, now became a subject of bitter controversy; it was maintained that the *elegerit*—'*quas vulgus elegerit*'— could not refer to the future : the kings are to uphold the old law, the law which the people had chosen, not the laws which the people should choose. On the other hand, it was even urged that the terms of the oath excluded the king from all share in legislation—that without perjury he could reject no bill passed by two Houses. Neither contention would harmonize with past history ; on the one hand the old oath was a not indistinct declaration that there were to be no laws save those chosen by the community of the realm ; on the other hand the contention that the king was no part of the community was wild. However, when such opposite views were taken of the king's obligation, the time for war had come.

The oaths of Charles II and James II seem to have been just those which Charles I had taken. Immediately after the Revolution a new oath was provided by a statute (1 William and Mary, c. 6) which recites that the old oath was framed in doubtful words and expressions with relation to ancient laws and constitutions at this time unknown. The most important phrase is this—the king promises to govern the people of England and the dominions thereto belonging according to the statutes in parliament agreed on, and the laws and customs

---

[1] The question is discussed by J. Wickham-Legg, *The Coronation Order of King James I*, London, 1902, pp. xcvi—cii.

of the same; thus 'the statutes in parliament agreed on' take the place of *leges quas vulgus elegerit*.

By another clause in the oath the king has to swear that he will maintain to the utmost of his power the true profession of the gospel and the protestant reformed religion established by law, and preserve unto the bishops and clergy of the realm and the churches committed to their charge, all such rights and privileges as by law do or shall appertain unto them. Another obligation is laid upon the king by the Bill of Rights and by the Act of Settlement: on the first day of his first parliament he must make the declaration against transubstantiation, the invocation of the saints and the sacrifice of the mass. The clauses which deprive him of his crown in case he holds communion with the Church of Rome or marries a Papist, have already come before us.

B. *Constitution of Parliament.*

We turn to speak of the composition of parliament. The number of the lords spiritual, the mode of their appointment, has not been changed: they are now a small minority in the Upper House. But though we have here to chronicle that things are as they were, still we must remember that there has been a period during which the bishops have had no place in parliament. The royal assent to an act excluding them was given on 13 Feb. 1642—this was one of the last concessions extorted from Charles. They were not restored by the Convention Parliament, but were restored by the second parliament of Charles II in 1661. They took their seats on 20 Nov., after an interval of nineteen years.

The number of temporal peers has greatly increased. To Elizabeth's last parliament, 1597, 56 were summoned. To James's first parliament, 1604, 78. To the first parliament of Charles I, 97. To the parliament of 1661, 142. To that of 1685, 145. The grant of a peerage has been used as a political reward. As to the mode of creating peers there is little to be added to what has already been said. It has, however, been decided that a peerage cannot be bound up with the possession of a tract of land; peerage by tenure is regarded as extinct. Also it has now become the quite definite rule that a summons by name to parliament, followed by an actual sitting, confers a hereditary peerage. However, for a long time past all peers have been created by letters patent.

Here again we have to remember that there has been a short breach of continuity, not indeed in law, but in fact. During the Civil War the number of lords who attend parliament is small—it becomes thirteen or thereabouts. On the eve of the king's trial on 4 Jan. 1649, the commons voted that 'the commons of England in Parliament assembled do declare that the People are under God the original of all just power, and that whatsoever is enacted or declared for law by the commons in Parliament assembled, hath the force of law ...although the consent and concurrence of the King or House of Peers be not had thereunto.' On 6 Feb. the lords sat for the last time. On 19 March the commons passed an act for abolishing the House of Peers. On 25 April, 1660, the lords reappear once more in the Convention Parliament, after an interval of eleven years. Their case must be distinguished from that of the bishops. The bishops were deprived of their seats by a statute passed by king, lords and commons; it required a statute to recall them: the temporal lords were excluded simply by the act of the commons, an act which so soon as the Restoration was agreed on, was regarded simply as null and void.

The numbers of the House of Commons have grown. In the first parliament of James there were 467 members. In the Long Parliament (1640), 504. In the parliament of 1661, 507; in 1679, 513. The causes of the increase have been various. In 1672 a statute admitted two knights for the County Palatine of Durham, and two citizens for the city. Except in this respect the representation of the counties remains unaltered. We have seen that under Edward VI, Mary, Elizabeth, and James, the number of borough members was increased by royal charter—thus it was hoped that a House favourable to the crown might be returned. Charles I added, or restored, I think, eighteen borough members[1]. Charles II exercised

---

[1] 'Restoration' is the right word. The nine boroughs restored to parliamentary rights under Charles I were however restored by resolution of the commons not by royal charter. Porritt, *The Unreformed Parliament*, vol. I, p. 382.

this prerogative but once, he gave Newark two members. This is the last exercise of this prerogative, and it did not pass quite unquestioned. For a long time past the commons had looked jealously on this power. They had claimed to themselves the right of deciding whether a borough had the right to send members—and most of the additions made by Charles I to the House were by way of reviving boroughs which, according to the decision of the House, had once returned members, but had discontinued the practice of sending them. The right to send members was now becoming a coveted right, and boroughs sought to show that they had exercised this right in remote times. The representation of the two Universities is due to James I. The prerogative of increasing the number of borough members was never taken away—but it was last exercised in favour of Newark in 1677 —and after the Restoration the House of Commons would have resented its exercise: though it is curious to observe that the excellent whig, John Locke, agreed that if the House would not reform itself, the king might reform it[1]. Thus the number of members became finally fixed at 513; 24 for Wales, 80 for the English counties, 4 for the Universities, the rest for the English boroughs; these, with the 45 Scottish members added under Anne, and the 100 Irish members added under George III, brought up the total to 658. This was the number in 1832.

Though from the legal point of view this is no precedent, still we do well to observe that in the parliament of 1656, the third of Cromwell's parliaments, Scotland and Ireland are represented[2]. It consists of 459 members: 375 English, 24 Welsh, 29 Scottish, 31 Irish.

The electoral qualifications remain what they have been. In the counties the electors are still the forty-shilling freeholders. In the boroughs there is the utmost variety. On the whole, the tendency has been towards vesting the right to elect representatives in an oligarchic governing body. In many cases the crown procured a surrender of an old charter and granted

---

[1] *Civil Government*, c. XIII.

[2] Irish and Scottish members sat in the Barebones Parliament (1653) and again, in accordance with the provisions of the Instrument of Government, in the Parliament of 1654.

a new. Under Charles II a plan was conceived for hastening this process. An attack was made on the charters of the city of London, and they were declared to be forfeited. It was a principle of law that if a charter was abused it was forfeited, and it was alleged that the citizens of London had in some not very important respects abused their corporate powers. Their charter was declared to be forfeited. In terror at this judgment many of the boroughs of England surrendered their charters, and received new charters vesting the right of election in governing bodies nominated by the king[1]. By these means James II obtained a very subservient parliament. After the Revolution—in 1690—the judgment against the city of London was declared void by statute. Some of the boroughs which had surrendered their charters and taken new ones, got back their old charters on the ground that the surrender was unlawful, but this was not always the case—in some instances the surrenders were adjudged lawful. Altogether, therefore, the constitution of very many boroughs had become oligarchic. After the Revolution many of them fall under the influence of great land-owners and become pocket boroughs. Already in William's day the distribution of seats presents many of those anomalies which are abolished in 1832. Shortly after the Revolution Locke wrote thus—'We see the bare name of a town, of which there remains not so much as the ruins, where scarce so much housing as a sheep-cote, or more inhabitants than a shepherd is to be found, sends as many representatives to the grand assembly of law makers as a whole county, numerous in people and powerful in riches. This strangers stand amazed at[2].'

The power of determining all questions as to contested elections, the House of Commons has now got into its own hand—and it jealously resents any interference by the king, the House of Lords, or the courts of law. Too often its decision is simply the result of a party division.

As to the qualification of those elected. The act of Henry V is still on the statute book, and it requires that the knights and burgesses shall be resident in the shires and towns

---

[1] Porritt, vol. I, pp. 393—6, 399—405.
[2] *Civil Government*, c. XIII.

which they represent; it will not be repealed until 1774, but since the days of Elizabeth it has been habitually disregarded. There is no property qualification—though we are on the eve of getting one—for in 1710 (9 Anne, c. 5) a statute is passed providing that a knight of the shire must have an estate of land worth £600 per annum, a burgess one worth £300.

Of late there has been a great noise against the number of place-men in parliament—at present there is no law against them—but the Act of Settlement (1700, 12 and 13 Will. III, c. 2) has lately provided 'that so soon as the House of Hanover shall come to the throne, no person who has an office or place of profit under the king, or receives a pension from the crown, shall be capable of serving as a member of the House of Commons.' This momentous clause never came into force: it was repealed in 1705 before the House of Hanover came to the throne. Had it ever come into play it must have altered the whole history of the House of Commons; no minister of the king would ever have been able to sit there. Macaulay says that the result would have been to make the House of Lords the most august of senates, while the House of Commons would have become little better than a vestry[1]. The plan in 1707, by a statute which still is the fundamental law on this subject, was that the acceptance of an old office, i.e., one created before 25 October, 1705, should vacate the seat, but that the office holder should be capable of reelection, while on the other hand no holder of a new office, an office created since that date, should be capable of sitting at all[2]. The clause in the Act of Settlement, to which we have just referred, is a good reminder that our modern system of ministerial government is modern; in 1700, let us repeat it, parliament ordains that there shall be no ministers in the House of Commons.

C. *Frequency and Duration of Parliaments.*

And now as to the frequency of parliaments. It is impossible to speak in general terms; each parliament of the time that we are surveying has its own very peculiar history. The first parliament of Charles I met on 17 May, 1625, and

[1] *History of England*, c. XIX.
[2] New offices have however been created by subsequent statutes to which this disability does not attach.

was dissolved on 12 August, the commons protesting, and no grant of tonnage and poundage having been made. The second parliament met on 6 February, 1626, and was dissolved on 15 June without passing a statute; the king was at issue with both Houses as to their privileges. The third parliament met on 17 March, 1628, and sat until 26 June, when it was prorogued. It sat a second time on 20 January, 1629, and was dissolved on 10 March. To its first session we owe the Petition of Right. Then for hard on eleven years there is no parliament. The fourth (a short) parliament met on 13 April, 1640, and was dissolved on 5 May—after less than a month; the king had got no supply. On 24 September Charles had recourse to a *magnum concilium* of peers held at York— the last occasion on which such a body has met—but got nothing from it, save advice to summon a parliament. One was summoned; it met on 3 November, 1640, and became the Long Parliament. We may say that it remained in legal being for twenty years, that it was never lawfully dissolved until in 1660 a statute of the Convention Parliament declared its dissolution. But we may rapidly trace its history. It met on 3 November, 1640, and sat on steadily until 22 August, 1642, when the king's standard was raised at Nottingham, and long afterwards. In the meantime, however, before the war broke out, not only had it procured the attainder of Strafford, the exclusion of the bishops from the House of Lords, the abolition of the Star Chamber; but further two acts were passed which particularly concern us here. In the first place on 15 February, 1641, the royal assent was obtained to the Triennial Act (16 Car. I, c. 1). This enacts that a parliament shall be held in every third year; if the Chancellor does not issue writs, then the peers are to meet and issue writs for the election of the representatives of the commons, and if the peers make default, then the sheriffs and mayors are to see to the election. No parliament, again, was to be dissolved or prorogued within fifty days after its meeting. The old statutes of Edward III which directed that a parliament should be held in every year or more often if need be were not repealed[1]. But a more

---

[1] Gardiner, *Constitutional Documents of the Puritan Revolution*, 2nd ed., pp. 144—55.

momentous concession was extorted on 17 May, 1641; the king gave his assent to a bill which declared that the present parliament shall not be dissolved unless it be by act of parliament to be passed for that purpose; nor shall it be prorogued or adjourned unless by act of parliament, and the houses shall not be adjourned unless by themselves or their own order. Thus the parliament provided that it should continue to exist during its own good pleasure. It continued sitting during the Civil War, after 1649 as a parliament without lords. On 7 December, 1648, the army which had become masters of England, violently expelled (Pride's purge), or as the phrase went, 'secluded' the majority of the house, a hundred and forty-three members of the Presbyterian party. The Rump that was left at once proceeded to erect a court of justice for the king's trial. This Rump of the Long Parliament went on sitting until 20 April, 1653—in 1651 it had voted that it would continue sitting until November, 1654—but meanwhile Cromwell put an end to its prating.

On 4 July, 1654, there appears the collection of persons known as the Little Parliament or Barebone's parliament— 140 persons, not elected by the country, but nominated by the council of officers; it sat until 12 December, and then dissolved itself. On 3 September, 1654, met the second of Cromwell's parliaments, if we reckon the Barebone's assembly as the first; it was a body of 400 elected members, elected according to a scheme settled by the Long Parliament in 1650; there was some redistribution of seats, and the county franchise was extended to any persons having real or personal property to the value of £200. On 22 January, 1655, Cromwell dissolved this body. His third parliament met on 17 September, 1656; it offered him the kingly title which he refused; it instituted an upper house consisting of his nominees, and then fell quarrelling as to whether this was a House of Lords. On 4 February, 1658, he dissolved it; on 3 September he died. Power had been given him to appoint a successor to the office of Lord Protector, and it seems that he had appointed his son Richard, though by no formal instrument. On 27 January, 1659, a parliament met; the military council of officers could not get on with it, and on 22 April Richard dissolved it. On

7 May the officers restored the Rump, the members of the Long Parliament not excluded in 1653; again they were expelled, and again they were restored—the secluded members returned. On 16 March, 1660, this Long Parliament passed a bill declaring itself dissolved, and taking order for the holding of a new parliament on 25 April.

That parliament was the Convention Parliament, and of some of its doings we have already spoken. With the king's assent, for Charles was restored in May, it passed an act declaring the dissolution of the Long Parliament; it was dissolved on 29 December, 1660. Charles's second parliament met on 8 May, 1661, and was not dissolved until 31 December, 1678, having thus sat between seventeen and eighteen years.

During this time it held sixteen sessions. Really it was a much longer parliament than what is called the Long Parliament—which had not sat thirteen years before Cromwell packed it off, though it maintained a notional existence for seven years longer. On 6 March, 1679, Charles's third parliament met; it was prorogued in May, dissolved in July. His fourth parliament met on October 17 in the same year, but did not sit for business until October, 1680; it sat until January, 1681, when it was dissolved. The fifth and last is the Oxford Parliament, which met on 21 March, 1681: sat but for a week and was then dissolved. From March, 1681, until his death in February, 1685, Charles reigned without a parliament. But we must go back for a moment. We have seen that the first act of the Long Parliament (16 Car. I, c. 1) was a Triennial Act (1641), which provided machinery for the assembling of a parliament once in every three years: if the king neglected to summon it, it would meet without his summons. In 1664 this act was repealed as being in derogation of the king's just rights. Instead thereof it was enacted (16 Car. II, c. 1) that the sitting and holding of parliament shall not be intermitted or discontinued above three years at the most—but no machinery was provided for the assembling of a parliament in case the king should neglect his statutory duty of calling one. It supersedes, we may say, though it does not repeal the acts of Edward III as to parliament being held once in every year, or more often if need be: it is the king's statutory duty to call a parliament together once at least in every three years, but if he neglects to do this there is no lawful manner in which a parliament can come together. Twenty years afterwards Charles II, as we have just seen, violated the act. He dissolved the Oxford Parliament in March, 1681, and had not summoned another when he died in February, 1685.

James held but one parliament; it met 19 May, 1685, held two sessions in that year, was prorogued on 20 November, 1685, and never sat again for business, though it was not dissolved until July, 1687.

We have already spoken of the Convention of 22 January, 1689, which became the first parliament of William and Mary. One of the clauses of the Declaration of Rights incorporated in the Bill of Rights declared that for redress of grievances, and for the amending, strengthening and preserving of the laws, parliaments ought to be held frequently. The Triennial Act of 1664, however, was left standing. The second parliament met on 20 May, 1690; it held six sessions and was dissolved in the autumn of 1695. Meanwhile it had passed another Triennial Act—carefully to be distinguished from the acts of 1641 and 1664. It was passed in 1694 (6 and 7 William and Mary, c. 2). This act was directed not so much against intermissions of parliament, though it repeated what was already law, namely, that a parliament shall be holden once in three years at least, but against long parliaments: no parliament is to endure for more than three years—it is then to die a natural death. As to this present parliament, it is to cease on 1 November, 1696. William dissolved it when it was just about to expire. William had rejected this Triennial Act in 1693 ; this is one of the last instances of the royal assent being withholden. It remained in force until the Septennial Act was passed in 1715 (1 Geo. I, st. 2, c. 38). William met his third parliament in November, 1695 ; it sat again in 1696 and 1697. Another met in 1698, and sat again in 1699 and 1700. A fourth met in 1701, and was in existence on 3 March, 1702, when the king died. I think that in the whole course of English history it had only once happened that a reigning king had died during the existence of a parliament—he was

Henry IV[1]. It had, however, been accounted well-settled law that the king's death, the demise of the crown, would dissolve parliament ; just as it would deprive the judges and all officers of state who held their commissions from the king of their powers. But shortly before William's death, in 1696, an act had been passed to obviate this evil result—if the present king dies when there is a parliament, it is to continue in existence for six months, unless sooner dissolved by his successor ; if there is no parliament when he dies, the last parliament is to come together and be again a parliament. The grave possibility of a disputed succession led to this act. It applied only to the case of King William; in 1707 (6 Anne, c. 41, sec. 4) the rule was generalized. In 1867 (30 and 31 Vic. c. 102, sec. 51) it was enacted that the demise of the crown should have no effect on the duration of parliament, and thus the rule as to six months was abolished.

It will be needless hereafter to speak of the actual duration of parliaments. Since the Revolution the principle that parliament shall sit in every year, has been secured by very efficient means which will soon come before us. This is one of the great results of the period which is now under our consideration. Of the other results let us take a brief review under six heads.

D. *The Question of Sovereignty.*

The first question which a student of modern jurisprudence is likely to ask on turning to consider a political constitution is, Where is sovereignty? I have before now given my reasons why we should not ask this question when studying the Middle Ages—why we should understand that no answer can be given.

Gradually, and as a result of long continued struggles, the question emerges, and it is not settled without bloodshed.

In the middle of the century Hobbes, in his vigorous writings, had sharply stated the theory that a sovereign there must be—some man or body of men whose commands are laws—and though Hobbes had no great following, still this theory told on the world. Now I think that at the outset of our

---

[1] Henry VIII and James I died during the existence of a parliament.

period there were three claimants for sovereignty, (1) the king, (2) the king in parliament, (3) the law. As a matter of history the claims of king and parliament certainly seem to us the best founded. We have seen that the practical despotism of the Tudors had laid a terrible emphasis upon the enormous powers of parliament—there was nothing that parliament could not do—it could dissolve the ancient dual constitution of church and state, it could place the church under the king, it could alter the religion of the land, it could settle the royal succession, it could delegate legislative powers to the king, it could take them away again. I think that the statesmen of Elizabeth's reign, witness Sir Thomas Smith, had distinctly held that king in parliament was absolutely supreme, above the king and above the law. Still for the king there was a great deal to be said—more, as I think, than modern writers are inclined to allow, and this even apart from those theories of divine right which were generally held by the monarchical party. Those theories, which became current under James I, we must leave on one side ; they belong rather to the domain of political philosophy, than to that of constitutional law. It is more within our scope to observe that it must have been a hard feat to conceive of sovereignty as vested in the parliamentary assembly. Consider how very much that assembly depends for its constitution, for its very existence, on the king's will. It comes when he calls it, it disappears when he bids it go ; he makes temporal lords as he pleases, he makes what bishops he pleases, he charters new boroughs to send representatives. After all, is not this body but an emanation of the kingly power? The king does well to consult a parliament—but is this more than a moral obligation, a dictate of sound policy? As to old acts of the fourteenth century, a question of sovereignty cannot possibly be decided by an appeal to ancient documents.

The high-water mark of this theory is to be found in some of the judgments delivered in the Ship Money case. I will read a few sentences.

Crawley, J. 'This imposition without parliament appertains to the king originally, and to his successor *ipso facto* if he be a sovereign in right of his sovereignty from the crown.

You cannot have a king without these royal rights, no not by act of parliament.

Berkley, J.   Where Mr Holborne supposed a fundamental policy in the creation of the frame of this kingdom, that in case the monarch of England should be inclined to exact from his subjects at his pleasure, he should be restrained for that he could have nothing from them, but upon a common consent in parliament: he is utterly mistaken herein.   The law knows no such king-yoking policy.   The law itself is an old and trusty servant of the king's; it is his instrument or means that he useth to govern his people by.   I never read nor heard that *lex* was *rex*; but it is common and most true that *rex* is *lex*.

Vernon, J.   The king *pro bono publico* may charge his subjects for the safety and defence of the kingdom, notwithstanding any act of parliament, and a statute derogatory from the prerogative doth not bind the king and the king may dispense with any law in cases of necessity.

Finch, C. J.   No act of parliament can bar a king of his regality, as that no land should hold of him ; or bar him of his allegiance of his subjects; or the relative on his part as trust and power to defend his people ; therefore acts of parliament to take away his royal power in the defence of the kingdom are void ; they are void acts of parliament to bind the king not to command the subjects, their persons and goods, and I say their money too ; for no acts of parliament make any difference[1].'

Now this goes far indeed, but as it seems to me, from a lawyer's point of view, the fatal flaw in it is that it does not go far enough.   If the judges had grasped the modern notion of sovereignty, the notion which Hobbes was just giving to the world—had said the question really is, Who is sovereign? had answered boldly, 'The king is sovereign, it is to him (not to him and parliament) that this nation renders that habitual obedience which is the fact which constitutes the relation of subject and sovereign ; this is clear from the nation's prolonged acquiescence in breaches by the king of the plain words of statutes ; no act of parliament binds or can bind him, no, not

---

[1] *State Trials*, 13 Charles I, 1637, vol. III, pp. 826—1315.

though he himself assented to it yesterday; he is, in short, a perfectly absolute monarch.' Had they said this, it would have been difficult to find any logical flaw in their judgments. The law, it might be said, cannot determine who is sovereign. But the judges, bold though their language was, shrank from this assertion, an assertion which must have hurried on the Civil War. They spoke of cases of necessity—the necessity of levying money for the defence of the realm—they admitted that the king could not of his own will impose a tax to be spent on his personal pleasures, they spoke of certain, or rather some not very certain, royal rights as beyond the power of statute. 'Acts of parliament,' even Finch admitted, 'may take away flowers and ornaments of the crown, but not the crown itself[1].' This makes their position very weak—who is to decide what is an ornament and what a substantial part of the crown —the notion of a constitution above both king and parliament, limiting to royal acts a proper sphere, limiting to statutes a proper sphere, was nowhere to be found expressed in any accurate terms, and would satisfy neither king nor nation. The contest was to be between the sovereignty of a king, and the sovereignty of a king in parliament. We know how the contest was decided—by the Civil War and the Revolution. Of course, however, so long as Jacobitism survived, and certainly it survived in 1745, there survived the doctrine that the title of the king, and some at least of the powers of the king, are above statute. The fatal theoretic fault of Jacobitism was that it could not say, dared not say, the king is utterly above all law, law is but the king's command.

I have said that there was a third claimant for sovereignty, namely the law. If the lawyers of James I's day had been forced to consider Hobbes's theory, they would, I think, have denied the necessity for there being any man or body of men above the law. This, so far as one can discover it, was the position of the great typical lawyer Coke. It is always difficult to pin Coke to a theory, but he does seem distinctly to claim that the common law is above statute, and above prerogative—it assigns a place to both king and parliament,

[1] In the Ship Money case, *State Trials*, vol. III, p. 1235, Broom, *Constitutional Law*, p. 363.

and keeps them in it. Coke distinctly claims that the judges may hold a statute void, either because it is against reason and natural law, or because it trenches on the royal prerogative[1]. He alleges precedents for this—cases in which statutes have been held void. I do not think that they bear him out. I do not think that the judges of the Middle Ages had considered themselves free to question the validity of a statute on the ground of its being against natural law. As to the prerogative, Coke's case was somewhat stronger; and, as already said, I take it to have been the lawyer's doctrine of James's time, that the courts had power to decide that a statute was not law. If this theory had been generally accepted the judges would have become the ultimate lawgivers of the realm—in declaring law they would have made law, which they would have upheld even against statute. They did not expressly claim legislative power, they did not even conceive that this was their claim : they claimed to declare that law— law, common law, natural law (and this was, as we have seen, the old theory) had an existence of its own, independent of the will of man, even perhaps of the will of God. The difficulty before this theory was that the judges could not point out the limits to the power of statute with any reasonable accuracy. A statute might take away flowers and ornaments of the crown, but not the crown itself. Such language is far too vague to become a constitutional theory, and looking back at the statute book of the fourteenth, fifteenth and sixteenth centuries, it was indeed difficult to find any matter with which parliament had not meddled. The vigorous legislation of our medieval parliaments had rendered any theory of law above king, above king and parliament, an unworkable doctrine. It soon perished; year by year events showed that the struggle lay between sovereignty of king, and sovereignty of king in parliament. A poor relic of the theory lives on in Blackstone—the judges, he seems to think, might hold a statute void if it contravened the law of nature, but by Blackstone's day this had become an impracticable speculative tenet, and we may fairly say that it was destroyed by Bentham. However, let us remember that Coke held it.

[1] 8 *Rep.* 118.

E. *Legislation.*

We may then regard the seventeenth century as finally settling the sovereignty of England in king and parliament. But we must watch this process more in detail: and we will start with the ordaining, dispensing and suspending powers which the kings have claimed. We have seen that under James I the judges, who were no enemies to the prerogative, had held that a royal ordinance or proclamation could have but an extremely limited force—it could create no new offence—it could simply be used as a public announcement of the law, an intimation that the government was going to enforce the law. Here then the common law as declared by the judges was against the king—but practically so long as the Court of Star Chamber existed, the last word on the matter did not rest with the judges: that court would, and did, enforce proclamations. The proclamations of Charles I were far more numerous than those of his father. Prices were fixed by proclamation ; houses were demolished, shops were shut in order that the new cathedral of St Paul might appear to better advantage ; all persons who had houses in the country were directed to leave London. On 5 July, 1641, the act was passed which abolished the Court of Star Chamber, and with it fell the power of enforcing proclamations. One finds it said in later law books, in accordance with the opinion of the judges of James I, that an offence may be aggravated by being committed against a royal proclamation. This doctrine would seem to hold even in our own day : a judge in passing sentence might take into consideration the fact that the offence, riot, let us say, or unlawful assembly, had been publicly proclaimed an offence by the king : but obviously a power of issuing such proclamations is not of first-rate importance.

With regard to the dispensing and suspending powers, I can refer you to Sir William Anson[1]. The two powers are in theory distinct. Our law might give to the king power to dispense with statutes in favour of individuals specially named by him, and yet might well deny him the power of suspending

---

[1] *Law and Custom of the Constitution*, Part I, *Parliament*, 3rd ed., pp. 311—19.

a law so that persons in general might treat it as being non-existent. The claim to the greater power seems to have grown out of the claim to the lesser power, and the theory established at the Revolution by the Bill of Rights is that, while the suspending power had never had any legal existence, the king had lawfully enjoyed a certain, or rather, perhaps we ought to say, an uncertain power of dispensation. It was extremely difficult even for the most ardent parliamentarians to deny that a dispensing power had existed, though as to the definition of its lawful limits there was a very great uncertainty. From a very early time the king had taken on himself to dispense with statutes. In theory this power was closely connected with that power of pardoning, with which our king is still entrusted. We may indeed readily distinguish between the two—pardon relates to something that has already been done, dispensation to something that is to be done in the future. Also to this day the queen, by her Attorney-General, has power to stop a criminal prosecution by entering a *nolle prosequi*. Every proceeding by indictment is in legal theory a proceeding by the queen, and if the queen refuses to prosecute, then the prosecution comes to an end. It should be remembered also that many of the medieval statutes imposed as punishments for offences not reaching the degree of felony, fines and forfeitures of which the king had the profit. It should be remembered also that a distinction between the king's public capacity and his private capacity, a distinction between the king and the crown is pretty modern and foreign to the Middle Ages. The royal revenue and the national revenue are all one; there is no such thing as national land, the king's lands are simply the king's lands, no matter by what title they became his. These things being remembered, it will not seem strange that the king should have exercised a power of dispensing with penal statutes. If any one breaks such a statute, who is wronged? The king; it is for him to prosecute, and the fines and penalties will be his. May we not say, *Volenti non fit injuria*; if the king chooses to say in advance that he will not consider himself wronged, that he will not exact those penalties which the statutes have given him, what harm is there in this? This power then of dispensing with statutes, seems to have provoked but little protest before the seventeenth century. In that century no lawyer, so far as I am aware, doubted its existence, and the Bill of Rights admitted that in some instances the exercise of it had been lawful. Certain lines had been drawn. It was, for example, a very general doctrine, that while the power extended to what were called *mala quia prohibita*, it did not extend to *mala in se*[1]. The king might permit a man to do what would not have been unlawful but for the statute; he could not permit him to do what apart from any prohibition would be wicked; might dispense with such a statute as those which forbad the holding of land in mortmain, but not with a statute which fixed a punishment for larceny or murder. Again we find in Coke the doctrine that the king can always dispense with a statute which trenches on the royal prerogative, yes, even though the statute itself declares that a dispensation shall be invalid. Coke more than once repeats this doctrine, which obviously points to prerogative above statute. He says that in Henry VII's day it was decided that the king might dispense with a statute, providing that the same person shall not be sheriff for more than a year, and which declared that a dispensation to the contrary should be invalid. The king, by his prerogative, was entitled to the service of his subjects as sheriffs and so forth; no statute could deprive him of this. The Year Book to which Coke refers does not seem to me to bear him out; such, however, was his doctrine[2]. It is only under James II that we hear much against dispensations, though the sale of them had long been a grievance. James seems to have used them with a settled purpose of practically annulling the statutes which excluded Papists from office. In this the court maintained him, and doubtless his success with dispensations set him on the project of suspending laws in a direct fashion. The line between the two powers that he claimed can be theoretically marked—the dispensation applies to this or that individual, a suspending of the statute would free all men, and yet, of course, the dispensing power might be so lavishly used that it would practically operate to suspend the laws. The

[1] Coke, *Case of Proclamations* XII, Report 76.
[2] ib. *Case of Non Obstante* XII, Report 18.

Bill of Rights condemned absolutely the suspending power; its condemnation of the dispensing power was qualified. 'The pretended power of dispensing with laws, or the execution of laws by regal authority, as it hath been assumed and exercised of late, is illegal.' It would have been going too far to declare that every exercise of the dispensing power had been illegal—many private rights and titles must have been acquired on the faith of dispensations. No attempt, however, was made to settle what dispensations had been legal: the words used were those which I have just read. As to the future, it was declared that no dispensation by *non obstante* of any statute shall be allowed, 'except a dispensation be allowed of in such statute, and except in such cases as shall be specially provided for by one or more bill or bills, to be passed during this present session of parliament.' There was some intention, at least among the lords, of passing an act defining in what cases dispensations should be valid; but the project fell to the ground—and so the words about a bill to be passed in the then session of parliament, never took effect. This is the last of the dispensing power.

As to the suspending power, the case of the seven bishops is the one great case. The question came but incidentally before the court. James II had issued the declaration of indulgence. By his royal prerogative (as the document runs) he declares it his royal will and pleasure that all and all manner of penal laws in matters ecclesiastical be immediately suspended. The clergy were required to read this declaration in church; the bishops petitioned, and their petition was the 'seditious libel' for which they were tried. Now the one precedent which could be produced for such a declaration, was a very similar declaration published by Charles II in 1673—a declaration of indulgence suspending the penal laws. But the commons had protested, and Charles had been compelled to acknowledge that the declaration was illegal. This precedent, therefore, so far from strengthening the case for the crown, could but weaken the case for James when he followed his brother's footsteps. At the bishops' trial the advocates make the best of their very bad case, but very bad it certainly was. Two judges charged the jury in favour of the crown, two in favour of the bishops. The two former seem to have had nothing to say for the declaration, save that the laws were the king's, and that he might do what he liked with them ; the bishops, as we all know, were acquitted. The only ancient record that was produced was from the reign of Richard II, and, as it seems to me, shows very plainly that even Richard did not believe himself to possess any such vast power as James now claimed[1]. The commons, expressing great confidence in the king, declared that the king, with the assent of the lords, might make such sufferance touching the Statute of Provisors lately passed, as should seem to him reasonable until the next parliament ; the commons, however, were to be at liberty to disagree to such sufferance in the next parliament, protested that this assent was a novelty, and was not to be drawn into consequence, and prayed that this protest might be recorded on the roll of the parliament. But in truth one can hardly speak of this declaration otherwise than as an open and determined attempt to override the law. The Bill of Rights dealt with the suspending power in a very summary way. 'The pretended power of suspending of laws, or the execution of laws by regal authority, without consent of parliament, is illegal.' This also is reckoned one of the ways in which King James did endeavour to subvert and extirpate the Protestant religion and the laws and liberties of this kingdom : namely 'By assuming and exercising a power of dispensing with and suspending laws, and the execution of laws without the consent of parliament ; also by committing and prosecuting divers worthy prelates for humbly petitioning to be excused from concurring to the said assumed power.'

F.   *Taxation and Control over Finance.*

At the beginning of our period the king has lately achieved a great victory in the financial sphere. The Court of Exchequer has decided in Bate's case, or the case of the Impositions, that the king may set a duty on imports. Even Coke thinks that he may do this, if it be not merely for the purpose of raising a revenue, but for the good of the realm ; he may prohibit importation, therefore *a fortiori* he may tax it.

[1] *State Trials*, XII, 375. For the precedent, *Rot. Parl.* 15 Ric. II. See also Broom, *Constitutional Law*, 2nd ed. pp. 406—506.

Parliament protested, and grew bolder the more it explored the records of the Middle Ages. None the less, imposts were set on all goods, and were collected. When Charles I met his first parliament, the commons refused to make that grant of tonnage and poundage for the king's life, which since the days of Henry V had been usual; they would grant it for but one year; the lords would not pass a bill for so restricted a grant; the king dissolved the parliament, and continued to levy tonnage and poundage and other imposts, without parliamentary sanction. Out of his second parliament he could get nothing; it was set upon impeaching Buckingham, and the king was set on saving him. Indirect taxation would not now suffice to meet the king's wants. He had recourse to a forced loan—the very sums which divers persons were to 'lend' him were specified. Five knights who refuse to contribute, Darnel, Corbet, Earl, Heveningham and Hampden, were committed to prison by the council. They applied for a habeas corpus, but could not get delivered; their case, famous as Darnel's case, will come before us under another heading.

In March, 1628, Charles had to face his third parliament, and on 7 June he gave his assent to the Petition of Right which turned it into a statute. The first of its four points concerns us here. It recites the *Statutum de Tallagio non Concedendo*, the statute of 1350 against forced loans, and the statute of Richard III against benevolences; it then recites that commissions have issued, by means whereof people have been required to lend money—and have been imprisoned for not doing so. It prays that no man hereafter be compelled to make or yield any gift, loan, benevolence, tax, or such like charge, without common consent by act of parliament. This request the king concedes.

As against anything that we could call direct taxation, these words are clear enough. That they were meant to strike at the customs duties, usually known as the impositions, which the king was levying without parliamentary consent, is by no means clear[1]. We have to remember that the Court of Exchequer had pronounced them to be lawful. As a matter of fact the king continued to levy them—some, Chambers for

---

[1] Gardiner, *History of England*, vol. VI, pp. 326—9. G. W. Prothero in *Eng. Hist. Rev.* vol. VI, p. 394—5 (April, 1891).

instance, refused to pay and were imprisoned. But during the long interval which now passed without a parliament (1629–40), the king had recourse to yet a new means of extorting money. In 1634 he required the seaports and maritime counties to furnish him with ships. Shortly after he demanded ship-money—money by way of composition for an equipment of ships—even from the inland counties. Hampden refused to pay. His case was heard by all the twelve judges in the Exchequer-Chamber[1]; seven decided against him, five were in his favour; but two of these took a merely technical point; only two, Cooke and Hutton, spoke decidedly against the king. Now that there were some ancient precedents which might be forced to support his case, could hardly be denied; but to say nothing of the *Confirmatio Cartarum*, and the *De Tallagio*, which parliament had lately treated as a statute, there was the recent Petition of Right. Whatever might be said of the customs duties, clearly this ship-money was a tax. The majority of the judges would not contest the applicability of these statutes—they fell back on prerogative above statute. I have already quoted some passages from their judgments— practically they say that the king is sovereign, and his commands are laws. The Long Parliament passed an act declaring the judgment void; the king gave his assent on 7 August, 1641. It declared that the writs for collecting ship-money were unlawful, and it condemned the practice of obtaining an extra-judicial opinion from the judges, a practice which had been resorted to in Hampden's case. Meanwhile the parliament had at last made grants of tonnage and poundage, and the king had, in giving his assent, declared that he was abandoning a right which his predecessors had ever considered their own. The act declared that it could not lawfully be levied without parliamentary grant. At the same time measures were passed to abolish the practice of forcing men to accept knighthood, or pay a fine—a practice of his

[1] There were two Courts of Exchequer Chamber, one created by 31 Ed. III, st. 1, c. 12 to hear appeals from the Court of Exchequer, the other, created by 27 Eliz. c. 8 to hear appeals from the Court of King's Bench. The Courts were practically amalgamated in 1830 by 11 Geo. IV, 1 Will. IV, c. 70, § 8. The Jurisdiction of the Exchequer Chamber was finally transferred to the Court of Appeal in 1873. 36, 37 Vict. c. 66, § 18. See W. S. Holdsworth, *History of English Law*, vol. I, pp. 108—10, 413.

ancestors which Charles had revived—and which parliament might well call useless and unreasonable, but could hardly call unlawful, and also to prevent the resuscitation of ancient forest rights, which had of late been oppressively used.

On the whole then, the victory in this matter of taxation was won, so far as such a victory can be won by acts of parliament, before the Civil War broke out.   Charles II had no need to raise revenue without the consent of parliament: he was liberally supplied.   But the duties which had been granted to him died with him, and James continued to levy them without parliamentary authority during the interval between his accession and the meeting of his parliament.   That interval was but two months, however, and his parliament was ready to condone what he had done.   However, when the Revolution came, this was reckoned up as one of his illegal acts in the Declaration of Rights and the Bill of Rights—he had levied money by pretence of prerogative for other time and in other manner, than the same was granted by parliament ; and it was declared that 'the levying of money for or to the use of the crown by pretence of prerogative without grant from parliament for longer time or in other manner than the same is or shall be granted, is illegal.'   This we may say is the last word on this matter—one great chapter of English history has been closed.

But controversy has been collecting round another point. Parliament has been claiming a control over the expenditure of the revenue.   We have to remember that throughout the Middle Ages the king's revenue had been in a very true sense the king's revenue, and parliament had but seldom attempted to give him orders as to what he should do with it.   However, sometimes, in particular under Henry IV, it had forced him to render accounts.   Under the Tudors, parliament hardly dared to meddle with such matters ; but in 1624 a precedent was set for an appropriation of supplies—the money granted by parliament was to be paid into the hands of commissioners named by the parliament, and was to be applied to the relief of the Palatinate.   A similar course was followed in 1641— but this might perhaps be accounted a revolutionary proceeding.   During the rebellion men became accustomed to see the national finances managed by a parliamentary committee. In 1665 a very large sum was to be granted for the Dutch war ; a clause was introduced into the bill which imposed the tax to the effect that the money was to be applied only to the purposes of the war. This precedent was followed in some, but not all, other cases under Charles II—it was not followed by the parliament of James II. After the Revolution it was invariably followed—money raised by taxation was appropriated to this purpose and to that, and a clause was inserted in the statute forbidding the Lords of the Treasury to use money for any other purpose than that for which it was appropriated. Before the end of William's reign, a certain annual sum is assigned to the king for his own use ; we begin to have what is afterwards called a civil list ; the residue of the money is voted for this purpose and for that—so much for the navy, so much for the army. Already under Charles II it had become apparent that such appropriation was to be no idle scheme ; the breach of an appropriation clause was one of the charges on which Danby was impeached. He was saved from punishment by a royal pardon—a matter which will come before us by and by. We shall also see how the appropriation of supplies secured as a matter of fact that parliament should meet every year.

Meanwhile, the commons had asserted, not merely that money bills must be first introduced in their house, but also that the lords cannot make amendments in them. This claim, it seems, cannot be traced beyond the Restoration, but we hear of it in 1661 and 1671. The lords gradually and reluctantly gave way about this matter—but a border warfare was long kept up between the two houses as to details. It is difficult to find any principle upon which this so-called privilege of the House of Commons can be founded. Before the end of William's reign the commons saw that this put a powerful engine into their hands for coercing the House of Lords. In 1701, in order to force the lords into passing a bill which annulled the grants which William had made out of the forfeited Irish lands, they tacked to this a money bill, a bill granting the Land Tax ; they sent up, that is to say, a single bill dealing with these two matters, and insisted that as it was a money bill, the lords could not amend it, could merely accept or reject it as a whole. The lords, thus forced into a dilemma, had to pass the bill, for they could not leave the king without money[1]. Thus the House of Commons became in practical power the superior of the two houses.

One curious little point remains to be noticed, namely, the taxation of the clergy. Ever since Henry VIII's day the clerical subsidies, though voted in the convocations, were confirmed by act of parliament. During the commonwealth the clergy were taxed along with the laity. After the Restoration the old plan was for a moment adopted—the convocations of 1661 taxed themselves; but in 1662 they were taxed by parliament. This theoretically great change was the outcome of no legislation, there was no fuss about it, merely a private arrangement between Lord Chancellor Clarendon and Archbishop Sheldon. From that moment, we may say, the clerical estate disappears finally. Convocations, however, still met, but in 1717 the Bangorian controversy, originated by the writings of Hoadley, Bishop of Bangor, was in flame; it was apparent that the clergy would censure Hoadley, a friend of the government. The convocations were prorogued by royal writ, and were never summoned again for business until 1861.

G.   *Administration of Justice.*

The greatest event that we have to notice under this heading is the abolition of the Star Chamber—accomplished by an act of the Long Parliament, to which the king gave assent on 5 July, 1641[2]. More and more the theory had grown, that it derived its only authority from the act of Henry VII, that all that it did beyond the authority of that statute was illegal. This theory was adopted by the act which abolished the court. It abolished the court commonly called the Star Chamber—it also forbad the council to meddle with civil causes—it abolished the jurisdiction of the Council of the Marches, and the Council of the North; it declared that no court should exercise the same or the like jurisdiction as had been exercised by the Star Chamber. On the same day, by

---

[1] Macaulay, *History of England*, c. xxv.
[2] Gardiner, *Constitutional Documents*, pp. 179—86.

another act, the Court of High Commission was abolished, and it was declared that no similar court should be erected for the future. This act used very large words as to the abolition of all ecclesiastical jurisdiction. During the commonwealth episcopacy disappeared. In 1661, after the Restoration, an act was passed, explaining that the old ecclesiastical courts were to retain their old powers—the act of 1641 was abolished save as far as related to the Court of High Commission. Loyal as was the parliament of 1661, it did not mean to have either the Star Chamber or the High Commission back again. However, in 1686 James II, in the teeth of these statutes, entrusted the whole government of the church to seven commissioners with large powers of suspending, depriving and excommunicating the clergy. His hardly disguised object was to force the Roman religion on the national church. It is one of the offences reckoned up against him in the Declaration and the Bill of Rights that he has issued and caused to be executed a commission under the great seal for erecting a court of commissioners for ecclesiastical causes : this is 'illegal and pernicious.'

The Chancery, though it had never been popular, and had at times been regarded as unconstitutional, escaped. Barebones' Parliament attempted to abolish it, but even Cromwell found that the Chancery lawyers were too much for him[1]. After the Restoration a new period opens in its history. Heneage Finch, Lord Nottingham, who became Chancellor in 1675, has been called the father of English Equity. Henceforth equity becomes a settled system of rapidly developing principles, a supplementary system of case law, giving additional remedies and enforcing additional duties—but a system of case law with precedents reported and respected.

Next we notice that the independence of the judges has been secured. Throughout the Stuart reigns judges have been dismissed if they withstand the king—too often they have been his servile creatures. All along they have held their offices *durante beneplacito*—during the king's good pleasure. At once after the Revolution the question is raised,

[1] For the attempts to reform the Law during the Commonwealth see F. A. Inderwick, *The Interregnum*, pp. 152—248.

and William's judges were commissioned *quamdiu se bene gesserint*—during good behaviour. He, however, refused his assent to a bill for making this a matter of law—but the point was secured by the Act of Settlement (12 and 13 Will. III, c. 2). So soon as the House of Hanover comes to the throne judge's commissions are to be made *quamdiu se bene gesserint*, and their salaries are to be fixed, but they are to be removable upon an address of both houses of parliament. This means that a judge cannot be dismissed except either in consequence of a conviction for some offence, or on the address of both houses.

Another important matter has been the power of committing to prison and the use of the writ of habeas corpus. The first question is, whether the king or king in council having committed a man to prison, it is a sufficient return to the writ that he was committed by the king's command. We have seen that the judges of Elizabeth's day had returned a very obscure, perhaps designedly obscure, answer[1]. The point was raised by Charles I in the interval between his second and his third parliament : five knights, Darnel, Corbet, Earl, Heveningham, and Hampden were committed to gaol for refusing to contribute to the so-called 'loan' that was being exacted. They obtained the habeas corpus, and the gaoler returned that they were imprisoned *per speciale mandatum domini Regis* signified to him by a warrant of the council. Darnel's counsel hardly contended that he should be set free —but did contend that he ought to be liberated on bail—and produced a great mass of precedents to show that the courts had repeatedly bailed prisoners about whom similar returns had been made. The judges refused to bail the prisoners, and sent them back to gaol. In doing this they had, I think, the weight of precedents, even of modern precedents, against them ; but practice had hardly been uniform, and we are not, I think, entitled to say that the judgment was plainly iniquitous. This was the second point dealt with by the Petition of Right. It recited the famous clause in Magna Carta *Nullus liber homo* etc. ; it recited what had happened in Darnel's case, and it prayed 'that no freeman in any such manner as is

[1] p. 274.

before mentioned be imprisoned or detained'; and to this prayer the king gave his assent. On 2 March, 1629, there was a disorderly scene in the House of Commons. The Speaker had the king's commands to adjourn the house. Eliot wished to read a remonstrance against the taking of tonnage and poundage without parliamentary sanction. The Speaker was held down in his chair. On 10 March the king dissolved parliament. A few days after he arrested some of those who had been engaged in the disorder, Eliot, Holles, Selden, Long and Strode. They sued out a writ of habeas corpus. On this occasion the return mentioned a cause for the arrest—they were arrested for notable contempts and for stirring up sedition. This was not a charge of felony or treason, and the judges seem to have had no real doubt that they ought to be bailed. However, they temporized and ordered the prisoners not merely to find bail for the present charge, but also to find sureties for future good behaviour. The prisoners refused to do this. The king afterwards liberated all but three. Against Eliot an information was filed in the King's Bench for words uttered in the House: against Holles and Valentine, for tumult and an assault on the Speaker. The further history of this case must come under the heading of parliamentary privilege.

The act of 1641 which abolished the Star Chamber did not deprive the council of the power of committing to prison; it deprived it of criminal jurisdiction, of power to hear and determine causes, but the power of committing to prison suspected persons in order that they might stand their trials in the ordinary courts was left to it, it was a power possessed by every justice of the peace. The act, however, provided that every person so committed should be entitled to a habeas corpus, and made some stringent regulations for forcing the court to decide at once whether they were bailable or no.

Thus at the Restoration, we may say, the general principles of the law were settled and needed no amendment; but events showed that they could be evaded. Between 1670 and 1679 the House of Commons attempted to get a new act dealing with this matter. In the latter year the famous Habeas Corpus act was passed (31 Car. II, c. 2). I know no subject on which it is more difficult to lecture briefly, because it is altogether made up of details, but roughly speaking the result is this—any person who stands committed for any crime except for treason or felony plainly expressed in the warrant of commitment, is to have the writ. He is to be able to get it in vacation time as well as term time. The chancellor or any judge to whom he applies must grant it, or incur a penalty of £500. The gaoler must make the return within a very brief time, or incur a penalty. No person is to be sent into prison out of the kingdom; anyone who breaks this rule is to incur the penalty of a *praemunire* and be incapable of pardon. Prisoners who are committed for treason or felony are to have a right to a speedy trial. The heavy penalties which judges and gaolers incur if they break this act are given to the injured person, may be sued for by him as debts; this scheme makes it impossible for the king to protect or pardon them, for the king has no power to forgive a debt due to his subjects. For further details I must refer you to Langmead or Hallam, or still better to the act itself[1].

One of the offences alleged against James II in the Declaration of Rights and Bill of Rights is that excessive bail has been required of persons committed in criminal cases to elude the benefit of the laws made for the liberty of the subjects: and it is declared that excessive bail ought not to be required. This is somewhat vague, but there was no more distinct provision. The law as to what offences were bailable, what not, was still in the main contained in the Statute of Westminster I (1275). As a general rule a person committed for a misdemeanour was entitled to bail; but in the course of the seventeenth and eighteenth centuries a number of exceptions were made to this.

To this period also we must assign the establishment of the principle that jurors cannot be fined or imprisoned or otherwise punished for a false verdict, or for a verdict against the judge's direction. The old process of attaint still existed: nominally it existed until 1825, when it was abolished; but it had fallen into disuse, and judges presiding at trials had taken

---

[1] Printed in Stubbs' *Select Charters*, pp. 517—23.

on themselves to fine and imprison jurors in a summary way for perverse verdicts. Apparently this practice began in the sixteenth century. In 1670 the Court of Common Pleas in Bushell's case decided that it was illegal, and set free jurors who had been imprisoned by justices of oyer and terminer at the Old Bailey. The abolition of the Star Chamber was, we must remember, the abolition of a court which habitually punished jurors for perverse verdicts. We may say that at the end of our period the principle is fully established that for a perverse verdict or a verdict against the judge's direction jurors cannot be punished—though the old process of attainting them before a jury of twenty-four (which seems never to have been applied in criminal cases) still maintained a nominal existence. A corrupt verdict would of course be a different matter—for this jurors might be indicted and tried in the regular way.

Meanwhile some other points of our judicial constitution were settled. The House of Lords had succeeded in establishing its right to hear appeals from the Court of Chancery and had failed in establishing a right to act as a court of first instance in civil matters. We have seen how the function of the House of Lords as a court of error had fallen into abeyance towards the end of the Middle Ages, and been revived under James I. During the reign of Charles I it pressed its claims further with little protest from the commons; it entertained appeals from the Chancery, and it exercised a jurisdiction as a court of first instance both in civil cases and in criminal cases which had nothing to do with privilege. When at the Restoration the time came for reestablishing the ancient constitution, this part of the constitution was in a somewhat undefined state and gave rise to some bitter quarrels between the two Houses of the parliament of 1661—Charles II's long parliament. The result I have described. In the case of *Skinner* v. *The East India Company* the lords attempted to act as a civil court of first instance. Both houses had gone great lengths, and when in 1670 the king intervened and persuaded the houses to rescind all their proceedings, the fruits of victory in this case were obtained by the commons—the lords tacitly abandoned their claim to an original civil jurisdiction. In

1675 they fell out again over the case of *Shirley* v. *Fagg*, a case in which the House of Lords had taken on itself to hear an appeal from the Chancery. In this case after long disputes the commons tacitly gave way, and the lords established their point. The truth seems to be that the commons were getting frightened by their own arguments. The historical investigations into which they plunged might show them that the claim of the House of Lords to an inherent power of hearing appeals from the Chancery was a new claim, but such investigations could only bring out into clearer relief the ancient doctrine that the only source of all jurisdiction is the king. They did not want to exalt the king's power, and they gave way without however conceding that they were in the wrong. Thus it came about that the House of Lords acquired a new domain for its judicial powers—it now sat as an appeal court from the Chancery; as the depository of the judicial power of parliament it was a court for correcting the errors in law of the courts of common law, it was a court for the trial of peers indicted for treason or felony, and lastly it was the tribunal for impeachments.

This is the era of impeachments. Do not think of impeachments as common events. During the whole of English history there have not, I think, been seventy, and a full quarter of all of them belong to the years 1640-1-2. Almost every case therefore has raised some new point. Perhaps the most important points are these—(1) can a commoner be impeached for felony or treason? The lords in *Fitzharris's case* (1681) decided that he could not—he was entitled to trial by jury in every capital case. The commons voted that this was a violation of the constitution of parliament. Fitzharris was indicted for treason in the ordinary way before the King's Bench and hanged. In 1689 however the House of Lords in the case of Sir Adam Blair and other commoners impeached for treason decided to proceed with the impeachment. Certainly in the reign of Charles I they had not objected to trying impeached commoners for treason. The question has not been raised since 1689, though it has often been discussed. I believe that the weight of legal authority is against the impeachment of commoners for treason or felony. Sir J. F.

Stephen lays down that a commoner cannot be impeached for treason or felony, but that there may be some doubt as to treason[1]. (2) It was at length decided in the case of Warren Hastings that neither a prorogation, nor a dissolution of parliament, will bring an impeachment to an end. About this the House of Lords in Charles II's reign had come to contradictory resolutions; in Danby's case (1679) it had held that a dissolution did not put a stop to an impeachment; in 1685 it reversed and annulled this resolution. Too often such matters have been decided by party votes. (3) Danby's case raised the important question, whether a royal pardon could stop an impeachment; the question was raised but not decided, for the impeachment was dropped. The Act of Settlement provides that a pardon shall not be pleadable to an impeachment, but does not prevent the king from pardoning after sentence—and three of the lords concerned in the rebellion of 1715 were pardoned after they had been impeached, found guilty and sentenced. As to the point raised in Danby's case, whether as the law stood a pardon would stop an impeachment, it was a very new point, and on general principles I am far from being satisfied that the commons had the best of the argument. The question would seem to be whether an impeachment was more analogous to an indictment, which could always be stopped by the king's pardon, or to an appeal of felony which, being regarded as a private suit, was beyond the royal power.

Another change to be noted is this. We remember that if a peer is indicted for treason or felony he is tried if parliament be in session by his peers in the House of Lords, but if parliament be not sitting, then by the Court of the Lord High Steward. The king, since the steward's office had ceased to be hereditary, made some peer High Steward for the occasion, who summoned a number of peers, not fixed by law, to hold the trial[2]. This of course enabled the king or his steward to pack the court. An act of 1696 altered this in case of treason, but not in case of felony, by ordering that all peers

---

[1] *History of Criminal Law*, vol. 1, p. 146.
[2] See above, p. 171.

should be summoned twenty days before the trial. I believe, however, that in no case has this provision taken effect; the last trial in the Court of the High Steward is said to be that of Lord Delamere for treason in 1686. Parliament has sat so regularly year by year that there has been no need for such a court, and since the end of George II's reign there have, I believe, been but four cases of the trial of peers in parliament otherwise than on impeachment. These are Lord Ferrers for murder in 1760, Lord Byron for murder in 1765, the Duchess of Kingston for bigamy in 1776, and Lord Cardigan for murder in 1841[1].

This same act of 1696 introduced various important modifications into the procedure in cases of treason. The indicted person was to have a copy of the indictment, might make his defence by counsel, and produce witnesses who were to be examined on oath. He was only to be convicted if there were two witnesses to the same treason, he was only to be prosecuted within three years after the alleged treason. He was to have a copy of the panel, that is, of the names of the persons summoned as jurors, two days before the trial, in order that he might consider whom to challenge. In all these respects a number of exceptions in favour of persons accused of treason were made from the general law. It was not until 1702 that an accused felon could produce witnesses who could be examined on oath, and it was not until 1836 (6 and 7 Will. IV, 114) that he was suffered to make his defence by counsel.

The evil practice of passing acts of attainder has not yet fallen into disuse. It was by an act of attainder that Strafford perished in 1641. It was by an ordinance of the two Houses, to which the king's assent had of course not been obtained, that Laud perished in 1645. In 1660 the turn for the regicides came; such of them as were already dead or beyond the seas were attainted of high treason by act of parliament. In 1696 Sir John Fenwick was attainted for the attempt to assassinate William III. This is the last instance of an act

---

[1] Lord Russell was tried for bigamy in 1901. Lord Halsbury (Lord Chancellor) presided as Lord High Steward. There were also present about 160 Peers, including all the Law Lords who generally hear appeals, and eleven Judges.

passed to inflict the punishment of death for an offence already committed; but minor punishments have been inflicted by similar means in later days.

One more remark. The act which abolished the Star Chamber did not of course abolish the council. It was still after the Restoration the body consulted by the king when he wanted advice, though already the practice is springing up of consulting only a few of its members, a practice which in course of time has given us the modern cabinet. But the act just mentioned did not deprive the council even of all judicial power. It was forbidden to take cognizance of any matter of property belonging to the subjects of this kingdom; but it retained jurisdiction as a court of last resort in admiralty matters, and in all matters civil and criminal arising in the king's lands beyond the seas. From very small beginnings, a jurisdiction over the Isle of Man and the Channel Islands, this power steadily grew as conquest and colonization gave the king new lands beyond the seas. Thus the Privy Council became an ultimate tribunal for a vast empire—not for England, not for Great Britain, but for all other lands of the king in all corners of the globe—a marvellous jurisdiction now exercised by the judicial committee of the Privy Council.

H. *Privilege of Parliament.*

Over the privileges of parliament there has been severe fighting. In the first place as regards freedom of speech we have Eliot's case. A few days after the dissolution of 1629 Eliot and others were arrested and committed to the Tower. They obtained writs of habeas corpus, and the returns to those writs stated that they had been committed for notable contempts and for stirring up sedition. The judges had to consider whether they should be bailed or no, and seemingly there was no real doubt that by law bail ought to be allowed —but they temporized and demanded from the prisoners not merely bail for the present charge, but also sureties for future good behaviour. The attorney-general then brought forward a criminal charge against three of them, against Eliot for words spoken in the House, against Holles and Valentine for a tumult on the last day of the session. The others were liberated. The prisoners pleaded that as the alleged offences were supposed to be committed in parliament they ought not to answer for them in another court. They relied much on Strode's case and the act of 1512 (4 Hen. VIII, c. 8), passed respecting him ; this they contended was a general act. The judges held that it only applied to suits against members of parliament prosecuted in the Stannary courts, and arguing that the King's Bench has power to punish crimes wherever committed, sentenced the prisoners, who refused to plead any other plea, to be imprisoned during the king's pleasure. When the Long Parliament met the commons protested against this as a breach of privilege. After the Restoration, the parliament, however loyal, was not disposed to retract its claim of privilege. In 1667 both Houses agreed in declaring that Strode's act was a general act declaratory of the ancient and necessary rights and privileges of parliament and that the judgment against Eliot, Holles and Valentine was illegal. What is more, Holles, who was still alive, caused the judgment to be brought before the House of Lords by writ of error, and the House in its judicial capacity reversed the judgment. We must not however suppose that the reversal of this judgment established the principle that nothing done in parliament by any of its members can be punished as a crime in a court of law. It was conceded that had the charge been merely that of committing a riot in the House, the King's Bench might have taken cognizance of the case ; but words spoken in parliament it could not punish. We may take it to be law that an ordinary crime, such as theft committed by a member in the House, might be punished in the ordinary courts in the ordinary way. Since the Restoration there has not, I believe, been any attempt made by any court of law to punish a member for words spoken in the House. The Declaration and Bill of Rights proclaim that the freedom of speech and debates or proceedings in parliament ought not to be impeached or questioned in any court or place out of parliament.

The attempt to arrest the five members must also be noticed. Charles had determined to accuse five members of the House of Commons of high treason. This he did, not by causing them to be indicted in the ordinary way, but by preferring a set of charges against them in the House of Lords. For such a proceeding there seems to have been no warrant, at least in later times. Only by an impeachment preferred by the commons could a commoner be brought to trial before the lords for any crime, and, as we have seen, it might be doubted whether a commoner could even be impeached for treason or felony—thus he would be deprived of trial by jury. Then the king in person attempted to arrest the five members in the House of Commons, while the House was sitting. Now a member of parliament has no privilege of freedom from arrest on a charge of treason or felony—indeed, according to later authorities, he has none on a charge of any indictable offence. You should therefore understand that outside the House Pym and his fellows might have been arrested; perhaps they might lawfully have been arrested within the walls of the House, if the House had not been sitting. But the attempt to arrest them while they were sitting as members of the House, we may probably reckon as a distinct breach of the law; at any rate it was an extremely high-handed act, intended to overawe the House: it made the Civil War almost certain.

After the Restoration members of Parliament enjoyed the privilege of freedom from arrest in all civil cases. We must remember that imprisonment in civil cases was at this time very common; debtors were imprisoned by way of execution, and when an action was begun against a man he might very commonly be at once arrested and compelled to find bail for his appearance in court, or otherwise remain in prison—so this privilege was a very important matter. It was carried to great lengths—the members claimed freedom from arrest not only for themselves but for their servants, and they claimed that their property should be privileged from execution. These extensive claims which were admitted in the seventeenth century were gradually curtailed by statute; they had become serious obstructions to the ordinary course of justice. A statute of 1700 began this process of curtailment; statutes of Anne and George III (1770) carried the process further[1]

[1] 2 and 3 Anne, c. 18. 10 George III, c. 50.

The servants and the property of members were no longer privileged—nothing was left but the freedom from arrest for members themselves, a matter which the abolition of imprisonment for debt has in our own day made of small importance.

As to the power of punishing persons for contempt, the two Houses vied with each other in extending its limits. It was freely exercised to protect the members of the Houses from assault and insult—under William III he who makes any insulting remark about any member of the House runs a great chance of incurring its displeasure and being imprisoned by its order. But further it becomes dangerous even to trespass on a member's land or to fish in his waters. During the latter half of the eighteenth century the Houses gradually abandoned their claim to avenge all manner of wrongs done to their members—but of this abandonment hereafter; during William's reign the claim of privilege was at its height.

A more justifiable use of the power of the House consisted in the punishment of attacks directed not against individual members but against the House as a body. But even in this sphere the power was intemperately used. A notorious instance has just occurred. In 1701 the majority in the Commons' House has been slow to grant supply. The grand jury of Kent present a respectfully worded petition begging them to grant the king the money urgently needed for the prosecution of the war. The House voted that this petition was scandalous and an attempt to destroy the constitution of parliament, and it committed some of the petitioners to prison. It does not seem that they appealed for protection to the courts of law; parliament was soon prorogued and they were delivered. By this time it had apparently become settled doctrine that the House of Commons could not imprison a person save during the session, so that a prorogation would set its prisoners free. They have not since the Revolution attempted to keep a man in prison beyond the limits of the session. On the other hand, the House of Lords has imposed fines and committed persons to prison for a term of months or of years.

Whether a person imprisoned for contempt could get any aid from a court of law, could get a court of law to entertain the question whether a contempt had been committed was, we may say, at this time somewhat doubtful. Suppose the prisoner obtained a writ of habeas corpus and the gaoler returned that he was imprisoned by order of one of the two Houses for a contempt, would the judges be at liberty to investigate the question whether the alleged acts amounted to a contempt? In 1677 the House of Lords committed Lord Shaftesbury and three other peers for words spoken during a debate. Shaftesbury applied for a writ of habeas corpus, but the judges held that they could not inquire into a commitment by the lords of one of their body. In 1680 the commons treated certain persons known as 'abhorrers' in a very arbitrary fashion. They brought actions against the serjeant-at-arms who had imprisoned them—he pleaded the command of the House; but the judges on this occasion over-ruled the plea. After the Revolution the commons took this matter up and summoned two of the judges to the bar. One of them, Pemberton, made some show of argument, but afterwards gave way and admitted that the command of the House would justify the officer in making the arrest.

Thus stands the question at William's death. Soon afterwards (Patey's case, 1705) the judges came to the opinion that they could not investigate the legality of a commitment for contempt. If the House committed a man for contempt and said no more, the courts could do nothing for him. Thus each of the Houses gained a power of arbitrary imprisonment which had been denied to the Court of Star Chamber. The judges of the last century seem to me to have been almost as subservient to the Houses as their predecessors of the Stuart times were to the king. And so the matter rests at the present day: if either House commits a man, whether he be a member or no, for contempt, there is no tribunal in which he can raise by writ of habeas corpus the question whether a contempt has really been committed.

I. *Military Affairs.*

Turning now to military affairs we have to recall the fact that before the days of Charles I proclamations of martial law had not been utterly unknown. Not to go back to the

Wars of the Roses, Elizabeth had issued such a proclamation in 1588 and again in 1595. James had followed the example in 1617, 1620, 1624. Probably we ought to say of them that they were illegal, though in this matter we may be prejudiced by what then was future history. Charles I early in his reign had recourse to such commissions. It became always clearer that there must be a standing army and that a standing army could only be kept together by more stringent rules and more summary procedure than those of the ordinary law and the ordinary courts. Another grievance was the billeting of soldiers. In 1628 the king had to assent to the Petition of Right. After dealing with the forced loan and the imprisonments by the king's command, it recited that 'of late great companies of soldiers and mariners have been dispersed into divers counties of the realm and the inhabitants against their wills have been compelled to receive them into their houses... against the laws and customs of this realm.' Then it recalled the words of Magna Carta, *Nullus liber homo,* and recited the commissions of martial law; these it declared to be wholly and directly contrary to the laws and statutes of the realm. It prayed that the king would be pleased to remove the said soldiers and mariners, 'and that your people be not so burdened in time to come, that the commissions of martial law might be revoked and annulled and that no such commissions might be issued for the future.' This of course settled the law, and no expedient for evading it could be discovered. The judges had to inform the king's generals that soldiers who offended must be tried by the ordinary courts; that only when an army of the king was in presence of the enemy could there be any place for martial law. Coke in one of his latest books lays down that to put a man to death by martial law is murder[1].

Meanwhile the king and parliament began to quarrel about another and a still more vital point. In whom was the command of the military forces of the kingdom vested? I think that historians and lawyers must agree that it was in

---

[1] 3 Inst. 52. Reference may be made to Dicey, *Law of the Constitution,* 6th ed. c. VIII, and App. XII; also to *The Charge of the Lord Chief Justice to the Grand Jury in the case of the Queen* v. *Nelson and Brand,* ed. F. Cockburn, 1867.

the king. It would have been necessary to go back to very remote and revolutionary times for a precedent of an attempt by parliament to wrest this power from the king's hands. However Charles was suspected, and perhaps justly suspected, of desiring to use the army for the overthrow of the parliamentary constitution ; and in 1642 the Houses asserted that the power of the militia (as it was called) was or at all events ought to be in their hands. This, as is well known, was one of the immediate causes of the Civil War; the king was required to consent to a bill putting the militia, as the old county forces were now called, beyond his control. That the militia and all fortified places should be in such hands as parliament should appoint was one of the Nineteen Propositions tendered to him at York in June, 1642. During the war which followed both sides had recourse to martial law for the government of their armies[1].

I need not remind you how after this England came under the domination of the army, parliament itself becoming the despised slave of the force that it had created. At the Restoration the very name of a standing army had become hateful to the classes which were to be the ruling classes. In 1661 a statute (13 Car. II, c. 6) declared that the 'sole supreme government of the militia and of all forces by sea and land is, and by the laws of England ever was, the undoubted right of the king and his predecessors, and that neither house of parliament could pretend to the same.' The old county force was remodelled by this act. But loyal as the parliament might be, it would not trust even a king with such an engine of tyranny as a standing army. The Convention Parliament passed an act disbanding the army; the king assented; he also had some reason to dread a standing army. The act of disbandment, however, sanctioned the continuance of 'the Guards and Garrisons.' The garrisons were to be placed in the condition in which they existed in 1637, and out of the residue of the soldiers the king was to be at liberty to retain a guard. The number of this guard was not specified. Throughout the reign and on to the Revolution no more than this was legalized. Controversy constantly broke

[1] Gardiner, *Constitutional Documents*, pp. 245—61.

out between king and parliament as to military matters. It was extremely difficult to prevent the king's guards living at free quarters, though the billeting of them was undoubtedly illegal. This practice had been declared illegal by the Petition of Right, and the old prerogatives of purveyance and preemption with which it was nearly connected had been abolished along with the military tenures. The king could impress no cart for military transport, he could buy no hay, straw, victual, or other thing save by free bargain. Anyone who attempted to exercise these old prerogatives was liable to an action for treble damages at the suit of the party grieved ; anyone who attempted to stop such an action was liable to the punishments denounced by the statute of *praemunire*. Also it was difficult for the king to keep his soldiers in hand. In time of peace no punishment, at least no punishment extending to life or member, could be inflicted on them except in the ordinary course of the common law. On the other hand it was practically very difficult to prevent the officers from proceeding according to what they conceived to be the justice of martial law. However, in 1666, articles of war were issued providing for the trial of even capital offences by court martial; also forbidding that any civil magistrate should imprison a soldier save for treason, or for killing or robbing a person not being an officer or soldier. Seemingly the officers who sat on such courts martial must have risked their necks.

Soon after this Clarendon was impeached, 'for that he hath designed a standing army to be raised and to govern the kingdom thereby; and advised the king to dissolve parliament and to lay aside all thoughts of parliament for the future, to govern by a military power and to maintain the same at free quarters and contributions.' But to keep a standing army of any considerable size without supplies from parliament was impossible, and parliament was beginning to appropriate its supplies and to impeach those who infringed the clauses of appropriation. Already, in 1666, a subsidy was granted ; £30,000 and no more was appropriated to the pay of the guards, the residue was to be spent in the war. In 1667 Charles declared that he was going to war with France ; parliament granted but appropriated ; war was not made; parliament passed an act for disbanding the army, an act which contains an important clause directed against the practice of billeting—important because it shows that the Petition of Right was not observed. Money was appropriated for the disbanding of the army. Seymour was impeached for having misappropriated these supplies—using them to retain instead of to disband the soldiers. Danby, the Lord Treasurer, was impeached ' for that he had traitorously endeavoured to subvert the ancient and well-established form of government in this kingdom, and the better to effect that his purpose, he did design the raising of an army upon a pretence of war against the French king, and to continue the same as a standing army within this kingdom ; and to that end he has misappropriated money, whereby the law is eluded, and the army is yet continued.' Nevertheless Charles and James after him in one way and another kept the army on foot. James seems to have had above 16,000 men. After Monmouth's rebellion courts martial sat to administer martial law upon the soldiers. I have before me[1] the record of one of these courts martial. Peter Teat and Peter Innes of Captain Bedford's regiment are tried by eighteen officers under one of the articles of war lately issued which says that ' No officer or soldier shall use any traitorous words against the sacred person of the king's most excellent majesty upon pain of death.' They are condemned to be hanged.

The Bill of Rights declared that one of James's offences had been that he had raised and kept a standing army in time of peace without consent of parliament, and quartered soldiers contrary to law; and further that the raising or keeping a standing army within the kingdom in time of peace, unless it be with consent of parliament, is against law. The words ' in time of peace ' should be noticed ; they certainly seem to imply that in time of war the king may keep a standing army even without the consent of parliament.

But before the Bill of Rights the first Mutiny Act had already been passed (1 William & Mary, c. 5). The troops favourable to James were to be shipped off to the Low Countries. When they reached Ipswich a mutiny broke out. It was

---

[1] Clode, *Military Forces of the Crown*, vol. I, p. 477.

necessary to take rapid action, and a bill was hurriedly passed through parliament. It is a very brief affair to this effect: any soldier in the king's service who shall excite or join in any mutiny or sedition in the army or shall desert shall suffer death or such other punishment as by a court martial shall be inflicted. Then follows a few sentences as to the constitution of courts martial. It is provided that nothing in this act shall exempt any officer or soldier from the ordinary process of law; also that it shall not affect the militia forces, that it shall only be in force until the 10th Nov. next, that is for about half-a-year, that nine out of thirteen officers constituting a court martial must agree in passing sentence of death. That is the whole sum and substance of the first mutiny act. The only crimes that it sends to a court martial are mutiny, sedition, desertion; and in no case is an officer or soldier exempted from the ordinary law. It should be added that though parliament was in haste, it was careful to state in the preamble that the raising or keeping a standing army within this kingdom in time of peace, unless it be with consent of parliament, is against the law. Also that no man may be forejudged of life or limb or subjected to any kind of martial law, or in any other manner than by the judgment of his peers, and according to the known and established laws of this realm. By this time of course it was the orthodox belief of all men that trial by jury was the *judicium parium* of the Great Charter.

From this time forward it became the regular practice to pass temporary mutiny acts. For a while this was not done with perfect regularity. On several occasions during the reigns of William and Anne there was for a few months no mutiny act in force. Sometimes on the other hand the act was to endure for two years. But very soon the practice became settled of passing the act for one year only and of passing such an act in every year. All along through the last century it was regarded as something exceptional, an evil of which we should get rid, if once we had a settled peace. And so for two centuries, year by year, the statute book was burdened by annual mutiny acts which always tended to become longer and longer.

PERIOD V.

Sketch of Public Law at the Present Day.

1887–8.

Preliminary.

On passing to our new point of view, it at once strikes us that our horizon is enormously widened. The parliament sitting at Westminster is no longer the parliament of England, it is the parliament of Great Britain and Ireland. But even this, its title, does not express the whole of the vast territory which is subject to its legislative power. It can make laws for the whole of that huge collection of lands which it is convenient to call the British Empire, but which we must formally style the United Kingdom of Great Britain and Ireland, its colonies and dependencies.

Let us very briefly recount the stages whereby new lands have been brought into connexion with that system, the history of which we have been tracing, and let us note the legal bonds which bind these lands together.

First as regards Wales. Its incorporation in the realm of England is an old story, partly accomplished by Edward I, partly by Henry VIII. The great monuments are the *Statutum Walliae* of 1284, which declared that Wales was not merely a feudal dependency of the English throne but was annexed to England *tamquam pars corporis ejusdem*, and the statute of 1535 which provided seats in parliament for representatives of the Welsh counties and boroughs and introduced the whole body of English law into Wales. So thoroughly had Wales become a part of England that a statute of 1747 laid down the rule that in acts of parliament the name England should be deemed to include Wales.

On the death of Elizabeth King James VI of Scotland became King James I of England; but there was no union of the two countries; they had nothing in common but their king; the parliament at Westminster could not make laws for Scotland, nor could the parliament at Edinburgh make laws for England. The English judges did indeed hold in Calvin's case, 1608, that a person born in Scotland after James had become king of England was not an alien in England, nor subject to the many disabilities to which aliens were then subject, in particular the inability to hold English land. But still the two nations were two distinct nations with two governments. James himself wished for a closer union; he wanted to be king of Great Britain; but his subjects were not prepared for this—he was merely king of England and king of Scotland. Under the Protectorate a closer union was realised; the Restoration, however, brought back the old state of affairs; Charles was king of England and king of Scotland.

The union was effected on 1 May, 1707. Queen Anne became queen of Great Britain. The Act of Union provided that the two kingdoms should become one kingdom by the name of Great Britain, and that there should be not only one king, but one parliament for the two. Sixteen of the Scottish peers were to be chosen by their fellows to represent the Scottish peerage in every parliament; and the Scottish shires and boroughs were to send forty-five members. The two lands, the two nations, were subjected immediately to the same supreme legislative assembly; the English parliament ceased to exist; the Scottish parliament ceased to exist; there was a parliament of Great Britain. It became and is to this day the established rule that every act of this parliament applies to both England and Scotland. If an act is not to apply to Scotland, the act says so expressly; if it is only to apply to Scotland, it says so expressly.

This, however, does not imply that the two countries became subject to the same laws. England kept and still keeps her common law in so far as it has not been abrogated by statute; and English statutes passed before the Union are still in force in England in so far as they have not been abrogated by later statutes. To the same extent Scotland keeps her own common law and her own old statutes. And Scottish law differs considerably from English law. In particular, as regards private law, the Scots attribute an authority to Roman law which it does not enjoy on this side the border. In the sixteenth century it had obtained a footing in Scotland, while from England it had been excluded owing to the early concentration of justice in our king's courts and the activity of our ancient parliaments[1]. So the Scots retained and retain to this day a system of courts which is very different from the English. Still since 1707 the two countries have been subject to one legislative body, fully competent to modify or to abrogate any rules whether of Scottish or of English law.

The Act of Union laid down certain rules as 'fundamental and essential conditions of the union.' Of these the most important related to the two churches of Scotland and England; their doctrines and discipline as established by law were to be inviolably preserved, and each king on his accession was to swear to maintain them. The fundamental and essential character of these provisions is insisted on with so much emphasis that we may say that the act goes near to an attempt to make law which no future parliament shall alter— goes near to such an attempt, but is not definitely guilty of it. It soon became the established doctrine that these provisions, like every other part of the law of England and Scotland, could be repealed by the parliament of the United Kingdom. Blackstone writing some fifty years after the union says this distinctly—'An act of parliament to repeal or alter the Act of Uniformity in England, or to establish episcopacy in Scotland, would doubtless in point of authority be sufficiently valid and binding; and notwithstanding such an act the union would continue unbroken[2].' We have no irrepealable laws; all laws may be repealed by the ordinary legislature, even the conditions upon which the English and Scottish parliaments agreed to merge themselves in the parliament of Great Britain.

[1] See Maitland, *English Law and the Renaissance*, Cambridge, 1901.
[2] *Commentaries*, Introduction, § 4 note.

To Irish history let us devote some little time. In 1169 some English or Norman barons, Robert Fitzstephen, Maurice Fitzgerald, Richard de Clare, known as Strongbow, landed in Ireland, and began to take part in the quarrels of the Irish chieftains. Henry II, fearing the establishment of an independent Norman state across St George's channel, went thither himself and obtained a submission from the barons and the Irish chiefs: they did homage to him. An English settlement was formed in the eastern part of the island. It was divided into counties; the king granted charters to its boroughs, he appointed sheriffs and justices of assize. John took the title of *dominus Hiberniae*. The English settlement was regarded as subject to the English common law, and so soon as John granted the Great Charter at Runnymede, it was sent over to Ireland and published there[1]. The growth of a parliamentary constitution in Ireland, i.e. among the English settlers, was parallel to the growth in England. In 1295 knights of the shire are returned to a parliament held by the viceroy; burgesses appear there, though not it is said until Edward III's reign. We have Irish statutes of 1310, but from that year they are lost until 1429[2]. The colony, however, constantly shrank—the colonists were constantly falling away into the barbarism of the native Irish tribes. The authority of the English king over Ireland reached at length its lowest point in the reign of Henry VII, when it was confined to the four counties of 'the pale,' Dublin, Louth, Kildare and Meath and a few seaport towns. The Anglo-Irish had taken the part of the House of York and had endangered Henry's crown by supporting pretenders. In 1495 he obtained from the Irish parliament a statute known by the name of his viceroy as Poynings' law. It provided that the statutes 'lately' made by the English parliament should hold good in Ireland. Whatever may have been the meaning of the word 'lately,' the construction put upon it was that all English statutes

---

[1] For the 'solemn and authoritative introduction into Ireland of the English system of procedure' in 1227 see Maitland in *Engl. Hist. Rev.* July 1889, pp. 516—18.

[2] Record however exists of legislation for 1297, 1320, 1324, 1351, 1366, 1394, 1402, 1409—10, see *Statutes and Ordinances and Acts of the Parliament of Ireland*, ed. H. F. Berry, Dublin, 1907.

earlier in date than Poynings' Act were law in Ireland. It also provided that no parliament should be held in Ireland until the viceroy should have certified to the king all such acts as were to be passed, and such acts had been confirmed by the king and his council. Thus the king and his English privy council obtained a check upon all proposals for legislation in Ireland. Thenceforward the authority of the king began slowly to revive and extend itself. In 1541 Henry VIII abandoned the old title Lord of Ireland for that of King of Ireland; he was also Supreme Head on Earth of the Church of Ireland. The attempt of Elizabeth to force the reformed English liturgy upon a country in which the Protestant doctrines had made no way led to rebellions, the rebellions to repression. The power of James I was at least nominally acknowledged throughout the whole island. It was all divided into shires; the franchise was given to many boroughs, the number of members in the commons' house was brought up to 232 in 1613. Unfortunately the English persisted in the attempt to force a new religion upon the country, and vast tracts of land which had been forfeited by the treason of rebellious lords were parcelled out among English colonists without regard for the rights of the Irish landowners. There followed the rising of 1641 and the terrible reconquest of the country by Cromwell. Vast quantities of Irish land passed into the hands of the Cromwellians, and at the Restoration many of their titles were confirmed. Under James II the Catholic Irish very naturally took the king's side; they were again repressed by William; and then there was another great confiscation and redistribution of lands.

During the reigns of William and Anne the severest laws were passed by the Irish parliament for the suppression of the Catholic religion. Catholics were excluded from parliament, and in 1715 were deprived of the electoral franchise which they had hitherto exercised. Meanwhile a dispute broke out as to the relation between the English and the Irish parliaments. That Ireland was subject to the king there was no doubt; he happened to be king of England, but he was also king of Ireland—but was Ireland subject to the English parliament? could the English parliament make statutes for

Ireland? The dispute becomes prominent under William III. The English parliament passed an act for Ireland, the Irish parliament reenacted it with some alterations. The English lawyers, including Coke, had for some time past argued for the supremacy of the English parliament. The medieval precedents were not very decisive. The English theory was this—that Ireland was a colony, and that a colony was subject to the legislature of the mother country. This general doctrine was indisputable English law—even the English colonists in America admitted that in a general way they were subject to the parliament at Westminster, though they were soon to deny that taxes could be imposed upon them by the English legislature. The proposition that Ireland was an English colony was much more disputable. In 1719 the question was brought to a head by a dispute between the two Houses of Lords. Each asserted its right to act as a court which could correct the errors of the Irish courts of law. A declaratory act was then passed (6 Geo. I, c. 5) by the English parliament to the effect that the English parliament has full power to make laws to bind the people of Ireland and that the Irish House of Lords has no power to reverse or affirm the judgments of the Irish courts. This act, being acquiesced in, definitely subordinated the Irish to the English parliament. Poynings' Act also remained unrepealed, and was so interpreted that the parliament had little more than a power of accepting or rejecting the proposals of the crown.

In 1782 the act of 1719 was repealed, and in 1783 the English parliament passed a statute declaring that the right of the people of Ireland to be bound only by laws enacted by the king and the Irish parliament is established, and shall at no time hereafter be questioned or questionable. No appeals were to be brought from the Irish to any English courts. Poynings' law also was repealed by the Irish parliament. For eighteen years Ireland was no more subject to England than was England to Ireland. The causes of this concession of Irish independence, and of the union of 1800, lie beyond our domain: but understand that it was the union of two independent kingdoms, not the absorption of a dependent kingdom. The union took effect on 1 Jan. 1801. There was no longer a kingdom of Great Britain and a kingdom of Ireland; there was a United Kingdom of Great Britain and Ireland. So again there was a parliament for the United Kingdom, in which the Irish peers were represented by twenty-eight of their number chosen by them for life, and by four bishops sitting according to a scheme of rotation, and the Irish commons by a hundred members. Every statute of this parliament applies to the whole of the United Kingdom unless some part of it is specially excepted. As on the occasion of the union with Scotland, articles were agreed on by the two parliaments; but these articles possess no particularly essential or irrepealable nature. This we may see from the fate of what was probably regarded as the most important of them—the churches of England and Ireland were united in one church, 'The United Church of England and Ireland,' and the continuance of this United Church was declared to be an essential and fundamental part of the union. In 1869 the union of the two churches was dissolved, and the Irish church was declared to be no longer an established church.

The laws in force in Ireland differ from those in force in England, but the differences are not so great as those which separate English from Scottish law. The acts of the Irish parliament are still in force in so far as they have not been repealed by statutes of the United Kingdom; but the basis of Irish law is English common law, which has been received ever since the days of Henry VIII. In one respect Ireland is kept a little more distinct from England than is Scotland. From the earliest time the king has had a representative in Ireland, a viceroy, lord-deputy, or lord-lieutenant, and the lord-lieutenant has had a council corresponding to the council of the English king. In 1800 these institutions were not destroyed —there still is a lord-lieutenant, and he has a council; practically, however, this does not mean any great degree of separation; the executive government of Ireland like that of England and of Scotland is *de facto* under the control of the cabinet. Just at one point, and that the highest, the judicial constitutions of the three countries are united. The House of Lords serves as a court of last resort for English, Irish and Scottish cases.

The Isle of Man and the Channel Islands are not parts of the United Kingdom, though king and parliament can make laws for them. The statutes made by parliament do not affect them unless they are specially mentioned, or it is evident from the context that they were within the purview of the legislature. The appeal from their courts is not to the House of Lords, but to the King in Council. The interest of these small dependencies lies in this, that the relation between them and England formed a precedent for the treatment of the vaster dependencies which have gradually collected round the United Kingdom.

As regards these greater dependencies, we can say but little ; we may, however, apprehend certain very general principles. First we have to note a distinction as to the mode in which territories have been acquired—we must distinguish colonization on the one hand from cession or conquest on the other. When a new country is colonized by Englishmen, they are conceived to carry with them all such part of the English common law and all such existing statutes as are applicable to their circumstances ; to distinguish what is and what is not applicable is the work of the courts which the king may establish among them, an appeal lying from those courts to the King in Council. The king cannot legislate for them ; on the other hand, king and parliament can legislate for them ; but the presumption is that a statute applies only to the United Kingdom, it does not extend to the colonies unless they are mentioned or it is plain that the statute was meant for them. As regards territories conquered by the king's armies or ceded to him by a foreign power, the act of conquest or cession does not alter their law. The king can legislate for them and *a fortiori* the king in parliament can legislate for them—but they retain their old law, French or Spanish or Dutch or whatever it may be, until new laws are made for them by the king with or without the concurrence of parliament. The king also may grant to them representative institutions of their own—may establish in them legislative assemblies—and when such a grant has been made he cannot revoke it. Over all these territories however obtained, whether by colonization or cession or conquest, whether they have representative assemblies of their own or no, king and parliament are supreme; but it is not considered that a statute applies to them unless the intention of the legislature that it should do so appears on the face of the statute. The distinction as to the mode of acquisition affects not the ultimate supremacy of king and parliament, but the power of the king to make laws without the consent of parliament—in a land obtained by cession or conquest he can make laws unless statute has said that he cannot: in what in the strictest sense is a 'colony' he has no such power.

As is well known, it was the attempt of the British parliament to tax the American Colonies which led to the War of Independence and the formation of the United States. Already in 1766 we have an act (6 Geo. III, c. 12) which recites that several of the houses of representatives in His Majesty's colonies and plantations in America "have of late, against law, claimed to themselves the sole and exclusive right of imposing taxes upon His Majesty's subjects in the said colonies and plantations": it is then declared that "the said colonies and plantations in America have been, are, and of right ought to be subordinate unto, and dependent upon the imperial crown and parliament of Great Britain"; and that the king and parliament of Great Britain have and of right ought to have full power and authority to make laws and statutes to bind the colonies and people of America in all cases whatsoever. I believe that I am right in saying that the colonists did not deny the general rule that the British parliament might legislate for them, but disputed only its right to tax them. The British parliament did not abandon its claim until it was forced to acknowledge that the United States were free, sovereign, and independent: though during the progress of the struggle it promised by an act of 1778 (18 Geo. III, c. 12) that it would not tax North America or the West Indies for the purpose of obtaining a revenue. The adverse issue of the war with the United States did not lead to any abandonment of the general principle. Our parliament claims to legislate for all lands which are subject to the crown of Great Britain, and the claim is no idle claim. To give but one instance, an instance on a great scale; in 1833 by an act of the parliament of the United

Kingdom (3 and 4 Will. IV, c. 73) slavery was abolished throughout the colonies; and though compensation was provided for the slave owners, this of course was a vast interference with the rights of private property. From time to time parliament makes laws for the colonies, thus the Copyright Act extends to them. The presumption of the courts, as already said, is that a statute does not extend to them, and therefore if parliament does mean to legislate for them, it generally says so in so many words. Even the right or power to impose taxes has never been abandoned, though it is not exercised. Students of Austin's Jurisprudence may find some interest in noticing this case: the sovereign body habitually refrains from making laws of a certain class and must suspect that if it made such laws they would not be obeyed.

As to the constitutions of the colonies. Subject to the general power of the British parliament there is considerable variety—for some the king can legislate, others have representative assemblies of their own. In these last the constitutional organization is modelled after that of the mother country—a royal governor represents the king, and the legislative assembly consists of two houses; but the upper house is not, like our House of Lords, a hereditary assembly. Their acts require the assent of the governor as representing the crown—this gives them a temporary validity—but they are liable to be disallowed by an order of the King in Council; not being sovereign, their legislative powers are limited: their statutes may be void. In this they differ from the statutes of the parliament of the United Kingdom, which cannot be void. However (at least in general) no attempt has been made to enumerate or specify the subjects about which a colonial legislature may legislate, or may not legislate. The general rule is laid down by an act of 1865 (28 and 29 Vic., c. 63): every law made by a colonial legislature is valid for the colony except in so far as it is repugnant to any *act of parliament* extending to the colony. This gives the colonial legislatures liberal powers, for the number of acts of parliament which extend to the colonies is not very great. Still a colonial judge or (on appeal) the judicial committee of the Privy Council may have to say 'this colonial act is void, for it is repugnant to an act of parliament which extends to the colony.'

As to the laws in force in the colonies, of course they vary greatly. In most of them the basis is English common law ; but in some it is French law, in others Roman-Dutch law, that is to say, Roman law as expounded by the jurists of Holland. Past history decides this matter : territories acquired by conquest or cession from foreign states have generally been allowed to keep their old laws. Then on the top of this basis of common law, whatever it may be, come those acts of the British parliament which affect the colony, and the acts of the colonial legislature.

The Judicial Committee of the Privy Council (of the constitution of which hereafter) is the supreme court of appeal for all the king's lands outside the United Kingdom. The business that comes before it is of the most miscellaneous character; the world has never seen a tribunal with such world-wide powers. It has to administer Mohammedan law and Hindoo law, French law, Dutch law, English law ; it has often to consider whether the legislative acts of colonial legislatures are valid or invalid, for instance, it may have to say that a statute of the Canadian parliament is invalid as repugnant to a statute which the parliament of the United Kingdom has made for Canada.

It is impossible in a few words to say much that is profitable about India, only let us remember this : that the parliament of the United Kingdom which we are about to describe is supreme over India, can, and in matters of the highest importance sometimes does, legislate for India.

In speaking then of king and parliament we are no longer speaking of what in strictness of language are merely English institutions ; the parliament represents the United Kingdom, and king and parliament have supreme legislative power over territories which lie in every quarter of the globe. Of this parliament we must speak. Below it there are many institutions, some of which are specifically English, specifically Scottish, Irish, Canadian, Australian, Indian ; for example, the judicial systems of England, Ireland and Scotland are distinct from each other, though at the supreme point they unite in the House of Lords. It is of great importance to distinguish those institutions which like the kingship and the parliament are (we can hardly avoid the term) imperial institutions, from those which like the High Court of Justice are specifically English, and I strongly advise you not to use the words England and English when you mean what is larger than England and more than English. When we have dealt with the institutions which have power over all the British dominions, we shall, being Englishmen in an English university, deal with some purely English institutions, as with the High Court of Justice, not with the Scottish Court of Sessions—but let us keep this distinction firmly in our minds ; if we are Englishmen, we are also subjects of a sovereign whose power extends over millions and millions of men who are not English.

Let me illustrate this by one further remark. There are two conceptions which are of great importance to students of international law: the one nationality, the other domicile. Now there is no such thing as English nationality, and there is no such thing as British domicile. The Englishman, the Scot, the Irishman, the Canadian, the Australian—all of these have a nationality in common ; if there be war between the United Kingdom and a foreign power, say France, all of them are enemies of the French, any of them who side with the French are traitors. But there is no such thing as British domicile— because there is no one system of private law common to all the British dominions ; a man is domiciled in England or Scotland or New Zealand, and to a very large extent the law under which he lives varies with his place of domicile. If I abandon my English domicile, and become domiciled in Scotland, this will have most important legal results for me, but my nationality remains what it was. So by England let us mean England, a land which consists of fifty-two counties.

There is another distinction which we must now keep constantly in view: we are lawyers dealing with law, but an account of our present mode of government which spoke only of legal rules would be an extremely inadequate and indeed a quite unintelligible account. To take the capital instance: everyone knows that the constitution of the cabinet is a matter of the utmost importance—indeed a great part of our political life is determined by the constitution of the cabinet for the time being—but most people know and everyone ought to know that the cabinet is a body unknown to the law: as a body it has no legal powers, rights or duties. We have then to distinguish at every step what is matter of law, from what is not matter of law, from what is matter of custom or convention. The two are intimately intertwined; as Mr Dicey has shown in his excellent lectures on the Constitution[1] (which I take this opportunity of strongly recommending to your notice) the customs or conventions of our constitution derive their force, a force which is often felt to be quite as strong as the force of law, from the fact that they are so much mixed up with law that they could hardly be violated without a violation of law. We must therefore keep this distinction before us, and whenever we come to a rule ask ourselves whether it be law or no, ask ourselves what would happen if it were broken—would anybody be punished, and if so how, or would there merely be a general outcry that a departure had been made from sound constitutional precedent?

The necessity for this caution is due in a large measure to our careful conservation of forms. Our queen to-day has by law almost all the power that Henry VII had by law; we know that as a matter of fact our present kingship is radically different from the kingship of the fifteenth century ; but law has done little to take away powers from the king. When we have insured by indirect methods that such powers shall not be exercised without the approval of parliament, we have considered that enough has been done—we have not cared to pass a statute saying in so many words that such powers have ceased to exist. Whatever may be thought of the wisdom of this course, it renders the task of lecturing on our modern constitution a very difficult task. One is constantly brought face to face with the question—what is it lawful for the king to do? what might he not lawfully do if he wished to go as near as possible to breaking the law? To find an answer is often hard or impossible. Since the Revolution our

[1] *Lectures Introductory to the Study of the Law of the Constitution* by A. V. Dicey, 6th ed. London, 1902.

kings have seldom gone near to breaking the law in serious matters—by all manner of indirect means they have been practically restrained from breaking the law, therefore we have no modern precedents, and are thrown back on ancient precedents, the applicability of which to the changed circumstances of modern times can often be very plausibly disputed. The law then as to the extent of the royal prerogative in many directions is often very vague, and often we have to solace ourselves with the reflection that any attempt to exercise the prerogative in these directions is extremely improbable.

A. *The Sovereign Body.*

I. *The Kingship.*

The succession to the throne is settled by the Act of Settlement upon the heirs of the body of the Electress Sophia, being protestants. It is needless to say that under these terms a woman can succeed. A queen has all the powers of a king. The husband of a reigning queen has no powers, he is not king unless an act of parliament makes him so. Philip of Spain, Mary's husband, bore the title of king, Anne's husband was simply Prince George of Denmark. Queen Victoria's husband was simply Prince Albert of Saxe-Coburg-Gotha until 1857 when the queen conferred on him the title of Prince Consort. He had no legal powers.

'The king never dies,' in other words under the Act of Settlement, and for some centuries before it, the heir begins to reign at the moment of the ancestor's death. The coronation therefore does not seem to be a legally necessary ceremony. The terms of the coronation oath are however fixed by statute—this statute passed immediately after the Revolution has come before us already[1]. The Act of Union with Scotland further required an oath to maintain the two established churches. George III thought that this oath stood in the way of his giving his assent to a bill removing the disabilities of the Roman Catholics; but it seems only intended to give a religious sanction to the king's duty of maintaining the churches according to the law in force for the time being,

[1] p. 287.

and not to hamper his conscience when considering a proposed change in the law : the queen's oath did not stand in the way of the disestablishment of the Irish Church. The king is also bound by the Act of Settlement either at his coronation or on meeting his first parliament, whichever happens first, to make a declaration against transubstantiation and other distinctively Roman doctrines prescribed by the Act of Settlement. He is also bound by the Act of Settlement to join in communion with the Church of England as by law established. He forfeits his crown if he holds communion with the Church of Rome, professes the Popish religion, or marries a papist ; the crown then passes as if he were dead to the next heir. There is no clause saying that he forfeits the crown if he ceases to be a member of the English Church, if, for instance, he becomes a Wesleyan Methodist.

Under the Royal Marriage Act, 1772 (12 Geo. III, c. 11), the marriage of any descendant of George II is invalid unless the royal consent has been obtained ; but this does not apply to the issue of princesses married into foreign families, and is subject to a proviso that a descendant of George II when of the age of twenty-five may signify to the privy council his intention of marrying without the king's consent, and unless within twelve months both houses of parliament object to the marriage, then he may lawfully marry.

There is, I think, no way in which a reigning king can cease to reign save by his death, by holding communion with the Church of Rome, professing the Popish religion or marrying a Papist, and possibly by abdication. I cannot regard the events of 1327, 1399 or 1688 as legal precedents. I can deduce no rule of law from them : they seem to me precedents for a revolution, not for legal action. If we had a very bad king, we should very probably depose him ; but unless he consented to an act of parliament depriving him of the crown, the deposition would be a revolution, not a legal process. Even the king's power to abdicate, except by giving his assent to a statute declaring his abdication may, as it seems to me, be doubted.

For the case of an infant king or a king incapable of transacting business our common law makes no special provision. Its doctrine seems to be that the king is never under

age and never incapable : he can always give his assent to
acts of parliament.   This doctrine has in the past given rise
to some curious fictitious transactions ; but ever since the end
of the Middle Ages a royal minority has always been foreseen
and provided for in advance by statute.   Thus in 1830 a
statute was passed (1 Will. IV, c. 2) to the effect that if
William died while the Princess Victoria was under the age
of eighteen years, the Duchess of Kent was until the queen
reached eighteen years to be her guardian, and was to exercise
all the royal powers, save that she was not to have power to
assent to any act altering the Act of Settlement or the Act
of Uniformity.   This act did not take effect because the queen
had attained eighteen before her uncle died.   A similar act
was passed in 1840, making Prince Albert regent if the queen
should die leaving an heir under the age of eighteen, the
regency to continue until the heir should be eighteen.   There
is now no such act in force, and there is no immediate necessity
for one.   It seems a common belief that a king attains full
age at eighteen or at some other age different from the usual
twenty-one ; but this is a mistake.   By common law a king
is never under age, but statutes passed on various occasions,
none of which are now in force, have chosen eighteen as
the age at which a regency shall come to an end.   For an
actual case of regency due to the king's infancy we have to
go back to the case of Edward VI.

Our law makes no provision for a case in which the king is
disabled from transacting business by mental or bodily illness.
The question arose in 1788, but not in its most aggravated
form for a parliament was in existence, so there was no need
to decide how a parliament could be summoned.   Parliament
was in existence but it stood prorogued, and according to
precedent when a parliament is prorogued it cannot proceed
to business until the session has been opened either by the
king in person or by commissioners appointed by him.   On
this occasion parliament met and proceeded to discuss what
was to be done.   Some maintained that the Prince of Wales
(afterwards George IV) had a right or at least a legal claim
to be regent.   This contention, however, in accordance with
past history was overruled—in accordance with past history,

for the precedent of Henry VI's infancy might be regarded as conclusive of this point. It being decided, however, that the prince was to be regent by act of parliament, the question arose how such an act could be passed. The Chancellor affixed the Great Seal to a commission for opening parliament; a regency bill was introduced, and it was intended that the royal assent should be fictitiously given to this bill by commission under the Great Seal. But before the bill was passed the king recovered and no further proceedings were necessary. The same difficulty occurred again in 1810. The king became incapable, this time for good and all, at a moment when parliament stood prorogued. The precedent of 1788 was followed. The Houses agreed that the parliament should be opened by commission under the Great Seal, and the Chancellor affixed it. A regency bill was introduced; it was carried through both houses, and a fictitious royal assent was given to it by commission under the Great Seal. The commission asserted that it was issued by the king himself, by and with the advice of the lords spiritual and temporal and commons in parliament assembled. The royal authority was to be exercised by the Prince of Wales, subject to certain restrictions as to the creation of peerages, the grant of offices and the like. These are the only modern precedents for the treatment of cases for which our common law makes no provision. Obviously the difficulty would be greater if there were no parliament in existence.

As regards 'the royal family,' a term of very vague import, there is little to be said. A king's wife, a king or queen's eldest son and eldest daughter, and the wife of the eldest son, enjoy a certain protection, if such it may be called, under the old statute of Edward III defining the crime of high treason. The eldest son of a reigning king or queen is born a peer of the realm, he is born Duke of Cornwall, he is not born to the title of Prince of Wales. All other sons and daughters of the king or queen are born commoners, and such they continue unless and until peerages are conferred upon them. A certain honorary precedence is given to certain members of the king's family by an act of 1539—31 Hen. VIII, c. 10—an act for the placing of lords, but this is a trifle.

II.   *The House of Lords.*

The House of Lords at present consists of about 540 members and is thus ten times as large as under the Tudors[1]. First as to the bishops.   Two archbishops and twenty-four bishops have seats in it.   When we last saw it all the English bishops sat there, including those whose sees were created by Henry VIII, or all except the Bishop of Sodor and Man, who has never had a seat, and whose absence is accounted for by the fact that in times past he was not a bishop of the English church; it was only under Henry VIII that his bishopric was made part of the province of York.   No new see was created until 1836 ; in that year the see of Ripon was created by Order in Council, and the bishop had a seat in parliament, but at the same time the two sees of Gloucester and Bristol were fused together so that the number of bishops was not increased.   Manchester was created under act of parliament in 1847, Truro and S. Albans in 1877, Liverpool in 1880, Newcastle in 1882, and Southwell in 1883, all under acts of parliament which provided that the number of bishops having seats in the House of Lords should not thereby be increased[2]. The statutory rule now is that the two archbishops, the bishops of London, Durham and Winchester, and twenty-one other bishops—the first in order of seniority—have seats, the others have no seats.   There are now six bishops without seats exclusive of the Bishop of Sodor and Man who never sits[3].

Between 1801 and 1869 under the Act of Union the Irish Church was represented by one archbishop and three bishops, who sat there according to a scheme of rotation.

The mode of making bishops remains just what it was in Elizabeth's time ; the chapters always elect the royal nominee ; if they did not the king would be able to appoint by letters patent under the act of Henry VIII.

---

[1] The number in Jan. 1913 was 636.

[2] Wakefield was created in 1888, Bristol in 1897, Birmingham and Southwark in 1904.

[3] There are now (1913) ten bishops exclusive of the Bishop of Sodor and Man without seats : i.e. Southwark, Carlisle, Worcester, Gloucester, Llandaff, Rochester, Ely, Truro, Newcastle, Chichester.

The vast increase that has taken place in the House of Lords is therefore an increase in the number of temporal peers. It would be a great mistake to suppose that there are many very ancient peerages in existence. Counting English, Scottish, and Irish peerages there are not a hundred which can be traced as far as the Middle Ages, and about half of these have been merged in newer and higher titles. A year now seldom goes by without the creation of half-a-dozen new peers. The power of creating new peers is obviously an important engine in the hands of a minister. During the last century peerages were lavishly created for political purposes. Under Anne in 1711, twelve peerages were created at once in order to secure a majority in the House of Lords. The lords resisted this, and by the peerage bills of 1719 and 1720 they sought to limit the king's power of creating new peers by a provision that when six more had been created the maximum number was to be reached. The king himself was willing to consent to this, but the bill was rejected by a large majority in the House of Commons, and thus a great change in our constitution was averted. In much more recent times the power of creating new peers has been used for a great end. In 1832 the House of Lords was practically coerced into the passing of the Reform Bill by the knowledge that if they again rejected it the king was prepared to consent to the creation of eighty new peerages. Thus a threat to create new peerages may be a potent political instrument; but for obvious reasons a minister would shrink from using it save in an extreme case—he could not see the end of his action; he would be creating heritable rights, and the political opinions of heirs are not always those of their ancestors. For centuries past, as we have seen, the invariable mode of creating peers has been by letters patent; usually they confer the dignity and the consequent right to a writ of summons on the grantee and the heirs of his body, but occasionally other forms of grant are adopted. As we have already seen in 1856 the House of Lords maintained that the grant of a peerage merely for the life of the grantee would not entitle him to a seat in parliament: that was the result of the Wensleydale case. A few ancient baronies created by writ are still in existence.

We have now to notice that a peer may be a peer of England or of Scotland or of Ireland or of Great Britain or of the United Kingdom. When Scotland and England were united Scotland possessed a large peerage of its own. There were, I think, 154 Scottish peers and but 168 English[1]. The plan adopted was this—only sixteen Scottish peers were to sit in the House of Lords. These sixteen were to be elected by the whole body of Scottish peers to represent them for a single parliament. All the Scottish peers, however, were to enjoy the other privileges of peerage, the freedom from arrest and the right to be tried before the House of Lords. Since the Act of Union the king has not been able to create a purely Scottish peer, or for the matter of that a purely English peer: the peers created were (if not peers of Ireland) peers of Great Britain, who, as such, would have hereditary seats in the House of Lords. Thus the number of Scottish peers who are to elect the sixteen representatives could not be increased and has steadily dwindled: for to say nothing of the extinction of peerages by failure of heirs, many Scottish peers have been promoted to peerages of Great Britain, and when this happens the peer so promoted having himself a hereditary seat in the House of Lords is no longer eligible to serve as a representative of the Scottish peerage. Such promotions have become so frequent that the day seems coming when there will be no more than sixteen peers of Scotland and they will be able to elect themselves. I believe that there are now only about thirty-two peers of Scotland who are peers of Scotland and no more[2].

On the union with Ireland a plan in some respects similar, in others dissimilar, was adopted. The Irish peerage was to be represented in the House by twenty-eight representatives, elected however for life. It was provided that one new Irish peerage might be created whenever three Irish peerages had become extinct until the number was reduced to a hundred, and that then it *might* be kept up at that figure. Sir William

---

[1] See Pike, *Constitutional History of the House of Lords*, pp. 360, 368.

[2] The number of such Peers has now (1913) sunk to nineteen, for of the eighty-six Scottish Peers, fifty-one have Imperial titles, while sixteen are elected to the Imperial Parliament.

Anson[1] says that it was provided that the number should never fall below a hundred, but that seems to me a distinct mistake (39 and 40 Geo. III, c. 67, art 4, ' it shall and may be lawful '). The king therefore since the Act of Union has had, and he still has, a certain limited power of creating Irish peers ; the other peers that he creates are peers of the United Kingdom with hereditary right to be summoned to parliament.

An Irish peer who is not a representative peer is capable of being elected a member of the House of Commons for any place in Great Britain, but not in Ireland ; while he has a seat in the House of Commons he is treated for many purposes as a commoner ; he has no right to be tried by the peers ; the other Irish peers whether representative peers or no have such a right. On the other hand a Scottish peer, even though he is not a representative peer, is disqualified from sitting in the House of Commons.

In 1876 a new class of peers was created, namely Lords of Appeal in Ordinary. By the Appellate Jurisdiction Act of that year (39 and 40 Vic. c. 59) power was given to the queen to appoint at once two Lords of Appeal in Ordinary, and on the happening of certain events the number might be raised first to three and then to four ; there are now four. The persons to be appointed were to have certain qualifications prescribed by the act, namely to have held certain high judicial offices or been barristers or advocates for a certain number of years ; they are paid salaries ; and it is their duty to take part in the judicial proceedings of the House of Lords. Under the act of 1876 they hold their offices during good behaviour, but are to be removable upon an address presented by both Houses of parliament. Their dignity was not to be inheritable ; but so long as they held office they were for all purposes to be peers of the realm and members of the House of Lords, capable of sitting, debating and voting as well when the House was acting as a legislative assembly as when it was acting as a court of law. Much stress was laid upon the fact that they were not to be life peers, but official peers ; their position was compared to that of the bishops. However a few years afterwards one of the lords first appointed, Lord

---

[1] *Law and Custom of the Constitution, Parliament*, 3rd ed. p. 197.

Blackburn, resigned his office. Under the act of 1876 he would thereupon have ceased to be a peer, but by an act of 1887 (50 and 51 Vic. c. 70) it was decreed that the Lord of Appeal in Ordinary might continue a member of the House of Lords during the remainder of his life, notwithstanding a resignation of his office. Thus in fact these peerages have become rather life peerages than official peerages.

As to the causes which may disqualify a man from sitting and voting in the House of Lords I may refer you to what Sir William Anson says about alienage, bankruptcy, infancy, felony, and a sentence of the House[1]. We ought of course to distinguish a disqualification from sitting and voting from a forfeiture of the peerage. Down to modern times it was possible that a peerage might become extinct for good and all owing to the commission of a treason or a felony. Owing to successive mitigations of the law beginning with an act of 1814 (54 Geo. III, c. 145), it is now-a-days, I think, practically impossible that a peerage should become extinct in this manner; but I am not sure that it is absolutely impossible. Suppose a peer committed treason or felony and was outlawed for it, the peerage would, I think, be forfeited; but in practice the process of outlawry has become obsolete.

III. *The House of Commons.*

Now as regards the members of this House we have to ask how many there are, by whom they are elected, who may be elected, how they are elected.

(1) We have watched the fluctuations of numbers in the English parliament down to the end of William III's reign: we left them at 513. On the union with Scotland in 1707, 45 Scottish members were admitted into the parliament of Great Britain. On the union with Ireland in 1801, 100 Irish members were admitted into the parliament of the United Kingdom. Thus the number became 658. The new Reform Acts have made but little difference in the total number of members or their allotment among the three kingdoms. There are now 670, 495 for England (in which I always include

[1] *Law and Custom of the Constitution, Parliament,* 3rd ed. pp. 211—13.

Wales), 72 for Scotland and 103 for Ireland ; the greatest change is that the number given to Scotland has risen from 45 to 72.

(2) The history and the present state of the law touching the qualification of voters in counties and boroughs is a complicated matter if one attempts to study it at all thoroughly. I strongly recommend to you Sir William Anson's chapter on the subject, which seems to me a very good elementary statement[1]. There is also an article on the recent act, the act of 1884, by Sir William Anson in the first number of the *Law Quarterly Review*, which, I think, will be of assistance to you in unravelling a tangled skein. I intend to speak at some length of this matter, and I shall not follow Sir William Anson's treatment, not because it is not good—perhaps it is the best possible—but because it would be idle for me to repeat what is in a book which is, or should be, in your hands, and because it is desirable that we should look at every point of the law from several different points of view.

The intricacy of the law is due to the fact that, after having remained almost unaltered for a period of four centuries, it has three times during the last sixty years been radically reformed. I refer, of course, to the Reform Act of 1832 and the Representation of the People Acts of 1867 and 1884. The changes made by these acts have been very great, but the law as a whole has never been codified or restated ; one has still to consider the law as it stood before these acts and to see exactly in what respects it has been modified by them, also to see how the earlier acts have been patched and tinkered by the later.

One more word of preface. You will find that all through our history the qualification of the voter has depended in some manner or another on his relation to what, loosely speaking, we may call real property (some land or tenement, or again, some dwelling-house) situated within the county or borough. Now we have to consider what *sort* of a tenement will do, whether a dwelling-house is necessary, whether a warehouse in which nobody sleeps is sufficient, whether land without buildings is enough (again, whether an incorporeal

[1] *Law and Custom of the Constitution, Parliament,* 3rd ed. c. v.

hereditament such as tithes or a freehold office will give the vote), and also what must be the value of the tenement, whether 40 shillings or £12 or £50, and how the value is to be measured, is it measured by rental, or is it measured by the assessment to poor rates? but (and to this I draw attention) we must also consider what is the requisite relation between the voter and the tenement. Different relations have been required at different times, by different statutes, for different purposes. Sometimes the relation is proprietary, the voter must have an estate or interest of a particular kind in the tenement: a freehold estate may be necessary, or again a copyhold estate may be enough, or a leasehold interest. And again, lines have been drawn between various estates of freehold. Sometimes again, proprietary right is not enough, there must also be possession: it will not, for example, suffice that you are entitled to a rent-charge, it is required that you be in possession of it. Or again, the statute may insist not on proprietary right but upon occupation, and occupation again is an idea which has required a great deal of definition at the hands of the courts. Does a servant occupy his master's house which has been left in his sole charge while his master lives elsewhere? Does an undergraduate, does a fellow of a college occupy what we call 'his' rooms in college, or are they occupied by the college, by the corporation? Again, the statutes sometimes insist on something more than occupation: the voter must be an inhabitant occupier, and I may occupy a house that I do not inhabit. In reading the acts, then, one must carefully observe how they describe the relation between the man and the thing, whether they call for proprietary right, or for possession, or for the two together, or for occupation or for residence. Lastly, some of the statutes have made the payment of rates an essential part of some of the qualifications, and this has been done in a perplexing way.

Now the county and borough franchises have always been, and still are, distinct things depending on different rules. The last statute, that of 1884, has introduced much more uniformity than there formerly was. Still, however, one cannot speak of them in the same breath; a qualification which would serve for a county will not always serve for a borough, nor *vice versa*. However, in the historical sketch that I am now to begin I shall treat them together, (that is to say) the sketch will naturally fall into four periods : (*a*) before 1832, (*b*) before 1867, (*c*) before 1884, (*d*) after 1884, and in each period I shall speak first of the county, then of the borough franchise. The history of the Scottish and Irish franchises differs in many details from that of the English, though on the whole it has followed the same general course. I fear that here we can say no more of it. As regards the English counties we must go back to the act of 1430 (8 Hen. VI, c. 7) : the knights of the shire are to be chosen in every county by people dwelling and resident in the same counties whereof every one of them shall have free land or tenement to the value of 40 shillings by the year at the least above all charges. An act of 1432—10 Hen. VI, c. 2— explained that the freehold was to be within the county for which the election was to be made. It may be doubted whether the object of these measures was to exclude from the election any large class of persons who had habitually taken part in them ; but the result was to establish a qualification by property, and one which at first was fairly high, though, owing to the change in the value of money, it became very low. You will observe that the act of 1430 required of the voter not only freehold, but also residence within the county. This requirement however—I do not exactly know how or when—fell into oblivion, and was swept away as long obsolete by a statute of 1774 (14 Geo. III, c. 58). At the same time a still older requirement that the elected knights and burgesses should be resident in their counties and boroughs, a requirement as old as 1413 (1 Hen. V, c. 1), was abolished : this also had long been disregarded. The qualification for county electors thus came to be definitely a qualification by property, the having free land or tenement, the having freehold to the value of 40 shillings. Observe that any freehold estate of the requisite value would give the franchise, even an estate for life or *pur autre vie*. In 1832 the main objection to the county qualification was not that it was too high, but that it was extremely capricious ; a leaseholder or copyholder, no matter how valuable his interest, had no vote ; on the other hand, a rent-charge of 40 shillings for life was enough ; votes have been claimed in respect of freehold pews, and, it is said, in respect of freehold graves. This, of course, made the manufacture of qualifications an easy matter. Several statutes of the last century attempted to guard against this abuse. In particular an act of 1745 (18 Geo. II, c. 18, sec. 5) required that the voter should be in actual possession or in receipt of rents and profits of his freehold estate for twelve months, unless that estate came to him by descent, marriage, marriage settlement, devise or promotion to a benefice or office. The idea was this : that if you acquire title by such means as these, it is needless to insist on *possession* ; if, on the other hand, you acquire it by sale or by gift *inter vivos*, there is danger of an attempt to manufacture votes, and so a certain length of possession is required in order to prove the good faith of the transaction.

You should further understand that until 1832 no list of voters was prepared beforehand. Since the Reform Act the qualifications by property, occupation and so forth are not strictly speaking qualifications entitling one to vote—they are qualifications entitling one to be placed on the register of electors, and the only qualification that (in strictness) entitles one to vote is the fact that one is a registered elector. Until 1832 the would-be voter appeared at the poll, tendered his vote, and then and there swore an oath prescribed by statute to the effect that he had the requisite qualification—that he had freehold, was in possession and so forth. The procedure now is quite different—no one can vote who is not on the register of voters, and on the other hand the register is for many purposes, though not for all purposes, conclusive that the persons whose names are there are entitled to vote.

As to the boroughs, before the act of 1832 the requisite qualification varied from borough to borough—there was no general law, statutes had hardly meddled with the matter, each borough had its own history, and the matter was settled for it either by the terms of its charter, or by ancient usage. Sir William Anson has a few pages on this subject which seem to me so extremely good that if I went over the same ground I could only paraphrase them[1]. The qualifications though they were very various fell into several great classes. First there was tenure. A few towns which by charter had been made counties of themselves had adopted the county qualification. There are, I believe, now seventeen towns (besides London) which are counties of themselves, or counties corporate[2]. In some of these the county qualification was adopted—namely, forty-shilling freehold. In some other towns burgage tenure gave the franchise. Burgage was a variety of socage found in some ancient boroughs, important in the Middle Ages, for the burgage tenement was generally devisable by custom long before freeholds in general were made devisable by statute. Residence, qualified in this way or in that, constituted a second head. I believe that if there was no charter and no usage to the contrary, the right was considered to be vested in 'the inhabitant householders,' and so if any qualification can be spoken of as the common law qualification, it is this. Very often indeed the right might be exercised by those who paid scot and lot, or to be more exact, who paid scot and bore lot. This phrase refers to a participation in the ancient local burdens—'scot' refers to the money payments; 'lot' to work done in person—men were compellable, for instance, to fill municipal offices: to be mayors, aldermen, constables, and so forth—those liable to burdens of this sort bore lot. In modern times liability to poor rate was taken as the general test—the person who was rated was deemed to pay scot and lot. Sometimes the right was vested in those who by a queer mistake came to be called potwallers, or even potwallopers; the mistake arose from reading an old fashioned W as a B— the word is really potboilers. Here the constitution was democratic indeed: even householding was unnecessary; the sole dominion of a single room having a fire-place in it was

---

[1] *Law and Custom of the Constitution, Parliament*, 3rd ed. pp. 103—5.

[2] The Local Government Act of 1888 (51 and 52 Vict. c. 41) created forty-four county boroughs in addition to the seventeen already existing and provided that any town might be constituted a county borough by order of the Local Government Board on attaining a population of 50,000. At the census of 1901 there were sixty-seven county boroughs.

enough. In a third great class of boroughs the persons entitled to vote were the freemen, that is, the members of the municipal corporation which had been created by charter; freedom of the borough, membership of the corporation, was acquired in many ways; some were born free, others obtained freedom by marriage, or by really or nominally serving as apprentices of some freeman in his craft or trade; the freedom of the borough might in some places be given or sold. In London, membership of one of the trading companies, the livery companies, became necessary. Lastly there were what were often known as the close boroughs; in these the right to vote was restricted by royal charter to the governing body of the borough—often a small knot of aldermen who elected their own successors. Such charters were the outcome of the efforts on the part of Tudors and Stuarts to obtain more manageable parliaments—not too successful, for these boroughs often fell under the influence of the great landowners and became pocket boroughs.

Such, put briefly, was the state of things before the first Reform Act. Now as to the English counties, that act altered the old and introduced several new qualifications. The old qualification was the forty-shilling freehold. As to this, it required that the person claiming to be registered should either (1) be in actual occupation of the tenement in respect of which he based his claim, or (2) have an estate of inheritance in it, or (3) should have acquired his estate by marriage, marriage settlement, devise or promotion, or (4) should have an estate worth £10 a year. To put the matter another way, it deprived of the franchise freeholders whose freeholds were worth 40 shillings but less than £10, if their freeholds were (a) not estates of inheritance, (b) not acquired by marriage, marriage settlement, etc., and (c) not in their own actual occupation. But of course the more important change was that the act invented several quite new qualifications. It entitled to the vote (1) any person seised at law or in equity of any land or tenement of copyhold tenure, or any tenure other than freehold for life or for any greater estate of the clear yearly value of £10 or upwards; (2) any person entitled as lessee or assignee to any lands or tenements for a term of years originally created for a period of 60 years or more of the clear yearly value of £10; (3) any person entitled as lessee or assignee to any lands or tenements for a term of years originally created for a period of not less than 20 years of the clear yearly value of £50; (4) every person who occupies as tenant any lands or tenements for which he shall be liable to a rent of not less than £50.

Thenceforwards then the classes of voters were (*a*) the forty-shilling freeholders, but as we have already seen the forty-shilling freehold would not in all circumstances give the vote: £10 was required in certain circumstances of those whose estates were but for life; (*β*) the £10 copyholders; (*γ*) the £10 long leaseholders; (*δ*) the £50 short leaseholders; (*ε*) the £50 occupiers. An occupation franchise was a quite new thing in the counties; the person occupying a tenement at a rent of £50 was to have the vote no matter what the character of his tenancy. Observe also that in this case the amount of rent payable was made the important thing—he was to be liable for a yearly rent of not less than £50.

As to the boroughs the act greatly simplified the complicated state of affairs which was then in existence. It introduced one uniform qualification into boroughs: the claimant must occupy as owner or tenant any house, warehouse, counting-house, shop, or other building of the clear yearly value of £10, he must occupy for twelve months next before the fixed day, he must (if a poor rate has been made) have been rated and have paid his rates, and he must have resided for the last six months within the borough or within seven miles of it; note the difference between residence and occupation. From 1832 to 1867 this was the uniform qualification in all boroughs, generally spoken of as the £10 occupation franchise. As to the old qualifications, which I may remind you varied from borough to borough, the act in a general way saved the existing rights of persons who were entitled to vote but imposed upon them certain restrictions. This saving we need not consider for its force must now be spent. But, and this is more important, it saved permanently certain qualifications as regards boroughs in which those qualifications already existed. These, I may say once for all, are still saved, though owing to more recent extensions of the franchise they are no

longer of much moment. The qualifications saved were these:
(1) the qualification of freeholding or burgage holding in those
towns being counties of themselves in which such qualification
already existed; (2) the qualification by being a freeman, or
by being a burgess, or by being a freeman or liveryman in
those boroughs in which these qualifications already existed.
But the qualification by being a freeman of the borough, or
a burgess of the borough, that is by being a member of the
municipal corporation according to its then constitution, was
put under restrictions; residence in or within seven miles of
the borough was required, and for the future freedom of the
borough was not to confer a title to a vote unless acquired
either by birth or by servitude. In some boroughs therefore
one still meets with persons who are entitled to be registered
as freemen.

For the boroughs then the Reform Act introduced one
uniform qualification; some other qualifications it preserved
where it found them, but only where it found them, and that
in a very modified form.

Parenthetically we may notice that the Parliamentary
Reform of 1832 was followed almost immediately by the
Municipal Reform of 1835. Practically and with the exception of London the municipal constitution of all the boroughs
was remodelled on one uniform plan. Every person who
occupies a house, warehouse, shop, or other building in the
borough for which he pays poor rates, and who resides within
seven miles of the borough, is entitled to be enrolled as a burgess, a member of the corporation; the municipal corporation
consists of the burgesses thus enrolled. Before the act the
members of the corporation, the freemen as they were called,
were often very few. In Plymouth, where the population
was 75,000, the number of freemen was 437 and 145 of them
were non-resident. In Ipswich less than two per cent. of the
inhabitants enjoyed corporate privileges, and of that two per
cent. a large number were paupers. I have said that the
qualification by freemanship has been to some extent retained; but you should understand that the man who is
burgess of a borough under the Municipal Corporations Acts
has not as such any right to a vote. It is probable now-a-

days, owing to more recent extensions of the parliamentary franchise, that the burgess will have a vote for the borough if indeed the borough returns a member. But this is not necessarily the case. A municipal borough is not as such entitled to be represented, many municipal boroughs have now no members of their own ; again, the geographical limits of what is called the parliamentary borough may well be different from those of the municipal borough, and again, though these limits coincide, yet a burgess may have no vote in a parliamentary election, while one who is no burgess may have a vote; the lodger for instance has now a vote, but is not entitled to be enrolled as a burgess. The two things must be kept distinct. The main right of the burgess as such is that of voting in the election of town councillors who manage the affairs of the borough.

We come to the act of 1867. As to the counties this did in the main two things. (1) You will remember that in several cases the act of 1832 required that the qualifying tenement should be of the yearly value of £10; this was the case as to estates for life except in certain circumstances, as to copyhold estates, and as to long leaseholds, that is, terms originally created for 60 years or more. In all these cases the new act substituted £5 for £10, thus lowering the property qualifications. (2) In the second place, it lowered the occupation qualification, or speaking more strictly it introduced a new occupation qualification ; the person entitled must have been for the last twelve months the occupier as owner or tenant of a tenement of the rateable value of £12, must have been rated to the poor rate—if any has been made—and must have paid his rates. The then existing qualification by occupation consisted, you will remember, in the occupation of a tenement at a rent of £50; this was not swept away; the new qualification was placed by its side, and it is quite possible, at least in theory, that a man should be paying a rent of £50 for a tenement rated at less than £12. In the counties then the act of 1867 lowered some of the qualifications by property, and it introduced a new qualification by occupation—occupation of a tenement worth £12 rateable value.

In the boroughs the changes were yet larger. Two quite new qualifications were introduced beside the occupation qualification of 1832—what are generally known as the household and the lodger franchises were created. The former can be claimed by a man who has been for a year an *inhabitant occupier* as owner or tenant of *any dwelling-house* within the borough, has been rated to any poor rate made during that period and has paid his rates. The latter can be claimed by any man who for a year has occupied as lodger the same lodgings of the clear yearly value of £10, if let unfurnished, and who has resided during the whole qualifying year. The qualification in these cases you observe consists not in mere occupation but in inhabitance or residence ; one must be the inhabitant occupier of the dwelling-house ; one must reside in the lodgings, and while the lodgings must be worth £10 a year any dwelling-house will do. So large a definition of a dwelling-house has now been given by statute, one so much larger than the ordinary meaning of the word, that it is sometimes very difficult to mark off the inhabitant occupier of a dwelling-house from the lodger who resides in lodgings.

The act of 1884, to which we now come, is a very clumsy document. What it does however, broadly stated, is this :— it extends to the counties the £10 occupation franchise, the household qualification, and the lodger qualification which had been introduced into the borough in 1867. The household qualification, you will remember, is that of the inhabitant occupier of a dwelling-house of any value, however small. The lodger qualification is that of a lodger who occupies and resides in lodgings of the value of £10. But both for counties and for boroughs the household qualification is extended or, if you please, a new qualification is created by a provision as to servants. If a man (A) himself inhabits any dwelling-house by virtue of any office, service or employment, and the dwelling-house is not inhabited by any person (B) under whom such man (A) serves in such office, service or employment, he (A) shall be deemed to be an inhabitant occupier of such dwelling-house as tenant. You see for what sort of case this section provides : my gardener who as such lives in a cottage of mine, paying no rent but getting less wages in consequence, is to have a vote : but for this section he would have had none; my butler who lives in the house that I inhabit will still have no vote. Then again the occupation qualification in the counties and boroughs was remodelled. The same qualification is to serve for both, namely occupying any land or tenement of a clear yearly value of £10. This lowered the qualification in counties where the requisite value had been £12 rateable value. It extended the qualification in boroughs where up to that time the tenement which would give this qualification was not any land or tenement, but any house, warehouse or other building. It thus made the occupation qualification much the same in counties and in boroughs ; not however quite the same—a condition of residing in or within seven miles of the borough is imposed on the borough voter, from which the county voter is free.

Broadly speaking then the result is this—there are three qualifications which prevail throughout all England, whether the place be in what for this purpose is called a county, or in what for this purpose is called a borough ; these are (1) the qualification of the inhabitant occupier of a dwelling-house, (2) that of the occupier as lodger of lodgings of the value of £10, (3) that of the occupier of any land or tenement of the value of £10. Besides these we have in the counties the property qualifications—including the old forty-shilling freehold qualification, which has been subjected to certain restrictions, the £5 copyhold qualification, and the £50 and £5 leaseholder qualifications.

It remains to be noticed that the Reform Acts, especially the last, have effected a very great change in the whole scheme of representation. Nominally we can still divide members into borough members and county members—and the distinction is still of some importance, because, as we have just seen, certain qualifications still exist in what are called counties, which will not serve for what are called boroughs. But in truth any talk about counties and boroughs is apt now-a-days to be misleading.

In the first place, since 1832 parliamentary organization has been quite separate from municipal organization. The so-called borough member now often sits for a district which has no municipal organization. This since 1884 is very frequently the case. The larger towns have been cut up into districts, each of which returns a member to parliament for itself. Thus take Liverpool: no member sits for the municipally organized borough of Liverpool, a member sits for the Abercromby division of Liverpool, another for the Everton division, another for the Exchange division, and so forth; so East Manchester has its member, and North-East Manchester, and so forth. The counties again have been cut up into districts. Cambridgeshire as a whole has no members, but the Chesterton Division of Cambridgeshire has its member, and the Newmarket Division, and the Wisbech Division. Again, often it happens that the area which returns members is larger or smaller than the area which has a municipal constitution. In short the tendency of the act of 1884 was to split up England into electoral districts, some known as divisions of counties, some known as boroughs or divisions of boroughs, which shall, roughly speaking, have equal populations. This principle was not rigorously carried out, some respect was had to already existing arrangements, but still a large step was made towards a parcelling out of England into equal electoral districts.

The ancient idea of the representation of communities, of organized bodies of men, bodies which, whether called boroughs or counties, constantly act as wholes, and have common rights and duties, has thus given way to that of a representation of numbers, of unorganized masses of men, or of men who are organized just for the one purpose of choosing members.

A list of the electoral qualifications should be followed by a list of the causes of disqualification. The disqualified classes are women, infants, peers (not being Irish peers with seats in the House of Commons), returning officers and persons concerned in the election as agents, clerks, messengers or the like, aliens, persons of unsound mind, persons convicted of treason or felony until they have served their terms of punishment or been pardoned, and persons convicted of certain electoral malpractices, persons in receipt of parochial relief or other alms; the exact extent of this disqualification by receipt of alms is not very well ascertained.

Until lately a good many persons were disqualified by statute in consequence of their employment in governmental posts, in particular revenue officers and policemen, but the disqualification of revenue officers was removed in 1868, and that of policemen in 1887, and I think that there can now be hardly anyone disqualified by reason of his employment, except returning officers and the agents and canvassers, etc., of the candidates. The clergy seem to have voted at least ever since the time when they ceased to be taxed by their convocations.

(3) As to the qualification of members returned. I will take them almost in Sir William Anson's order, with the view of making a few additional remarks. I pass by (1) infancy, (2) insanity, (3) want of British nationality, (4) peerage, (5) clergy; the clergy of the established churches of England and Scotland are excluded, so also the clergy of the Romish church: ministers of other religious bodies are not excluded. Women are excluded—Sir William Anson appears to have forgotten this, but there can be no doubt that this is common law. The fact that peeresses have never sat in the House of Lords seems by itself conclusive. I do not think that a woman has ever been elected to the House of Commons. Bankrupts are disqualified by statute. Persons convicted of treason or felony and sentenced to death, penal servitude, or imprisonment with hard labour, or imprisonment for more than a year, are incapable of sitting until they shall have suffered the punishment or been pardoned. This by statute of 1870, but it seems that common law would exclude convicted traitors and felons. It remains to speak of religion, office and property.

The history of parliamentary oaths and religious disabilities is very intricate, and I am not at all certain that I have got it straight. But it begins in 1562 with the statute 5 Eliz., c. 1, 13, which required every member of the House of Commons to take the oath of supremacy—to swear that the queen is only supreme governor of this realm as well in spiritual as in temporal causes, and that no foreign person or potentate has any authority ecclesiastical or spiritual within this realm. In 1609 an oath of allegiance was added (7 Jac. I, c. 6), to the effect that the king is lawfully king, and that the pope has no power to depose him. In 1678 (30 Car. II, stat. 2, c. 1) to these oaths was added a declaration against transubstantiation, the invocation of saints and the sacrifice of the mass: and the two oaths and this declaration were required of lords as well as commons. The doors of both Houses were thus effectually closed to members of the Roman church; some of them might be ready to take the two oaths which related to church government, but the declaration as to doctrine was utterly incompatible with their most fundamental beliefs. Immediately after the Revolution the two oaths of allegiance and supremacy were altered in form, the first was to be merely this, 'I will be faithful and bear true allegiance to King William and Queen Mary'; the second was 'I do abhor as impious and heretical the damnable doctrine and position that powers excommunicated by the Pope or any authority of the see of Rome may be deposed or murdered by their subjects or any whatsoever, and I declare that no foreign prince or person hath or ought to have any jurisdiction or authority ecclesiastical or spiritual within this realm.' The declaration against transubstantiation was still maintained. An act of 1701 added a third oath, known as the oath of 'abjuration,' it is long and of a more political character: the swearer abjures all allegiance to the pretended Prince of Wales, and promises to maintain the royal succession as fixed by the Bill of Rights and the Act of Settlement, and this he does upon the true faith of a Christian.

The persons who were thus excluded were members of the Roman Church, persons who objected to oaths, and persons who were not Christians: Quakers we may say, and Jews. In 1696 (7 and 8 Will. III, c. 27) the oaths of allegiance and supremacy were required of the electors as well as of the elected; and the electors had also to take the oath of abjuration. In 1696 Quakers were permitted to make an affirmation instead of taking an oath. On the accession of George I, the oaths were slightly altered. Catholics then could not sit in either House until 1829, and properly speaking they could not vote in parliamentary elections, but the business of tendering oaths to the voters had made elections so very long, that it was not gone through unless the candidates required it, and statute (1794, 34 Geo. III, c. 73) permitted this omission, so I daresay that Catholics did vote. The Catholic Relief Act of 1829 (10 Geo. IV, c. 7) substituted another oath which Catholics could take—they had to swear allegiance, and also that the pope had no *civil* jurisdiction or authority within this realm, and that they would not subvert the church establishment or exercise any privilege to weaken the Protestant religion in this kingdom. The Catholics who would take this oath were thus enabled to sit in either House, and vote at parliamentary elections: Catholics in holy orders were, however, expressly excluded from the Commons' House. In the previous year, 1828, a great measure of relief had been given to all non-conformists, by what is generally called the repeal of the Test and Corporation Acts (the Test Act was not wholly repealed), but this does not concern us, the Protestant dissenter had not been excluded from parliament nor from voting in parliamentary elections, but he had been excluded from many offices by a requirement that he should take the sacrament. This requirement, ever since 1727, had been evaded by the passing of annual bills indemnifying those office-holders who had failed to take the sacrament. In 1828 a declaration was substituted for the sacramental test, a declaration to the effect that the declarant would not use his privileges to the injury of the established church. The necessity of making such declaration was removed in 1868 (31 and 32 Vic., c. 72). But to return to parliamentary tests.

All oaths to be exacted from an elector disappeared in 1832 under the Reform Act, except an oath as to his identity—that he was the person named on the register. In 1858 (21 and 22 Vic., c. 48) the old oaths of allegiance, supremacy and abjuration were swept away, and a new form devised, to the effect that the swearer will bear true allegiance to the queen, and maintain the succession fixed by the Act of Settlement, and that he declares that no foreign power, prelate or potentate has any jurisdiction or authority, ecclesiastical or spiritual, within the realm. The special oath for Roman Catholics, as settled in 1829, was still maintained. Another act of the same year, 1858 (21 and 22 Vic., c. 49), enabled either House to

dispense, in the case of a Jew presenting himself as a member
of that House, with the words 'in the true faith of a Christian.'
This was a compromise: for some years past the House of
Commons had been sending up bills for the relief of Jews to
the House of Lords, which rejected them.   The commons
admitted Jews; the lords could exclude them.   In 1866 the
parliamentary oath was simplified (29 Vic., c. 19), it became
an oath to be faithful to the queen, and to maintain the royal
succession as fixed by the Act of Settlement; there were no
words about the pope, and 'the true faith of a Christian'
disappeared; Catholics and Jews could take the oath required
of other members.   In 1868 the oath was once more simplified,
it was cut down to this, 'I will be faithful and bear true
allegiance to Queen Victoria, her heirs and successors, according to law, so help me God.'   What is more, failure to take
the oath does not vacate the seat, it subjects the member to
a penalty of £500 every time he votes.   The results, as worked
out in Bradlaugh's cases, are lucidly explained by Anson[1].   In
1888 (51 and 52 Vic., c. 46) an act was passed which enabled
any person to substitute for an oath a solemn affirmation, if he
objects to being sworn, and states as the ground of such
objection, either that he has no religious belief, or that the
taking of an oath is contrary to his religious belief.

And now as regards office, the only common law disqualifications seem to have been those of the sheriffs (who might
not sit for their own shires) and the judges of the three common
law courts, and these have been swallowed up in statutory
disqualifications which comprise all returning officers, and
almost all persons who can be comprised in the term judges:
this includes the judges of the High Court of Justice and the
Court of Appeal, the County Court judges, and the police
magistrates.   A recorder may not sit for the town of which
he is recorder; a revising barrister may not sit for any place
comprised within his district.   On the other hand, the unpaid
magistrates, the justices of the peace, are not excluded.
Judges are not excluded from the House of Lords—very
frequently the Lord Chief Justice is made a peer.

[1] *Law and Custom of the Constitution, Parliament*, 3rd ed. pp. 87—9.

As regards other offices legislation has been very complicated. As showing the view taken by parliament at the
beginning of the last century, we may start with the broad
principle laid down in the Act of Settlement, that no person
who has an office or place of profit under the crown shall be
capable of serving as a member of the House of Commons.
This rule was to come into force so soon as the Hanoverian
House should come to the throne. But before it could take
effect it was repealed in 1705 by a Statute (4 Anne, c. 8)
which in substance laid down the rule which was repeated
in 1707 by 6 Anne, c. 41, an act still in force, and the
foundation of all subsequent legislation. What it says is in
short this, that no person having any office or place of profit
under the crown, created since 25 Oct. 1705, shall be capable
of being elected or sitting in the House of Commons; secondly,
if any member shall accept any office of profit from the crown,
his election shall be void, and a new writ shall issue as though
he were dead, provided, nevertheless, that he shall be capable
of reelection. This then divided offices into new offices and
old offices, the holding of a new office was to be utterly
incompatible with a seat in the House; not so an old office :
a person accepting such an office is to vacate his seat, but be
capable of reelection. Offices are 'new' or 'old,' according as
they were or were not created since the 25th Oct. 1705.

I need hardly pause to point out how different would have
been the history of parliament, had the clause in the Act of
Settlement become a permanent part of the law of the land.
Our modern ministerial system would have been impossible,
and the House of Lords, to which the king would have called
his ministers, would have become far more important than the
House of Commons. The act of Anne is the basis of much
intricate legislation. Parliament, in enabling the king to
create a new office,—and owing to the appropriation of supplies,
it has been very difficult for the king to create a new office
without act of parliament—Parliament I say has generally
provided in express words into which of three classes the
office shall fall : (*a*) shall it be wholly incompatible with a seat
in the House of Commons ? or (*b*) shall acceptance of it vacate
a seat, but the holder be eligible for election? or (*c*) shall it not

render its holder ineligible, nor even make him vacate his seat if he has one? Out of these miscellaneous statutes one can get a rough general rule; but, of course, in every particular case one must go to the statute book, must ask whether the office be new or old, and whether any express provision has been made about it. The rough general outcome is this, that the holders of the high offices of state can sit in the House, but acceptance of such an office vacates the seat. On the other hand the holders of subordinate offices in the civil service of the crown are in general absolutely disqualified from sitting in the House. Our present system demands that the heads of the great departments, those who collectively form the ministry, shall be in parliament and answer for the business of their departments. I say our system demands this; our law, of course, does not demand it; there is no law to the effect that ministers must be in parliament, and sometimes for a short while a minister cannot find a seat, but the business of the nation could not be carried on in the wonted way unless almost all the ministers were in parliament, and if they could not find seats, they would soon have to resign their offices. On the other hand the subordinate officers of the civil service are excluded by law, and the consequence is that we have a permanent civil service, a body of civil servants unidentified with any particular policy— were they in parliament they might easily fall out with their superiors, and we should have the whole civil service changing with the ministry. Such is the general outline. Military and naval officers are not excluded from the House of Commons. As to pensioners and contractors it is needless to speak.

As to the property qualification. We have seen that at times during the Middle Ages attempts were made to secure that the so-called knights of the shire should really be knights, or at least notable esquires. This demand, however, seems to have become obsolete in the sixteenth century, and there was no property qualification during the seventeenth century. In 1696 a bill for establishing a qualification of real property passed both Houses; at the Revolution the landowners had become the ruling class: but the king refused his consent to the bill. A more successful effort was made in 1710, when a statute (9 Anne, c. 5) was passed, establishing that a member must have an estate in land, worth per annum for a county member £600, for a borough member £300. This remained law until after the Reform Act; but in 1838 (1 and 2 Vic., c. 48) a change was made; the qualifying income was still to be of the old amount, but it might be derived from personal as well as real property. In 1858 (21 and 22 Vic., c. 26) the property qualification disappears altogether. The consequence is that a man may be qualified to sit in the House of Commons, though he is too poor to have a vote in a parliamentary election.

(4) As regards the mode of electing members, the chief point to notice is the passing of the Ballot Act in 1872 (35 and 36 Vic., c. 33), down to which time elections were open. The Ballot Act was a temporary act passed for but eight years, but it has since been kept alive by annual acts, and I suppose that we must regard it as having become in fact a permanent part of the constitution. The claims of the ballot had been pressed in parliament for some forty years before it was adopted.

The registration system was, as already said, introduced by the first Reform Act. No one can vote whose name is not on the register, and in general (but this does not seem quite true) every one can vote whose name is on the register. The register is annually revised by barristers appointed for the purpose by the judges, revising barristers who hear claims and objections. In 1843 (6 and 7 Vic., c. 18) an appeal from the decision of the revising barrister on points of law was allowed to the Court of Common Pleas. The appeal now lies to the High Court of Justice, and thence with its permission to the Court of Appeal.

(5) The power of determining a disputed election is a different matter. We have seen that in the days of James I the House of Commons claimed and won this power as one of its privileges. In the eighteenth century it was shamefully misused for party purposes. The question whether a member was duly returned or no became a question of confidence in the government. In 1770 the famous Grenville Act was passed which committed this power to a committee of thirteen members, constituted by a process which was some slight security for impartiality (10 Geo. III, c. 16). Some further improvements were made in 1839, but the House showed itself

very unwilling to surrender what it regarded as a privilege. At last, however, in 1868, an act was passed (31 and 32 Vic., c. 125) which made over the matter to the Court of Common Pleas. The jurisdiction is now exercised by the High Court of Justice. There are several different grounds on which an election return may be questioned. Thus it may be alleged that the majority of lawful votes was not in favour of the candidate returned, and in that case it may be questioned whether some of the persons who actually voted were lawfully entitled to vote. As regards some matters the register will apparently be conclusive, as regards other matters it will not: thus a person's vote might be struck off on the ground that he was an infant or an alien, but not on the ground that he had no proper qualification by property, occupation or residence[1]. Or again the election may be disputed on the ground of bribery. The legislation against bribery and other corrupt practices is now very complicated and minute, and is hardly a subject for elementary study. Bribery was a common law offence, and an election might be made void on the score of bribery without any aid from statute law. Bribery became common after the Restoration. Legislation against it begins in 1696, but the parliaments of the last century were never in earnest against bribery, and were extremely jealous of any interference on the part of the courts of law with any matters connected with parliamentary elections. Something was done in 1762, and something more serious, after the lapse of eighty years, in 1841. Our modern law is to be found chiefly in three acts belonging respectively to 1854, 1863 and 1883—whether even the last is severe enough remains to be seen.

The right to wages, four shillings *per diem* for the knight of the shire, two shillings for the burgess, has never been expressly abolished—it was still exacted in the seventeenth century—but we may well doubt whether the redistribution of seats has not tacitly abolished it.

(6) A member of the House of Commons may cease to be a member by death, by a resolution of the House declaring him insane, by becoming an alien or a peer, by taking orders,

---

[1] Stepney Election Petition, 1866, 17 Q. B. D. 54.

by conviction for corrupt practices or for certain other crimes (we have noticed these disqualifications), by remaining bankrupt for six months, by acceptance of office. A member has no power to resign his seat. It is well known, however, that this rule is evaded; the member who desires to resign is granted the stewardship of the Chiltern Hundreds or some other nominal office under the crown, and this under the act of Anne vacates his seat. Possibly the office would be denied him if he sought it in order to escape expulsion.

The House has an undoubted power of expelling a member, and the law does not attempt to define the cases in which it may be used. If the House voted the expulsion of A.B. on the ground that he was ugly, no court could give A.B. any relief. The House's own discretion is the only limit to this power. Probably it would not be exercised now-a-days, unless the member was charged with crime or with some very gross misbehaviour falling short of crime, and in general the House would wait until he had been tried and convicted by a court of law. In 1856 a member who had been indicted for fraud and who had fled from the accusation was expelled.

During the seventeenth century, when the House expelled a member, it often declared him incapable of being re-elected. This of course was a considerably greater exercise of power than mere expulsion. In 1769 the House expelled John Wilkes for a libel. He was immediately re-elected without a contest: then the House resolved that having been expelled he was incapable of sitting during the present parliament, and declared the re-election void. Again he was elected, and again the election was declared void. As the passions of the House cooled it came to the conclusion that it had acted illegally, and in 1782 the resolution of 1769 was expunged from the journals as subversive of the rights of the whole body of electors of this kingdom. We may take it then as certain that the House has no power to declare a man ineligible. Without being expelled a member may be suspended from sitting in the House for a certain time; of late years this power has been not infrequently exercised.

IV. *Frequency and Duration of Parliament.*

As regards the frequency of parliaments, there is still in force one statutory enactment. There are altogether five acts to be remembered. First there are the two old acts of Edward III (1330 and 1362) about annual parliaments. These were practically overridden, though not definitely repealed by the three later acts that I have to mention; and just lately they have been repealed as obsolete; the act of 1362 was repealed in 1863, the act of 1330 in 1881 (44 and 45 Vic., c. 59). Then there is the act of 1641 (16 Car. I, c. 1), which provided that a parliament should be holden at least in every third year, even though not summoned by the king. This was repealed in 1664 by 16 Car. II, c. 1, as contrary to the king's just rights, and instead thereof it was enacted merely that the sitting and holding of parliaments shall not be intermitted above three years at the most. This again was repealed in 1887 by 50 and 51 Vic., c. 59, as unnecessary on account of the act of William and Mary, which I am about to name. The act of William and Mary (6 and 7 W. and M., c. 2, 1694), which settled the duration of parliament at three years, provided also that a parliament shall be holden once at least in every three years; and this provision is still in force, and is the only enactment touching the frequency of parliaments that is in force, if we except the vague words of the Bill of Rights, that parliaments ought to be held frequently.

As a matter of fact, however, we know that parliament sits every year. I think that a parliament has sat in every year since the Revolution. We know also why this is necessary— (1) the maintenance of a standing army is only legalized for a year at a time, (2) supply is only granted to the crown sufficient for one year's expenditure. In this case therefore practical necessity lays down a rule more stringent than that which stands upon the statute book.

As to the duration of parliaments we must note a change. The first limit set to the power of the crown in this direction was, if we neglect the act of the Long Parliament which rendered that assembly indissoluble without its own consent, the Triennial Act of 1694 (6 and 7 Will. III, c. 2), which laid down the rule that no parliament should endure for longer than three years. The Septennial Act of 1715 substituted seven for three years. It has been noticed that this act is an excellent illustration of the supremacy of parliament : a parliament summoned for three years by its own act declared that it might sit for seven years—if for seven years why not for seventy? Various schemes for shortening the duration of parliament have from time to time found favour—some have advocated triennial, others annual parliaments—at the present moment we hear little of them[1].

The king without breaking the law can dissolve a parliament whenever he pleases. Any restraints that there are on this power are not legal restraints. We are not likely to see it abused. The king must have supplies, to get supplies he must have a parliament, there can be no good in his dissolving a parliament unless he believes that it does not fairly represent the wishes of the nation.

In 1867 the continuance of parliament was made independent of the demise of the crown. If when the king dies a parliament is in existence it will continue in existence just as though nothing had happened, but of course may be dissolved by the new king (30 and 31 Vic., c. 102). The first step in this direction was taken in 1696 (7 and 8 Will. III, c. 15)— parliament was to endure for six months after the king's death, unless sooner dissolved by his successor.

V. *Privileges of Parliament.*

The privileges of the two Houses occupy a large space in our books of constitutional law and history. Their importance in the past has been great; their importance in the present we are apt, I think, to overrate. Let us briefly see what they come to; for a fuller account I can refer you to Sir William Anson.

---

[1] The proposal to limit the duration of parliament to five years formed part of the scheme shadowed out by the Prime Minister on June 24, 1907, and was embodied in the Parliament Act of 1911.

(1) Freedom of speech. Freedom of speech as against the crown was, we may say, secured at the Revolution; since then there have been no legal proceedings by the crown against members for words uttered in the House. During the last century, however, the king did occasionally as a matter of fact take notice of opposition to his wishes, and make things unpleasant for the opponents by depriving them of offices. This it was difficult to prevent, the offices were held during the king's good pleasure, and he was not bound to give a reason when he exercised the legal power of dismissal. We are not very likely to hear of any repetition of such proceeding at the present day. At the present day it may be more important to notice that this freedom of speech holds good not only against the crown, but against private individuals also. A member speaking in either House is quite outside the law of slander. He may accuse any person of the basest crimes, may do so knowing that his words are false, and yet that person will have no action against him. Had he uttered the words elsewhere he might have had to answer for them in a court of law, but for what he says in the House he cannot be sued. In 1837 an attempt to extend this privilege from words uttered in the House to words printed by the authority of the House gave rise to the famous case of *Stockdale* v. *Hansard*, and to a violent collision between the Commons and the Court of King's Bench. Messrs Hansard, by order of the House of Commons, printed a report of the inspectors of prisons, which contained some defamatory words about Stockdale. He sued Hansard: and he failed because the jury thought that the words were true; but Hansard had in the first instance set up the order of the House as a complete defence, and Denman, C.J., and the other judges of the court, held that it was no defence: the order of the House of Commons would not justify anyone in publishing a libel. Stockdale brought another action; the House of Commons took offence, resolved that there was a breach of privilege, and refused to let their printer put in any defence but the order of the House; Stockdale obtained a verdict for £600 damages, and the sheriffs of Middlesex levied that amount. Then the House committed the sheriffs to prison, as also Stockdale and his solicitor. The sheriffs obtained a

writ of habeas corpus before the King's Bench. The serjeant-at-arms who had them in custody returned that they were imprisoned under a warrant of the Speaker for a contempt of the House of Commons. Upon this the judges held that they had no power to set the prisoners free, and so the wretched sheriffs remained in prison for doing what the court declared was their legal duty. Thereupon a bill was introduced to settle this disputed privilege for the future; and it passed into an act which provides that no civil or criminal proceedings can be taken in respect of any defamatory matter contained in any paper printed by the order of the House. This settled one point; as to the point raised by the committal of the sheriffs we must speak again.

Of course the principle that a member speaking in the House may speak ill with impunity does not involve the principle that I, or anyone else, may safely report his speeches. However, it has been decided that the editor of a newspaper may publish fair and honest reports of what has been said in parliament and cannot be sued for this, though he reports remarks which are untrue and defamatory. This was decided in 1868 in *Wason* v. *Walter* (L.R. 4, Q.B. 73), an action brought against the editor of the *Times* for reporting some words uttered by Lord Chelmsford in the House of Lords which accused the plaintiff of falsehood and malignity.

We ought here to remember that during the whole of the last century the Houses insisted that no one was entitled to publish reports of their proceedings, and committed to prison those who broke the rule. This perhaps we ought to regard as in its origin a measure of self-protection against the crown; so long as the Houses had to dread the action of the crown, they did well to insist that their proceedings should be secret. To this day reports are made on sufferance and published on sufferance. The House at any time may order strangers to withdraw; the House may at any time resolve that its proceedings shall not be reported, and commit to prison as for a contempt all those who report them. However, save in some extraordinary emergency, we are not likely now-a-days to find either of the Houses desiring to hide its light under a bushel.

(2) Freedom from arrest is now no very important matter, because this immunity does not extend to imprisonment on the charge of an indictable offence, and in 1869 imprisonment for debt was abolished. There are still some cases in which a person may be imprisoned in the course of civil proceedings, as for not paying trust monies which he has been ordered to pay by a court of justice, and in these cases a member of parliament would enjoy a special immunity; but this is no great matter.

In the case of members of the House of Commons this privilege is enjoyed during the session of parliament, and for 40 days before and 40 days after. On the other hand a peer, as I understand, enjoys this immunity at all times. Sir William Anson[1] seems to deny this, and to confine the privilege 'within the usual times of privilege of parliament' (whatever that may mean), but certainly the old rule was that 'the person of a peer is for ever sacred and inviolable' (as Blackstone phrases it), and I know not how it has been altered; further Irish and Scottish peers who have no seats in the House of Lords enjoy this privilege: it is indeed rather a privilege of the peerage than a privilege of parliament.

(3) The power of punishing for contempt. First as to the extent and nature of the punishment. The House of Lords has, it seems, power to fine and to imprison, and it can imprison for a specified term which may endure beyond the duration of the session. Thus in 1850, two days before a prorogation, it committed two persons to prison for a fortnight. I do not think that it has of late exercised its power of imposing a fine, but we cannot deny that the power exists. On the other hand it seems that the House of Commons cannot impose a fine; it has not done so since 1666, and any imprisonment that it inflicts comes to an end with the end of the session. Of the power of expelling or suspending its own members we have already spoken.

In the second place, for what offences can the House inflict this punishment of imprisonment? Our answer must be that it is the power of the House to inflict it in a quite arbitrary

---

[1] *Law and Custom of the Constitution, Parliament,* 3rd ed. p. 226.

way. In the last century it was established by decisions of the law courts that if a prisoner committed by the House obtained a writ of habeas corpus, and the return to the writ was that he had been committed for a contempt of the House, the court would inquire no further but would remand the prisoner to his gaol. Some precedent for this doctrine was to be found in the fact that the superior courts have long exercised a power of summarily committing persons for contempt, and a commitment made by one of them could not be questioned in another; thus if the prisoner had been committed for contempt by the Court of Common Pleas, it would have been useless for him to obtain a writ of habeas corpus in the King's Bench: on its appearing that he had been committed by the Court of Common Pleas for contempt, the judges of the sister court would have refused to inquire whether any contempt had actually been committed. Still it will strike you that each House has by this means obtained just that power of arbitrary imprisonment, which was wrested from the council of Charles I. This, however, was established by a series of decisions in the last century, and is not now to be doubted. Possibly if the House in its warrant for commitment stated the facts of the case a court of law would consider whether they constituted a contempt; but if it says merely that A.B. is committed for contempt, A.B. will appeal to the law courts in vain. We have seen this in the case of the sheriffs of Middlesex: they had to remain in prison, though in the view of the Court of King's Bench they had only done what it was their legal duty to do. Again a person so committed would have no action against the officers of the House who arrested him.

Thus it would seem that the House has a legal power to turn into a contempt just what it pleases, and the same may be said of the superior courts of law. Still we may inquire how this power has been actually exercised: and on the whole it has of late been exercised temperately enough save in some moment of irritation, such as that which occurred when the House of Commons was at issue with the Court of King's Bench over the case of *Stockdale* v. *Hansard* and committed the sheriffs of Middlesex.

Sir Erskine May divides breaches of privilege into four classes: (1) disobedience to general orders or rules of either House, (2) disobedience to particular orders, (3) indignities offered to the character of proceedings of parliament, (4) assaults or insults upon members or reflections upon their character and conduct in parliament or interference with officers of the House in discharge of their duties[1]. His instances of the first class consist almost entirely of publications of debates at a time when this was forbidden by general rules of the House. In the second place we have the neglect of orders directing persons to come and be examined before the House or before a committee, and breaches of other similar orders. In the third class we have libellous reflections on parliament. The last case that he gives is from 1819, when Mr Hobhouse was sent to prison by the House of Commons for 'a scandalous libel containing matter calculated to inflame the people into acts of violence against the legislature and against this House in particular.' Then as to attacks on individual members: assaults on members on their way to or from the House have been punished, also libels on members. In the past this power has been liberally used, but the more modern doctrine is that in order to be a contempt of the House the libel must be a libel on the member in his character of member: to accuse a member of having taken a bribe for his vote, would doubtless be treated as a contempt; on the other hand if one accused a member of bigamy he would probably be left to use his legal remedy, an action for slander or libel. Then to obstruct the officers of the House in the execution of their duties, and again to tamper with witnesses who are to give evidence before the House are treated as contempts.

To a certain extent the House acts according to rules; precedents are collected and to some extent respected, but too often we see questions of privilege treated as party questions, and then the House, whatever it may think of itself, becomes truly contemptible. That it has a very dangerous power in its hands is obvious.

I do not think it convenient (though this is sometimes done) to treat as matters of privilege the special functions of

[1] *Constitutional History of England*, vol. II, c. 7.

the two Houses, such e.g. as the special function of the House of Commons in relation to money bills or the special function of the House of Lords as a court of law. These are the outcome of rules of constitutional law, and stand on a different footing from the matters that we have been considering. The same may be said of the power of the House of Commons to decide all matters relating to disputed elections, a power which, as we have seen, it has recently made over to the courts of law.

VI. *The Work of Parliament.*

We have now to see what the work of parliament is. Doubtless its most important work is that of making statutes. But this is not all that it does. I leave out of sight for a time the judicial power of the House of Lords as a court for the trial of peers, and as a court to which appeals can be brought from the lower courts ; also I leave out of sight the procedure by way of impeachment—these matters are better treated in connexion with the administration of justice. But we ought to notice that the Houses of parliament do a great deal of important work without passing statutes or hearing causes. In the first place they exercise a constant supervision of all governmental affairs. The ministers of the king are expected to be in parliament and to answer questions, and the House may be asked to condemn their conduct. The legal power which enables the Houses to insist that ministers shall answer what are deemed to be proper questions is in the last resort the power of withholding supplies, or of refusing to legalize the existence of a standing army. Of course it is needless to have recourse to these powers—their exercise would throw the whole business of the country out of gear—still there those powers are and a ministry could not long exist if it had not the confidence of the House of Commons or refused to give such information as the House thought itself entitled to have. Then again by means of committees the Houses now exercise what we may call an inquisitorial power. If anything is going wrong in public affairs a committee may be appointed to investigate the matter ; witnesses can be summoned to give evidence on oath, and if they will not testify they can be committed for contempt. All manner of subjects concerning the public have of late been investigated by parliamentary commissions; thus information is obtained which may be used as a basis for legislation or for the recommendation of administrative reforms.

But the chief function of parliaments is to make statutes. We have observed the history of the legislative formula; for two centuries it has been accurately preserved, 'Be it enacted by the king's most excellent majesty by and with the advice and consent of the lords, spiritual and temporal, and commons in this present parliament assembled and by the authority of the same.' The essence of the statute seems to be the concurrence of the king, the House of Lords and the House of Commons. Each House we know has a well-settled order of business: thus it requires that every bill shall be read three times[1]. This procedure is in part defined by the standing orders which each House makes for itself, partly by tradition. In its main outlines this procedure is ancient; thus we can trace the three readings to the end of the Middle Ages, but it is not a procedure imposed by law. Each House has a very large liberty of regulating its own procedure, and just at present we constantly see the House of Commons engaged in this task. But not only has each House the power of making rules for itself, we must add that a disregard of its rules will not vitiate the statute. A court of law, we may safely say, would never go into the question whether an act has been passed in disregard of the usual formalities. The furthest that it would go would be to insist that the whole act had received the consent of king, lords, and commons; it would never for example permit the question to be raised whether a bill had been read three times—the rule which requires three readings, ancient and punctually observed though it may be, is no rule of law. On the other hand the assent of the king and the two Houses to the whole act in its ultimate form seems essential. Some delicate questions might arise as to this in case the officials of the House made mistakes. Suppose a bill carried through the House of Commons; the lords make amendments in it; it ought then to go back to the commons

---

[1] This principle has been modified by the Parliament Act of 1911 (1 and 2 Geo. V, c. 13) which provides that under certain circumstances bills may become statutes without the consent of the House of Lords. See Appendix.

in order that they may consider whether they will assent to the bill thus amended. But suppose that this step is omitted; that the bill is then presented to the king and that he gives his assent. Is this bill a statute? I take it that it is not; but the question how far a court of law would hold itself bound by a statement on the bill that it had received the assent of king and both Houses, whether it would permit a litigant to dispute this statement, is a somewhat difficult question. Such mistakes have occurred more than once in the present reign. Thus in 1844 there were two Eastern Counties Railway bills in parliament; one had passed all its stages, the other was still pending in the House of Lords, when by mistake the queen expressed her consent to the latter instead of to the former. The mistake was discovered, and another act was passed declaring that the bill to which assent had been given should not be deemed to have received the royal assent. Other mistakes of a similar kind have been similarly corrected. I may explain that a vellum copy preserved in the House of Lords is the ultimate evidence of a statute. Perhaps a court of law would allow a litigant to prove that as a matter of fact this document had never received the consent of king, lords and commons; but I am not sure of this.

For a long time past political theorists have insisted on the distinction between legislation and the other functions of government, and of course the distinction is important though it is not always easy to draw the line with perfect accuracy. But it seems very necessary to notice that the power of a statute is by no means confined within what a jurist or a political philosopher would consider the domain of legislation. A vast number of statutes he would class rather as *privilegia* than as *leges*; the statute lays down no general rule, but deals only with a particular case. This is particularly noticeable in the last century. The Revolution had, once for all, put an end to the ordaining and dispensing powers of the king, and parliament sought to do the work itself by means of statutes. If we take up any volume of eighteenth century statutes we find it very bulky. Apparently parliament got through much more work then than it gets through in our own day. But on inspection we find that anything that in the strictest sense can be called legislation, any alteration of the general rules of law, was much rarer then than it is in our own day, rarer than it was in the days of the three first Edwards. I take up a list of the statutes of 1786. There are 160 so-called public acts, and 60 so-called private acts. But listen to the titles of a few of the public acts: an act for establishing a workhouse at Havering, an act to enable the king to license a playhouse at Margate, an act for erecting a house of correction in Middlesex, an act for incorporating the Clyde Marine Society, an act for paving the town of Cheltenham, an act for widening the roads in the borough of Bodmin. Fully half of the public acts are of this petty local character. Then as to the private acts, these deal with particular persons: an act for naturalizing Andreas Emmerich, an act for enabling Cornelius Salvidge to take the surname of Tutton, an act for rectifying mistakes in the marriage settlement of Lord and Lady Camelford, an act to enable the guardians of William Frye to grant leases, an act to dissolve the marriage between Jonathan Twiss and Francis Dorrill. Then there are almost countless acts for enclosing this, that and the other common. One is inclined to call the last century the century of *privilegia*. It seems afraid to rise to the dignity of a general proposition; it will not say, 'All commons may be enclosed according to these general rules,' 'All aliens may become naturalized if they fulfil these or those conditions,' 'All boroughs shall have these powers for widening their roads,' 'All marriages may be dissolved if the wife's adultery be proved.' No, it deals with this common and that marriage. We may attribute this to jealousy of the crown: to have erected boards of commissioners empowered to sanction the enclosure of commons or the widening of roads, to have enabled a Secretary of State to naturalize aliens, would have been to increase the influence and patronage of the crown, and considering the events of the seventeenth century, it was but natural that parliament should look with suspicion on anything that tended in that direction.

As time has gone on parliament has become much less suspicious of the crown, because 'the crown' has come to mean a very different thing from what it meant in the last century. The change is a gradual one, but I think we may say that it becomes very apparent soon after the Reform Act of 1832. Parliament begins to *legislate* with remarkable vigour, to overhaul the whole law of the country—criminal law, property law, the law of procedure, every department of the law—but about the same time it gives up the attempt to *govern* the country, to say what commons shall be enclosed, what roads shall be widened, what boroughs shall have paid constables and so forth. It begins to lay down general rules about these matters and to entrust their working partly to officials, to secretaries of state, to boards of commissioners, who for this purpose are endowed with new statutory powers, partly to the law courts. I will give a few examples of what I mean. In the last century the administration of the poor law was altogether a local affair entrusted to the parochial overseers of the poor and the county justices. By the great Poor Law Reform Act of 1834 certain poor law commissioners were given very large statutory powers of regulating this matter for the whole kingdom. Later statutes gave them ever greater powers. In 1871 these commissioners gave place to the Local Government Board, which exercises very great powers over local affairs. A vast number of things that in the last century could only have been done for the parish of Little Peddlington by a statute can now be done without statute under an order, or with the sanction of the Local Government Board. Then again in the last century, if an alien wished to become naturalized he had to go to parliament for a statute. In 1844 a general statute was passed giving power to the Home Secretary to grant certificates of naturalization: thus recourse to parliament was rendered unnecessary. Then again in the last century there was no court which had power to dissolve a marriage. The ecclesiastical courts could pronounce a divorce, *a mensa et thoro*, could decree, that is to say, that the husband and wife need not live together, but in order to dissolve their union and set them free to marry again, recourse to parliament was necessary, and acts dissolving the marriage between X and Y were by no means uncommon. In 1857 however a new Court for Divorce and Matrimonial Causes was created, and was empowered to dissolve marriages whenever certain facts should be proved.

These are but a few examples of a general tendency which has been at work for the last fifty years, a tendency we may say on the part of parliament to confine itself to the work of legislation, of framing general rules of law, and to entrust the power of dealing with particular cases to the king's ministers, to boards of commissioners, to courts of law. Still parliament has not renounced and, according to our accepted theory of sovereignty, could not renounce the power of dealing with particulars, and in certain cases it still habitually exercises that power. The most important instance of this is to be found in the appropriation of supplies. When a supply of money is granted to the king, parliament proceeds to appropriate that supply with great minuteness, to say, that is, how much of it may be spent for this purpose, how much for that. Thus in 1886 it appropriated £2,902,900 for the payment of seamen and marines, £964,400 for their victuals and clothing, £11,477 for the maintenance of the British Museum and the Natural History Museum, £2,100,000 for public education, £1,000 as a gratuity for the widow of a certain distinguished public servant. Now an act saying to the queen, 'You may spend £1,000 in giving a gratuity to Lady A' is certainly not in the jurist's sense a law, it is no general rule, but this minute appropriation of supplies is a most important part of the work of every session, and it is effected by statute; the same formula is used as though a general law were being made: it is enacted " by the king's majesty with the advice and consent " etc. Nor must you suppose that this instance, though it is the most important, stands alone. To take another very common case: a railway company wants the power to compel landowners to sell the land necessary for the construction of its line; it must go to parliament for a statute. There is no general statute which empowers such companies to force the sale of land, but parliament in each case authorizes this particular company to compel the sale of those particular lands. Parliament has kept this matter in its own hands. Again it is not very often now-a-days that private persons succeed in obtaining or desire to obtain special acts of parliament dealing with their particular cases: formerly the tenant of a settled estate used sometimes to desire to sell the estate, and this he could not do without the aid of a statute; recent legislation as to settled estates has made it much easier to deal with settled estates, and private estates acts have become very unusual; still they are sometimes wanted, and are sometimes passed.

The power of a statute to descend to particulars receives its most striking and terrible illustration in an act of pains and penalties, an act inflicting punishment upon some particular person for some particular act. We have before this spoken of acts of attainder[1]. The last instance, I believe, of capital punishment being thus inflicted was that of Sir John Fenwick, who was executed in 1697. He, no doubt, was guilty of high treason in taking part in the plot to assassinate William III, but it was impossible to get two witnesses against him, and as you remember two witnesses are necessary in case of high treason. So instead of being tried in a court of law, he was attainted by act of parliament. Since then there have been other acts inflicting punishment, but never I think the punishment of death; thus Atterbury was banished in 1720. Now-a-days such acts would be very properly condemned, but even within quite recent times individuals have been disfranchised by act of parliament on account of bribery. In 1876 certain voters for the City of Norwich were thus disfranchised.

An act then can punish; so also it can absolve from punishment. Acts of indemnity are occasionally passed freeing this or that person from the penal consequences of what they have already done. Thus a year or two ago it was discovered that certain lords had sat in the Upper House without taking the oaths, and had thereby incurred very heavy money penalties. Acts were passed absolving them from the consequences of their inadvertence[2]. A curious little act of 1887 has just met my eye. The Duke of Connaught was Commander-in-chief of the Presidency of Bombay. Under a statute of 1793, if any Commander-in-chief in India comes home to Europe, he thereby resigns his office. The duke wished to be present at the Queen's Jubilee. An act of parliament was passed

---

[1] See above, pp. 215—16, 319—20.
[2] 43 and 44 Vict. Private Acts.

enabling him to do this without forfeiting his command[1]. A statute about so trivial a matter is, I think, a good illustration of the supremacy of parliament. If it can do the greatest things, it can do the least also; if it can make general laws for a vast empire, it can make a particular exception out of them in favour of a particular individual. The one thing that it cannot do is to prevent its own repeal.

To what extent parliament actually and habitually exercises this vast power—what can be done without an act of parliament, for what purposes an act is necessary—these are questions which can only be fully answered by stating the whole law of England. For instance, can a company lay a tramway through the streets of Cambridge without obtaining an act of parliament, and if so, can it use steam engines to draw its carriages? To answer such questions, one must look to the statute book and see what parliament has said about tramways. Generalizations, we shall find, are dangerous things; we cannot describe in wide terms the sort of acts which parliament passes; we must read, and read patiently, the acts that it has passed.

B.   *The 'Crown' and 'The Government.'*

We know however as a matter of fact that a great deal of the utmost importance is done towards governing the kingdom that is not done by parliament; indeed in common talk we constantly make a contrast between parliament on the one hand, and what we call the government on the other. What then is this government? The answer to this question, if it is to be true, must be both long and difficult. The reason is this. During the last two centuries there has grown up an organization which is not a legal organization. Of course, I do not mean that it is an illegal organization; rather I should prefer to say that it is an extra-legal organization; the law does not condemn it, but it does not recognize it—knows nothing about it. I mean the organization to which we point when we use such terms as 'the Cabinet,' 'the Ministry,' 'the Government,' 'the Prime Minister,' 'Mr Gladstone's second

[1] Duke of Connaught's Leave Act, 1887, 50 Vict. c. 10.

Ministry,' 'Lord Salisbury's administration.' This certainly is a most curious state of things, that the law should not recognize what we are apt to consider an organ of the state second only in importance to the parliament. The only explanation that can be given is a historical explanation. We must go back to William III's time.

We may start with this. William III as king of England had very great powers. The revolutionary settlement, in particular the Bill of Rights, set certain limits to those powers. The king was to be distinctly below statute; he was to have no power to suspend statutes or to dispense with statutes; he could not by his proclamations create any new offence; he could not keep a standing army in the realm in time of peace without consent of parliament; parliament had begun to appropriate supplies; the military tenures were gone; he had no powers of purveyance and preemption; he could not try men by martial law; the judges were no longer to hold office during his good pleasure; the courts of politicians whereby the Tudors and two first Stuarts had enforced their will were gone; there was no Star Chamber, no High Commission. Still the king's legal powers were great: it was a goodly heritage that was settled on King William. Indeed, as we have seen, there was a plausible case for holding that the Revolution was a restoration, a restoration of the ancient constitution as it stood in the days of the Lancastrian kings. All the old prerogatives existed save in so far as they had been expressly abolished by statute, and they were wide, and it was intended that William should exercise them. It was no honorary president of a republic that the nation wanted, but a real working, governing king—a king with a policy—and such a king the nation got.

Then the king has a council, a privy council; from a remote time this has been so; we can trace back the history of this council at least as far as the beginning of Henry III's reign. It has already four or five centuries of definite history and is very well known to the law. Before this I have tried to point out, however, that the constitution and the functions of the council have always depended to a great degree on the will of the king. The councillors are councillors only during

the king's pleasure. Only during minorities or during brief
revolutionary periods has parliament determined who shall be
councillors. And again no law compels the king to take or
even to ask the advice of his councillors. Great as are the
powers that the council exercises under the Tudors and the
Stuarts they are in law, at least generally, the king's powers,
the royal prerogatives—powers which the king might lawfully
exercise himself were he capable of discharging personally
the vast business of government. A privy councillor as such,
though the law knows him, has hardly any legal powers.

We notice also that the act which abolished the Star
Chamber weakened the council; not merely did it deprive
the council of almost all its judicial powers, but by so doing
it rendered regular meetings of the council less necessary
to the king. Charles II has a council whom it is needless to
keep together in permanent session; there is now no judicial
work for it to do; while as to the work of advising the king
upon the exercise of his prerogatives, no law compels the
king to seek the advice of all his councillors[1]. As a matter
of fact Charles does not seek their advice on all occasions:
he has business on hand which can be trusted to very few,
and he trusts very few. Something like an inner circle of
advisers is formed consisting of a few privy councillors who
hold some of the highest offices in the state. Men speak
of it as the Cabal; it so happens that the initial letters of
the names of its members make this word: Clifford, Ashley,
Buckingham, Arlington and Lauderdale. The privy council
is at this time a large body, consisting of some fifty members—
too large a body for united action. Sir William Temple evolved
a plan for reforming the council and restoring it to the position
that it had formerly held, that is to say, the position of a body
whom the king does really consult; but the plan broke down.
Under William it became obvious that there was a circle of real
councillors within the wider circle of nominal councillors, and
this inner circle gradually acquired the name of the Cabinet
Council—the council held in the king's own cabinet. This
was looked on with considerable suspicion by the parliamen-

---

[1] See E. I. Carlyle, "Committees of Council under the Earlier Stuarts,"
English Historical Review, Oct. 1906, pp. 673—86.

tarians of the time, and one more attempt was made to restore
the privy council to its lost position. When in 1700 it became necessary to settle the crown on the House of Hanover,
it was enacted by the Act of Settlement, that so soon as that
house should succeed to the throne ' all matters and things
relating to the well-governing of this kingdom which are
properly cognizable in the privy council by the laws and
customs of this realm shall be transacted there, and all
resolutions taken thereupon shall be signed by such of the
privy council as shall advise and consent to the same.' It
was feared that a Hanoverian prince would be in the hands
of foreign favourites, and it was desired that everyone who
gave the king counsel should do so under his hand, so that
his responsibility for the advice might be brought home to
him. What would have been the effect of this clause had
it ever taken effect, it is hard to say ; for it seems to say
no more than that things which by law ought to come before
the council ought to come before the council. My impression
is that whatever ancient usage may have required, law did
not require the king to consult his privy council about the
exercise of his prerogatives. And this became apparent afterwards. However the clause in question never came into force.
It was repealed in 1705 before the House of Hanover came
to the throne. That it would not work had, I suppose,
become apparent. During Anne's reign men became more
and more familiarized with the existence of a cabinet, and
the abandonment of the attempt to exclude placemen from
the House of Commons made possible our modern system
of government.

A great deal however remained to be done before that
system would assume the shape which is familiar to us ; but
before we trace the process any further we must turn back to
consider the position of those whom I will call the high officers
of state. All along there have been such officers. It would,
I think, be interesting could we take the history of each
office: for this, of course, we have not time; still a few
things should be remembered. In very ancient times the
chief officers of the king are the officers of his household : his
steward, his butler, his chamberlain, his marshal or the like.

Their activity spreads outwards from the household over the kingdom, and the greatest men of the kingdom are proud to hold offices which in their origin we may call menial. In the German Empire the Count Palatine of the Rhine was steward, the Duke of Saxony was marshal, the King of Bohemia cup-bearer, the Margrave of Brandenburg chamberlain. Soon after the Norman Conquest we see similar high officers in England, and their offices are hereditary. The high stewardship is hereditary in the House of Leicester, the office of constable in the descendants of Miles of Hereford, and that of chamberlain in the family of Vere and the butlership in that of Albini[1]. But in England owing to the strength of the Norman kingship, we may state as a general rule that an office which becomes hereditary becomes politically unimportant: it becomes an office of show and ceremony. Two of the most ancient offices still exist: the Earl of Norfolk is Marshal of England, the office of Lord Great Chamberlain is held jointly by Lady Willoughby d'Eresby and Lord Carrington. The offices of Lord High Steward and Lord High Constable fell into the king on the accession of the House of Lancaster. Since that time these offices have not been granted out as hereditary offices. They are, I believe, granted for the purpose of coronations and similar pageants, and when a peer is to be tried by his peers a high steward must be appointed for the occasion—a fact that may remind us that the king's steward would very naturally have been the president of the king's court just as the lord's steward presided in the court of the manor. These great offices of the first rank, however, have long been so purely honorary that we find a reduplication of offices; even the household work which would naturally be done by these officers is done by another set of officers. Thus besides the hereditary Lord Great Chamberlain who does nothing and is paid nothing, there is a Lord High Chamberlain, who has duties in the king's household and is paid a salary. Beside the hereditary Earl-Marshal, there is a non-hereditary Master of the Horse. So again there is a Lord Steward of the Household whose office is not hereditary, and who receives a salary.

[1] Stubbs' *Constitutional History*, vol. I, § 119.

But it is not these officers of the oldest and highest rank who acquire governmental functions. Another group of officials collects round the Norman king, and their offices are not hereditary. Foremost among them is the justiciar, *capitalis justitiarius Angliae.* His office comes to an end before the death of Henry III, and its extinction leaves as the two chief officers of the realm the Lord Chancellor and the Lord High Treasurer. Throughout the later Middle Ages, the Chancellor and Treasurer are the king's right-hand men. Other offices grow up. Under the Tudors a Lord President of the Council is sometimes appointed, and under the Stuarts this office becomes more permanent. Then, as we have already seen, confidential clerks begin to intervene between the king and his chancellor. There is the Lord Keeper of the Privy Seal, who already in Henry VIII's reign ranks next to the Chancellor, Treasurer, and Lord President. Then the king's secretary intervenes between the king and his privy seal, and in 1601 he becomes 'our principal secretary of estate.' The growth of the Court of Chancery has an important influence on the distribution of offices; the Chancellor with his increasing burden of judicial duties cannot be always at the king's side. Sometimes there are two Secretaries of State (Henry VIII appoints a second in 1539), sometimes even three; under Charles I it becomes the regular rule to have two, until 1708, when, on the occasion of the union with Scotland, the number was increased to three. There are now, as we shall see hereafter, five. On a somewhat lower level stood the Chancellor of the Exchequer, also the Lord High Admiral.

Occasionally we find that some of these offices are put into commission; thus instead of a Lord Chancellor, the great seal is entrusted to commissioners. At the beginning of George I's reign the office of Lord High Treasurer was put into commission, and it has remained in commission ever since. It is executed by certain persons who are collectively Lords Commissioners for executing the office of the Lord High Treasurer, or as they are generally called the Lords of the Treasury; the one who is first named in the patent of appointment is the First Lord of the Treasury. So also on the accession of William III, the office of Lord High Admiral was put in commission; it was revived for a short while in Anne's reign. Her husband, George of Denmark, was Lord High Admiral. It was revived again for a few months in 1827, when the Duke of Clarence became Lord High Admiral. But except during these intervals it has been in commission, executed by Lords Commissioners for executing the office of Lord High Admiral, that is to say, by a First Lord of the Admiralty and several other lords. Now these servants of the king, more especially the older of them, were known to the law, to the common law. They had legal powers. The king could not have got on without them. For instance, the Chancellor had become a judge; with the assistance of a Master of the Rolls and certain Masters in Chancery he had to discharge the ever increasing business of a great court. Take another and more important instance: in Elizabeth's reign the judges had to consider whether a certain sum of money had been lawfully issued out of the king's exchequer; they laid down two propositions: (1) that no money could be lawfully issued without the king's own warrant; (2) that such a warrant would not be sufficient, it must be sealed with the great seal or with the privy seal; the king's command by word of mouth is not enough, the king's command signed by his own hand and countersigned by his secretary is not enough—the great, or at least the privy, seal must be attached. And so in other cases, the courts would take no notice of the king's command unless formally sealed. A mass of laws grew up about this matter; for some purposes the great seal was indispensable, for others the privy seal would do, for others again the signet kept by the secretary: in a few cases the king's oral command would be enough—thus undoubtedly he could dissolve parliament by word of mouth. This doctrine of the seals practically compelled the king to have ministers entrusted with the seals who could be called in question for the use that they made of them. We must not think, even now-a-days, of 'the seals of office' as mere ceremonial symbols like the crown and the sceptre; they are real instruments of government. Without a great seal, England could not be governed. Every corporation, this University for instance, has as perhaps you know a common seal, and a great many things can only be done by the use of the common seal. It is somewhat the same with the seals of office: courts of law take notice of these seals, and insist that they must be affixed.

We return now to the growth of the Cabinet. The inner circle of councillors which grows up within the Privy Council consists of a few holders of these high offices. With their aid, the king can exercise all the powers with which the law entrusts him. They keep the various seals of office, and if they will affix them, then the king's business can be done. Certain things, it is true, must according to settled usage be done by Order in Council, that is, by an order made by the king at a meeting of the Privy Council. Thus from a remote time it has been the practice that the summoning of a parliament shall be determined on at a council. The writs of summons recite that by the advice of his Privy Council, the king has determined to call a parliament. Settled usage, I say, requires this—it might be too much to say that it is required by law—but at any rate, law does not require that all the members of the council shall be summoned to a meeting. A meeting of the king with just a few of its members selected by him is a meeting of the Privy Council, and a resolution passed at such a meeting and published is an Order in Council.

We now see how it is legally possible for the work of government to fall into the hands of a small number of the council—those members who hold the high offices of state and who have control over the seals of office. If the king has with him the Chancellor, the Treasurer or First Lord of the Treasury, the Lord Privy Seal, and the Secretaries of State, he can get his work done without consulting the mass of privy councillors. If, for any purpose, an Order in Council is required, a meeting of the king with just these few intimate advisers will be a good enough meeting of the Privy Council at which Orders in Council can be made. So much as to the legal possibility of cabinet government.

Still cabinet government, in our modern sense, is but slowly perfected; our idea of it involves several principles which were by no means acknowledged principles in the days of William III, which hardly obtained complete recognition until late in the last century. In the first place there has been a further change in the mode of conducting business. William and Anne were habitually present at the meetings of the Cabinet Councils, which also, as we have just seen, were legally meetings of the Privy Council. But then there comes a change. George I ceased to attend the meetings of the Cabinet. He and George II could not speak English, and felt little concern as to the internal policy of England; they were more concerned for Hanover. The Cabinet then begins to meet without the king's presence. The results of its discussions are, when this is necessary, conveyed to the king by one of the ministers. If an Order in Council is wanted, then a few ministers are got together, and what is formally and legally a meeting of the Privy Council is held under the king's presidency. But the business of such a meeting becomes merely formal; it is held in order that it may register a foregone conclusion, a conclusion debated in the Cabinet and communicated to the king. George III, though he had a will of his own and strong views of policy, did not interfere with this arrangement. At the deliberative meetings of the Cabinet Council the king was not present; the formal meetings of the Privy Council at which he was present were not meetings for debate or discussion, but merely meetings at which the king would give his formal assent and authority to matters which had been already before the Cabinet and about which the king's pleasure had been already taken.

Then again we must notice the growing solidarity of the Cabinet. This solidarity (I can find no better word for it) we may analyze into three principles: (1) political unanimity, (2) common responsibility to parliament, (3) submission to a common head.

(1) Only by degrees does it come to be considered that the king ought to choose all his ministers from one of the two great parties. The ministries of Anne's reign are partly Whig, partly Tory. The Whig administration of Sir Robert Walpole sets the precedent for party ministries and thenceforward, though there are occasional aberrations, the bonds of party are drawn tighter. Of course there may be coalition ministries, but then a coalition ministry has a policy of its own, though it does not happen to be the policy of either of the two great

permanent parties, the existence of which we have come to regard as natural.

(2) Connected with this is the principle of common responsibility to parliament, by which is meant that the ministry, if defeated, will resign in a body. This principle was not fully admitted until the last century was far advanced. We may find one minister resigning because he cannot get on with parliament, while his colleagues retain office; quarrelling with him is not quarrelling with them, nor are they in honour bound to support his cause. We must remember in this context that the presence of ministers in the House of Commons was long disliked by the House. So far from wishing to have ministers there to answer for their doings, the House struggled to exclude them. But the ideal changed; the House wished to have the ministers before it—became accustomed to have them before it—to support them, to attack them, to regard them as a whole, to regard them not merely as the representatives of the king, but also as the representatives of a party, so that a defeat of a minister would be a defeat of a party.

(3) Such organization of a ministry almost of necessity involves some degree of subordination and very slowly it becomes acknowledged, not by law, but by parliamentary practice that there is among the ministers a Prime Minister, one who has a certain amount of authority over his fellows, one who, to a certain extent, stands between them and the king. But this is the gradual outcome of practice. Walpole, for example, though, as a matter of fact, he had great authority over his colleagues, protested against being called Prime Minister, and to this day the law knows no such person[1]. Lord Salisbury, we say, is Foreign Secretary and Prime Minister; to the law he is merely one of H.M. principal Secretaries of State, and whatever power he may have over his colleagues is not legal power—he has no more legal power to give them orders than they have to give him orders; he has no more power to dismiss them than they have to dismiss him. Still, before the end of the last century constitutional practice required that there should be a Prime

---

[1] The Prime Minister was granted precedence next after the Archbishop of Canterbury by royal warrant dated Dec. 4, 1905, and appearing in the *London Gazette* of Dec. 5. The warrant does not constitute an office, but grants precedence to the person holding a particular position.

Minister, and in the present century his ascendency has become still more marked.

Then again, we have to notice the growth of the principles, which of course are no principles of law: (1) that the king is bound (at least in all grave matters) to act on the advice of his ministers, (2) that he must choose his ministers, or rather his first minister, in accordance with the will of the House of Commons. We cannot trace step by step the process whereby the king's personal will and pleasure has come to count for very little in our government. The reigns of the two Hanoverians, George I and George II, had much to do with it. George III's attempt to govern as well as to reign was, we may now say, a retrograde attempt; it is improbable that we shall see such an attempt in the future. The process of which we are speaking is a very gradual process, and it is very difficult to say with any accuracy how far it has gone. Few indeed are the people who really know how much or how little the queen's own wishes affect the course of government. I strongly suspect that her influence is rather underrated than overrated by the popular mind. Persons in general do not know how vast a mass of business is brought before her, how many papers she has to sign with her own hand. Still there is no doubt that it is expected of her that in all grave matters she should accept the advice of her ministers. It much rather concerns us as legal students to see how this non-legal rule is intimately connected with legal arrangements. Without parliament's consent, given year by year, no standing army can be kept on foot. Without the grant of supplies the king will have no money, or at any rate not enough money to enable him to carry on the work of government. Thus parliament, and in particular the House of Commons, has a most efficient check upon the king's action. An attempt to keep in office ministers who could not command a majority in the House of Commons would speedily fail: the House could refuse to renew the Army Act, or refuse to grant supplies. An attempt to overrule ministers who commanded such a majority might be met in a similar fashion. The most important choice that a king can have to make is now the choice of a Prime Minister; the other ministers are practically chosen for him by the Prime Minister, and even here he seldom has much choice. It is even laid down as constitutional practice that when a ministry resigns, the king ought to offer the premiership to the person named by the outgoing minister.

We here find ourselves among rules which most clearly are not rules of law ; we may call them rules of constitutional morality, or the customs or the conventions of the constitution. We find them of every degree of stringency and of definiteness: on the one hand there are rules so stringent and so definite that they practically operate as rules of law ; on the other hand there are rules which have hardly yet obtained general recognition, and the very existence of which is disputable. For instance, we may now take it as a well-settled understanding that when a bill has passed both Houses of parliament, the king will not withhold his assent. The last occasion on which such assent was withheld occurred so long ago as Queen Anne's reign, when she rejected a Scottish Militia Bill. We now expect the royal assent as though it were a mere matter of course, and (to say the least) the circumstances would have to be of a very extraordinary character which would allow the king to withhold his royal assent without a breach of a well-settled constitutional understanding. On the other hand, we seem to see a rule growing up to the effect that the House of Lords ought not persistently to resist the will of the House of Commons about matters of first-rate importance. At present this rule, if rule we may call it, is of a very vague character ; we have to use in expressing it such elastic terms as 'persistently' and 'matters of first-rate importance,' and our view as to the existence of the rule is likely to be affected by our political opinions : if we be Tories we shall perhaps deny it, if Radicals we shall affirm it : if we try to be impartial we shall have to say something very loose: as, for instance, that this rule has been observed more or less for some time past and seems to be growing stricter. An instance of a more definite rule, which yet is no rule of law, is that the lords are not to make changes in a money bill, but must accept it as a whole or reject it as a whole. As an illustration of a very debateable matter, we may take the power of the House of Commons to make use of this rule as to money bills for the purpose of forcing other measures through the Upper House. Is it unconstitutional for the commons to, as the phrase goes, tack a bill granting money to the crown to another bill to which the lords object, and thus to put the lords in the dilemma of having either to pass the obnoxious bill or to leave the crown without money? There are a few instances of this having been done, and more of its having been threatened; I do not think that it has actually been done since William III's reign. The lords contend that such a proceeding is unconstitutional—the commons might take a different view. There is no impartial tribunal before which such questions can be brought, no tribunal which even pretends to be impartial. In each particular case there is likely to be a brisk party conflict, but slowly understandings are established. And thus it is as to the personal wishes and opinions of the king: they have come to count for little, but for how much few of us can say.

But we must not confuse the truth that the king's personal will has come to count for less and less with the falsehood (for falsehood it would be) that his legal powers have been diminishing. On the contrary, of late years they have enormously grown.

The principle being established that the king must govern by the advice of ministers who are approved by the House of Commons, parliament has entrusted the king with vast powers—statutory powers. Many governmental acts, which in the last century would have required the passing of an act of parliament, are now performed by exercise of statutory powers conferred on the king. Acts which give these powers often require that they shall be exercised by order in council. Thus in addition to his prerogative or common law powers the king now has statutory powers. All this, coupled with the delegation of other powers to this minister and that, is the result of a new movement which began about 1830.

These brief remarks about history are intended as an introduction to an examination of the present state of affairs. We have to enquire how what we may loosely call the government is organized, and we must carefully distinguish between rules of law and rules which, however binding they may be considered, are not rules of law and could not be enforced by any legal proceedings.

We have to begin with describing the present constitution of the Privy Council, the Cabinet, the Ministry.

(1) The Queen has a Privy Council and in some sort is obliged by law to have one, not indeed quite directly, but the legal pressure amounts to necessity, for many things which must be done (if government is to go on at all) can only be done by the Queen in Council. This is the result (for the most part) of statutes passed within the last fifty years, a mass of statute law growing rapidly year by year. One statute we may specially note:

The Act of Union with Scotland provides that there shall be but one Privy Council for Great Britain.

(2) The legal composition of the Council is as follows. No number is fixed; no legal *quorum* is demanded; the Queen of her own will can make any man (not an alien) a privy councillor. Summons and oath make the privy councillor— in substance he swears to advise the king to the best of his discretion. From the form of oath, which is very ancient, little is to be learned. The privy councillor swears to keep the king's counsel secret, to avoid corruption, to do all that a good counsellor should do. He is dismissible at pleasure, without cause assigned.

(3) In actual composition the body consists of some two hundred and fifty members—about half peers and half commoners.

It contains all present and past cabinet ministers, a few members of the royal family, two Archbishops and the Bishop of London, a number of the highest judges and ex-judges, and a number of persons selected on grounds of military, political, scientific, literary and even philanthropical services. Certain offices carry with them a constitutional claim to a seat in the privy council: a cabinet minister is always called to the council board, also the lord chief justice, the lord justices (a relic of former time), the Archbishops and the Bishop of London. *De facto* councillors are not dismissed;

indeed it probably would not be considered constitutional (i.e. it would raise an outcry) to dismiss them except for crime or gross immorality. It follows from the composition of the body that if the Privy Council really met, it would do no business for it would comprise members of both political parties: Salisbury, Gladstone, Hartington, Morley, Chamberlain, Randolph Churchill.

(4) The queen is not bound by law nor by any constitutional understanding to summon all her councillors; on the contrary, modern constitutional understanding requires of her that she shall summon but a small selection of them. A privy councillor made so as a mere honour—e.g. an ex-judge—goes to the council board once to take the oath, and he never goes again. Perhaps it may be said that he has a constitutional (it can hardly be a legal) right to be heard, if he has advice to give. Perhaps it would be considered that the queen ought not to refuse him an audience; but obviously, if this right were really insisted on, our constitution would soon be topsy-turvy: as, for instance, if, while the present ministry remains in power, Gladstone insisted on constantly having the queen's ear. Possibly a formal meeting of the whole Privy Council would be summoned at the beginning of a new reign[1]. Again, a meeting might be summoned in some extraordinary national emergency. A full meeting was held in 1839 when the queen's approaching marriage was announced.

(5) But a meeting of the Sovereign with any of the Privy Council (subject to such understandings as may exist with regard to a *quorum*, the presence of the Clerk of the Council, or the books of the Council[2]) has enormous power. It is the constitutionally correct and in some cases the legally necessary mode of exercising the common law powers, 'prerogatives' of the crown. It is the statutory means of exercising many—most, and those the most important—of the statutory powers of the crown.

---

[1] At the accession of King Edward VII a full meeting was summoned at St James Palace Jan. 23, 1901, and attended by four Royal Dukes, two Archbishops, the Lord Chancellor, the Lord President and 97 other Lords of the Council.

[2] An accurate record is kept of the proceedings of the Privy Council, though it is not in terms described as 'Minutes.' I owe this information to the kindness of Mr Almeric Fitzroy, the Clerk of the Council.

(6)　It is legally requisite that the Sovereign should have certain high officers of state, a Lord Treasurer, for instance, or commissioners for executing his office, a Lord Chancellor or Lord Keeper of the great seal or commissioners entrusted with the great seal, at least one Secretary of State. It is legally requisite, because it would become utterly impossible to govern England lawfully without such officers, impossible, for instance, to get a penny out of the Bank of England without the commission of a high crime. This is true in a less degree of the Board of Trade, the Local Government Board, the committee of Council for Education ; grave public affairs would be in a mess if these bodies were non-existent for a month. This is the result of modern statutes.

(7)　A certain number of these high officers of state are said to constitute 'the cabinet': these, together with other officers, are said to constitute 'the ministry.' Neither of these terms is known to the law. No official document constitutes the cabinet. Some officers are always (by practice) members of the cabinet, for instance, all Secretaries of State, the first Lord of the Treasury, the Chancellor, the Chancellor of the Exchequer, the first Lord of the Admiralty. As to other officers, the practice varies: the Postmaster-General, the President of the Local Government Board, the President of the Board of Trade, the Lord Privy Seal, the Chancellor of the Duchy of Lancaster are generally members of the cabinet. In practice every member of the cabinet holds a legal office : most members hold extremely important legal offices ; even when it is wished to have the presence of some one who is past work, he is given an office—though one to which few duties are annexed—the Chancellorship of the Duchy or the like.

(8)　The truth that the cabinet is unknown to law must not be converted into the falsehood that it is a meeting of persons who have no legal powers. Each cabinet minister is a privy councillor, each is a high officer, each has usually large legal powers. But the legal powers of a cabinet meeting are only the sum of the legal powers of its members. The cabinet has no corporate powers.

(9)　The cabinet is a selection out of a larger body of

'ministers'; the 'ministry' consists of those holders of office under the crown who according to constitutional usage are expected to be members of one or other House of Parliament and to act together. Recall the law as to the qualification for the House of Commons. Office under the crown either does or does not disqualify from a seat in Parliament; the law must be sought in a variety of statutes; but the general result is that only those holders of civil (as distinct from military) offices under the crown can sit who are intended and expected to act together and to form a coherent body in parliament.

There seem to be forty or fifty such offices. A ministry consists of forty to fifty men, of whom fifteen to seventeen form the cabinet[1]. As instances of ministerial offices which are not cabinet offices we may cite the law officers of the crown, the Attorney-general and Solicitor-general for England and for Ireland, the Attorney-general and Solicitor-general for Scotland, the junior lords of the Treasury, the junior lords of the Admiralty, the first Commissioner of Works and public buildings, the Paymaster-general, the two Secretaries to the Treasury, the political secretaries representing the Home Office, Foreign Office, India Office, Colonial Office, War Office, the Board of Trade, the Local Government Board, the Secretary to the Admiralty. The general idea is that each great department of State shall have one representative in each House: thus if the Secretary of State for Foreign Affairs be in the Lords, the political Under-Secretary will be in the Commons.

It is a general rule, though not of course a rule of law, that all ministers should be in one House or the other. The case of the Naval Lords appears to be the sole exception.

Further there are some understandings, though less distinct, as to which House shall contain a particular minister. The Chancellor of the Exchequer must be in the Commons; a rule seems to be growing up that the Home Secretary must be there likewise. And it is a legal rule that not more than four under-secretaries of State may sit in the Commons[2].

Again it is a general rule that other offices in the civil service are to be permanent and not political; but this is a

---

[1] The number of the cabinet in 1913 is 21, the number of the ministry 59.
[2] 21 and 22 Vict. c. 106. See also 27 and 28 Vict. c. 34.

constitutional understanding not law. When there is a change of ministry, but a few officials are changed, though these are the highest.

It is just worth noting that the highest officers of the Household are changed—the Master of the Horse, the Master of the Buckhounds, the Mistress of the Robes—but this is a relic.

(10) The quasi-corporate character of the 'cabinet' and of the 'ministry' is entirely extra-legal. One minister is not legally answerable for what another does: he is answerable of course for aiding and abetting, answerable as accessory before or after the fact, but probably responsibility does not go beyond this: 'probably,' for who shall say what might happen upon an impeachment? but the question might quite conceivably be raised upon an indictment in an ordinary court of law, and there seems no principle in our law which could hold A guilty because he was a member of the cabinet at the time when another member B committed some crime in the execution of his office.

Still the law not very indirectly compels harmony among ministers; this is noticeable in particular as to Secretaries of State who are fungible—if Secretary X were always revoking (as legally he might) the orders given by Secretary Y, there would soon be an intolerable confusion. However unity is secured in the main by extra-legal rules; rules which require that ministers shall either agree with their colleagues or resign, which require that as regards important practical questions ministers shall have the same policy. These rules, though they have grown more strict since the beginning of the century, are and must be pretty vague; there is no impartial tribunal to enforce them. It does not belong to us to discuss them: their sanction is a vote of want of confidence, and beyond that the impossibility of carrying on business in the teeth of such a vote.

So also the cabinet is expected to meet, to discuss measures, to have a policy. The meeting of the cabinet is perfectly informal; it receives no summons from the Sovereign; the Sovereign is never present; no record is kept.

The Prime Minister is unknown to law; nor is the premiership annexed to any particular office.

(11)   All these high officers of state, indeed all officers of state, hold office legally *durante beneplacito*. But the queen is expected to choose a Prime Minister who will command the confidence of the House of Commons; and to appoint his nominees to office. Ministers expect to collectively resign their offices if they cannot command a majority in the House of Commons. A defeated minister has the choice between resigning, and counselling a dissolution of parliament. As to when he may counsel a dissolution, no very precise rule can be laid down. All we can say is that, according to modern precedent, he is not bound to await a conflict with parliament, in which he will certainly be defeated.

Officers of state, or the queen's executive servants, not being members of the ministry, hold office *durante beneplacito*; still *de facto* their tenure is very permanent; they do not 'go in and out with the ministry'; they cannot (as a rule) sit in the House of Commons, and are expected not to take any very active part in party politics.

(12)   Now let us consider the relation of these informal extra-legal bodies to the Privy Council.

The Government of the country is carried on chiefly by the exercise of statutory powers: to some small extent by the exercise of prerogative powers.

Statutory governmental powers are most miscellaneous: we might classify them (*a*) according to the nature of the work to be done, as whether it be that of issuing general rules (subordinate legislation) or that of giving particular orders, or (*b*) according to the mode in which the power is to be exercised. It is with (*b*) that we are now concerned.

Of these statutory powers there are two great groups:— though classification is difficult, and in every particular case the statute must be consulted and punctually obeyed.

(i)   Powers given to the Queen in Council: 'it shall be lawful for H.M. by Order in Council.'

(ii)   Powers given to one of the high officers of state, or to some combination of them: 'it shall be lawful for one of H.M. principal secretaries of state.'

(13)   Roughly speaking, the most important powers are given to the Queen in Council—but this is only a rough statement.

How are they to be exercised? By the queen at what is legally a meeting of her Privy Council. The queen holds such meetings from time to time. Summonses are sent out by the Lord President of the Council to a few privy councillors. It is, I believe, usual to get six members to attend, just a few of the cabinet ministers; sometimes one of the queen's sons; as already so often said, no one has a right to be summoned[1]. The business, I believe, is of the most formal kind, the orders have been prepared by the minister whose department they concern, if of importance they have been discussed in the cabinet; their nature is explained to the queen, who says 'approved'; there is, I believe, no debate. The order is drawn up and signed by the Clerk of the Council, a permanent officer: such is an Order in Council.

The use of requiring a formal meeting of this sort is, I take it, that to any Order in Council several members of the cabinet must almost necessarily be committed, if not legally, at least constitutionally. When power is given (say) to a Secretary of State to issue rules, orders and regulations as to the discipline of the police, and he exercises this power, it might be difficult, even in parliament, to hold the Chancellor of the Exchequer in any sense answerable for what his colleague had done if he chose to repudiate the act: it would, I imagine, be much more difficult for any cabinet-minister to deny responsibility for an Order in Council. Here, however, we go beyond the law.

The form of an Order in Council is as follows:

October 4, 1887.

At the court at Balmoral the 15th day of September, 1887.

Present,

The Queen's most Excellent Majesty in Council.

Whereas under certain statutes the Ecclesiastical Commissioners have prepared a scheme for making new parishes.

---

[1] Mr Almeric Fitzroy, the Clerk of the Council, kindly informs me that so far as he is aware, no rule has been laid down as to the *quorum* necessary for Orders in Council; but that in practice the rule embodied in an Order of Feb. 20, 1627 has been followed. It requires the presence of three of the Lords of the Council. The presence of the Clerk of the Council is necessary, as it is his attestation which affords legal proof of the document.

And whereas the scheme has been approved by H.M. in Council. Now therefore H.M. by and with the advice of her said Council is pleased to order and direct that the said scheme shall come into force on a certain date.

C. L. PEEL.

The *London Gazette* is *prima facie* evidence of an Order in Council. Such orders are very different from statutes; judges are not bound to take judicial notice of them.

The various powers which parliament has delegated may be classified according to their nature.

(1) Power of laying down general rules which shall have the force of law—much is now done in this way: thus the Home Secretary has power to issue general orders as to the discipline and pay of the police, the Local Government Board has power to issue general rules as to the government of workhouses, etc. In other words they exercise powers of subordinate legislation. The validity of these rules may be questioned, they may be *ultra vires* and so invalid.

(2) Power of issuing particular commands: thus supposing that a sanitary board will not make proper sewers, the Local Government Board, on being satisfied of such default, may order the sewers to be made and order the defaulting authority to pay cost.

(3) Power to grant licenses for this and that: thus the Home Secretary may license a person to practise vivisection, may license a Jesuit to remain in England.

(4) Power to remit penalties: not uncommonly given.

(5) Powers of inspection: factories, mines, stores of explosives.

(6) Inquisition: holding inquiries into explosions, railway accidents, etc.

We will now take a brief survey of the powers of the various high officers of state, taking them one by one. Our sketch must be very brief and imperfect, but still it may serve to give us some insight into the real practical working of English public law.

1. First we have the Treasury. There are five lords commissioners for executing the office of Lord High Treasurer: a

First Lord (Mr Smith, Cabinet), the Chancellor of the Exchequer (Mr Goschen, Cabinet) and three junior lords (Mr Herbert, Col. Walrond, and Sir Herbert Maxwell)[1]. Legally they have, at least for the most part, equal powers. During the eighteenth century the Lords of the Treasury used to meet as a board and transact business as a board, and the practice of holding formal meetings was maintained until some forty years ago[2]. The supreme control fell more and more into the hands of the Chancellor of the Exchequer, and now the junior lords are in the view of parliament very distinctly his subordinates. The First Lord does very little official work. Very commonly he is Prime Minister; at the present moment he is not Prime Minister, but he is the recognized leader of the House of Commons; he devotes himself, I believe, rather to a general superintendence of the government business in the House of Commons than to the exercise of those legal powers which he has as a Lord of the Treasury. Now acts of parliament frequently say that this that and the other matter shall or may be done by 'the Treasury.' An act of 1849 declares this to mean that the requisite document shall be signed by two of the Commissioners[3]. Such a document is required for a vast number of purposes. To take one of the most important: when parliament has granted a supply to the king no money can come out of the Exchequer except in obedience to a warrant under the royal sign manual countersigned by two Lords of the Treasury; not a sixpence of the money voted by parliament can lawfully be spent until the king has signed a warrant, and this is countersigned by the Lords of the Treasury (29 and 30 Vic., c. 39). I doubt whether it is generally known how many documents the queen has to sign : were she to lose the use of her hand for a month a great deal of public business would soon be in utter confusion. In 1830 George IV found it difficult to write, an act of parliament had to be at once

---

[1] Written in 1887–8.

[2] 'Since 1856 the meetings have been discontinued,' Anson, *The Crown*, p. 172.

[3] By the Interpretation Act of 1889 (52 and 53 Vict., c. 63) the expression 'The Treasury' is defined to mean 'the Lord High Treasurer for the time being or the Commissioners for the time being of H.M. Treasury.'

passed authorizing the use of a stamp to be affixed in his presence to documents which required the use of the royal sign manual. In 1811, when George III lost his wits, the difficulty was much more serious; the ministers could get no money because the king could not sign the necessary warrant: parliament had to pass a resolution authorizing and commanding the issue of money; and it may be doubted whether even this resolution, to which the king, of course, could not consent, made the issue legal. But not only is the sign manual necessary, the counter-signature of two Lords of the Treasury is necessary also. That is one illustration of the powers of the Treasury, but very generally you will find that nothing whatever can be done which in any way involves the expenditure of public money without the consent of the Treasury: this is required by law, by statute. Then it is the duty of the Chancellor of the Exchequer to present to the House of Commons the estimates of expenditure and to make proposals for grants by which such expenditure shall be met, to recommend the imposition and the remission of taxes.

2. We turn next to H.M. principal Secretaries of State. There are now five. During the greater part of the eighteenth century there were but two, though for a while there were three. In 1801 we have three: one for Home Affairs, one for Foreign Affairs, one for War and the Colonies. In 1854 a fourth was appointed, War being separated from the Colonies. In 1858, when an end was put to the East India Company, a fifth Secretary of State was appointed to look after Indian Affairs. We of course freely talk of the Home Secretary, the Foreign Secretary and so forth, but this division of labour is hardly known to the law. The language of statutes generally is 'it shall be lawful for one of H.M. principal Secretaries of State.' Legally any one of the five secretaries may exercise that power—the subject matter of the act will decide who shall really exercise it, thus if the act relates to the Colonies then it will be exercised by the Colonial Secretary. However, to this rule there are exceptions. I know of one instance in which a statutory power is given to the Secretary of State for the Home Department (23 and 24 Vic., c. 34, an Act to amend the Law relating to Petitions of Right).

Now each Secretary of State has very large powers—a few given him by the common law, a vast number given to him by statute. Thus it seems certain that a Secretary of State may by the common law commit to prison on suspicion of treason or any treasonable offence, i.e. commit for trial. This is no great matter now-a-days and the power is not exercised, because it is easy enough to take the suspected person before a justice of the peace. But it made a great noise in the eighteenth century in connection with the proceedings against Wilkes. Lord Halifax, the then Secretary of State, was guilty of issuing warrants which the courts of law held to be illegal: e.g. a warrant to seize, not A. B., but the author of a particular seditious libel, No. 45 of the *North Briton*, and a warrant to seize the papers of A. B., suspected of being the author of a seditious libel. However, the Court of Common Pleas had somewhat reluctantly to hold that the Secretary of State had power to issue a warrant for the arrest of A. B., suspected of a treasonable or seditious offence: how he had acquired that power was much questioned, but it had been exercised during the earlier part of the century, and its existence could not be denied. This power, however, is a small matter, though it has made much noise, compared with the vast powers with which the Secretary of State has been entrusted by modern statutes.

A few examples may be given of the powers entrusted by statute to the Home Secretary.

By the statute instituting the modern police force, 1839, (2 and 3 Vic., c. 93, s. 3) the Secretary may from time to time issue rules for the government, pay, clothing and accoutrements of the constables. The County force cannot be increased or diminished without leave of the Secretary. So too in the government of prisons, he possesses enormous powers: thus he may make rules as to classification of prisoners, and may interfere in particular cases, substituting one kind of hard labour for another.

Again he has received vast powers over the regulation of factory labour and the regulation and inspection of mines and collieries. The attempt, characteristic of modern times, to protect the economically weaker classes has given rise to statutes which bristle with powers entrusted to the Secretary of State. Thus, for instance, his license is required for vivi-section (1876, 39 and 40 Vic., c. 77).

Again, he is empowered to grant certificates of naturaliza-tion, a discretionary power. Notice this 'devolution' of a power once kept by parliament in its own hand.

These are instances of statutory powers: but the Home Secretary is also the proper adviser of the crown as to the exer-cise of certain prerogative powers: for instance, that of pardon.

Perhaps the Home Secretary is more interesting to us than other secretaries; but they also have many statutory powers of the utmost importance. Thus, to take but one example: the act which put an end (1858) to the government of India by the East India Company provided that 'all the powers and duties then exercised or performed by the East India Company should in future be exercised and performed by one of H.M. principal Secretaries of State.'

To a large extent the powers of these *four* Secretaries consist in this, that it is for them (each in his own department) to advise the queen as to the exercise of powers which by law are her powers, either ancient prerogative powers or more modern powers given to her by statute. Still (especially in the case of the army) we find powers given expressly to the Secretary for War.

All Secretaries are invariably in the cabinet: each has a parliamentary Under-Secretary, who is a minister but without a seat in the cabinet.

3. The Admiral's office is in commission: a first lord (cabinet) and three junior lords, two 'naval'—not necessarily in parliament—and one 'civil,' in parliament; all of them in the 'ministry.'

This is a really deliberative board.

4. Of the Lord-Lieutenant of Ireland and his principal secretaries, one of whom is often in the cabinet, we have no time to speak; nor of the new Secretary (not of State) for Scotland, created in 1885 to exercise for Scotland powers theretofore exercised by the (Home) Secretary and some others taken from various English departments. More interesting to us are: the Board of Trade, the Local Government Board, the Education Department, the Board of Agriculture.

5. The Board of Trade is in form a committee of the Privy Council, consisting of a President and certain *ex officio* members. The First Lord of the Treasury, the Chancellor of the Exchequer, the Secretaries of State, the Speaker of the House of Commons, and the Archbishop of Canterbury. But all its powers can legally be and are exercised by the President, who practically is the Board. These powers are vast and most various : in particular as to railways, and as to merchant shipping, as, for instance, the detention of unseaworthy ships. The whole of our mercantile marine has by an elaborate code been placed very much under the governance of the Board of Trade. Then again since 1883 the working of the bankruptcy law has been placed in the hands of official receivers, appointed and dismissible by and answerable to the Board of Trade.

6. The Local Government Board, created by an act of 1871, consists of a President and of certain *ex officio* members (Lord President of the Council, Secretaries of State, Privy Seal and Chancellor of Exchequer), but all its powers can be exercised by the President with the counter-signature of his secretary or assistant secretary. Thus it is a board only in name[1].

Manifold statutory powers in the working of our poor law and sanitary law have been conferred upon it.

The Poor Law Amendment Act of 1834, declared central control to be necessary and lodged it in the hands of three Poor Law Commissioners. Then (1847) came the Poor Law Board consisting of a number of high state officials headed by a President. Finally in 1871 this Board was merged in the newly-constituted Local Government Board.

In a most general way all paupers are placed under its 'rules, orders and regulations.' It exercises strict control over the local administrators—boards of guardians ; can give them orders, and (within wide bounds) can legislate for them.

So too with regard to the sanitary system : the great code of 1875, the Public Health Act, is worked in districts by 'local sanitary authorities' who are much controlled by the Local Government Board.

---

[1] 34 and 35 Vict., c. 70.

7. The Education Department is also in form a committee of the Privy Council: a 'Committee of the Council for Education.' More recently it has received the title of 'Education Department.' It consists of the Lord President of the Council and the Vice-President of the Committee, and certain *ex officio* members, e.g. the Chancellor of the Exchequer. The powers of the committee are practically exercised by the Lord President (for whom duties have thus been found) and the Vice-President[1]. The great system of Public Elementary Education introduced in 1870 is placed under control of this department, which thus has very large statutory powers, both of giving particular orders and of laying down general rules.

8. In 1889 (52 and 53 Vic., c. 30) a Board of Agriculture was created[2], consisting of a President of the Board, the Lord President of the Council, the Secretaries of State, the First Lord of the Treasury, the Chancellor of the Exchequer, the Chancellor of the Duchy. Here also the powers are really wielded by the President.

9. Of the other high officials of state the Postmaster-General possesses many statutory powers and sometimes sits in the cabinet, the Lord Privy Seal has merely formal duties, while the Chancellor of the Duchy has now little work, for though the old Palatine Court is kept up, the judicial work is done by a Vice-Chancellor who is a judge.

10. Lastly (though he is highest in rank) the Lord Chancellor, of whom more hereafter, is always a member of the cabinet. It is curious that one who is the highest of judges is a member of the cabinet, a politician actively engaged in party warfare, who 'goes in and out with the ministry.' It is curious: it is a reminder that in the past judicial and governmental functions have been much blended.

An an illustration of the actual working of our government system we cannot do better than take the Municipal Corporations Act, 1882 (45 and 46 Vic., c. 50), our best specimen of a code; we find powers given to the Queen in Council, to a

[1] The Committee of Council for Education was superseded by a Board in 1899. 62 and 63 Vict., c. 33.

[2] Since 1903 the Board of Agriculture and Fisheries.

Secretary (Home) of State, to the Treasury, to the Local Government Board.

Sec. 23. A Town Council may make bye-laws, not to come into force for forty days: a copy to be sent to the Secretary; if within that time it is disallowed by the queen with the advice of her Privy Council it is not to come into force.

Sec. 28. Accounts to be sent to the Local Government Board, which is to lay an abstract before Parliament.

Sec. 30. If two-thirds of a Town Council agree to petition for the division of the borough into wards, it shall be lawful for H.M. by Order in Council to fix the number of wards. Thereupon the Secretary shall appoint commissioners to determine the boundaries; the scheme of boundaries to be sent to the Secretary, who is to submit it to H.M. in Council for approval.

Sec. 62. Day for electing auditors of borough accounts is 1 March or such other day as the Town Council with the approval of the Local Government Board shall appoint.

Sec. 105. We come to the borrowing powers of the Town Council: here the 'approval of the Treasury' is necessary; so for leases and sales of corporate land.

Sec. 154. Administration of justice. It shall be lawful for the queen from time to time to assign to any persons H.M. commission to act as justices of peace [this implies the action of the Lord Chancellor].

Sec. 161. If a stipendiary magistrate be wanted, the Town Council may petition the Secretary to make an appointment, and thereupon it shall be lawful for the queen to appoint a barrister of seven years' standing.

Sec. 162. If the borough wants a separate Court of Quarter Sessions, the queen on petition to H.M. in Council may grant the court.

Sec. 164. The Table of fees of the Clerk of the Peace is to be submitted to the Secretary of State for confirmation.

Sec. 210. Grant of new charters. On petition of the inhabitants the queen by the advice of her Privy Council may grant a charter, but the petition must first be referred to a committee of the Lords of H.M. Privy Council, so that objections may be heard.

etc.　　　　　　　　etc.

My object in saying so much of the statutory powers by means of which our government is now-a-days conducted, is to convince you that the traditional lawyer's view of the constitution has become very untrue to fact and to law. By the traditional lawyer's view I mean that which was expressed by Blackstone in the middle of the eighteenth century, and which still maintains a certain orthodoxy. According to that view, while the legislative power is vested in king and parliament, what is called the executive power is vested in the king alone, and consists of the royal prerogative. Now most people know that this is not altogether true to fact—they know that the powers attributed to the king are really exercised by the king's ministers, and that the king is expected to have ministers who command the confidence of the House of Commons. Still I think that they would say that this was a matter not of law, but of convention, or of constitutional morality—that *legally* the executive power is in the king, though constitutionally it must be exercised by ministers. But the point that I wish to make is that this old doctrine is not even true to law. To a very large extent indeed England is now ruled by means of statutory powers which are not in any sense, not even as strict matters of law, the powers of the king. Let us take an instance or two. Look at the police force, that most powerful engine of government. That force was gradually created by means of a series of statutes ranging from 1829 to 1856. To some extent it was placed under the control of local authorities, of the justices of the peace in the counties, of watch committees in the boroughs: but a power of issuing rules for the government was given—to whom? not to the queen, but to one of H.M. principal Secretaries of State, which means in practice the Home Secretary. It is not for the queen to make such regulations: it is for the Secretary. So as to the administration of the poor law. In 1834, when the law was remodelled, a central authority was created with a large power of issuing rules, orders and regulations as to the relief of the poor. This power was given, not to the king, but to certain poor law commissioners, and it has since been transferred to the Local Government Board. Look again at the powers of regulating the mercantile marine created by the great Merchant Shipping Act of 1854 or the powers relating to public elementary education given by the act of 1870. These are not given to the queen—they are given in the one case to the Board of Trade, in the other case to the Education Department[1].

How vast a change has taken place since Blackstone's day we may see from a very interesting passage in his book, Book 1, chap. IX.[2] He has a chapter on the Subordinate Magistrates. In this he speaks of sheriffs, coroners, justices of the peace, constables, surveyors of highways, and overseers of the poor. He prefaces it with these words, 'In a former chapter of these commentaries we distinguished magistrates into two kinds: supreme, or those in whom the sovereign power of the state resides; and subordinate, or those who act in an inferior secondary sphere. We have hitherto considered the former kind only, namely the supreme legislative power or parliament, and the supreme executive power, which is in the king; and are now to proceed to inquire into the rights and duties of the principal subordinate magistrates. And herein we are not to investigate the powers and duties of his majesty's great officers of state, the lord treasurer, lord chamberlain, the principal secretaries or the like; because I do not know that they are in that capacity in any considerable degree the objects of our laws or have any very important share of magistracy conferred upon them: except that the secretaries of state are allowed the power of commitment in order to bring offenders to trial.' Now that is a very memorable sentence, and on the whole (though perhaps it is a little exaggerated) I think that it was true in Blackstone's day. The lord treasurer, the secretaries of state, were of course very important persons—perhaps quite as important then as now—but the law knew them not, or merely knew them as persons who advised the king in the use of his prerogatives. The law gave powers to sheriffs and coroners, to surveyors of highways and overseers of the poor; it gave few powers to

[1] The Merchant Shipping Act of 1854 is now superseded by the Merchant Shipping Act of 1894.

[2] Sir William Blackstone's *Commentaries on the Laws of England* were published in 1768—9.

the high officers of state, to the men who for good and evil had really the destinies of England in their hands : the powers that they in fact exercised were in law the king's powers. But I know no proof of the power of Blackstone's genius so striking as the fact that the sentence that I have just quoted should be repeated now-a-days in books which profess to set forth the modern law of England. Does not our law know these high officers of state ? Open the statute book, on almost every page of it you will find 'it shall be lawful for the Treasury to do this,' 'it shall be lawful for one of the Secretaries of State to do that.'

This is the result of a modern movement, a movement which began, we may say, about the time of the Reform Bill of 1832. The new wants of a new age have been met in a new manner—by giving statutory powers of all kinds, sometimes to the Queen in Council, sometimes to the Treasury, sometimes to a Secretary of State, sometimes to this Board, sometimes to the other. But of this vast change our institutional writers have hardly yet taken any account. They go on writing as though England were governed by the royal prerogatives, as if ministers had nothing else to do than to advise the king as to how his prerogatives should be exercised.

In my view, which I put forward with some diffidence and with a full warning that it is not orthodox, we can no longer say that the executive power is vested in the king : the king has powers, this minister has powers, and that minister has powers. The requisite harmony is secured by the extra-legal organization of cabinet and ministry. The powers legally given to the king are certainly the most important, but I cannot consent to call them supreme. To be able to declare war and peace is certainly an important power, perhaps the most important power that the law can give, and this belongs to the king. But the power to make rules for the government of the police force is also an important power, and this our law gives to a secretary of state. The one power may be vastly more important than the other, but it is in no sense supreme over the other. The supremacy of the king's powers, if it is to be found anywhere, must be found in the fact that the ministers legally hold their offices during his good pleasure.

There is one term against which I wish to warn you, and that term is 'the crown.' You will certainly read that the crown does this and the crown does that. As a matter of fact we know that the crown does nothing but lie in the Tower of London to be gazed at by sight-seers. No, the crown is a convenient cover for ignorance : it saves us from asking difficult questions, questions which can only be answered by study of the statute book. I do not deny that it is a convenient term, and you may have to use it ; but I do say that you should never be content with it. If you are told that the crown has this power or that power, do not be content until you know who legally has the power—is it the king, is it one of his secretaries : is this power a prerogative power or is it the outcome of statute ? This question is often an extremely difficult question, and one of the difficulties by which it is beset is worthy of explanation.

We find that there is often great uncertainty as to the exact limits of the royal prerogative. Since the settlement of 1688 very little has been done towards depriving the king by any direct words of any of his legal powers. Those powers were great, and they were somewhat indefinite. Very seldom has any statute expressly taken them away, very seldom has any statute said in so many words 'it shall not be lawful for the king to do this.' But without directly destroying these prerogative powers statutes have created a large number of powers dealing with the same matters, some given to the king, some to one or to another of his great officers. Such modern powers have been definite and adapted to the wants of modern times, and they have been freely used. On the other hand the old prerogative powers have become clumsy and anti-quated, and have fallen into disuse : the very uncertainty as to their limits has made them impracticable. Still they have not been expressly abolished, and to the legal student the question must often occur whether they are or are not in existence. Remember this, that we have no such doctrine as that a prerogative may cease to exist because it is not used. On the other hand we shall often find that it would be extremely difficult to use these prerogative powers without doing something definitely unlawful.   Let me give a few examples.

What an outcry there would be if the queen were to attempt to debase the coinage.   Probably such an attempt would cost her her throne.   Nevertheless Sir M. Hale was of opinion that the king had power to debase the coinage, and with the decided cases before us it is difficult to say that he was in the wrong.   Even Blackstone was not certain that this power did not exist[1].   Well, so far as I am aware, that power has never been expressly taken away by statute.   We may say pretty confidently that the power does not exist, but why?   Not because it has been expressly taken away, not because it has fallen into desuetude, but because for a very long time past statutes have fixed the amount of gold and silver in the coins : thus by statute a sovereign is to weigh $123\cdot27447$ grains, and is to be eleven-twelfths gold and one-twelfth alloy.   So long as such statutes exist the prerogative power of regulating the coinage cannot be used, but it is not until we have gone through those statutes and seen how they deal with the whole matter that we are entitled to say that the prerogative is superseded.

Take a more difficult case.   Can the king erect new courts of justice?   Most indubitably this power was exercised in the Middle Ages.   Nothing was commoner than for the king by his charter to grant to some town or some lord of a manor the right to hold a court.   Even when in the seventeenth century the Courts of Star Chamber, of the Council of Wales, of the Council of the North, had become hateful burdens, no one seems to have questioned the king's power of erecting new courts of common law.   A distinction was drawn between courts of common law and other courts : he might not create a new court of equity.   Has the queen then now-a-days a power to create new courts?   It has never been expressly taken away, and I believe we must say that it exists.   I take this from a recent judgment, 'It is a settled constitutional principle or rule of law, that although the crown may, by its

[1] See above, p. 260.

prerogative, establish courts to proceed according to the common law, yet it cannot create any new court to administer any other law; and it is laid down by Lord Coke in the Fourth Institute that the erection of a new court with a new jurisdiction cannot be without an act of parliament' (*In re* Bp. of Natal, 3 Moore, P.C. (N.S.) 152). As a matter of fact this prerogative power of erecting new courts has not been used in England for a very long time past. In recent years the whole country has been covered by a network of new local courts—the (so-called) new county courts. But this was not done under an exercise of the prerogative, but by virtue of powers given to the Queen in Council by a statute of 1846 (9 and 10 Vic., c. 95) which regulated the jurisdiction of these new courts. There are two reasons why this prerogative has fallen into disuse. (1) Owing to modern changes in the law a court which could administer nothing but common law would be a somewhat useless and very clumsy affair. (2) Owing to the appropriation of supplies the queen would have no money with which to pay the judges of new courts unless she took it from her privy purse. Still we cannot say that the prerogative is gone; at any moment it might become important. In the first part of the eighteenth century courts were established in India by virtue of the royal prerogative, and as regards the colonies I am not sure that the power has not been exercised for them in much more recent times. In 1827 the law officers advised the king that the extent of his power to create a new court in Canada was very doubtful, and that it would be wiser to obtain an act of parliament.

Often enough this difficulty must occur to anyone who is studying our constitutional law. He will be told that a prerogative power exists; then he will find a modern statute taking no notice of that prerogative, but enabling the king, or some one of the high officers, to exercise a more limited power. Then the question will occur to him—how far does this modern statutory power take away the old prerogative power? You will understand the difficulty better from an example. The great Municipal Reform Act of 1835 (now represented by the **Municipal** Corporations Act, 1882, 45 and 46 Vic., c. 50) empowered the king to create in any borough a separate Court of Quarter Sessions for that borough. It laid down rules as to the exercise of that power, for instance, the court was to be held by a recorder, who was to be a barrister of five years' standing, and to hold office during good behaviour. No notice was taken of the prerogative power of erecting new courts. Now suppose that the queen creates a Court of Quarter Sessions which does not exactly comply with the language of the statute—has she power to do this? Not by statute; but how about the prerogative power? We have to consider, and it may be a very delicate question, how far the act has *tacitly* curtailed the royal prerogative. In practice such questions may seldom arise—the queen's advisers are careful to keep within the limits of the statutory powers—but for the student, for the lecturer, the difficulty is very great. He will hardly dare to say that in no conceivable case could the old prerogative power be used and used lawfully. This comes of our great civility to the king; we have seldom said to him 'you may not do this,' we have said, 'you may do *that*,' and then left to ourselves or our judges the problem of deciding how far the 'may' necessarily implies a 'may not.'

One more illustration of a simpler kind. We find it laid down that if the king, under his great or his privy seal, prohibits a man from leaving the realm, or enjoins him to come back from foreign parts, and this command is disobeyed, the disobedience may be punished by fine and imprisonment. I believe that we must say that this is the law, though for a long time past it has not been used, and though any use of it except in very extraordinary circumstances would surprise the nation and create a great outcry. Thus our course is set about with difficulties, with prerogatives disused, with prerogatives of doubtful existence, with prerogatives which exist by sufferance, merely because no one has thought it worth while to abolish them.

C. *Classification of the Powers of the Crown.*

Still we must do our best, and I will venture to suggest the following classification of the powers of 'the crown' (by which phrase I understand the powers of the king and the powers of the high officers of state):

1. Powers relating to the constitution, assembling and dissolving of parliaments, and of assenting to statutes.

2. Powers relating to foreign affairs, to peace and war, etc.

3. Powers of appointing and dismissing officers, civil and military, executive and judicial.

4. Powers relating to the collection and expenditure of the revenue.

5. Powers relating to military and naval forces.

6. Powers connected with the administration of justice.

7. Powers connected with maintenance of order.

8. Powers connected with social and economic affairs, such as public health, education, trade, etc.

9. Powers connected with religion and the National Church.

I will now say a few words as to the powers of the first three of these classes; the others we will treat if time serves when we try to view as a whole the Fiscal System, the Military System, the Administration of Justice, the Police, Social and Economic Government, and the National Church.

1. As we have already seen, the king's power of summoning, proroguing, dissolving parliament, is very large. I will not go over this ground again. Briefly the law comes to this, that a parliament cannot be kept in existence beyond seven years. At the end of that period it would be dissolved without the king's action; on the other hand the law requires that a parliament shall sit once in every three years, but does not provide any machinery whereby a parliament can come into being without royal summons, should the king disobey this rule.

Then, without the king's assent, no bill can become law. A statute is enacted by the king, by and with the advice and consent of the lords, spiritual and temporal, in parliament assembled, and by the authority of the same. It is only since 1445 that these last words, 'by the authority of the same,' become a regular part of the legislative formula. Go back half a century further, and acts are passed by the advice of the lords at the petition of the commons. But to this day the form makes the statute the act of the king. To speak of his power as a veto is hardly correct; the bill will not become law if he merely abstains from interfering, it will not become law unless he expressly assents. The last occasion on which that assent was withheld, was in 1707, when Anne withheld it from the Scotch Militia Bill. William III had withheld it on several important occasions. It seems to me that circumstances might be conceived in which the king's ministers might advise him to refuse consent, and yet escape general condemnation, as on the sudden outbreak of a war or some similar unforeseen emergency.

Really, however, in a working sketch of the constitution it is more important to notice that the king has a considerable power in constituting one of the two Houses. If the bishops are not royal nominees, this is merely because a bare form of election by the cathedral chapters is kept up. The king again can create as many temporal peers as he pleases, but the hereditary principle makes any recourse to this power for the purpose of packing the House an objectionable measure. A threat, however, of using it, has on more than one occasion proved effectual, and without doing anything that is thought at all strange, a modern cabinet can use this prerogative to reward or shelve its followers, and to divide the members of the ministry between the two Houses.

2. Next, I should place the prerogative of making war and peace. This power, of the utmost importance, belongs to the king. Without the consent of parliament he can direct the invasion of a foreign country. Of course, parliament has a certain check on this power. It might refuse to vote the necessary supplies. What is more to the purpose, it insists on knowing from the king's ministers what are the relations between the king and foreign governments, on having diplomatic correspondence laid before it, and so forth. Still it takes no act of parliament to make a war, even a war of aggression,

and practically a ministry has a great deal of power as regards foreign affairs, and might even force a reluctant nation into a war from which it would be impossible to withdraw. This is really a great matter.

Stephen (following Blackstone) says that to make a war completely effectual it is necessary that it be publicly declared, and duly proclaimed by the sovereign's authority[1]. I believe that to be misleading, and that neither English law, nor what is called International Law, requires any formal declaration of war[2]. I believe that an English court would hold that there was war so soon as the queen had authorized acts of hostility.

Close to this power of making war and peace, Blackstone speaks of the power of making treaties, and says what seems to me very untrue. 'It is also the sovereign's prerogative to make treaties, leagues and alliances with foreign states and princes. For it is by the law of nations essential to the goodness of a league, that it be made by the sovereign power; and then it is binding upon the whole community; and in England the sovereign power, *quoad hoc*, is vested in the king. Whatever contracts therefore he engages in, no other power in the kingdom can legally delay, resist or annul[3].'

Now in contradiction to this we may, I believe, say that a treaty made by the king has in general no legal effect whatever[4]. The king, as just said, can make peace and can make war, and the making of either will of course have important effects: whether an act be a laudable attack on a public enemy, or mere piracy, is one of the many questions that might thus be decided. Also it seems certain that as an incident to a treaty of peace, the king may cede territory, may at all events cede territory acquired by him during the

---

[1] H. J. Stephen, *New Commentaries on the Laws of England*, 14th edn. vol. II, p. 495 allows that 'the modern practice is by no means uniform.'

[2] A Convention was signed at the Hague Conference in 1907 according to which 'the Contracting Powers recognise that hostilities between themselves must not commence without previous or explicit warning in the form either of a reasoned declaration or of an ultimatum with conditional declaration of war.' *Parl. Papers, Miscellaneous*, No. 1, 1908.

[3] *Commentaries* I, c. 7 § 11.

[4] This view was upheld by the Privy Council in Walker v. Baird, LR. AC. 1892, p. 491.

war[1]. Exactly how far this power extends is a somewhat debateable matter, and I think it very doubtful whether the queen can cede land subject to the British parliament, except in a treaty of peace; could she sell Jersey, Guernsey, or Kent to France? I much doubt it. When in 1782 it became necessary to recognize the independence of the American Colonies, an act of parliament was passed authorizing the king to make peace and to repeal all statutes relating to those Colonies[2]. But as to the more general principle put forward by Blackstone and Stephen, its unsoundness can be easily proved by reference to the law about extradition. The common law of England, at least for a long time past, has been that though the king bound himself to surrender criminals, still the treaty could not be carried out, save by virtue of an act of parliament. Suppose that under such a treaty a person was arrested and brought before one of the courts by habeas corpus; the treaty would have been treated as waste-paper—the king has no power to send men out of the country, and cannot give himself power by making a treaty. This has been law at least all through the nineteenth century. It is fair to Blackstone to say that the point was not so clear in his own day. The Court of Exchequer seems to have thought that the king might hand over fugitives. However, there is no doubt about the matter now. Our earliest extradition treaties were individually sanctioned by parliament. The general act, 1870 (33 and 34 Vic., c. 52), now in force, enables the queen, by Order in Council, to apply that act in the case of any foreign state with which she has made an arrangement for reciprocal extradition. This is a good instance of a power given to the queen by act of parliament, one of those royal powers which we do not usually call prerogatives. I take extradition as one example, but the general principle is quite unsound. Suppose the queen contracts with France that English iron or coal shall not be exported to France—until a statute has been passed forbidding exportation, one may export and laugh at the treaty. Still,

---

[1] For recent cases and debates bearing on the cession of territory, see Ilbert, *Government of India*, 2nd edn. p. 207.

[2] 22 Geo. III, c. 46: see Forsyth, *Cases and Opinions in Constitutional Law*, pp. 182—4, on the general question of the power to cede territory. F. W. M.

though this is so, we must remark that the king has here a very substantial power, though it does not operate directly on the law. It would obviously be a serious step, were parliament to refuse to pass the laws necessary for carrying out a treaty already concluded. The honour of the nation might be already pledged. The interrogation of ministers in parliament, perhaps, is a sufficient guard against this danger.

In this context the power to send and receive ambassadors deserves notice. It has some important legal effects. An ambassador accredited to the queen occupies a very privileged place. To a large extent he, his family, his suite and his servants, are placed outside the ordinary civil and criminal law of the country, it being unlawful and criminal to arrest them, or to exercise any compulsory process against them. In this matter the English courts receive what they consider to be the best doctrines of International Law. But the arrest of an ambassador, or of any servant of his, publicly registered as such, is punishable under a statute of 1708 (7 Anne, c. 12). That statute was passed in consequence of the ambassador of Peter the Great having been arrested for debt, and it denounces a very severe punishment against those who are guilty of like acts in the future. The exact limits of the privilege are not in all respects well defined, and are, I think, best discussed as a topic of International Law.

A brief note on the treatment by our law of aliens may not be out of place. By the common law, and down to 1870, an alien could not hold real property in England. The common law allowed him to hire a house for his own habitation, and an act of 1844 (7 and 8 Vic., c. 66), allowed him in certain circumstances to take a lease for 21 years at the longest. He was incapable of inheriting land, and if he purchased land the king became entitled to it—might turn him out, and take the land to himself. On the other hand the alien could hold movable goods, could deal with them freely, and bring actions for debts or for wrongs done to his person or his goods. In 1870 the law was changed by the Naturalization Act (33 and 34 Vic., c. 14), which declared that real and personal property of every kind in the United Kingdom might be acquired, held, and disposed of by an alien, as though he were a British subject; but he was not qualified to be the owner of a British ship, and the act did not qualify him for any office, or for any parliamentary, municipal, or other franchise. I believe that, as regards all that we can call private law, property, tort, contract and so forth, we have no need now-a-days to distinguish between subject and alien, save in that one matter of the ownership of British ships. On the other hand I think we may say that as a general rule our common law, still in force, excludes aliens from political offices and political rights, and the act of 1700 settling the succession to the crown expressly declares that no alien can be a member of the Privy Council, or of either House of Parliament. But an alien can gain even political rights by ceasing to be an alien : by becoming naturalized.

An act of parliament might of course turn an alien into a subject, and until lately acts having the object of naturalizing this or that foreigner were not uncommon. A statute, however, was necessary ; it seems to have been established at an early time, certainly before Coke, that the king without parliament could not turn an alien into a subject for all purposes. He might for some, but not for all. This doctrine gave rise to the class of persons known as denizens—intermediate between subjects and aliens. The denizen was so made by the king's letters patent, i.e. by an act done by the king without parliament. The limit to the royal power (as I understand it) was this : the person whom the king made a denizen of his realm became capable of acquiring lands by purchase or devise, and of holding them when acquired, and in general he became a subject of the realm, but the king could not make him capable of inheriting. An act of parliament might of course do even this, and Naturalization Acts (I believe) usually did it, but the king could not do it. This is worthy of notice as a good illustration of a matter of which I have already spoken. Neither now nor at any time past can we say with any exactness that the function of the English parliament is purely legislative, that of the English king purely executive. Parliament habitually passed acts naturalizing this person and that by name ; if we call these acts legislative, how are we to refuse the same term to letters patent, which do almost exactly the same thing? The line between making A. B. a denizen and naturalizing him is not the line between executive and legislative functions. The act of 1870, amending the previous act of 1844, has provided a mode whereby persons may be naturalized without special act of parliament, but has expressly preserved the queen's power of granting letters of denization. I should imagine that such power is seldom if ever used, for it is easy to become naturalized. British nationality can now be granted by a Secretary of State. The applicant must have resided in the United Kingdom for five years, or have been in the service of the crown for five years, and must intend when naturalized to reside in the United Kingdom, or to serve under the crown. The Secretary has an absolute discretion in giving or withholding the desired certificate, and need assign no reason for refusal. The oath of allegiance must be taken. If the certificate be granted, then the naturalized alien shall, within the United Kingdom, have all political and other rights and privileges to which a British subject is entitled[1].

3. I think it well to notice separately that almost all those who have any governmental or judicial powers of any high order are appointed by the queen; if their powers are of a judicial kind, they generally hold office during good behaviour; if their powers are not judicial, they generally hold office merely during the queen's good pleasure and no reason need be assigned for dismissing them. I think it well to notice this separately, for it is these powers of appointment and dismissal which give to our scheme of government the requisite unity. The privy councillors hold their places during good pleasure, so do those high officers of state who form the ministry. It is not usual to remove a privy councillor, and as regards the choice of ministers, the king is practically obliged to suit himself to the will of the House of Commons. But the legal power is absolute; and it is just because the legal power is absolute that our system of party government is possible.

I mention this power of appointing and dismissing the

[1] A criticism of the Act may be found in the Report of an Inter-departmental Committee on the Naturalization Laws, 1901.

high officers of state by itself because it is so very important, but of course the king has a very general power of appointing not only those whom we speak of as collectively forming the ministry, but all or almost all of those who hold public offices of first-rate importance. Blackstone calls him the fountain of honour, of office and of privilege. As regards mere honours, it were needless to say much; the making of knights and baronets, the invention of new orders of knighthood, the conferring of ceremonial precedence, is no very great matter; and as to the power of making peers, which is of considerable importance, we have already spoken. But look at the whole legal structure of society, and we shall generally find that the holders of important public offices are appointed by the king and very commonly hold their posts merely during his pleasure. I do not think it possible to lay down any sweeping principle about this matter: the terms and mode of appointment vary very greatly. Thus almost all persons who have any judicial duties to perform are appointed by the king, but that is not universally true; the county court judges are appointed by the Lord Chancellor under statutory power. Again, we may say that since 1700, it has been the general policy of the legislature to secure the independence of the judges by making their tenure of office tenure during good behaviour. The judges of the superior courts hold during good behaviour, but can be dismissed on an address presented by both Houses of Parliament. The tenure of the county court judges is rather different: they can be removed by the Lord Chancellor for inability or misbehaviour. On the other hand the justices of the peace, whose duties may perhaps be said to be in part judicial, in part executive, hold only during good pleasure and can be dismissed without the assignment of any cause. It is, on the other hand, the general policy of our modern law that executive officers shall hold only during good pleasure, shall be dismissible without the assignment of any cause. But we must look to the statute book about each office, and not rely very confidently on any general principle. For instance, take the Comptroller and Auditor-General: we do not call him a judge; still it has been thought of exceeding importance that he should be a very independent person, and looking to the act under which he is appointed (1866, 29 and 30 Vic., c. 39), we find that he holds during good behaviour subject to removal on an address presented by both Houses of Parliament. We must remember too that we cannot state this general policy as a rule of common law; formerly the king had a very large power of granting offices on what terms he pleased; down to William III's reign, we find the judges appointed *durante beneplacito*; on the other hand a large number of executive offices, as we should call them, places in the Exchequer and so forth, were held for life or for several lives. To take one more instance: a county police force is under the command of a chief constable. Now *a priori* we cannot tell whether or no this officer is appointed by the king; were we to guess that he is, we should guess wrongly, for he is appointed by the justices in quarter session. The extent to which what I may call the subordinate government of the country is under the control of the king, the central government, the extent to which it is ordered by local authorities, the quarter sessions, the municipal counties, the constitution of these local authorities—these are matters regulated in various ways by countless acts, which can only be studied in detail. A great vague phrase such as 'The executive power is in the king and is exercised by the ministry' gives us no help whatever.

D. *The Fiscal System.*

We turn to say a little of our fiscal system—of the collection and expenditure of the royal or the national revenue. The first point that we have to seize in dealing with this subject historically is that in old times the national revenue was very really the king's revenue, or, to put it another way, there was no national revenue; whatever money came to the king's hand was his to deal with as he pleased, whether it consisted of the rents of his demesne lands, or the profits of the feudal tenures, or the outcome of the aids or subsidies granted to him by the great council of the nation. The crown lands were the king's lands; what is more, the king's lands were the crown lands—a distinction between the king's private capacity and his public capacity was not yet observed. Before the Norman Conquest there was indeed land which was conceived of as belonging to the people, the folk-land; and the king himself could make no part of it his own without the consent of the wise[1]. But at the Conquest this simply becomes *terra Regis*, and very probably the Conquest did but hasten the end of a process that had already gone far. In later days we find the practical denial of any distinction between the property which the king has, as king, and the property that he has, as man, carried to its logical extreme. 'If,' says Coke, 'the king purchaseth lands of the custom of gavelkind and die leaving divers sons, the eldest son shall only inherit these lands[2].' So on the death of Edward VI all his fee simple lands, however acquired, descended to the Lady Mary, to the exclusion of her half-sister the Lady Elizabeth. All the lands of the king, by whatever title acquired, were his to grant away as he pleased; on the other hand, he could not devise them by his will. The notion that the king was in any sense a trustee for the nation of these lands grew up but very slowly; rather the notion was that the king had a large property of his own, and that he ought not therefore to come begging of his subjects except on special occasions. No distinction was taken between land which the king had bought with money out of his own pocket and land which came to him by way (for example) of escheat. Nor was this singular; other persons besides the king got lands by way of escheat. Complaints against the king's lavish grants to his favourites are from time to time loud, but they do not issue in prospective legislation; they issue in acts of resumption—acts enabling or obliging the king to resume the lands granted away by himself or his predecessors. Thus in 1450 a general act of resumption was passed, by which all grants made since the accession of Henry VI in 1422 were annulled. A similar act was passed in 1473 under Edward IV. In 1485, immediately after the Battle of Bosworth, the grants made by the kings of the House of York were annulled. This was, I believe, the last precedent[3] for an act of resumption

---

[1] See above, p. 57.   [2] *Co. Lit.* 15 *b*.
[3] Some lands granted to abbeys in the reign of Queen Mary were resumed by 1 Eliz. c. 24.

when in 1700 William III was compelled to assent to an act
annulling all his grants of Irish land. The passing of this
act is described at the very end of Macaulay's history ; it is
perhaps the most noteworthy example of the practice known
as ' tacking a money-bill '—the assent of the House of Lords
to a measure which may well seem to us extremely unjust
was extorted by the addition to the bill of clauses granting
the land tax ; the lords, it was contended, could not amend
this money-bill, while to reject it would have been to deprive
the crown of the means of carrying on government. It was,
I believe, this incident which led to the first prospective restraint on the king's power of granting away his lands. On
the accession of Anne an act was passed (1 Anne, c. 1) which
restricted the queen's power of alienation to the granting of
leases, which in general were not to be for more than 31 years
or three lives, and were to reserve the ancient rent or a reasonable rent. Now even this act drew no distinction between
lands belonging to the queen in her public, and those belonging
to her in her private capacity. It placed the same restriction
on the alienation of any of her lands. It is just another
century before the distinction, to which I have referred, finds
expression in the statute book. This was done in 1800
by 39 and 40 Geo. III, c. 88. By a process which I shall
describe hereafter, a distinction had by this time been made
between that part of the royal revenue that was devoted to
the support of the king's household and of the honour and
dignity of the crown of Great Britain and the great bulk
of the revenue which was to be used for what we may loosely
call national purposes, and since the accession of George III
the revenue of the crown lands had come under the latter
head. It was at least a serious question whether lands which
King George had bought out of what may be styled his own
pocket-money were not subject to that restraint on alienation
that was imposed in 1701. So in 1800 parliament enabled
the king to hold land in a private capacity. Land purchased
by him out of money devoted to his privy purse was to be
held by him with all that liberty of alienation that a subject
has ; he was, for example, to have power to devise them by
his will. However a good many other statutes have been

required to make this matter clear, and I think that it is not until 1862 that we find in the statute book such a phrase as 'the private estates of Her Majesty.' I am not very sure that one part of the old law does not yet prevail. The king, it used to be said, could have no heir but the heir to the crown. I have given you Coke's illustrations of this and I cannot find that the rule has been altered; so that if the queen died intestate and if according to the usual canons of inheritance, three daughters would be her co-heiresses; the eldest would inherit not only the crown of Great Britain but also Osborne House or whatever private estates in fee simple the queen had at her death. But I will not say this confidently, for there are many long acts of parliament.

I mention these things in order to show how slow and how recent has been the growth in our law of that distinction between the national revenue and the king's private pocket-money which we naturally suppose to exist. It has taken many statutes to get this matter clear. It becomes clear gradually as parliament takes upon itself to appropriate the supplies that it grants, to say that they are only to be used for certain definite purposes. Of the early history of this appropriation of supplies we have already said something. In 1665 Charles II asked a very large sum of money for the Dutch war, and consented that a clause should be inserted in the act declaring that the money raised under that act should be applicable only to the purposes of the war. This was an important concession, and similar appropriations were afterwards made during his reign. Since the Revolution the practice has, I believe, never varied; in granting money to the crown, parliament has appropriated the supply to particular purposes more or less narrowly defined.

At this point it becomes necessary to remember that the king had a very considerable revenue which was not granted to him by parliament. This is what Blackstone speaks of as the king's ordinary revenue as contrasted with that extra-ordinary revenue which arises from taxation[1]. He classifies it thus: first there are revenues of an ecclesiastical kind, the

---

[1] *Commentaries*, vol. I, c. 8.

custody of the temporalities of bishops, the first-fruits and tenths, and some minor matters. Next come the rents of the demesne lands, the profits of tenure, wardships and marriages (abolished at the Restoration), also the prerogatives of purveyance and preemption (abolished at the same time), the profits of the royal forests; the profits of the king's ordinary courts of justice, fines, forfeitures, amercements; royal fish; wreck of the sea; royal mines; treasure trove; waifs, estrays, deodands, escheats, idiots. Many of these sources of income must always have been trifling, others became trifling in course of time, but still in the seventeenth century the king had a considerable revenue which was all his own; he required no grant from parliament to help him to this, and to dictate to him how he should spend this would have been a strong measure; in such case he might plausibly have complained that he was treated more harshly than the meanest of his subjects, who would be suffered to spend his own income in his own way. The crown lands were still of considerable value and much profit could be made of the feudal rights, also of purveyance and preemption.

Now at the Restoration the most profitable sources of this hereditary revenue were abolished. You will have been accustomed to consider the abolition of the military tenures as an incident in the history of the law of real property. It is far more than this: it is a great event in the history of the royal and national revenue. It was necessary to compensate the king for the loss of income that he was to sustain; 'and now,' says the act, 'to the intent and purpose that his Majesty his heirs and successors may receive a full and ample recompence and satisfaction' for the abolished rights, 'be it enacted that there shall be paid to the king's Majesty his heirs and successors for ever hereafter in recompense as aforesaid' the rates and duties following. The act then imposes certain excise duties on beer, cider, spirits and so forth. Now this is the hereditary excise, given to the king, his heirs and successors for ever as a valuable consideration for abolition of the military tenures. This then gave to the king a source of ordinary and hereditary revenue consisting of a tax. Also it imposed a perpetual tax, and this was a new thing. The indirect taxes, the customs, tonnage and poundage had indeed been granted to the king for life from the time of Henry VII to that of James I, but only for life; and, as you will remember, parliament had refused to grant them to Charles I for more than a year. The direct taxes, the subsidies, tenths and fifteenths were granted for the occasion only.

But it is not of the manner of taxation that I would at this moment speak, but rather of the gradual separation of what, using unlawyerly terms, we may call the king's private pocket-money from the national revenue. When William III came to the throne he had the hereditary excise, also he had what remained of the old hereditary revenue. Parliament granted to him and Mary a further excise for their joint lives and the life of the survivor. This revenue was the king's and unappropriated. In 1698 a step was made. I think we may say that for the first time the notion of a civil list appears on the statute book. It is intended, says the act, that the sum of £700,000 a year shall be supplied to his majesty for the service of his household and family, and for other necessary expenses and occasions. A new tax, a tonnage and poundage, is granted to the king for his life, but it is provided that if the revenue arising from certain sources there mentioned, including the crown lands, many of the smaller prerogatives, the hereditary excise, the excise which William has for his life and the tax now granted him shall in any year exceed the £700,000, then no more than that sum is to be issued or applied to any use or purpose without the authority of parliament (9 and 10 Will. III, c. 23). A somewhat different arrangement was made in 1700, and on the accession of Anne we find again that certain sources of revenue are declared to be for the support of her majesty's household and the honour and dignity of the crown. These are in the main such as I have lately mentioned, the old prerogative rights, the crown lands, the hereditary excise, and certain excise and customs duties which are granted to Anne during her life. A similar arrangement was made on the accession of George I, but with this addition that besides the sources of revenue thus set apart for him, he was to have a further sum of £120,000 for the service of his household and family, and his necessary expenses and occasions. This sum was to come out of the produce of certain taxes which were to be massed together to form what was to be called 'the aggregate fund.' It was intended that the king should thus have at his command an income of £700,000. A very similar arrangement was made on the accession of George II, but parliament promised that the sum at his disposal should be £800,000 per annum. On the accession of George III another large step was made, for the king gave up for his life the greater part of the hereditary revenues of the crown including the crown lands, many of the minor prerogatives and the hereditary excise. In return a sum of £800,000 was to be paid to him yearly out of 'the aggregate fund.' In 1780, however, his majesty had to come to parliament for the payment of his debts. Parliament insisted on a more economical management of what had come to be called his civil list revenues, and forbad him to charge them with pensions beyond a limited amount. It divided the payments that were to be made out of such revenues into eight classes; and we can learn from the act in question that these were still of a miscellaneous nature: the second consists of the salaries of the judges, the third of the salaries of the ambassadors, the fourth of tradesmen's bills. George IV again on his accession gave up the same hereditary revenues that George III had given up. In return he was to have £850,000 out of what had now become the Consolidated Fund. This sum still included the salaries of judges, ambassadors, commissioners of the treasury; but there is now set apart, as what is to be the king's pocket-money in the narrowest sense, £60,000 per annum. William IV gave up what his brother had given up and he gave up somewhat more, namely the *droits* of the admiralty and the *droits* of the crown; in return he was given what seems much less, namely £510,000 per annum; but at this time the civil list was relieved of the salaries of judges and ambassadors. The queen again gave up what her uncle had given up, and was to receive £385,000 a year out of the Consolidated Fund. Besides this she was given a power of granting pensions to a certain limited amount—£1200 in each year.

I have been obliged to deal with these details in order to

explain what the law now is as to the hereditary revenues. If the queen were now to die the Prince of Wales would become entitled to these revenues, including the hereditary excise. This is curious, for the hereditary excise is not now collected. As an expedient for raising money, it has long since been superseded. But when William IV died, the queen immediately became entitled to it; the officers of the inland revenue proceeded to collect it, and had not the queen consented to give it up, it would be collected now under the act of Charles II which abolished the military tenures. As a matter of fact, a few months after her accession she gave her consent to the act settling a revenue upon her, and that act remitted all money which had become due for the hereditary excise. If the Prince of Wales now came to the throne this would happen over again: what he would be entitled to would be the hereditary revenue, including the excise—a tax which would have to be collected under the provisions of the act of 1660, 12 Car. II, c. 24. This may well seem rather absurd. It seems as if parliament had considered that a king could not, even with parliament's concurrence, deprive his successors of their hereditary rights, or that at all events it would not be fair to ask a king to do it[1].

Practically, then, we have come to have a king with a salary. The sum of £385,000 was to be paid yearly out of the Consolidated Fund for the purposes of the civil list, but the queen has had and still has a limited power of granting pensions payable out of the Consolidated Fund, and in consequence of the exercise of this power the civil list payments now amount to something more than £400,000 a year. Even this sum, however, is to a certain extent appropriated by the act passed on the queen's accession. Thus, for example, £131,260 is assigned for 'salaries of her majesty's household and retired allowances.' Only £60,000 is allotted to H.M.'s privy purse, and we may say that this is the only sum paid by the nation to the queen over which she has an absolutely unfettered power. I do not mean that this is all that the queen

---

[1] By the Civil List Act of 1901 (1 Ed. VII, c. 4) the hereditary revenues were again directed to be paid into the Exchequer and to form part of the Consolidated Fund.

receives—she holds, for instance, the Duchy of Lancaster, and has not surrendered the revenue arising from her ducal rights, and it may be that there are some minor prerogatives of the crown the revenue of which has not been surrendered : the revenue derived from the first-fruits and tenths of the clergy has long been given up (as you may read in Blackstone) to form Queen Anne's bounty for the augmentation of the maintenance of the poorer clergy. Still we have come to this, that the 'royal revenue,' using that phrase in its large sense, is now hard on £90,000,000 a year, out of which less than half a million is devoted to the queen's civil list, and £60,000 to the queen's privy purse. And yet to give the name royal revenue to the whole ninety millions is not foolish. All of it is granted by parliament to the queen, though appropriated to particular services ; none of it comes out of the Exchequer without a warrant under the queen's sign manual[1].

Let us now take a brief view of the legal aspect of the national finance at the present day. We have to consider how this large revenue of £90,000,000 is obtained, and how it is spent. First a few words about the Consolidated Fund and about the National Debt. Back in the Middle Ages we find our kings large borrowers ; they pledge, or profess to pledge, what they can; sometimes the proceeds of taxes not yet collected, sometimes the crown lands, sometimes the crown jewels ; in the days of Edward I and Edward II some of the taxes are farmed by Italian merchants. Practically in the end the nation has to pay; this is one of the king's expedients of practically forcing parliament to grant him money; his debts must be paid, or his credit among foreigners will be ruined. Under Henry VIII parliament does a scandalous thing: it declares that the king need not pay his debts. At all times it is difficult enough to get money from the king—one cannot sue him. A flagrant case occurs under Charles II. The London goldsmiths (the goldsmiths of those days were

---

[1] The revenue raised in 1905–6 was over 144 millions. By the Civil List Act of 1901 (1 Ed. VII, c. 4) the Civil List was fixed at £470,000 appropriated as follows: Privy Purse £110,000; Salaries of Household £125,800; Expenses of Household £193,000; Works £20,000; Royal Bounty, Alms and Special Services £13,200; Unappropriated £8000.

also the bankers) had lent Charles about £13,000, and he had pledged for the repayment of this sum part of his revenue. Suddenly the Exchequer was shut against them. It was not convenient to pay them their principal; they must be content with the interest. Perpetual annuities were granted to them and charged on the hereditary excise. The annuities were paid for four years and then further payment ceased. Even when William and Mary had come to the throne it was extremely doubtful whether these bankers had any remedy except by petition of right, and to that remedy they could not come except by the king's fiat. Thus it was evident enough that if money was to be borrowed for national purposes upon good security, that security must be something other than the king's word, or the king's letters patent. In 1692 there was pressing need for a large sum for the French war, and in that year it is usual to date the foundation of a national debt, a debt contracted upon the security of act of parliament. A million was to be borrowed. New duties were to be imposed for ninety-nine years upon beer and other liquors. These duties when collected were to be brought into the Exchequer to a separate account and were to form a fund for paying annuities to the creditors. Life annuities were to be granted; each subscriber of £100 was to have an annuity of £10 (which was to be reduced to £7 in 1700) for life. But there was an element of gambling in the transaction; as the annuitants died their annuities were to be divided among the survivors until only seven should be left; after that whatever fell in was to be for the use of the king. The act directed the officers of the Exchequer to pay the annuities out of the produce of the tax devoted to this purpose, gave an action for treble damages against any officer who disobeyed the act; so the creditor would lend no longer upon the security of the king's word, but upon the security of an act of parliament. You will observe that only a particular fund was pledged, not the revenue in general, only certain excise duties. You will observe also that the lenders were not to see their principal again: instead of this they took life annuities with a benefit of survivorship.

Now it is not for us to trace the growth of the national

debt; enough that it grew rapidly; at the accession of Anne it amounted to above 16 millions, at that of George I to above 54 millions, at the Peace of Paris in 1763 to above 138 millions. During the peace it fell to 128 millions, during the American War it grew to 249 millions; in 1817 after our long wars with France it was above 840 millions; it has since been reduced to a little below 698 millions[1]. But during the earlier part of the period, over which I have just ranged, it would be more correct to speak of the national debts than of the national debt. We have seen that in 1692 certain specific taxes, excise duties, were imposed, and their produce was charged with the payment of certain annuities. This device was repeated over and over again in a manner most perplexing to anyone who goes to the statute book for his information. Often the return given to the lender took the form of a perpetual annuity, payable to him, his executors, administrators, or assignees, but redeemable at any time[2]. In 1752 (25 Geo. II, cap. 27) two great masses of annuities charged upon various taxes were consolidated with the consent of the proprietors; the taxes on which they were charged were to be carried to a common fund, and these various annuities were to be paid out of it. The annuities thus consolidated came to be known as the consolidated 3 % bank annuities, and the consolidated 3½ % bank annuities.

Other measures towards simplifying finance were taken at various times: thus the produce of certain taxes was brought into one fund known as the aggregate fund; but still the whole matter was enormously complicated until 1787 (27 Geo. III, c. 13), when a very great act (very great in every sense) was passed; a very large part of the revenue had been raised by indirect taxes, customs duties and excise duties, which were levied under a vast multitude of acts of parliament; these were swept away and new duties were imposed in their place. But all or most of the old duties had been pledged for the payment of annuities; it became necessary to provide for these. The whole produce of the

---

[1] In 1912 the Net Debt stood at £718,406,428.
[2] See for instance 12 Geo. I, c. 2.

new taxes, the revenues of the crown lands (which George III, as you will remember, had surrendered), the revenue of the Post Office, in short, I believe that I am right in saying, almost all that could be called royal revenue was to be brought into one consolidated fund, and out of this the various annuitants were to be paid.   Since that time the Consolidated Fund has been the central point of English finance; whatever is received in the way of royal revenue forms part of that fund, and statutes direct how the annuities which are held by the public creditors shall be paid out of that fund.   A similar measure was taken in Ireland, and in 1816 the Consolidated Fund of Great Britain and the Consolidated Fund of Ireland were consolidated into the Consolidated Fund of Great Britain and Ireland.

The Consolidated Fund of Great Britain is then the public revenue or royal revenue of Great Britain, as collected under the laws in force for the time being.   No creditor, therefore, of the nation can say that he has any legal interest in this or that mode of taxation.   Taxes, as we know, are frequently readjusted—an old duty is abolished—this is no breach of faith ; he trusts that parliament will always keep sufficient taxes imposed for the payment of his annuity; he trusts that parliament will not repeal (or, if it repeals, will substantially re-enact) the laws which direct that his annuity shall be paid out of the Consolidated Fund for the time being.

The greater part of our national debt consists of perpetual but redeemable annuities.   The person who had £1000 consols was entitled to be paid £30 per annum for ever ; he was not entitled to be paid £1000 ; but the queen had power at any time to redeem the annuity by paying him £1000—to redeem the debt at par.   The full title of what we briefly call £1000 consols is a sum of £1000 consolidated 3 °/₀ bank annuities. It was this power of redemption which enabled the Chancellor of the Exchequer in 1888 to reduce (as we say) the interest on the national debt ; he could say to the holders of these annuities 'We shall redeem you by paying you off at par, or if you prefer it you can have certain new annuities which will bring you in $2\frac{3}{4}$ °/₀ instead of 3 °/₀.'   These are 'bank' annuities because the Bank of England is charged with the business of paying them, and they are transferable by entry in books kept by the bank. Of the Bank of England I should like to say more, but can only say this, that though it is a banking corporation composed of private individuals, so that you or I might be lucky enough to be members of it, still its position is unique. In return for extremely valuable privileges granted to it by charter and acts of parliament it has come under a large number of public duties. The same may be said of the Bank of Ireland. Our government banks with these banks. The various commissioners who are charged with the duty of collecting the taxes, pay what they collect into an account at these banks called 'The account of Her Majesty's Exchequer.' Sums sufficient to meet the payments becoming due from the Consolidated Fund to the national creditors are drawn from this account and paid to the chief cashier, who is bound to see to the payment. This operation involves the action of the Treasury and of the Comptroller and Auditor-General, but no act of parliament, no vote of the House of Commons, is required.

A word of explanation as to the terms funded and unfunded debt. Debt is funded when the indebted nation is not under any obligation to pay the principal of the debt, but is merely bound to pay the interest for ever, or until it chooses to pay the debt. The man who has £100 of our debt has no right to £100 in cash; he has a right to £2. 15s. per annum for ever, subject to the nation's right to pay him £100 and so extinguish his annuity. The holder is liable to be paid off at a year's notice. Any vote or resolution of the House of Commons signified by the Speaker in writing inserted in the *London Gazette* and affixed on the Royal Exchange in London, shall be deemed sufficient notice. But besides the funded debt there is always a certain amount of unfunded debt. Money is borrowed upon what are called exchequer bills for short and definite times, and under these the creditor is entitled to receive his principal at a certain time and meanwhile to receive interest.

Now let us look at the revenue which forms the Consolidated Fund. It is hard on ninety millions. By far the greater part of it consists of the produce of taxes and govern-

ment monopolies.   Less than half-a-million comes from the
crown lands ; there are the dividends on shares in the Suez
Canal, and there are certain miscellaneous receipts ; but the
great sources of revenue are taxes and monopolies.   I say
'and monopolies,' for about £9,000,000 come from the Post
Office, and the Post Office, as our Cambridge colleges have
lately been reminded, has a monopoly of carrying letters.
The great heads of revenue are customs producing about
twenty millions, excise twenty-five millions, stamps twelve
millions, income-tax twelve millions, house-tax and land-tax
near three millions[1].   Now by far the greater part of this large
sum is raised under permanent acts of parliament.   It requires
no annual act.   If parliament had not sat this year it would
still have been levied.   If you take up any recent volume of
statutes you will find that only a small part of the existing
burden of taxation is imposed by anything in that book.   I
think that at present there are only two taxes which would
come to an end if an act of parliament did not reimpose them,
namely, the income-tax and a duty on tea.   All the taxing
that parliament now does in any one year is generally done by
a single act.   I have the act of 1885 before me.   It is a short
act.   It continues for one year a customs duty on tea at the
rate of 6d. per lb.   It makes a few alterations in the permanent
excise duties.   It imposes the income-tax for one year at the
rate of 8d. in the pound.   It imposes an entirely new tax
upon the property of corporations.   All this can be done by
a few brief sections.   The machinery for collecting taxes is
permanent.   There are commissioners of customs at the head
of one department, commissioners of inland revenue at the
head of another; the manner in which taxes are to be assessed
and collected, the duties of excise officers and customs officers
are set forth in permanent acts.   It is a simple thing to say
that for yet another year a customs duty of 6d. per lb. shall
be charged on tea ; that the income-tax shall be levied at
this or that rate.   But what it is most desirable to understand

---

[1] Nearly 145 millions was raised for the financial year, 1907–8.   The chief
heads of revenue (in millions) were : Customs 32 ; Excise 30; Stamps 7¾; Income
Tax 31 ; Estate Duty 14; Post Office 17 ; House Duty and Land-tax 2½; Telegraph
Service 4.

is that parliament does not annually vote the taxes. If parliament never sat again, still under acts of parliament now in force a great quantity of taxes would be collected; the commissioners of inland revenue, the commissioners of customs, the postmaster-general, would continue to pay in vast sums of money to the account of her majesty's exchequer.

And money would flow out of the Exchequer also, to the amount of something like twenty-five millions a year[1]. Under permanent acts of parliament certain payments become due from the Consolidated Fund, and there are officers charged with the duty of seeing that these are paid. By far the greatest item here consists of the interest on the national debt; this would be paid though parliament never sat; then there is the queen's civil list, and a mass of judicial and other salaries which parliament has made permanently payable. It has been thought undesirable that the question whether Mr Justice A.B., or the comptroller and auditor-general, shall be paid his salary, should be annually submitted to a vote. On the other hand it has been the policy of late years not to charge upon the Consolidated Fund the salary of any executive officer or the cost of any government office, but to bring all such matters annually under the review of parliament.

No payment can be made out of the Consolidated Fund without the authority of an act of parliament. Some payments, as we have just seen, including the large item of interest on the debt, are provided for by permanent acts. And now as to other payments. These are provided for by acts which grant supply to the queen, and then appropriate the supply so granted. The form of a supply act is this: 'We, your Majesty's most dutiful and loyal subjects, the Commons of the United Kingdom of Great Britain and Ireland, in Parliament assembled, towards making good the supply which we have cheerfully granted to your Majesty in this session of Parliament, have resolved to grant to your Majesty the sum hereinafter mentioned, and do therefore humbly beseech your Majesty that it may be enacted, and be it enacted by the Queen's most Excellent Majesty by and with the consent and advice of the Lords Spiritual and Temporal and Commons in

[1] Now (1913) over 36 millions.

this present Parliament assembled, and by the authority of
the same as follows: The Commissioners of her Majesty's
Treasury for the time being may issue out of the Consolidated
Fund and apply towards making good the supply granted to
her Majesty for the service of the year ending 31 March, 1886,
the sum of £45,361,227.' The appropriation clause takes this
form: 'All sums granted by this act are appropriated for
the purposes and services expressed in the schedule annexed
hereto.' Turning to the schedule we find that the appropriation
is pretty minute. There are sums great and small. These
are instances:

For wages, etc., to 59,000 seamen and marines...	£2,728,100
For the expense of dockyards and naval yards at home and abroad	£1,639,300
For the volunteer corps' pay and allowances ...	£606,000
For the maintenance and repair of Marlborough House	£7,120
For the cost of erecting a monument to the late Major-General Charles George Gordon ...	£500
For her majesty's foreign and other secret services	£50,000

Now observe first that this is supply granted to the queen;
none of it will go out of the Exchequer without the sign
manual, and the warrant of the Commissioners of the Treasury.
Parliament does not grant money to the seamen and marines,
or to the sculptor who makes a monument to General Gordon.
Of course all this might be done, but it is not done; it is
thought very undesirable that it should be done. Money is
granted to the queen; it is placed at the disposal of her and
her ministers. But she and they are not bound by law to
spend it, at least not bound by the Appropriation Act. Of
course if the queen's advisers withdrew all ambassadors from
foreign courts, or disbanded the navy or the like, they might
be severely blamed and possibly they might be impeached.
But statute does not say to the queen 'You shall spend so
much on your embassies, so much on your navy.' Rather its
language is: 'Here is money for this purpose and for that;
spend it if you please; we trust the discretion of your
advisers; the account of the expenditure will be presented

to us, and votes of censure may follow. This, however, applies only to expenditure within the limits laid down by the act: here is two and a quarter millions for warlike stores, £100,000 for the royal parks, one hundred guineas for expenses connected with the observation of the transit of Venus; if more is drawn out for any of these purposes, someone will have committed a crime, indeed in all probability several persons will have conspired to commit a crime[1].' I may here remark that soldiers, sailors, and civil servants are servants of the queen and of no one else, generally dismissible at a moment's notice and without cause assigned. The pay, salaries, pensions, for which they serve, are paid to them on behalf of the queen, and at least in general they can bring no action for their pay against the queen's ministers; the contract is with the queen, and the remedy on it is a petition of right. The fact that parliament has voted a supply to the queen for the payment of such salaries or pensions does not give them a remedy against the lords of the treasury or the secretaries of state who are charged with the expenditure. No one can say, 'Under the Appropriation Act, the secretary of state for war, or the lords of the admiralty, have received money which they hold upon trust for me.'

In speaking of the grant and appropriation of supplies I have somewhat unduly simplified the course of business. Only one Appropriation Act is passed in each year, and that near the end of the session; that provides for the whole estimated expenditure of the then current year. But before the whole of the estimates can be considered it often is necessary that the queen should have money. Early in the session the House of Commons forms itself into a committee of supply and begins going through the estimates. The minister in charge of the business proposes grants one by one, as, for instance, that a sum not exceeding £10,000 be granted to her majesty for the object specified in the estimate.

---

[1] This is emphasized by a now usual clause, which empowers the treasury in case of necessity to use money appropriated to one military purpose for another military purpose. In 1883-4 advantage was taken of this; an act of 1885 declares that what was done was lawful. On the other hand even at a pinch money appropriated to the navy cannot be applied to the army. F.W.M.

The House also forms itself into a committee of ways and means and therein considers how the supply thus voted shall be raised : it votes that so much money be granted out of the Consolidated Fund towards making good the supply voted to her majesty.   This resolution is then embodied in a bill passed early in the session.   For instance I take up the statutes of 1885.   On the 28th of March an act obtains the royal assent ; it states that the Commons towards making good the supply voted to Her Majesty have granted the sum hereinafter mentioned, and that it is enacted by Queen and Parliament that the Commissioners of the Treasury may issue out of the Consolidated Fund and apply towards making good the supply voted to Her Majesty for the year ending 31 March, 1886, a sum of ten millions odd.   The act contains no further words of appropriation ; merely says that the Commissioners of the Treasury may apply this sum towards making good the supply that has been voted : this supply however has been voted, as I have already described, for specific purposes.   On 21 May another act of the same kind is passed granting another thirteen millions.   On 14 August we have the Appropriation Act.   It grants another forty-five millions.   Then it proceeds to appropriate the whole of these three sums of ten, thirteen, forty-five millions, and it appropriates them retrospectively.   It says that all sums granted by the two acts of March and May, and the present act, are appropriated and shall be deemed to have been appropriated as from the date of the passing of the first of those acts, for the purposes expressed in the schedule to the present act.   This, however, is rather a detail of business.

E. *The Military System.*

We have traced the legal history of our military system down to the reign of William III.   From that time onward it becomes the history of an act passed in every year—known as the Annual Mutiny Act—an act legalizing the existence of a standing army consisting of a certain specified number of men for one year more.   The practice of passing a whole Mutiny Act in every year was continued until 1879.   In that year an act of a different kind was passed and in 1881 a new edition of this act was passed. This act of 1881—the Army Act of 1881—now governs the army. But it is an act of a very peculiar character—it always requires another act to keep it in force—and in every session of parliament a brief act is passed renewing the act of 1881. This was but a change in parliamentary procedure, the principle is still preserved that the army shall be legalized only from year to year.

I have said that the legal history of the British army from the days of William III to the present time is chiefly the history of these annual mutiny acts. We sometimes talk about the Mutiny Act being re-enacted, but do not be deceived by this into thinking that the same act was passed year after year. The acts grow and grow in bulk, and become always minuter and more precise. The first Mutiny Act is a trifling little thing. I think that I have stated to you the whole of its sum and substance. The act of 1881 is a vast code, has 193 sections and takes up more than 60 octavo pages. Now to trace this process of growth would take a very long time; I can only ask your attention to a few salient points. In the first place we always have the solemn recitals 'Whereas the keeping of a standing army in time of peace within the United Kingdom of Great Britain and Ireland without the consent of parliament is against law,' 'And whereas no man can be forejudged of life and limb, or subjected in time of peace to any kind of punishment within this realm by martial law, or in any other manner than by the judgment of his peers and according to the known and established laws of the realm.' The words 'in time of peace' in this last recital were not in the earliest mutiny acts; their presence certainly seems to suggest that in time of war the subjects of this realm might be punished by something called martial law. That is a point to which I shall return. As to the judgment of one's peers, that I think has become sorry old nonsense. A subject of this realm can be sent to prison by one stipendiary magistrate—I fail to see how he gets the judgment of his peers in any sense in which he would not get it were he tried by court martial.

Then the modern acts specify the precise number of soldiers that may be kept. It is adjudged necessary by the queen and parliament that a body of forces should be continued for the safety of the United Kingdom and the defence of the possessions of Her Majesty's Crown and that the whole number of such forces should consist of 142,194 men. The queen, I take it, is not in the least bound to keep that number; it is a maximum.

Next we will notice that the act expressly empowers the queen to make Articles of War for the better government of officers and soldiers. The act does not constitute by any means the whole of our military code—there is besides a large body of Articles of War. If you wish for an example (I have before this mentioned others) of delegated legislative powers I know of no better than this—for the queen is empowered to legislate for the better government of officers and soldiers and she can create new offences. But the act goes on to mark the limit. No person by such articles is to be subject to any punishment extending to life or limb, or to be kept in penal servitude, except for crimes which are by this act expressly made subject to such punishment as aforesaid or be subject, with reference to any crimes made punishable by this act, to be punished in any manner which does not accord with the provisions of this act. Now probably there is a certain (or I had better say uncertain) prerogative power for making articles for the government of the army. The earlier Mutiny Acts only deal with mutiny and similar crimes, crimes which they punish with death, but during the reigns of William and Anne Articles of War were issued dealing with minor offences, and the legality of these seems to have been admitted by parliament. What the limit to the prerogative power was supposed to be I am not certain, probably life and limb. Historically, as it seems to me, there are difficulties in drawing any line. The annual acts protested that no man should be subjected to any kind of punishment by martial law—if the king could order that drunkards be flogged, why not that mutineers be hanged? In the act of 3 George I, however, the king was expressly empowered to make articles for the better government of his forces as well within the realm as without, and to inflict pains and penalties to be pronounced by courts martial. This became, I believe, a standing clause in the act. Gradually parliament expressly dealt with more and more offences, going always into smaller details, and thus in effect the scope of Articles of War was limited—for it was established as early as 1728 that the king could not impose by articles a graver punishment than that which the Mutiny Act had imposed. Also the king was advised by his law officers in 1727 that he could not commute the sentence pronounced by a court martial under the act —could not substitute flogging for death.

Now though an express power of making articles is given by the annual acts this would not take away any previously existing prerogative; so, on the whole, we ought probably to believe that when parliament has legalized a standing army, has said that the queen may keep soldiers in her pay, she has, if nothing more be said, a power of making regulations for their government, a power extending to the denunciation of punishments short of life and limb. The modern acts, however, give her expressly a power which is more limited; her articles may not inflict penal servitude or vary the punishments for the many offences for which the act itself provides.

As to what these offences are I cannot go into many particulars. There are a considerable number of offences for which death may be inflicted. For instance, anyone who ' misbehaves or induces others to misbehave before the enemy in such a manner as to show cowardice' may be sentenced to death. Some offences there are which are punishable with death if committed while on active service, but are not so punishable if committed in other circumstances. Desertion is a case in point; anyone who, while on active service, deserts or attempts to desert can be sentenced to death. Anyone who deserts while not on active service can get no severer punishment than imprisonment. As to disobedience the rules are these: he who disobeys, in such a manner as to show a wilful defiance of authority, any lawful command given personally by his superior officer in the execution of his office, is liable to suffer death; he who disobeys any lawful command given by his superior officer is liable, if he commits the offence while on active service, to penal servitude, if otherwise to imprisonment. The punishments which can be inflicted are death, penal servitude for five years, imprisonment for two years, for officers cashiering, for soldiers discharge with ignominy, forfeiture, fines, stoppages. Flogging has lately disappeared ; a maximum punishment of 300 lashes was fixed in 1812, of 200 lashes in 1832, in 1867 it was confined to a few offences, in 1868 it was abolished altogether in time of peace. In the act of 1879 it appears for the last time—25 lashes may be inflicted for certain offences if committed on active service. It is not to be found in the act of 1881.

Hitherto we have been dealing with what we may call military offences. Now as to other offences, crimes against the general law of the land, the policy of these acts has for a long time past been not to exempt the soldier from the ordinary rules and the ordinary processes of the law. You may have noticed this when I was speaking of the first of all the Mutiny Acts. The principle is laid down broadly in what is now the standing act. 'A person subject to military law when in his majesty's dominions, may be tried by any competent civil court for any offence for which he would be triable if he were not subject to military law.' What is more, he can seldom be tried by court martial for an offence against the ordinary civil law—never within the United Kingdom ; but outside the United Kingdom, and if more than a hundred miles from any town in which there is a competent civil court, he may be tried for treason, treason-felony, murder, manslaughter or rape. When the jurisdictions of courts martial and ordinary courts overlap, the fact that the offender has been punished under the military law is no bar to criminal proceedings against him, but the court is ordered to take his previous military punishment into consideration when awarding sentence. As regards debts and other civil causes of action, one can sue a soldier and have execution against his property, but his person is exempt unless the sum due be above £30. This does not mean very much, now that imprisonment for debt has been abolished.

The act contains elaborate rules as to the constitution of courts martial ; their procedure is for the most part left to regulations made by the queen and signed by a secretary of state. The act, however, provides how a prisoner may challenge his judges, and provides also that the ordinary English rules of evidence shall be observed.

One great branch of the act then deals with these matters and the like. It enacts a military penal code, and provides special courts for enforcing that code. Another large branch deals with billeting and the impressment of carriages. Billeting has been found necessary, and year by year the section about it in the Petition of Right is solemnly suspended. But the burden is not, I think, very heavy. Soldiers can only be billeted on those whom, roughly speaking, one may call keepers of public-houses—victualling houses is the statutory word. The prices to be paid for accommodation are fixed from time to time by parliament, and the act goes into detail; indeed it chronicles small beer, for not more than two pints thereof need be provided for any soldier per diem. So carriages, carts, horses may be impressed for the transport of regimental baggage, all to be practically paid for at parliamentary rates.

There is a third great branch of the act which deals with enlistment. Now parliament for a long time left the king to make what terms he pleased with his soldiers. Gradually, however, clauses as to enlistment make their way into the Mutiny Acts. Their object was to provide that the recruit should really understand what he was about, and not sell himself half-drunk into a life-long service. Similar clauses appear still ; the recruit must be taken before a justice of the peace, sign a declaration and so forth. But of late parliament has interfered with the terms of the enlistment in order to carry out a policy of short service. The act of 1881 says that a person may be enlisted for a period of twelve years, or for such less period as may be from time to time fixed by the queen, but not for any longer period. There are also clauses providing for passing men into the reserve. This reserve 'it shall be lawful for Her Majesty in council' to call out, 'in case of imminent national danger or of great emergency by proclamation, the occasion being first communicated to parliament if parliament be then sitting, or if parliament be not then sitting, declared by the proclamation.' But though the soldier engages for a term of years, the queen is not bound to keep him for that term, he can always be dismissed without cause assigned; this applies to all officers and soldiers alike from the general commanding in chief downwards.

It is, I believe, a common mistake that since the Revolution we have no such thing as impressment or conscription for the army. Of course no permanent law provided for it, because there was no permanent law for the army. Also it is true that this means of raising a force was only made lawful in times of war, and was applied in a limited way. But in the first place it was at times applied to insolvent debtors. Imprisoned debtors were discharged on condition of their enlisting or finding a substitute. This seems to have been done on many occasions during the eighteenth century. Then again convicted criminals were released upon condition of their enlisting. This was, I believe, done until the end of the Peninsular War. Thirdly, conscription was applied to the pauper class. In 1703 justices are to raise and levy such able-bodied men as have not any lawful calling or employment, or visible means for their maintenance or subsistence, and hand them over to the officers of the queen's forces. Similar acts were passed during the reigns of George II and George III, the persons liable to be impressed were 'all such able-bodied, idle and disorderly persons, who cannot upon examination prove themselves to exercise and industriously follow some lawful trade or employment, or to have some substance sufficient for their support and maintenance.' I believe that clauses directing the impressment of able-bodied paupers were in force until 1780. A British army of the eighteenth century must have been largely composed of bad characters, insolvent debtors, criminals, idle and disorderly persons. The army was never popular; the soldiers, as a class, were despised. For a long time past we have depended for supplies of men upon voluntary enlistment.

Now under the acts of parliament, and within the limits which they set, the command, government, disposition of the army is in the queen. Probably it is within this military sphere that the personal will of the king has been most efficacious within what we may call recent times. Even to this day a very great mass of military business is, I believe, brought under the queen's own notice, and her sign manual is required for many purposes. But down to 1793 there was no Commander-in-chief, or rather the king himself really and truly commanded the army. A general might be appointed for a time to conduct a campaign on the continent; but the true head of the army was the king. What led to the appointment of a Commander-in-chief was, it seems, the use for political ends of the king's power of appointing and dismissing officers. It was thought that in such matters he ought to act on the advice of one who was primarily a soldier, and who stood outside party politics. On the other hand the disposition, the general administration of the army has always been falling more and more into the hands of a political minister, a member of parliament and of the cabinet. This is a particularly complex piece of history, and I must shirk it. Until the beginning of the Crimean War responsibility was much divided between a Secretary at War, who was not a Secretary of State, and the Secretaries of State. At that time the office of Secretary of State for War was created, and a few years afterwards the much older office Secretary at War was abolished. The legal necessity of his counter-signature as an authentication of the queen's orders, even when such orders are addressed to the Commander-in-chief, secures that his advice shall be taken in all matters relating to the disposition of the forces, and he has to answer in parliament for the advice he gives. The Commander-in-chief is trusted with a large power as to the discipline of the forces, appointment and promotion. A political minister ought not, it is thought, to interfere with these matters; but the highest appointments, the command in chief on foreign service, have the approval of the Secretary of State, and in important cases become 'cabinet questions.' As to the employment of troops in war, I believe we may safely say that the Secretary of State must always become responsible for this, and that his signature is legally necessary. But the relations between the Horse Guards and the War Office are delicate and intricate, and I cannot pretend to have studied them closely[1].

[1] This dualism ceased when by Orders in Council of 29 Dec. 1887 and 21 Feb. 1888, the whole administration of the army was centred in the Commander-in-chief,

And now we must go back to the Restoration to take up the tale of the militia. The necessity for a standing army was denied, thing and name were hateful, the ancient force was to be reorganized. The Statute of Winchester was still in force, the old principle was to be revived. First, however (1662), the act recited that 'the sole and supreme power, government, command and disposition of the militia, and of all forces by sea and land is, and by the laws of England ever was the undoubted right of his majesty and his royal predecessors, kings and queens of England ; and that both or either of the Houses of Parliament cannot, nor ought to pretend to the same.' Now the original plan of this militia is something of this kind. The king appoints a Lieutenant for each county, who with the king's approval appoint Deputy-Lieutenants. They at a meeting (this comes to be called a lieutenancy meeting) are to charge the inhabitants of the county with the duty of finding men and armour according to this scale : Anyone with a revenue of £500, or with £6,000 in goods, must find one horse, horseman, and armour, and so in proportion if his wealth be greater ; anyone who has less than this, but has a revenue of £50 or £600 in goods, must find a foot soldier and arms. This county force the Lord-Lieutenant is to command ; the subordinate officers are to be commissioned by him, unless the king shall exercise a reserved power of making the appointments ; these officers the king can dismiss. Ordinarily the force can only be called out for a certain very limited quantity of exercise in the year : once a year for four days there is a general muster and exercise of regiments ; four times a year for two days at a time there may be an exercise of single companies and troops. No person can be forced to serve in person, but must send a sufficient man and pay him a certain statutory maintenance, twelve pence per day for a foot soldier ; ammunition the county must provide ; if the force is called

himself responsible to the Secretary of State for War. The authority of the Commander-in-chief was somewhat abridged by Orders in Council of 21 Nov. 1895, and the office itself was abolished after the Boer War in 1904, when an Army Council was created by Letters Patent. All powers exercised under the royal prerogative by the Secretary of State for War and the Commander-in-chief were transferred to the Council, which in 1908 consists of seven members including the Secretary of State for War and the Chief of the General Staff.

into actual service the king is to pay wages, but these have to be advanced in the first instance by the persons who are charged to provide the men.   Now the object for which this force can be employed is this: the Lord-Lieutenant may call it together, and in case of insurrection, rebellion, or invasion, may conduct and employ it for suppressing of all such insurrections, and rebellions, and repelling of invasions according as he shall from time to time receive directions from the king.   For this purpose the force may be led into any part of England, but this act 'is not to be deemed or taken to extend to the giving or declaring of any power for the transporting of any of the subjects of this realm, or any way compelling them to march out of this kingdom, otherwise than by the laws of England ought to be done.'   A force of this kind the opinion of the day considered the proper force to protect the kingdom against invasion and rebellion.   The curiously aristocratic nature of the force will not escape your notice. It is to be provided by and officered by the landowners of the county.

The statutes of Charles II remained the basis of the militia law during the first half of the eighteenth century. The force which it created must have been a very clumsy and very costly force, and despite all the grand things that were said of it, it hardly became an effective institution.   In 1757 (30 Geo. II, c. 25) all the earlier statutes were swept away, and the force was reorganized—there was fear of a French invasion. All men between eighteen and fifty, except certain specially exempted classes, are liable to serve, or to find substitutes who will serve as privates in the militia.   The quota, however, of men for each county is fixed by statute ; thus for Huntingdonshire it is 320, for Middlesex 1,600.   This requisite quota is to be obtained in each county by ballot.   Within the county the apportioning of numbers, first to hundreds (or lieutenancy sub-divisions) and then to parishes, is accomplished by the Lieutenant and Deputy-Lieutenants at lieutenancy meetings, and they look after the ballot.   A man drawn in the ballot or his substitute must serve for three years : the amount of exercise that can be required of him is minutely defined.   In case of actual invasion or imminent danger thereof, or in case of rebellion, the king (notifying the occasion to parliament if parliament be then sitting) can draw out and embody all the militia, and place them under general officers. The force can then be obliged to serve in any part of the kingdom. When the militia is thus embodied, the militiaman is to receive the pay of a regular soldier, and will come under the Mutiny Act and the Articles of War. No provision was made for the pay of the militia during training and exercise. This was an intentional omission, it made necessary an annual act for pay and clothing, and thus gave the House of Commons a control similar to that which it had over the regular army. The power of the crown in the appointment of officers was somewhat increased, but an officer was to have a fairly high property qualification—£50 a year for an ensign, £200 for a captain, and so forth.

In 1786 again a clean sweep was made by 26 Geo. III, c. 107; this is a long and intricate militia code of 136 sections. The general plan of the force, however, remains that settled in 1757. This again gave way in 1802 to a new code of 178 sections. I can only say that the plan remains much the same. Very rarely indeed had the militia been drawn out and embodied. It was embodied during the Seven Years' War, again between 1778 and 1783, again between 1792 and 1803. Each embodiment is marked by a new code. In 1815 an act was passed empowering the king to embody it because of the war with France. A profound peace followed. The ballot was suspended, and I believe that even the annual exercising of voluntarily enlisted militiamen was very generally suspended. Then in 1852 there was a new terror, and consequently a new act. It did not sweep away the previous acts, indeed the act of 1802 is still, to a considerable extent, the basis of the law. It endeavoured to make the militia a more flexible and serviceable force. The number of men is fixed at 80,000, but in case of actual invasion or imminent danger thereof the queen may direct that 40,000 more be raised. In this case she must first communicate the reason to parliament, if there be a parliament sitting; if parliament be prorogued she must summon it to meet within fourteen days—that, by the way, is a case in which statute orders the queen to call parliament together. The quotas for the counties are now to be fixed by Order in Council; the numbers are to be raised by voluntary enlistment, but if this fails to produce the requisite total, then the ballot is to be resorted to. In the main the old law as to the obligation to serve or find a substitute is kept on foot. The whole, or part of the force, can be exercised for twenty-one days in a year. By Order in Council, however, the time may be extended to fifty-six days; by similar means the county force can, if necessary, be exercised out of its county. The law as to embodying the militia for actual service remains much as before. Many alterations are made as to the appointment and qualification of officers, tending to give the commissions rather to real soldiers than to the landed gentry.

However, the ballot really remained in suspense. It was suspended by an act of 1829 for a year, and I believe that it then became the practice to pass a similar act in every year. In 1865 an act of this kind was passed, and since then the practice has been to include the act of 1865, which suspended the ballot, in the Expiring Laws Continuance Act. But even while that act remains in force the ballot may be introduced by Order in Council. This was actually done in 1830, and the balloting clauses remained in play until February, 1832. I believe that since then there has been no ballot. The bounties and pay are high enough to procure what is considered a sufficient number of men.

There have been a great many more changes, culminating in an important Consolidation Act of 1882 (45 and 46 Vic., c. 49). Briefly the result is this: all the duties and powers of the Lords-Lieutenant, over or in relation to the militia, are taken from them. These are now exerciseable by the queen through a Secretary of State, or any officers to whom the queen may, by the advice of a Secretary of State, delegate such duties or powers. The officers are commissioned directly by the queen, but the Lieutenants have still a certain power of recommending for first appointments. There is now no permanent statute fixing the number of the militia. It is lawful for her majesty to raise and keep up a militia consisting of such number of men as may from time to time be provided by parliament. Militiamen are to be enlisted voluntarily for some term not longer than six years.   They go through six months' preliminary training ; then they are liable each year to be exercised for twenty-eight days, but by Order in Council this can be extended to fifty-six.   The force can be embodied for actual service by Royal Proclamation in case of imminent national danger or great emergency.   In that case, if parliament be prorogued, it must be summoned to meet within ten days; the force can then be kept embodied until the queen disembodies it by proclamation.   It can be sent into any part of the United Kingdom, but not out of it ; though with their own consent the men may be sent to Gibraltar or Malta.   As well when they are training, as when they are embodied, the officers and men are under the Mutiny Act.

As you will see, the militia while keeping its name has by slow degrees—every step can be traced on the statute book— become something utterly different from what it was in the seventeenth, even in the eighteenth century.   In truth it is very like a second standing army.   Owing to the fact that England is an island, we have never taken kindly to compulsory military service; the consequence is that we have two professional armies.   The old ballot clauses of 1802 are still hanging over our heads, but they would be rusty machinery for the present day.   The militia is now quite as much under the control of the crown as is the regular army.   The Lord-Lieutenant has ceased to be a military officer, the militia has now but little to do with any organization of the county[1].

---

[1] Under the Territorial and Reserve Forces Act of 1907 (7 Ed. VII, c. 9) County Associations were established for the purpose of raising a Territorial Force for home defence.   Under Pt III, § 33 of the Act the Army Council was empowered to form Special Reservists into regiments, battalions and other military bodies, as provided in the Reserve Forces Act of 1882.   The old Militia Battalions do not form part of the Territorial Force, and are quite independent of the County Associations.   They form 'Special Reserve Battalions' of the Line regiments to which they severally belong and are liable to active service with the regular Battalions whenever and wherever required.   Their officers are 'Special Reserve Officers' of the regular army.   The old Militia therefore has ceased to exist in name, in fact and in law, for though with the exception of twenty-three suppressed Battalions, the old Militia Battalions have been transferred to the new 'Special Reserve,' they are no longer liable only for service in the United Kingdom and Ireland, nor are they enlisted on the old Militia basis.   The Volunteer Territorial Force (which includes Yeomanry and Volunteers) is more akin to the ancient

The treatment which the navy has received at the hands of parliament has been curiously different from that of the army. While the statute book bristles with acts about the army, acts about the navy are very few. I can only notice a very few points.

In the first place it has not been asserted that the maintenance of a standing navy even in time of peace, without the consent of parliament, is against law. In point of fact parliament has long since acquired just as much power over the navy as over the army. This power has been acquired by means of appropriation acts. In 1885, for example, a sum of $2\frac{3}{4}$ millions odd was appropriated for the wages, etc. of 59,000 seamen and marines, so much for victuals and clothing, so much for the expenses of dockyards, and so forth. This has practically obliged the king to have in parliament a minister who will state the needs of the navy, and the manner in which money is spent. But no act of parliament is necessary to legalize the very existence of a royal navy. As to discipline: this was long regulated by a statute made immediately after the Restoration (13 Car. II, c. 9). This having been several times amended was replaced by an act of 1749 (22 Geo. II, c. 33). This code, with some amendments, remained in force until 1860, when it was replaced by another. The act now in force is the Naval Discipline Act of 1866 (29 and 30 Vic., c. 109). It covers much the same ground as the act which regulates the discipline of the army: defines offences and imposes punishments. In the past there was this difference, that while the military penal code was to be found largely in Articles of War made by the crown, ever since the Restoration there has been a statutory naval penal code defining offences and awarding punishments. But for some time past there has really been little difference in this respect, for the Army Acts have always been becoming more detailed and precise. The act now in force for the army expressly provides for all or most of the offences which can be considered as very serious, and so takes them out of the sphere of articles made by the

fyrd. Whether or no the Ballot Act (42 George III, c. 90) could be legally put in force to obtain men for the 'Special Reserve' or for the Territorial Army, whose conditions of service more resemble those of the old Militia, is very doubtful.

queen. On the other hand the Naval Act has a very general clause, which provides for the punishment of any act, disorder or neglect, to the prejudice of good order and naval discipline not hereinbefore specified ; and again, it provides that when no punishment is mentioned in the act, an offence against the act may be punished according to the laws and customs in such cases used at sea. There is, however, this difference, that the Naval Act provides for offences against the ordinary criminal law. A sailor of the royal navy who commits murder or larceny or any other crime on sea, or on land outside the United Kingdom, can be tried by a court martial administering the ordinary criminal law of England. It is only in quite rare circumstances that a soldier can be tried by court martial for one of the common crimes.

But to students of the history of law the most interesting thing about the navy is impressment. The history of the word itself is very curious—doubtless pressing suggests the notion of compulsion, physical restraint—and doubtless for a very long time past people have had this notion in their minds when they talked about impressment, pressing sailors, the press-gang and so forth. But it is, I believe, quite well established that the word originally bore a quite different sense. In the National Debt Act of 1870 (33 and 34 Vic., c. 71, sec. 14), one may read that the money issued for the payment of dividends is to be paid to the chief cashier of the bank by way of imprest. It is from *impraestare*—think of the French word *prêter*—money is imprest when it is advanced for a specific purpose ; and 'imprest money' was the sum advanced or given to soldiers and mariners upon enlistment. Now the impressment of marines for the purposes of the royal navy had been clearly recognized as legal by statutes going back to the reign of Richard II. And in 1743 in *Rex* v. *Broadfoot* it was contended by Sir Michael Foster, that ' the right of impressing mariners for the public service is a prerogative inherent in the crown, grounded upon common-law and recognized by many acts of Parliament.' Broadfoot had killed one of a press-gang while engaged in pressing seamen under a legal warrant executed in an illegal manner, for the warrant stated that its execution could only be entrusted to a commissioned officer, and this was not done. Foster admitted that the press-gang were not acting in terms of their warrant, and so were engaged in attempting to make an illegal arrest; but he thought it well to discuss the whole subject, and produced a long array of authority in favour of the legality of pressing.   Afterwards both Mansfield and Kenyon upheld its legality, and there can now be no doubt at all, to press sailors into his service is one of the king's prerogatives.   It has never been taken away.   I cannot say when last it was used; it is not used in time of peace; but we should be rash in saying that it would never be used in case of a great naval war: at any rate there the power is, and parliament has left it alone.   It has been so long disused that there is some difficulty in saying who might be impressed. However, I believe it certain that they must in some sense be sailors—they must use the sea.   There is an act of 1740 still in force, which exempts persons above forty-five years of age, or below eighteen; persons who use the sea are by the same act exempted for two years after the beginning of their first voyage[1].

F.   *Administration of Justice.*

It is important at the outset of legal study to have some notion of the history of the courts and of their procedure, for a large portion of our law is not statute law, but case law— 'common law' and 'equity'; and case law cannot be read unless we know a little of the courts.

We must first dismiss with a few brief words what is perhaps the most important court held in England, because (save in some comparatively minor matters) it is not a court for England—the Judicial Committee of the Privy Council.

The act which abolished the Court of Star Chamber did not deprive the Privy Council of all jurisdiction.   In particular

---

[1] 2 Ric. II, stat. 1, c. 4; 2 and 3 Phil. and Mary, c. 16; 2 and 3 Anne, c. 6; 4 and 5 Anne, c. 19; 7 and 8 Will. III, c. 21.   For *Rex* v. *Broadfoot, State Trials,* XVIII, p. 1323 ff.   For Mansfield's judgment in *Rex* v. *Tubbs* (1776) Cowper, *Reports,* II, p. 512 ff.   For Kenyon in *Ex Parte Fox, State Trials,* V, 276.   For the whole subject Broom, *Constitutional Law,* pp. 111—114.   Robertson, *Statutes Cases and Documents,* p. 344.

it remained the supreme Court of Appeal for all the king's lands beyond the seas. This was then a small matter; the king's lands beyond the seas were the Isle of Man, the Channel Islands, a few struggling colonies. Now it has become a very great affair, as the king by cession, conquest, and colonization, has acquired new lands in every quarter of the globe.

Until 1833 this jurisdiction was, in fact, exercised by such members of the Privy Council as had held high judicial offices. In that year a committee was created by statute, consisting of the members who should be holding, or have held, certain high judicial offices, and this committee was to do the judicial work. In 1871 four paid members were appointed, and they, together with the Chancellor, do almost all the work of the Court. According to a scheme at present at work, these four members will also be the four Lords of Appeal in Ordinary, and thus the two supreme tribunals of the empire, the Privy Council and the House of Peers, will for practical purposes consist of the same members.

Practically this committee is a court of law, but administrative forms are in some respects maintained. Its 'judgment' is not technically a judgment, but advice to the queen, whereupon an Order in Council is made, affirming or reversing the judgment of the colonial court, against which appeal is made. Only one opinion is expressed—secrecy is insisted on. These features form a curious reminder of the time when judicial and governmental functions were intimately blended, and the same council advised the king on acts of state and judicial business.

The Council does a little work for England—is the Court of Appeal from the ecclesiastical courts—and until 1875 from the Court of Admiralty; but the business of the ecclesiastical courts has become small for a reason soon to be given.

Turning to the English courts, we must first distinguish between civil and criminal jurisdiction—some courts have both jurisdictions, some only one.

Now with respect to civil jurisdiction our whole judicial system has been recast within the nineteenth century.

Let me recall the leading dates in this process:

1846. Formation of new County Courts.

1857. Transfer to new Courts of ecclesiastical jurisdiction in testamentary and matrimonial causes—(1) Court of Probate, (2) Court of Divorce.

1875. Fusion of all superior courts of law and equity (except House of Lords) into a new supreme court.

1876. Reformation of the House of Lords as a judicial tribunal.

a. The Civil Courts. There is one court of first instance for the whole of England, with an unlimited competence in all civil cases—the High Court of Justice. From this an appeal lies to the Court of Appeal. From this again an appeal lies to the House of Lords. These courts are central and superior.

Besides these there are some five hundred 'county courts' which are local, inferior, and of limited competence, and from them an appeal lies to the High Court.

First we will speak of the county courts. We have already spoken of the centralization of justice and of the great work that it did for us in the past, giving us a common law. But owing to the decay of the old local courts this extreme centralization produced many evils. The system was too costly and dilatory for small causes, and often amounted to an absolute denial of justice. Attempts were made to correct this evil in the eighteenth century by the creation of petty courts here and there, 'courts of conscience,' or 'courts of requests,' before which (without trial by jury) debts might be recovered. But no general reform was attempted until 1846, when a new system of courts was created throughout the land. To these new courts was transferred such remnants of contentious jurisdiction as were possessed by the old county courts—those county courts which played so important a part in the earlier Middle Ages. But though the new courts are called 'county courts,' they really have little to do with the county system. The 'old county courts' still have a theoretic existence, though not as judicial tribunals, thus the coroners are elected in what is a county court of the old type which all freeholders may attend; and I am not sure that to this day, even with our system of vote by ballot, the members for a county are not supposed to be elected in what is theoretically a county court of the old type.

These new so-called county courts have been steadily growing in importance. Parliament has frequently given them fresh powers[1]. They exercise a civil jurisdiction limited in two ways—(1) by the amount at stake, (2) by geography.

(1) Ordinarily (but there are some large exceptions) the amount claimed must not exceed £50.

(2) They are local courts. The defendant must (ordinarily) be sued in the court of the district within which he dwells or carries on business.

In many cases a plaintiff has a choice between the county court and the High Court; in some he must go to the county court, and suitors are discouraged (by rules about costs) from taking to the High Court matters which might have been heard in the county court.

The county court is presided over by a judge; there are about fifty county court judges, each of whom therefore has generally several districts. The judge is appointed by the Lord Chancellor from among barristers of seven years' standing; he can be removed by the Chancellor for inability or misbehaviour; he is disqualified from practising as a barrister and from sitting in the House of Commons; his salary is charged on the Consolidated Fund.

In most cases either of the parties to the action can insist on having a question of fact tried by a jury of eight. But trial by jury in a county court is very uncommon; generally the judge decides both fact and law.

From the judge's decision on any point of law, but not from his decision of matter of fact, there lies an appeal to the High Court of Justice. With the leave of the High Court, but not without, there is an appeal to the Court of Appeal and so to the House of Lords.

A few other local courts survive. The most important is the court held by the Vice-Chancellor of the County Palatine of Lancaster. But all England has now been brought within this system of new county courts, and almost every year they gain something in dignity and importance as parliament gives them new powers. Their business is entirely civil business.

---

[1] The County Courts Act of 1888 (51 and 52 Vict., c. 43) is the last comprehensive measure dealing with these courts.

We have already noticed how beside the old courts of common law, there grew up in later Middle Ages a court administering equity; how equity obtained a large field for itself by the invention of uses and trusts; and how equity became a fixed body of rules to be discovered in the decisions of the Chancellors.

I believe that we may think of equity as becoming a fixed and well ascertained body of law towards the end of the seventeenth century; perhaps 1688, the year of the Revolution, would be as good a year as any to name. Lord Nottingham, who became Lord Keeper in 1673 and shortly afterwards Lord Chancellor, has been called the father of equity, and seems to have done much towards defining the jurisdiction By the middle of the next century Blackstone could explain, though explanation was still necessary, that courts of equity, like other courts, were bound by fixed rules and were not free to do just what might seem to be fair and right to their judges. 'The system,' he writes[1], 'of our courts of equity is a laboured connected system, governed by established rules, and bound down by precedents from which they do not depart, although the reason of some of them may perhaps be liable to objection.' He then mentions some rules which he thinks irrational (for instance, the husband is allowed curtesy of a trust estate, but the widow is not allowed dower). 'All these, he says, 'and other cases that might be instanced, are plainly rules of positive law supported only by the reverence that is shown and in general very properly shown to a series of former determinations.' Blackstone, like other common lawyers, was not very fond of the chancery. The view of the thinking English lawyer of his time seems to have been that the chancery was a necessary evil, though they were unwilling to confess what may seem to us the truth, namely that trial by jury was becoming an antiquated form of trial inadequate to meet the complicated problems which arise under modern law.

I propose now to say a little about the domain of modern equity; and first about the courts and their procedure. At the beginning of the eighteenth century there were but two judges in the Court of Chancery, the Chancellor [or Lord Keeper] and

[1] *Commentaries*, vol. III, p. 433.

the Master of the Rolls; and the Master of the Rolls was not competent for all business. In early times the Chancellor was assisted by certain persons known as Masters in Chancery; they sat in court as his assessors and did some of the subordinate work under his supervision. Of these the Master of the Rolls was the foremost and gradually, as it seems, he became more and more an independent judge. In the reign of George II his functions became the subject of a smart controversy; it was affirmed and denied that he was more than a delegate of the Chancellor. An act of parliament of the same reign set this question at rest (3 Geo. II, cap. 30). The Master of the Rolls became an independent judge, but there were a good many matters that he could not hear, and a case which had been before him might be taken before the Chancellor for a rehearing. In 1813 a Vice-Chancellor was created; in 1841 two more Vice-Chancellors, though the third Vice-Chancellorship was not made permanent until 1852. In 1851 the Lords Justices of Appeal were appointed. The final constitution of the court when it was abolished in 1875 was this: there were four judges of first instance, viz. the three Vice-Chancellors and the Master of the Rolls. From the decisions of any of these there lay an appeal to what had come to be called the Court of Appeal in Chancery. Of this there were three judges, viz. the Chancellor and the two Lords Justices[1]. From the Lord Chancellor and from the Court of Appeal in Chancery the appeal was to the House of Lords. I have already noticed how near the end of the seventeenth century the House of Lords asserted and established its right to entertain appeals from the Chancery[2]. Such an appeal, unlike a writ of error, might reopen all questions, as well questions of fact as questions of law. In the Chancery what has been called 'the one-judge' system prevailed. A suit was begun before the Master of the Rolls or one of the Vice-Chancellors and every step in the suit was taken before him; and he sat by himself. This

[1] The Chancellor by himself, or the two Lords Justices together, would be competent for all appeals; some matters might come before a single Lord Justice. The Lord Chancellor might sit as a judge of first instance, though it became rare for him to do so. F.W.M.

[2] See above, pp. 316—7.

was in sharp contrast to the procedure of the common law courts where a question of law was usually argued before and determined by all the judges of the court. Then again there was no jury in the Court of Chancery; it had not the power to summon a jury. Sometimes it would send an issue of fact to be tried in a court of common law by jury; this was at one time a pretty frequent practice, but it grew rarer as time went on, and at last very rare indeed. Usually the judge determined all questions both of fact and of law. It was also the practice before 1852 that if a question of mere common law (law as opposed to equity) arose in any suit— and such a question might well arise incidentally—to send a case for the opinion of one of the courts of common law. That practice was abolished by statute in 1852 (15 and 16 Vic., c. 86, sec. 61). It is well worth mention as showing how distinct law and equity had been. The Chancellor was not supposed to know common law, nor were the judges of the older courts supposed to know any equity. After 1852 the chancery judges could decide questions of pure common law if they arose during the progress of a suit.

The first step in the commencement of a suit (it was a *suit* in equity, an *action* at law) was the filing of a bill addressed to the Lord Chancellor; this stated the matters whereon the plaintiff relied and prayed the desired relief. Then followed the obtaining of a writ of subpoena. Now this differed very materially from those writs original at the common law of which I have lately spoken. It did not give the defendant any knowledge as to what was the complaint against him; it did not mention any cause of action. There was but this one simple and perfectly general form of writ instead of the many different forms of writ whereby actions were begun. This from the first made equity a flexible system; so to speak, it left room for growth; and indeed when contrasted with the procedure of the common law the procedure of equity was comparatively formless. I do not mean that chancery pleading did not require great technical skill—that would be quite untrue—but there were not a fixed number of definite forms between which a choice had to be made. In 1852 a certain change was made which rendered

needless the issue of a writ of subpoena; the defendant was
to be served with a printed copy of the bill, in which there
was an indorsement directing him to appear, but into this
I need not go. The generality of the writ from the earliest
time is the point to which I ask attention. Also it should be
noticed that until a comparatively recent time there was no
need that the plaintiff should specify the relief that he wanted;
a prayer just for such relief as the nature of the case might
require was sufficient, and the plaintiff could be given any
relief to which he was entitled by the facts alleged and proved.
This was afterwards changed, still it remained the practice to
the end to pray for general as well as special relief, and much
could be granted in answer to this general prayer. All this
was very different from what went on in the common law
courts where a plaintiff might fail fatally because he had sued
in Trespass when he ought to have sued in Case or in Trover.

One other point of procedure is of very great importance.
The chancery had for the most part borrowed its procedure
from the ecclesiastical courts. The defendant was required
to answer the matters alleged against him in the bill, and to
answer upon oath. The statements of the bill were turned into
an interrogative form, and the defendant had to answer the
questions thus put to him fully and in detail. Now here is a
great contrast to the common law procedure, and I have no
doubt that here was one cause for the great unpopularity of
the Court of Chancery at an early time; the defendant, it
was said, was forced to accuse himself. It is still the general
rule of our criminal procedure that the accused cannot be
questioned, and indeed cannot give evidence even if he wishes
to do so, though some exceptions have already been admitted
and the rule seems to be upon its last legs[1]. But until very
lately what is still true of criminal procedure was true also
of civil cases. Any person interested in the question was
incompetent to testify; this included of course the plaintiff
and the defendant, they could not give evidence. This rule
was abolished bit by bit by a series of statutes extending from

---

[1] In 1898 (Act to amend the Law of Evidence, 61 and 62 Vict., c. 36) every
person charged with an offence, and the wife or husband of the person so charged
was allowed to give evidence at every stage of the proceedings.

1833 to 1853. The first great alteration took place in 1843, when interested persons other than the parties, their husbands and wives, were rendered competent witnesses (6 and 7 Vic., c. 85). In 1851 (14 and 15 Vic., c. 99) the parties, except in criminal proceedings, were made competent and compellable to give evidence; a later act of 1853 (16 and 17 Vic., c. 83) dealt with the evidence of husbands and wives. It is very necessary to remember this in reading old cases—not so very old either, forty years old—we have become so very much accustomed to seeing parties as witnesses that we easily forget that this is only under modern statutes. Now the rule against interested witnesses prevailed in the chancery as well as elsewhere, and the parties could not give evidence in their own favour. Still the defendant had to answer the bill upon oath, and could thus be obliged to give evidence in the plaintiff's favour. This was not indeed regarded as a giving of evidence; it was a sworn answer (answer was the technical word) to the charges made against him in the bill. Well then in the chancery you could (to use the proper term) 'obtain discovery' from the plaintiff; you could, to use a slang phrase, 'scrape his conscience.' I believe that here we have one of the causes why the chancery came to be known as a court of conscience; the defendant could be obliged to reveal what he knew—to make sworn confession. Indeed at almost every point chancery procedure differed radically from common law procedure. Sometimes it seems as if the mere fact that one rule prevailed in the old courts was a sufficient reason why another should prevail in the new. Nor is this mere fancy. The chancery had been obliged to keep very clear of the province of the other courts; any open usurpation of their powers would have been resented, and if ever there was what might fairly have been called usurpation it was concealed by a difference of terminology. The two procedures were so distinct that a lawyer seldom knew much about both: this emphasized and exaggerated the differences between the two bodies of substantive rules, the body known as common law and that known as equity.

Equity in the course of the eighteenth century became a great body of rules supplementing the common law, enforcing certain obligations which common law did not enforce, giving certain remedies which the courts of common law did not and could not give. The main illustration of a purely equitable obligation is the duty of a trustee and person who holds property upon trust for another. Of any such obligation the courts of common law knew nothing.

Again, the Court of Chancery gave new remedies for common law rights, e.g. injunction and specific performance of contracts. You build a wall darkening my ancient lights: the Court of Common Law will give me money damages, the Court of Equity will enjoin you to pull the wall down. You contract to sell me land and refuse to carry out your contract: the Court of Common Law will give me money damages, the Court of Equity will command you to fulfil your contract, and in case you disobey will put you in prison.

It is easy to see how awkwardness would arise from such a dual system. In order to get complete justice I may have to go to two courts.

Mitigations of the evil were introduced in the nineteenth century. It was settled, for instance, that the Court of Common Law might grant injunction, and the Court of Equity might give damages. But at length it was determined to abolish the dual system. This was effected by the Judicature Act, which came into force in 1875 and amalgamated all the old courts, i.e. Chancery, King's Bench, Common Bench, Exchequer, Court of Admiralty, Court of Probate, Court of Divorce.

The Court of Admiralty had a long history of its own—from the close of the Middle Ages.

The Court of Probate and the Court of Divorce were created in 1857, and the old jurisdiction of the ecclesiastical courts over testamentary and matrimonial causes was transferred to them, together with some new powers, such as that of completely dissolving a marriage.

In place of these we have the High Court of Justice and the Court of Appeal.

The High Court of Justice is a court of first instance for all England with unrestricted competence in all civil actions, capable of administering and bound to administer both law and equity in every case.

Originally it had five divisions—Chancery; King's Bench; Common Bench; Exchequer; Probate, Divorce and Admiralty. But an Order in Council, 16 Dec. 1880, fused the Common Bench and Exchequer in the King's Bench Division. We have therefore now three divisions—Chancery; King's Bench; Probate, Divorce and Admiralty.

To each of these divisions certain business is specially assigned. Often a plaintiff has a choice; sometimes there is but one division to which he ought to go. But this distribution of business is an utterly different thing from the old distinction between courts of law and of equity. Any division can now deal thoroughly with every action; it can recognize all rights whether they be of the kind known as 'legal' or of the kind known as 'equitable'; it can give whatever relief English law (including 'equity') has for the litigants. They can no longer be bandied about from court to court. Also it is regarded as a mere matter of convenience which might be altered at any time by rules made by the judges. Its chief practical import is that in cases of a kind specially assigned to the Chancery Division there can be no trial by jury without leave of the judge. In other cases either of the parties can insist that any question of fact that there may be shall be tried by jury. But really trial by jury in civil cases is becoming less and less common. Very usually both parties are willing that all questions whether of law or of fact shall be disposed of by the judge.

From the High Court, in almost all cases, lies an appeal to the Court of Appeal and thence again to the House of Lords. All questions of law (and often of fact) may be reopened.— There is no jury in Court of Appeal or House of Lords.

The number of judges is small—twenty-nine for High Court and Court of Appeal together, including the Chancellor[1]. All (except the Chancellor) are appointed by the crown; paid by salaries charged on the Consolidated Fund; may not sit in the House of Commons; hold office during good behaviour, but can be removed by the sovereign on an address presented by both Houses.

---

[1] The number is now (1908) thirty-three.

From almost every judgment or order of the Court of Appeal appeal lies to the House of Lords.

We have seen how in the Middle Ages the House of Lords became a court capable of correcting errors of the lower courts of common law, and how in the seventeenth century it successfully asserted the right to hear appeals from the Chancery.

It is well, however, to note the discrepancy between law and actual practice. In the eighteenth century it became customary for the lords to leave their judicial business to be done by such only of their number as were distinguished lawyers. So late as 1844 some 'lay lords' were with difficulty restrained from voting on difficult questions of law arising out of the trial of Daniel O'Connell. We have come to regard it as a 'constitutional' rule that only the law lords are to sit, and now by a statute of 1876 there must be three law lords present—but the rule is only a 'constitutional' not a 'legal' rule—every lord who has a right to sit and vote when the House is about its legislative business, has also a right to sit and vote when the House is acting as a Court of Appeal, though this right is not exercised.

The act of 1876 introduced lords of a new kind, lords of appeal in ordinary—salaried and holding office during good behaviour, but dismissible on address presented by both Houses. Their dignity is not hereditary. At present there are three such lords—there will hereafter be four along with the Chancellor—and with some help from other law lords they do the judicial business of the House.

b. *The Criminal Courts.* Punishable offences fall into two classes—indictable and non-indictable.

A vast quantity of petty offences are by statute punishable upon summary conviction—this means trial without jury before two justices (or one police magistrate).

We have traced the history of this jurisdiction[1]. It grows rapidly during the eighteenth and nineteenth centuries. Statute after statute prescribed that this and that petty offence might be summarily punished by the justices. At last, in 1848, a statute was passed regulating the procedure.

[1] See above, pp. 232—6.

The courts in which this jurisdiction is exercised are often spoken of as Petty Sessions.

The punishments inflicted by these courts can seldom exceed three months imprisonment and for the most part consist of fines of varying amount. The province of this summary justice is variegated. At the one end of the scale there are what would commonly be called the smaller crimes —assaults, small thefts, malicious injuries to property; at the other, disobediences to statutory rules framed to secure some economic or social good, as, for instance, public health, education, the well-being of factory children, a revenue from excise and customs and the like: between these poles lie the breaches of good order, such as disorderly drunkenness and vagabondage in its various forms, the pettier kinds of dishonesty—adulteration, the use of false weights and measures, cruelty to animals, some electoral malpractices and other particulars not to be classified. How vital a part of our system this summary justice has become may best be shown by figures. In 1883 the number of persons convicted by juries did not amount to 12,000, while more than 80,000 sentences of imprisonment were passed by justices without any trial by jury[1].

Generally, but not always, there is an appeal to Quarter Sessions and questions of law can be brought before the High Court.

In some large towns this work is now done by paid justices of the peace known as police magistrates, or stipendiary magistrates. The system was gradually introduced into London by statutes beginning in 1792, and since 1835 a municipal borough may have a stipendiary magistrate if it chooses to ask for one and pay for one. These magistrates are appointed by the queen, and hold office like the other justices of the peace merely during good pleasure.

The graver offences (felonies and misdemeanours) can be punished on an indictment. Indictment (as already said) is still in form an accusation made by a grand jury. An indictment may be the first step in a prosecution. As a matter of fact grand jurors do not now proceed upon their own knowledge. Someone prefers a bill of indictment, and

[1] Of 61,463 persons tried for indictable offences in 1905, 49,138 were tried summarily. *Judicial Statistics, England and Wales*, Pt. I.

they, after hearing evidence for the prosecution, but not for the defence, decide whether there is sufficient cause for putting the accused upon his trial : if so, they find the bill a true bill, if not, they ignore it.   The grand jury must consist of not less than twelve, not more than twenty-three.

'Any person may present a bill to a grand jury, accusing any other person of any crime whatever'—this is the general rule to which as yet hardly any exception has been made[1].   Thus anyone may prefer a bill against one of the queen's ministers.

An indicted person will be tried—unless he cannot be found, in which case he may (theoretically) be outlawed.   An outlawry, however, would be a tedious process conducted by the sheriff; the outlaw, in case of felony or treason, would be in the same position as if he had been tried, and even in case of misdemeanour his goods would be forfeited.   Outlawry is not used now—indeed is not worth using.

There are other means besides indictment of bringing a man to trial for an indictable offence—but these are of limited applicability.

(1)   A verdict of a coroner's jury of manslaughter or murder is equivalent to indictment.

(2)   So too is a criminal information by Attorney-General or the Master of the Crown Office in case of misdemeanour.

A person thus accused by indictment, inquest, or information, is tried by a petty jury.

The criminal courts are (1) Quarter Sessions, (2) the High Court of Justice.

Quarter Sessions are not competent to try quite the worst offences, such as murder, treason, and some others—perjury, forgery, libel, etc.   They are constituted, as of old, by justices of the peace—who are the judges of law—while a jury decides questions of fact.   An elected chairman presides[2].

Since 1875 all the other courts which try indictable offences are theoretically branches of the High Court of Justice —this is a reform of a highly technical character.   Prisoners are tried either before the High Court in London, or at the Central Criminal Court, or before Commissioners of Assize, Oyer et Terminer, Gaol Delivery; but such Commissioners

---

[1] Mr G. J. Talbot, K.C., reminds me that a very considerable inroad on the old principle was made by the Vexatious Indictments Act of 1859.
[2] In Quarter Session boroughs the Court is a recorder.

(though they are not in all cases permanent judges of the High Court) hold the High Court of Justice in the various shire towns. To explain this would take us too far.

In these criminal cases there is properly speaking no appeal. But (1) occasionally the High Court will grant a new trial after a conviction for misdemeanour : it does not grant a new trial in case of felony, or after an acquittal for misdemeanour. (2) There is a procedure by writ of error whereby (with the Attorney-General's consent) cases can be taken to the Court of Appeal and thence to the House of Lords : but this procedure can only be used in very few cases —it can only be used when there is an ' error apparent on the record.' It is difficult to describe without going into details what errors are 'apparent on the record' and what not, but the main matter is this, that no error made by the judge in charging the jury will appear on the record, and a wrong or even perverse verdict cannot be thus corrected. In truth writs of error are extremely rare[1]. (3) On a conviction (but not an acquittal) the judge may, if he thinks fit, reserve a question of law (but not of fact) for a Court for Crown Cases Reserved which will consist of five or more judges of the High Court. Lastly the king can pardon a criminal, either absolutely or upon condition, and this power, wielded by the Home Secretary, is sometimes used as a means (a clumsier means there could not be) for practically nullifying an unsatisfactory verdict[2].

It should just be noticed that the House of Lords has other judicial functions besides that of acting as a Court of Appeal, functions which, were they exercised at all, would, I take it, even at the present day, be exercised by the whole body of the House, and not merely by the law lords. (1) As of old a peer accused of felony or of treason must be tried by his peers. He cannot even (it seems) elect to be tried by a jury as a commoner would be[3]. (2) There might be an impeach-

---

[1] By the Criminal Appeal Act, 7 Edw. VII, c. 23, § 20, writs of error were abolished.

[2] In 1907 (Criminal Appeal Act, 7 Edw. VII, c. 23) a Court of Criminal Appeal was established. A person convicted on indictment may appeal on any ground of appeal which involves a question of law alone. If a question of fact alone or of mixed law and fact is involved he must obtain the leave of the Court of Criminal Appeal or the certificate of the judge who tried him. The powers and authority of the C.C.R. are now vested in the Court of Criminal Appeal, and its old procedure by case stated may still be used in certain cases.

[3] See above, pp. 169—71.

ment—a procedure of which we have already spoken[1].   Since
the death of William III there have been but nine ; in the
nineteenth century but one, that of Lord Melville in 1805; the
most famous case of course is the trial of Warren Hastings
which dragged on its weary length at irregular intervals for
seven years.   It seems highly improbable that recourse will
again be had to this ancient weapon unless we have a time of
revolution before us.   If a statesman has really committed a
crime then he can be tried like any other criminal : if he has
been guilty of some misdoing that is not a crime, it seems far
better that it should go unpunished than that new law should
be invented for the occasion, and that by a tribunal of
politicians and partizans; for such misdoings disgrace and
loss of office are now-a-days sufficient punishments.   Lastly a
modern House of Commons will hardly be brought to admit
that in order to control the king's advisers it needs the aid of
the House of Peers.   However there the old weapon is—an
accusation by the commons of England at the bar of the
House of Lords.

We have said that indictment may be the first step in
prosecution ; but, as a matter of fact, this is not usual.
Generally before the accused is indicted, he is subjected to a
magisterial examination and is committed to prison to await
his trial or else he is bailed.   Magisterial examination, of
which we have already traced the historical beginnings in
statutes of Philip and Mary, has now become a preliminary
trial[2].   Both prosecutor and accused may produce witnesses—
have power to compel the attendance of witnesses.   The
accused is not questioned, is not bound to say anything,
receives 'the usual caution.'   The procedure is regulated by a
statute of 1848 (11 and 12 Vic., c. 42).   An application for a
writ of habeas corpus is a ready means for bringing before the
High Court any question as to the legality of an imprisonment.
The famous act of 1689 was made yet more efficient by an
act of 1816.

Of substantive criminal law we must say but a very few
words.   At the beginning of the last century the number of

---

[1] See above, pp. 317—8.
[2] See above, p. 232.

capital crimes was very large; it has been diminished by a series of acts beginning in 1827 and extending to 1861. In that year it was reduced to treason, murder, piracy with violence, and setting fire to dockyards and arsenals. As regards treason the basis of our law is still the statute of 1352 on which we have already commented[1]. The process of glossing its elastic language about 'imagining the king's death,' and 'levying war against the king,' went on during the eighteenth century. And in 1795 an act was passed, which is still in force, giving statutory authority to several of the interpretations which judges had put upon the old act. At the end of the eighteenth century there was a great outcry against what were called the constructive treasons—the doctrines whereby judges had stretched the words of the statute of Edward III beyond their natural meaning. Those doctrines, however, seem still to be law, though some of the offences which they declare to be treason can now be dealt with under a statute of 1848 as felonies subjecting the offender to a maximum punishment of penal servitude for life.

The old classification of indictable crimes as treasons, felonies and misdemeanours is still maintained and has some procedural consequences. A trial for felony differs in some respects from a trial for misdemeanour. But owing to the abolition of the punishment of death in all, except a very few, cases, it has lost most of its old meaning and is now little better than an absurdity—a misdemeanour is now often punished more severely than a felony. But of all these matters you will have to learn a great deal more when you come to study criminal law. I think, however, that a lecturer on constitutional law is bound to try to bring out the relation between what we call 'the government' and the administration of justice.

  c. Government and Justice. Notice: (1) The independence of the judges. Of the terms of their appointment we have already spoken: they hold office on good behaviour but are liable to be removed on an address presented by both Houses. The Lord Chancellor is a curious exception to the

---

[1] See above, pp. 226—8, 319.

general rule. Again, since their salaries are charged on the Consolidated Fund, their conduct does not come before parliament year by year. Further, for a judge to give an opinion as to a case which was to come before him judicially would now be considered distinctly wrong. Coke condemns the practice in the *Institutes*, though it had been common, and he himself had given opinions to the crown. We have also heard Coke assert the doctrine that the king, though he is the source of all justice, cannot act as a judge. Since the fall of the Star Chamber no king has sought to do this.

(2) The crown has no control over civil justice. The process of the superior courts runs in the queen's name—' Victoria Dei Gratia etc. commands the defendant to appear '—but a plaintiff obtains such a writ as a matter of right and the queen herself could not prevent its issue. So when the plaintiff has obtained judgment, execution follows as a matter of course; he obtains a writ commanding the sheriff, e.g., to sell the goods of the defendant to satisfy the debt. The writ runs in the queen's name—' Victoria D.G. etc. commands the sheriff to an execution '; but Victoria cannot stop the issue of the writ. The sheriff would be bound to execute it, even if he had a command to stop from the queen's own mouth or from a Secretary of State. And a sheriff who disobeyed the writ would be liable not merely to criminal proceedings (which the queen might stop) but to civil proceedings at the suit of the party damaged.

Again, the royal power of pardon does not extend to civil proceedings. If A owes B a debt, the queen has no power to forgive the debt. So if A assaults or libels B, the queen cannot forgive A, or stop B from suing A. This is so, even when the wrong is a crime as well as a tort (civil injury). Thus in the case of false imprisonment, which is both a wrong and a crime—the queen can pardon the crime, but not the tort. The importance of this can be seen if we suppose the person guilty of false imprisonment to be a Secretary of State, for the queen cannot prevent his being sued. Heavy damages have before now been recovered against a Secretary of State—the crown could not protect one of its most eminent servants.

(3) On the other hand legally the crown has a considerable control over criminal proceedings. (i) It can pardon any crime before or after conviction. This power is exercised for the king by a Secretary (Home) of State. A may commit a brutal murder, the king can pardon him and so stop any trial. An explanation of this wide legal power may be seen in this, that during the Middle Ages there were two methods of proceeding against a felon—the appeal brought by the person injured by the crime, for instance, the person whose goods were stolen, or the next kinsman of the murdered man—and the indictment, a royal procedure at the king's suit. The king by pardon might free a man from indictment, but not from appeal. But appeals of felony have long been disused and were abolished in 1819 (59 Geo. III, c. 44). Thus the king can completely pardon any crime. The one limit to the efficacy of a pardon is that imposed by the Act of Settlement (1700), namely, that a pardon cannot be pleaded to an impeachment. In Danby's case, 1678, it had been questioned whether an impeachment could be prevented by a pardon; it had been contended that an impeachment should be considered as analogous rather to an appeal of felony than to an indictment at the king's suit. We must, I think, take it as the result of that case that, as the law then stood, an impeachment could be prevented by a pardon—but the Act of Settlement altered the law. A pardon then cannot stop an impeachment—it cannot be pleaded as a bar to an impeachment—but there is nothing to prevent the king from pardoning after the impeached person has been convicted and sentenced, and some of the Scottish lords who were impeached for the rebellion of 1715 received pardons.

The legal power of pardon then is very extensive indeed. The check upon it is not legal but consists in this, that the king's secretary may have to answer in the House of Commons for the exercise that he makes of this power.

The king has no power to commute a sentence. When we hear of sentences being commuted, what really happens is that a conditional pardon is granted: a condemned murderer is pardoned on condition of his going into penal servitude. It is a nice question whether he might not insist on being hanged.

(ii) The king's Attorney-General has power to stop any criminal prosecution without pardon. All criminal proceedings (now that appeals are abolished) are in law at the suit of the king—*Rex* v. *A. B.* If the king's Attorney-General states that he will not prosecute (enters a *nolle prosequi*) then proceedings are at an end, though other proceedings may be begun. This power is sparingly exercised to stop prosecutions which are obviously vexatious. The safeguard consists in this, that the Attorney-General is expected to be a member of the House of Commons, and according to usage a member of the Ministry, though not of the Cabinet. Any use he may make of this power might thus be called in question : he could not use it for political purposes without the approval of the House of Commons.

On the whole, though the crown has thus by law a complete control over criminal justice, the prosecution of offenders has hitherto been left very much in the hands of the public. The king has had officers, 'law officers,' Attorney-General and Solicitor-General, charged with the duty of bringing the greatest offenders to justice, but it is in the power of any man to begin a criminal prosecution by presenting a bill of indictment to a grand jury, and as a matter of fact, until very lately, it has generally been left to those who have suffered by crime to bring an ordinary criminal to justice. This work is now falling more and more into the hands of a Director of Public Prosecutions, an officer first appointed in 1879, but we have as yet made no large inroad on the general principle, that any person may prefer a bill of indictment against any other person accusing him of any crime. The assent of the Director of Public Prosecutions has been required in certain libel cases by an act of 1881, but that, I think, is as yet the only exception. This principle is an important one : if I think that the Home Secretary has been guilty of any criminal offence, e.g. of bribery or extortion, I can present a bill to a grand jury—simply as a member of the public, and although the alleged crime has done me personally no harm—and it would be a very serious step for an Attorney-General to shelter his colleague by stopping a prosecution, unless it was obviously frivolous. A principle of law is not unimportant because we never hear of it; indeed we may say that the most efficient rules are those of which we hear least, they are so efficient that they are not broken. No person, even though he be a minister of the crown, can commit an indictable offence without running the risk of some member of the public beginning a prosecution against him.

(iii) And now as to proceedings against the king. Here we meet the maxim that 'the king can do no wrong.' This we may translate thus, 'English law does not provide any means whereby the king can be punished or compelled to make redress.' I think that you ought to distinguish quite clearly this proposition of English law from the doctrine of some writers on jurisprudence, that a subject can have no right against the sovereign, that the sovereign can have no legal duty to the subject. I confess that this doctrine seems to me merely a matter of words. Suppose, to take the simplest case, that an absolute monarch declares it his will that his subjects may sue him for any money they lend him, shall we say, is it convenient to say, that, while this law remains unaltered, it gives the subjects a right against their sovereign? I believe that in the United States a citizen can sue the sovereign people. But at any rate one should not, as Blackstone does, identify this speculative doctrine with our English rule. Our king is not in the jurist's sense sovereign, there is no reason in the nature of laws, rights, remedies, why our king should not be liable to be sued, and even to be prosecuted. As a matter of fact the Judicial Committee of the Privy Council has lately held that according to the law in force in Ceylon the crown can be sued (9 Ap., Cas. 571); it is said that kings of Scotland were sued by their subjects; it has been said that our Henry III was sued by his subjects, but this is extremely doubtful, and I do not think that our law has ever known any mode of suing the king, save the petition of right and some similar proceedings which are mere appeals to the king's conscience.

Proceedings on a petition of right are now regulated by an act of 1860 (23 and 24 Vic., c. 34). The petition is presented to the Secretary for the Home Department, and by him it is submitted to the queen. If she thinks fit she grants her fiat that right be done, and then there is in effect a lawsuit between the petitioner, or suppliant as he is called, and the Attorney-General. We may regard it as a constitutional usage, but certainly not as a rule of law, that the queen ought not to withhold her fiat. The scope of this remedy by petition of right seems in former times to have been limited to cases in which the king was in possession of some hereditament, or some specific chattel to which the suppliant claimed a title. The judgment, if favourable to the suppliant, was that the king's hands be removed and possession be restored to the suppliant—*quod manus domini regis amoveantur et possessio restituatur petenti, salvo jure domini regis.* In 1874, seemingly for the first time, the question was decided whether this remedy could be employed as a remedy for a breach of contract. In *Thomas* v. *Reg.* (L.R. 10, Q.B. 31) the suppliant asserted that he had invented a certain system of heavy artillery, and that in consideration of his placing his invention at the disposal of the royal ordnance department, the Secretary of State for War had promised that a reward should be given him, the amount of which was to be determined by the Board of Ordnance. He asserted further that this promise had been broken. The Attorney-General, for the sake of argument, admitted that the Secretary for War had authority to make this contract as agent for the queen; so the legal point was argued whether the petition of right could be used as a remedy for breach of contract. Blackburn delivered a very learned judgment holding that, despite the apparent narrowness of the old precedents, which dealt solely, or almost solely with demands for specific lands, the petition of right was a remedy applicable to breaches of contract. Judgment could be given in the suppliant's favour to the effect that he was entitled to a particular sum by way of damages. Now in these days breach of contract is likely to become the most common and useful field of the petition of right. The queen and her officers are no longer in the habit of seizing land upon all manner of pretences; there are few pretences available, escheat is very rare, but contracts with high officers of state, who contract on behalf of the queen, are by no means rare, and often involve large sums of money. On such contracts the subject, the other contractor, has a remedy. The court can only declare that he is entitled to such and such relief, e.g. to £10,000 damages; no execution can issue against the queen. Still it is obvious that a very strong moral pressure can thus be brought to bear on the queen's advisers. It would be a very unpopular thing were they to advise the queen to prevent any really arguable question coming before a court of law, but still more unpopular to deny the suppliant that redress to which he had been declared entitled by the judgment of a court.

(iv) We can hardly lay too much stress on the principle that though the king cannot be prosecuted or sued, his ministers can be both prosecuted and sued, even for what they do by the king's express command. We often say that in this country royal immunity is coupled with ministerial responsibility: but when we speak of ministerial responsibility we too often think merely of the so-called responsibility of ministers to parliament. Now that is an important matter; it is an important matter that our king cannot keep in office advisers who have not the confidence of the majority of the House of Commons—in the last resort this impossibility could be brought home to him by a refusal to grant supplies, or a refusal to renew the Army Act. But let us look at the matter a little more closely. Strictly speaking, ministers are not responsible to parliament; neither House, nor the two Houses together, has any legal power to dismiss one of the king's ministers. But in all strictness the ministers are responsible before the courts of law and before the ordinary courts of law, and they are there responsible even for the highest acts of state; for those acts of state they can be sued or prosecuted, and the High Court of Justice will have to decide whether they are legal or no. Law, especially modern statute law, has endowed them with many great powers, but the question whether they have overstepped those powers can be brought before a court of law, and the plea 'this is an official act, an act of state' will not serve them. A great deal of what we mean when we talk of English liberty lies in this.

G. *The Police System.*

We must speak briefly of the system by which order is maintained, and suspected persons are brought to justice, even though we can take but a superficial view of what has come to be a great department of law.

The decline and fall of sheriff's office has already been traced down to the seventeenth century[1]. During the whole of our period this process of decay is continued, the sheriff loses function after function. We know the High Sheriff now-a-days as a country gentleman, who (it may be much against his will) has been endowed for a single year with high rank, and burdened with a curious collection of disconnected duties, the scattered fragments of powers that once were vast. He receives the queen's judges on their circuits, he acts as a returning officer in parliamentary elections for his county, he executes civil judgments, and has to see to the hanging of those who are appointed to die. He has lost almost all other duties. Long ago the institution of justices of the peace gradually deprived him of all penal jurisdiction, and in 1887 the court in which he exercised that jurisdiction—the sheriff's tourn—was formally abolished (he had, I think, ceased to hold it for quite two centuries); in 1846 such civil jurisdiction as the old county court had was transferred to the so-called new county courts; in 1865 he was relieved of the custody of prisoners, except those appointed to die. I think that I have mentioned what now are his main duties. Civil execution is the most important of them, i.e. the seizing and selling of lands and goods in order to satisfy the judgments of civil courts. Such duties are performed for him by an under-sheriff, but the sheriff is answerable for the mistakes of his subordinates. Some fees and percentages are payable for this work, but the sheriff has no salary, and is always a loser by his office. He is still appointed by the king, who chooses the sheriffs (pricks the sheriffs) from a list settled at a meeting, at which some of the judges and some of the ministers are present, and under the old statutes, of which we have formerly spoken, he can hold office but for one year[2].

---

[1] See above, pp. 232—4.
[2] See Maitland, *Justice and Police.*

We have seen how in old times it was one of his main duties to pursue and arrest malefactors, and also how this work fell more and more under the control of the Justices of the Peace, the arrests being actually made by the parish or township constables under warrants of the justices. The old system of parish or township constables lingered on far into the nineteenth century. During the eighteenth century, this and that big town obtained a special act for the creation of a paid force of watchmen, and London began to get a force of paid constables in 1792, a force which gradually increased in size and was placed more and more directly under the control of the Home Secretary. But for England at large, the only constabulary was that old parish or township constabulary of the early history of which we have spoken. So late as 1842 an effort was made to put new life into the old system. By an act of 1842 (5 and 6 Vic., c. 109) the general principle was put upon the statute book that every able-bodied man resident within any parish, between the ages of twenty-five and fifty-five, rated to the poor rate at £4 or more, was liable to serve as constable for the parish ; but certain classes were specially exempted, and the list of exemptions was long. Lists of persons liable to serve were to be laid before the justices, and they were thereout to appoint so many constables for each parish as they should think fit; substitutes were allowed ; and a man who had served in person or by substitute was exempt from serving again until every other person liable to serve had taken his turn ; he was not bound, as a general rule, to act outside his parish ; he might earn certain fees, but otherwise was unpaid. Thirty years later, in 1872, the new police forces having been created in the meantime, a statute ordained that no parish constables should be appointed for the future, unless the justices at Quarter Sessions should think fit. The act of 1842 can still be put in force if need be; the able-bodied man, not specially exempted, is liable to be constable for his parish or to find a substitute ; but practically this statute is never put in force. Then there is another act of 1831 in force, which enables the justices, in case of any reasonable apprehension of riot or felony, to force men to serve as special constables. A Secretary of State has even greater powers—he can oblige the exempted classes to serve as special constables ; we must not regard this power as obsolete, on occasions it would doubtless be used.

But gradually a new police force was called into being. The Metropolitan force was created in 1829 by an act introduced by Sir Robert Peel. In 1839 the City of London force was created. In 1835 occasion was taken of the great reform of the municipal boroughs, to insist that every such borough should have a paid police force. In 1839 the counties were permitted, in 1856 they were compelled, to create paid county forces. Thus by the beginning of 1857 the whole of England had been brought within the new system.

There is no one police force for the whole of England, but rather a number of distinct local forces. Part of the expense (if the force is reported as efficient) is paid by the nation, part is paid by the counties and boroughs. The various forces are annually reviewed by royal inspectors, who report to the Home Secretary, and only, if their report is favourable, does the nation contribute to the expense. There are some very considerable differences between the various forces. Thus in the Metropolitan district there is very perfect centralization, no 'local authority' has anything to do with the system. A Commissioner and two Assistant Commissioners, holding office during the queen's good pleasure, regulate and command, appoint and dismiss the constables, but a supreme supervisory control is reserved to the Home Secretary.

But take a county force : the Home Secretary can make general rules as to the government, pay and clothing of constables ; but the justices in Quarter Sessions, with the Secretary's consent, determine the number of the force, and appoint and can dismiss the chief constable[1]. The chief constable has the general command of the force, subject to the lawful orders of the justices in Quarter Sessions, and he at his pleasure can dismiss any of his subordinates.

[1] Under the Local Government Act of 1888 (51 and 52 Vict., c. 41) the County police was placed under the general control of the Standing Joint Committee of Quarter Sessions and the County Council. The control over individual constables is however retained by the Quarter Sessions and even by individual justices. See Jenks, *An Outline of English Local Government*, pp. 179—81.

Let us then consider briefly the position of a police constable, he has peculiar duties and peculiar powers, and is subjected to a peculiar discipline. Take this last point first. The peculiar discipline to which he is subject is not nearly so stringent as that of military law; we have no court martial for the policeman. A county constable can be dismissed at the will of the chief constable. The chief constable, if he thinks him remiss or negligent in his duties, can reduce him in rank, or fine him one week's pay. On a summary conviction for neglect or violation of duty, he can be fined £10 or condemned to a month's hard labour; but on the whole he has been left much to the general law, and if guilty of any offence against it, can be treated like another offender.

Now looking at his powers and duties, we find that he has in the first place powers and duties concerning the arrest of offenders. It is his duty to execute warrants for arrest issued by the justices, and in so doing he is protected. Unless there is some flagrant illegality apparent in the warrant he is bound to obey it, and safe in obeying it. But then without any warrant he may, in certain cases, arrest suspected persons. What those cases are, you will have to learn some day when you study criminal procedure. You will find that in this respect every person, every member of the public has certain powers, but that a constable has greater powers. The distinction between felonies and misdemeanours here plays a large part. For example, there are a number of misdemeanours for which a man may be arrested without warrant, if he is caught in the act by a constable, while a person not a constable would not be safe in arresting him. You must remember this, that it does not follow that because I have committed a crime therefore I can be arrested without warrant either by anyone, or by a constable. If I have committed murder anyone may arrest me without a justice's warrant, if I am drunk and disorderly a constable may arrest me without a warrant; but if my crime is perjury or bribery, it will be unlawful to arrest me without warrant. He who does so, whether he be a constable or no, does an unlawful act, does me a wrong; and he does a dangerous act, for I may lawfully resist him, his attack is unlawful and my resistance is lawful.

Now it is in these peculiar powers of arrest, and in the duty to exercise them, that lies the chief difference between the constable and the private man—he may lawfully make arrests which the private man cannot make lawfully. But statutes have gradually been heaping other powers and duties upon police constables, e.g. empowering them to enter public-houses to detect violation of the Licensing Acts. If it occurs to parliament that steam thrashing-machines are dangerous things that ought to be fenced, then it passes an act saying that 'any constable may at any time enter on any premises on which he has reasonable cause to believe that a thrashing-machine is being worked contrary to the provisions of this act, for the purpose of inspecting such machines.' Examples might be indefinitely multiplied.

We may pass to a few words about the provision that our law makes for the maintenance of order in extreme cases, and we may start with this, that it is the common law right and duty of all persons, whether constables or no, to keep the peace, and according to their power to disperse, and if necessary arrest, those who break it. From an early time the common law was supplemented by statutes, statutes of the Tudor reigns which made it felony for twelve persons or more to continue together riotously for an hour after they had been ordered to disperse by a justice of the peace. These statutes were temporary, and expired at the death of Elizabeth; in 1714 they were replaced by the famous Riot Act (1 Geo. I, st. 2, c. 5), which is still in force. It makes it felony for twelve rioters to continue together for an hour after the reading of a proclamation by a magistrate ordering them to disperse. It then requires the magistrates to seize and apprehend all persons so continuing together, and it provides that if any of them happen to be killed, maimed or hurt in dispersing, seizing or apprehending them, the magistrates and those who act under their orders shall be held guiltless. This act then gives to the magistrate and those who act under his orders special protection in case rioters remain together for an hour after the reading of the proclamation (commonly but erroneously called the reading of the Riot Act), but it does not say, nor does it mean, that force, if necessary armed force, may not be used until then.

As regards the employment of soldiers for the purpose of putting down riots, we have no special statutes, it is left to the common law and to the Riot Act. The general principle seems to be this, that the soldier, like every other citizen, is bound to do what in him lies to preserve the peace, and if necessary to suppress unlawful force. 'The military subjects of the king,' said Tindal, C. J., 'like his civil subjects, not only may but are bound to do their utmost of their own authority to prevent the perpetration of outrage, to put down riot and tumult, and to preserve the lives and property of the people[1].' Our law does not even say that military officers must not act without the command of the civil magistrates ; it is prudent not to do so; but in a great emergency a military officer is entitled, nay bound, to suppress unlawful force by force. A person may be indicted for not doing what he could to suppress a riot : magistrates can be, and have been, indicted for neglect of their duty of preserving the peace.

In connexion with this subject a few last words should be said of martial law. We have already seen that under the provisions of the Army Act which is called into force year by year we have among us a large number of persons who are living under a special law. This law is to be found partly in the Army Act itself, partly in articles which can be made from time to time by the queen in exercise of powers given by that act ; and it seems probable that, apart from the act, the queen has some, not very well defined, power of making Articles of War for any troops that she is lawfully keeping. This special law for soldiers is administered by tribunals known as courts martial, and is frequently spoken of as martial law ; but in the act it is called 'military law,' and it seems very desirable that we should adopt that term rather than the other. For at times the belief has prevailed that there is some other body of rules known as martial law, some body of rules that the king or his officers could in cases of emergency bring into force by way of proclamation and apply to persons who are not soldiers and who therefore are not subject to that special code of military law of which we have just been speaking.

[1] Charge to the Grand Jury of Bristol in 1832. *State Trials*, N.S., vol. III, p. 5. See also Dicey, *Law of the Constitution*, 6th edn., Note VI, pp. 460—2.

Now it may, I believe, be pretty confidently denied that there is any such body of rules. In the first place you will remember that the Petition of Right, after reciting that commissions under the great seal had of late been issued to certain persons to proceed ' according to the justice of martial law,' declared that such commissions were illegal, and prayed that no commissions of the like nature should issue in the future. Then again our annual acts legalizing the army declare that ' no man can be forejudged of life or limb or subjected to any punishment within this realm by martial law in time of peace.' The words ' in time of peace,' which were not in the earliest Mutiny Acts, certainly seem to suggest that in time of war men may be punished by martial law. But we can find a sufficient meaning for them by saying that in time of war *soldiers* may be punished by martial law; that is to say, apart from the Army Acts the crown would have some power in time of war of maintaining discipline in its troops by regulations similar to those of our present military code. It must be confessed however that a parliament—an Irish parliament after the rebellion of 1798—has spoken of martial law as though it were some known body of rules that might in times of great emergency be applied to persons who are not soldiers—that there can be such a thing as a proclamation of martial law. If however we ask, where are we to find this body of rules? what is martial law? we shall hardly get an answer to our question. When considered the matter seems to resolve itself into this—it is the right and duty of every subject to aid in the suppression of unlawful force; it is more especially the right and duty of magistrates and peace officers of all degrees to do so. The common law defines, though from the nature of the case not very exactly, the occasions on which force may be repelled by force, and the amount of force that can be used ; and in great emergencies it may become necessary that even death should be inflicted, and deliberately inflicted, for the suppression of disorder. A proclamation of martial law can have no other legal effect than this—it is a proclamation by the king, or by persons holding office under the king, announcing that a state of things exists in which it has become necessary that force shall be repelled and suppressed by force; it is a warning that the part of our common law which sanctions such repulsion and suppression, has come into play. A court of law, an ordinary court of law, may afterwards have to judge whether really there was a legal justification for these high-handed acts which were done in the name of peace and order; but doubtless it might, and in appropriate circumstances would, take into consideration the fact that those who suffered by such acts had had full notice that they were about to be done. But suppose one of the rebels captured, there is no court that can *try* him save the ordinary criminal courts of the country. In particular circumstances it might perhaps become necessary to shoot him in order that he might not escape or be rescued, and undoubtedly in such a case, if time permitted, it would be well for those who had him in custody to satisfy themselves that he was a rebel. But any inquiry that they might make about this could not have the effect of a trial before a competent tribunal; it would be a wise precaution, but not a judicial proceeding having force as such. He would not really be tried and condemned by any body of rules known as martial law—we know not where to look for any such body of rules—if lawfully put to death, he would be put to death under a rule of our common law, which justifies the suppression by force of unlawful force. As to the whole of this matter see the opinion of Edwin James and Fitzjames Stephen in the case of Governor Eyre (Forsyth, *Cases and Opinions on Constitutional Law*, p. 551)[1].

H. *Social Affairs and Local Government.*

There is a vast domain of our public law at which we ought to take a brief glance; we ought to know at least that it exists, that its boundaries are being extended year by year, and that it is constantly becoming of greater importance. The title which I have chosen, 'Social Affairs and Local Government,' is, I fear, not very satisfactory, but you will gain a notion of what I mean as time goes on.

[1] See also Dicey, *Law of the Constitution*, 6th edn., Note XII, pp. 502—19.

And first a few words as to the organs of local government. We have already said a little about the history of the justices of the peace. Instituted in the reign of Edward III, their functions have from that time to the present become ever more and more miscellaneous. At the present day their Quarter Sessions are a court for the trial of criminal cases; two justices can form a court of summary jurisdiction to punish any of those thousands of petty offences which can now be punished without trial by jury; they hold the preliminary examination of persons accused of indictable crimes, they can commit the accused to prison or bail him for trial. We have seen also how they have a control over the constabulary, and how they are bound to keep the peace and suppress riots. These functions of theirs fall under the headings—The Administration of Justice and The Police System. But they acquired other functions of the most miscellaneous character. Already in Elizabeth's day, Lambard, who wrote an excellent book on the office of the justices, expressed a fear that they were being overladen with work, that their backs would be broken by these 'not loads, but stacks of statutes[1].' His 'stacks of statutes' would seem very small to our eyes. During the last two centuries parliament has continued to heap work upon the justices. The Commission of the Peace had become the one vigorous and healthy local institution. The old communal courts of the hundred and the shire had fallen into utter decay; they had become at best courts for petty debts held by the under-sheriff. A non-representative assembly of freeholders was an antiquated institution quite unsuited to the wants of the time, and no attempt was made to introduce representative government into local affairs. The municipal corporations again were becoming utterly unfit for any governmental work. With the view of getting favourable parliaments the Tudor and Stuart kings had spoilt the constitution of the boroughs; by their charters they had vested the local government along with the parliamentary franchise in small oligarchical bodies—mayor, aldermen and councillors—who had the right to fill up the

---

[1] Lambard, *Eirenarcha*, Book I, c. 7.

vacancies in their own bodies. These bodies became hopelessly corrupt; some belonged to the crown and returned to parliament the nominees of the ministry; others belonged to great landowners, Whig or Tory, and returned their candidates; others sold themselves from time to time in open market. The justices, on the other hand, were competent members of the ruling class, and nothing was more natural than that a parliament of landowners (and remember that in the eighteenth century members of the House of Commons had to be landowners) should trust them with all manner of duties and governmental powers; some to be exercised in their Quarter Sessions, others to be exercised by a justice or two justices out of Quarter Sessions.

A word about the appointment and qualification of justices. They were and still are appointed by the king (in practice by the Lord Chancellor), who usually acts upon the recommendation of the Lord Lieutenant of the county. They held and still hold office merely during good pleasure. Gradually, however, we have come to expect that a justice will not be removed save for some misconduct. If George III dismisses justices on political grounds, we look back upon this as an unconstitutional act. From of old it has been required that justices should have landed property in the county; in 1439 (18 Hen. VI, c. 11) the minimum value was fixed at £20 per annum. This in the eighteenth century had become very low, and in 1732 was raised to £100 per annum, because as the act (5 Geo. II, c. 18) says 'the constituting of persons of mean estate to be justices of the peace may be highly prejudicial to the public welfare.' Not until 1875 (38 and 39 Vic., c. 54) was this relaxed, and then only to the extent that the *occupation* of a dwelling house assessed at £100 per annum should also be a qualification[1]. In the Middle Ages the justices (like members of parliament) were not unpaid, they were entitled to four shillings a day at Quarter Sessions; but this sum having become small, like the wages of the members, was not demanded, and practically the office became honorary: in 1855 the payment was abolished.

[1] The property qualification of county justices has now been removed by the Justices of the Peace Act of 1906, 6 Ed. VII, c. 16.

Thus the local government of England came to be government by country gentlemen. But observe that there was nothing feudal or patrimonial in it. The country gentleman did not do justice or govern the county in his own name or as a landlord; he was one of the justices assigned to keep the king's peace; the justices were expected to obey orders sent to them in the king's name by the Secretary of State, and the courts of law, which were never very friendly to the summary jurisdiction, were very ready to entertain complaints as to any irregularities committed by the justices.

By degrees the justices of the county became very numerous. In the Middle Ages the demand is that there shall be some six or eight in every shire. In Elizabeth's day this was already far exceeded. At the present time there are, I believe, more than eight hundred in Lancashire, and even Rutland has twenty-five, but about one-half of these are but titular justices; they have not taken the requisite oaths and so become acting magistrates.

Much about their governmental powers we shall not be able to say; still we shall return to them hereafter. Meanwhile we have to notice that in the days of the great Reform Bill a new current of legislation sets in which has gone on flowing ever since—the creation of representative local institutions.

The first great achievement that we will notice is the municipal reform of 1835. All the boroughs in England, except London and a few small places which we need hardly notice, were reformed and were reconstituted according to a uniform model, and power was given to Queen in Council to give the same constitution to other towns as yet unincorporated. We have now about two hundred and fifty incorporated boroughs—'municipal boroughs.' I have before this asked you to notice that the parliamentary and municipal organizations have now fallen quite apart. In the later Middle Ages, after the representation of towns in parliament had begun, every borough returned its two burgesses to parliament; you will remember what the sheriff's instructions were, he was to send two burgesses from every borough. In course of time indeed this became the test whether a town was a borough or no; those towns were boroughs which sent members to parliament. Now-a-days the two things are quite distinct; a borough fully constituted for municipal purposes may send no members to parliament; and again members, who are known as borough members, may be returned by a district which is not under the government of any municipal corporation. We distinguish then between the 'parliamentary borough' and the 'municipal borough.' The former is but an electoral district; it is of the latter that we have to speak. Now the municipal constitution is briefly this. The corporation consists of the mayor, aldermen and burgesses; thus the proper style of the corporation of Cambridge is 'the mayor, aldermen and burgesses of Cambridge.' In case of a city (generally a municipal borough which is also a bishop's see) we speak of citizens instead of burgesses. Every person who occupies a house or other building for which he or she pays rates is entitled to be a burgess, and becomes so on having his name put upon the burgess roll. Women may be burgesses. The main right of the burgess is to vote in the election of the town council. The government of the borough is vested in the mayor, aldermen and councillors. The number of councillors is fixed upon the incorporation of the borough. The councillors are elected by the burgesses and hold office for three years; since 1872 the election has been by ballot. The number of aldermen is one-third of the number of councillors. They are elected by the council, and hold office for six years. The mayor is elected by the council, and holds office for a year. This governing body, consisting of mayor, aldermen and councillors, has very considerable powers; it manages the property of the corporation (which in some cases is considerable); it must maintain a proper police force; it must see to the paving and lighting of the town, and so forth; and it enjoys some legislative power, for it may make such bye-laws as seem meet for the good rule and government of the borough and for the prevention and suppression of nuisances. A fine of £5 is the heaviest punishment that it can denounce for the breach of its bye-laws. Power, however, is given to the Queen in Council to disallow any bye-law in whole or in part.

The extent to which the borough is exempted out of the jurisdiction of the county justices varies somewhat from borough to borough; some boroughs have a separate commission of the peace and a court of Quarter Sessions held by an officer known as the Recorder. Others have a commission of the peace but no court of Quarter Sessions. Others again have no separate commission of the peace, but in every borough the mayor is *ex officio* a justice and remains so for one year after he has ceased to be mayor. Then again some boroughs maintain their own police, while others are ' policed by the county.' Into these variations we must not go. What we are concerned to observe is the growth of democratic, representative government. Under the act of 1835 in all the great towns of England, except London, there was erected a body consisting of persons elected by the ratepayers and by the representatives of the ratepayers which was armed with many governmental powers.

Another great step was made one year earlier, in 1834. The administration of the poor law, which down to this time had been carried on partly by parochial officers, overseers of the poor, partly by the justices of the peace, had for a long time past become very unwise and extravagant. A thorough reform was necessary if England was not to be made bankrupt by its paupers. The country was mapped out into districts, consisting of a number of parishes, which were to be united for many purposes of the poor law : of these ' Poor Law Unions ' there are now about 650. Each Union has a Board of Guardians of the Poor. The justices of the peace resident in the Union are *ex officio* guardians, and besides there are a number of cted guardians. They are elected by the ratepayers according to a scheme of plural voting ; a voter may have from one to six votes according to his property qualification : property rated at less than £50 gives one vote, property rated at £100 two votes, and so on up to six[1]. The constitution therefore of a Board of Guardians is not so democratic as that

---

[1] By the Local Government Act of 1894 (56 and 57 Vict., c. 73, sec. 20) *ex officio* guardians were abolished, and each elector was entitled to give one vote and no more for each of any number of persons not exceeding the number to be elected.

of a municipal corporation. The Board has very large powers in administering relief of the poor within the district of the union. But I want you to observe that every reform of local government has hitherto meant an addition to the powers of the central government. A large control over the whole poor law system was in 1834 given to certain Poor Law Commissioners; they had wide powers of checking the actions of the guardians, and even of legislating; they could issue rules, orders and regulations as to all matters relating to the relief of the poor. It was expected that the commission would only be necessary for a time, but it was renewed and renewed again and developed first into the permanent Poor Law Board, and then into the existing Local Government Board, which as we have seen is but nominally a board, for its President, a cabinet minister, can and habitually does exercise all its most multifarious powers. These two processes have been going on side by side; on the one hand we get new organs of local government, on the other hand we get new organs of central government, the organs of central government being some or other of those high officers of state who according to constitutional usage form the cabinet.

The elaborate system of sanitary law which exists in our own days we can carry back only to 1848. The main stages in its development are marked by acts of 1848, 1858 and 1875; it is now represented chiefly by a great statutory code, the Public Health Act of 1875. Throughout England local sanitary authorities have been created. In some places they are the municipal corporations, in others again the guardians of the poor, in others again they are Boards of Health elected by the ratepayers for the purpose. The central authority is the Local Government Board. Then we have the great educational system introduced by the act of 1870. It is worked by school boards and school attendance committees elected by the ratepayers and controlled by the Education Department, a board consisting of cabinet ministers whose powers are exercised chiefly by the Lord President of the Council, and the Vice-President of the Department[1]. Then

[1] The Education Act of 1902 abolished the School Boards and entrusted Education to the 'local Education authority,' i.e. the Council of a County or

again we have elected Highway Boards and elected Burial Boards[1].

As a general result we have a pretty wild confusion not easily to be described in elementary lectures. For one thing we may note that each of these systems of which we have spoken had a geography of its own. In 1834 when the new Poor Law was passed and the country was mapped out into Poor Law Unions the fatal mistake was committed of disregarding the old territorial divisions, the county boundary. Often a Union extends into two or more counties. We have now one geography for civil justice, another for criminal justice, another for police, another for poor law, another for sanitary law and so forth.

Perhaps we have lived to see the beginning of the end of this disorder. I refer to the great Local Government Act of 1888 (51 and 52 Vic., cap. 41). The result of this has been to add to the number of the organs of local government by creating County Councils. The constitution of the boroughs has been taken as a model for the counties. Each county has a Council elected by the ratepayers, and to this Council have been transferred all or most of those powers of the justices of the peace that we can in any sense call administrative. The government of the county police force is given to the Council and the court of Quarter Sessions jointly, and is to be exercised by a joint committee. On the whole we may say that it is intended that the Council shall be the governmental assembly of the shire, while the justices both in and out of Quarter Sessions keep all those powers which can be called judicial. I need not, however, warn you again that these are not the words of the statute book; it goes into

County borough, and also (but only for elementary purposes) to the Council of a borough with more than 10,000 and to the Council of an Urban District with more than 20,000 inhabitants.

[1] The Local Government Act of 1894 created Parish Councils and District Councils. The Parish Council is empowered to adopt the Burial Acts, and where the area of a Burial Board is identical with that of a rural parish, the Burial Board will merge in the Council. The District Councils inherit the functions formerly discharged by the Highway and Sanitary Boards. An Urban District Council may also by consent or by Order in Council become the sole burial authority within its district.

minute details, and in England it would often be hard enough to say on general principles whether a power was to be deemed administrative or deemed judicial. But this (it is expected) is by no means all that the County Councils will in course of time do for us. Listen to this clause (sec. 10): it is an extremely good instance of the way in which parliament legislates for us now-a-days, 'It shall be lawful for the Local Government Board to make from time to time a provisional order for transferring to County Councils any such powers, duties, and liabilities of H.M. Privy Council, a Secretary of State, the Board of Trade, the Local Government Board, or the Education Department, or any other government department, as are conferred by or in pursuance of any statute and appear to relate to matters arising within the county and to be of an administrative character.' Such a provisional order will require an act of parliament to put it in force. The hope, I suppose, is that some measure of decentralization will become possible, a hope which can only be fulfilled if the County Councils prove themselves capable and honest. For the moment, however, this act only adds to the existing confusion; we have one new 'local authority,' but the older local authorities still exist: the guardians of the poor, the school boards, the sanitary authorities, the highway boards and so forth. It may be that some day a lecturer will be able to state in simple and general terms the chief outlines of our local government; but that time has not come yet. That between the township or parish and the shire there should be some intermediate district is an idea which crops up again and again in all our legislation and schemes of legislation: it is, we may say, the old idea of the hundred. Some day it may become possible for a lecturer to say England is divided into shires, the shire into hundreds, the hundred into townships; each township, each hundred, each shire has one and only one organ of local government appropriate to itself: but that time seems far distant.

This you will say (and I will not contradict you) is a very poor lecture, but I do think it worth our while just to see that there are these vast tracts of modern constitutional law, though we can do little more than barely state their existence. I say of constitutional law, for it seems to me impossible so to define constitutional law that it shall not include the constitution of every organ of government whether it be central or local, whether it be sovereign or subordinate. It must deal not only with the king, the parliament, the privy council, but also with the justices of the peace, the guardians of the poor, the Boards of Health, the School Boards, and again with the constitution of the Treasury, of the Education Department, of the Courts of Law. Naturally it is with the more exalted parts of the subject that we are chiefly concerned; they are the more intelligible and the more elementary: but we must not take a part for the whole or suppose that matters are unimportant because we have not yet had time to explore them thoroughly. Year by year the subordinate government of England is becoming more and more important. The new movement set in with the Reform Bill of 1832: it has gone far already and assuredly it will go farther. We are becoming a much governed nation, governed by all manner of councils and boards and officers, central and local, high and low, exercising the powers which have been committed to them by modern statutes.

It may, I think, be instructive in this context to say a few words as to the active duties which our law lays upon the generality of Englishmen, instructive because I think that their extent is often neglected by students of jurisprudence. By active duties I mean duties which consist in the doing of something, and not in the leaving of something undone. Now the great mass of our ordinary criminal law is made up of prohibitions, of the imposition of negative duties; its language is 'Thou shalt do no murder,' 'Thou shalt not steal,' and so forth. It does not say 'Thou shalt succour thy neighbour in distress'—I commit no crime by not pulling my neighbour out of the water, though thereby I could save his life without wetting my feet. So again our law as to civil injuries, 'Torts' as we call them, consists of prohibitions—I am not to assault or slander or defraud my neighbour, trespass on his land or damage his goods. Generally it takes some contract or some special relationship or some office to create an active duty. In the greater number of cases in which anyone is bound actively to do something, he is bound because he has agreed to be bound. In some other cases he is bound because of a standing relationship between him and the person for whose benefit he must act, such a relationship, for instance, as that of father and child. So again there are duties arising out of the holding of a public office. But there are cases in which active duties are cast by law upon a person irrespective of any contract, of any special relationship, or of any public office.

First there is a comprehensive duty or class of duties consisting in the payment of taxes and rates. Think for one moment how great a group of duties we have here. If your imagination fails you, flatter yourselves that you are young and happy. The generality of Englishmen have to pay first the taxes which parliament directly imposes, and then the rates which it empowers local boards and so forth to raise. During the nineteenth century the system of local taxation has rapidly grown ; one can be taxed by many different bodies, for many different purposes, for the relief of the poor (that is an old matter), the maintenance of a police force, the improvement of sanitary conditions, for public education, for the erection of town halls, public baths, public libraries, and very many other purposes. But it is not on duties that can be discharged by the payment of money that I would at this moment dwell. There are other active duties : some ancient, some modern, some imposed by the common law, some by statute.

From military duties we are practically free. We have already traced the history of this matter. There is no power to force men to serve as soldiers except under the ballot clauses of the Militia Act which are suspended year by year. There is a prerogative power of pressing sea-faring men for the royal navy, but this has not been exercised for a long time past. The Englishman is still by statute bound to serve as a parish constable or find a substitute if he is between twenty-five and fifty-five years of age, and is rated to the poor rate at £4 or more, and does not belong to certain special exempted classes : the power of forcing men to serve as parish constables might be put in force if the justices at Quarter Sessions thought fit, but as a matter of fact owing to the creation of the professional police forces it is found unnecessary. But one may be forced to serve as a special constable if occasion requires for a particular occasion, and the (Home) Secretary can order that even the exempted classes may be sworn in. These matters are regulated by a statute of 1831.

Then again the common law requires everyone to give active aid to a parish constable in the apprehension of offenders: within recent years a man has been indicted and convicted for not aiding the police when they called for his assistance (*R*. v. *Sherlock*, I. C.C.R., 20)[1]. We may probably lay down a more general rule and say that it is the legal duty of every subject to do all that in him lies to suppress a riot, and that one might be indicted for neglecting this duty. Again in general one is not under any legal duty to reveal a crime that has come to one's knowledge—so long as there is no aiding and abetting, no harbouring of the criminal, so long as one simply does nothing one is guilty of no offence. But it is laid down in the books that high treason is an exception: if I know that high treason has been committed and do not within a reasonable time give information thereof, I commit the crime known as misprision of treason and may be imprisoned for life.

Then look at jury service: of old this was incumbent on the freeholders. Under modern acts it is cast upon those who occupy houses of a certain value or have interests in land of a certain value; speaking generally the person liable to jury service must be a householder rated at £20 or have an interest in land worth £10 or £20 according to the nature of the interest; but all burgesses are bound to serve on the jury at the Quarter Sessions for the borough.

Then again one of the public duties that our law enforces is the duty of giving evidence. A person can be compelled to testify in criminal proceedings and in civil actions and also in many proceedings of many kinds which are inquisitorial rather than judicial. For instance one may be summoned as a witness not only before the ordinary law courts, before ecclesiastical courts, courts martial, but also before either

---

[1] Sherlock was fined five pounds by the Quarter Sessions at Lewes 2 July 1865. The Court for Crown Cases Reserved affirmed the conviction.

House or a committee of either House of Parliament ; or again to take examples of what is becoming common, before the persons appointed by the Board of Trade to investigate the causes of a railway accident, or by the Home Office to investigate the causes of an explosion. If one thus summoned will not attend, he can generally be punished for a contempt in a very summary way. In civil actions a witness need not appear unless a reasonable sum is tendered to him for his expenses, but no such tender is necessary in a criminal proceeding.

Then again it is a very general, if somewhat antiquated, doctrine of the common law that a person is bound to serve the crown in all manner of offices. We see this chiefly applied in the cases of sheriffs : a person who has sufficient land in the county to qualify him for the office (a very vaguely defined amount) is bound to serve if he be appointed and can be fined if he refuses. This is, I think, but an instance of a general principle which exists, though it is seldom put in force. Could a man be punished for refusing to become Chancellor of the Exchequer or Secretary of State ? It is absurd to consider such a case, but I imagine that he could. But in particular cases statute has stepped in to enforce this doctrine: a qualified person elected to serve as an officer of a municipal corporation can be fined for not accepting the office, thus one elected to the office of mayor may be fined £100.

But now glance for one moment at the active duties which modern statutes have cast upon Englishmen in general. An Englishman has a child born to him ; within 42 days (says an act of 1874: 37 and 38 Vic., c. 88) he must register its birth at the proper office, if he does not he can be fined. Within three months, says an act of 1867 (30 and 31 Vic., c. 84), he must have that child vaccinated, otherwise he can be fined. Then, says an act of 1876 (39 and 40 Vic., c. 79), 'it shall be the duty of the parent of every child to cause such child to receive elementary instruction in reading, writing and arithmetic, and if such parent fail to perform such duty he shall be liable to such orders and penalties as are provided by this act.'

I take these instances of active duties not to be discharged by the payment of money, because it seems a stronger thing to command a man to do something than to prohibit him from doing something. I want to warn you against taking too narrow a view of the field of modern English law, and in so doing I may be of some service to you in your study of general jurisprudence. Do not imagine that English law is exhausted by those departments of it that you can study here—the law of crimes, the law of property, torts, and contracts, and that part of constitutional law which is concerned with king and parliament. No, there are vast departments of law lying outside these boundaries; some of them belong to constitutional law, others perhaps may be called administrative law; for the most part they are statutory and of recent creation, the work of the last fifty years: but their importance is very great. For turn from active duties to negative duties, duties which consist in forbearance only and see how we are surrounded by prohibitions: the list of offences for which one may be punished summarily by justices of the peace is enormous. Then if one takes up any business or employment, if one begins to build a house or thinks to open a lodging-house, or keep a trading-ship or be a baker or a chimney-sweep, straightway one comes in contact with a mass of statutory rules, and if one keeps all the rules expressly laid down by statute still one is not safe, one may come across the rules, orders and regulations which some Secretary of State or central board has been empowered to make or the bye-laws of a municipal borough or of a local sanitary authority. And then you may have to consider whether you are bound by those rules or that bye-law: for remember that the Secretary of State or the municipal corporation has no unlimited power of legislation ; it is but a delegated power, and if the rule or bye-law is not authorized by the power you may break it with impunity, and the judges will say that it is invalid. If you take up a modern volume of the reports of the Queen's Bench division, you will find that about half the cases reported have to do with rules of administrative law; I mean with such matters as local rating, the powers of local boards, the granting of licenses for various trades and professions, the Public Health Acts, the Education Acts and so forth. Now these matters you cannot study here ; they are not elementary, they are regulated by volumes upon volumes of statutes. Only do not neglect their existence in your general conception of what English law is. If you do, you will frame a false and antiquated notion of our constitution. That constitution does not now-a-days consist merely of king and parliament, privy council, courts of law and some purely executive officers, such as sheriffs, obeying their commands. We have changed all that since the first Reform Act. The governmental powers, the subordinate legislative powers of the great officers, the Secretaries of State, the Treasury, the Board of Trade, the Local Government Board, and again of the Justices in Quarter Sessions, the Municipal Corporations, the Guardians of the Poor, School Boards, Boards of Health and so forth ; these have become of the greatest importance, and to leave them out of the picture is to make the picture a partial one-sided obsolete sketch.

J. *The Church.*

We ought to devote a little time to the history and the present position of the church, looking of course at its legal side. We speak of the church as being established by law. This phrase has a correct meaning, still it may suggest a wrong view of history, it may suggest that at some time or another the state chose out one among a number of competing faiths, established it and endowed it. Of course this is not true : the church has a continuous history from a time when there were no competing faiths, when the idea of choosing a religion would have seemed a profane absurdity. The medieval theory of the relation between church and state seems this, that they are independent organisms consisting nevertheless of the same units. Every man, we may say, is a member of both—except indeed the Jews, whose position in England before they were banished by Edward I, was altogether anomalous ; they were not members of the church, but then they were hardly in any sense members of the state—they lived under special laws of their own protected by the kings, to whom they were financially useful, against the very general hatred of the people ; they are an exception which illustrates the rule.   But though consisting of the same units, church and state were not one ; each had its laws, its legislature, its courts of justice, its proper sphere of action.   Their relation to each other constituted a standing denial of that theory of sovereignty which has become orthodox in our own times.   And it is well for students of jurisprudence to observe that such a denial does not mean anarchy.   From time to time there were disputes between the two powers ; it is sufficient to recall the quarrel between Henry II and Archbishop Thomas ; and through several centuries there is a constant border warfare going on between the temporal and the ecclesiastical courts as to the exact limits of their several domains—but normally the relation between the two powers is that of peace.

I spoke of the two organisms as consisting of the same units ; this, however, is not quite true, and only perhaps because it was not quite true was a prolonged continuance of the situation possible.   The English church was but a branch or member of the church catholic and Roman.   King and parliament might be supreme over the English state, but the provincial convocations were not supreme over the English church ; they acknowledged the authority of the Pope and general councils of the church.   To a large extent the English church claimed and enjoyed what we may describe as Home Rule, and about certain matters a quarrel with the See of Rome was maintained from century to century ; in particular the Pope was constantly striving to interfere with ecclesiastical appointments in a way which English churchmen as well as English statesmen warmly resented.   For full a hundred and fifty years before Henry VIII broke with the Pope the English parliament had been legislating at intervals against what it regarded as the usurpations of the See of Rome—interferences with rights of patronage, and all this without a suspicion of heresy or schism.

Let us look briefly at the relation between the two organisms as it was at the end of the Middle Ages.   In the first place we notice that the rulers of the church have a place in the supreme body of the state.   The bishops and abbots constitute a good half of the House of Lords.   Their position in that body is, however, somewhat ambiguous; if they are prelates of the church they are also tenants in chief of the crown, and many abbots have shaken off the duty of going to parliament by the plea that they are not tenants in chief. Then again the inferior clergy are summoned to parliament by the *praemunientes* clause; they do not attend, but they tax themselves in the two principal convocations, usually making a grant proportioned to that which the commons have made in parliament. In these convocations they enjoy a certain power of legislating as to spiritual matters, of making canons, and these canons can be enforced against the laity as well as the clergy in the ecclesiastical courts.

These ecclesiastical courts have a manifold jurisdiction. In the first place there is the discipline of the clergy, and this is a wide field—for not only is the purely ecclesiastical discipline within their cognizance, but we have to remember that they are the only courts which can punish an ordained clerk for felonies, murder, robbery and so forth—to treason, it is said, the benefit of clergy does not extend. Then again they have large fields of jurisdiction which do not seem to us very spiritual—all testamentary causes including the distribution of the goods and chattels of intestates are within their sphere, and again all matrimonial causes. Not content with this they have long sought to obtain a general jurisdiction in matters of contract; in this they have failed, the temporal courts have warned them off that field, but in consequence have been obliged to enlarge their own notions of the law of contract. Besides all this these courts exercise a very wide jurisdiction over what we may call immorality—forms of social misdoing to which the lay courts pay no heed, such as fornication and incest. In the medieval law of the lay courts we find no such headings as slander and libel; these matters are dealt with as sins by the tribunals of the church.

The means which these courts have of enforcing their decrees are in theory spiritual. Over the clergy they have large powers, being able, for example, to degrade a clerk from his orders. Over the laity they exercise authority by means of penance and excommunication. In the last resort, however, the secular arm gives them its aid. If the excommunicated person remained contumacious for forty days, this was signified to the king's court, which then issued a writ commanding the sheriff to imprison him until he should satisfy the claims of the church.   Excommunication itself had very serious legal consequences, for the excommunicated person was unable to bring any action even in the temporal courts: it was a sufficient answer to him to say 'You are excommunicated.' In this respect his condition was no better than that of an outlaw.

The existence of these ecclesiastical courts involved the existence of a considerable class of ecclesiastical lawyers, canon lawyers, familiar with the jurisprudence of those courts —a jurisprudence which was distinct from that of the lay tribunals.   It included the body of canon law published in the *Decretum* of Gratian and its successive supplements, the more recent canons of general councils and the canons published by the English archbishops in their provincial convocations.   Canon law was taught in the universities ; the common law was not ; its students acquired their learning in London, in the Inns of Court, societies of common lawyers which had gradually grown up and provided more or less efficiently for legal education[1].

As to heresy, for a long time we had practically no law, for we had no heretics.   Probably it was considered that a heretic, if one occurred, would be properly burned ; in 1222 we hear of a deacon being burned—he had turned Jew for the love of a Jewess[2].   But practical law against heresy we had none and needed none until the rise of Lollardy at the end of the fourteenth century.   In 1382 we have our first statute against heresy—heretics are to be kept in prison until they satisfy the claims of the church.   An act of 1401 went further —a heretic who refused to abjure was to be publicly burned. In 1414 a further act was passed ; it made heresy an indictable offence—but the accused person is to be tried in the bishop's court.   It was under this statute that most of the executions of the fifteenth and sixteenth centuries took place.

[1] See Maitland, *Roman Canon Law in the Church of England.*
[2] See Maitland's witty article, *The Deacon and the Jewess or Apostacy at Common Law*, in the *Law Quarterly Review* for April 1886.

We have also to think of the church as being endowed : but this phrase again must not lead us astray—there never was any body of men called the church which held property. First and last the church has never been a corporation, holding or capable of holding property. 'Church property,' if we allow ourselves that phrase, consisted and consists of the various properties of a large number of different persons : e.g. the Bishop of Ely as such had land, the Abbey of S. Albans as such had land, the parson of Trumpington as such had land—a very large part indeed of the land in this country was held by religious houses, though from Edward I's day onward the statutes of mortmain had prevented the increase of that quantity ; but any land belonging to these religious houses belonged to them and to them only. And as with land so with tithe—in a remote age the general Christian duty of devoting a tenth of one's property to the service of God had become defined as a burden on land ; this piece of land owed tithe to the parson of the parish church, or its tithe had been appropriated to some monastery, but there was no body, no corporation, entitled to the aggregate of the tithes of England.

As regards ecclesiastical patronage we have to remember that at an early time this had come to be regarded as property. The right to appoint the parson of a church, or rather to present him to the bishop for appointment, the advowson of the church (*advocatio ecclesiae*) was freely bought and sold ; often it belonged to the lord of the manor, but it might be held separately from the manor. Over this form of property, for such we must call it, the royal courts claimed jurisdiction, and already in the twelfth century they had made good their point. Thus the line between the spiritual and the ecclesiastical jurisdictions was not drawn just where we might expect to find it. The provision of a parson for the parish we might regard as a religious trust. On the other hand we might think that testamentary causes had little about them that was spiritual ; but in the Middle Ages all litigation regarding wills was matter for the courts Christian, while over the right to present to ecclesiastical benefices the king's courts exercised an exclusive jurisdiction.

The great series of events which we know as the Protestant

Reformation altered profoundly the relation between church and state; still it would be easy for us to exaggerate the extent of the definite legal changes. The old legal organization of the church with its bishops, its convocations and its courts, was for the most part preserved, though it was brought under subjection to king and parliament. We have only time to deal very briefly with subsequent history. I will make an attempt to sum it up under several headings.

In the first place we have the subjection of the church to the state. In 1534 Henry VIII, having wrung from the clergy a reluctant promise that they would never make any new canons without the royal assent, this rule was confirmed by statute (25 Hen. VIII, c. 19). In the next year it was declared by statute that the king our sovereign lord, his heirs and successors, kings of this realm, shall be taken, accepted, and reputed the only supreme head in earth of the Church of England (26 Hen. VIII, c. 1). These acts, I think we may say, mark the moment at which the church was brought under the state. At the same time the Church of England was severed from the Church of Rome. It had already been made unlawful to pay to the Pope the annates and first-fruits which he had been accustomed to receive, appeals to Rome from the ecclesiastical courts were forbidden, the English chapters were to elect as bishops the persons recommended by the king; if they would not do so, the king was to have power to make the appointment by letters patent. The smaller monasteries were dissolved in 1536, the greater in 1539: the effect that these measures had upon the constitution of the House of Lords we have already observed[1]. The result of these measures at a time when the doctrines of the church were being called in question was that in 1539 parliament found itself legislating about religious doctrine—legislating this time in a conservative sense. The Act of the Six Articles made it highly penal to deny certain articles of the faith, in particular the real presence. Henry did not intend that his political measures should lend to any renunciation of catholic dogma or catholic ritual. But under Edward VI the reforming party got the upper hand. In 1548 we have the

---

[1] See above, p. 238.

first Act of Uniformity—a certain book of common prayer
has been drawn up and is to be used in all churches. Any
parson who does not use the book or uses any other form of
liturgy is to be punished in a lay court—on a third conviction
he is even to be imprisoned for life. All other books of
prayer are to be destroyed ; all images in churches are to be
destroyèd ; bishops are to be appointed simply by letters
patent. Religion has now become an affair of statute. But
the power which makes statutes can unmake them, as the
reformers learned under Mary. The legislation of the two
last reigns was swept away, and the reformers were heretics
who could be proceeded against under the Lancastrian statutes.
That legislation was restored under Elizabeth, except that
she did not assume, nor have her successors assumed, the title
'Head of the Church,' and except also that bishops were to be
made under the act of Henry VIII which preserved the form
of capitular election, not under that of Edward VI which
abolished it. The reign begins with Acts of Supremacy and
Uniformity. The former is called an 'Act to restore to the
Crown the ancient jurisdiction over the Estate, Ecclesiastical
and Spiritual,' and among other things it founded the Court of
High Commission and imposed on all ecclesiastics an oath ac-
knowledging the queen's supremacy and renouncing all foreign
authority. The Act of Uniformity imposed a book of common
prayer—to use any other liturgy was made highly penal.
In substance this act (1559) has fixed the law from that time
to the present day. The present prayer book, however, is one
ordained by a statute of 1662—by the Act of Uniformity passed
after the Restoration—a revised edition of the earlier prayer
book. You should therefore understand that a clergyman of
the Church of England in reading the service is performing a
statutory duty ; it would be penal for him to read any other
service. In 1871 it was thought desirable to alter the lectionary
of the service ; the new lectionary was introduced by statute,
34 and 35 Vic., c. 37 ; it is a schedule to an act of parliament.
It is under a special proviso of the act of 1662 that the
University sermon can be preached without any reading of
the book of common prayer. I say this in order to illustrate
the fact that the church services are statutory. There is no

body which has any power to alter them except king and parliament.

This leads us to speak of the convocations. In Henry VIII's day parliament began to pass statutes confirming the grants of the clergy—the clerical subsidies[1]; but the convocations continued to grant their taxes until the Civil War and began the practice again after the Restoration. In 1662 the practice was quietly abandoned, and parliament began to tax the clergy directly. During the reign of William III a quarrel broke out between the upper and lower houses of the convocation of Canterbury. The two houses took different views of ecclesiastical policy, but the exact point of dispute was the question whether the archbishop could prorogue the houses. The quarrel went on until 1717 when the two houses were at issue over the Bangorian controversy. They were never again summoned for business until 1861—though between 1717 and 1741 formal meetings were held. Thus for a whole century and more the Church of England (if any such body can be said to exist) had no representative assembly, no power of making rules for itself. The convocations cannot now meet without the royal summons; they can make no canons without the royal assent. And further, since the days of James I it has been the doctrine of the law courts that canons even when they have received the royal assent are not binding on the laity. Thus the legal powers of the convocations are extremely limited; they may discuss and deliberate, but they can do very little.

In reviewing the present position of the church it would be necessary to chronicle that the bishops, or rather some of the bishops, sit in the House of Lords, that no clergyman can sit in the House of Commons, but that there is nothing to prevent him from voting in a parliamentary election. As regards the disqualification from being elected, we have to remember that the clergy are still summoned to parliament under the *praemunientes* clause. In 1801 Horne Tooke, a clerk in holy orders, having been elected, search was made for precedents; they were considered obscure and inconclusive; the House refused to declare that Tooke was incapable of sitting but passed an act (41 Geo. III, c. 63) disqualifying

[1] See p. 240.

clergymen for the future. At the same time it disqualified the clergy of the Scottish Church. In 1829 when Roman Catholic laymen were admitted by the Catholic Emancipation Act (10 Geo. IV, c. 7), the Roman Catholic clergy were expressly excluded. These disqualifications are somewhat anomalous, for there is nothing to prevent the minister of a congregation of Protestant nonconformists from sitting. In 1870 (33 and 34 Vic., c. 91) persons in the orders of the established church were enabled to solemnly renounce their orders and so free themselves from disability.

We turn to another portion of our subject. From the time of the Reformation onwards a long attempt is made to force people to accept the doctrines and worship of the church as defined by statute. The gradual abandonment of this attempt constitutes the history of toleration. Starting in Elizabeth's day we find one set of statutes directed against the Catholics, and another against the Puritans. In 1562 the oath of supremacy, which declared the queen to be the only supreme governor of this realm, as well in all spiritual or ecclesiastical causes as temporal, was required of members of the House of Commons: it might be tendered to all persons who had taken a degree in the University, to all schoolmasters, to all barristers, and to various other classes; to refuse it once was to incur the penalty of *praemunire*, to refuse it a second time was high treason. In 1571 new treasons were invented: thus to call the queen a heretic was treasonable, to publish any papal bull was treasonable, to reconcile any of the queen's subjects to the See of Rome was treasonable. In 1580 to celebrate mass was made a crime, and to hear mass. Everyone was to attend the church service upon pain of forfeiting £20 per month. In 1585 the Jesuits and seminary priests were expelled: for them to remain here was high treason. As to the Puritans, the rigorous action of the Court of High Commission served to expel them from ecclesiastical benefices, and in 1593 there is direct legislation against them; persons who frequent irregular conventicles are to be imprisoned until they conform. Under James there was fresh legislation against popish recusants, that is to say against all persons who refused to take an oath declaring that James was lawfully king, and that the Pope had no power to depose him. Such a person was deprived of most of his civil rights, and was almost in the position of an outlaw. The legislation against Catholics was infinitely more severe than the legislation against Puritans. Still the latter had many grievances in that they were excluded from ecclesiastical benefices by the Act of Uniformity, which was rigorously enforced. Then, as we know, for a time Puritanism gained the upper hand, and again at the Restoration it fell. The time then comes for laws against the Protestant nonconformists. All the while, however, the terrible code against the Catholics remains unrepealed, though under Charles II and James II breaches of it are connived at by the king, and sanctioned by virtue of the dispensing power. The great acts of Charles II's reign which we have to notice are five in number. The Corporation Act, 1661, obliged all holders of office in municipal corporations to receive the sacrament according to the rites of the Church of England. The Conventicle Act of 1664 made it penal for any person to attend a conventicle, that is, any meeting for religious worship at which five persons were present besides the household. Three months imprisonment was the punishment for the first offence. The Five Mile Act of 1665 made it unlawful for any nonconformist minister to come within five miles of a corporate town upon pain of a £40 fine, and no nonconformist might teach in any public or private school. The Test Act of 1673 imposed the sacramental test on all persons holding any office of trust. The Parliamentary Test Act of 1678, directed against Roman Catholics, imposed the declaration against transubstantiation upon members of both Houses, and thus for the first time excluded Roman Catholic peers from the House of Lords.

Meanwhile the old law as to the burning of heretics had passed away. Its history is particularly complicated and confused, owing to the rapid fluctuations of religious opinion during the age of the Reformation. On Elizabeth's accession the old statutes of Henry IV and Henry V were repealed; some Anabaptists were burnt in her reign, and an Arian was burnt in 1612 under James I; but it is doubtful whether these proceedings were lawful, and in particular Coke gave his opinion against the execution of 1612[1]. The question was whether the common law—the old statutes being repealed— had any procedure against heresy. This case of 1612 is believed to be the last case of anyone being executed as a heretic. In 1677, under Charles II, an act was passed (29 Car. II, c. 9) which abolishes whatever power there may have been of burning heretics. We must carefully distinguish the trial of a man for heresy, from his trial under any of the statutes directed against Papists; the Catholics who for one reason and another suffered death under Elizabeth and James, were tried by the ordinary legal tribunals for offences created by statute.

Immediately after the Revolution the Penal Code against Protestant dissenters was very much mitigated by the Toleration Act of 1688 (1 Will. and Mary, c. 18). There was a slight reaction in favour of persecution under Anne, which produced the act against occasional conformity of 1711 (10 Anne, c. 6), and the Schism Act of 1713 (13 Anne, c. 7), but the latter was repealed five years afterwards in 1718 (5 Geo. I, c. 4). In 1728, just after the accession of George II, a practice was begun of passing every year an act indemnifying those holders of offices who had failed to take the requisite oath or to receive the sacrament—a curious English practice. It amounts to saying 'We will not repeal the law, but it is understood that nobody need keep it, for every year an act will be passed indemnifying those who have not kept it.'

I can best illustrate this part of the subject by referring to Blackstone's *Commentaries*, vol. IV, p. 53. Blackstone, writing in the middle of the eighteenth century, still treats nonconformity as being in a general way an offence—he calls it the crime of nonconformity—and then describes how of late exceptions have been made to a general rule. For instance it is still, as a general rule, a statutory offence under acts of Elizabeth and James not to go to church; he who absents himself forfeits one shilling for every Sunday, and £20 if he absents himself for a month, but an exception has been made in favour of dissenters by the Toleration Act; they may absent themselves

[1] Coke, *Reports*, XII, 93. See on the whole question, Stephen, *History of Criminal Law*, vol. II, pp. 437—69.

provided (1) they be neither Papists nor Unitarians, (2) they have taken the oaths of allegiance and supremacy and subscribed the declaration against transubstantiation, (3) they repair to some registered place of worship. So again dissenting preachers are exempted from the acts which prohibit them from teaching if they have subscribed the Thirty-nine Articles except three and part of a fourth, that is, except those which relate to the government of the church and infant baptism; they are also exempted by a still newer act of 1779, if instead of subscribing the Articles they will profess themselves Christians and Protestants. Toleration of any profession of faith, other than that of the established church, is still the exception, not the rule. However, by this time the more orthodox sects of Protestant nonconformists enjoyed liberty of worship and teaching. The annual Indemnity Acts enabled them to hold office, and there had never, I think, been anything which excluded them from voting in parliamentary elections, or sitting in either House of Parliament.

With the Catholics it was still far otherwise. Catholicism had been treated not as a mere religious error, but as a grave political danger, and considering the risings of 1715 and 1745, we are perhaps not justified in condemning that treatment. How enormously severe the law was, will appear from the following passage from Blackstone[1]: 'Papists may be divided into three classes—persons professing popery, popish recusants convict, and popish priests. 1. Persons professing the popish religion, besides the former penalties for not frequenting their parish church, are disabled from taking lands either by descent or purchase after eighteen years of age, until they renounce their errors; they must, at the age of twenty-one, register their estates before acquired, and all future conveyances and wills relating to them; they are incapable of presenting to any advowson [or granting to any other person any avoidance of the same], they may not keep or teach any school, under pain of perpetual imprisonment; and if they willingly say or hear mass they forfeit the one 200, the other 100 marks, and each shall suffer a year's imprisonment. Thus much for persons,

[1] *Commentaries*, vol. IV, p. 55.

who, from the misfortune of family prejudices or otherwise, have conceived an unhappy attachment to the Romish Church from their infancy, and publicly profess its errors. But if any evi industry is used to rivet these errors upon them, if any person sends another abroad to be educated in the popish religion, o to reside in any religious house abroad for that purpose, o contributes to their maintenance when there, both the sender the sent and the contributor are disabled to sue in law o equity, to be executor or administrator to any person, to take any legacy or deed of gift, and to bear any office in the realm and shall forfeit all their goods and chattels and likewise al their real estate for life. And where these errors are also aggravated by apostasy or perversion, where a person is reconciled to the See of Rome, or procures others to be reconciled, the offence amounts to high treason. 2. Popish recusants, convicted in a court of law of not attending the service of the Church of England, are subject to the following disabilities, penalties and forfeitures, over and above those before mentioned. They are considered as persons excom municated; they can hold no office or employment; the must not keep arms in their houses, but the same may be seized by the justices of the peace; they must not come within ten miles of London on pain of £100, they can bring no action at law or suit in equity; they are not permitted to travel above five miles from home unless by licence, upo pain of forfeiting all their goods; and they may not come to court under pain of £100....A married woman, when recusant shall forfeit two-thirds of her dower or jointure, may not be executrix or administratrix to her husband, nor have any part of his goods, and during the coverture may be kept i prison, unless her husband redeems her at the rate of £10 month or the third part of all his lands. And lastly, as *feme-covert*, a recusant may be imprisoned; so all others mus within three months after conviction, either submit an renounce their errors, or if required so to do by four justice: must abjure and renounce the realm, and if they do not depar or if they return without the king's licence, they shall be guilt of felony, and suffer death as felons without benefit of clergy ...But (3) the remaining species or degree, viz. popish priest.

are in a still more dangerous condition, for by 11 and 12
Will. III, c. 4, popish bishops or priests celebrating mass or
exercising any part of their functions in England, except in
the houses of ambassadors, are liable to perpetual imprisonment.   And by 27 Eliz., c. 2, any popish priest born in the
dominions of the crown of England, who shall come hither
from beyond sea (unless driven by stress of weather and
tarrying only a reasonable time), or shall be in England
three days without conforming and taking the oaths, is guilty
of high treason ; and all persons harbouring him are guilty of
felony without the benefit of clergy.'

Such were the laws against Catholics in the middle of the
eighteenth century, the result of a series of statutes extending
from the reign of Elizabeth to that of George II.   It is
customary for writers to become eloquent over the acts against
Protestant nonconformists—the Corporation Act, Five Mile
Act, Conventicle Act—they were trifles when compared with
the rigorous laws against the Catholics.   In Blackstone's day
they were seldom enforced, still they existed.

From both Houses of Parliament Catholics were excluded
by the declaration against transubstantiation.

The greater part of this rigorous code was repealed in
1791 (31 Geo. III, c. 32), or rather all Catholics were exempted
from it upon taking an oath, which it was possible for them to
take, renouncing the Pope's civil power and the doctrines that
faith need not be kept with heretics, and that princes excommunicated by the Pope might be deposed or murdered.   A
Catholic who would take this oath was freed from civil
disabilities, might worship in his own way in a registered place
(which, however, might not have a steeple nor a bell), and
could not be prosecuted for not attending church.   He might
hold most offices in consequence of the annual indemnity acts.
He was still, however, unable to sit in either House of Parliament, because the declaration against transubstantiation was
required of all members.   In strictness of law he could not
vote in a parliamentary election, because all electors on
presenting themselves to vote might be required to take an
oath declaring that the Pope had no spiritual jurisdiction
within this realm ; an oath which, though not so stringent as

the declaration against transubstantiation, a conscientious Catholic could hardly take. As a matter of fact, however, I suspect that Catholics did vote, for the oath seems to have seldom been tendered; owing to the lengthy process of swearing the electors, an act of 1794 said that this form was only to be gone through if a candidate required it, and then at his own expense. Catholic emancipation came in the year 1829 (10 Geo. IV, c. 7). Catholics might vote in parliamentary elections, sit in either House and hold any lay office (except those of Regent, Chancellor and Lord-Lieutenant of Ireland) on taking an oath of allegiance in which there was nothing offensive to their religious principles. The subsequent history of parliamentary oaths we have already traced. However, as I have explained, the act of 1791 did not repeal the old laws against Catholics, it merely exempted from their terms those who would take a certain oath. It was not until 1846 (9 and 10 Vic., c. 59) that those laws were swept off the statute book.

Meanwhile full relief had been given to the Protestant nonconformists. The provisions of the Test and Corporation Acts, which were obnoxious to them, were repealed in 1828 (9 Geo. IV, c. 17), though the work was not quite accomplished until 1868 (31 and 32 Vic., c. 72): between those two dates a declaration was required of office-holders to the effect that they would not use their offices to injure or weaken the Church of England.

The legislation by which disabilities have been first imposed and then removed is very complicated, but at the present moment we may, I think, say that religious liberty and religious equality is complete. These, however, are vague phrases, and we ought to render them more precise. I mean by them:

(1) That the profession of any religion or of no religion is no offence. This, however, is subject to what I shall hereafter have to say as to blasphemy, and as to the procedure of the ecclesiastical courts against heresy.

(2) That every form of public worship is permitted There are provisions as to the registration of places of worship but these, however, hardly derogate from our proposition There are also some statutory clauses still in force against

Jesuits and other religious orders of the Church of Rome, requiring that they should obtain license to reside in the United Kingdom: whether they are practically applied I cannot say; they are laid down in the Emancipation Act of 1829, and are severer than most people imagine: it is a misdemeanour for a Jesuit to come into this realm without the license of a Secretary of State.

(3) The profession of any form of religious belief is not a condition for the existence or exercise of civil rights. On the whole, I think we may say that this certainly is so, though it is only of quite late years that a person having no religious belief has been able to give testimony before a court of justice. Until 1869 a person who would not take an oath could not give evidence unless he was a Quaker—Quakers had been relieved much earlier. In that year he was enabled to substitute a declaration for an oath, on satisfying the judge that an oath would have no binding effect on his conscience. We may note also a disability in respect of advowsons. Roman Catholics cannot present to livings in the established church. This, however, is hardly an exception, though it is curious, for it seems that an atheist may present.

(4) The profession of any form of religious belief is not a condition for the existence or exercise of political rights. This is generally true—but there are some exceptions and one very notable exception. The king forfeits the crown by becoming or marrying a Papist, also the king is directed to join in communion with the established church. It seems however that the king would not commit a forfeiture by becoming a Baptist.

Again it would appear that there are two offices which cannot be held by Roman Catholics, those namely of Lord Chancellor of England, and Lord-Lieutenant of Ireland. A statute of 1867 (30 and 31 Vic., c. 75) provides that the Lord Chancellor of Ireland may be Catholic.

It remains to qualify our proposition as to the lawfulness of publishing opinions about religion:

(a) Blasphemy is a common law misdemeanour. Until lately there was good ground for contending that any publication was blasphemous if it denied the main doctrines of

Christianity; this had been so laid down in several cases
But it seems now that we must qualify it by adding tha
publications intended in good faith to propagate opinions o
religious subjects, which the person who publishes then
regards as true, are not blasphemous, if they are expressed in
decent terms.

(*b*) Under Stat. 9 and 10 Will. III, c. 32 (1698) it is a
misdemeanour for anyone who has been a Christian to deny
by writing, printing, teaching or advised speaking the Christian
religion to be true or the Old and New Testaments to be o
divine authority. The offender upon a first conviction i
disabled from holding any office or employment, ecclesiastical
civil or military. On a second conviction he must be im
prisoned for three years. This act had long lain dormant or
the statute book, when an attempt, which failed, was made
to put it in force against Bradlaugh[1].

(*c*) Mere heresy or schism is in all probability to this day
an ecclesiastical offence, i.e. an offence to be punished in the
ecclesiastical courts, and for it a man might be imprisoned for
six months. I am not aware, however, that a layman has been
prosecuted for heresy for the last century and more. Bu
this leads us to another part of our subject: the history o
the ecclesiastical courts.

The act of the Long Parliament which abolished the
Court of High Commission used such very general words that
if it did not abolish the old ecclesiastical courts, it practically
deprived them of their power. At the Restoration, however
by statute passed in 1661 (13 Car. II, c. 12) it was 'explained
that this was not the desired result : the Court of High Com
mission was not to be re-established, but the old ecclesiastica
jurisdiction of the old ecclesiastical courts was to be exercisec
as of old. A few years afterwards (1677, 29 Car. II, c. 9) the
act was passed which forbad the burning of heretics, but i
was expressly added that nothing contained in that act shoulc
take away the jurisdiction of the ecclesiastical judges in case
of atheism, blasphemy, heresy or schism, or any other damnable
doctrines and opinions, but that they may punish the same

---

[1] *Reg.* v. *Bradlaugh and others*, 1883. Cox, *Criminal Law Cases*, vol. xv
p. 218 ff.

by excommunication, deprivation, degradation and other ecclesiastical censures.

There were then ecclesiastical courts—an elaborate structure of them, with appeal lying from the lower to the higher; an archdeacon's court for each archdeaconry, a bishop's court for each diocese, an archbishop's court for either province: the final appeal being under an act of Henry VIII (1534, 25 Hen. VIII, c. 19) to the king who was to appoint judges, 'judges delegate,' to hear the cause. This structure of courts with little modification still exists. The greatest change is that in 1832 (2 and 3 Will. IV, c. 92) the jurisdiction of these judges delegate was transferred to the Judicial Committee of the Privy Council, which was formed in the next year. Under an act of 1876 the ultimate appeal is to the Judicial Committee, certain bishops sitting as assessors of the judges according to a rota of seniority settled in 1876.

But though these ecclesiastical courts still exist their power has very much declined. Let us take up the main heads of the old ecclesiastical jurisdiction one by one.

(i) In the first place they were, as so often said, the courts for matrimonial and testamentary causes: and this brought them a great deal of work. Every will of personal property had to be proved in the bishop's or archbishop's court. This large jurisdiction they retained until 1857, when it was taken from them and vested in two new courts: a Court for Divorce and Matrimonial Causes, and a Court of Probate, courts which in 1875 were merged in the High Court of Justice.

(ii) They had, and theoretically still have, a considerable penal jurisdiction over laity as well as clergy, in what we may call cases of irreligion and immorality: a power to correct the sinner *pro salute animae* by means of penance and excommunication. Throughout the Middle Ages this power was largely used, and it has never been expressly taken away. However it has long been considered an established principle that the ecclesiastical courts were not to try men for temporal offences, i.e. offences punishable in the king's courts. Now many of the graver offences, with which the ecclesiastical courts once dealt, have by statute been made crimes punishable by the lay tribunals, and in this way the courts Christian

have lost jurisdiction. Bigamy is a case in point; until 16c
it was only an offence against ecclesiastical law : in that yea
it was made a felony. Until 1855 the ecclesiastical court
punished defamatory words : in that year their jurisdiction i
this matter was abolished by a statute (18 and 19 Vic., c. 41
which speaks of it as grievous and oppressive, so I suppos
that it was exercised. But they probably still have power i
cases of adultery and of fornication. To these must be adde
heresy and schism. This jurisdiction is expressly saved b
the act which abolished the writ *de haeretico comburendo*.
is not exercised ; but seemingly it exists. As to the weapor
which these courts have at command—over the laity these a1
penance, and in the last resort excommunication. Excom
munication, as already said, involved a number of civil di
abilities, and if the excommunicated person would not submi
the king's writ issued *de excommunicato capiendo*, and he wa
imprisoned until he satisfied the church. In 1813 (53 Geo. II
c. 127) the law was altered ; excommunication was no longer t
have any disabling effect, but the court pronouncing th
sentence of excommunication was to have power to imprisc
the excommunicate for any term not exceeding six month
It would seem then that the heretic, schismatic, fornicato
adulterer or other offender (the catalogue of offences w
cannot lay down with any certainty) may be tried by th
ecclesiastical court, excommunicated and imprisoned for si
months.

(iii) These courts have had a power, never very extensiv
in some matters relating to the endowments of the churche
in particular tithes and church rates. They could compe
for instance, the payment of tithes, if the right to the tith
was not disputed, but their sphere was a limited one: from a
early time, as we have already said, the king's courts regarde
ecclesiastical endowments and ecclesiastical patronage
belonging to their own province. And practically the sphe
of the courts Christian has become very limited indeed, a seri
of modern acts having provided summary remedies for th
recovery of tithes, and of the rent-charge into which tith
have been commuted: while as to church rates, the compulso
church rates were abolished in 1867 (31 and 32 Vic., c. 10

There are a good many small miscellaneous matters relating to the fabrics of the churches which are subject to these courts, but as a matter of fact the greater number of these courts do no business whatever from year's end to year's end.

(iv) However it must not be forgotten that their power over the clergy is large and real.   They can suspend a clerk in orders from ministration, and they may deprive him of his benefice if he has one.   The legal position of a clerk in the orders of the Church of England differs radically from that of the priest or the minister of any other religion.   The one, we may say, has in the strict sense of the term a legal status, the other has not.   The duties of the clerk in holy orders are directly imposed upon him by law; if, for instance, he is bound not to perform publicly any service save those authorized by the book of common prayer, this is no matter of contract or of trust, it is a matter of status, and there are special courts which can enforce those duties.   Otherwise is it with the Catholic priest or the Wesleyan minister, the law imposes no duty upon him as such.   If he has contracted to preach those doctrines or perform those ceremonies and none other, an action may lie against him for breaking his contract.   If the trustees or owners of a chapel have engaged him to teach one set of dogmas, he will not be allowed to use that chapel for the propagation of another set of inconsistent dogmas.   Before now the Court of Chancery has had to decide that a non-conformist minister had no right to use a chapel, because he was engaged to preach the doctrine of universal depravity and was not preaching it.   So an English temporal court might have to decide whether a Roman priest was preaching ortho-doxy or heterodoxy, i.e. whether he was doing what he was paid for, or putting a particular building to its right use.   But all this is matter of contract or of trust, matter of private law, and the court would receive evidence as to what are the orthodox doctrines of the Roman Church or of the Particular Baptists.   Otherwise with the clerk in English orders—contract or no contract, trust or no trust, he has both negative and positive duties: he must not preach heterodox doctrines, he must not use ceremonies not authorized by the prayer book; if he has a church he must perform the church services, he must bury, he must marry, and the courts do not require *evidence* as to the doctrines that he is to teach, or the ceremonies that he is to perform : the standard of orthodox dogma and orthodox ritual is directly fixed by law.

Once more I call your attention to the fact that there is no body having power to alter that standard, other than the statute-making body, king and parliament. This gives to the Church of England a very unique position. Indeed I do not think that we can for legal purposes define the Church of England as consisting of a body of persons, or as represented by a body of persons. It is no corporation, it is no self-governing body of persons, consequently it has no rights and no duties. As already explained it has no property : there is no land, for instance, which belongs to the Church of England—there is glebe of this parish church, and of that parish church. Further the benefit of the organization is not confined to any definite body of persons : the parishioner has a legal right of attending the services in his parish church, until comparatively recent times it was his legal duty to attend them, even from the Holy Communion he can only be excluded for one among several definite causes, known to the law; the clergyman who refused to receive him would have to prove the existence of one of those causes. We may speak if we will of the church as a legal organization, but we must not think of it as of a legal person or as a definite body of persons.

K. *The Definition of Constitutional Law.*

We will end our cause by raising a question which perhaps in your opinion ought to have been raised and discussed long ago, namely, How are we to define constitutional law ? I have thought it best to postpone the discussion until this our last moment, because it seems to me that we cannot profitably define a department of law until we already know a good deal of its contents. I hope that I do not undervalue that study of general jurisprudence which holds the first place in the programme of the law tripos ; still you will by this time have learnt enough to know that a classification of legal rules which suits the law of one country and one age will not necessarily suit the law of another country or of another age. One may perhaps force the rules into the scheme that we have prepared for them, but the scheme is not natural or convenient. Only those who know a good deal of English law are really entitled to have any opinion as to the limits of that part of the law which it is convenient to call constitutional.

Now my first remark must be that this question is on the whole a question of convenience. It is not to be solved by any appeal to authority. The phrase, constitutional law, is of course a very common phrase, but it is not a technical phrase of English law. I am not aware that it has ever been used in the statute book or that any judge has ever set himself to define it. If we had a code which called itself a code of constitutional law, then the definition might be a matter of authority, it would be thrust upon us by the legislature; but we have nothing of the sort, and are therefore free to consider what definition would be convenient and conformable to the ordinary usage of the term.

Now there is one use of the word constitutional which we must notice in order that we may put it on one side. Occasionally it is contrasted with legal: we are told for example that a minister's conduct was legal but not constitutional. We have seen that our rules of law touching public affairs are very intimately connected with rules touching public affairs which are not rules of law, rules which are sometimes called rules of constitutional morality, or constitutional practice, the customs of the constitution, the conventions of the constitution, or again constitutional understandings. It is to a breach of rules of this latter class, rules which are not rules of law, that we refer when we say that a man's conduct though legal was not constitutional. He has broken no rule of law, but he has broken some rule of constitutional usage, some convention of the constitution: no court of law will punish him or take any notice of his misdoing, still he has broken a rule which is generally kept and which in the opinion of people in general ought not to be broken. But this usage of the word can hardly help us when our object is to determine what part of the law is to be called constitutional; it merely tells us that according to common opinion certain rules are constitutional which are not rules of law.

Now I will place before you two accredited definitions or descriptions of constitutional law; the one comes from Austin, the other from Professor Holland. Austin's opinion will be found in a note at the end of the *Outline of the Course of Lectures*[1]. Having defined 'public law' as the law of political conditions, he subdivides 'public law' into 'constitutional law' and 'administrative law'; and he writes thus: 'In a country governed by a monarch, constitutional law is extremely simple: for it merely determines the person who shall bear the sovereignty. In a country governed by a number, constitutional law is more complex: for it determines the persons or the classes of persons who shall bear the sovereign powers; and it determines moreover the mode wherein such persons shall share those powers. In a country governed by a monarch, constitutional law is positive morality merely: in a country governed by a number, it may consist of positive morality, or of a compound of positive morality and positive law.

'Administrative law determines the ends and modes to and in which the sovereign powers shall be exercised: shall be exercised directly by the monarch or sovereign number, or shall be exercised directly by the subordinate political superiors to whom portions of those powers are delegated or committed in trust.

'The two departments therefore of constitutional and administrative law do not quadrate exactly with the two departments of law which regard respectively the *status* of the sovereign and the various *status* of subordinate political superiors. Though the rights and duties of the latter are comprised by administrative law, and are not comprised by constitutional law, administrative law comprises the powers of the sovereign in so far as they are exercised directly by the monarch or sovereign number.

'In so far as the powers of the sovereign are delegated to political subordinates, administrative law is positive law,

[1] *Jurisprudence*, ed. 1873, vol. i, p. 73.

whether the country be governed by a monarch or by a
sovereign number. In so far as the sovereign powers are
exercised by the sovereign directly, administrative law in a
country governed by a monarch is positive morality merely :
in a country governed by a number it may consist of positive
morality, or of a compound of positive morality and positive
law.'

Let us try to make this clearer by examples. The one
object of constitutional law, according to Austin, is to define
the sovereign. In a monarchical state it is extremely simple
and is not in the strict sense law. Thus on a subsequent
page Austin says that from the days of Richelieu to those
of the great Revolution the king of France was sovereign in
France[1]. 'But in the same country, and during the same
period, a traditional maxim cherished by the courts of justice
and rooted in the affections of the bulk of the people determined the succession to the throne : it determined that the
throne, on the demise of an actual occupant, should invariably
be taken by the person who then might happen to be heir
to it agreeably to the canon of inheritance which was named
the Salic law.' This then, in his opinion, was the whole
substance of the constitutional law of France : the heir male
of S. Louis is to be sovereign, and in the strictest sense
this was no rule of law, it was only a rule of positive
morality. Austin's view, as you probably know, is that in a
monarchical state the succession to the throne cannot be fixed
by law, positive law : when the king dies law dies with him ;
sovereignty is not a matter of law, it is a matter of fact : the
people by accepting, tacitly accepting, Louis XV on the death
of Louis XIV obey no law; they raise up a new sovereign; the
rule which they observed in accepting the great-grandson of
the late king was no rule of law ; they would have broken no
law, had they instead accepted a bastard or a foreigner or
anyone else. In such a case constitutional law then consists
of some simple rule, probably some canon of descent, and
even that is not in strictness law.

As to administrative law in a monarchical state; it defines

---

[1] *Jurisprudence*, ed. 1873, vol. I, p. 275.

the powers of the sovereign and the powers of the political subordinates. In so far as it deals with the powers of the sovereign, it is not in strictness law : no law can limit the powers of the sovereign. If it be generally expected by the French nation that Louis XIV will only exercise his powers in these or those ways this expectation can constitute no rule of law, it can at best give rise to positive morality. But as to political subordinates—ministers, judges, intendants—the rules which, for the time being, define who they shall be and what powers they shall have, will be true rules of law—positive law— though rules which the sovereign monarch might at any time abolish. This then is the sphere of administrative law.

But turn from France of the eighteenth century to England of our own day. Constitutional law determines the persons or the classes of persons who shall bear the sovereign powers ; it determines, moreover, the mode wherein those persons shall share those powers. Now Austin himself had, as I dare-say you know, a curious doctrine about the sovereignty of this realm; instead of holding that the sovereign body consisted of the king, the lords and the representatives of the commons assembled in parliament, he held that it consisted of the king, the lords and the electors : he treats the members of the House of Commons as mere delegates of the electors. This seems to me a singularly profitless speculation. Suppose that the present parliament were to make a statute contrary to the strongest wishes and well-founded expectations of those who elected it ; doubtless that statute would be law ; the courts would treat it as law and would not for one instant permit a suggestion that parliament had exceeded its powers by betraying (if you will) the trust that was imposed in it. I am obliged to notice this point in passing, but it is of no very great importance to us at the present moment; for which-ever view we take, whether Austin's which places sovereignty in king, lords and electors, or the commoner and saner view which places it in king and parliament, the mass of rules that will be covered by his definition of constitutional law will be much the same. It is to determine the persons who shall bear the sovereign powers and the mode wherein those persons shall share those powers. It must determine then, in the first place, who is to be king. The act which settled the succession to the throne on the heirs of the body of the electress Sophia, being Protestants, is clearly a part of constitutional law. The rule that a king will forfeit his crown by marrying a Papist is clearly a rule of constitutional law. Whatever law we have as to regencies will be constitutional law. Then all the law as to the composition of the House of Lords will be constitutional law. Again all the law as to the qualifications of voters for members of the House of Commons must in any case be constitutional law. Accepting the ordinary doctrine that our sovereign body consists of king and parliament, all the law as to the qualifications of members of the House of Commons will be constitutional; but Austin, I think, can hardly include it within his definition, for according to him it is not the representatives but the represented who form part of the sovereign body, and the rules as to how many delegates the electors may choose, and what must be the qualification of those delegates, would seem to be no part of the law that defines the composition of the sovereign body. But any way you will see that Austin's definition of constitutional law is very narrow: it only includes those rules which determine the composition of the sovereign body. All rules as to the appointment and powers of officers who are subordinate to the sovereign are excluded: they are relegated to the department of administrative law. Thus Austin's constitutional law would, I take it, say nothing of the Privy Council, of the Treasury, of the Secretaries of State, of the judges, still less of justices of the peace, poor law guardians, boards of health, policemen: all these are topics not of constitutional but of administrative law. Even the procedure of the sovereign body itself is a topic not of constitutional but of administrative law.

For my own part, I regard this definition as far too narrow, by which I mean that it excludes a very great deal of what is ordinarily called constitutional law, and most certainly any student set to study constitutional law would be ill-advised if he were to trust that his examiners would not go beyond Austin's definition. To take one instance; the question whether the king has power to tax without the consent of parliament would be very generally treated as a grave and typical question of constitutional law, but it does not fall within Austin's definition; it might be admitted that the sovereign power was possessed by king and parliament, or by king, lords and electors in certain shares, and yet the question would be possible whether law gave the king a power of imposing customs duties.

Let us turn to Professor Holland. Having divided law into public and private, he subdivides public law into six departments, the first of which he calls constitutional and the second administrative. Of constitutional law he writes thus[1]:

'The primary function of constitutional law is to ascertain the political centre of gravity of any given state. It announces in what portion of the whole is to be found the 'internal sovereignty,' '*suprema potestas*,' '*Staatsgewalt*,' or as Aristotle called it, τὸ κύριον τῆς πόλεως. In other words it defines the form of government.' 'The definition of the sovereign power in a state necessarily leads to the consideration of its component parts....It prescribes the order of succession to the throne, or, in a Republic, the mode of electing a President. It enumerates the prerogatives of the king or other chief magistrate. It regulates the composition of the Council of State, and of the Upper and Lower Houses of Assembly, when the assembly is thus divided; the mode in which a seat is acquired in the Upper House, whether by succession, by nomination, or by tenure of office, the mode of electing members of the House of Representatives; the powers and privileges of the assembly as a whole, and of the individuals who compose it and the machinery of law-making. It deals also with the ministers, their responsibility and their respective spheres of action; the government offices and their organization; the armed forces of the State, their control and the mode in which they are recruited; the relation, if any, between Church and State; the judges and their immunities; the relations between the mother country and its colonies and dependencies. It describes the portions of the earth's surface over which the sovereignty of the state extends, and defines

[1] *Jurisprudence*, 10th ed., p. 359.

the persons who are subject to its authority. It comprises, therefore, rules for the ascertainment of nationality, and for regulating the acquisition of a new nationality by naturalization. It declares the rights of the state over its subjects in respect of their liability to military conscription, to service as jurymen and otherwise....The contents of the constitutional branch of law may be illustrated by reference to a draft piece of legislation, which enters far more into detail than is usual in such undertakings. The draft Political Code of the State of New York purports to be divided into four parts, whereof "The first declares what persons compose the people of the State, and the political rights and duties of all persons subject to its jurisdiction ; the second defines the territory of the State and its civil divisions ; the third relates to the general government of the State, the functions of its public officers, its public ways, its general police and civil polity ; the fourth relates to the local government of counties, cities, towns and villages." '

Now this can hardly be called a definition of constitutional law, rather it is a string of particulars. I have no doubt, however, that Professor Holland has general usage on his side in giving the term a far wider meaning than that which Austin put upon it. But he has to meet this difficulty, that he includes so much under constitutional law that he seems to leave little to come under his head of administrative law. His general idea, however, is given in these words : ' The various organs of the sovereign power are described by constitutional law as at rest; but it is also necessary that they should be considered as in motion, and that the manner of their activity should be prescribed in detail. The branch of law that does this is called administrative law, ' *Verwaltungsrecht* " in the widest sense of the word[1].' I think that we catch his idea if we say that, while constitutional law deals with structure, administrative law deals with function. If this idea were pursued, then constitutional law would tell us how a king comes to be king, and how he can cease to be king, how a man comes to be a peer of the realm, when, where and how

[1] *Jurisprudence*, p. 363.

men are elected to the House of Commons, how parliament is summoned, prorogued, dissolved, how men become privy councillors, secretaries of state, judges, justices of the peace, aldermen, poor law guardians—for constitutional law deals not only with the structure of the sovereign body, but also with the structure of inferior bodies possessing legal powers of central or local government. But if we ask what can these bodies and these officers do, what are their functions, then, according to the general idea, we should be sent to administrative law; thus, if we ask what are the royal prerogatives, what are the privileges of the House of Commons, what powers has a secretary of state, a justice of the peace, a town councillor. But if, with this idea before us, we attempted to state the law of England, or, I should imagine, the law of any other country, we should probably find ourselves involved in many difficulties. For instance, it is certainly the duty of constitutional law to state how, when, and by whom, parliament can be summoned and prorogued. Attempting to do this, we immediately find ourselves describing one of the king's prerogatives. It is certainly the duty of constitutional law to define the composition of the House of Lords, but immediately we have to state another of the king's prerogatives—the power of making peers. So again, if we have to describe the structure of the ministry, we must deal with the functions of the king in appointing and dismissing ministers; while if we descend to inferior organs, such as municipal corporations and boards of guardians, we shall have to speak freely of the functions of the local government board and the secretaries of state. In short, it is impossible to describe the structure of some organs without describing the functions of others, for it is among the most important functions of some organs, especially the higher, to determine the structure of other organs. Thus, taking the view that constitutional law deals with structure, not with function, we still cannot get through our constitutional law without describing very many functions of the highest organs; we have, for instance, to describe many of the royal prerogatives, the functions of the king. The question then arises whether it is convenient to break up so important a topic as the royal prerogatives, in order to deal with some parts of it under the heading of constitutional law, and to relegate other parts to various sub-heads of administrative law.

Professor Holland is alive to the inconvenience of such a course of procedure. He expressly includes an enumeration of the king's prerogatives under constitutional law, also he includes under the same head the whole topic of parliamentary privileges, and I venture to think that he is right in so doing. A book on constitutional law, which did not deal with royal prerogatives and privileges of parliament, would, I think, be generally considered as worse than imperfect. This brings him to abandon, for the sake of convenience, the general idea with which he started, namely, that constitutional law deals with structure, and administrative law with function. His ultimate opinion seems to be that constitutional law deals with structure and with the broader rules which regulate function, while the details of function are left to administrative law.

So far as I am aware, this is in accordance with common usage, though we certainly use the term constitutional law now in a wider and now in a narrower sense, and we shall look in vain for any such term as administrative law in our orthodox English text-books. But I may illustrate the difficulty of drawing convenient lines. It would be generally allowed that the law as to parliamentary elections is a most important part of constitutional law: that, for instance, the extension of the county franchise, from the 40 shilling freeholders to many other classes, constituted a great change in our constitutional law. Then again it would be allowed that the introduction of the ballot was another great change—that members of the House of Commons are elected by secret voting is, I take it, distinctly a rule of constitutional law. But then our law has minute provisions as to how the registers of voters are to be made up and revised, and again it has minute provisions as to the conduct of the election, the custody of the voting papers and so forth; in order to secure secrecy it descends to very small details. Now shall we call all these small rules, rules of constitutional law? Would our code of constitutional law describe all the duties of revising barristers and returning officers? That, I think, is a question of convenience, a question which the maker of a complete code of English law would have to consider very carefully, but still a question of convenience, a question to be solved by the art of draftsmanship. One of the points that he would have to consider would be the desirability of avoiding repetitions. Very possibly he would find it convenient to bring under the head of constitutional law the broad rules which settle the qualification of electors, and leave the details as to the making and revision of the registers to come under some chapter of administrative law. Very possibly he would find it convenient to state, as a rule of constitutional law, that elections are to be made by secret voting, and to place the description of the process of election, the rules which regulate the conduct of returning officers, under some chapter of administrative law.

In this country such questions would be questions of convenience, because our constitutional law has no special sanctity. It would not be so everywhere. Some countries have constitutions which cannot be altered by the ordinary legislature. In such countries it is, of course, a fact of immense importance that a particular rule is, or is not, a rule of the constitution; if it is not, it can be repealed by the legislative assembly, if it is, then to repeal it may require an appeal to the people, or there may be no recognized mode of repealing it at all. But here in England that part of the law which we call constitutional has no special sanctity. The hours, during which an election may be held, are fixed by statute, the succession to the throne is fixed by statute; neither the one nor the other could be altered except by statute, but the same statute might alter both, the one as easily as the other. So, I repeat it once more, the demarcation of the province of constitutional law is with us a matter of convenience. I do not think that we have any theory about it which can claim to be called orthodox. I think that Austin's definition is decidedly too narrow. I think that Professor Holland's description is fairly conformable to our ordinary usage, but that the line between the constitutional and the administrative departments is one which it is very hard to draw.

And as with constitutional law so with constitutional

history. This title was, I believe, a new one when Hallam chose it for his great work, and it was liable to misconstruction. By this time it is well rooted in our language, but there seems to be no great room for difference of opinion as to its meaning. But I think that we can see a steady tendency, very manifest in the great work of Stubbs, to widen the scope of the term in one direction, to narrow it in another. On the one hand we no longer conceive that the historian of our constitution has done his duty when he has told us of kings and parliaments; at least, as regards early times, we expect him to speak of the courts of law, of the sheriffs, of local government, of hundred courts and county courts. On the other hand we expect him to give us a history of results, rather than a history of efforts and projects. If we look at May's book we find it to be to a large extent a history of efforts and projects: it is full of proposals to alter the law, of the strife between Whigs and Tories—the struggle over the Reform Bill for example. Some people seem to think that a bill loses all its importance at the very moment when it becomes law, that it ceases to be a subject for constitutional history, or indeed for history of any kind, when the last division has been taken. But that surely is a perverse view, and I hope that it is becoming an old-fashioned view: political struggles are important, but chiefly because they alter the law. Constitutional history should, to my mind, be a history, not of parties, but of institutions, not of struggles, but of results; the struggles are evanescent, the results are permanent. That is, I think, the view taken by the latest and greatest of the historians of our constitution, and I hope the day may come when someone will take up the tale where Stubbs has dropped it, and bring the history of our constitution down to modern days, as a history of institutions, a history of one great department of law, and of its actual working.

It will perhaps occur to you that I am making an apology, for I have spoken a great deal about modern statutes, and not a word of Whigs and Tories, Liberals and Conservatives. Well, I know that a great many apologies might be required of me, but not, I think, for this. I have been trying to turn your thoughts away from what I think to be an obsolete and inadequate idea of the province of constitutional history, I have been asking you to set your faces towards the rising sun. And the sun will rise, not a doubt of it.

The practical application of these remarks should be obvious. The student who is set to read English constitutional law will, if he be prudent, take a wide view of his subject. Even if his sole object be to obtain marks in an examination, he will do well to recognize the fact that the limits of constitutional law are not strictly defined, and that his examiners may not be disposed to make them narrow. And when he is asked to study constitutional history as well as constitutional law, the expedience of wide reading will be the more apparent. Regarding the matter historically we may say that there is hardly any department of law which does not, at one time or another, become of constitutional importance. Go back for a moment to the Middle Ages. If we are to learn anything about the constitution it is necessary first and foremost that we should learn a good deal about the land law. We can make no progress whatever in the history of parliament without speaking of tenure, indeed our whole constitutional law seems at times to be but an appendix to the law of real property. It would be disastrous therefore, as well as stupid advice, were I to tell you that you could read constitutional history without studying land law—you cannot do this, no one can do it. And then again, turn to the seventeenth century and the great struggle between king and parliament ; this truly is a constitutional struggle in the strictest sense of the word, it is a struggle for sovereignty, but how can you study it without knowing something of criminal law and criminal procedure? At more than one moment the whole history of England seems to depend on what it is possible to describe as a detail of criminal procedure—the question whether ' He is committed to prison *per speciale mandatum domini regis*,' is or is not a good return to a writ of habeas corpus. How can we form any opinion about that question unless we know something about the ordinary course of criminal procedure? A modern code-maker would very possibly not put the provisions of the Habeas Corpus Act into that part of the code which dealt with constitutional law—he would keep it for the part which dealt with criminal procedure—still we can see that the history of the writ is very truly part of the history of our constitution; if the king had been able to commit to prison without giving any reason, he would have had at his command a potent engine for controlling parliament, and might have succeeded in his effort to make himself an absolute monarch.

I have some little fear lest the study of what we call general jurisprudence may lead you to take a false view of law. Writers on general jurisprudence are largely concerned with the classification of legal rules. This is a very important task, and to their efforts we owe a great deal—it is most desirable that law should be clearly stated according to some rational and logical scheme. But do not get into the way of thinking of law as consisting of a number of independent compartments, one of which is labelled constitutional, another administrative, another criminal, another property, so that you can learn the contents of one compartment, and know nothing as to what is in the others. No, law is a body, a living body, every member of which is connected with and depends upon every other member. There is no science which deals with the foot, or the hand, or the heart. Science deals with the body as a whole, and with every part of it as related to the whole. Who, at this moment, can vote in parliamentary elections? Begin answering that question, and you begin to talk about freeholders, copyholders, leaseholders; but you cannot talk about them with much intelligence unless you understand some real property law. Life I know is short, and law is long, very long, and we cannot study everything at once; still, no good comes of refusing to see the truth, and the truth is that all parts of our law are very closely related to each other, so closely that we can set no logical limit to our labours.

APPENDIX

By the Parliament Act of 1911 (1 and 2 Geo. V, c. 13) it is provided

1.   That if a Money Bill (subsequently defined as 'a Public Bill which in the opinion of the Speaker of the House of Commons contains only provisions dealing with all or the following subjects'—a list follows) is sent up to the House of Lords at least one month before the end of the session and is not passed by the House of Lords without amendment within one month after it is sent up, the Bill shall, unless the House of Commons direct the contrary, be presented to the King and become an Act of Parliament on the Royal Assent being signified notwithstanding that the House of Lords have not consented to the Bill.

2.   That if any Public Bill (other than a Money Bill or a Bill containing any provision to extend the maximum duration of Parliament beyond five years) is passed by the House of Commons in three successive sessions (whether of the same Parliament or not) and having been sent up to the House of Lords at least one month before the end of the session is rejected by the House of Lords in each of those sessions, the Bill shall on its rejection a third time by the House of Lords, unless the House of Commons direct the contrary, be presented to the King and become an Act of Parliament on the Royal Assent being signified thereto, provided that two years have elapsed between the date of the second reading in the first of these sessions in the House of Commons and the date at which it passes the House of Commons in the third of these sessions.

3. That a Bill shall be deemed to be rejected by the House of Lords if it is not passed by the House of Lords either without amendment or with such amendments only as may be agreed to by both Houses.

4. That the House of Commons may in the passage of such a Bill through the House in the second and third sessions *suggest* amendments without inserting them in the Bill. If these amendments are agreed to by the House of Lords, they shall be treated as amendments made by the House of Lords and agreed to by the House of Commons.

5. That the duration of Parliament should be reduced from seven to five years.

The general effect of these provisions is (1) to deprive the House of Lords altogether of its power of amending or rejecting Money Bills, (2) to restrict the House of Lords to a suspensive veto in respect of Bills (other than Money Bills or Bills to prolong the duration of Parliament), as may be passed by the House of Commons in three successive sessions during the first two years of Parliament, (3) to enable the country to pronounce more rapidly upon the action of a ministry so passing bills into statutes in defiance of the opposition of the Second Chamber.

INDEX.